Microsoft® Office Visio® 2003 Inside Out

Mark H. Walker and Nanette Eaton

PUBLISHED BY
Microsoft Press
A Division of Microsoft Corporation
One Microsoft Way
Redmond, Washington 98052-6399

Library of Congress Cataloging-in-Publication Data

Walter, Mark H.
    Microsoft Office Visio 2003 Inside Out / Mark H. Walker, Nanette Eaton.
       p. cm.
    Includes index.
    ISBN 0-7356-1516-0
    1. Computer graphics. 2. Microsoft Visio. 3. Business--Data processing. I. Eaton, Nanette J. II. Title.

    T385.W345 2003
    006.6'8682--dc22   2003065173

Printed and bound in the United States of America.

4 5 6 7 8 9   QWT   8 7 6 5

Distributed in Canada by H.B. Fenn and Company Ltd.

A CIP catalogue record for this book is available from the British Library.

Microsoft Press books are available through booksellers and distributors worldwide. For further information about international editions, contact your local Microsoft Corporation office or contact Microsoft Press International directly at fax (425) 936-7329. Visit our Web site at www.microsoft.com/mspress. Send comments to mspinput@microsoft.com.

Acquisitions Editor: Alex Blanton
Project Editors: Sandra Haynes and Kristine Haugseth
Technical Editor: Chris Russo

Body Part No. X10-08615

Contents at a Glance

Table of Contents

Part 1
Introduction to Visio 2003

Chapter 1
Getting Started with Visio 2003   3

Table of Contents

Chapter 10
Visualizing an Organization   283

Chapter 11
Displaying Relationships and Processes in Block Diagrams   307

Chapter 12
Tracking Projects and Schedules   323

Chapter 13
Adding Impact to Microsoft PowerPoint Presentations
345

Part 4
Inside Scaled Drawings

Chapter 16
Measuring and Dimensioning with Precision   421

Chapter 17
Using CAD Drawings in Visio   471

Chapter 18
Laying Out Floor and Site Plans   497

Part 5
Inside Database and Software Diagrams

Chapter 19
Diagramming and Documenting Databases   553

Part 6
Inside the Visio Platform

Chapter 22
Drawing and Editing to Create New Shapes   637

Chapter 23
Defining Styles, Patterns, and Colors   681

Chapter 24
Connecting Diagrams and Databases   711

Chapter 25
Making Shapes Smart   735

Part 7
Inside Technical Diagrams

Chapter 26
Managing Facilities with Space Plans   757

Table of Contents

Appendix B
Template and Stencil Reference 851

Acknowledgments

Visio has graced my computer since it had version numbers like 4.0. I've always enjoyed using it, but I never fully comprehended its power and versatility until Microsoft asked me to write and revise this book. In the course of combing through over nine hundred pages of text, I've come to appreciate the magnificent depth of the software and, more importantly, its ease of use.

Nevertheless, despite that ease of use, this book would have never happened without the aid, advice, input, and support of a lot of people. Thanks to Alex Blanton for trusting me to revise the book. Thanks to Sandra Haynes and Kristine Haugseth for their neverending patience and good humor. Speaking of good humor, I sincerely appreciate both the technical editor, Chris Russo, and the copy editor, Teresa Horton. Both grinned and bore my frequent mistakes, and caught my technical and grammatical miscues. In fact, the entire book development team at nSight, Inc., was invaluable. Also invaluable were the book's first author, Nanette Eaton, and the Visio 2003 Product Manager, Jorie Wackerman. Jorie frequently called in the experts on her team, including, but not limited to, Susan Raisi, Kathy Shoesmith, Jeff Hannibal, Chang Oh, Darrin House, Bill Holt, Jon Price, Shawn Schoenrock, Mark Nelson, Mai-lan Tomsen Bukevec, Dan Clay, Matt Winterowd, Gary Klapel, Cynthia Shelly, and Richard See.

My helpers were almost too many to list, so if I leave someone out here it isn't intentional. Thanks to everyone, and see you next year!

We'd Like to Hear from You!

Our goal at Microsoft Press is to create books that help you find the information you need to get the most out of your software.

The INSIDE OUT series was created with you in mind. As part of an effort to ensure that we're creating the best, most useful books we can, we talked to our customers and asked them to tell us what they need from a Microsoft Press series. Help us continue to help you. Let us know what you like about this book and what we can do to make it better. When you write, please include the title and author of this book in your e-mail, as well as your name and contact information. We look forward to hearing from you.

How to Reach Us

E-mail: nsideout@microsoft.com
Mail: Inside Out Series Editor
              Microsoft Press
              One Microsoft Way
              Redmond, WA 98052

Note: Unfortunately, we can't provide support for any software problems you might experience. Please go to http://support.microsoft.com *for help with any software issues.*

About the CD

The companion CD that ships with this book contains many tools and resources to help you get the most out of your *Inside Out* book.

What's On the CD

Your *Inside Out* CD includes the following:

- **Complete eBook**   In this section you'll find the an electronic version of *Microsoft Office Visio 2003 Inside Out*. The eBook is in PDF format.

- ***Computer Dictionary, Fifth Edition*** **eBook**   Here you'll find the full electronic version of the *Microsoft Computer Dictionary, Fifth Edition*. Suitable for home and office, the dictionary contains more than 10,000 entries.

- **Microsoft Resources**   In this section, you'll find information about additional resources from Microsoft that will help you get the most out of the Microsoft Office System. Building on the familiar tools that many people already know, the Microsoft Office System includes servers, services, and desktop programs to help address a broad array of business needs.

- **Extending Visio**   In this section, you'll find great information about third-party utilities and tools you use to further enhance your experience with Visio 2003.

The companion CD provides detailed information about the files on this CD and links to Microsoft and third-party sites on the Internet. All the files on this CD are designed to be accessed through Microsoft Internet Explorer (version 5.01 or higher).

> **Note**   Please note that the links to third-party sites are not under the control of Microsoft Corporation, and Microsoft is therefore not responsible for their content, nor should their inclusion on this CD be construed as an endorsement of the product or the site.
>
> Software provided on this CD is in English language only and may be incompatible with non-English language operating systems and software.

Using the CD

To use the companion CD, insert it into your CD-ROM. Accept the license agreement that is presented to access the starting menu. If AutoRun is not enabled on your system, run StartCD.exe in the root of the CD or refer to the Readme.txt file.

System Requirements

Following are the minimum system requirements necessary to run the CD:

- Microsoft Windows XP or later or Windows 2000 Professional with Service Pack 3 or later
- 266-MHz or higher Pentium-compatible CPU
- 64 megabytes (MB) RAM
- 8X CD-ROM drive or faster
- Microsoft Windows–compatible sound card and speakers
- Microsoft Internet Explorer 5.01 or higher
- Microsoft Mouse or compatible pointing device

Note System requirements may be higher for the add-ins available on the CD. Individual add-in system requirements are specified on the CD. An Internet connection is necessary to access the some of the hyperlinks. Connect time charges may apply.

Support Information

Every effort has been made to ensure the accuracy of the book and the contents of this companion CD. For feedback on the book content or this companion CD, please contact us by using any of the addresses listed in the "We'd Like to Hear From You" section (page xxv).

Microsoft Press provides corrections for books through the World Wide Web at *http://www.microsoft.com/mspress/support/*. To connect directly to the Microsoft Press Knowledge Base and enter a query regarding a question or issue that you may have, go to *http://www.microsoft.com/mspress/support/search.asp*.

For support information regarding Office 2003, you can connect to Microsoft Technical Support on the Web at *http://support.microsoft.com/*.

Conventions and Features
Used in This Book

This book uses special text and design conventions to make it easier for you to find the information you need.

Text Conventions

Convention	Meaning
Abbreviated menu commands	For your convenience, this book uses abbreviated menu commands. For example, "Choose Tools, Track Changes, Highlight Changes" means that you should click the Tools menu, point to Track Changes, and select the Highlight Changes command.
Boldface type	**Boldface** type is used to indicate text that you enter or type.
Initial Capital Letters	The first letters of the names of menus, dialog boxes, dialog box elements, and commands are capitalized. Example: the Save As dialog box.
Italicized type	*Italicized* type is used to indicate new terms.
Plus sign (+) in text	Keyboard shortcuts are indicated by a plus sign (+) separating two key names. For example, Ctrl+Alt+Delete means that you press the Ctrl, Alt, and Delete keys at the same time.

Design Conventions

 This text identifies a new or significantly updated feature in this version of the software.

Tip Tips provide helpful hints, timesaving tricks, or alternative procedures related to the task being discussed.

Cross-references point you to other locations in the book that offer additional information on the topic being discussed.

Caution Cautions identify potential problems that you should look out for when you're completing a task or problems that you must address before you can complete a task.

Note Notes offer additional information related to the task being discussed.

Inside Out

This statement illustrates an example of an "Inside Out" problem statement

These are the book's signature tips. In these tips, you'll get the straight scoop on what's going on with the software—inside information on why a feature works the way it does. You'll also find handy workarounds to different software problems.

Troubleshooting

This statement illustrates an example of a "Troubleshooting" problem statement

Look for these sidebars to find solutions to common problems you might encounter. Troubleshooting sidebars appear next to related information in the chapters. You can also use the Troubleshooting Topics index at the back of the book to look up problems by topic.

Sidebar

The sidebars sprinkled throughout these chapters provide ancillary information on the topic being discussed. Go to sidebars to learn more about the technology or a feature.

Part 1
Introduction to Visio 2003

1

Getting Started with Visio 2003

Microsoft Office Visio Standard 2003 and Microsoft Office Visio Professional 2003 provide a broad range of diagramming possibilities that help people visualize and communicate ideas, information, and systems. You don't need to be a professional illustrator or drafter to get professional results with Visio. Whether you need a simple flowchart or a multiple-page, highly detailed technical drawing, you can get up to speed quickly by dragging and dropping predefined shapes. Visio includes thousands of SmartShapes symbols that allow you to easily assemble business diagrams, technical drawings, and information technology models, and more symbols are available at *http://www.microsoft.com/visio*. Automatic layout and alignment tools provide design assistance that ensures professional results.

As a member of the Microsoft Office System, Visio is designed to complement Microsoft Office Excel 2003, Microsoft Office Word 2003, and Microsoft Office PowerPoint 2003, and let Visio users share their drawings and collaborate with fellow workers using the software's Review feature and Microsoft's SharePoint technology. Visio diagrams stand alone or increase the impact of your Office documents. This chapter introduces key concepts and the different versions of Visio, lists new features, and helps you get started working efficiently with this powerful application.

What Is Visio?

Some people might think that only artists can—or need to—draw. Visio can help you toss that belief out the door. Visio is a business and technical drawing and diagramming program that anyone can use to communicate concepts, procedures, product information, specifications, and more. Most of us respond to visual images on the Web and in the reports and e-mail we see every day, even when the accompanying text doesn't grab our attention. Images such as charts, tables, process flows, floor plans, Venn diagrams, and so on use text and symbols to convey information at a glance. You could call this type of image an information graphic, and a good one can clarify an idea and help you understand even complex concepts more quickly. Visio is designed to help you convey information visually—without requiring that you know how to draw.

Visio does this by solving your diagramming needs with categories that include ready-to-use templates that set up a page appropriately and open stencils that contain predrawn shapes. For example, Visio includes several flowcharting templates, as Figure 1-1 shows. If you start with the Basic Flowchart template, Visio displays a new, blank drawing page and opens several stencils that contain the shapes you need to create a flowchart. You drag a shape from the stencil onto the page, which has a grid that helps you align your diagram. You might have heard this process referred to as *drag and drop*. That is the fundamental idea behind everything you do in Visio. Perhaps even more important is the idea of connecting shapes. When you drag additional shapes onto the page to create a diagram such as a flowchart, special lines called *connectors* connect the shapes and stay attached when you move shapes around. By arranging and connecting shapes on the page, you can rapidly assemble a diagram that you can drop into another document, such as a report or presentation slide; save as a Web page; or print.

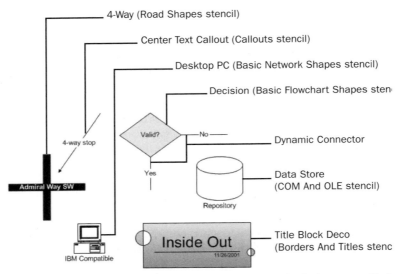

Figure 1-1. Visio provides you with diagramming tools that are specific to the type of drawing you choose to create.

When you talk about dragging shapes, it sounds pretty simple. However, this simplicity is deceptive. The built-in solutions you'll find in Visio range from straightforward block diagrams to complex relational data models. The advantage to you is that no matter what type of information you want to present visually, Visio has a way of getting it done.

Inside Out

Learning the Visio language

The Visio team has conducted much usability research in past years that indicates a consistent theme: Visio often overwhelms new users with the number of new terms they have to learn. Even if you're very comfortable with other Microsoft Office applications, you can expect to wrestle a bit with Visio terminology at first. Part of the difficulty is that the term *template* is often used interchangeably with *drawing type* in different documents and on the Web site. Moreover, the part of the Visio screen where stencils appear is labeled *Shapes*, and shapes themselves are sometimes called *SmartShapes symbols*, *masters*, or *master shapes*. If you're confused, you're not alone—but don't worry. As you use Visio, you'll pick up the lingo you need to know. This book tries to use the terms *templates*, *stencils*, *shapes*, and *master shapes* consistently. A shape is an object—be it a simple triangle or "intelligent" window schedule—that may be placed on a Visio drawing page. A stencil is a logical grouping set of shapes that may be used together to make a Visio drawing, for example, the Basic Shapes stencil. A master shape is the shape that resides on a stencil. It may not be changed, although a copy of it may be saved to a custom stencil and subsequently altered. A template is a logical group of stencils that give a user all the tools that he or she needs to produce a drawing, for example, the Basic Diagram template, which includes the Basic Shapes, Borders and Tiles, and Backgrounds stencils.

Two Versions: Visio Standard and Visio Professional

Visio comes in two flavors: Visio Standard 2003 and Visio Professional 2003. The two versions differ in their intended audience, which is reflected in the number and type of templates and shapes they include. Visio Standard is intended for business professionals who need to communicate visually about their organization's people, projects, and processes. The following visual solutions are included:

- **Block Diagram**   Includes the Basic, Block, and Block with Perspective templates. These are useful for showing all types of relationships and hierarchies and provide the basic arsenal of information graphics tools.

- **Brainstorming**   Includes the new Brainstorming diagram that allows you to capture, arrange, and expand ideas generated by a group or yourself. These diagrams display hierarchical relationships and allow exportation to Word for a more linear view, or to an Extensible Markup Language (XML) file for reuse elsewhere.

- **Business Process**   The new Business Process category provides a collection of templates you can use for specific business process documentation efforts, including Six Sigma, SAP, and International Organization for Standardization (ISO).

- **Building Plan**   Provides a quick way to design accurate, to-scale office and furniture layouts.

- **Charts and Graph** Formerly Forms and Charts. Includes templates for designing business forms; creating quick pie, line, and bar charts and graphs; and creating marketing diagrams.
- **Flowchart** Includes templates for creating audit diagrams, basic flowcharts, cause and effect diagrams, cross-functional flowcharts, mind mapping diagrams, total quality management (TQM) charts, and workflow diagrams.
- **Map** Includes templates for creating simple street maps and attractive 3-D maps.
- **Network** Includes shapes designed to resemble common network topology and devices. Useful for planning and documenting small to medium-sized networks.
- **Organization Chart** Includes intelligent shapes that "know" their position in an organization, so that reporting structures stay in place. You can even use the Organization Chart Wizard to automatically build a chart from a spreadsheet or database without having to draw a thing.
- **Project Schedule** Includes templates for creating PERT charts, Gantt charts, timelines, and calendars, so you can keep your projects on track.

Visio Professional is intended for technical professionals—IT personnel, database and software programmers, and engineers—and includes many industry-specific solutions. If you have Visio Professional, you have all the templates and shapes that are included with Visio Standard as well as the following solutions geared specifically for the technical audience:

- **Building Plan** Includes templates for creating plan-view drawings of corporate offices and industrial manufacturing facilities. Designed for space planners and building engineers, this solution lets you create floor plans, home plans, plant layouts, reflected ceiling plans, site plans, and the building services schematics that support them.
- **Database** Includes templates for communicating database designs using multiple notations intended for database professionals. With the Database Model Diagram template, you can even reverse engineer and get support for leading client/server and desktop databases.
- **Electrical Engineering** Includes a variety of templates used by electrical engineers for creating electrical and electronic schematics, wiring diagrams, and logic diagrams.
- **Mechanical Engineering** Includes templates for diagramming fluid power control systems and hydraulic or pneumatic circuits as well as part and assembly drawings.
- **Network** Includes further templates for creating high-level, logical diagrams and for designing local area networks (LANs), wide area networks, wiring closets, server rooms, and telecommunications structures. In addition, you can create diagrams of Microsoft Active Directory, Novell Directory Services (NDS), and other LDAP-based directory structures.
- **Process Engineering** Includes templates for assembling detailed piping and instrumentation diagrams (P&IDs) and process flow diagrams (PFDs) used by many chemical and industrial engineers.

- **Software**   Includes templates for major object-oriented software notations, including the full Unified Modeling Language (UML) 1.2 notation. In addition, you can diagram data flows, Windows user interfaces, COM and OLE objects, and more.
- **Web Diagram**   Includes templates for automatically mapping Web sites and conceptual shapes for planning new designs.

 Note   Although the disc comes stuffed with almost every imaginable solution, more templates, including prepopulated "starter" templates for those who wish to construct their own custom templates are available at *http://www.microsoft.com/visio*.

With everything from block diagrams to UML software models, Visio satisfies a wide range of diagramming needs for a diverse audience. This book covers both products, which means that some chapters won't apply to you if you have Visio Standard. You'll see a note when the information in a chapter applies to Visio Professional users only.

Microsoft Office Diagram Gallery vs. Visio

The Microsoft Office Drawing Toolbar and Diagram Gallery deliver straightforward drawing tools right in the Office System applications such as Excel, Word, and PowerPoint. You can use these tools to create simple drawings and sketches in your Office documents, so why fire up Visio at all? It's a question of scale. For that quick, two-step process chart, use the tools in the Office System. For anything more complex, it's probably more efficient to use Visio, a dedicated drawing application—and you can more easily reuse the results.

Drag-and-Drop Diagramming with Shapes

If you're new to Visio, you might think shapes look a lot like clip art. In fact, shapes have built-in intelligence—their "smarts"—that makes them work in uniquely appropriate ways. For example, you can use auto-routing lines to connect process shapes in a flowchart. When you move a process shape, all the lines stay connected and reroute around other shapes as necessary, as Figure 1-2 shows. What a huge time savings that represents! The truth about shapes is that you shouldn't notice how smart they are, because they just work the way you expect them to.

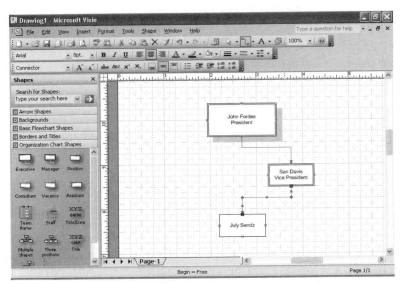

Figure 1-2. When you drag a shape that's connected to other shapes, Visio's built-in "intelligence" takes care of the connections for you and reroutes lines automatically.

Shapes are smart in other ways, as well. For example, door shapes in an office layout can swing in or out by using a single command; valve shapes can rotate into place automatically on a pipe; milestone shapes can shift position on a timeline as you adjust dates. These are just a few examples. The type of drawing you create determines the type of shape smarts you'll see. On one hand, this means that Visio can seem inconsistent. Techniques that work with brainstorming shapes might not apply to organization chart shapes. On the other hand, a template and the shapes it provides are designed to make it easy for you to create a specific type of drawing. Visio is not a fixed menu; it's more like a buffet table with many options for combining great ingredients.

Diagramming in Visio Standard vs. Modeling in Visio Professional

Is Visio the ideal tool for busy business users who want to assemble great-looking graphics in no time? Yes. Is Visio the ideal tool for modeling real-world systems and tracking detailed component specifications? Yes. Are we talking about the same product? Yes! It's a matter of perspective. The diagrams you can create with Visio Standard tend to be conceptual diagrams—shapes that show connections and relationships, as in flowcharts and timelines. Visio Professional includes more modeling capability. Shapes represent real-world objects with attributes, such as 10-foot walls that enclose office number 4N171, which is occupied by Sam Abolrous, whose title is vice president.

Why would you need to understand the difference between diagramming and modeling? If you only ever use Visio to create one type of diagram, it doesn't matter and you can ignore this section. However, if you use several Visio templates, you will probably discover that you need different methods for working with different types of diagrams, and this can make Visio seem hard to use. Despite the "drag-drop-done" philosophy, which says that you just click shapes into place and Visio practically draws for you, some Visio templates do not work that way. If you know this up front, maybe you won't be quite so frustrated when you can't seem to get a shape to look or work the way you want.

One of the primary goals of this book is to help you work successfully in any Visio diagram type, regardless of a solution's idiosyncrasies. It can help to think of each different diagram type as a separate application with unique rules.

What's New in This Release

In this, the second Visio release since it joined the Microsoft Office team, you'll find a lot that's familiar, but also much that is new. As previously mentioned, there are several new template categories, including Brainstorming, Business Process, and Charts and Graph (formerly Forms and Charts). Visio 2003 includes the following new shapes and templates:

- Brainstorming shapes
- Business Process shapes
- New Calendar template and shapes
- Improved Organizational Chart
- Improved Space Plan including Visio smart tags Improved Timeline template that includes an expanded Timeline shape
- Basic Network Diagram template with new shapes that include 22 predefined definitions to generate shape reports
- Detailed Network Diagram template with improved shape appearance
- Rack Diagram for laying out rack space requirements
- Improved Web Site Map template
- Windows XP User Interface template
- Improved Electrical Engineering and Building Plan shapes

The following new features enhance the way you work in Visio:

- **Search for shapes** Now you can search for shapes right from the Visio Shapes window. In fact, if you are online, Visio will even search the Web. You can drag any of the shapes that you find onto your drawing and drop them.
- **Personalized shape management** You can use the new My Shapes folder to save shapes to either a custom stencil or the supplied Favorites stencil.
- **New rotation handles** Visio shapes have been given Office-style rotation handles, so that they can be rotated without selecting the rotation tool.
- **Multiple shape selection techniques** There are three ways to select multiple shapes: You can hold the Shift key to select multiple shapes, use the Lasso tool, or click and drag around the shapes.

- **Color schemes**   The templates that include color schemes now include new options to allow the customization of those schemes. You can make some pretty attractive presentations this way.

- **New task panes**   There are several new task panes that, by default, dock to the right edge of the drawing page. Of course you can position the panes wherever you like by clicking on the left side of the pane header bar and dragging the pane to a new position. Briefly, the new panes are listed here. We cover them in greater detail as we move through the book.

  - **Getting Started**   Displays most recently used drawings.
  - **Help**   Use the table of contents or search for help.
  - **Clip Art**   Displays available clip art.
  - **Research**   Research information on the Internet or your own computer.
  - **Search Results**   Displays results of latest research.
  - **New Drawing**   You can choose to start a new drawing or select a previously saved drawing.
  - **Shared Workspace**   You can share a drawing using SharePoint.
  - **Reviewing**   Mark up or review the comments of others on a review copy of the drawing.

Collaboration in Visio 2003

There is no denying that two heads are better than one. Microsoft understands that, and has done everything possible to make all the Office System applications, including Visio 2003, more collaboration friendly. New collaboration features include the following:

- **Document workspace**   Using Microsoft SharePoint Team Services, users can create document workspaces that allow multiple users to review and modify a document in real time.

- **Review**   Use the Track Markup feature (under the Tools menu) to make and view proposed changes in a drawing. You can e-mail drawings by clicking the E-mail button on the toolbar.

- **Microsoft Office Visio Viewer 2003**   With the new Visio viewer, people can view Visio drawings through Microsoft Internet Explorer. The viewer can be downloaded from the download section at *http://www.microsoft.com*.

- **SVG**   Visio now supports Scalable Vector Graphics (SVG), a new standard for graphics formats.

- **Tablet computer support**   Visio now supports inking on the tablet PC. Hence you can provide input into Office documents with your own tablet pen.

- **Ink**   Ink allows you to create hand-drawn shapes and insert them or modify and review Visio drawings.

What You Won't Find in This Release

The Visio team is constantly striving to make Visio a better product. Part of that improvement plan entails dropping features that are either antiquated or seldom used. Other features are improved and morph in to more highly capable features. Below is a list of features that have been discontinued in Visio 2003.

Table 1-1. Features No Longer in Visio

Deleted Feature	Status
Data Flow Model Diagram Explorer (Visio Professional)	This has been removed from the Data Flow Model Diagram Template. The Model Explorer has been retained in the UML Model Diagram template.
Directory Services Directory Navigator (Visio Professional)	No Longer Supported
Form Template	Removed
Import Project Data Wizard	It is no longer possible to import Microsoft Office Excel data, txt, or mpx files into a timeline. Nor is it possible to convert data between a timeline and a Gantt chart using the Import Project Data Wizard. You can, however, still import Microsoft Office Project data using the new Import Timeline Data Wizard. You can still use the Import Project Data Wizard (on the Gantt Chart menu) to create Gantt charts.
Import Flowchart Data Wizard and Organization Chart 5.0 conversion utility	Removed
VNE Sampler (Visio Professional)	Removed

Additionally, the following file types and converters are no longer converted.

- Adobe Illustrator (AI)
- ABC Flow Charter 2.0/3.0/4.0 (AF2/AF3/AF4)
- CorelDRAW 3.0–7.0 (CDR)
- CorelFLOW (CFL)
- Computer Graphics Metafile (CGM)
- Corel Clipart Format (CMX)
- Microstation (DGN)
- MicroGrafx Designer 3.1 (DRW)
- MicroGrafx Designer 6.0 (English only) (DSF)
- Encapsulated PostScript (EPS)
- Initial Graphics Exchange Specification (IGS)

- ZSoft PC Paintbrush (PCX)
- Mac Clipboard (PICT)
- PostScript (PS)
- Text files (TXT)
- Comma Sep. Value (CSV)

Starting with the Diagram Type You Want

Many people approach Visio as they would Word or Excel and expect a blank page to appear. With Visio, though, you're better off starting with a template. The page might still be blank at first, but at least by basing it on a template, the appropriate set of shapes will appear. It's easy to select the template you want, because when you start Visio, the Choose DrawingType pane shows you previews of the types of diagrams typically created with a particular template, as Figure 1-3 shows.

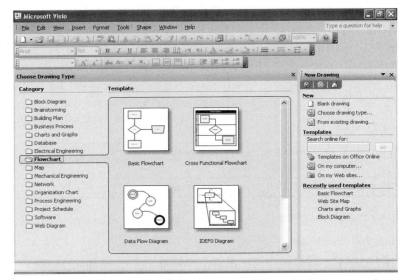

Figure 1-3. When you start Visio, you can preview sample diagrams for each template within a category.

> **Tip** Choose a drawing type
>
> When you're working in Visio, you can display the Choose Drawing Type pane without closing and reopening the program by selecting File, New, Choose Drawing Type. A shortcut to the categories of templates is to select File, New, and then click a category to display a submenu of templates.

Starting with a Template

You can start Visio with a new, blank drawing, which opens only a drawing page and no stencils. However, starting with a template provides important advantages that help you work more efficiently:

- A template can help you solve formatting and design problems in advance. It sets up the appropriate size and orientation of the page for the type of diagram you want to create.

- A template opens the stencils that contain the shapes you'll need to use. It includes diagram-specific styles for formatting the shapes.

- A template displays rulers and a grid on the drawing page and sets them appropriately for the type of diagram. Templates with "US Units" in the name start a page that displays a ruler with inches; otherwise, metric units are used.

- Some templates add special-purpose menus and toolbars. The only way to create certain types of diagrams in Visio and take advantage of timesaving features is to start with the appropriate template.

- Prepopulated starter templates come with draft content already on the page. These can be downloaded from Microsoft Office Online.

For all these reasons, you're almost always better off using a template. It sets up your working environment for you, so all you have to do is add shapes and text.

To start a diagram with a template, follow these steps:

1 On the Start menu, click All Programs, Microsoft Office, and then click Microsoft Office Visio 2003.

2 In the Choose Drawing Type pane, select a drawing type under Category.

   Pictures of specific diagram types appear in the area under Template. Each picture represents a sample diagram created using that template.

> **Note** When you install Visio, you have the option to install metric versions of the templates and add-ons. If you choose this option, you'll see two copies of each template in the Choose Drawing Type pane: one labeled "(US Units)" and one not. The only difference is whether the page is set up for United States units (inches) and page size or metric units and page size.

3 Select the picture that represents the diagram type you want to create.

   Visio opens a new drawing page. Stencils containing shapes appropriate for that diagram type appear on the left, as Figure 1-4 shows.

> **Note** Visio templates establish other page settings that can vary from diagram to diagram. For example, some templates adjust the way shapes snap into position, how they glue to one another, whether drawing pages have backgrounds, and more. This book discusses template-specific settings in the chapters that cover different diagram types.

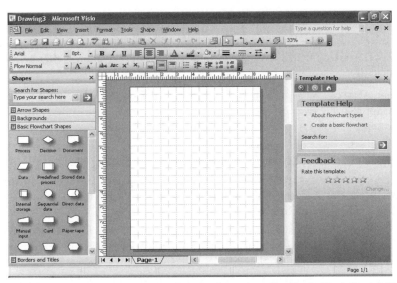

Figure 1-4. If you start a new diagram based on the Basic Flowchart (US Units) template, Visio opens a letter-sized drawing page with three stencils.

Starting in the New Drawing Pane

The Choose Drawing Type pane is a great way to learn about Visio's offerings, but after you've created a few diagrams, you might prefer to work in the New Drawing task pane, shown in Figure 1-5. The task pane shows you diagrams you've opened, templates that you've used recently, and options for starting a new diagram based on a template.

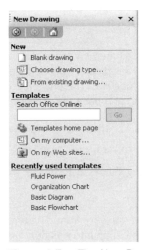

Figure 1-5. The New Drawing task pane provides shortcuts for creating new diagrams and opening existing ones.

Inside Out

New drawing task pane

The New Drawing task pane repeats options that are available in the Choose Drawing Type pane and from the File menu and toolbars, so it might seem redundant. If you prefer not to see the New Drawing task pane press Ctrl + F1 or select View and remove the check next to Task Pane. Then you can use the File menu to choose a drawing type. However, the task pane has other uses. You can use it to display search options for locating files, researching the Internet, or a reviewing pane. To do so click the drop-down arrow on the task pane's title bar, and then select how you wish to use the pane.

Touring the Visio Window

When you first open a new drawing, you see the menus and toolbars across the top, stencils along the side, rulers around the page, and the status bar below. In fact, a great deal of visual information is presented all at once, and much of it has built-in help in the form of Screen-Tips. Pause your mouse over a toolbar button or a shape, and a small box or balloon containing a helpful tip appears, as shown in Figure 1-6.

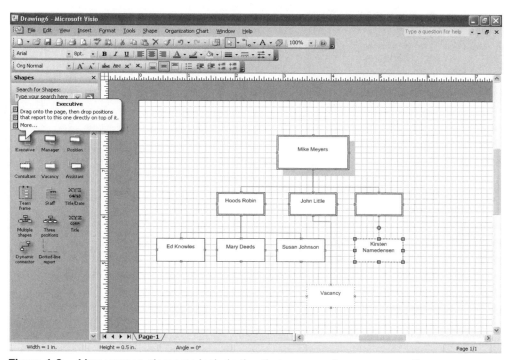

Figure 1-6. Many screen elements include tips that appear when you pause the mouse over an item. A shape's tip describes a shape's purpose.

You can even hover the mouse over a shape for tips on what the shape is and how best to employ it. In fact you can directly access Visio 2003 Help from most shapes by clicking the "More" link in any shape that has one. Doing so opens the help window.

Like other Office programs, Visio displays only the most commonly used commands in the drop-down menus. To see the complete list, point to the double-arrow at the bottom of the menu, and after a moment, the full menu appears. As you use commands, Visio adds them to the menu. To work with the full menus all the time, click Tools, Customize. On the Options tab, select the Always Show Full Menus check box.

Another important element of the Visio window is the status bar located across the bottom of the screen. As you work, changes you make to shapes are reflected on the status bar. For example, in Figure 1-7, the status bar states that the selected shape is 55 feet from the left side of the page, 65 feet from the right side of the page, 39 feet from the bottom, and 49 feet from the top. Note that the default scale in a Visio floor plan is 1" = 10'.

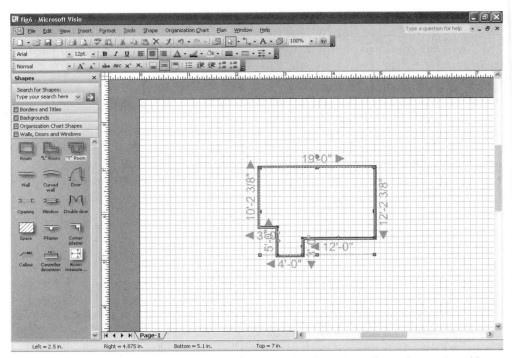

Figure 1-7. As you drag a shape on the drawing page, the status bar tells you its exact position.

Tip Customize the Visio desktop

Stencils don't have to be green, pages don't have to be white, and the page background (or pasteboard) doesn't have to be light blue. To customize any of these colors, choose Tools, Options, and then click the Advanced tab. Under Color Settings, you can choose different colors for stencils, pages, and other objects. Choices you make here change the Visio working environment until you choose different colors. You can also alter color schemes (i.e., the colors of lines, shadows, etc.) by right-clicking in the document page. Select Color Scheme, and then choose your color pattern.

Using the Toolbars for Drawing and Formatting

Many of the most common editing tasks have a shortcut on the Standard and Formatting toolbars that Visio displays by default. The Standard toolbar contains many of the same buttons that you see in other Microsoft Office programs. The Formatting toolbar contains style lists and options for formatting the appearance of text, lines, and fill—the interior color of shapes. You can use the Customize command on the Tools menu to add and remove commands from toolbars so that the shortcuts you use most are at hand.

Visio has a toolbar for most every task. To choose the toolbars you want to work with, click View, Toolbars. A check mark appears beside the toolbars that are displayed. Click to display the toolbar you want. If you want to turn off the display of a toolbar, click a checked toolbar. You can also create a custom toolbar by clicking View, Toolbars, and then Customize. Click the Toolbars tab, select New, and then type a name for the toolbar, and click OK. Add the menu commands you wish, and then close the dialog box.

What if you prefer to display toolbars vertically? You can *dock* and *float* toolbars (and other windows) by dragging them where you want. Toolbars are docked when they are attached to the side of the window. Usually they're docked along the top, but you can drag them to an edge or the bottom of the Visio window. When you float a toolbar midscreen, it displays a title bar, as you see in Figure 1-8.

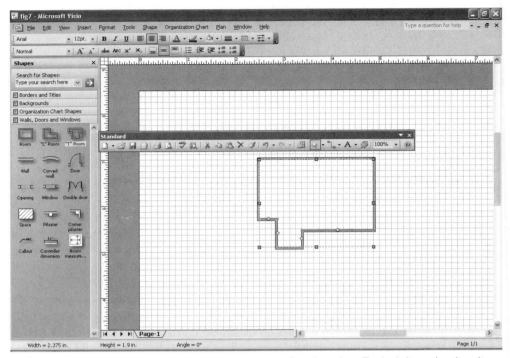

Figure 1-8. You can drag a toolbar to a more convenient location. To dock it again, drag it back to the top, bottom, or side of the Visio window.

Tip To close any Visio window, click the "X" in the upper right corner. To close a stencil right-click its title bar, and then click Close.

Working in the Visio Drawing Page

The quickest way to fill a blank drawing page is to drag shapes onto it. When you start a diagram with a template, Visio typically opens several stencils, which Visio docks on the left side of the screen. To bring a stencil to the top of the stack, click its name. The stencil that was on top is minimized, as Figure 1-9 shows. You can drag an individual stencil window to a new location on the screen, or you can drag the entire Shapes pane and dock it in a new location, as Figure 1-10 shows. To move the stencil back to its original position, drag the Shapes title bar to the left side of the window; Visio automatically docks it against the side of the window. Rather than drag a stencil, you can right-click the Shapes title bar, and then click Float Window. You can resize a floating stencil by dragging a side or corner.

Figure 1-9. To display a stencil, click its name on the stencil window's title bar.

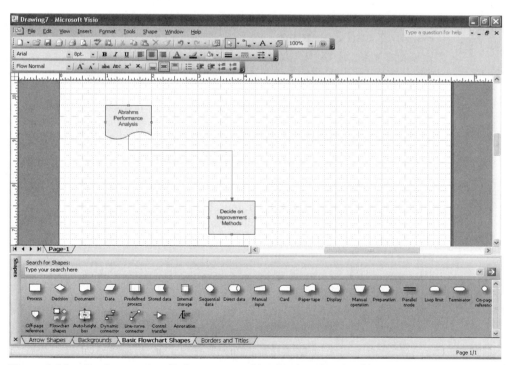

Figure 1-10. Dock your stencils in a new position by dragging the Shapes title bar to the top, side, or bottom of the Visio widow.

Stencils typically display three master shapes across and several down, although you can adjust this arrangement. The term *master shape* (or *master*) is used to differentiate between the shape as it appears in a stencil and the copy of it that you drag onto your page. You can resize the Shapes area to display more or fewer master shapes at a time: point to the border between the Shapes area and the drawing page. The pointer becomes a two-headed arrow, indicating that you can drag the window's right border to resize it.

Troubleshooting

The Shapes window splits the stencil windows in two

Because Visio can dock a window anywhere you drag it, if you inadvertently drag a stencil by its name, it can end up below the other stencils in a separate pane. To dock the stencil with the others, drag it into the middle of another stencil. At lower screen resolutions (such as 800×600), you might find it easier to use a two-step process: Drag the stencil into the middle of the drawing page, and then release the mouse button so that the stencil floats. Then, point to its title bar, drag it back into the Shapes window, and drop it in the middle of the open stencil.

Panning and Zooming

Zoom

To get a good look at a diagram, you can zoom in close or zoom out to see the entire page. When you start a new diagram, Visio displays the full page. If you look at the Zoom list on the Formatting toolbar, you'll see the percentage of zoom. To get a close-up view, click the drop-down arrow on the Zoom list, and then choose a larger percentage. At 100% view, shapes appear on the screen at approximately the same size they appear when printed. Understand, however, the higher your monitor's resolution the smaller the shapes will appear on the screen, but this will have no effect on the printed page.

When you're working in a large diagram, you can use the Pan & Zoom window to see where you are in the big picture, as Figure 1-11 shows. To display this window, click View, Pan & Zoom Window. Visio docks the window alongside the drawing page, but you can move it to a location or dock it with the stencils as you can do with any window in Visio. In the Pan & Zoom window, a red selection box highlights the area currently displayed on the drawing page. You can do the following:

- Drag a side or corner of the red box to resize it, thereby changing the level of zoom on the drawing page.

- Drag to create a new selection box in the Pan & Zoom window, which effectively displays a new area of the drawing page and zooms in.

- Drag the box to display a new section of the drawing page. To do so move your pointer into the box and hold down the left mouse button. When the pointer changes to a four-way arrow you may drag the box.

- Drag the slider on the right side of the Pan & Zoom Window to change to size of the area viewed.

Getting Started with Visio 2003

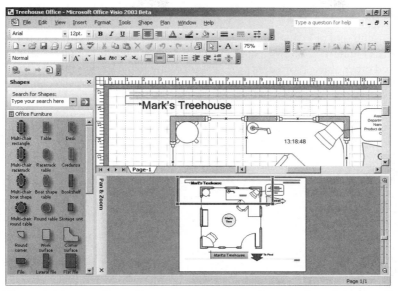

Figure 1-11. In a large diagram, you can get a close-up view of the drawing page by zooming and maintain a bird's-eye view in the Pan & Zoom window.

Tip Use the AutoHide icon (which looks like a pushpin) to allow windows to tuck out of sight when not in use. When you point to the window, it scrolls open again.

Although the Pan & Zoom window is great for providing the big picture, you can also use keyboard shortcuts for moving around a drawing page and quickly zooming in and out as Table 1-2 shows.

Table 1-2. **Keyboard Shortcuts for Panning and Zooming**

Shortcut	Effect
Press Shift+Ctrl+left mouse button	Zooms in
Press Shift+Ctrl+right mouse button	Zooms out
Press Shift+Ctrl+drag with the left mouse button	Zooms in on a selected area
Press Shift+Ctrl+drag with the right mouse button	Pans the drawing page

Note In Visio, the zoom level at which you view and work on a drawing is independent of the scale you set for a drawing page. Whatever your drawing scale, you might still need to zoom in on a portion of a drawing to move shapes exactly or do other precise work. For example, you can change the magnification from 50% to 200%. We discuss setting your page's drawing scale in subsequent chapters, but briefly stated, you may set the scale by selecting File, Page Setup, and then clicking on the Drawing Scale tab.

Microsoft Office Visio 2003 Inside Out

Viewing Shapes and Pages in the Drawing Explorer

Another useful tool in Visio that provides an alternative view of your diagram is the Drawing Explorer, as Figure 1-12 shows. For some diagram types, it helps to see a hierarchical list of shapes and other objects sorted by page. The Drawing Explorer provides this view. To display it, click View, Drawing Explorer Window. In the Drawing Explorer, you can add, delete, and edit items in your drawing. You can even use it to locate shapes—when you click a shape that's listed in the Drawing Explorer, Visio also selects it on the drawing page, making it more visible.

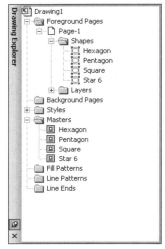

Figure 1-12. The Drawing Explorer provides a hierarchical view of the shapes, pages, and other objects in your diagram.

You can display the Drawing Explorer for any diagram type in Visio. However, some solutions include their own explorer windows for organizing information on the page. For example, a P&ID includes a Component Explorer that works specifically with that solution's shapes. These special-purpose explorer windows are described elsewhere in this book.

Note If you find audible feedback useful, you can have a sound play when a Visio window, such as the Drawing Explorer or Pan & Zoom window, opens and closes. To do this, use the Sounds, Speech, And Audio Devices (in Microsoft Windows XP), Sounds And Multimedia (in Microsoft Windows 2000) or Sounds (in Microsoft Windows 98) option in Control Panel. In the Sound Events or Events box, select Restore Up or Restore Down under Windows. Click the drop-down arrow on the Name box, select a sound, and then click OK. This global change affects all programs. In other words, opening and closing any window will play the sound.

Merging Windows

If you work with drawing types that require the use of several view windows, consider taking advantage of a great feature. You can *merge* windows, such as the Drawing Explorer and Pan & Zoom windows, which means to tuck one window inside another. Visio displays page tabs so that you can switch between windows, as Figure 1-13 shows. To merge windows, drag a window by its title bar into the center of a docked window. You can merge any anchored window, which includes the Custom Properties window, Drawing Explorer window, Pan & Zoom window, Size & Position window, and some template-specific windows. To initially display any of these windows, choose the appropriate command from the View menu.

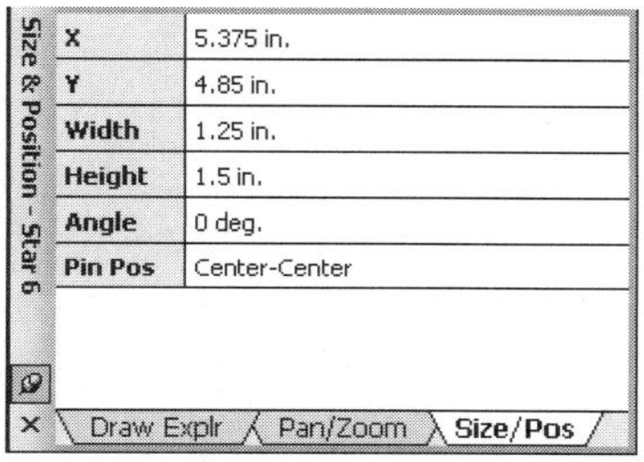

Size & Position - Star 6		
	X	5.375 in.
	Y	4.85 in.
	Width	1.25 in.
	Height	1.5 in.
	Angle	0 deg.
	Pin Pos	Center-Center

Draw Explr / Pan/Zoom \ Size/Pos

Figure 1-13.   To conserve screen real estate, you can merge docked windows.

Tip   **Dock windows**

The Shapes window where stencils are stored is a handy location for docking other windows while you work. For example, point to the title bar of a window, such as the Pan & Zoom window discussed previously. Drag to the Shapes window, and then release the mouse. Visio arranges the window above or below the stencils so that all the tools you work with appear together.

Finding the Information You Need

As you work in Visio, you can display detailed task information in Help and find answers to specific questions by using the Answer Wizard. On the menu bar you can type a question in the Type A Question For Help box, as Figure 1-14 shows. When you press Enter, Visio lists possible topics of interest. If you are connected to the Internet, Visio will also search Microsoft online for answers to your question. When you click a topic, the Help window opens. You can dock it alongside the drawing page or float it on top for greater readability.

Figure 1-14.   Type your question in the Type A Question For Help box on the menu bar and press Enter to start the Answer Wizard.

Using Online Help

There are several ways to display the Help window without going through the Answer Wizard. You can do the following:

- Choose Help, Microsoft Visio Help, and then click the Table of Contents link, as Figure 1-15 shows.

75%

Help

- Click the Help button on the Standard toolbar.

- Press the F1 key.

NEW FEATURE!

- Type your question in the search window of the Task pane.

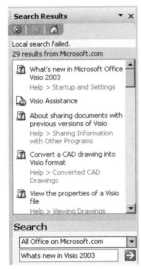

Figure 1-15. You can dock or float the Visio Help window.

You can locate information by searching for a keyword in the Search box, or you can click on the Table Of Contents link to scan topics.

Template Help

For each template, you can get help on the most efficient way to draw, the best way to use and combine shapes, how to perform specific actions using shape and page shortcut menus, how and when to access wizards that automate tasks, and more. To get help on a particular template, press F1, click the Table Of Contents link, and Creating Drawings to expand the list. Expand the drawing type you want, and then choose the type and name of the template you want.

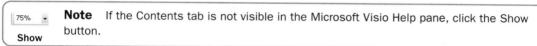

Note   If the Contents tab is not visible in the Microsoft Visio Help pane, click the Show button.

Tip   To display generic information about how to use shapes, right-click a shape, and then choose Help.

Dialog Box Help

If you are in a dialog box and need help, many of them will provide a help button which you can click, as Figure 1-16 shows. The Help pane opens with context-sensitive help—that is, details about each option in the dialog box.

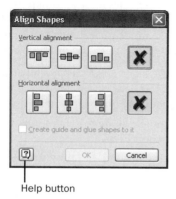

Help button

Figure 1-16.   When you choose a command that displays a dialog box, you can find out what each option does by clicking the Help button.

Sources of Other Information

Questions frequently arise while you work. If typing a question in the Search box doesn't help, try the following Web resources:

- For the latest Visio shapes, you can type a shape title in the Search box of the Shapes pane. It can search a Web-based database of Visio shapes and locate what you need.

- For tips about working efficiently in Visio, see the Microsoft Office Web site (*http://www.office.microsoft.com*).

- For articles about known issues and technical problems, search the Microsoft Knowledge Base (*http://www.search.microsoft.com*).

Information for Network Professionals

If you're using Visio Professional, the Visio Network Center Web site links you to more information about network diagramming tools. Microsoft very much wants Visio Professional users to know about the Microsoft Visio Enterprise NetworkTools add-on, which includes shapes and solutions that ease network documentation. On the Visio Network Center site, you'll find new tools, up-to-date network equipment shapes, and advanced network solutions.

Information for Visio Developers

Visio is a graphical development platform that includes Microsoft Visual Basic for Applications and can be modified using Microsoft Visual Basic .NET. For example, corporations can build business-integrated applications for asset tracking, sales force automation, automated scheduling, data visualization, and so on by integrating Visio with their systems. Although this book is not specifically intended for the developer audience, technical information about Visio development tasks appears in several places in the product and on the Web:

- Programmers and others who want to extend Visio can use the Developer Reference. To display it, click Help, Developer Reference. The Reference includes a complete Automation and ShapeSheet reference and information about programming with Visio.

- *Developing Microsoft Visio Solutions* is the complete guide to creating shapes and programming with Visio. It's available from Microsoft Press.

- The Visio Developer Center (*http://msdn.microsoft.com/visio*) provides technical articles, code samples, and more.

Troubleshooting

Shape names are not readable on stencils

If you display only the shape icons, no text labels appear. To turn on your text labels again, right-click the stencil's title bar. In the shortcut menu that appears, click Icons And Names.

If the problem is that the text is just too small to be read easily, you can try spacing the icons apart more or changing the colors to improve the contrast. The font size of the label itself can't be changed. Click Tools, Options, and then click the View tab. Try adjusting the options under Stencil Spacing as well as the Stencil Text and Stencil Background options under Color Settings.

Opening Visio Documents

In Visio, you can open diagrams, stencils, templates, and workspace files. Each is represented by a different file extension:

- VSD is a Visio drawing file.
- VSS is a Visio stencil file.
- VST is a Visio template file.
- VSW is a Visio workspace file.

75% ▾

Open

Most of the time, you use the Open command or toolbar button to open a drawing file (.vsd). This section focuses on different ways to open diagrams.

> For details about opening and saving Visio files in XML format, see "Visio and XML File Formats," page 616.

Opening an Existing Diagram

Visio includes the same Open dialog box as Microsoft Office (see Figure 1-17), so with the Places bar of shortcuts, you can quickly locate frequently used folders and documents. Not only can Visio 2003 open documents and diagrams created in Visio 2002 and earlier versions of Visio, but Visio 2000 can open diagrams created in Visio 2002 and Visio 2003.

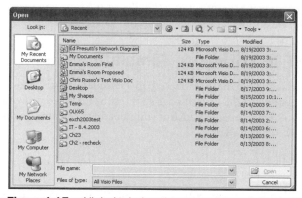

Figure 1-17. Visio includes the same Open dialog box as other Microsoft Office 2003 programs.

To open an existing drawing file, follow these steps:

1 Click the Open button on the Standard toolbar to display the Open dialog box. You can instead choose File, Open or press Ctrl+O.

2 In the Look In list, open the folder that contains the file or files you want to open. Visio displays the folder's contents.

3   Click a file to select it. To open more than one drawing file, press Ctrl and then click the files you want.

4   Click Open.

Opening a Recently Used Diagram

The quick way to find a diagram you worked on recently is to look on the File menu, which lists the most recently opened diagrams at the bottom of the menu. Click the file name to open the diagram. You can also use the New Drawing task pane to locate recently opened files. This is a good technique to use when you're starting Visio, because the Choose Drawing Type pane appears with the New Drawing task pane. If you're working in Visio and want to display it, choose File, New, Choose Drawing Type. In the New Drawing task pane, you'll see the diagrams you've worked on under the Open A Drawing heading. If you don't see the drawing you want listed, click More Drawings. Visio displays the Open dialog box, so you can locate the file you want.

Opening Another Visio File Type

Besides drawing files, Visio can open stencils, templates, workspaces, and files in other formats as well. Choose File, Open. The key is to use the Files Of Type drop-down list that appears at the bottom of the Open dialog box. Click the drop-down arrow to display a list of the types of files that Visio can open. Select a file format. Then, in the Look In list, open the folder that contains the file you want to open. Only the files of the type you selected are displayed, making it easy to locate and select the one you want. Then click Open.

Opening a New Drawing File Without a Template

You can open a new Visio drawing file that's not based on a template. Visio creates a new diagram with a blank drawing page and the default page settings for unscaled drawings. It's like starting with a fresh slate. No stencils are opened, but you can add them later. To do this, click Ctrl+N, or choose File, New, New Drawing.

Opening Stencils

When you want to work with more shapes, you can open additional stencils. There's a practical limit to the number of stencils you can open, although it depends on your screen resolution. The screen can become pretty crowded with more than about seven stencils, and it gets a little tougher to find the particular shape you want. However, you can open as many stencils as you need. The easiest way is to use the Shapes button on the Standard toolbar. If you click the button, a menu of diagram types appears, and you can point to a type to display its stencils, as Figure 1-18 shows.

Figure 1-18. The quickest way to open another stencil is with the Shapes button on the Standard toolbar.

If you prefer working with menus, choose File, Stencils, Open Stencil to display the Open Stencil dialog box, where you can locate any stencil, including ones you create.

Inside Out

Saving your stencils

If you create your own stencils, they will appear on Visio's stencil lists in the Open Stencil button and dialog box if you save them in the right folder. Visio automatically looks for stencil (.vss) files in the C:\Program Files\Microsoft Office\Visio11\1033\Solutions folder and its subfolders.

For details about creating stencils, see "Saving Customized Shapes as Masters," page 619. For details about opening stencils for editing, see "Opening Stencil (.vss) Files," page 612.

Opening Older Versions of Microsoft Visio Files

You can open files created in any previous version of Microsoft Visio Standard, Visio Professional, Visio Technical, or Visio Enterprise, including Visio 1, 2, 3, 4.x, 5.x, 2000, or 2002. To do this, choose File, Open, locate the drawing file you want to open, and then click Open.

Another great feature is that any drawing file you create with Visio 2003 can be opened by other Visio users—regardless of the version of Visio they have. They might not be able to see every drawing element, however. For example, Visio 5 and earlier versions do not include many of the windows on the View menu, such as the Pan & Zoom window.

> **Tip** If you use Windows Explorer to locate a Visio drawing file (.vsd) created in an older version of the product, you can double-click the file name. Visio 2003 automatically opens with the old drawing.

Troubleshooting

Opening a Visio drawing file causes a message about macros to appear

When you open a drawing file that includes a VBA macro, VB .NET macro, or other programming code, Visio displays a message to warn you about its contents, as Figure 1-19 shows. Usually the macros are needed to enable interactive features of the drawing. This message is a new safeguard feature of Visio to protect the user against viruses. If you know that the drawing file came from a reputable source, click Enable Macros. Visio probably requires the macro to run the built-in shape intelligence.

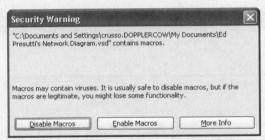

Figure 1-19. If you open a Visio drawing file that includes a built-in macro, as many Visio drawings and templates do, this message appears.

If you frequently open drawing files created in older versions of Visio, you might want to disable the message. This requires lowering your security settings. To do this, click Tools, Macros, Security, and then select the Low security option. Note, however, that this eliminates the virus protection provided by a higher security setting, and could lead to the introduction of harmful viruses into your computer.

Searching for a File to Open

The task pane includes a powerful search tool that you can use to find the files or folders you need without leaving your Visio diagram. You can locate text in a document and find files or folders, regardless of where they are stored—your local hard disk, a network folder, or Microsoft Office Online. To display the task pane, click View, Task Pane. Click the Task Pane's drop-down menu and select New Drawing. The task pane's Search options appear as Figure 1-20 shows.

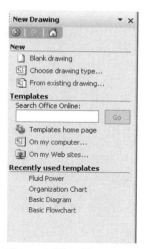

Figure 1-20. The task pane (View, Task Pane) helps you locate documents based on the text they contain.

You can do the following:

● In the Search Text box, type one or more words—text in the document, keywords, or other file properties. Use an asterisk character (*) to replace groups of characters and a question mark (?) to replace a single character. Click Tips For Better Search Results for help.

Tip The more words you type in the Search Text box, the more specific your search results will be.

● Click On My Computer or On My Web Sites to browse the folders on your computer or LAN. You can click Templates Homepage to browse the templates on Microsoft's templates home page.

Opening a File in a Document Management System

If you work with a document management system (DMS) that supports the Open Document Management API (ODMA) standard, you can retrieve and store Visio drawings and diagrams with it. If Visio detects the presence of an ODMA 1.5–compliant system on your computer, you can choose File, Open to open your drawing file, and the DMS Open dialog box appears instead of the Open dialog box. If you use another method of opening your file, such as pressing Ctrl+O, you won't be able to save to the DMS. If the DMS Open dialog box does not appear, you might need to register Visio with your DMS. Refer to the documentation that came with your DMS.

Creating a Diagram

The easiest way to create drawings is to drag master shapes from stencils and drop them on the drawing page. This is called drag-and-drop drawing. If you start your drawing based on a template, the shapes you need are docked on the left side of the Visio window. To assemble your diagram, you add shapes, connect them if necessary, and adjust the layout. To add a professional touch, you can apply quick formatting touches, such as a background or color scheme.

Not all drawings and diagrams go together in this way, but most of the business diagrams do. If you have Microsoft Office Visio Professional 2003 and are creating a floor plan, process engineering diagram, database model, UML diagram, or Web site map, you should refer to the chapters about those diagram types for direction. This chapter describes the fundamental techniques for working with Visio shapes and pages that apply to most diagram types.

Adding Shapes to a Diagram

The fastest way to create a drawing in Visio is to drag a master shape from a stencil onto the drawing page. Dragging means that you point to a shape with the pointer tool, hold down the left mouse button, and then move the mouse. Release the mouse button to drop the shape into place. As you drag, Visio snaps the shape to the nearest grid line. *Snapping* is the subtle tug you feel as you drag a shape. A *grid line* is one of the faint, nonprinting vertical or horizontal lines that Visio displays by default on the drawing page. Together, snapping and grid lines help you align shapes perfectly.

Visio can snap shapes to other objects, and you can control the degree of "tug" Visio uses when snap is active. For details, see "Snapping Shapes for Automatic Alignment," page 436.

Inside Out

Altering your snap settings

Snapping can get in the way of some tasks. For example, if you don't want to align to the grid, or you're trying to draw a freeform curve, you might find it easier to do so if snapping is turned off. Choose Tools, Snap & Glue, clear the Snap check box under Currently Active, and then click OK. While you're in the dialog box, you might also change what your shapes snap to by selecting the appropriate boxes under the Snap To header. To turn snapping back on, reverse the procedure by selecting the Snap check box in the Snap & Glue dialog box. If the Snap & Glue toolbar is visible (View, Toolbars, Snap & Glue), you can do the same thing by clicking the Toggle Snap button.

Identifying Parts of a Shape

When a shape is selected, Visio provides a lot of visual feedback in the form of green squares and circles, yellow diamonds, and blue X's, as Figure 2-1 shows. What are these colorful markers for? In essence, they tell you how the shape works. The important parts of a shape are as follows:

- **Selection handles (the green squares)** When you click a shape, you *select* it, which means that the next action you take applies to the shape. If you see selection handles it means that a shape is selected. You can drag a selection handle to size a shape. Drag a corner selection handle to size it proportionally. (Lines do not have corner selection handles.)

- **Rotation handles (the green circles above most shapes)** You can rotate most shapes in Visio. In other words, you can change their angle on the drawing page. In past versions of Visio this required the Rotation tool, but no longer. Now to rotate a shape you merely need to select the shape, place your cursor over the rotation handle and drag the handle to reposition the angle of the shape.

- **Connection points (the blue X's)** When you connect shapes, connection points tell you where to *glue* connectors and lines. Glue keeps shapes together so that they stay attached when moved. You can add connection points to the inside, outside, or perimeter of a shape, and you can hide them from view (View, Connection Points).

- **Control handles (the yellow diamonds)** Some shapes have built-in intelligence in the form of control handles that you can drag to adjust the shape's appearance. Control handles vary in what they do. For details, see "Control Handles" later in this chapter.

Creating a Diagram

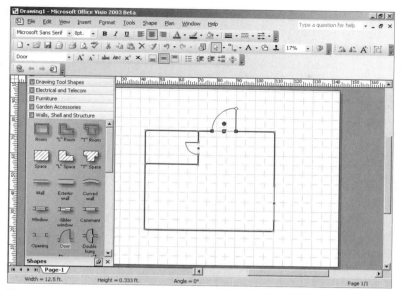

Figure 2-1. The types of handles on a shape indicate how the shape can be used. Not all shapes have connection points or control handles.

Tip Changing the center of rotation

Shapes rotate around their center of rotation. This point is shown as a small green circle within the shape. You can, however, change where this center of rotation is located and thus change the point about which the shape rotates. To do so click and drag the circle to a new location.

Using 1-D and 2-D Shapes

Visio shapes fall into two broad categories (shown in Figure 2-2) that affect how you can move and resize them:

- *1-D shapes* have endpoints and are often used as connectors between two 2-D shapes. They sometimes, but not always, look like lines. You can drag an endpoint in any direction to rotate and stretch the shape.

- *2-D shapes* have up to eight selection handles, including corner handles that you can use to resize the shape.

Chapter 2

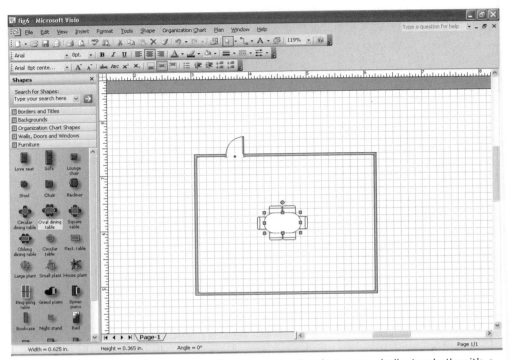

Figure 2-2. When you select a shape, the type of handles that appear indicate whether it's a 1-D or a 2-D shape.

Control Handles

Some shapes have control handles that provide unique editing options. Control handles work differently depending on the design and purpose of a shape. For example, you can use a control handle to move the built-in lines on a Predefined Process shape, change the shadow depth on a 3-D box, or pull a connector directly out of a shape, as Figure 2-3 shows. The way to tell what a control handle does is to pause the pointer over the handle until Visio displays its ScreenTip.

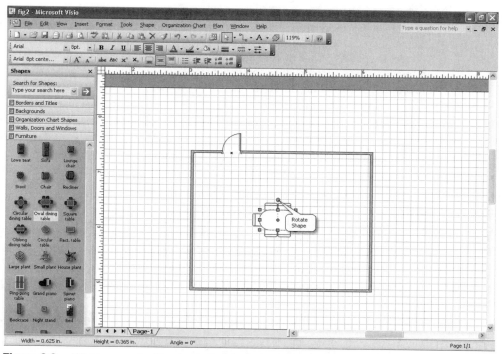

Figure 2-3. When you select a shape that includes a control handle, you can pause the mouse over the handle to display a ScreenTip.

Connecting Shapes as You Add Them

The fast way to assemble any connected diagram, from a flowchart to a network diagram, is to connect shapes as you work. Visio provides several techniques for connecting shapes that make specific drawing tasks faster and the diagram easier to create. Table 2-1 summarizes the ways you can connect shapes. When you connect shapes, you're not just drawing a line between them. You're gluing the shapes so that when one moves, the other goes with it. Visio shows you when you're gluing a connector to a point or a shape—a red box appears around the point or the shape, as Figure 2-4 shows.

Connector tool

You typically use the Connector tool on the Standard toolbar to draw connectors between shapes. *Connectors* are a special type of line that automatically finds the best route between shapes. For example, in a flowchart, if you move a process shape that's connected to a decision shape with a connector, the connector is automatically rerouted. In fact, there's so much intelligence built into connectors that there's an entire chapter about it in this book.

For details about connectors and routing, see Chapter 3, "Connecting Shapes."

Table 2-1. Techniques for Quickly Connecting Shapes

Task	Technique
Connect shapes as you add them to the drawing page	Click the Connector tool, and then drag and drop flowchart shapes. Visio glues the currently selected shape to the last shape dropped on the page.
Connect shapes in an organization chart	Drop a shape on top of the shape it reports to. For example, drop a manager shape on top of an executive shape; drop a position shape on top of a manager shape. Visio creates connectors automatically.
Connect shapes between two specific points	Click the Connector tool, and then drag from the connection point on one shape to a connection point on the second shape. As in the above examples, if you move shapes, the connector reroutes to stay attached to the same two points.
Connect shapes between the closest two points	Click the Connector tool, and then point to the center of one shape until you see a red box around the entire shape. Then click and drag to the center of the second shape until you see a red box around the center of that shape; release the mouse button. As above, if you move shapes, the connector reroutes between the closest two points.

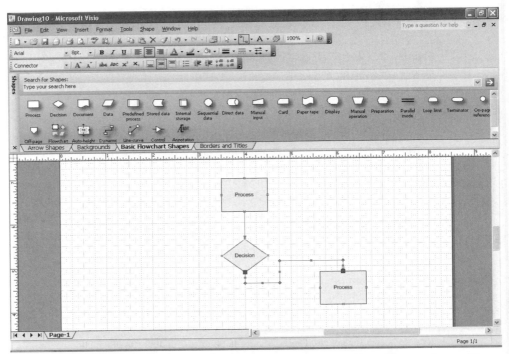

Figure 2-4. You can create connections between shapes or specific points on shapes. The difference lies in how the connector moves when you rearrange the shapes.

Finding the Shape You Want

Dragging shapes from stencils works great as long as you can find the shape you want. What if you don't see the right shape, though? Fortunately, there's a great new tool for locating shapes. In Visio 2002 users could locate shapes using the Find Shape command under the File menu. Now the Shapes window on the left of the screen includes a Search For Shapes text box at the top, as Figure 2-5 shows. Simply type in your search request, press enter, and Visio searches all your installed stencils for shapes based on the keyword that you typed. The first time you conduct a search Visio asks if you would like to use the Indexing Service. If you agree your searches will be faster, but it may periodically degrade your system performance as the computer searches your hard drive and indexes files. If you're connected to the Internet, Visio can look for new Visio shapes on the Web—both from Microsoft and third-party vendors.

Figure 2-5. The Search For Shapes text box lets you search for shapes among the stencils installed on your local hard drive as well as the Web if you're connected to the Internet.

It helps to narrow the scope of your search by typing as many applicable keywords as possible. For example, if you type *bus* as the search word, you'll get dozens of results ranging from the School Bus shape to the Bus Network shape.

Chapter 2

Inside Out

Shape search tips

The Search For Shapes text box searches for shapes based on keywords that are stored with the shapes. If you know a shape's name, it might not be relevant—the name is not necessarily a keyword. You're better off thinking of descriptive terms for the shape you want. In addition, Search For Shapes is very literal and only matches whole keywords based on the exact text you type. So if the plural form of a word does not work, try its singular form. You cannot use wildcard characters.

When you click the green arrow next to the Search For Shapes text box, Visio hunts through the stencils on your hard disk and, if you're connected, on the Web. If it finds shapes that contain the keywords you typed, they're displayed below the text box in the familiar template form (three columns of multiple shapes). The results include an icon and name, as Figure 2-6 shows. To use a shape, drag it from the Find Shapes pane onto your drawing page.

Figure 2-6. The Search For Shapes command displays results in a template-like results pane.

 You can alter how and where Visio searches for the shapes on your computer. Click Tools, Options, and then click the Shape Search tab. Modify your search parameters and then click OK to save the changes and close the box.

Note A Web search locates only those shapes that are intended for Visio product. In other words, if you have Visio Standard, the Search For Shapes command won't locate Visio Professional shapes.

Troubleshooting

Search For Shapes doesn't locate a shape that's used in a diagram

Search For Shapes looks only at the stencils installed with Visio and on the Web. If you want to locate a shape that's in your diagram somewhere, use the Find command on the Edit menu.

Laying Out Shapes on the Page

Pointer tool

To move a shape, drag it. When you point to a shape with the Pointer tool, the pointer changes to a four-headed arrow as Figure 2-7 shows, indicating that you can drag the shape. If you're working in a connected diagram, such as a flowchart or network diagram, you have to be a little more careful about dragging shapes. Depending on the type of shape, you'll see different results:

- If you move a 2-D shape that's connected to other shapes, the shape and everything glued to it are repositioned.

- If you move a connector that's glued to other shapes, you'll disconnect the shapes.

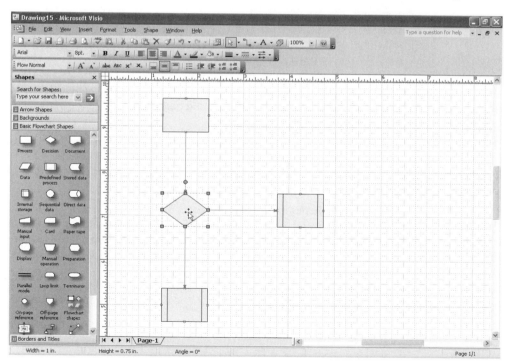

Figure 2-7. When you point to a shape, the pointer displays a four-headed arrow, indicating that you can drag it.

Chapter 2

For some diagram types, it's helpful to know where each shape is located with respect to the entire page. You can see this level of detail in the Size & Position window, as Figure 2-8 shows. To display this window, choose View, Size & Position Window. In the Size & Position window's boxes, you can view a shape's exact dimensions and position, and enter new values as well. The options in this window vary depending on whether you select a 1-D or 2-D shape.

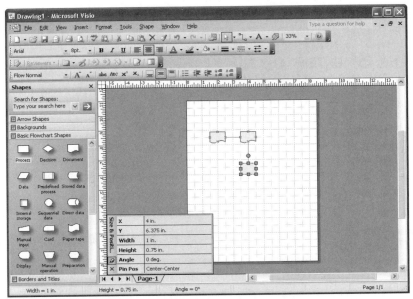

Figure 2-8. For a selected shape, the Size & Position window indicates its exact size (width and height), position (x and y), and angle on the page.

For details about using the Size & Position window, see "Positioning Shapes Precisely," page 436.

Moving Shapes

To help you arrange shapes on the drawing page, Visio includes many layout and alignment tools. In general, only a few prove useful for a given diagram type, which is why there are so many. If you're laying out walls in an office plan, for example, you need different tools than if you're arranging workstation shapes in a network diagram. Table 2-2 summarizes the options.

Table 2-2. Layout and Alignment Tools

Option	What It Does	What It Applies To
Guides	A nonprinting reference line that you drag from a ruler into the drawing window to help position shapes precisely. Click on a ruler and drag onto the drawing page to position a new guide.	Any diagram or drawing
Rulers	The horizontal and vertical rulers around the drawing page. As you move a shape, its position is shown on the rulers, which reflect the drawing file's units of measure. If you don't see the rulers, make sure Rulers is checked on the View menu.	Any diagram or drawing, but especially to-scale drawings
Dynamic grid	Reference lines that appear when you drag a shape near another shape to show you perfect alignment. To display, choose Tools, Snap & Glue. On the General tab, check Dynamic Grid, and then click OK.	Any diagram or drawing
Drawing aids	More advanced versions of the dynamic grid that display geometric reference lines. To display, choose Tools, Snap & Glue. On the General tab, check Drawing Aids; on the Advanced tab, select the aids you want (in the Shape extension options window), and then click OK.	Technical drawings
Lay Out Shapes command	Automatically arranges shapes and routes connectors between them. Choose Shape, Lay Out Shapes to see options.	Conceptual diagrams that are connected, such as flowcharts, organization charts, and network diagrams

Tip Move a shape without resizing it

To make sure you move a shape when you drag it without stretching a side accidentally, make sure the shape is not selected, and then point to the middle. When you see the four-pronged cursor, drag the shape.

If it's a very small shape, zoom in first (press Shift+Ctrl+left mouse button).

Selecting Multiple Shapes

When you want to move an entire row of shapes or apply the same color to several shapes, you can use one of several multiple-selection techniques. The technique you choose depends on whether the shapes you want to select are side by side or scattered across the drawing page. To select several shapes at once, you can use any of the following methods:

- **Shift+click**   Select the first shape, hold down the Shift key, and then click to select other shapes one at a time. Visio draws a box around the group of selected shapes, and each shape is outlined in magenta. You can also select multiple shapes by dropping the menu below the Pointer Tool, choosing the Multiple Select Tool, and clicking on each shape that you wish to select.

- **Drag**   Click the Pointer tool on the Standard toolbar, and then drag a rectangle that encloses all of the shapes that you want to select.

- **Select All**   Choose Edit, Select All to select all the shapes on the page.

- **Select By Type**   Choose Edit, Select By Type, and then check the type of object that you want to select, such as shapes, groups, or guides.

- **Keyboard shortcut**   Press Ctrl+A to select every shape in the drawing.

- **Lasso Tool**   Drop the menu below the pointer tool and select the Lasso tool. Draw the lasso around the area that you wish to select.

To cancel the selection for a shape in a multiple selection, Shift+click the shape.

Tip   **Select multiple shapes**
If you frequently drag a rectangle around shapes to select several at once, you can widen the selection rectangle so that shapes partially within the rectangle are also selected. To do this, choose Tools, Options. On the General tab, click the Select Shapes Partially Within Area check box.

Troubleshooting

A shape cannot be selected

The problem could be that what appears to be a shape is really a group, or the shape could in fact be protected against selection. Sometimes both factors come into play, when a protected shape is part of a group. It's a tricky way for shape designers to prevent you from making changes to a shape when the change could affect how the shape works. Try this: select the shape, and then choose Format, Protection. If the From Selection option is checked, that's the cause of the problem. The From Selection lock prevents you from selecting a shape. Clear the check box, and then click OK.

If that's not the problem, perhaps your shape is a group. Select it, and then choose Format, Special. If the Type field says Group, you've got a group. Click Cancel to close the Special dialog box. Usually, if you click a group once, you select the group. If you click a second time (do not double-click), the shape that's beneath the pointer in the group is selected. Alternatively, you may also edit a group by clicking Edit, Open {Group Name}.

For details about groups, see "Working with Groups," page 668.

Using Stacking Order

Shapes have a *stacking order* on the page that determines which shape appears to be in front, as Figure 2-9 shows. The first shape you draw or drop on the page is at the back of the stack; the most recently created shape is at the front. Stacking order makes a difference when you align and distribute shapes and perform some other tasks. For example, Visio aligns multiple shapes to the top shape. To change a shape's stacking order, choose Shape, Order, and then click the command you want. Table 2-3 describes the Order commands.

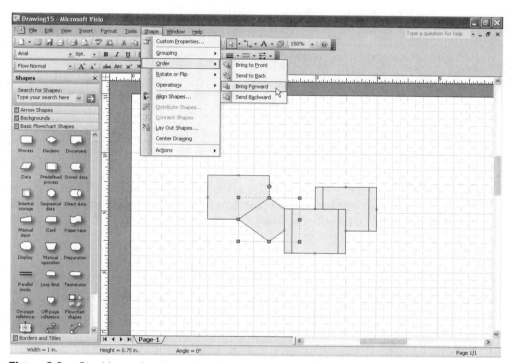

Figure 2-9. Stacking order determines how shapes overlap. To change a shape's order, select it, and then use the Order commands on the Shape menu.

Table 2-3. Changing a Shape's Stacking Order

Order Command	Effect
Bring To Front	Moves a selected shape in front of all others on the page.
Send To Back	Moves a selected shape behind all others on the page.
Bring Forward	Moves a selected shape one step closer to the front of the stacking order.
Send Backward	Moves a selected shape one step back in the stacking order.

For details about the **Align Shapes and Distribute Shapes** commands, see "Aligning Shapes to Each Other," page 449.

Flipping and Rotating Shapes

You can move a shape by rotating it, flipping it across a vertical or horizontal axis, or reversing its ends, as Table 2-4 shows.

Table 2-4. Moving a Selected Shape

Task	Technique
Rotate shape 90° to the left	Press Ctrl+L.
Rotate shape 90° to the right	Press Ctrl+R.
Flip shape vertically	Press Ctrl+J.
Flip shape horizontally	Press Ctrl+H.
Flip a line shape to reverse its ends	Choose Shape, Operations, Reverse Ends.

Tip Nudge a shape

To move a shape a very small amount, you can *nudge* it. Nudging moves a shape one pixel—which might be the very increment you need to straighten out a bent line or get two shapes to align perfectly. To nudge a shape, select the shape, and then press the Up, Down, Left, or Right Arrow key.

Grouping Shapes

Consider grouping shapes that you use together regularly. A group can be formatted, moved, and sized as a single shape, but you can also format and edit the shapes in a group individually. You can group any shapes on the same drawing page, regardless of their distance from each other. To create a group, select the shapes you want, and then press Shift+Ctrl+G. Or choose Shape, Grouping, Group.

When you want to work with the shapes individually, you can *subselect* them. Special selection handles appear around the shape, as Figure 2-10 shows. In general, when you click a group, you select the group. When you click a second time, the shape under the pointer is subselected. Then you can move and format the individual shape without breaking the group. If you do want to break the group association, you can *ungroup* it: select the group, and then press Shift+Ctrl+U; or choose Shape, Grouping, Ungroup.

Creating a Diagram

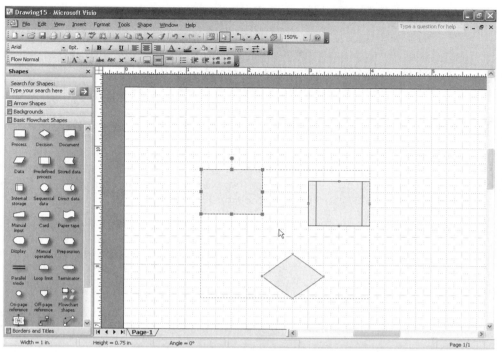

Figure 2-10. When you subselect a shape in a group, Visio displays special selection handles.

 Troubleshooting

Subselecting a shape in a group causes gray box handles to appear

If gray boxes appear around a shape you subselect, it means that the shape is locked against sizing or rotating. However, you might still be able to apply other formats to the shape, such as fill color. If you still can't edit the shape as desired, you have options.

For details, see "Editing Locked Groups," page 673.

Many Visio master shapes are groups, which can be a little deceiving. Perhaps you try to apply fill color to a shape and nothing happens. Is that shape really a group? There is a way to find out. Select a shape, and then choose Format, Special. If the Special dialog box displays Type: Group, you're working with a group. That means you have access to some unique methods for controlling the shapes within the group.

For details about creating and editing groups, see "Working with Groups," page 668.

Editing Multiple Shapes at Once

Visio includes a back door for editing all the shapes in a drawing file that are based on the same master shape. You can make sweeping changes to your diagram by editing just one shape on the *document stencil*, a window in your drawing that contains a copy of each master used on the drawing page. For example, you can change the look of every Manager shape in an organization chart by editing the Manager master shape on the document stencil. To see the document stencil in your drawing, choose File, Shapes, Document Stencil.

Here's the big benefit to anyone who wants to make quick changes: when you edit a master on the document stencil, every copy of that master in your diagram inherits the changes. So, for example, if you change the line style of the Manager master on the document stencil of an organization chart drawing, every copy (or instance) of the Manager shape in your organization chart will be updated with the same line style.

Visio displays the document stencil on top of any other stencil windows you have open, as Figure 2-11 shows. To edit a master shape in the document stencil, right-click the master shape, and then click Edit Master, Edit Master Shape. Visio opens a drawing page window for the master shape, where you can make the changes you want as you would to any shape. When you're done, click the Close Window button on the master drawing page window, and when prompted to update the master, click Yes. You can also right-click on the master shape, choose Edit Master, and choose to edit either the master shape icon or the master shape properties.

> For details about the document stencil and its relationship to the Visio file format, see "Mastering Visio Documents," page 609.

Figure 2-11. Every drawing includes a document stencil that contains a copy of the shapes used in that drawing.

Creating a Diagram

> **Tip** **Format multiple shapes with styles**
> Another timesaving technique for modifying multiple shapes at once is to use styles. If you use styles in Microsoft Office Word 2003 to change the look of your documents, you're a good candidate for using Visio styles, which work much like those in Word. The main difference is that Word styles specify text formats, and Visio styles can specify text, line, and fill formats. You can apply a style to a shape, and then, when you want to change the look of all shapes formatted with that style, you can simply change the style definition. All the shapes that use the style will then be reformatted with the new attributes. For details, see "Understanding Text, Line, and Fill Styles," page 681.

Chapter 2

Adding and Editing Pages

For many diagrams, it's helpful to show details on additional pages or to spread out information across several pages. To add pages to a diagram, choose Insert, New Page. The Page Setup dialog box appears and displays the Page Properties tab. If you simply click OK, you'll create a new page that inherits the settings of the page currently displayed in the drawing window. You don't necessarily have to know more than that until it comes time to print, and that's when it really helps to understand the way that Visio deals with pages. You can review page setup options at any time by choosing File, Page Setup as Figure 2-12 shows. These options affect how much room you have for your diagram and how it will print.

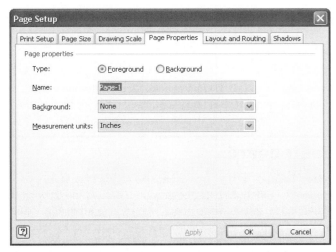

Figure 2-12. When you insert a page, you can give it a name, change its size and orientation, and specify other properties. In a multiple-page diagram, each page can have different properties.

> **Tip** You can also insert a page without using the drop-down menu. Simply right-click on the page tabs at the bottom of the drawing screen and choose Insert Page.

Microsoft Office Visio 2003 Inside Out

If you start your diagram with a template, a number of decisions have already been made for you about the size and orientation of pages. Each page in a drawing file can be sized and oriented differently. When you insert a new page, you can choose its attributes and give it a name, which appears on the page tab at the bottom of the Visio window, as Figure 2-13 shows. To move among pages, click a page tab.

Here's what the three main tabs of the Page Setup dialog box do:

- On the Page Properties tab, you can give the page a name, choose its measurement units, and change the depth of shadows cast by shapes when you use the Shadow command.

- On the Drawing Scale tab, you can set a scale for the page, such as in an office layout, floor plan, or other drawing that represents real-world measurements.

- On the Page Size tab, you can change the page orientation and preview how the page compares with the size and orientation of the paper currently specified for your printer.

The Page Setup dialog box also includes tabs for Print Setup, where you decide how your page will print; Layout And Routing, where you decide how your shapes will be laid out and how connectors will route; and Shadows, where you set the parameters for how shadowed shapes will display shadows.

> For details about setting up a drawing scale, see "Setting Up Measurements in a Diagram," page 421.

Figure 2-13.   When you insert a page, you can change its size, its orientation, and other properties. In a multiple-page diagram, each page can have different properties.

About the Pasteboard

If you've ever used a page layout or design application like Adobe PageMaker, you might be familiar with the concept of a pasteboard. It's the gray area around the drawing page. In Visio, you can use this area as useful storage space when you're arranging shapes on the page. Each page has its own pasteboard. You can drag shapes to the pasteboard that you want to keep around but don't want to print or use just yet in a diagram. You don't hear much about the pasteboard in Visio, but it's useful nonetheless.

Adding, Rearranging, and Removing Pages

You can work with the page tabs to quickly add pages, change their order, or remove pages you no longer need. Table 2-5 summarizes the techniques.

Table 2-5. Adding, Rearranging, and Removing Pages

Task	Technique
Add a page	Right-click a page tab, and then click Insert Page. Choose settings in the Page Setup dialog box, and then click OK to insert a new page after the one that's displayed.
Remove a page	Right-click the page tab for the page you want to remove, and then click Delete Page.
Rearrange pages	Right-click any page tab, and then choose Reorder Pages. In the Page Order box, select a page, and then click the Move Up or Move Down button to change its order in the list. Click OK.

Tip Add pages in Drawing Explorer

You can also add a page in the Drawing Explorer. If the Drawing Explorer is not visible, choose View, Drawing Explorer Window. Right-click the Foreground Page folder or Background Page folder, and then choose Insert Page, which opens the Page Setup dialog box and displays the Page Properties tab.

Using Background Pages

Each Visio drawing or diagram contains at least one page: its *foreground* page. A drawing might also contain one or more *background* pages. You can assign background pages to other pages in the Page Setup dialog box. A background page appears behind another page, like the bottom page in a stack of transparencies. Whatever's on the bottom shows through on the top page. In Visio, a background page can include borders, titles, company logos, or other shapes that you want to reuse, as Figure 2-14 shows. What's especially convenient is that you can assign one background page to more than one page so that the shapes on the background page show up in as many of your drawing's pages as necessary.

Chapter 2

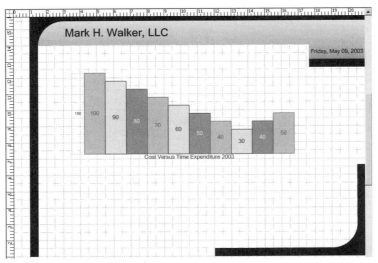

Figure 2-14. You can use a background page for consistent design elements, such as a logo, that appears on multiple pages of a drawing file.

Follow these steps to create a background page and assign it to a foreground page:

1 Right-click a page tab, and then click Insert Page.

2 On the Page Properties tab, click Background. In the Name box, type a name for the background page, and then click OK.

3 Display the page to which you want to assign the background, and then choose File, Page Setup.

4 Click the Page Properties tab. In the Background box, click the drop-down arrow to display the list, select the name of the background page you just created, and then click OK.

Resizing Pages

You can use the Page Setup command to change the size of a drawing page, but there's a satisfying, visual method of resizing pages by dragging that's worth checking out. This method is especially useful when you need to quickly enlarge the page to fit a diagram that's expanded. When you resize a page, you're changing the size of only the drawing page on display. In a drawing file with several pages, you have to resize each page separately.

Dragging to Resize a Page

Zoom

To resize a page by dragging, click the Pointer tool on the Standard toolbar. Zoom out so that you can see the whole page. For example, in the Zoom list, click Page. Point to an edge or near corner of the drawing page, and then press the Ctrl key so that a double-headed arrow appears, as Figure 2-15 shows. Now you can drag the page edge to the desired size. If you want to verify the size of the page you've just created, you can glance at the rulers or choose File, Page Setup, click the Page Size tab, and then see the results. If you place the cursor too

Creating a Diagram

close to the page's edge the rotation cursor appears. Don't panic, just slide your cursor down the edge of the page until the double-headed arrow cursor appears, and then resize the page.

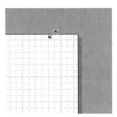

Figure 2-15. You can drag any edge of the drawing page to resize it. You must press the Ctrl key while you drag.

Tip If you watch the ruler as you drag, you'll see a dotted line that shows you the page size.

Specifying the Page Size

You can specify an exact page size by choosing File, Page Setup. Click the Page Size tab, shown in Figure 2-16. You can use a predefined size, type a custom size, or choose Size To Fit Drawing Contents, which automatically adjusts the page size to fit your diagram. Click OK to apply the settings.

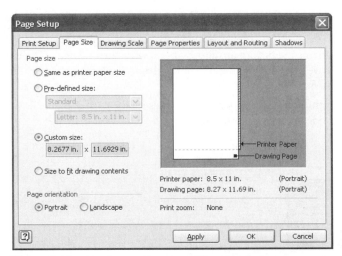

Figure 2-16. To change the size of the drawing page, use the Page Size tab of the Page Setup dialog box.

Note Changing the page size can affect the way your diagram prints. For details, see "Printing Diagrams of Any Size," page 242.

Microsoft Office Visio 2003 Inside Out

Rotating Pages

Just as you can drag to resize a page, you can drag to rotate a page. The difference is primarily in the tool you use. In most business diagrams, there's no particular reason to rotate a page. The feature is really intended for technical drawings, where it's often useful to provide alternative views of an image. For example, in an architectural design, you might want to see your plan in an orthogonal view (that is, displayed at a 90-degree angle). You can do this by rotating the page. All rotation does is move the page with respect to the rulers.

Before you rotate a page, zoom out so that the entire page is visible. In the Zoom list on the Standard toolbar, choose Page.

You used to need the Rotation tool to turn a drawing, but now, to rotate a page move the Pointer tool to a corner of the page and press and hold Ctrl. The cursor changes into the rotational indicator. Click and hold the left mouse button and drag the corner in the direction in which you want to rotate the page.

Tip   Move the ruler's zero point

Visio rotates a page around its *zero point*, which is the lower left corner of the page. However, you can move the zero point by pressing Ctrl as you drag the blue crosshair at the ruler intersection. For details, see "Changing the Zero Point," page 432.

Quickly Formatting Shapes and Diagrams

When you think about what makes up a shape's format, it helps to understand the following two attributes of a shape (shown in Figure 2-17):

- Its *line*, which forms the border around 2-D shapes or the line of a 1-D shape. You can change the line weight (its thickness), color, pattern (such as dashed or dotted lines), and line end (such as an arrowhead).
- Its *fill*, which is the color and pattern of a shape's interior. Of course, a 1-D shape such as a connector doesn't have an interior.

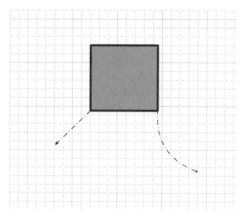

Figure 2-17.   The square is a 2-D shape formatted with a fill pattern and thick line weight. The lines are 1-D shapes formatted with line ends and patterns.

You can format individual shapes to change their appearance, or you can change the look of an entire diagram all at once with timesaving formatting tools. For example, you can apply an attractive background and border to your diagram, as Figure 2-18 shows. The following sections describe other techniques for quickly formatting shapes and diagrams.

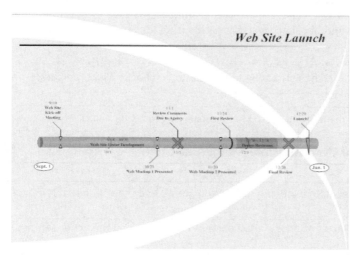

Figure 2-18. You can format individual shapes or use backgrounds, borders, and color schemes to format entire diagrams at once.

Inside Out

Creating Line and File Patterns

Can't find the pattern you need? You can create your own. For example, many technical diagrams require industry-standard line and fill patterns to convey information.

For details, see "Creating Your Own Line and Fill Patterns," page 693.

Formatting with the Formatting Toolbar

One way to change the way a shape looks is to select the shape and then select an option from the Formatting toolbar, shown in Figure 2-19. The Formatting toolbar contains more tools than might be apparent at first glance. Some buttons include a drop-down arrow that indicates a list of additional formatting options. If you click the drop-down arrow on the button, you'll see the options. If you click the button, you'll apply the last format that was selected.

Figure 2-19. You can quickly change text, line, and fill attributes for shapes with the tools on the Formatting toolbar.

For example, to make the connecting lines of a network diagram thicker, select a line, and then click the drop-down arrow on the Line Weight button to display a drop-down list of line weight options. Click the one you want to apply to the selected shape.

Format Painter

To format several shapes at once, select all the shapes you want to format, and then format them as you would any shape. For sample techniques, see Table 2-6. You may also copy a shape's format to another shape (or shapes) by using the Format Painter button on the Standard toolbar.

> **Tip**   If you don't see the Formatting toolbar buttons, choose View, Toolbars, Formatting.

> For details about formatting with styles, see "Understanding Text, Line, and Fill Styles," page 681.

Table 2-6. Formatting Multiple Shapes at Once

Task	Technique
Format all the shapes in a group	Select the group, and then choose a format, such as line or fill color.
Format several shapes at once	Select all the shapes, and then choose the format you want them all to have.
Quickly repeat formatting	Format one shape, select other shapes, and then press F4.
Copy a shape's format to another shape	Select a formatted shape. Click the Format Painter button on the Standard toolbar. Click a shape to paste the format.
Copy a shape's format to several shapes	Select a formatted shape. Double-click the Format Painter button on the Standard toolbar. Click each shape to which you want to copy the formatting. To stop formatting, click the Format Painter button again or press Esc.

> **Tip**   Hide shape borders
>
> If you don't want the edges of a shape to stand out, you can remove its border (in Visio terms, its line). To do this, select the shape, click the drop-down arrow on the Line Pattern button on the Formatting toolbar, and then choose No Line. Or use the Line command on the Format menu.

Chapter 2

Troubleshooting

A shape cannot be stretched or resized

If you select a shape and gray box handles appear, the shape has been protected against resizing. The shape might be designed specifically not to resize because it's based on an industry-standard size. Or the shape might include a custom property that you should use to resize it. If this is the case, right-click the shape, choose View, Custom Properties to display the Custom Properties dialog box, and see whether there are options for changing the shape's size. You might also want to right-click on the shape, then select Format, Protection to see the shape's enabled protections.

You can remove locks by using the Protection command on the Format menu or by right-clicking as just described. Just be aware that a shape might not interact correctly with other shapes if you remove its locks. Usually they are there for a reason. However, you can always press Ctrl+Z to reverse the effects of your action if the results aren't what you expected.

Troubleshooting

A shape won't accept formatting

There could be several reasons for this problem. Try these solutions:

- **Is the shape a group?** Select it, and then choose Format, Behavior. If the Group Behavior options are available (not dimmed), you've got a group. Groups have special formatting behavior. Typically, you can subselect a shape in a group, and then apply a format, such as fill color, to that shape only. For details, see "Editing Shapes in a Group," page 671.

- **Is the shape locked?** Visio shapes can be protected against formatting. When you try to apply a style to a protected shape, you might see an error message or you might see nothing at all. For details, see "Formatting Locked Shapes," page 687.

Formatting with the Format Commands

Sometimes it's easier to format shapes with the commands on the Format menu. In the Line and Fill dialog boxes, you can apply several formats at once, which can be more efficient than clicking one toolbar button after another. To see line formatting options, select a shape, and then choose Format, Line. The Line dialog box appears, as Figure 2-20 shows. When you format a line, you can change its line pattern, such as dotted or solid; line weight, or thickness; color and transparency; line cap, making the ends rounded or square; and line ends. Line ends are a little tricky in that you have to remember which end of the line is the beginning (the handle with the ×) and which is the end (the handle with the +). You can also round shape corners.

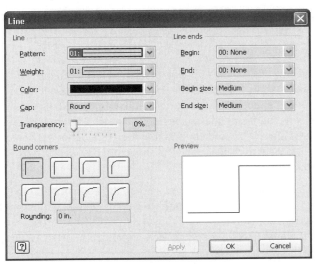

Figure 2-20. To apply multiple line attributes at once, use the Line dialog box, which lets you preview the effect of an option.

To see fill formatting options, select a shape, and then choose Format, Fill. The Fill dialog box appears, as Figure 2-21 shows. If you choose a pattern, the Pattern Color options become available so that you can choose the color that applies to the pattern alone. The Color options apply to the area behind the pattern. You can also apply a shadow to a shape in the Fill dialog box. The depth of a shape's shadow is a function of the page properties, which means that all the shapes on a page have the same shadow depth. To change it, choose File, Page Setup, and then click the Page Properties tab to see the Shape Shadow Offset option.

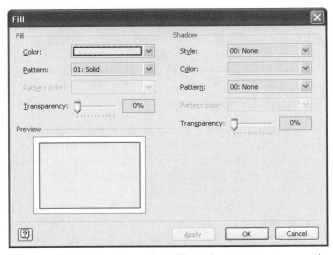

Figure 2-21. To apply multiple fill attributes at once, use the Fill dialog box.

Chapter 2

> **Tip** **Reverse the direction on arrow points**
>
> If you apply an arrowhead or other line end to a line and it points the wrong way, you can quickly remedy the situation by reversing the line's ends. To do this, select the line, and then choose Shape, Operations, Reverse Ends. When you select a line, you see its endpoints, which indicate its beginning and end and tell Visio which way to apply line ends. The beginning endpoint is marked with an ×. The ending endpoint (for lack of a better expression) is marked with a +.

Working with Color Schemes

The quickest way to add overall polish to a business diagram is to apply a *color scheme*. Visio includes several schemes of coordinated colors that you can apply automatically to all the shapes in your diagram. For example, you can apply the Coffee color scheme to a flowchart to instantly update all the shapes with different shades of brown and tan. To apply a color scheme, right-click on a page and select Color Schemes to display the Color Schemes dialog box, as Figure 2-22 shows. Choose a scheme and click Apply to see the results. If you don't like the colors, choose a different scheme, and then click Apply again. When you find the one you like, click OK.

> **Note** If you don't see the Color Schemes command, you're working in a diagram that is not designed to support color schemes. If you drag a shape from another drawing that does not support color schemes on to one that does, they might not display the color schemes properly.

Figure 2-22. The Color Schemes dialog box lets you apply a set of coordinated colors to an entire diagram.

> **Tip** You can press Ctrl+Z to undo the results of the Color Schemes command and return to the colors you had before.

You cannot apply a color scheme to some drawing types. Color schemes are intended for use with business diagrams, such as flowcharts, organization charts, timelines, and calendars. Most of the technical diagram types in Visio Professional do not support color schemes. The following templates include shapes that are designed to work with color schemes:

Audit Diagram	Calendar	Marketing Charts And Diagrams
Basic Shapes	Cause And Effect Diagram	Organization Chart
Basic Flowchart	Charts And Graphs	PERT Chart
Basic Network	Cross-Functional Flowchart	SDL Diagram*
Block Diagram	Data Flow Diagram*	Timeline
Block Diagram with Perspective	Gantt Chart	TQM Diagram
Brainstorming Diagram	IDEF0 Diagram*	Work Flow Diagram

* Available in Visio Professional

Even if your diagram type does not support color schemes, you can still use the Tools, Color Palette command to make numerous colors available in a drawing. This technique gives you a varied palette for even the advanced software, engineering, or database diagrams of Visio Professional.

> For details about how Visio works behind the scenes when a color scheme is applied, see "Working with Color in Visio," page 706.

⚙ Troubleshooting

The Color Schemes command is missing or nothing happens when a color scheme is applied

The Color Schemes command appears when you right-click only when you're working in a diagram type that supports color schemes. Otherwise, you can choose Tools, Color Palette to add colors to a diagram, but the shapes in the diagram won't automatically take on the color scheme.

Color schemes are designed primarily to work with business diagrams. The Color Schemes command has no effect on shapes in office layouts, directional maps, and most of the engineering, network, software, and database shapes specific to Visio Professional.

Applying Transparent Colors

Transparent colors are a great formatting option in Visio. Lines, fills, and even text can have transparent color so that objects beneath show through. The trick is to use the commands on the Format menu—the toolbar buttons apply only solid colors. Select a shape, and then choose Text, Line, Fill, or Shadow from the Format menu. A Transparency slider adjusts the level of transparency for the color selected in the Color box, as Figure 2-23 shows. You can use the slider, or type a number in the box, such as 50 for 50 percent transparency—the higher the percentage, the more transparent the color.

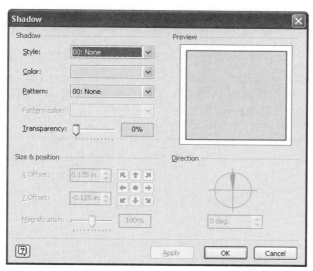

Figure 2-23. Like the Fill, Line, and Text dialog boxes, the Shadow dialog box includes an option for making a shape's color transparent.

 Inside Out

Setting shape shadows

Transparent colors are especially useful for creating shadows behind shapes. You can apply a shadow to a selected shape with either the Fill or Shadow command on the Format menu. To change the amount of shadow that appears, choose File, Page Setup; click the Page Properties tab; and then specify the amounts in the Right and Down boxes for Shape Shadow Offset.

Adding Backgrounds and Borders

You can add a background to your diagrams for instant polish. When you drop a background shape onto a diagram, Visio fills the background of the page with an attractive design.

If the Backgrounds stencil is not open, click the Open Shapes button on the Standard toolbar, and then click Visio Extras, Backgrounds. Drag a shape from the Backgrounds stencil onto your page. Visio automatically adds a background and sizes the background shape to fill the entire page.

 Inside Out

Background shapes create background pages

Technically, Visio inserts a new background page when you add a background shape to a foreground page, applies the background shape to it, and then assigns the background page to your current foreground page. That's why you might notice a new page tab after using a background shape—it's for the new background page.

Connecting Shapes

With Microsoft Office Visio 2003 drawings and diagrams you can communicate all sorts of information about ideas, processes, organizations, layouts, and even buildings. And as you've already seen, the basic building blocks you use to create your drawings are the shapes provided on Visio stencils. Connectors are drawing elements that indicate why the shapes are there and what they are doing. Shapes and connectors together give the complete picture. Connected drawings are meaningful drawings.

The previous chapter introduced a few of the methods for connecting shapes. This chapter provides an in-depth look at connectors so that you can revise connected drawings more easily and take advantage of the automated layout features in Visio.

Adding Connectors to Your Diagrams

There are about as many ways to connect shapes in Visio as there are types of Visio drawings. Most drawing types have their own unique visual language, and you'll find a multitude of connectors and connector behaviors in Visio that are meant to accommodate the needs of each drawing. Visio even includes an entire stencil that contains nothing but connectors.

Despite the variety of connectors, most are nothing more than a line that attaches to one shape at one end and another shape at the other end. For example, in a flowchart, the connector is the line that goes from a process shape to a decision shape, as Figure 3-1 shows. In a network diagram, the connector is the line that connects a printer to a hub. In the first case, the line represents the order in which you do things. In the second case, the line represents an actual network connection. In both cases, the connection tells us something important about the relationship between two shapes. In some drawings, such as database and software model diagrams in Visio Professional, connectors actually trigger the transfer of data between the shapes they are connected to.

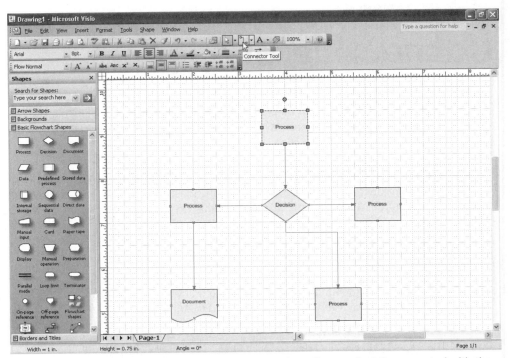

Figure 3-1. Connectors provide additional flexibility in a diagram that lines created with the Line tool don't.

Using Connectors and the Connector Tool

In Visio, the terms *connector* and *1-D shape* are almost synonymous. Whatever term you use, connectors exist so that you can attach lines to 2-D shapes in Visio. To put it simply, a connection happens when you drag an endpoint of a 1-D shape onto a connection point of a 2-D shape. The two ends of a connector aren't interchangeable—as with any line, there's a beginning and an end, and Visio stores information about which is which, in essence giving the line directionality.

Both 1-D and 2-D shapes provide visual cues that show you where connections can be made (before you connect) and what type of connection has been made (after you connect). On a 2-D shape, each point at which a connection can be made is marked with a connection point, the blue ×. On a 1-D shape, the ends are marked with square endpoints, which you see when the shape is selected.To help show the direction of the connection, the two endpoints on a 1-D shape are different, as Figure 3-2 shows. The *begin point* of a 1-D shape has a × symbol inside the square. The *end point* has a + symbol inside the square. Either endpoint can be attached to any connection point on a 2-D shape.

> **Tip** If a shape's connection points aren't visible, select Connection Points on the View menu.

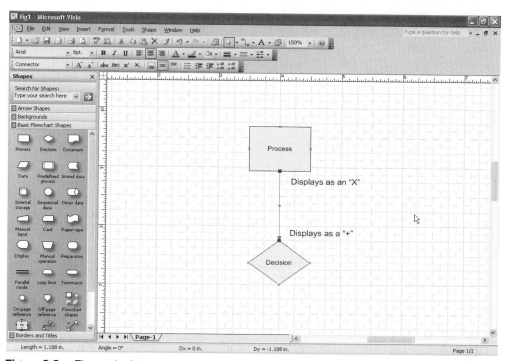

Figure 3-2. The endpoints on connectors are designed to connect to the connection points on 2-D shapes.

Connectors and other types of 1-D shapes are the only shapes that have begin and end points. The begin and end points provide visual feedback that a connection has been established, but they also indicate direction. Think of it this way: if your connector had an arrowhead on it, which way would it point, and why? When you add connectors to a drawing, connect or draw them so that they match the order of your shapes—attach the begin point to the first shape, and attach the end point to the next shape.

Using the Connector Shapes on Stencils

When you start a drawing with a template, Visio opens stencils containing the appropriate shapes and connectors for the drawing type. Many of the basic connector shapes—such as the Dynamic Connector and Line-Curve Connector shapes shown in the stencil in Figure 3-3—appear on multiple stencils to make them easy to find. You can use these shapes in any Visio drawing. Other stencils contain specialized connectors with advanced features and behaviors that support a specific drawing type.

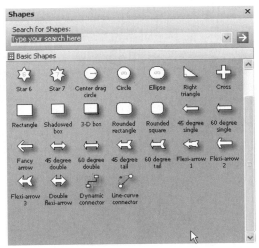

Figure 3-3.   Visio includes the Dynamic Connector and Line-Curve Connector master shapes on many stencils, because they work in any drawing type to connect shapes.

Follow these steps to use any connector shape on a stencil:

1   Drag the connector shape from a stencil onto the drawing.

2   Drag an endpoint of the connector to a connection point on a shape.

3   Drag the other end of the connector to a connection point on another shape.

 Tip   Pause your pointer over a connector shape on a stencil to find out what it does. You can also click the More link in the information box to call up general help on shapes and connectors.

Drawing Connectors with the Connector Tool

**Connector
Tool**

The Connector tool works like a drawing tool in that you can select it and then draw connectors between shapes. However, the connections you draw are smarter than plain old lines. Depending on how you position the tool as you drag, you can connect to a specific connection point on the shape or to the whole shape to create a *dynamic connector*—the same as the shape on a stencil. The difference in how you draw with the Connector tool affects the way you work with shapes afterward, as follows:

● If you connect to a point, Visio makes sure the connector remains attached to that specific point when you rearrange shapes. This type of connection is called *point-to-point* or *static* and is appropriate in electrical wiring schematics, logic diagrams, or any diagram where a specific point has meaning.

● If you connect to the whole shape, Visio can move the connector to a different point when you rearrange shapes. This type of connection is called *shape-to-shape* or *dynamic* and is suitable for workflows, Gantt charts, or other conceptual diagrams.

Connecting Shapes

Follow these steps to use the Connector tool to manually draw connections between shapes:

1 Drag the 2-D shapes you want in your drawing onto the page, and then move them into position.

2 Select the Connector tool on the Standard toolbar, and then create a point-to-point or shape-to-shape connection as follows:

- For a point-to-point connection, position the Connector tool over a connection point on the first shape. When a red square appears around the point, drag to a connection point on the second shape.

- For a shape-to-shape connection, position the Connector tool over the center of the first shape until you see a red border around the entire shape. Drag to the center of the second shape.

When you release the mouse, Visio displays red handles to show that the shapes are connected. The handles differ in appearance depending on the type of connection, as Figure 3-4 shows.

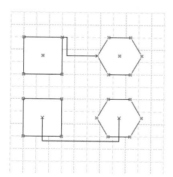

Figure 3-4. The shapes on top have a point-to-point connection. The shapes on the bottom have a shape-to-shape connection.

Drawing Specific Connectors with the Connector Tool

With the addition of one step, you can use the Connector tool to create any sort of connector that appears on a stencil. By default, when you connect shapes using the Connector tool, you create a dynamic connector. However, you can use the Connector tool in tandem with a connector shape on a stencil to draw that shape instead.

67

Follow these steps to use the Connector tool to draw a different connector type:

1   Drag the 2-D shapes you want in your drawing onto the page, and then move them into position.

2   Select the Connector tool on the Standard toolbar.

3   Click once on a connector master shape in the stencil window. For example, click the Line-Curve Connector shape.

4   On the drawing page, draw a connector from shape to shape as described in the previous procedure.

    The tool draws the type of connector you selected on the stencil instead of the default dynamic connector.

> **Tip**   As long as the Connector tool remains selected on the Standard toolbar, shapes you drag from the stencil to the drawing page will be connected automatically.

Changing the Type of Connection

If you need to change the point to which a connector is attached or change the type of connection altogether, you can do this by disconnecting and reconnecting shapes: simply drag the glued endpoint slightly away from the shape to disconnect it, and then drag the endpoint back over the shape's center to reattach as a shape-to-shape connection or to a particular connection point to reattach as a point-to-point connection.

> **Tip**   Create a shape-to-shape connection
> One way to ensure that you're creating a shape-to-shape connection is to hold down the Ctrl key as you drag an endpoint (or the Connector tool) over a shape. This technique is handy for connecting shapes that are small or complex or for shapes that have a connection point in the center area.

Troubleshooting

Shapes won't stay connected, and the handles don't turn red

The basic technique for connecting shapes is to drag the endpoint of a connector to a connection point on a 2-D shape. Dragging the entire connector or line might result in a connection if the endpoint comes near a connection point. However, dragging a 2-D shape over to the connector won't work. Some shapes that look like connectors are really 2-D shapes. Make sure you're using a 1-D shape with a begin point and an end point as a connector.

> **Note** You might notice that the Stamp tool, which is used to duplicate images on your page, has been removed from the Connector drop-down menu. You can display it by clicking Toolbar Options, Add Stamp Tool.

Dragging Connectors from Shapes

Some shapes include a connector built into the shape, such as the Ethernet shape in a network diagram and the tree shape shown in Figure 3-5. You can drag a control handle on the shape to pull a connector directly out of the shape and attach it to another shape. With these shapes, you can move only one end of the connector; the other end is already attached to the shape.

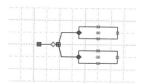

Figure 3-5. Some shapes, such as the Multi-Tree Sloped shape on the Blocks stencil, have control handles with connectors that you can attach to other shapes.

 Inside Out

Control handle tips

Control handles are your clue that a shape does something special—but you generally can't tell what that is just by the shape's appearance. A control handle might configure a curve, reposition a text block or other component, or associate a shape with another shape. When you see a control handle, pause your pointer over it to display a ScreenTip about what it does.

Connecting a Series of Shapes All at Once

When you want to create shape-to-shape connections throughout a diagram, let Visio connect shapes for you. You can use the following technique for enormous layout flexibility, because it works well with the automated tools described in the next section. To connect a series of shapes, select them one by one in the order you wish to connect them. For example, select shapes from top to bottom or from start to finish. Once the shapes are selected, choose Shapes, Connect Shapes.

Laying Out Shapes Automatically

Many of the drawing types in Visio incorporate automated layout behavior so that you don't have to manually rearrange connectors and shapes. For example, the dynamic connector can route itself around shapes that get in the way and find the best point to connect to shapes. It will also jump over other connectors that cross it. At some point, you will probably encounter the results of the built-in layout and routing behavior—which behaves logically for the most part, but yields surprising results occasionally. Understanding how layout and routing works will make your drawings easier (and more fun) to revise.

The language for describing this behavior is a little peculiar. For example, almost all shapes can be detected by connectors and "routed around." In Visio-speak, shapes with this attribute are called *placeable*, which means simply that Visio recognizes they are there and tries to route lines around rather than through them. The route that a connector can take varies depending on whether you create point-to-point or shape-to-shape connections, as Figure 3-6 shows. Most of the time, when a connector has extra bends or seems to have taken a circuitous route to a shape, the explanation lies with the type of connection that Visio is trying to preserve.

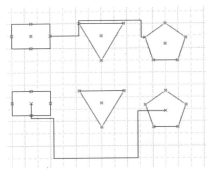

Figure 3-6. To maintain a point-to-point connection, a connector must bend to avoid the triangle. With a shape-to-shape connection, the connector can move.

Here's how can you ensure good results when connecting shapes:

- Create shape-to-shape connections whenever possible.
- Make sure the begin point and end point on a connector align with the direction of the diagram you're creating.
- Make sure that endpoints are properly connected. When you select a connector, its endpoints turn red if they're connected to another shape.

Tip You can alter the routing of connectors by clicking on a connector's handle. Drag the handle where you wish the connector to route, and there you have it: a rerouted connector.

Setting Up Shapes for Automated Layout

The shapes provided on the stencils for connected drawing types are already set to perform automatic layout and routing tasks. When you attach a connector to a 2-D shape, Visio makes that shape placeable by default, which means that as you move shapes, connectors can take the best new route to the shape. You can enable and disable placeable status for any shape you create by using the Placement tab in the Behavior dialog box, as Figure 3-7 shows.

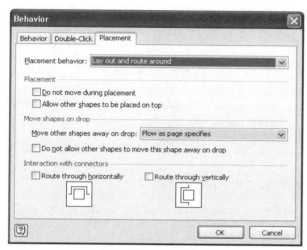

Figure 3-7. To control a shape's layout behavior, select the Lay Out And Route Around option, and then specify the settings you want.

Follow these steps to access the placement settings for any shape:

1 Select a 2-D shape, and then choose Format, Behavior.

2 Click the Placement tab.

3 To disable placement behavior, select the Do Not Lay Out And Route Around option in the Placement Behavior list. Otherwise, select Lay Out And Route Around to make the following options available:

- **Placement** Select Do Not Move During Placement to prevent a shape from moving at all when you use the Lay Out Shapes command. Select Allow Other Shapes To Be Placed On Top to allow Visio to place other shapes on top of the selected shape, if need be, during automatic layout.

- **Move Shapes On Drop** Use this option to specify a shape's *plow* behavior, which controls how a shape reacts to the proximity of other shapes. As the name suggests, you can use this setting to allow a shape to plow all other shapes out of its way when it's placed near them, or if they get too close.

- **Interaction With Connectors** Use these check boxes to allow connectors to route straight through a shape (either horizontally or vertically), rather than around them.

Chapter 3

71

Note You can make a shape immune to the plow settings of another shape by selecting the Do Not Allow Other Shapes To Move This Shape Away On Drop check box. Shapes for which this option is set don't move when other shapes are dragged onto the page, regardless of the other shapes' settings.

Troubleshooting

All the options are unavailable on the Placement tab in the Behavior dialog box

If you select a 1-D shape or connector when you choose the Behavior command, the options on the Placement tab are unavailable, because only 2-D shapes are placeable. Connectors, by contrast, are routable. If you select a 2-D shape and the options are still unavailable, see which option is displayed in the Placement Behavior box. If Let Visio Decide is selected, all the other options are unavailable. Choose Lay Out And Route Around to make the rest of the options available.

Setting Layout Style, Depth, and Routing

With the Lay Out Shapes command, you can rearrange the shapes on your page in a completely new layout style and vary the spacing between shapes. For example, you can easily flip a vertical flowchart to change a top-to-bottom style to a bottom-to-top orientation, as Figure 3-8 shows.

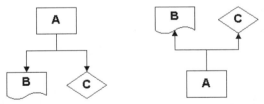

Figure 3-8. With the Lay Out Shapes command, you can change the placement style for an entire diagram.

You can change the placement and connector styles separately for a diagram. Placement options affect the way Visio can lay out 2-D shapes. Connector options specify the style and direction of lines used between shapes. In theory, the combination of placement and connector options provides an enormous variety of layout styles, from tree to radial to circular patterns. In practice, only a few settings are relevant for a particular diagram type. For example, the radial placement style works well only for diagrams with connectors that have no implied direction, as in some network drawings. For best results, use the same placement and connector direction. In other words, don't mix a vertical placement direction with a horizontal connector direction. The results might be awkward.

To set the layout and routing style for a diagram, choose Shape, Lay Out Shapes. As you make selections in the Lay Out Shapes dialog box, the preview gives you an idea of the intended outcome, as Figure 3-9 shows. However, the results on the drawing page can vary depending on the direction of your connectors and whether your shapes use point-to-point or shape-to-shape connections.

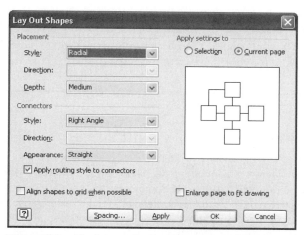

Figure 3-9. To change the layout, depth, and routing style in a connected diagram, choose Shape, Lay Out Shapes.

In the Lay Out Shapes dialog box, you can set the following Placement options:

- **Style**   Select an option to place shapes in a radial, circular, or traditional flowchart/tree pattern.

- **Direction**   Select an option to orient shapes from top to bottom, bottom to top, left to right, or right to left. Specifically, the shape at the begin point of a connector is placed in a position relative to the shape at the end point.

- **Depth**   Select an option to fit a number of shapes optimally on the page. Specifically, Depth refers to the number of levels (as in a hierarchy) of a diagram. Choose Shallow to group shapes well, even if that means taking up more space. Choose Deep if space is tight. Medium is the compromise setting between the two. If you have few shapes, or extra space on the page, you might not see a difference between these settings.

To customize the routing behavior of connectors, you can choose the following Connectors options in the Lay Out Shapes dialog box:

- **Style**   Select an option to determine the path connectors take between shapes. Although some styles are associated with a particular drawing type, you can select any style you like.

- **Direction**   Select an option to change where connectors attach to shapes. For example, choose Left To Right to attach connectors to the left and right sides of 2-D shapes. In most cases, this setting should match the Placement Direction setting.

Chapter 3

73

- **Appearance**   Use this setting to specify straight or curved connectors.
- **Apply Routing Style To Connectors**   With this option you can apply settings to all the connectors on your page. Clear this check box to change shape placement options without affecting the connectors.
- **Align Shapes To Grid When Possible**   Select this check box to lay out shapes and route connectors at regular intervals based on the settings in the Layout And Routing Spacing dialog box.
- **Enlarge Page To Fit Drawing**   Select this check box to allow Visio to increase the page size if the optimal layout for your shapes requires more room.

Inside Out

Undoing unwanted shape layout

If you're unclear about the effect a particular combination of placement and connector options might have on your diagram, you're not alone. Shape layout involves many variables, which makes it difficult to predict the exact outcome of the Lay Out Shapes command. Even people who have used Visio for years usually recommend an experimental approach to the Lay Out Shapes command—try an option, see what it does, and then press Ctrl+Z (Undo) if you don't like the results. Note that the preview box gives an indication of the results of your selection, but you never know exactly how it will look until you apply the results.

Customizing Shape Spacing and Connector Routing

When you work in a multiple-page diagram, you can specify different layout and routing settings for each page. The Lay Out Shapes command works in combination with a page's settings to control the way shapes and connectors are displayed. You can adjust the shape spacing and the connector routing to control Visio's behavior with more finesse.

Adjusting Shape Spacing

If you want to crowd more shapes on a page or provide more space between connected shapes than Visio does by default, you can adjust shape spacing. Shape spacing comes into play when your diagram includes placeable shapes. Only placeable shapes move in response to the Lay Out Shapes command. To set spacing options for a page, choose File, Page Setup. On the Layout And Routing tab, click Spacing to display the Layout And Routing Spacing dialog box, as Figure 3-10 shows. Table 3-1 describes each option.

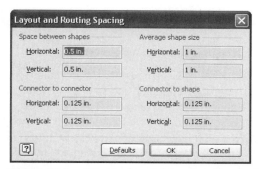

Figure 3-10. Use the Layout And Routing Spacing dialog box to adjust horizontal and vertical spacing for shapes and connectors.

In earlier versions of Visio, the spacing options are called *block size* and *avenue size* because of the way they specify a map-like grid. Shapes are like city blocks, and the routes a connector can take when you use the Lay Out Shapes command are the avenues. It might help to envision blocks and avenues when you adjust the settings in this dialog box.

Table 3-1. Layout and Routing Spacing Options

Option	Description
Space Between Shapes	Specifies the amount of space between placeable shapes when you use the Lay Out Shapes command.
Average Shape Size	Determines the "block" that Visio uses to calculate optimum shape layout and the placement of reference lines when the dynamic grid is displayed.
Connector To Connector	Specifies the minimum amount of space between parallel segments of connectors.
Connector To Shape	Specifies the minimum amount of space between connectors and shapes.

Tip   If your drawing contains shapes of various sizes, you might need to experiment with the average shape size. If your shapes vary significantly, using a smaller average shape size could yield better results.

Chapter 3

Troubleshooting

The Lay Out Shapes command doesn't lay out certain shapes in the diagram

Only placeable shapes respond to the Lay Out Shapes command. If you create your own shape, and it isn't placeable, the connectors can't detect it and so won't route around it. To make any shape placeable, select the shape, choose Format, Behavior, and then click the Placement tab. For Placement Behavior, select Lay Out And Route Around. This setting enables the shape to take part in Visio's automatic layout and routing features. You can clear this check box for any shape to prevent connectors from routing around it.

Adjusting the Connector Path Manually

If a connector takes one too many bends in its route through your diagram, you can adjust its path. A dynamic connector includes vertices on each corner (marked with a green diamond) and a midpoint on each segment (marked with a small green square with a darker green × in it), as Figure 3-11 shows. To change the position of a line segment, drag a vertex or midpoint.

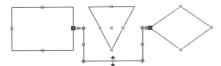

Figure 3-11. To change the path of a connector, drag a vertex or midpoint.

Note Some Visio connectors, such as the Line-Curve Connector, have a yellow control handle in the middle of a segment. The control handle provides another way to change the connector's path. On a Line-Curve Connector, the control handle adjusts the curvature of the line.

Displaying Line Jumps on Crossing Connectors

Where connectors cross in a diagram, you can specify the style of *line jump* that Visio uses, such as the arc shown in Figure 3-12. Line jumps make it easier to see the route a connector takes. To accommodate the needs of different business and technical drawing types, Visio includes several styles of line jump, including gap, square, and multisided options. You can customize the look of line jumps for all the connectors in your diagram or for an individual connector.

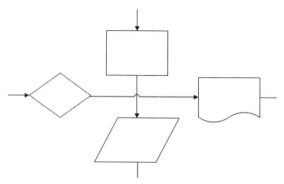

Figure 3-12. You can specify whether Visio displays a line jump where connectors cross.

Follow these steps to specify the line jump style:

1 Do one of the following:

   ■ To specify the style for the entire diagram, choose File, Page Setup, and then click the Layout And Routing tab.

   ■ To change an individual connector, select the connector, and then choose Format, Behavior and click the Connector tab.

2 Under Line Jumps, select an option from the Style list.

3 Click OK.

Adding Connection Points to Shapes

A connection point on a shape shows where you can glue connectors. You can add new connection points to any shape, whether it's a Visio shape or one you have created yourself. You can also move an existing connection point to another location on the shape. Perhaps the most difficult part about adding and moving connection points is finding the tool you want. The Connection Point tool is stashed below the Connector tool, as Figure 3-13 shows.

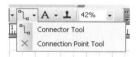

Figure 3-13. The Connector tool appears at the top of the list by default, but if you choose the Connection Point tool, Visio places it on the toolbar.

Tip   When you hold down the Ctrl key, the Connection Point tool displays a small blue crosshair symbol, which can help you pinpoint an exact location on your shape.

Follow these steps to move an existing connection point:

1 Click the Connection Point tool on the Standard toolbar.

2 Click any connection point on a shape. (Don't use the Ctrl key.) The connection point turns magenta to show that it's selected.

3 Drag the selected connection point to a new location on the shape. For exact placement, watch the status bar, which displays the pointer's position.

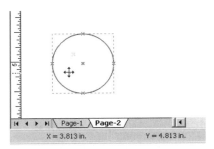

Using Different Types of Connection Points

In some connected drawings, it's more common to glue 2-D shapes to each other than to join them with connectors, and in many technical drawings, connection points provide meaningful information about the objects or components they connect. For example, in a piping and instrumentation diagram, an indicator on a signal includes different types of connection points, as Figure 3-14 shows. To support a variety of connection behavior, Visio offers three types of connection points in all. Unless you're creating your own shapes and require sophisticated connection behavior, you can ignore connection point types. Visio shapes are already designed to connect correctly.

Figure 3-14.   The indicator shape includes both inward (marked with an ¥) and outward (marked with a square) connection points.

So why bother with different types of connection points? They can tell you something about a diagram's contents. In a diagram that represents a physical system, such as the pipes and valves in a processing plant, you want the shapes to mimic the constraints in the real world. Some components receive connections, and others initiate them. Visio tries to duplicate this information with the different types of connection points. Here's what they mean:

- **Inward connection points** An *inward* connection point (the default type you create with the Connection Point tool) pulls the endpoints of 1-D shapes in toward itself to make a connection. It also pulls in and connects to an *outward* connection point, but it won't be attracted to another inward connection point. This type of connection is marked by the familiar blue × you see on most of the shapes in Visio Standard.

- **Outward connection points** An *outward* connection point looks like a small blue square and reaches out to attach to an *inward* connection point on another shape. This type of connection point can be used to make a point on a 2-D shape attach to an inward connection point on another 2-D shape. However, two outward connection points won't join to each other.

- **Inward and outward connection point** An *inward and outward* connection point acts as a sort of universal connection point. It is used on shapes to allow them to connect to any other connection point, in any direction. The symbol for this connection point looks like an outward connection point on top of an inward connection point—which, in effect, is what it is.

Changing Connection Point Type

When you add a connection point to a shape, you create an inward connection point by default. However, you can use the connection point's shortcut menu to change its type, as Figure 3-15 shows.

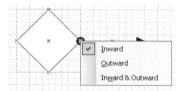

Figure 3-15. You can change the type of connection point on a shape.

To change the type of a connection point on any shape, click the Connection point tool on the Standard toolbar. Now you can right-click a connection point (it turns magenta), and then choose Inward, Outward, or Inward & Outward.

Changing the Angle of Connection

When you connect shapes at their connection points, Visio connects the shapes end to end, with their edges flat against each other. What if you want shapes to connect at an angle to each other? You can set the *angle* property for a connection point to rotate shapes when they are connected. This technique represents an advanced option primarily intended for shape designers who want to create shapes that automatically create appropriate connections.

By default, the angle of most connection points, and any connection points you add yourself, is set to 90 degrees. For example, if you have a corner desk shape and a work surface shape, you want the angle of their connection points to be 90 degrees so that the ends connect at an angle. However, shapes can connect at any angle you specify. If your company likes annotations to be rotated to 30 degrees, for example, you can design shapes that include a rotated connection point angle.

Follow these steps to change connection point angle:

1 Choose Tools, Options, and then click the Advanced tab.
2 Select the Run In Developer Mode check box, and then click OK.
3 Click the Connection Point tool.
4 Click the connection point (it turns magenta) to display a rotation arrow, and then drag the arrow to the angle you want, as Figure 3-16 shows.

Figure 3-16. When you run in Developer mode, a rotation arrow appears when you select a connection point.

Controlling Connections with Glue

Glue is what keeps connectors attached to shapes. When a connector is glued to a shape, Visio displays the connector's endpoints in red. By default, Visio can glue shapes to guides and 1-D shapes and connectors to connection points. However, you can prevent Visio from connecting shapes with glue, and you can specify other points where Visio can glue shapes, with the options in the Snap & Glue dialog box, as Figure 3-17 shows. For example, you can also glue connectors to the edges of a shape.

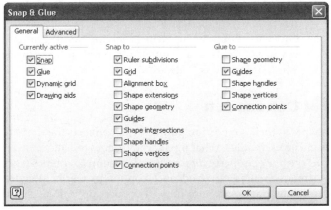

Figure 3-17. Choose Tools, Snap & Glue to control the glue settings that Visio uses when you connect shapes.

Follow these steps to prevent Visio from connecting shapes with glue:

1 Choose Tools, Snap & Glue.

2 Under Currently Active, clear the Glue check box.

3 Click OK.

Follow these steps to specify where Visio can glue shapes:

1 Choose Tools, Snap & Glue.

2 Under Glue To, select the options you want from the following:

- **Shape Geometry**   Select this check box to glue 1-D shapes to any point on a shape's edge.
- **Guides**   Select this check box to glue 1-D and 2-D shapes to guides.
- **Shape Handles**   Select this check box to glue 1-D shapes to the selection handles on another shape.
- **Shape Vertices**   Select this check box to glue 1-D shapes to the vertices on another shape.
- **Connection Points**   Select this check box to glue 1-D shapes to the connection points on another shape.

> **Note**   The options you specify in the Snap & Glue dialog box affect all the pages in your drawing file.

Glue in the ShapeSheet Window

In case you want to create your own shapes or are just curious, Visio records the type of glue that's used in the GlueType cell of a connector's ShapeSheet. Glue type corresponds to the connection type. For example, a point-to-point connection uses point-to-point, or static, glue. A shape-to-shape connection uses dynamic glue. When you reconnect shapes using a different type of connection, you change the value of the GlueType cell. A value of 0 means static glue; a value of 3 means dynamic glue.

Chapter 3

Adding Text to Shapes and Diagrams

Microsoft Office Visio 2003 was designed with the idea that any shape can have text, and all you do to insert that text is click and type. Text appears attractively formatted exactly where you need it. In theory, you should never have to think much about text in Visio except to consider what you want to say. Visio takes care of the rest.

In practice, most people spend a lot of time formatting and positioning text in their diagrams, because most diagrams contain a lot of text. In this chapter, *text* refers to lists, labels, notes, callouts, legends, tables, titles or title blocks, and so on. Visio includes many shapes that are specifically intended for adding formatted text to a diagram. For example, title block shapes on the Borders And Titles stencil make it easy to add preformatted titles to a diagram, and callout shapes are great for annotating a diagram.

Still, you'll probably find yourself wanting to adjust the built-in formatting of a shape's text, or maybe you can't find an existing shape to use for your purpose. Maybe you just want to understand why Visio doesn't work like Microsoft Word, or why some shapes don't obey the usual click-and-type rule. This chapter provides the details you need to work with text in Visio.

Adding Text

Although some shapes have special behavior, you can usually add text to any shape by selecting the shape and typing. You don't even have to choose the Text tool first to add text to a shape. Visio always places the text you type in a shape's *text block*. The text block might be on top of, beside, or below the shape, but it is part of the shape nonetheless, as Figure 4-1 shows.

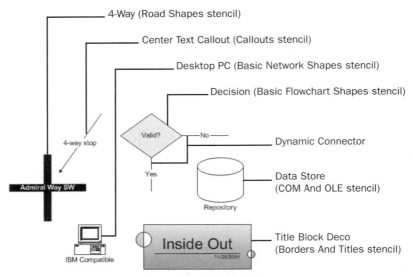

4-Way (Road Shapes stencil)

Center Text Callout (Callouts stencil)

Desktop PC (Basic Network Shapes stencil)

Decision (Basic Flowchart Shapes stencil)

Dynamic Connector

Data Store
(COM And OLE stencil)

Title Block Deco
(Borders And Titles stencil)

Figure 4-1. These built-in shapes position and format text appropriately—centered on the shape, below the shape, and so on. To add text to a shape, select the shape, and then type.

In general, to type text in any shape, follow these steps:

1 Select a shape.

2 Start typing.

   Visio zooms in to show you the text you're typing at 100 percent view. If you misspell or type a word that Visio doesn't recognize, the word appears with a wavy, red underline.

   Don't worry if you type more text than the shape can contain. You can adjust the shape size, text block size, or font size later.

3 When you're finished, press the Esc key, or click outside the text block.

> **Tip** When your goal is to add text, it doesn't matter which tool you use to select a shape—the Pointer tool, the Text tool, or a drawing tool.

How Visio Fits Text to Shapes

Visio doesn't place limits on the amount of text you can type in a shape's text block. The nice thing about this feature is that you can keep typing and worry about formatting later. If the text doesn't fit, you can do any of the following:

**Pointer
tool**

● Resize the shape to encompass the text. To do this, click the Pointer tool, click the shape, and then drag a selection handle.

Text Block tool

- Move the text block out of the way of the shape. To do this, click the Text Block tool, click the shape, and then drag the text block to a new position.

- Format the text using a smaller font. There are several ways to do this, but the quickest is probably to select the shape, and then choose a smaller value from the Font Size list on the Formatting toolbar.

Later sections in this chapter provide details about formatting and resizing text and text blocks.

To disable automatic zooming and the spelling checker as you type, follow these steps:

1 Choose Tools, Options, and select the General tab of the Options dialog box.

2 To turn off text zooming, in the Automatically Zoom Under box, type 0.

3 To turn off the spelling checker, click the Spelling tab, and then clear the Check Spelling As You Type check box.

4 Click OK.

Troubleshooting

Text appears smoother than in Visio 2000, but it's not as legible at different zooms

When you zoom out to see more of your page, text in the diagram might not be legible, even if the same text was legible at that zoom when viewed in Microsoft Visio 2000. New Visio users who need to see the entire drawing page at a time might wonder why it's so hard to read text at all. For example, perhaps you want to use the 50 percent zoom so that you can see more of a flowchart at once, yet still be able to read the text in your shapes.

A couple of factors are responsible. Visio uses a display technology called GDI+ that enhances font resolution on the screen by smoothing curves and edges with a technique called anti-aliasing. You can disable text anti-aliasing behavior, which makes text look the way it did in Visio 2000 and might make your text more legible when you zoom out. To do this, select Tools, Options. Click the View tab, and then select the Faster Text Display (Aliased) option.

Chapter 4

Visio includes a third text option on the View tab of the Options dialog box. You can now also choose Clear Type Text Display. This is best used for computers with LCD displays such as laptops.

Note Unlike Microsoft Word, Visio does not include grammar checking.

Troubleshooting

When you type in a shape, Visio zooms in so that the text is legible, but then when you work in the drawing, you can't read the text anymore

Let's say that you're using 12-point Arial text in your shapes. If you're used to working in Word, you know that 12-point type is plenty big enough to read. And it seems very readable when you first type in Visio until you click away and display the entire drawing, when the text is no longer big enough to read.

Zoom

What's happening is that Visio automatically zooms to show you your shape at 100 percent size when you type in it, which means that your 12-point type looks like 12-point type. When you click away from the shape or press Esc, Visio returns to the magnification that you were using for your drawing. If you just started your diagram, Visio is probably displaying the full page so that you can see all of your drawing, but at this zoom level, 12-point text is not legible. You can use the Zoom list on the Standard toolbar to zoom in and out in your drawing to see shapes and text up close. Regardless of the zoom level, when you print your diagram, that 12-point type will be printed at exactly that size.

Using the Text Tool

You can type anywhere on a page when you use the Text tool. For example, if you want to type a note in a diagram, you can select the Text tool, click where you want the text to appear, and then start typing, as Figure 4-2 shows. You can also drag with the Text tool to create a text block in the size you want.

A ▾

Text tool

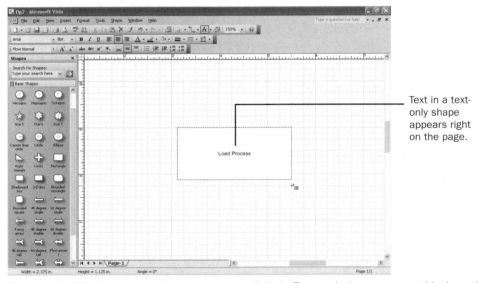

Text in a text-only shape appears right on the page.

Figure 4-2. To add text anywhere on a page, click the Text tool, drag out a text block, and then type. The text wraps as you type according to the width of the text block you dragged.

Inside Out

Text-only shapes

When you use the Text tool to type on the page, you are in fact creating a shape—a *text-only shape*, also referred to as independent or freestanding text. This technical detail explains in part why the way you add and edit text in Visio is different from other Microsoft Office programs. In addition, you can format text-only shapes like other shapes. Although a text-only shape has no line or fill by default, you can add them by selecting the text-only shape, and then choosing an option from the Formatting toolbar, or by right-clicking the shape and selecting Format, Fill or selecting Format, Line to change the border.

To add text anywhere on a drawing page, follow these steps:

1 Click the Text tool on the Standard toolbar.

2 Drag on the drawing page to create a text block of the size you want.

3 Start typing.

Visio zooms in to show you the text you're typing at 100 percent view.

4 When you're finished, press the Esc key, click the Pointer tool, or click outside the text block.

Visio creates a text-only shape and formats your text using the default settings. Unless you change these settings, the default format is centered, Arial, 8-point text.

Tip To center text on a page easily, click the Text tool, drag to create a box the width of the drawing page, and then type. Visio centers the text within the text box, so if the box is the width of the page, the text is centered horizontally within the page.

Understanding Text and Text Blocks

When you add text to a shape, the text always appears in a text block. However, the size, shape, and location of a text block can differ from those of its shape. In other words, the text block's geometry and position do not have to conform to the shape it's in. This is a really powerful idea, because it gives you complete control over where text appears in relation to a shape.

Text Block tool

If you want to see a shape's text block, click the Text Block tool, and then click the shape. If you draw a shape, its text block has the same boundaries as the shape itself. For example, let's say you draw a rectangle. If you select the rectangle and then start typing, text appears centered in the rectangle pretty much as you'd expect. The rectangle's text block occupies the same area as the rectangle. However—and this is pretty cool—it doesn't have to appear this way. You can move, resize, and rotate a shape's text block without affecting its shape. You can even drag the text block outside of the shape. The text remains part of the shape, but its location in relation to the shape is up to you, as Figure 4-3 shows.

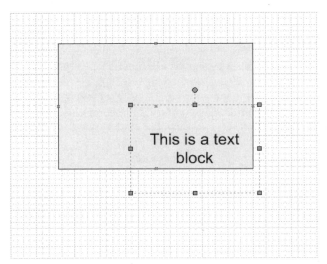

Figure 4-3. When you select a shape with the Text Block tool, Visio displays selection handles for the text block alone, which can differ in size, shape, and location from its shape.

Text Tools Explained

If you're used to working in a word processing program like Microsoft Word, you may find Visio's text behavior a little surprising. Here are a few fun facts about Visio text tools that you can take advantage of:

- As noted previously, it doesn't matter which tool you use to select a shape when you want to type text in it. If you've been drawing ellipses, you can keep using the Ellipse tool if you like, and then click a shape and start typing.

- When you select a shape with any tool other than the Text tool and start to type, your new text automatically replaces the existing text.

- If you click a shape with the Text tool, Visio places an insertion point (a blinking I-beam cursor) in the text.

- You can also select a shape and press F2 to begin typing text.

If a shape already includes text and you want to add more, or select parts of the existing text, it's easiest to use the Text tool or select the shape and then press F2.

Inside Out

Sorry, one per customer

Despite appearances to the contrary, a shape can have only one text block. If you see a Visio shape that looks like it has more than one text block, such as a Title Block shape with a name and date, you're probably looking at a group.

When you use the Text tool to type on the page, the text is automatically placed in a shape without lines or fill—in other words, a text-only shape. Because a text-only shape is still a shape, you can format it, and its text block, as you would any other shape. You can even add lines or fill.

Some unlikely Visio objects turn out to have text blocks, as Figure 4-4 shows. For example, connectors and other 1-D shapes have text blocks, which allows you to add text to line, spline, arrow, or callout shapes. Even guides and guide points can have text. (Try it—drag out a guide, and while it's still selected, start typing.)

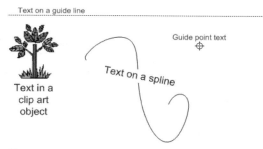

Figure 4-4.   Many objects in Visio can have text, including guide lines and guide points.

Viewing Text Blocks in the ShapeSheet Window

Just as a shape has width and height values that you can view and change in the Size & Position window, a shape's text block has width, height, and other properties that you can see in the ShapeSheet window. When you use the Text Block tool to move, rotate, or resize a text block, Visio records your actions in the cells of the Text Transform section. Most people need never display the ShapeSheet window, but shape programmers can take advantage of this architecture to write formulas that control text behavior. For example, one common type of text formula prevents a text block from moving or rotating when a callout shape is stretched. The text remains right side up regardless of the direction in which the line points.

For an introduction to ShapeSheet formulas, see "Writing ShapeSheet Formulas," page 740.

Chapter 4

Troubleshooting

Is there a way to distinguish "model space" text from "paper space" text as some CAD programs can do?

Visio doesn't display text the same way as CAD programs do. Text is displayed in your drawing using its printed size. When you zoom in and out, text looks larger and smaller, but only the view, not the text size, is changing. Changing the drawing scale also has no effect on text size, which is always measured in the real-world units of the printed page.

Understanding Text in Groups

Many Visio shapes are really groups, and often they contain text that you can customize. For example, many of the title block shapes in the Borders And Titles stencil are groups. Typically, groups work the way you expect them to, and text is added in an appropriate format and location. You don't have to think about it—except when you do. Maybe you see text on a shape that you want to change, but can't figure out how to get at it. In times like these, you've probably encountered a group. With a little background information about how groups handle text, you can better predict the text behavior of existing Visio groups.

Groups associate shapes in a unique manner that you can take advantage of in your own diagrams. For example, if you want a way to keep blocks of text together, and yet format each block differently, you should create a group. You create a group by selecting Visio objects, and then choosing Shape, Grouping, Group. Because the group itself is a separate object with a text block, it can have text. Each shape in the group can also have text. And each shape's and group's text can be formatted differently. In this way, you can have multiple text blocks in an object that appears to be one shape, as Figure 4-5 shows. You can subselect shapes in the group to type text in them. Only a group can have more than one text block, as you see in Figure 4-5: one for the text area and one for the title.

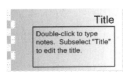

Figure 4-5. The Note Box shape from the Borders And Titles stencil is really a group.

To see a group's text block, select the group, and then press F2. Visio opens the group's text block. To type in one of the group's shapes, subselect the shape, and then type. Sometimes a group has been protected so that you can't add text to it. It's safe to assume that the shape designer had a good reason for locking the shape, but if you want to add text such protection can be frustrating. Fortunately, there are workarounds for this issue. For example, you can use the Text tool to create a text-only shape containing the text you want, drag it into place atop the group, and then group the text and the group. Or you can try to bypass the protections.

For details, see "Editing Shapes in a Group," page 671.

Tip How can you tell if you're typing in a group? Select the shape, and then choose Format, Special. You'll see Type: Group in the Special dialog box if the shape is a group.

Selecting and Editing Text

When you want to add, edit, format, copy, cut, or paste all or part of a shape's text, you first need to know how to select it, which Table 4-1 shows. You can move the insertion point by clicking anywhere in the text block or by using the arrow keys on the keyboard.

Table 4-1. Techniques for Selecting Text

Action	Tool	Technique
Select a text block	Text Block tool	Click the Text Block tool, and then click a shape.
Open a shape's text block and select all the text in it	Pointer tool	Do one of the following: Double-click the shape. Select the shape, and then press F2.
Display the insertion point	Pointer tool	Open the text block as described in the preceding row of this table, and then click once.
Display the insertion point	Text tool	Click a shape or text.
Select part of the text in a text block	Text tool	Click a shape, and then drag to select the text you want. Or click at the start of the text you want, hold Shift, and then click at the end.
Select a word	Text tool	Click a shape, and then double-click a word.
Select a paragraph	Text tool	Click a shape, and then triple-click a paragraph.

You select text when you're about to do something to it, such as copy, cut, or format it. Unless you want to work with individual words, you can simply select the shape, and then take an action. For example, to format a shape's text, you can select the shape, and then click a format. You don't necessarily have to use the Text tool to select the text you want to format.

For details, see "Formatting Text," page 110.

Note When you begin to type, Visio automatically zooms in on the drawing so that you can see what you are typing. To return to the original magnification, press the Esc key or click anywhere outside the shape or text block after you type the text.

Typing Special Characters

If you use the Insert, Symbol command in Microsoft Word or other Office programs, you might wonder how to add symbol and special characters in Visio. You can insert ANSI characters into text. The ANSI character set consists of 256 characters established by the American National Standards Institute. How ANSI characters look on-screen depends on which font you are using.

To type ANSI characters, follow these steps:

1 Make sure your keyboard's NumLock is enabled.

2 Hold down the Alt key. Using the keys on the numeric keypad, type **0**, type the numeric ANSI code for the character you want, and then release the Alt key. For example, to type an em dash (—), press Alt+0151, and then release the Alt key.

If you are using Microsoft Windows XP or Microsoft Windows 2000, you can also do one of the following: Click Start, All Programs (click Programs in Windows 2000), Accessories, System Tools, Character Map. Select the font you wish to use and then choose the special character. Select it and then copy it. Return to Visio and paste it where you like.

Cutting, Copying, and Pasting Text

You cut, copy, or paste text within Visio diagrams and between other programs. The commands you use will look familiar if you use other Microsoft Office programs, asTable 4-2 shows. Note that Visio 2003 allows you to copy text and its format so that you can paste it into another application. Visio pastes text in rich-text format, so formats are preserved.

Table 4-2. Techniques for Cutting, Copying, and Pasting Selected Text

Action	Tool on Standard Toolbar	Keyboard Shortcut
Cut	✂ Cut	Ctrl+X
Copy	📋 Copy	Ctrl+C
Paste	📋 Paste	Ctrl+V

The text you copy or cut in Visio is temporarily stored in the Windows Clipboard. It remains in the Clipboard until you cut or copy something else, which allows you to copy a shape or text once, and then paste it in multiple locations. (This is standard Windows behavior; it's not unique to Visio by any means.)

> **Tip** Instead of copying and pasting, you can duplicate shapes wholesale—text and all—with one command. Select a shape, and then press Ctrl+D (or choose Edit, Duplicate). Visio creates a copy and pastes it on the drawing page.

Copying Text from Other Programs

You can also copy text from another program and paste it into Visio. For best results, create a text-only shape, and then paste the text. For example, in Microsoft Word, select the text you want, and then press Ctrl+C to copy it. In Visio, click the Text tool, drag to create a text-only shape in the location you want, and then press Ctrl+V to paste the Word text. Visio pastes the text and its formats.

Deleting Text from a Shape

When you delete text from a Visio shape, you remove only the text, not the text block. You can't delete a text block, although a text block that doesn't contain any text isn't visible. If you delete all the text in a text-only shape, however, Visio also deletes the shape.

To delete text from a shape, follow these steps:

1 Click the Text tool on the Standard toolbar, and then click a shape.

   Visio places the insertion point in the shape's text block.

2 Select the text you want, and then press the Delete key.

3 Press Esc or click outside the shape to close the text block.

To delete a text-only shape, select the shape with the Pointer tool, and then press the Delete key.

Adding Text to Lines and Connectors

You can add text to any line or connector (that is, any 1-D shape). Where the text ends up depends on the shape. If you draw a line, select it, and then type, Visio places your text on the center of the line, as Figure 4-6 shows. To make the text more readable, you can adjust the size and position of the shape's text block.

Chapter 4

Figure 4-6. You can add text to any line you draw. By default, Visio centers the text on top of the line.

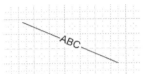

Figure 4-7. With the Format, Text command, you can choose a solid color to appear just behind the text to make it more readable.

> **Note** Because the background color fills in the area around the text, the color only appears when a shape contains text.

To put a solid background behind the text on a line, follow these steps:

1 Select a line, and then choose Format, Text.

2 Click the Text Block tab.

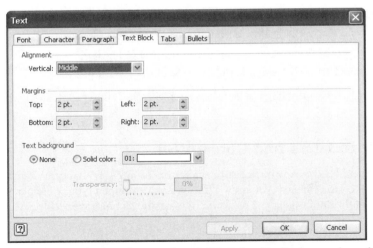

3 In the Text Background area, select Solid Color. To display a color other than white behind the text, choose a color from the list box.

4 Click OK.

Visio fills only the area behind the shape's text with the solid color you selected. If you type more text, the area of solid color is adjusted to fit.

Tip   You can apply this procedure to any shape with text, not just lines.

Repositioning Text on Lines and Connectors

If you're using one of the many line or connector shapes from a Visio stencil, as Figure 4-8 shows, you typically don't have to think about the text format. The Visio shape designer has done that for you, and you can just type and go. However, when you know the secrets to formatting text on lines, you can more easily customize the built-in connector shapes when you need to. For example, you can use the Text Block tool to move the location of the text on the line. To do this, click the Text Block tool, select the shape to display its text block, and then drag the text block to a new position. You can even drag the text block out of its associated shape.

Figure 4-8.   These shapes from the Callouts stencil are really just lines with specially formatted text (and a few SmartShape formulas thrown in for good behavior). Use callout shapes to annotate your drawings.

Editing Locked Lines and Connectors

Many of the Visio callout and line shapes are locked to prevent the text from rotating as the line is dragged. Locking ensures that the text stays right side up when viewed on the page. You can tell that a shape is locked when you select it with the Text Block tool—padlock handles will appear.

To rotate text on a locked shape, follow these steps:

1   Select the shape, and then choose Format, Protection.

2   The Protection dialog box appears, as shown in Figure 4-9. If the shape is locked to prevent rotation, the Rotation check box is selected.

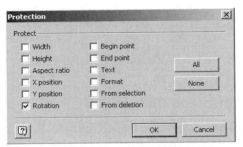

Figure 4-9. The Note Box Triangles shape on the Borders And Titles stencil is a group that contains two text blocks: one for the title and one for other information.

3 Clear the Rotation check box, and then click OK.

On the drawing page, the padlock handles no longer appear on the selected shape.

4 Click the Text Block tool, click the shape, and then drag a round corner handle to rotate the text block.

Adding and Editing Text in Groups

Because groups are composed of several shapes, each of which can have a text block, adding text can be a little more involved than with other shapes.

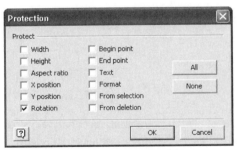

In theory, here's how you can add and edit text in a group:

1 Click the Text tool, click a group, and then start typing to add text to the group's text block.

When you start typing, Visio zooms to 100 percent view so you can see the text more easily.

2 If the group contains a shape with additional text that you want to edit, click the shape again to select it separately from the group, and then type.

3 To close the text box, press Esc, or click outside the group.

> **Tip** To place an insertion point in one of a group's shapes, subselect the shape, and then click the Text tool.

You can also use the Text Block tool to subselect shapes in a group and move or resize their text blocks.

Complications can arise when you're working with a Visio-designed group that has special behavior. Some groups include text that you cannot edit; others are locked against text entry altogether. The intention of the shape designers is to make the group behave properly, given its diagram context. Even so, if you want to add text to a locked or protected shape, you usually can—but the shape might not work the same afterward.

For details about groups and behavior options, see "Working with Groups," page 668.

Adding Text on a Layer

In many offices that routinely create drawings such as blueprints or other plans, files are passed around for review, and reviewers add text comments directly to the drawing on a separate layer. Sometimes this process is called "redlining" a drawing, because review comments traditionally appear in red for certain drawings. Anyone can take advantage of this useful method of marking up a diagram or drawing in Visio without affecting the diagram itself, as Figure 4-10 shows. When you add text to a layer, you can format that layer differently to make the text easier to see or hide it temporarily to view only the diagram. You can also print just the objects—including text—on a particular layer.

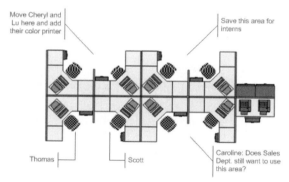

Figure 4-10. In this office layout, comments (which are shapes from the Callouts stencil) appear on a separate review layer so that text can be hidden or printed separately.

After you create a new layer specifically for your comments, you designate it as the *active layer*. If you haven't used layers in Visio before, this might sound a little abstract, but all it means is that any objects you add to the drawing, including callout shapes or other text, will automatically be assigned to the layer. You can assign a color to the active layer, so that your comments are easier to see. A layer color doesn't change a shape's original color, but as long as the layer color is enabled, the shape is displayed using that color.

Chapter 4

To create a separate layer for text, follow these steps:

1   In the drawing you want to add comments to, choose View, Layer Properties. The Layer
    Properties dialog box appears.

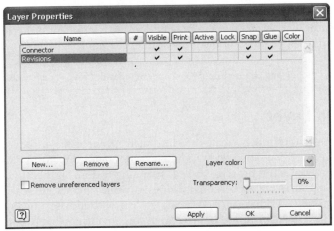

2   Click New. In the New Layer dialog box, type a name for the layer.

    For example, type **Review** or **Comments**.

3   Click OK to close the New Layer dialog box.

    In the Layer Properties dialog box, Visio adds the new layer to the bottom of the list of
    layers and selects it.

4   Click in the Active column for your new layer.

    A check mark appears next to the layer to show that it is the active layer for the
    drawing.

5   If you want your comments to appear in a particular color, click the drop-down arrow
    in the Layer Color box, and select a color.

    The color you choose will be used to display all shapes and text assigned to your com-
    ments layer.

6   Click OK, and then type comments or add shapes in your drawing.

    Shapes and text that you add are assigned to the comments layer and displayed in the
    layer color you selected.

After you've created a comments layer and added text to it, you can selectively hide, show, and
print your comments or change their color as follows:

●   If you want to hide the comments layer and view only the drawing, as Figure 4-11
    shows, choose View, Layer Properties, and then clear the check mark in the Visible col-
    umn for your comments layer. Click OK.

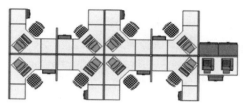

Figure 4-11.   By setting the comments layer to not visible, you can see your drawing alone, without the text.

- If you want to print only the comments, choose View, Layer Properties, and then clear the check mark in the Print column for every layer *except* your comments layer. Click OK, and then print the drawing.

- If you want to view the comments in a different color, choose View, Layer Properties, select your comments layer, and then choose a different color in the Layer Color list. If you no longer want to use a layer color, clear the check mark in the Color column for your comments layer, and then click OK.

- If you no longer want shapes and text to be assigned to your comments layer automatically, you must deactivate the layer. To do this, choose View, Layer Properties, and then clear the check mark in the Active column for your comments layer. Click OK.

Layers are also a powerful tool for organizing shapes in a drawing.

For details about using layers, see "Controlling Shapes with Layers," page 460.

Tip   If more than one person is reviewing a drawing, create a redlining layer for each reviewer and give each layer a different display color.

In fact, there might be times when you prefer to make comments and add a text layer to a drawing. However, when this is not the case, Visio 2003 adds the Markup feature common to many Microsoft Office programs. To access this feature, click Tools, Track Markup. This opens the Reviewing toolbar and the Review task pane.

To add a shape, drag it onto the drawing. Note that it is now a different color. This shows that it is a change. To insert a comment, click Insert Comment on the Review task pane. The markup is translucent, so you can easily see the original drawing beneath the markup.

Creating Tables and Lists

When you want to organize text into rows and columns or lists, you can manually format it using tabs or use one of several built-in shapes scattered among various stencils. Figure 4-12 shows a few examples of what's possible. If you just want several rows of aligned text without fancy borders or titles, it's probably quickest to tab between columns as you type. If you're looking for the type of nicely formatted tables that you can create in Word, your best bet is to use a table or chart shape from one of the stencils in the Forms And Charts solution.

Chapter 4

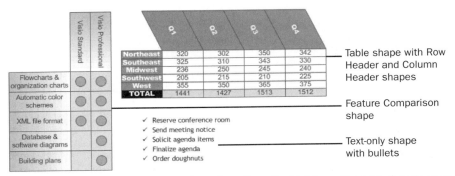

Figure 4-12. You can create a variety of preformatted tables with Visio shapes or create bulleted lists and other columns of tabbed text simply by typing.

As for formatting lists, Visio includes a Bullets button on the Format Text toolbar that works like its cousin in Word to quickly create bulleted lists. However, Visio does not offer a method for generating numbered lists automatically. The following sections tell you how to create tables and lists using different procedures.

Tabbing to Create Tables and Lists

The manual method of aligning text in tables and lists is to set tab stops, and then type text with tab characters in between columns. Setting tabs in Visio works in more or less the same way as it does in other Microsoft Office applications. The difference is that shape size can affect the margins of your text, which in turn affects where tabs align. Try to avoid resizing shapes after you've set tabs; it can make all your hard work look a bit strange.

Because text always appears in a shape, you need to consider the margins of the text block and perhaps also the shape's size when you set tabs. You set tab stops based on the text block width. The "ruler" you work with is in effect the width of the text block, and the zero point is the text block's left edge. This makes setting tabs in Visio quite different from setting tabs in a word processing program. For example, a tab stop at 0.5 inches is measured from the left edge of the text block—not from the edge of the shape, not from the edge of the page, and not from the 0-inch mark on the drawing page ruler.

It's easiest to figure out where to set tab stops if you first move the ruler's zero point to the left edge of the shape, as Figure 4-13 shows. The zero point is where 0 appears on the ruler, and typically it's the edge of the page, but you can move it to any position you like to make alignment and tabbing easier.

Chapter 4

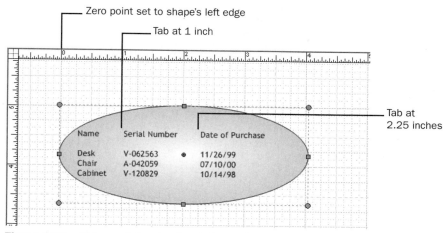

Figure 4-13.   Tabs and margins for a shape's text are measured from the left edge of the text block. For this ellipse, the left margin is indented 0.25 inch and tabs are set at 1 inch and 2.25 inches.

You can specify tab alignment as centered, left aligned, or right aligned, and you can align columns of numbers by their decimal points. You can set up to 10 tab stops for a text block, and the tab stops apply to entire paragraphs, not to selected text within a paragraph. This configuration makes Visio a little less flexible than Microsoft Word, but then, Visio wasn't designed to replace your word processor.

Tip   To set the ruler zero point, press the Ctrl key, and then drag from the vertical ruler to the left edge of the shape. Visio marks the horizontal ruler's zero at that point.

For conceptual Visio diagrams such as flowcharts and timelines, the rulers are marked in inches, just like the rulers in Microsoft Word. However, Visio drawings can be to scale, such as a floor plan or office layout, in which case the rulers might display feet, meters, or some other unit of measure. When you work in the Text dialog box to set tabs, you set tabs based on the position of text on the page regardless of the drawing scale. In this matter, Visio does work like Word.

Chapter 4

To set tab stops for a shape's text, follow these steps:

1　Select the text you want as follows:

■　If you want to set tabs for one paragraph of a shape, click the Text tool, and then select the paragraph.

■　If you want to set tabs for one shape in a group, use the Text tool to place the insertion point in the shape.

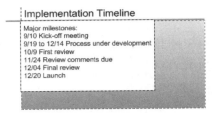

■　Otherwise, select a shape.

2　To move the ruler's zero point, hold down the Ctrl key, and then drag from the vertical ruler to the left edge of the shape or text block.

The zero point of the horizontal ruler is reset to the left edge of the text block.

3   Choose Format, Text, and then click the Paragraph tab.

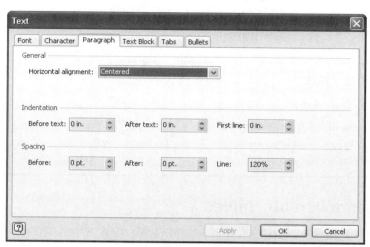

4   In the Horizontal Alignment box, select Left. In the Indentation boxes, set Before Text, After Text, and First Line to 0 in.

5   Click the Tabs tab, and then drag the Text dialog box so that you can see the text block.

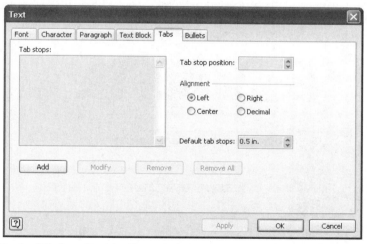

6   In the Tab Stop Position box, click the up or down arrows to set the first tab stop.

Because you moved the zero point, you can set tab stops in the Tab Stop Position box as the distance from zero.

7   Under Alignment, select an option, and then click Add.

8   Repeat steps 6 and 7 for each tab in your table. Or to set tab stops at regular intervals, in the Default Tab Stops box, enter the spacing you want between tab stops, and then click Add to set incremental tabs at the default spacing.

Chapter 4

9   Click OK in the Text dialog box.

Visio aligns the tabs at the tab stops you specified. You may reset the tabs by repeating steps 2 through 9 above.

Inside Out

Inside tab settings

Working with tabs in a scaled drawing is a little confusing. The units you see on the rulers do not reflect the units you must use in the Text dialog box to set tabs. For tab settings, enter unscaled measurements.

Using Shapes to Create Tables

Visio includes several prebuilt table shapes in different solutions that you can use to format rows and columns of text, as Figure 4-14 shows. Although you won't find a Convert Text To Table command like the one in Microsoft Word, you can use one of several table shapes that are already formatted. You just add the text. These shapes even work with a diagram's color schemes. The table shapes in Visio were designed for the Charts and Graphs solution, but they work just as well in other diagram types. Don't let the stencil name fool you. For example, you might be creating a network diagram, but you can still use the shapes on the Forms Shapes stencil to quickly assemble a table or grid-like form.

	Visio Standard	Visio Professional
Flowcharts & organization charts	●	●
Automatic color schemes	●	●
XML file format	●	●
Database & software diagrams		●
Building plans		●

	Q1	Q2	Q3	Q4
Norheast	320	302	350	342
Southeast	325	310	343	330
Midwest	236	250	245	240
Southwest	205	215	210	225
West	355	350	365	375
TOTAL	1441	1427	1513	1512

	Headcount	Status
Sales	576	• Regional differences • Revenue targets hit • Staffing on schedule
IT	342	– No issues –

Figure 4-14. You can create tables like these using Visio shapes.

To create tables like those shown in Figure 4-14, you can use the following built-in shapes and tools:

● **Grid, Row Header, and Column Header shapes on the Charting Shapes stencil (Charts and Graphs solution)**   You can specify the number of rows and columns you want in the table or grid. The Row Header and Column Header shapes drag into place.

- **Feature Comparison and Feature On/Off shapes on the Charting Shapes stencil (Charts and Graphs solution)** Although designed for marketing diagrams that compare products, the shapes work for any yes–no type of table. You can also type in the cells rather than using the Feature On/Off shape.

Follow these steps to create a table:

1 Open the stencil containing the table shape you want: click the Shapes button on the Standard toolbar, select Charts And Graphs and then select Charting Shapes.

   Visio adds the stencil to your drawing.

2 Drag the Grid shape from the stencil to the location on the page you want.

   The Custom Properties dialog box appears.

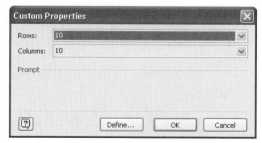

3 Click the arrows to enter the number of rows and columns you want.

   You can always add rows and columns to your table later.

4 Click OK.

5 If you want to change the cell width, you can grab a grid handle and expand or shrink the grid.

   Visio adds a table with your specifications to the drawing page.

6 If you want to use angled column labels, drag the Column Header shape from the Charting Shapes stencil into position over the first table column. Repeat this task for each column and resize as necessary to fit the column.

7 If you want to have separate row labels, drag the Row Header shape from the Charting Shapes stencil into position to the left of the first row. Repeat for each row and resize as necessary to fit the row.

8 To add text, click a row header, column header, or table cell, and then type.

Editing Table Shapes

When you use the Grid or Feature Comparison shape, the resulting table is actually a group. Because of this, tables are a little strange to work with at times. They are designed so that you click a cell, and then start typing. When you want to move the entire table, however, you must be careful not to select individual cells. The easiest thing to do is cancel all selections on the page (click a clear area), and then drag the table. Don't click to select it first; just drag.

To adjust the width of a column, you must select all the cells in the column (the easiest way is either holding down the Shift key and selecting each in turn or using the Multiple Select tool on the Pointer tool drop down menu) and resize them as a group. You may also select the entire table and resize it with its control handles.

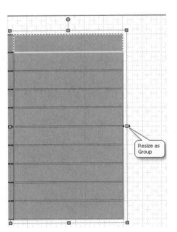

Figure 4-15. To adjust the width of a column in your table, select all the cells in the column.

Unlike column width, row height responds to your text's requirements automatically. Simply type the amount of text you want. Visio sizes the row to accommodate your text.

To add rows or columns to your table, right-click the table, and choose Set Grid, and then choose the total number of rows you want, as Figure 4-16 shows.

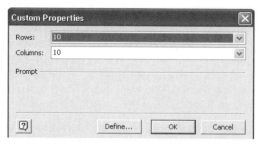

Figure 4-16. When you right-click a table shape, you may select Set Grid to display the Custom Properties box.

Formatting Table Shapes

You can format table shapes pretty much as you'd expect. Select the shapes you want to format, and then choose an option. It's probably best to either hold down the Shift key and select each in turn or use the Multiple Select tool on the Pointer tool drop-down menu.

Table shapes are designed to work with color schemes. If you apply a new color scheme to your diagram (using Tools, Add-Ons, Visio Extras, Color Scheme), the table, row header, and column header shapes are formatted with the new fill color. You can override the color scheme color by selecting the table or individual rows in it, and then choosing a new fill color.

Creating Bulleted and Numbered Lists

A bulleted list is just a list of text in which every line is set off with a symbol called a bullet. The easiest way to create a bulleted list is to select a shape with text and then click the Bullets button on the Format Text toolbar, as Figure 4-17 shows. The default bullet symbol is a dot, but you can specify a different character, such as check boxes, check marks, or diamonds. Visio remembers the bullet character you selected, and the next time you click the Bullets button, the same symbol is applied.

Figure 4-17. You can quickly format lists with a bullet character by using the Bullets button on the Format Text toolbar.

The Bullets button uses the default paragraph and tab settings to create hanging indents with the currently selected bullet symbol. If you're using a small font or typing inside a small

Chapter 4

shape, the space between the bullet symbol and your text might look too wide, but you can adjust the settings in the Text dialog box. When you select a shape and then click the Bullets button on the Format Text toolbar (View, Toolbars, Format Text), Visio makes every line in your shape that ends with a soft or hard return into bullet text. A hard return results when you press the Enter key; a soft return happens when you press Ctrl while pressing Enter to make a line break rather than a paragraph break. If you want only certain text to become bullets, use the Text tool to select the text you want, rather than selecting the entire shape.

You can specify a character to use for the bullet symbol. Visio uses the font applied to the rest of the text. When you use one of Visio's built-in bullets, you can change the text font without affecting the bullet character. When you change font size, however, bullet size also changes.

To create and format a bulleted list, follow these steps:

1 Select a shape with text, or click the Text tool, and then select a portion of text to make into a bulleted list.

2 Click the Bullets button on the Format Text toolbar.

 Visio creates a bulleted list using the default paragraph settings.

3 To use a different bullet symbol, select Format, Text, and then click the Bullets tab.

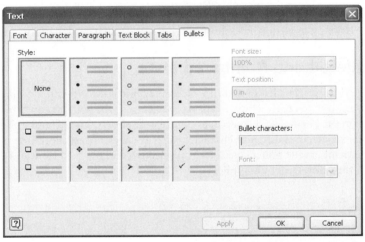

4 Select an option or type a character in the Custom box to use for the bullet symbol.

5 To adjust the spacing between bullet symbols and the list text, click the Paragraph tab.

6 If the space between the symbol and text is too wide, type a smaller value in the First box for the Indentation settings.

 The value in the First box sets the hanging indent for the list, so it's a negative number. For example, type -0.25 in. to indent the bullet character 0.25 inches to the left of the left margin.

7 If you change the First indentation value, click the Tabs tab, and then set a tab at the new position.

 For example, in the Tab Stop Position box, type 0.25 in., and then click Add.

8 Click Apply, and then view the results on the drawing page. Move the Text dialog box to the side if necessary.

9 Make additional adjustments to the indentations or tab stops if necessary. Click OK when you're satisfied with the results.

Tip   **Create a bulleted list**

Rather than typing and then formatting your text as a bulleted list, you can set up the formatting first. To do this, click in a shape where you want to start a list, click the Bullets button on the Format Text toolbar, and then type the list items.

Creating Lists with Custom Bullet Symbols

It's possible to use a custom bullet in one font and a different font for the rest of the text. To do so, select Format Text and click on the Bullets tab. In the Bullet characters window type the character that you wish to use as a bullet. In the Font window choose the font that you want from the drop-down window.

Creating Numbered Lists

Visio, unlike Microsoft Word, does not provide a way to number lists automatically. You have to type your text and the numbers and set tab stops with hanging indents. The process is admittedly tedious, especially when you've become accustomed to automatically numbered lists in other programs.

Tip   It is possible to cheat. You can create a numbered list in Microsoft Word, copy it, and then paste it into a Visio 2003 shape.

Follow these steps to create a numbered list:

1 Use the Text tool to type a number, press Tab, and then type your text.

Don't worry about the formatting yet. For example, type **1** (or **1.**, if you prefer), press Tab, type your text, and then press Enter. Repeat this process for each numbered line of text.

2 After you've typed your list, choose Format, Text, and then click the Paragraph tab.

3 In the Horizontal Alignment box, click Left.

4 In the Left box, type the left margin for the text (not the number).

For example, type **0.5 in.** to indent the text 0.5 inches from the left edge of the text block. Make sure the Left value provides enough space for the number and tab.

5 In the First box, type a negative value to set a hanging indent from the left margin.

For example, type **-0.5 in.** This creates the hanging indent for the number.

6 Click the Tabs tab, and then add a tab stop at the left margin position.

For example, type **0.5 in.** in the Tab Stop Position box, and then click Add. The value for the Tab Stop Position box should match the value for Left in step 4.

7 Click Apply, and then verify that the numbers are aligned correctly. To close the Text dialog box, click OK.

> **Tip** **Define a numbered list style**
> If you create numbered lists frequently, consider creating a style that contains the settings you want. To set such a style, select the shape containing a numbered list, and then select Format, Define Styles. In the Define Styles dialog box, click <New Style> in the Name list and type a new name for the style. Click Add. Clear the Line and Fill check boxes to make sure the style applies only the text formats. Then click OK. Visio uses the text settings of your selected shape as the basis for the new style. For details about styles, see "Creating and Editing Styles," page 688.

Formatting Text

The quickest way to format text is to click a button on the Formatting and Format Text toolbars, as Figure 4-18 shows. With the toolbar buttons, you can quickly change text size, color, font, style, indents, paragraph spacing, and bullets. These toolbars provide quick access to many of the options on the tabs of the Text dialog box (Format, Text). The Formatting toolbar is typically displayed when you start a new Visio diagram. To display the Format Text toolbar, choose View, Toolbars, Format Text.

Figure 4-18. Both the Formatting and Format Text toolbars contain shortcuts for formatting text. The Formatting toolbar has the advantage of including the font formatting buttons, but the Format Text toolbar includes shortcuts for changing margins and creating bulleted lists.

Although the toolbars provide an obvious way to format the appearance of text, they're not the only way. You can also format text using the following methods:

● **Choose a command on the Format menu** Sometimes it's easier to figure out what an option does when you see it in the context of related options. For example, when you choose the Text command, the options are grouped on the dialog box tabs according to the part of text that they affect: Font, Paragraph, Character, Text Block, Tabs, and Bullets.

● **Choose a style from the Text Style list on the Format Text toolbar** The Formatting toolbar also displays a style list, but that list includes fill and line styles as well as text styles. When you apply a style from the Text Style list, Visio applies the text formats specified by the style in much the same way as applying the Heading 1 style in Microsoft Word formats a line of text as a heading.

Whether you use the toolbar buttons or the commands of the Format menu, the effect of a formatting option depends on how you select the text:

- If you select a shape and then choose a formatting option, all of the shape's text is formatted with the option you chose.

- If you use the Text tool to select a portion of a shape's text, you can individually format characters, words, or paragraphs.

Format Painter

Because Visio always formats text as part of a shape, you can format more attributes than you might realize if your experience is with word processing programs. For example, the text block itself can have a background color, and you can specify alignment and margin settings that differ from the settings for a paragraph.

Tip   **Quickly copy text formatting**
If you like the text formatting of a particular shape, you can quickly transfer just the text formatting to another shape with the Format Painter button. To do this, select the formatted shape with the Text tool. Click the Format Painter button on the Standard toolbar, and then click the shape you want to format. Clicking the Format Painter button copies only text formatting—the font, size, color, style, alignment, spacing, and text block background—and applies it to the shape you want.

Changing the Text Font and Style

When you want to quickly change the appearance of text in a shape, you can change the font, size, or style. Most Visio shapes specify black, Arial text because it's readable and the Microsoft Windows operating system always includes the Arial font. But there's no reason for you to use a shape's default text formatting if you want to use something else. The only drawback to changing text appearance is that you might also have to tweak other settings. Visio's shapes are designed to accommodate a particular size and style of text. If you change the font or size, you might also have to adjust the text block or bump the font size up or down to get the same overall look.

The Text dialog box now inclues a fifth tab: Character. This tab allows you to alter the scale of your text (size relative to the shape), and the individual letter spacing.

Follow these steps to quickly format individual paragraphs, words, or characters:

1 Click the Text tool on the Standard toolbar, and then select the text you want to format. Or, to format all the text in a shape, select the shape.

2 Click one of the buttons on the Formatting or Format Text toolbar listed in Table 4-3. Or, choose Format, Text, click the Font tab, and then specify the options you want.

Table 4-3. Text Formatting Options

Tool	Name	What It Does
Arial	Font	Sets the font of selected text and has the same effect as choosing Format, Text, and then selecting an option in the Font box of the Font tab.
8pt.	Font Size	Sets text size and has the same effect as choosing Format, Text, and then typing a value in the Size box of the Font tab. Click the drop-down arrow and choose a size, or type a new value in the box.
B	Bold	Formats selected text in **bold**. Has the same effect as choosing Format, Text, and then selecting the Bold check box on the Font tab.
I	Italic	Formats selected text in *italic*. Has the same effect as choosing Format, Text, and then selecting the Italic check box on the Font tab.
U	Underline	Formats selected text with an underline.
A	Increase Font Size	Sets the font size to the next higher value in the Font Size list.
ABC	Decrease Font Size	Sets the font size to the next lower value in the Font Size list.
ABC	Strikethrough	Formats selected text with a line through it like ~~this~~; has the same effect as choosing Format, Text, and then selecting the Strikethrough check box on the Font tab.
ABC	Small Caps	Formats selected text in small capital letters like THIS.
x^2	Superscript	Formats selected text as a superscript.
x_2	Subscript	Formats selected text as a subscript.

Inside the Text Display in Visio 2003

If you used versions of Visio earlier than Visio 2002, you might have noticed that text looks smoother on the screen in Visio 2003. This is because since Visio 2002 the Visio engine includes a new graphics display subsystem (called GDI+ for those who like the details). This technology also makes lines and curves look smoother and generally sharpens the display of objects on the Visio drawing page.

The new display subsystem is one of many welcome improvements under the hood that came as part of the deal when Microsoft Corporation acquired the Visio product. Now Visio can use some of the same components that other Microsoft Office applications use, which makes Visio—and your diagrams—look better.

Formatting Paragraphs of Text

When you want to change the margins or alignment of text in Visio, you need to assess whether it's really the paragraph or the text block that needs to be changed. For example, when you draw a new shape and type in it, the text is centered. This alignment is actually two settings: a horizontal paragraph alignment that puts the text midway between the left and right sides, and a vertical text block setting that places the text midway between the top and bottom sides. Paragraph and text block alignment settings are displayed on tabs of the Text dialog box (Format, Text).

The distance that text appears from the edge of a shape is a factor of both the paragraph indentation and the text block margins. Paragraph indentation is measured from the margins of the text block. Text block margins are measured from the edges of the shape (if a shape and text block are the same size) or from the edges of the text block, as Figure 4-19 shows.

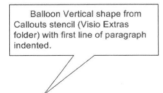

Figure 4-19. The first line of the paragraph in this shape is indented from the text block margins, which are measured from the edges of the text block.

One way to think about the difference between paragraph and text block settings is to realize that a text block is something like a page unto itself. Its margins are like the default margins of a page in a word processing application. Paragraphs can be indented from the page margins, just as Visio paragraphs are indented from the text block margins. Usually Visio specifies text block margins of 4 points all around, which ensures that the text you type in a shape doesn't butt up against the shape's outer edges. The final word on text alignment is that it has little to do with the rulers or where a shape sits on the page and everything to do with the text block.

Chapter 4

113

Changing Paragraph Alignment and Indentation

You can use the buttons on the Formatting and Format Text toolbars to change common paragraph alignment options and indents as Table 4-4 shows. However, to create hanging indents (as in a list), specify justified text, or change text block margins, you must use the Format, Text command.

To indent and align a paragraph, follow these steps:

1 Click the Text tool on the Standard toolbar, and then select the text you want to format. Or, to format all the text in a shape, select the shape.

2 Click one of the buttons on the Formatting or Format Text toolbar listed in Table 4-4.

Or, choose Format, Text, click the Paragraph tab, and then specify the options you want. For example, you can specify justified text (text with even left and right margins) in the Horizontal Alignment box, or set a hanging indent in the First Line box. Click Apply to see the effects of your settings.

> **Note**   Visio doesn't care which units of measure you use when entering indentation values for paragraphs in the Text dialog box. For example, you can type **72 pt.** or **6 pica** or **2.5 cm** to get a 1-inch margin.

Table 4-4. Adjusting Indentation and Margins

Tool	Name	What It Does
≣	Align Left	Aligns selected text to the left paragraph margin. This button has the same effect as choosing Format, Text, and then choosing Left for Horizontal Alignment on the Paragraph tab.
≡	Align Center	Centers text with respect to the left and right margins. This button has the same effect as choosing Format, Text, and then choosing Centered for Horizontal Alignment on the Paragraph tab.
≣	Align Right	Aligns selected text to the right paragraph margin. This button has the same effect as choosing Format, Text, and then choosing Right for Horizontal Alignment on the Paragraph tab.
⇤≣	Decrease Indent	Moves the left paragraph margin to the left. This button has the same effect as choosing Format, Paragraph, and then choosing a smaller Left value on the Paragraph tab.
⇥≣	Increase Indent	Moves the left paragraph margin to the right. This button has the same effect as choosing Format, Paragraph, and then choosing a larger Left value on the Paragraph tab.

Table 4-4. Adjusting Indentation and Margins

Tool	Name	What It Does
┷═ ┯═	Decrease Paragraph Spacing	Decreases the amount of space after the last line of one paragraph and before the first line of the next. This button has the same effect as choosing Format, Text, and then choosing Before and After options on the Paragraph tab.
┯═ ┷═	Increase Paragraph Spacing	Increases the amount of space after the last line of one paragraph and before the first line of the next. This button has the same effect as choosing Format, Text, and then choosing Before and After options on the Paragraph tab.

Changing Text Block Alignment

When you want to change the vertical alignment of text within a shape, change the text block alignment (Format, Text, Text Block). Most Visio shapes center text vertically within a text block, which feels counterintuitive when you're used to text starting at the top of a page and expanding downward as you type. You can align text to the top of a text block to reproduce this type of word processor behavior, as Figure 4-20 shows. Text block settings also affect the point from which the paragraph indents are measured. Usually, the default text block margins work just fine, but you can change them as needed. Text block margins affect all the text in a shape, whereas paragraph indents can apply only to selected paragraphs in a shape.

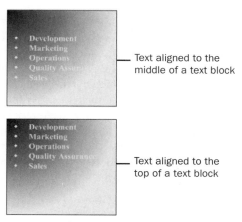

Text aligned to the middle of a text block

Text aligned to the top of a text block

Figure 4-20. Visio typically centers text vertically within a text block. As you type, the top and bottom margins remain equal. To add text in word processor fashion, use top alignment for the text block.

To change the margins between the text and the edge of the text block, do the following:

1 Select the shape you want to format.

2 Click one of the alignment buttons (listed in Table 4-5) on the Format Text toolbar.

Chapter 4

Or, choose Format, Text, click the Text Block tab, and then specify the options you want. For example, you can individually specify the top, bottom, left, and right margins for the text block. Click Apply to see the effect of your changes.

Table 4-5. Adjusting Text Block Alignment

Tool	Name	What It Does
≡	Align Top	Aligns text to the top margin of the text block. This button has the same effect as selecting Format, Text, and then choosing Top in the Vertical Alignment box of the Text Block tab.
≡	Align Middle	Centers text with respect to the top and bottom margins of the text block. This button has the same effect as selecting Format, Text, and then choosing Middle in the Vertical Alignment box of the Text Block tab.
≡	Align Bottom	Aligns text to the bottom margin of the text block. This button has the same effect as selecting Format, Text, and then choosing Bottom in the Vertical Alignment box of the Text Block tab.

> **Tip** Did you know that you can type in the Font Size box to enter a font size? For example, if you really want 9.5-point type, you can type **9.5** in the box and then press Enter.

Formatting Text with Styles

You can format a shape's text by applying a style, and if you've used styles in other programs like Microsoft Word, you know what timesavers they can be. Styles in Visio work mostly like the styles you might have used in Word, but with some critical differences. Namely, a Visio style can define formats for text, line, and fill, and most of the built-in styles apply all three. That makes it quick to ensure consistency across a number of shapes—apply one style, and voilà! All the line weights, fonts, and fill colors match. However, if all you want is to format text, the trick is to select a style from the Format Text toolbar, not the Formatting toolbar. Both toolbars include style lists, as Figure 4-21 shows, but you can apply only the text formats of a style when you use the Text Style list on the Format Text toolbar. This is important, because most of the built-in styles in Visio affect the text, line, and fill formats when applied to a shape.

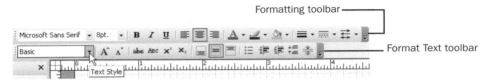

Figure 4-21.   Although you can apply a text style from either the Formatting or Format Text toolbar, you'll have more control when you use the Text Style list on the Format Text toolbar.

Part of the difficulty of using styles in Visio is that from one diagram type to the next, you don't know what the styles do until you apply them. By contrast, it's a little easier to use a text style in Microsoft Word, because the style name is formatted in the style (in Microsoft Office 2000 and later versions), and the style names are a little easier to predict. Heading 1 means a heading with more prominence than Heading 2. In Visio, style names differ from template to template. A "normal" text style in a network diagram is called Net Normal, whereas the equivalent style in a flowchart is called Flow Normal. If you like using styles, your best bet might be to define your own text styles. At least then you'll know what they do when applied.

Note A text style applies to an entire shape. You can't use a text style to format part of a shape's text. If you want to do something like this, create a group with two shapes, and then subselect the shapes to apply different styles.

Follow these steps to apply a text style:

1 Make sure the Format Text toolbar is visible. If not, select View, Toolbars, Format Text. Visio adds the Format Text toolbar to the top of the drawing window.

2 Click the Pointer tool, and then click to select a shape.
   Or press Shift while clicking to select multiple shapes to format.

3 On the Format Text toolbar, click the Text Style drop-down arrow to display the list of styles, and then choose the style you want.

   If the style includes line or fill formatting, Visio displays a message like the one shown in Figure 4-22. You can do one of two things:

   ■ Click Yes to apply all formatting to the shape (and risk the possibility of unexpected formatting).

   ■ Click No to apply only the text formatting.

Figure 4-22.   When you apply a style from the Text Style list on the Format Text toolbar, Visio asks whether you want to apply the style's nontext formatting.

All of the built-in Visio shapes have been formatted using styles. You can also define styles that specify the text formats you frequently use.

For details about how Visio styles work and how to define your own, see "Understanding Text, Line, and Fill Styles," page 681.

Setting a Default Format for All Text

A very handy technique for adding text to a diagram is to specify a default text format. This means that you specify all the font and paragraph settings that you want to use, and then when you use the Text tool to add text, it's formatted with the default settings automatically. If you use other drawing tools to create shapes and then type in them, they also use the default text formats you specify. However, when you type in an existing Visio shape, the text is formatted according to the shape's built-in styles.

Follow these steps to change the default formatting used by the Text tool:

1   Make sure nothing on the drawing page is selected, and then choose Format, Text.

2   On the tabs of the Text dialog box, select the options you want to use as the defaults, and then click OK.

    For example, suppose you want all text-only shapes you draw with the Text tool to use 12-point, Verdana text. In the Font box, select Verdana, and in the Size box, select 12 pt. You can also set paragraph margins on the Paragraph tab.

When you subsequently draw a shape with any of the drawing tools and add text to it, or add text with the Text tool, your new default settings are used.

Changing How Text Is Displayed On-Screen

Visio provides some options that let you control how text appears on the screen. For example, when you're zoomed out in a diagram that includes text, Visio *greeks* the text—that is, displays scratchy marks instead of discrete characters, which would be too small to read anyway. You can specify the size of text that Visio displays this way. By default, text that would appear smaller than 4 points in size is greeked. Perhaps you want to be able to read the text even when you are zoomed out, in which case you would decrease the point size of greeked text.

In addition, if system performance is a higher priority than display quality, you can disable the font smoothing behavior that Visio employs. This behavior is called *anti-aliasing*, which means that colors on the screen are dithered to make text look better. However, displaying anti-aliased text requires a certain amount of processor power that could be used for redrawing your page more quickly.

Follow these steps to adjust text display:

1 Choose Tools, Options, and then click the View tab.

2 To disable anti-aliased text, select Faster Text Display (Aliased) under Text Quality. Note that Visio 2003 includes a third type of text quality, Clear Type. This is an anti-aliased text display for LCD displays.

3 To change font greeking, in the Greek Text Under box, type a size in points.

4 Click OK.

Changing the Position of a Shape's Text

When you want to control the precise location of text with respect to a shape, you can rotate, size, and even move a shape's text block. A text block can appear anywhere. When you create a new shape, its text block is set to the same size as the shape, but that's not always the best location for text. In fact, in many Visio shapes, the text block appears below or beside the shape like a label. If shapes are crowded on a page, you can move text blocks to make labels more legible or rotate text used as an annotation. When you need to make text more readable and setting the margins isn't enough, it makes sense to move or resize the text block, as Figure 4-23 shows.

Chapter 4

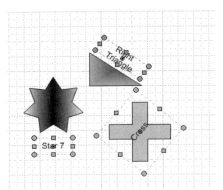

Figure 4-23. By selecting these shapes with the Text Block tool, you can see that the text block doesn't match the shape. You can move, size, and rotate the text block to adjust the position of a shape's text.

To work with the text block, use the Text Block tool on the Standard toolbar. It works in much the same way that the Pointer tool works on shapes, but affects only the text block.

Rotate Text 90° tool

When you want to rotate a shape's text, but not the shape itself, you can use either the Text Block tool on the Standard toolbar or the Rotate Text 90° tool on the Action toolbar (click View, Toolbars, Action to display the Action toolbar). Both tools rotate only the shape's text block. The Text Block tool lets you drag to any angle you want, whereas the Rotate Text 90° tool does what its name says.

To rotate, size, or move a text block, follow these steps:

1 Click the Text Block tool on the Standard toolbar, and then click a shape.

Selection handles appear around the text block. If the handles have an × symbol, the text block is part of a grouped shape.

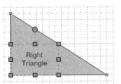

Tip If you can't see the text block handles easily, try dragging one of the handles to make the text block a little larger.

2 To resize the text block, drag a side, top, or corner selection handle.

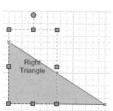

3 To move the text block away from the shape, drag it to a new position.

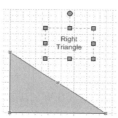

4 To rotate the text block, point to the round selection handle, which is set apart from the text block. The pointer becomes a rotation pointer. Drag to a new angle.

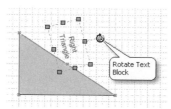

Most Visio shapes include a control handle that makes it easy to move and rotate the text block.

Follow these steps to quickly rotate a text block in 90-degree increments:

1 If the Action toolbar is not visible, select View, Toolbars, Action.

2 Select a shape.

3 Click the Rotate Text 90° tool. Visio moves the text block 90° counterclockwise.

Finding and Correcting Text

Visio can correct spelling or find and replace all uses of particular words. You can specify whether you want Visio to search a selection, a page, or the whole diagram. When you search for or check the spelling of text, Visio searches in all shapes, including these:

- Text-only shapes
- Data fields
- Stencils
- Custom property fields
- Text you enter in the Properties dialog box

Tip To search for shapes, type your criteria into the search window located above the Shapes window. You can locate shapes by using names or keywords. For details, see "Finding the Shape You Want," page 39.

Finding and Replacing Text

Finding and replacing text in a Visio diagram works a little differently from your typical word processing document. When Visio searches for text, it examines text in shapes, in text-only shapes, on stencils, in the Properties box, text within custom properties, shape names, user-defined cells (a type of ShapeSheet cell of interest to shape developers), and in data files. You can also search for special characters, such as tabs or line breaks.

When you search for a word or phrase in Visio using the Find or Replace command, you can define the scope of the search—selected text only, one page, or all pages in the diagram. Visio searches the text blocks of shapes for the text you specify. When you use the Find command, you can refine the search even more. Table 4-6 shows you the options for searching when you use the Find command.

Table 4-6. Table Options for Searching

Search Location	Description
Selection	Searches for text only in the currently selected shapes on the drawing page.
Current Page	Searches for text on the current page only.
All Pages	Searches for text on all pages of your diagram.
Shape Text	Searches the text blocks of all shapes, including text-only shapes.
Custom Property	Searches for text in the custom property fields of all shapes.
Shape Name	Searches the Name field of a master shape or instance of a master shape (that is, what you drop on the page). This option is best used when a stencil file is open for editing to check master shape names.
User-Defined Cell	Searches the formula text in the Value and Prompt cells of the User-Defined Cells section of the ShapeSheet spreadsheet for all shapes.

To search for a word or phrase, follow these steps:

1 Choose Edit, Find; or press Ctrl+F to open the Find dialog box.

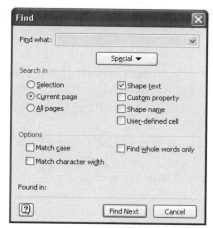

2 In the Find What box, type the word or phrase you want to search for. To search for a special character, click Special, and then select an option.

3 Under Search In, choose the options you want to control where Visio searches.

4 Under Options, select the matching options you want, and then click Find Next.

If Visio locates an occurrence of the search text in a shape, the text is highlighted in the diagram. If the search text is found in a shape name or user-defined cell, the name is displayed in the Found In section of the Find dialog box, and the shape is selected on your drawing page.

5 To edit the found text, click the Close or Cancel button to close the Find dialog box. Or click Find Next to find its next occurrence.

To replace a word or phrase, follow these steps:

1 Choose Edit, Replace to open the Replace dialog box.

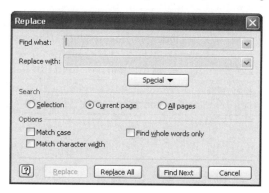

Chapter 4

123

2   In the Find What box, type the word or phrase you want to replace. To search for a special character, click Special, and then select an option.

3   In the Replace With box, type the new word or phrase you want to use. To replace the Find What text with a special character, click Special, and then select an option.

4   Under Search, select an option to control where Visio searches.

5   Under Options, select the match options you want.

6   To replace all instances of the Find What word or phrase, click Replace All. Otherwise, click Find Next to search for the next occurrence of the text.

    If Visio locates an occurrence of the search text in a shape, the text is highlighted in the diagram.

7   Click Replace to replace the selection with the text in the Replace With box, and then click Find Next.

    Visio displays a message when it has finished searching.

8   Click OK, and then click the Close button to close the Replace dialog box.

The commands on the Edit menu aren't the only commands for searching. Like other Microsoft Office programs, Visio includes a task pane for searching in other files on your computer or elsewhere, as well as the Find Shapes command for tracking down elusive shapes. Table 4-7 summarizes the commands you can use to search for text, files, or shapes.

Table 4-7. Commands for Searching in Visio and Beyond

Command	Description
Edit, Find	Searches for a word or phrase in a diagram.
Edit, Replace	Searches for a word or phrase in a diagram and then replaces it with a new word or phrase.
View, Task Pane	Opens the Basic Search pane, where you can search for text in other files, including Microsoft Office documents, on your computer, in network folders, at Microsoft.com, or in Microsoft Outlook. For details, see "Searching for a File to Open," page 30.
Search window above Shapes window	Type text into the window to search for shapes. For details, see "Finding the Shape You Want," page 39.

Checking Spelling

When you check spelling in a diagram, Visio examines the spelling of text in shapes, including text-only shapes, and data fields. Visio typically checks the spelling for shapes on the current page only, but you can specify to check selected text only or all pages in a diagram.

Follow these steps to check spelling in a drawing:

1 Choose Tools, Spelling, or press F7.

   If Visio encounters any words not found in its dictionary, it displays the Spelling dialog box.

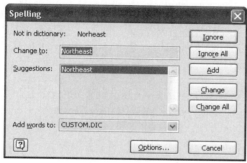

2 If the highlighted suggestion in the Change To box is correct, click Change to replace the misspelled word with this text. Or click Change All to replace every instance of the misspelled word throughout the drawing file. Otherwise, choose a word in the Suggestions box, or type the correct spelling in the Change To box, and then click Change.

3 If the unrecognized word is spelled correctly, click Ignore to continue the check. Or click Ignore All to ignore all instances of the word in the diagram and continue the check.

4 If you want to add an unrecognized word to Visio's spelling dictionary, click Add.

   For example, use the Add button to add your company's name to the dictionary so the spelling checker won't ask you about it every time.

5 Click Options to ensure that the spelling options are set the way you want.

   When Visio has finished checking spelling (or if it doesn't find any misspelled words), a message box appears indicating that it has finished checking.

6 Click OK.

By default the spelling checker checks all text in your drawing. That's all shapes and all text. You can limit the check by highlighting the text you wish to check and then pressing F7 (or the Spelling button on the Standard toolbar).

> **Tip** By default, Visio 2003 checks your spelling as you type. If a word is misspelled, Visio underlines it with a squiggly red line. Right-click the word to display a shortcut menu that includes suggested corrections of the misspelled word.

Chapter 4

Creating Your Own Dictionary

When you check spelling in a diagram, Visio compares words to its dictionary, a file called Custom.dic. You can add words to this dictionary as you check spelling, but for some diagrams with unusual or industry-specific terms, you might not want to pollute the built-in dictionary. For your personal vocabulary needs, Visio lets you create a *user dictionary* for storing words that you want the spelling checker to recognize. When the spelling checker encounters an unrecognized word you can add it to your user dictionary so that it won't be listed as a misspelling in the future.

Visio uses the *active dictionary* to check spelling. When you create a user dictionary, you add it to the list of active dictionaries. More than one dictionary can be active. Then, when you use the Spelling command, all the active dictionaries, including the user dictionary, appear in the Add Words To box. When you no longer want your user dictionary to appear in this box, you can remove it from the active list. Removing a dictionary doesn't delete it; it just prevents the dictionary from showing up in the Spelling dialog box, so you can't add words to it.

Note Visio saves dictionaries in the C:\Documents and Settings\<*user*>\Application Data\Microsoft\Proof folder or C:\Programs\Common\Proof folder.

Follow these steps to create a user dictionary and make it active:

1 Choose Tools, Options, and then click the Spelling tab.

2 Click Add next to the Custom Dictionaries box.

   The Add User Dictionary dialog box appears.

3 In the File Name box, type a name for the dictionary, and then click Open.

   In the Options dialog box, the dictionary name you created appears in the Custom Dictionaries box.

4 Click OK to close the Options dialog box.

   The user dictionary has been added to the diagram.

Follow these steps to add words to a user dictionary:

1 Choose Tools, Spelling.

2 When Visio encounters a word it doesn't recognize, click the Add Words To drop-down arrow, and then select the name of your user dictionary.

3 Click Add to add the word to the user dictionary.

To make a user dictionary inactive, follow these steps:

1 Choose Tools, Options, and then click the Spelling tab.

2 In the Custom Dictionaries box, select the name of your user dictionary, and then click Remove.

   Visio removes the user dictionary from the list. The dictionary file is not deleted.

3 Click OK.

> **Tip** To reactivate an existing user dictionary, click Add on the Spelling tab of the Options dialog box, locate the user dictionary in the Add User Dictionary dialog box, and then click Open.

Turning Off the Spelling Checker

Visio automatically checks your spelling as you type and displays a wavy, red underline under words that it doesn't recognize. Some people love an interactive spelling checker, and others loathe the interruption. If you're in the latter camp, you can turn off the spelling checker. That way, you can control when you want Visio to check your spelling—just press F7.

Turn off the automatic spelling checker as follows:

1 Choose Tools, Options, and click the Spelling tab.

2 Clear the Check Spelling As You Type check box.

3 Click OK.

Automatically Correcting Text as You Type

It used to be only the shapes were smart in Visio. Now text is smart, too, with automatic corrections. Visio 2003 includes many of the AutoCorrect and AutoFormat features that make Microsoft Word so nice for typing. Depending on the options you choose, Visio can automatically correct common typos and capitalization errors and format certain characters as you type. For example, if you start a new sentence with a lowercase letter, Visio can automatically replace it with an uppercase letter.

Visio can correct the following typos and formats:

- **Capitalization mistakes** When you type too many capital letters in a word, or too few at the start of a sentence or in the name of a day, Visio fixes the word. For example, *VIsio* becomes *Visio* and *tuesday* becomes *Tuesday*.

- **Caps Lock errors** When you accidentally press the Caps Lock key on your keyboard while typing, Visio continues to type in lowercase.

- **Formatting fixes** Visio swaps symbol characters for commonly typed letters. For example, some fractions (3/4) are converted to stacked fraction characters (¾), and two hyphens (- -) become an em dash (—).

What if AutoCorrect "fixes" a word that you typed exactly as intended? When AutoCorrect makes a correction that you don't want, you can press Ctrl+Z (or choose Edit, Undo) to undo the correction.

Both of these techniques can be an irritating interruption. You can instead define exceptions to the rules so that AutoCorrect applies its capitalization rules only to the words you want. Or you can disable the feature altogether and trust the spelling checker to catch your mistakes.

Chapter 4

Follow these steps to specify the AutoCorrect options you want:

1 Choose Tools, AutoCorrect Options.

The AutoCorrect dialog box appears and displays the AutoCorrect tab.

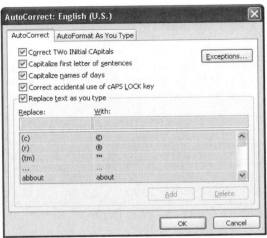

2 To set capitalization corrections, select or clear the first four check boxes in the dialog box.

3 To set formatting options, click the AutoFormat As You Type tab.

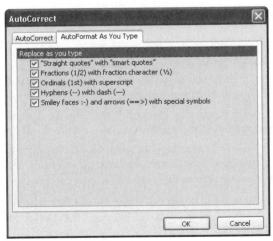

4 Select or clear the options you want, and then click OK.

> **Note** To disable AutoCorrect altogether, clear all of the check boxes in the AutoCorrect dialog box.

Chapter 4

Adding AutoCorrect Entries

If the list of built-in AutoCorrect entries doesn't contain the corrections that you want, you can easily add or edit AutoCorrect entries. For example, you can add an entry to automatically spell out the name of your company when you type an abbreviation.

Follow these steps to add an AutoCorrect entry:

1 Choose Tools, AutoCorrect Options.

The AutoCorrect dialog box appears and displays the AutoCorrect tab.

2 Make sure Replace Text As You Type is checked.

3 In the Replace box, type a word or phrase that you often mistype or misspell, or type the short form of a word that you want AutoCorrect to spell out.

For example, type **MS Press**.

4 In the With box, type the correct spelling of the word.

For example, type **Microsoft Press**.

5 Click Add. Continue adding entries, or click OK to close the AutoCorrect dialog box.

Specifying Exceptions to the AutoCorrect Rules

You can prevent AutoCorrect from making specific capitalization corrections. When you define an AutoCorrect exception, you specify letters that should not be capitalized. Defining an exception lets you keep the AutoCorrect feature enabled and yet avoid the irritation of undoing unwanted corrections. Otherwise, when AutoCorrect makes an unwanted correction, you must press Ctrl+Z (or choose Edit, Undo) to remove the entire correction and retype the word you want.

Follow these steps to define a capitalization exception:

1 Select Tools, AutoCorrect Options, and then click Exceptions.

The AutoCorrect Exceptions dialog box appears with the First Letter tab displayed.

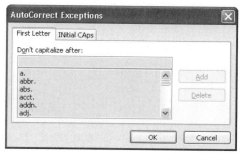

2 To prevent AutoCorrect from capitalizing a word you type after a specific abbreviation, type the abbreviation (including periods) in the Don't Capitalize After box. Click Add.

3 To prevent AutoCorrect from correcting a word that contains mixed uppercase and lowercase letters, click the INitial CAps tab. In the Don't Correct box, type the word, and then click Add. Click OK to return to the AutoCorrect dialog box.

Using Visio Shapes to Display Text

When you want to call attention to information in a diagram, you can use one of the many predesigned shapes for formatting notes, titles, and file information. Visio includes numerous *callout* shapes, which are lines with a text box that you can use to type notes. If you're working in a diagram that uses custom property fields to store information, you can use the *custom callout* shape to display property values. In addition, title and title block shapes help you display file information in your diagrams.

This section helps you locate some of the available shapes that you might not know about.

 In Visio 2003 you can insert Shape Screen tips that explain the function of any shape, or just help those viewing your work. To do so, select a shape and then click Insert, Shape Screen Tip. Type your tip into the Shape Screen Tip window and click OK to close the window. Now, whenever you hold your cursor over the shape, it will display the Shape Screen tip.

Annotating Diagrams with Callout Shapes

If you like to draw arrows on a diagram to call attention to important information, you can save time by using a callout shape. Callouts typically look like a line to which a text box is attached, but Visio includes many styles, as Figure 4-24 shows. You type your notes or exclamations in the box and then point the line in the appropriate direction. Some callouts can even be glued to shapes so that they stay in place, which is handy when you're still working on the layout of a diagram.

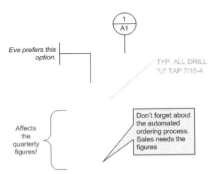

Figure 4-24. When you want to call attention to something in a diagram, use a callout shape.

A charming idiosyncrasy of Visio is that it includes a multitude of different shapes all with the name Callout. That makes it a little tough to use the Find Shapes command to search for a particular callout shape. However, the following list helps you locate many interesting callout and annotation shapes. And remember, it doesn't matter which stencil you took a shape from or what it's called. You might be laying out your house plan, but you can still use shapes from the Charts And Graphs solution. If the shape looks right, go ahead and use it.

Inside Out

Sending callouts to other Office files

You can drag callout shapes directly into other Microsoft Office files to annotate your documents with flair. Just tile your program windows so you can see both the stencils and the target document, and then drag and drop. The shapes are added to Office documents as embedded objects.

You'll find the biggest variety of predesigned callout shapes on the following stencils:

Open Stencil

- **Callouts stencil**   Use any of the dozens of callouts, starbursts, bracketed notes, and other great shapes to add text. To open this stencil, click the drop-down list arrow for the Open Stencil button on the Standard toolbar, and then choose Visio Extras, Callouts.

- **Charting Shapes stencil**   Use the Word Balloon, Callout, or Annotation shape to make notes on any diagram. To open this stencil, click the drop-down list arrow for the Open Stencil button on the Standard toolbar, and then choose Charts and Graphs, Charting Shapes.

- **Landmark Shapes stencil**   Intended for directional maps, this stencil contains a simple callout shape as well as a Direction and North symbol to keep readers oriented when viewing your diagram. To open this stencil, click the drop-down list arrow for the Open Stencil button on the Standard toolbar, and then choose Map, Landmark Shapes.

Visio Professional also includes a legacy stencil from days of yore, the Annotations stencil, which you can open from the Visio Extras folder. It contains callout and reference shapes used in technical drawings. However, if you open one of the building plans or engineering diagram types, the template probably opens a stencil with technical annotation shapes.

In general, to add a callout shape to a diagram, follow these steps:

1. Drag the callout shape you want to use from the stencil onto the drawing page near the shape you want to annotate.

2. With the callout shape selected, type the text you want.

3. If the callout isn't oriented in the direction you want, select it, and then choose Shape, Rotate Or Flip, Flip Horizontal.

4. To point the callout at another shape, drag the callout's endpoint (the selection handle with a +).

5. To glue the connector to a shape, drag the endpoint to a connection point on the shape.

   When the handle turns red, it's glued to the shape.

Chapter 4

131

> **Note** You won't be able to glue a callout to a shape unless glue is enabled in your diagram. To check, choose Tools, Snap & Glue. Under Currently Active, make sure Glue is selected.

You can format callouts as you would any other shape. To change the color of the callout's line, select the shape, and then click the Line Color button on the Formatting toolbar and choose a color.

For details about gluing shapes together, see "Controlling Connections with Glue," page 80.

Displaying Values in a Custom Callout

If you're working in a diagram that stores information with shapes in the form of custom properties, you can use custom callouts to automatically annotate shapes with property information. You might not even be aware that your diagram does include custom properties. Many shapes feature built-in properties. For example, flowchart shapes include custom properties for cost, duration, and resources; network equipment shapes and furniture include custom properties for manufacturer and part number or model name.

When you use a custom callout shape, you can display the value of a custom property field as the text on the callout. If you haven't been adding data to the custom properties, your fields are empty and there's nothing to display. But in diagrams that include this data, the custom callout shapes provide a quick and convenient way to display it, as Figure 4-25 shows.

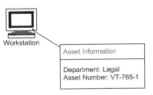

Figure 4-25. When you attach a custom callout shape to another shape that includes custom properties, you can display the properties, such as Department and Asset Number, in the callout.

> **Tip** To see whether your shapes already include property fields, choose View, Custom Properties Window to display the Custom Properties window.

Visio includes a couple of different styles for custom callout shapes, but they all work the same way. The callout shape includes a control handle that you drag to attach to another shape called the *target shape*. Visio then displays a list of the shape's properties, and you can choose the ones you want to display. You can specify whether you want both the property name and its value to appear in the callout and the order in which the properties are displayed. Visio draws a line automatically between the callout and the target shape, but you can choose not to display the line. The callout will still be associated with the designated target.

To display custom property information in a custom callout shape, follow these steps:

Open Stencil

1   If the Callouts stencil is not already open, click the drop-down list arrow for the Open Stencil button on the Standard toolbar, and then choose Visio Extras, Callouts.

Visio adds the Callouts stencil to the drawing window.

2   Scroll down in the Callouts stencil until you see the Custom Callout shapes, and drag the Custom Callout shape you want onto the drawing page.

3   Drag the yellow control handle on the callout shape to another shape in the diagram that contains custom properties.

When you release the mouse, the Configure Callout dialog box appears.

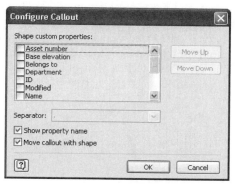

4   In the Shape Custom Properties list, select the properties you want to display.

Visio lists only the properties for the target shape. If no properties have been defined for the shape, nothing appears in the Shape Custom Properties list.

5   To change the order in which the properties appear in the callout, click the Move Up or Move Down buttons.

6   If you have selected more than one property, choose an option in the Separator box to indicate how you want Visio to separate each property in the callout.

For example, click <Return> to place each property on a separate line.

7   If you don't want to include the property name as well as its value in the callout, clear the Show Property Name check box.

If you leave this check box selected, Visio displays the property and its value; for example, *Serial Number: 10-320.*

8   If you want the callout to stay anchored when you move the target shape, clear the Move Callout With Shape check box.

If you move the target shape, the callout line stretches, but the text box stays anchored. If you select this check box, Visio moves the entire callout shape when you drag the target shape.

9   Click OK to add the properties to the callout shape.

Chapter 4

To change the appearance of the callout after you've configured it, you can do the following:

- To change any of the callout settings, right-click the callout shape, and then click Configure Callout.
- If you don't want a line connecting the callout text to the target shape to appear, right-click the callout, and then clear the Show Leader option.

Adding a Title Block to a Diagram

Visio includes a number of shapes for adding titles and file information to a diagram. Title blocks are the area traditionally used to specify important information on technical drawings, including blueprints, schematics, and mechanical drawings. The Borders And Titles stencil includes fun and informal title block shapes for identifying a diagram, its author, creation date, and so on. In addition, Visio 2003 Professional includes several styles of formal title block shapes that conform to appropriate standards for different paper sizes. Figure 4-26 shows title block shapes and both informal and technical title blocks created with Visio shapes.

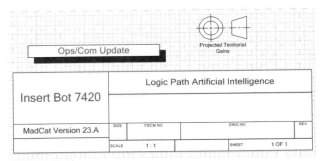

Figure 4-26. Visio includes an assortment of title blocks that you can use to provide identifying information in a diagram or technical drawing.

Many Visio templates open a stencil that contains appropriate text and title shapes. However, when you start a drawing from scratch, you need to open the stencils you want. Here are some places to look for preformatted title blocks:

- **Borders And Titles stencil**   This stencil contains more than 30 styles of border and title shapes, some of which display today's date automatically. To open this stencil, click the Shapes button on the Standard toolbar, and then choose Visio Extras, Borders And Titles.

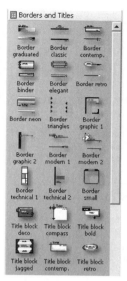

- **Title Blocks stencil (Visio Professional only)**   This stencil includes standard-sized title blocks as well as shapes that represent individual blocks (date, drawn by, description, and more). To open this stencil in Visio Professional, click the Shapes button on the Standard toolbar, and then choose Visio Extras, Title Blocks.

The ready-made title block shapes are actually groups. When you click a title block, the entire group is selected; then, you can click an individual shape to subselect it.To add your information, subselect a shape in the title block, and then type.

Most of the title blocks from the Borders And Titles stencil are designed so that if you just click and type, the text *Title* is replaced by your typing. However, when you use the title

Chapter 4

blocks from the Title Blocks stencil, it's better to subselect the individual block you want to type in.

Some title blocks include fields as placeholders for time, date, or file information, as Figure 4-27 shows. If you drag a title block onto the page and it displays today's date, then you know the shape includes a field. You want to take care not to overwrite the field when you add text, unless you intend to remove it. You can insert another field if you like or edit the field's format so that it displays the information differently.

For details, see "Creating Text Fields to Display Information," page 141.

Date field

Figure 4-27. The Title Block Elegant shape on the Borders And Titles stencil includes a field that displays the date in long form.

Note On the Borders And Titles stencil, some title blocks are smarter than others. For example, when you type a long title in the Title Block Contemp. shape, the shape is resized to accommodate all of your text. If you type a long title in the Title Block Jagged shape, the text can extend beyond the shape's borders. You have to stretch the shape manually to fit your title (or choose a smaller font size).

Tips for Formatting Title Blocks

This section applies primarily to the shapes on the Borders And Titles stencil, which are designed to add winsome flair to routine office diagrams. But perhaps you'd like that Title Block Retro shape a little better if the swooshes were green, or maybe Title Block Jagged would be perfect if only it didn't have the stripes. Or maybe you resized the title block and got strange results. It's easier to format the title block shapes than to resize them. Because the title blocks are groups, they consist of multiple shapes, some of which can be typed in, formatted, sized, and deleted, and some of which cannot.

To format a shape that's part of a group, you must subselect the shape. If you use the Pointer tool, you click once to select the group and then click a second time to subselect a shape in the group. Then you can use any of the formatting tools to change line, fill, and font color and other attributes.

Sometimes it's easiest to work with groups in the group window. This is a separate window that displays the shapes as if they were not grouped, as Figure 4-28 shows. When you click a shape in the group window, the shape is selected; you don't have to subselect it (unless the group includes a group, which sometimes happens). To open a group in the group window, select the group, and then choose Edit, Open <*group*> where <*group*> is the shape's name (at the bottom of the Edit menu). For example, the command name for the title block shown in Figure 4-28 is Open Title Block Small.

> **Tip** You may name a group. Select the group, and then click Format, Special. Type in the name of the group and click OK.

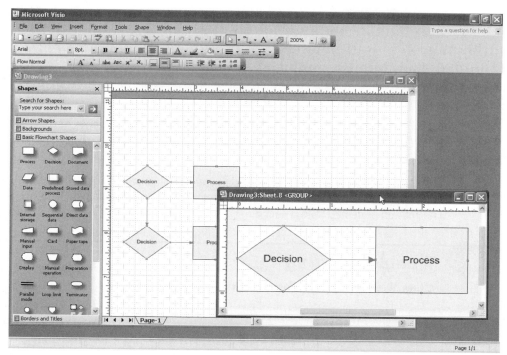

Figure 4-28. When you select a group and then choose Edit, Open, the group appears in a new window so that you can more easily work with individual shapes in the group.

Many of the individual shapes that make up a title block are locked. When you subselect the shape, padlock handles appear. Usually the shape has been locked to prevent you from resizing it, because the group contains SmartShape formulas that automatically control the size of the title block, and stretching a shape would interfere with the formulas. However, some shapes are also locked against deletion, but if you really want to delete a shape from a title block, you should be able to—but be aware that the group behavior might change as a result. If that happens, and you are unhappy with the consequences, you can simply drag a fresh title block from the stencil.

To see what kind of protection locks a shape has, subselect the shape, and then choose Format, Protection. The selected check boxes in the Protection dialog box indicate what is protected, as shown in Figure 4-29. If you clear a check box, you remove that lock. For example, you can clear the Deletion box so that you can delete a shape (such as the striped background on Title Block Jagged). If the shape has other locks, you'll still see the padlock handles even after you clear one of the locks.

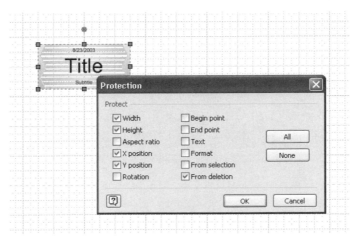

Figure 4-29. Padlock handles appear around a subselected shape in a group when a protection has been set for the shape. Here, the shape is protected against changing its width and height and protected from deletion.

Troubleshooting

A title block shape resizes unevenly when stretched

If you try to resize a title block and encounter obstacles—part of the title block resizes and part does not, or it doesn't all resize the same amount—you have encountered a side effect of width-height protection locks. Some of the title block shapes are rather inflexible and work best only at their original size with text no longer than the word *Title*. That seems like bad behavior for a SmartShape symbol, but you can work around it if you really want to use a particular shape. You can try unlocking all the shapes in the group so that they resize the way you want. Or you can ungroup the title block (Shape, Grouping, Ungroup) and reassemble it as you want. Visio warns you that the action will sever the object's link to its master. Click OK anyway. You can always drag another master shape onto the page if you want to start over with the original.

Creating a Custom Title Block for a Technical Drawing

You can assemble a customized title block for technical drawings using the shapes on the Title Blocks stencil, which is included only with Visio Professional. Title blocks usually appear in the same form in a variety of drawings. If you need a title block to conform to a particular standard, you can piece together a suitable title block from the shapes on this stencil.

A variety of block shapes include fields that display file and system information, such as file name, date, and page number. Visio uses the file and page properties to display this information in the field. You can use the frame shape to set up the border of the title block and then insert the block and other shapes as required. When you're done, you can group the shape (Shape, Grouping, Group) to make it easier to move and work with the title block.

In a technical drawing, or any diagram where you want the same title to appear on every page, you can drag a title block shape onto a background page. As long as your foreground pages are assigned to display the background, the title block will appear on every page. Another advantage of using a background page is that it frees you to change page settings, such as drawing scale, on the foreground page.

Saving a Customized Title Block

You can save a customized title block as a new master shape on a stencil, so that you can reuse it in other drawings.

Follow these steps to save a customized title block:

**Open
Stencil**

1   Open the stencil in which you want to save the title block. Do one of the following:
    - ■ To open an existing stencil, click the Shapes button on the Standard toolbar, and then locate and select the stencil you want.
    - ■ To create a new stencil, choose File, Shapes, New Stencil or click the Shapes button on the Standard toolbar and select New Stencil.

2   Drag the title block (or a copy) from the drawing page into the stencil's window.

    If you're dragging into an existing stencil open as read-only, Visio asks whether you want to edit the stencil to complete the operation. Click Yes.

    Visio creates a new master shape and an icon with a default name for the title block.

3   Right-click the new master shape, and then select Master Properties to enter a name and other options for the master. Click OK.

> For details about editing masters, see "Editing Masters," page 621.

> **Tip**   Add a title block to a template
> You can also create a template that includes the title block in the correct position, so that every time you start a drawing, the information you want is already there. For example, in a technical drawing, or any diagram where you want the same title to appear on every page, you can place the title block on a background page. Then use the Save As command to save the drawing as a template (.vst) file.

Adding Text to Headers and Footers

Headers and footers are text that runs along the top or bottom of the printed page. They don't appear when you view a diagram on the screen, but you can choose File, Print Preview to see them. In a header or footer, you can insert fields that automatically display page numbers, file name, current date and time, and other information, which you can format.

To set up headers and footers, choose View, Header And Footer. The Header And Footer dialog box appears, as Figure 4-30 shows. You can type the text that you want to appear, or you can choose one of several fields, which act as placeholders for information that Visio fills in for you. When you select a field, such as Current Date, Visio inserts a field code that it replaces with the information when you print the diagram. Field codes look like an ampersand (&) followed by a letter.

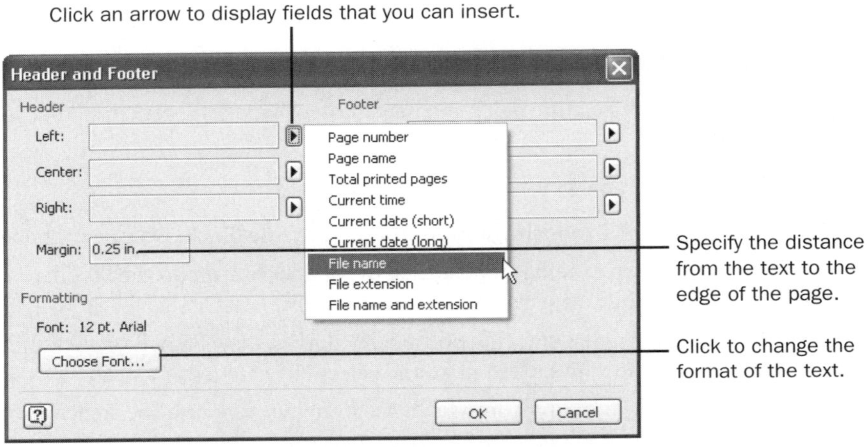

Click an arrow to display fields that you can insert.

Specify the distance from the text to the edge of the page.

Click to change the format of the text.

Figure 4-30.   You can set up headers and footers that print at the top or bottom of every page in a diagram.

To indicate the position for the header or footer text, type or insert a field in the Left, Center, or Right box. Visio prints the header and footer text using the font displayed in the Formatting area, which you can change by clicking Choose Font. The header and footer text is printed at the distance from the edge of the page specified by the Margin box.

To add text to a header or footer in a diagram, follow these steps:

1   Select View, Header And Footer. The Header And Footer dialog box appears.

2   Depending on where you want the text to appear, type in the Left, Center, or Right box under Header or Footer.

    For example, type **Confidential** in the Center box under Footer to display the text *Confidential* at the bottom center of every page when you print the diagram.

3   To insert a field, click one of the list arrows (Left, Center, or Right) under Header or Footer.

    A shortcut menu appears with a list of fields that you can insert.

4   Select a field.

    Visio inserts a code that will be replaced by the field information when you print.

Tip   Select the Page Number field to add automatic page numbering to your diagram.

5 To specify text formatting, click Choose Font.

6 The Choose Font dialog box appears, which looks like the Font tab of Visio's Text dialog box.

7 Select a font, style, size, and color option, and then click OK to return to the Header And Footer dialog box.

8 Click OK.

The text appears when you print the diagram.

Creating Text Fields to Display Information

You can insert a placeholder called a *field* into text that displays information such as dimensions, dates, and times. You can insert a field to show the date and time a drawing is printed, a shape's angle of rotation, or the result of a formula you write. Visio tracks a great deal of information in the form of shape and document properties, and this information is available to you to display automatically when you insert a field. Some Visio shapes already include fields, as Figure 4-31 shows. For example, title block shapes that display file name, date, and time or a dimension line that displays shape width can do so because that data is contained in a field. Fields are automatically updated when you change a drawing.

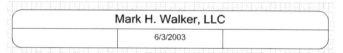

Figure 4-31. These shapes from the Forms Shapes stencil include fields that display file and page properties, such as author and date, automatically.

You can add as many fields to a text block as you want. Visio includes a variety of field types, such as date and time and document information, as Table 4-8 shows. In addition, if you know the syntax for ShapeSheet formulas, you can insert a field that displays the result of your formula.

Table 4-8. Types of Fields

Field Category	Description
Custom Formula	Lets you enter a ShapeSheet formula in the Custom Formula box. The formula's result is displayed in the field.
Date/Time	Uses information from the Windows Control Panel to display the date and time a file was created, revised, or printed or to display the current date or time.
Document Info	Uses information entered in the Properties box (File, Properties) to display the diagram's creator, description, directory, file name, keywords, subject, title, manager, company, category, or hyperlink base (for linked files).

Chapter 4

Table 4-8. Types of Fields

Field Category	Description
Geometry	Uses the shape's width, height, and angle information to display dimensions. The Width field is useful for dimension lines. The Angle field is useful for showing how far a shape is rotated from its original position.
Object Info	Uses information entered in the Special dialog box (Format, Special) to display the shape's internal ID; master used to create it; name; type (shape, group, bit map, and so on); and values of the Data 1, Data 2, and Data 3 fields.
Page Info	Uses information entered in the Page Setup dialog box to display the name of the background page and the number of pages in a diagram. The Page Number field is intended for displaying a page number on a page.
Custom Properties	Uses data entered in a shape's custom property fields to display shape information.
User-Defined Cells	Uses formulas entered in the Value and Prompt cells of a shape's User-Defined Cells ShapeSheet section.

When you insert a field, you can choose a format that determines how the field is displayed. Visio includes a field-formatting shorthand, which you can see in the Format area of the Field dialog box.

Among the more popular uses for fields are the following:

- **Insert page numbers in a diagram**   Use the Page Number field in the Page Info category.

- **Number selected shapes**   Use the ID field in the Object Info category. This one's a little tricky, because you have to select all the shapes you want to number, which means that the field replaces other text in the shapes. Visio numbers the shapes according to the order you added them to the drawing page.

- **Add the date you created the diagram**   Use the Creation Date field in the Date/Time category.

- **Display shape dimensions on a shape**   Use any of the fields in the Geometry category, which is a convenient way to update technical specifications in a drawing automatically, create dimension lines, or display the measure of the rotation angle.

Inserting a Field into Text

When you insert a field in text, Visio places the field at the insertion point. Make sure to add the appropriate spacing or punctuation around the field.

> **Tip**   Remember to add appropriate labels or phrases before or after fields. For example, type **Date:** and then insert a date field.

To insert a field into text, follow these steps:

1 Click the Text tool, click a shape, and then move the insertion point to where you want to insert the field.

The insertion point looks like a flashing I-beam. If you want the field to replace the text in the shape, just select the shape.

2 Select Insert, Field to display the Field dialog box.

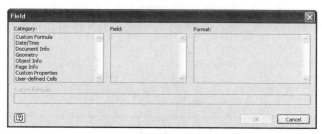

3 In the Category box, select a field category.

A list of fields for that category appears in the Field box.

> **Note** If you select the Custom Properties or User-Defined Cells category and nothing appears in the Field box, the shape does not include any custom property fields or formulas in user-defined cells.

4 In the Field section, select a field.

Format codes for the field are listed in the Format box.

5 In the Format box, select a format for the field information.

For example, if you select the Current Date field and select Long Date, the date appears as Thursday, November 15, 2001. If you select dd/MM/yy, the date appears as 15/11/01.

6 Click OK.

> **Tip** If the date and time seems incorrect, double-check your field parameters. A common mistake is setting the date and/or time to the Creation Date instead of the current date.

Editing Fields

Many ready-made Visio shapes include fields that display the date or other file information. You can edit these fields to change their display format or to display different information in the field. For example, some title blocks display the date in long form, such as Monday, September 10, 2001. You can edit the field to display the date in a different format, such as Sept. 10, 2001, or 9/10/01.

Chapter 4

To edit an existing text field, follow these steps:

1 Click the Text tool, click a shape, and then click a field.

   The field is selected. Note that you can't place an insertion point in a field. Instead, the entire field text is highlighted.

2 Choose Insert, Field.

   The Field dialog box appears and displays the current settings for the field.

3 To change the way the field is displayed, choose a new option under Format. Or choose a different field altogether by selecting an option in the Category and Field boxes.

4 When you've edited the field, click OK.

   Visio updates the shape.

Using Custom Formulas in Fields

If you're comfortable working with macro languages or have written ShapeSheet formulas, you might be interested in using the Custom Formula option to insert fields that display formula results. Typically, a custom formula includes either the FORMAT or FORMATEX function to format the formula results. The formula shorthand you use to format custom formulas is the same as that which Visio displays in the Format box of the Field dialog box. This shorthand, which Visio documentation calls a *format picture*, looks like a string of zeros, pound signs, and other characters and is used to specify the format for strings, numbers, currency, text, dates, and time.

For example, you can use a custom formula to display a shape's width using any units of measure you want. If you define a field using the Width field in the Geometry category, you're limited to displaying width in the default units of measure for the diagram. However, by creating a custom formula in a field, you can specify the units you want the result to display. If Width is in inches and you want to display it in centimeters, you would enter the following custom formula in the Fields dialog box:

```
= FORMATEX(Width,"0.00 u", "in.", "cm.")
```

If a shape is 1 inch wide, this formula displays its width as 2.54 cm.

For an introduction to formulas in Visio, see "Writing ShapeSheet Formulas," page 740. Also refer to the Developer Reference Help in your Visio product for details about working with functions and format pictures.

Chapter 5

Using Visio Diagrams on the Web

Need to communicate a new organization chart to everyone? Provide a floor plan that shows employees who sits where? If you have information to share with a large audience, the World Wide Web might be your most effective distribution medium, and Microsoft Office Visio 2003 includes many features that help you present your visual data effectively and quickly. When you combine the strengths of each Visio solution with its Web capabilities, you have a powerful tool for communicating ideas and information to anyone with access to your Web site.

You can export a Visio drawing or diagram as its own Web page or save it within an existing HTML template. You can also export a drawing as a graphic to include in any HTML file. You can even put the actual Visio drawing (in Visio or XML format) on your Web server so that other employees running Visio can open it in Microsoft Internet Explorer.

With the Visio viewer, even those without access to Visio can view Visio documents. The viewer is available at *http://www.microsoft.com/downloads*.

Using Microsoft's new SharePoint services, you can provide central locations for collaboration and sharing data. No, this isn't an integral part of Visio 2003, but it is an important tool in the Office toolbox.

Visio and the Web

Chances are your organization maintains a Web site on the Internet as well as an intranet site for internal communication. When you want to communicate processes, procedures, or other organizational information visually, you can save your Visio diagrams in a Web-compatible format to post on a Web site. Visio 2003 has the ability to save in a robust HTML format backed by XML.

When you save a Visio diagram as a Web page, you can take advantage of the following features:

- The Save As Web Page command on the File menu.
- Multiple shape hyperlinks to other pages, drawings, and URLs.
- A custom properties frame that displays shape data in a Web browser.

- For programmers, a documented application programming interface (API) for accessing the Save As Web Page functionality for batch conversion of files.

Earlier versions of Visio had several shortcomings that made its Save As HTML feature problematic. For some drawing types, the quality of the image maps that Visio created was poor. Large drawings—measured in terms of the number of shapes—sometimes couldn't be converted to HTML at all. The Save As Web Page command was introduced in Microsoft Office Visio 2002 to solve these issues and to provide a more consistent interface for Office users. Visio now supports raster images natively with its GDI+ display technology, which means drawings simply look better when converted for display on the Web.

> **Note** Visio no longer includes the option to create server-side image maps, which was a feature in the Export Options dialog box when you saved a Visio 2000 drawing as HTML.

Most of the impressive Save As Web Page options in Visio are compatible with Internet Explorer 6 and later browsers. You can't count on every viewer getting the full effect. However, those who use other browsers can still see the core of your page—the Visio drawing itself.

For details about Visio's support of XML, see "Visio and XML File Formats," page 616.

More Web Options in Visio Professional

Visio 2003 Professional can help you make your organization's Web site robust in other ways. For example, the Web Site Map template, included only with Visio Professional, makes it easy to diagram and troubleshoot Web sites on an intranet, Internet, or other network server.

For details about using Visio to diagram and troubleshoot a Web site, see Chapter 15, "Planning and Mapping Web Sites," page 393.

Linking Visio Shapes and Pages

You don't have to save your diagram as a Web page to create *hyperlinks*, which make it possible to jump from one shape or file to another. You can link a shape on one page of a diagram to a shape on another page that provides another view or more information. You can also link a shape to another Visio, Office, or other document, or even a Web address. Shapes can even contain multiple hyperlinks. And if you do add hyperlinks to shapes, and then save the diagram as a Web page, Visio preserves the links, which appear when you pause the pointer over a shape. In a diagram, hyperlinks that you define appear as options on a shape's shortcut menu, as Figure 5-1 shows.

Figure 5-1. When you define one or more hyperlinks, Visio adds the links to the shape's shortcut menu.

You can create, edit, and delete hyperlinks in Visio, and you can insert multiple hyperlinks for a single shape. If you need to link multiple shapes to a single destination, you can also copy a hyperlink or copy the hyperlink with its shape.

Hyperlink Icon

Tip When you point to a shape in Visio that contains a hyperlink, the pointer displays the hyperlink icon. Right-clicking the shape displays the link destination. Click on the destination to follow the hyperlink.

Linking to Another Shape, Page, Document, or Web Site

In Visio, a hyperlink links a specific shape or page to something else. Whether you want to link to another shape, page, document, or Web site, you must provide what Visio calls an *address*. As Figure 5-2 shows, the Hyperlink dialog box includes two types of addresses:

- **Address**   Specifies the URL of an Internet address or the file path for a document, including another Visio drawing file (.vsd), Office document, or any other type of file.
- **Sub-address**   Specifies a page and shape in the current Visio diagram, or an anchor (an <A> tag) within the body of the HTML page specified in the Address box.

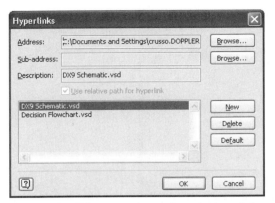

Figure 5-2. When you choose Insert, Hyperlinks, you can link to Internet addresses, files, or other pages in the current drawing file.

It's a little confusing to think of a shape or page in your diagram as a subaddress, but that's how the Hyperlink dialog box works. By default, Visio uses a *relative path* for the address, which means that Visio stores the location of the link's target (the page, file, or Web address) relative to the location of the drawing file. The advantage to you is that when you can link your drawing file to another file, you can move the files to a new folder without breaking the link. The opposite of a relative link is an *absolute link*, which specifies the exact location of a linked file (that is, its drive, folder, and file name). With an absolute link, you can move the drawing file that contains the hyperlink, and the link will not break.

The Hyperlink dialog box includes another option, the Default button, which you can use to specify a default hyperlink when a shape has more than one.

Linking to a Web Site

Follow these steps to create a hyperlink to a Web site:

1   Select a shape. Or, to add a hyperlink to a page, make sure nothing is selected.

2   Choose Insert, Hyperlinks or click the Insert Hyperlink button on the Web toolbar (you can also press Ctrl+K).

3   If you know the exact URL you want to use, type it in the Address box. Otherwise, click Browse to the right of the Address box, and then choose Internet Address to start your browser. (You must be online.) Locate the site you want, and copy its address. Switch to Visio, and then paste the URL in the Address box.

4   To link to a specific location on the page, type the anchor name or fragment identifier in the Sub-Address box. For example, type **#Sales** to specify the anchor link defined as <A href="#Sales">.

5   To change the name that appears on the shortcut menu for the hyperlink, type the text you want in the Description box.

6   Click OK, or click New—and repeat steps 1–5—to add another hyperlink.

Linking to a File

Follow these steps to create a hyperlink to a Visio, Office, or other file:

1 Select a shape. Or, to add a hyperlink to a page, make sure nothing is selected.

2 Choose Insert, Hyperlinks or click the Insert Hyperlink button on the Web toolbar (you can also press Ctrl+K).

3 Click Browse next to the Address box, and then click Local File.

4 In the Link To File dialog box, make sure the appropriate file type is selected in the Files Of Type list, navigate to the file you want to link to, and then click Open.

> **Note** If you haven't saved the file you want to link to, it won't appear. You must save the document before you can link to it.

5 To change the name that appears on the shortcut menu for the hyperlink, type the text you want in the Description box.

6 If you want to link to the file by its exact file path rather than by a relative path, clear the Use Relative Path For Hyperlink check box.

7 Click OK, or click New to add another hyperlink.

Linking to a Page or Shape

You can create a link from a shape on one page to another page, and even zoom in to a specific shape on that page. To link to a shape, you must use a unique name. You can easily find that name and use it to refer to the shape. A shape's name is displayed when you choose Format, Special or in the title bar of the Custom Properties window when you've selected the shape. Follow these steps to create a hyperlink to a shape or page in the current drawing file:

1 Select a shape. Or, to add a hyperlink to a page, make sure nothing is selected.

2 Choose Insert, Hyperlinks.

3 Click Browse next to the Sub-Address box to display the Hyperlink dialog box.

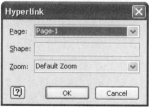

4 In the Page list, select the name of the page you want to link to.

5 If you want the link to go to a particular shape, type the name of the shape in the Shape box.

6 To change the zoom level when the page is displayed, choose an option in the Zoom list. This option is particularly useful if you're linking to a specific shape.

7 Click OK to return to the Hyperlinks dialog box.

8 To change the name that appears on the shortcut menu for the hyperlink, type the text you want in the Description box.

9 Click OK, or click New to add another hyperlink.

Using a Relative Path

When you use a relative path, Visio uses the location of the current drawing file as the basis for finding the linked file. If you want to specify a relative path for the hyperlinks in the Visio drawing that is not based on the location of the drawing file, specify it in the file's properties. After closing the Hyperlinks dialog box, choose File, Properties, and then type the base path you want to use in the Hyperlink Base box, as Figure 5-3 shows.

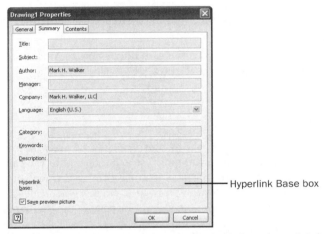
— Hyperlink Base box

Figure 5-3. You can specify a relative path for a hyperlink by choosing File, Properties.

The relative path for a Visio drawing file used to be specified in the Options dialog box on the File Paths tab. It has been moved to Tools, Options, Advanced, File Paths. Visio uses this information to search for stencils, templates, and other Visio files. To define a new relative path for a Visio file, choose Tools, Options, Advanced, and then click File Paths. Type a new path in one or more of the boxes.

Adding a Hyperlink Navigation Shape

Visio includes hyperlink navigation shapes so you can make it easier for viewers to navigate your Visio drawings on the Web. Visio includes three hyperlink navigation shapes on the Borders And Titles stencil, as Figure 5-4 shows. The buttons work like any other hyperlink in Visio. The only difference is that when you drag a Hyperlink shape onto the drawing page, the Hyperlinks dialog box opens so that you can specify a Web page, file, page, or shape. To activate the link, you must right-click the shape to display the shortcut menu that includes the link.

Chapter 5

Figure 5-4. When you use the Hyperlink Circle 2 (at left), Hyperlink Button, or Hyperlink Circle 1 shape from the Borders And Titles stencil, you can select the icon that appears on the button.

 Inside Out

Make any shape a navigation shape

You can make any shape a navigation shape by adding a hyperlink to it and typing the appropriate label. You aren't required to use these navigation shapes; they are merely a convenience and can give your drawing a more consistent look.

The hyperlink shapes don't include text labels, because they're designed to be iconographic—and you can choose the icon that appears. However, you can type a label for the hyperlink shape as you would for any shape. Select the shape, and then type. You can reposition the label with the shape's control handle. To change the icon for a hyperlink shape, right-click the shape, choose Change Icon, and then select an option in the Icon Type list. Table 5-1 shows the icons that you can display.

Table 5-1. Hyperlink Shape Icons

Icon	Icon Type	Icon	Icon Type
	Back		Forward
	Directory		Help
	Down		Home
	Info		Photo
	Mail		Search
	None		Up

Modifying or Deleting a Hyperlink

After you've created a hyperlink, you might need to modify it—perhaps the linked file has been moved or renamed, or you want to change the magnification for a linked shape. Anything you can specify when you create a hyperlink can be changed just as easily.

Follow these steps to modify or delete a hyperlink:

1 Select the shape or the page that contains the hyperlink, and then choose Insert, Hyperlinks.

2 If the shape contains multiple hyperlinks, select the link you want to change in the list of links at the bottom of the dialog box.

3 To delete the hyperlink, click Delete in the Hyperlinks dialog box.

4 To modify the hyperlink, make the changes you want.

5 Click OK.

Copying Hyperlinks

When you add a hyperlink to a shape or page, you can copy the shape or page and then paste it in Visio with the hyperlink intact. Even better, you can paste just the hyperlink to add it to another shape or page. For example, if you want the same home page hyperlink to appear on each page of a multiple-page diagram, you can copy and paste the hyperlink. You don't have to manually insert a new hyperlink each time.

Follow these steps to copy a hyperlink to other Visio shapes:

1 Select a shape that contains a hyperlink, and then press Ctrl+C to copy it.

2 Select a new shape on the same page, on another page, or in another Visio drawing file.

3 Choose Edit, Paste As Hyperlink.

Microsoft Office 2000 and later applications also include the Paste As Hyperlink command, which means that you can paste the hyperlink from a Visio shape into Word, for example, to create hyperlinked text. To paste a hyperlink into a document in another application, choose Edit, Paste As Hyperlink. Only the shape's text (if it has any) and its hyperlink are pasted. To paste just the shape, choose Edit, Paste Special, and then choose a file format. The shape is pasted but not its hyperlink.

Troubleshooting

When you click a link to a Visio diagram, Internet Explorer opens instead of Visio

If you click a link to a Visio drawing file on a Web site, Internet Explorer can open the Visio drawing file. This behavior might seem strange if you were expecting Visio to start. However, you can edit Visio drawings within Internet Explorer and even drag shapes from stencils. If you don't see the Visio toolbars and menus, click the Tools button on the Internet Explorer toolbar to display them. When Internet Explorer opens a Visio drawing, you can edit a diagram while retaining the advantages of the Web environment. For example, you can use the Forward and Back buttons to display other Web pages and other Office documents.

Exporting Visio Diagrams for Use on the Web

Anyone with a Web browser can view your Visio diagrams—including the data stored with shapes—when you save the drawing file as a Web page. Saving a diagram in Web format isn't much different from saving it in Visio format, although you have more options. However, all you really have to do is choose File, Save As Web Page, type a file name, and then click OK. Visio creates one or more Web pages and all the supporting files and graphics, which you can open in a browser such as Internet Explorer, as Figure 5-5 shows.

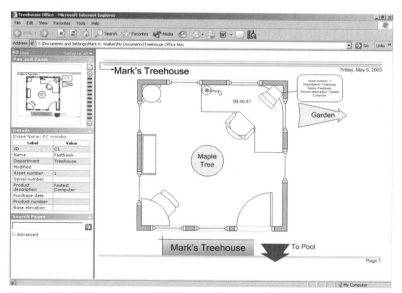

Figure 5-5. Visio creates a Web page from your diagram that includes the shapes' custom properties. You can pan the drawing with the scroll bars, change the zoom level, and use the shapes' hyperlinks.

The Save As Web Page command is easiest to use if you have Internet Explorer 6 or later, because the default options are set to work with the latest Microsoft browser. However, Visio automatically customizes certain settings and disables others when it detects Netscape Navigator or an earlier version of a browser that does not support Vector Markup Language (VML) and XML. For these browsers, the Visio diagram remains visible, but hyperlinks and custom property data might not be.

Files Created by the Save As Web Page Command

When you use the Save As Web Page command, Visio creates all the files necessary to display the contents of the drawing in a Web browser. If you have developed Web pages, you know how many files it takes to display even one page. As a result of the Save As Web Page command, you could have a dozen or more files associated with the HTML page that Visio creates. Visio creates the root HTML file in the location you specify. All the other files that are required for the drawing are stored in a subfolder unless you specify otherwise.

Visio creates a subfolder with the same name as the root HTML file but appends "_files" to the folder name. The addition of "_files" to the folder name allows the folder and files to follow each other. That is, if you delete the root *.htm file, the subfolder is also deleted, and vice versa. After Visio generates a Web page, you cannot rename the root *.htm file.

For each page in the drawing, Visio creates an HTML file that defines the frames, a VML graphics file that contains the diagram's shapes and text, and—if you request it—an alternate graphics file containing the same data in a format you select for browsers that don't recognize VML. Visio also creates all the necessary supporting files, including cascading style sheets (.css files), and other features you've requested, such as scroll bars, page tabs, magnification (zoom) options, and custom property data. Most of these features require Internet Explorer 6 or later to work as expected.

Visio creates standard HTML files that you can edit in an HTML editor or in any text-editing application, such as Windows Notepad. If you modify or move any of the HTML files, you might need to modify the pointers to graphic files.

Creating Web Pages from Visio Diagrams

Everything starts with the Save As Web Page command on the File menu, which opens a modified version of the Save As dialog box, as Figure 5-6 shows. You can provide a file name, click Save, and be done with it, or you can click Publish to customize the page options.

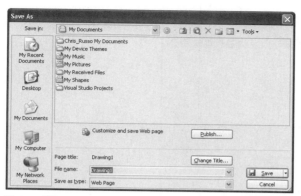

Figure 5-6. When you choose File, Save As Web Page, this dialog box appears.

> **Note** If you choose File, Save As, and then specify Web Page as the file type, the options for saving Web pages are added to the Save As dialog box.

Follow these steps to save a drawing as a Web page:

1 Choose File, Save As Web Page.

2 From the Save In list, open the folder in which you want to save the file. In the File Name box, type a name for the Web page.

3 To customize the title that will appear on the title bar when the page is displayed in a browser, click Change Title. In the Page Title box of the Set Page Title dialog box, type a title, and then click OK.

Chapter 5

4 To define the attributes of the Web page in greater detail, click Publish.

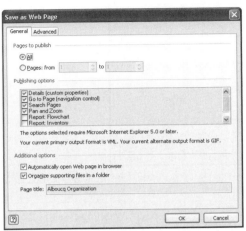

5 On the General tab, specify which drawing pages to publish, whether to display the custom property viewer, and whether to use the Go To Page (Navigation Control), Search Pages, Pan And Zoom, and Report: Inventory options.

6 Under Additional Options select the Automatically Open Web Page In Browser check box to open the page in your browser after saving. Select the Organize Supporting Files In A Folder check box to put the files in a folder as described earlier.

7 To specify a graphic format other than VML, click the Advanced tab, and then specify a graphic format in the Output Formats list. If you want to specify an alternate format other than GIF, select the Provide Alternate Format For Older Browsers check box, select the format you want from the drop-down list.

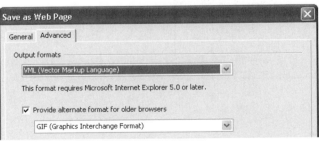

8 In the Display Options section, specify the target monitor screen size.

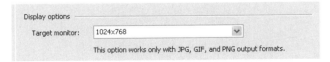

9 Select where you would like to host the page in the Host As Web Page drop-down list. Under Style Sheet, choose a style for your Web page.

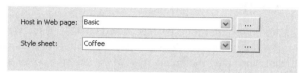

10 Click OK to save the Web page. Visio will also automatically open your Web browser so you can view the results.

Displaying Shape Data in a Frame

When Visio saves a diagram as a Web page, it also saves any custom property data stored with the diagram's data. This information appears in a frame when you view the resulting Web page in Internet Explorer 6 or later. If the shapes include custom properties, as many do, Visio will display them in a frame with your Web page—even if you haven't stored data with the shape's properties. As you Ctrl + Click different shapes on the Web page, the custom property data is displayed in a frame on the left side of the browser window, as Figure 5-7 shows.

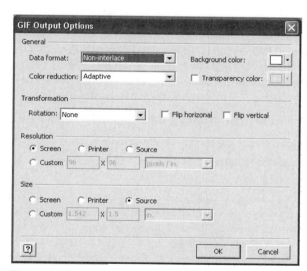

Figure 5-7. Custom properties appear in a frame by default when you save a diagram as a Web page.

Chapter 5

157

VML Graphics in Browsers Other Than Internet Explorer

VML is an emerging standard for Internet drawings based on XML. Because it provides good-quality vector images for the Web, VML is the default format for the images Visio exports with its HTML files, including the image map of the drawing page. VML graphics offer the scalability and precision that come with vector graphic formats, which isn't available with raster formats such as GIF or JPEG. For example, the quality of VML graphics is not compromised when browsers zoom in on them. Because VML graphics are vector-based, they also download more quickly than raster-based Web graphics.

When you export your HTML file, you can choose an alternate graphic format for browsers that do not support VML. The alternate graphic file is referenced in the HTML file, and that's what viewers using other browsers will see. By default, GIF is the alternate format. To change that, or to change the primary format from VML, click Publish in the Save As dialog box, and then click Format Options on the General tab to make the necessary changes.

If you don't use VML graphics, you won't see the option to change the zoom level of the drawing in the browser; therefore, that option is never available in browsers that do not support VML.

If you open the Visio-generated Web page in a browser that does not support frames, only the diagram will appear. Depending on the browser, a message might appear first saying that the page requires features not supported by the browser. If you don't want this message to appear, you can disable the custom property frames when you generate the Web page.

Follow these steps to prevent Visio from adding a custom property frame to your Web page:

1 Choose File, Save As Web Page, and then click Publish.

2 On the General tab, click Publishing Options.

3 Specify other settings as desired, and then click OK.

Tip When you display a Visio Web page with custom properties, a shape's details (that is, its custom properties) can be displayed by Ctrl+clicking on the shape. The details will remain visible until you Ctrl+click on another shape.

Viewing Multiple Hyperlinks in a Shape

If you're using Internet Explorer 5 or later, you can view and use multiple hyperlinks in a shape on a Web page, as Figure 5-8 shows. If you're using a different browser, you might see the hyperlinks but not be able to use them.

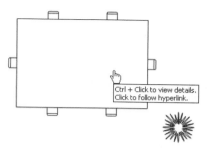

Figure 5-8. If a shape includes hyperlinks, they'll appear when you point to the shape in Internet Explorer 5 or later.

Troubleshooting

An error appears when you try to rename a file created by the Save As Web Page command

Visio links all the supporting files to a root file, *.htm. If you rename this file, the following message appears:

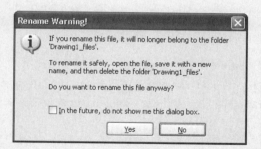

This message lets you know that the links between the root file and its supporting files will be broken. If you try to display the page in your browser, graphic elements might be missing, or you might see an error informing you that the page cannot be displayed. Visio looks for the supporting files based on the root file's name. If that name changes, the Web page can't be displayed correctly. You can use the Save As Web Page command again to specify a different file name when you generate the Web page.

To follow a link when a shape includes more than one, click the shape. The links appear in a list next to the shape. You can then select the one you want, as Figure 5-9 shows.

Chapter 5

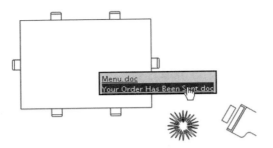

Figure 5-9. If a shape includes multiple hyperlinks, you can find the one you want by clicking the shape and choosing from the list that appears.

Troubleshooting

In Netscape Navigator, multiple hyperlinks appear on the shape but they all jump to the same place

Some browsers do not support multiple hyperlinks. However, you can specify a default hyperlink in Visio that will be used as the link's target in browsers that support only one link per shape. That way, you can keep all the hyperlinks you have added to a shape but make sure that users with other browsers will see the link you specify. To do this, you need to edit the hyperlink in Visio before you save the diagram as a Web page.

Follow these steps to specify a default hyperlink:

1 Select a shape with multiple hyperlinks in Visio, and then choose Insert, Hyperlinks.

2 In the box that lists the hyperlinks, select the one you want to be the default link, and then click Default.

3 Click OK.

Embedding a Visio Drawing into an Existing Web Page

Most organizations use a consistent design template for the pages of their Web sites. You can insert the Web pages that Visio creates into an existing HTML template that you can specify when you use the Save As Web Page command. Visio includes a sample template, Basic.htm, that you can copy and customize, or you can use one you already have. The critical piece of information that a template must include is the following HTML tag, which you place wherever you want the Visio drawing to appear on the Web page:

```
<IFRAME src="%%VIS_SAW_FILE%%">
```

This tag refers to the HTML output file that Visio creates for the drawing (SAW for Save As Web). When Visio creates a Web page, it embeds the drawing information into an inline frame using an <IFRAME> tag. The Basic template includes a default version of the <IFRAME> tag with specified dimensions. You can open the Basic template and make changes or copy the information to an existing HTML file and then customize the <IFRAME> tag to control the width, height, border, and other attributes of the inline frame. By default, Visio installs the Basic template (Basic.htm) in C:\Program Files\Microsoft Office\Visio11\1033\ . If you save your template in the same folder, it will appear as an option in the Save As Web Page dialog box, as Figure 5-10 shows.

> **Note** The <IFRAME> tag works best in Internet Explorer 3 and later and Netscape Navigator 6.

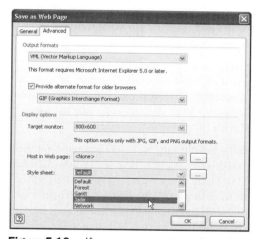

Figure 5-10. If you save a custom theme in the Visio directory structure, it appears as an option on the Advanced tab.

After you create a template file, follow these steps to apply it:

1 In Visio, choose File, Save As Web Page, and then click Publish.
2 On the Advanced tab, select the template you want to use from the Host In Web Page drop-down list.
3 If your theme doesn't appear, click Browse to locate and select the file.
4 Specify other settings as desired, and then click OK.

Chapter 5

Troubleshooting

Visio displays HTML code instead of graphics

When you use the Save As Web Page command and specify to use an HTML template, Visio displays the HTML coding instead of your diagram if the template doesn't include the requisite <IFRAME> tag.

In your HTML file, insert the following tag where you want the Visio diagram to appear:

```
<IFRAME src="%%VIS_SAW_FILE%%">
```

Using a Visio Diagram as a Web Graphic

If you want to use your Visio diagram as part of a larger Web site, or you plan to distribute it electronically without including the custom property data, you can save it in a graphic format. When you save a portion of your diagram or the entire diagram as a graphic, Visio creates a new file—your original drawing file isn't changed.

Visio supports three Web graphic formats: Joint Photographic Experts Group (JPEG), Graphics Interchange Format (GIF), and Portable Network Graphics (PNG). Almost all browsers display JPEG and GIF images; earlier browsers might not display PNG images. When you save a Visio drawing, or shapes in a Visio drawing, in a graphic format, no custom property data or hyperlinks are saved with the graphic.

To save a Visio drawing as a Web graphic, you use the Save As command on the File menu and then specify the format you want in the Save As Type box. When you click Save, you'll see a dialog box similar to the one shown in Figure 5-11 with options that affect the way the graphic file will be saved. You can specify resolution, image size, transformation, and color options. You can also choose whether the image will be interlaced or not. *Interlaced* images appear in the Web browser in stages, as more information is downloaded; *noninterlaced* images appear all at once. For JPEG images, the options are *progressive* and *baseline*. Progressive JPEGs are like a smoother version of an interlaced GIF, but not all Web browsers support them.

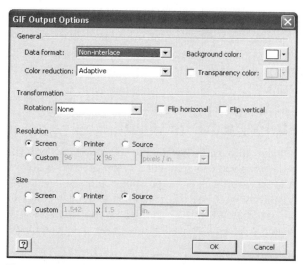

Figure 5-11. When you save shapes or a diagram in a Web-compatible graphic format such as GIF, you can specify options for how the image is downloaded and displayed.

Note An interlaced GIF can be displayed by a browser that does not support the interlaced format (the image is displayed normally); however, a progressive JPEG will not load at all in a browser that does not support the progressive format.

 Inside Out

Creating a VML Graphic

Although Visio supports the VML format for the Web pages it creates, you can't save a drawing in VML format when you use the Save As command. However, you can still create a VML graphic in a slightly roundabout way: Save your diagram as a Web page, and then use the VML graphic (*.vml) that Visio creates in the subfolder for that page.

Chapter 5

Most Visio drawings retain their integrity and appear sharpest when saved as GIF images rather than as JPEG or PNG images. However, the best graphic format to use depends on the kind of drawing you're saving and how you will use it. For example, .tif or .bmp formats usually work best if the file will be used as part of printed matter. If you have the time, save your diagram in different graphic formats and select different options, and then compare quality and file sizes to see which one best meets your needs.

Tip Add a Visio graphic to a Web page

To include an exported Visio graphic in a Web page, add the <IMG> tag to the HTML file for the page. For example, if your exported graphic is named Drawing1.gif, store it in the same folder as the HTML file and then include the line <IMG SRC="Drawing1.gif"> in the HTML file.

Automating Web Page Generation

Visio exposes its Web functionality through its API so that you save Visio files as HTML programmatically. There are two ways you can go about it. Visio exposes a Component Object Model (COM) object that anyone using an automation-compliant language can create. The main interface is IVisSaveAsWeb. The easier method is through a command-line interface, where you embed a call to the RUNADDONWARGS function onto a shape's Event section in the ShapeSheet window. An example call to the add-in looks like this:

```
=RUNADDONWARGS("SaveAsWeb","/target=c:\temp\mypage.htm /quiet
/prop /startpage=1 /endpage=3 /altformat /priformat=vml
/secformat=jpg /openbrowser")
```

Although it's beyond the scope of this book to explain how to write programs that work with Visio, you can refer to the Developer Reference (choose Help, Developer Reference) in Visio. In addition, Microsoft has made the documentation for this interface available on its Web site. See *http://msdn.microsoft.com* for the latest information.

Storing Data in Diagrams

Besides the great visuals you get from a drawing or diagram, you can use Microsoft Office Visio 2003 to store a great deal of information. Most diagram types are designed to include data in the form of customizable shape properties called custom properties. Custom properties provide a data-entry interface for a shape. For example, organization chart shapes can store data about employees, such as name and job title. Network shapes can store data about devices and equipment, such as manufacturer and model number. You don't have to take advantage of these properties; your drawings and diagrams can remain just as they are. But if you want to provide a deeper layer of information about your drawing's contents—information that can be extracted in reports and other forms—you can store data as custom properties.

This chapter describes how to use and revise the built-in custom properties that come with many Visio shapes and how to create new properties. In addition, this chapter describes the reporting tools that can be used for any drawing or diagram that contains custom property data.

Working with Shapes, Data, and Custom Properties

During Visio's development cycles, the product's designers realized that the drawings could have value beyond their worth as graphical representations. Part of what makes a Visio drawing valuable is the investment of time taken to create it, but a more significant part of a drawing's value comes in the form of important, job-critical information that can be stored right in the drawing. When you view the shapes in a drawing as meaningful conveyors of information, rather than simply graphics, you can use Visio to model systems and processes. In this sense, for example, an organization chart is not just a chart, but also a visual representation of an employee database, and shapes can serve as records in that database complete with specific fields of data, such as employee name, title, date of hire, and so on. In Visio, a *custom property* is the means by which you associate valuable data with a shape.

You can see whether a shape has custom properties by displaying the Custom Properties window. When you select a shape on the page, the shape's properties are displayed, as Figure 6-1 shows. Some custom properties operate like fields that you type in; others are set up to provide a list of options. When you click in the latter type, an arrow appears, indicating that you can open a drop-down list of choices.

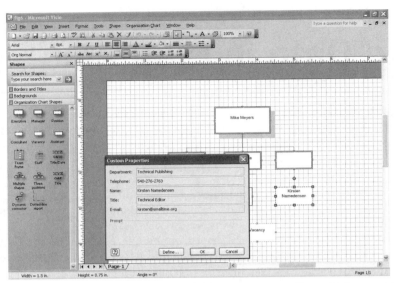

Figure 6-1. Many Visio shapes include custom properties, which you can define to store valuable information with a drawing.

Why would you want to go through all the effort of using a drawing as a data-entry form? Typing in custom property fields is bound to be time consuming. And when you look at a drawing, you don't necessarily know whether there's more data behind the shapes. The answer lies in what you can do with the data once you've entered it. Visio can automatically generate reports based on custom property data. You can display the results in a table in your drawing or save them as an external report file in HTML or XML format. Information about reports is covered later in this chapter.

In addition, you can automate the process of adding data to and extracting it from custom properties. Visio can read comma-delimited text files and a variety of databases, and custom property information can be exported. By connecting diagrams and the shapes in them to live sources of data, your drawing becomes a visual representation of your database. Companies have used Visio to set up visual network inventories, manufacturing parts databases, and other mission-critical systems where a diagram provides a recognizable and easy-to-use interface for business data.

For details about linking custom properties to existing data, see Chapter 24, "Connecting Diagrams and Databases," page 711.

Using Shapes with Custom Properties

Visio shapes that include built-in custom properties do so for one of two reasons:

- To provide configurable options that affect the shape's appearance. These options allow one shape to represent several different types of symbols. For example, in an office layout, the 110-volt outlet shape can represent the symbol for a standard, dedicated, or split-wired outlet. You choose which one by using the Outlet Type custom property. Other shapes let you configure them, such as the bar graph shape, which includes a custom property for setting the number of bars.

- To provide a means of associating data with a shape. For example, you can track model numbers for equipment and furniture in an office or network layout.

This chapter is concerned primarily with the second use of custom properties—tracking data in diagrams. However, some shapes include both types of custom properties, as Figure 6-2 shows. For example, the outlet shape includes blank custom properties Base Elevation. You can enter data for this field if you want to track this type of information in an office layout or floor plan, or you can leave it blank. The shape looks the same on the page either way.

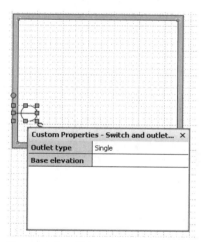

Figure 6-2. This outlet shape includes custom properties for configuring the symbol (Outlet Type) as well as optional properties for tracking data (Base Elevation).

 Inside Out

Inside custom properties

For Visio shape designers, custom properties are often the easiest way to build intelligence into shapes. That's why custom properties perform double duty—they're used to configure and store data with shapes. When the designers want a single shape to represent multiple symbols, as with the single or duplex outlet shape, they can provide the options to you most easily in the Custom Properties window.

Most shapes include at least a few custom properties for configuring that shape. A few diagram types include shapes with no custom properties at all. Other diagram types are specifically designed for tracking data, such as the organization chart shapes, and often include special commands or wizards to help you set up the data. In the chapters of this book that focus on specific diagram types, you'll find information about shapes with special custom properties.

Creating Properties in Master Shapes

How is it that some shapes already include custom properties? The explanation lies in how shapes inherit information from masters when you drag them from stencils onto the drawing page. You can create and save custom properties with master shapes, which is what the Visio shape designers have done, as Figure 6-3 shows. By dragging a shape on the page, you create a copy of the master shape that inherits all the master's custom properties (as well as other attributes). To use the custom properties, all you have to do is enter data.

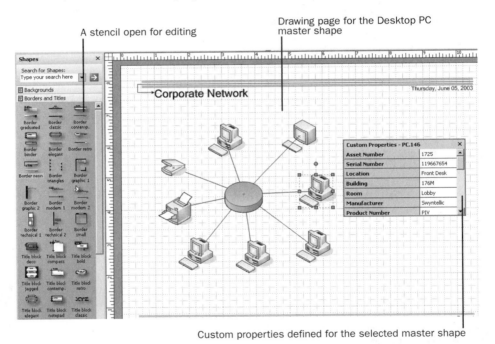

Figure 6-3. When custom properties are defined for a master shape, every time you drag that master onto the drawing page, your shape will include the same set of properties.

Because shapes inherit properties from the master shapes, it makes sense that when you want to edit or add custom properties, you work with the master shapes. You have to decide, though, which stencil to edit:

- Edit a Visio stencil file as Figure 6-3 shows when you want to add, edit, or remove custom properties for all drawings that use shapes from that stencil.

- Edit a document's stencil as Figure 6-4 shows when you want to add, edit, or remove custom properties for the shapes you've used in one drawing.

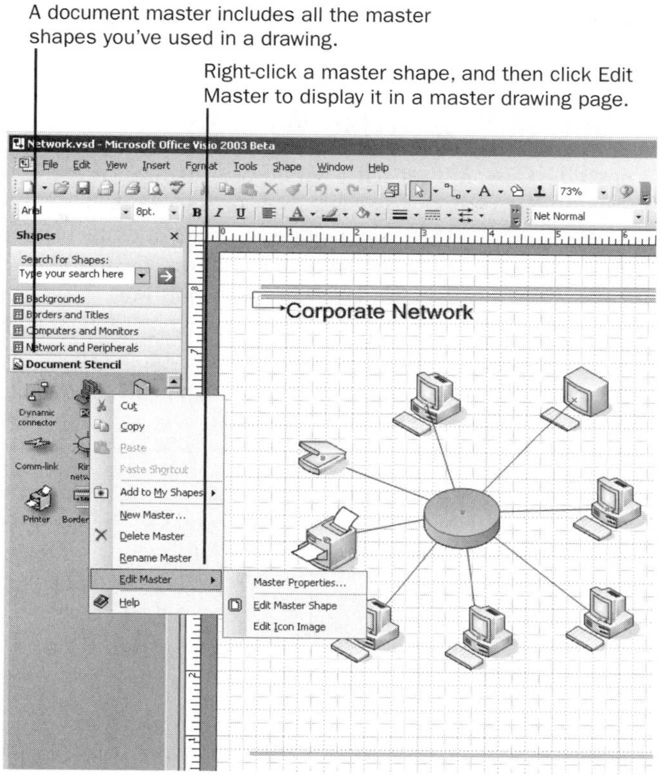

A document master includes all the master shapes you've used in a drawing.

Right-click a master shape, and then click Edit Master to display it in a master drawing page.

Figure 6-4. To edit custom properties in a way that affects only the shapes in a drawing, you can edit the master shapes on the document stencil.

Note In Visio 2003 you cannot edit the master stencils that ship with the software. You may add shapes to a custom stencil, such as My Shapes (described below), or edit the shapes on a document stencil, but you may not edit the master stencil.

In Visio 2003 you can right-click any shape in a master or document stencil, and choose the Add To My Shapes options. This allows you to add it to a stencil named My Shapes (or anything else you like).

This is a big decision because it affects where your changes are saved—with a reusable stencil file or just in your drawing. If you don't want to affect the shapes for all future uses, you clearly don't need to add the edited shapes to the My Shapes or any other custom stencil that you have created. In that case, you edit the document stencil in your drawing file. The

Chapter 6

document stencil stores a copy of each master shape you've used in a drawing. By editing the master shapes on the document stencil, all the shapes in your drawing that are based on those masters will be updated. In this way, you can add, edit, and delete custom properties and affect all the shapes in your drawing.

> For details about document stencils and the Visio file format, see "Mastering Visio Documents," page 609.

Customizing the Custom Properties Window

When you first open the Custom Properties window, Visio docks it against a ruler. However, you can place the window just about anywhere by dragging its title bar. The window can float on the drawing page and outside the Visio window, or it can dock against an edge of the page, below the drawing page in its own pane as Figure 6-5 shows, or in the stencil area. Table 6-1 lists the techniques for locating the Custom Properties window.

> **Tip** You may dock windows within windows. For example, you may dock the Custom Properties window with the Pan & Zoom window. Each window then displays a tab at the bottom of the window that you may select to display the window.

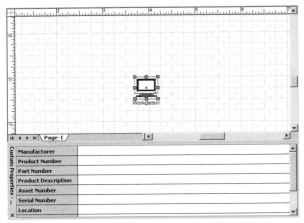

Figure 6-5. To prevent the Custom Properties window from obscuring your diagram while you work, you can dock the window below the drawing page.

Table 6-1. Arranging the Custom Properties Window

Task	Technique
Display the Custom Properties window	Choose View, Custom Properties Window.
Set the Custom Properties window to automatically move out of your way	Click the pushpin icon or right-click anywhere in the Custom Properties window, and then select Auto-Hide.

Table 6-1. **Arranging the Custom Properties Window**

Task	Technique
Keep the window open at all times	Click the pushpin icon or right-click in the Custom Properties window, and then deselect AutoHide.
Make the Custom Properties window float on the drawing page	Drag the window by its title bar away from its docked position, or right-click anywhere inside the Custom Properties window, and then choose Float Window.
Dock the Custom Properties window	Drag the title bar of the Custom Properties window into the stencil area, against the side of the drawing page, below the drawing page, or right-click anywhere inside the Custom Properties window and then choose Anchor Window.

Inside Out

The Custom Properties window and page properties

If no shapes are selected, the Custom Properties window lists any properties that are defined for the page. In general, page properties are used only by a Visio solution to configure the page for a particular diagram type. For example, the Gantt template uses page properties to set up default task information.

Tip   **Play a sound when the window opens**
You can have sounds play when the Custom Properties window opens and closes. To add sounds, open Windows Control Panel, choose Sounds, and then define a sound for the Restore Up and Restore Down event. Note that these changes will affect all Windows programs, not just Visio 2003.

Displaying Properties for One Shape

You can display the custom properties temporarily for one shape by right-clicking the shape, as Figure 6-6 shows, and then selecting Properties. This won't work for all shapes. Only shapes that are designed for tracking data or for setting configuration options include the Properties command on their shortcut menus. When you display shape properties this way, Visio opens the Custom Properties dialog box, as Figure 6-7 shows. You can then enter data and click OK to close the dialog box.

Chapter 6

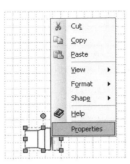

Figure 6-6. When you right-click some shapes with custom properties, the Properties command appears on their shortcut menus. Not all shapes include this command.

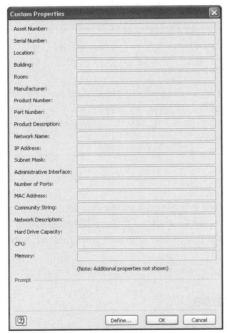

Figure 6-7. You can work in a shape's Custom Properties dialog box instead of the Custom Properties window, but both include the same set of properties. This dialog box is for a shape from the Basic Network Shapes stencil.

Creating Configurable Custom Properties

Can you create custom property fields that provide configurable options, such as the built-in Visio properties that display a drop-down list of options? The answer is yes, if you're willing to write a program to do so.

It's beyond the scope of this book to describe exactly how to write such a program, but it starts with the Custom Properties section of a ShapeSheet, where you can write formulas that link a shape's geometry or style attributes to its custom properties. In that way, you can design shapes that respond to user input in the Custom Properties window. In addition, you can use an external program to create custom properties and get and set custom property values. For details, refer to the developer reference (Help, Developer Reference) or search for Visio information on *http://msdn.microsoft.com*.

Accessing Custom Properties Through the ShapeSheet

If you want to study the way Visio shapes use custom properties, look in the ShapeSheet window. As Figure 6-8 shows, the Custom Properties section includes all the information you see in the Custom Properties window, plus a few additional options that shape programmers can take advantage of. For example, the Invisible cell lets you define a custom property that does not appear in the Custom Properties window—something you might want to do if you used an external program to control shape properties.

Custom Properties	Label	Prompt	Type	Format
Prop.ShapeClass	"ShapeClass"	No Formula	0	No Formula
Prop.ShapeType	"ShapeType"	No Formula	0	No Formula
Prop.SubShapeType	"SubShapeType"	No Formula	0	No Formula
Prop.Manufacturer	"Manufacturer"	No Formula	0	No Formula
Prop.ProductNumber	"Product Number"	No Formula	0	No Formula
Prop.PartNumber	"Part Number"	No Formula	0	No Formula
Prop.ProductDescription	"Product Description"	No Formula	0	No Formula
Prop.AssetNumber	"Asset Number"	No Formula	0	No Formula

Figure 6-8. Cells in the Custom Properties section of the ShapeSheet show the labels and values that you see in the Custom Properties window.

You can define custom properties and their values in the ShapeSheet window, but unless you're using a program to automate the process, you're better off working with the tools in the drawing page. However, the way Visio references ShapeSheet cells affects the way certain custom property options are displayed in other parts of the user interface. For example, let's say you define a custom property called Name. Visio adds a row to the Custom Properties section of the ShapeSheet called Prop.Name. When you're creating reports or exporting data, sometimes you'll see your property listed as Name and sometimes as Prop.Name. If you're writing ShapeSheet formulas that refer to the custom property cells, you must use proper ShapeSheet syntax. For example, to refer to the value of the Name custom property in a formula, you type **Prop.Name.Value** where .Value tells Visio to look in the Value column of the Name row of the Properties section.

For details about ShapeSheet syntax, see "Writing ShapeSheet Formulas," page 740.

Chapter 6

Entering Data in Shapes

A shape becomes a data-entry form when you enter values, or data, for its custom properties. In the Custom Properties window, the *label* is the name of a particular property, and the *value* is the information you type or select for a given property. The part of the custom property where you type is sometimes referred to as a *field*, because custom properties work like database fields. For example, in an office plan, you can enter a value for a furniture shape's Manufacturer property to create a visual record of purchase orders. In an organization chart, you can enter telephone numbers to create a visual employee phone list, as Figure 6-9 shows. After you enter values for custom properties, you can extract them in a report, as described later in this chapter.

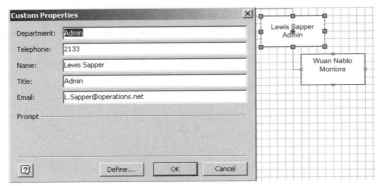

Figure 6-9. In this organization chart, shapes include a custom property for employee telephone extension. By entering data in the Telephone field, you can create a visual phone list.

> **Tip** When you're entering values for a number of shapes, dock the Custom Properties window under or along the drawing page so that you can see all the properties and shapes. Then you can click a shape to see its properties.

To enter data for a shape's custom properties, follow these steps:

1. Select a shape.

2. If the Custom Properties window is not already open, choose View, Custom Properties Window.

   If no custom properties have been defined for the shape, you'll see a message to that effect in the Custom Properties window.

3. Click in a custom property field, type a value, and then press Enter.

   If you click in a field and an arrow appears, the custom property is meant to provide configurable options for the shape. Depending on the shape, you might be able to type in the field. For example, the Wall Thickness custom property for wall shapes displays a drop-down list of options, but you can also type any value for thickness. Wall Height displays a similar set of options.

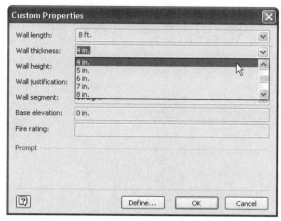

4   When you've entered values for a shape, select a new shape on the page to display its values.

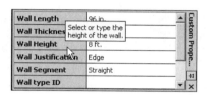

Tip   Display Help for a Custom Property
If you aren't sure what to enter in a custom property, display the property's prompt, which tells you what the field is for. To display a prompt in the Custom Properties window, point to the property label. In a shape's Custom Properties dialog box, the prompts are displayed at the bottom of the dialog box.

Defining Custom Properties

If you want to track information with your drawings, you probably also want to customize the custom properties. Perhaps your company uses a specific nomenclature for fields that you want your drawing to reflect. Or maybe you want to remove some custom properties to streamline data entry. You can add and remove custom properties as well as edit their labels and the format used to display the values. Visio features two ways of accessing custom properties:

● Through the Custom Properties window, which lets you work with the properties of a single shape or master shape.

● By editing custom property sets, which is described later in this chapter. This lets you define multiple properties at once (that is, a custom property set), which can be applied to multiple shapes at once.

Chapter 6

Whether you work with individual shapes in the Custom Properties window or create custom property sets, you will encounter the Define Custom Properties dialog box, as Figure 6-10 shows. Working with this dialog box can be a little tricky, because as soon as you specify an option, it's applied to a property.

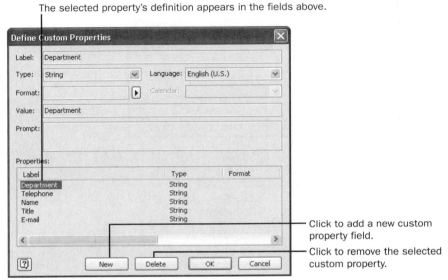

The selected property's definition appears in the fields above.

Click to add a new custom property field.

Click to remove the selected custom property.

Figure 6-10. You can change the definition for an existing custom property in the Define Custom Properties dialog box; for example, you can type a new label, which then appears in the Custom Properties window.

The options in this dialog box let you define the properties that appear in the Custom Properties window, as Table 6-2 shows. If you're working with a shape that already has custom properties, the existing properties are listed at the bottom of the Define Custom Properties dialog box in the Properties box. When a property is selected in this box, the dialog box displays its definition in the fields on top, so if you make changes to one of the options, the change is immediately reflected in the custom property's definition.

Table 6-2. Options in the Define Custom Properties Dialog Box

Option	What It Does
Label	Provides the name of the property as you want it to appear in the Custom Properties window.
Type	Lists Visio data types that you can specify for a value. If you aren't sure what to choose, select String.
Format	Specifies a format for the type of data. The options change depending on the type you select. Not all property types have formats that you can choose. When you select an option, a format code appears in the Format box that tells Visio how to display the property's value.

Table 6-2. **Options in the Define Custom Properties Dialog Box**

Option	What It Does
Value	Shows the current value of the property or lets you set an initial value for a new property. If you leave it blank, an empty field is displayed in the Custom Properties window.
Prompt	Provides an instructional or descriptive prompt about the property. Prompts are optional, but they're useful for describing the purpose of the custom property. Your prompt text appears as a ScreenTip in the Custom Properties window or in the Prompt area of a shape's Define Custom Properties dialog box.
Properties	Lists the custom properties that are already defined for a shape. If you select a property from the list, you can then change the Label, Type, Format, Value, and Prompt settings, and your changes are immediately applied to the custom property definition.
New	Creates a new custom property and initializes the Label, Type, Format, Value, and Prompt options so that you can define the new property.
Delete	Deletes the custom property selected in the Properties box.

Defining Custom Properties for Individual Shapes

If you really want to revise the custom properties for one shape in one drawing, you can do so. You can edit shape properties directly in the Custom Properties window or Custom Properties dialog box without affecting any custom property sets that have been defined for the shapes. The changes you make are saved only with the drawing. If the shape is based on a master shape, your changes to the shape do not affect the master or any other instances of the master you've dragged onto the drawing page.

Tip Change a shape
If you want to change all shapes in a drawing, edit the shape's instance on the document stencil. If you want to change the shape for all future uses, right-click the shape and add it to My Shapes. You may then edit the shape from the My Shapes stencil. Whenever you wish to use the edited shap in a drawing, open the My Shapes stencil (by clicking File, Shapes, My Shapes) and drag the shape onto the page.

To add or edit custom properties for one shape, follow these steps:

1 Select a shape on the drawing page.

2 If the Custom Properties window is not already open, choose View, Custom Properties Window.

   If no properties have been defined for the shape, Visio displays a message to that effect in the Custom Properties window.

3 Right-click anywhere in the Custom Properties window, and then choose Define Properties.

Chapter 6

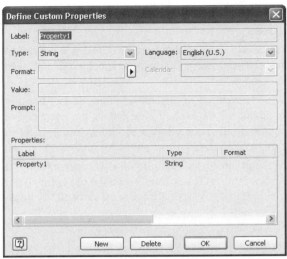

4 If the shape already includes custom properties, in the Properties box, select the property you want to edit, or click New.

When you select an existing property, its settings are displayed in the dialog box. As soon as you change a setting, the new specifications are applied to the selected property.

5 Define the new property, or revise the selected property, by typing or selecting the values you want for Label, Type, Format, Value, and Prompt. For details about these options, see Table 6-2.

6 When you've defined the property, do one of the following:

- Select a new property to edit in the Properties box.
- Click New to define a new custom property.
- Click OK to close the Define Custom Properties dialog box.

Visio adds the properties to the shape, which you can see in the Custom Properties window.

Defining Custom Properties for Master Shapes

One time when it is handy to add or edit an individual shape's custom properties is when you're working in a custom stencil. You might apply a set of custom properties to all the shapes in the stencil and then edit a particular master shape in the custom stencil to customize its properties. The procedure is basically the same as the one for a shape on the drawing page. The difference is in the first couple of steps, in which you open a custom stencil and edit a master.

> **Note** You may not edit the master shapes on the stencils that ship with Visio 2003. To edit a master you must first right-click the master and then save it to My Shapes or any other custom stencil that you have created. To create a stencil choose File, Shapes, New Stencil. No fuss, extremely little muss.

To add or edit custom properties for a master shape on a custom stencil, follow these steps:

1 Open the custom stencil containing the master shape you want to edit by doing one of the following:

   ■ To edit a master shape on an existing custom stencil, right-click the stencil's title bar, and then choose Edit.

   ■ To edit the copy of a master shape used by the shapes in a drawing, choose File, Stencils, Document Stencil to open the document stencil.

2 Right-click a master shape in the stencil, and then choose Edit Master to open the shape in a new drawing window.

3 If the Custom Properties window is not already open, choose View, Custom Properties Window.

4 Select the master shape.

   If the shape includes custom properties, they are displayed in the Custom Properties window. Otherwise, Visio displays the "No Custom Properties" message in the window.

5 Right-click anywhere in the Custom Properties window, and then choose Define Properties.

6 Select the property you want to edit, or click New.

   When you select an existing property, its settings are displayed in the dialog box. As soon as you change a setting, it's applied to the selected property.

7 Define the new property, or revise the selected property, by typing or selecting the values you want for Label, Type, Format, Value, and Prompt. For details about these options, see Table 6-2.

8 When you've defined the property, do one of the following:

   ■ Select a new property to edit in the Properties box.

   ■ Click New to define a new custom property.

   ■ Click OK to close the Define Custom Properties dialog box.

When you're ready to save your changes to the master shape, click Close Window in the master shape's drawing window. Make sure you click the correct button. Don't click the Visio window's Close button. Visio displays a message asking whether you want to update the master.

Chapter 6

If you edited the document stencil, the message differs slightly.

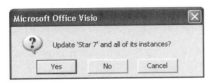

9 Click Yes.

If you edited a document stencil, all the shapes in the drawing that are based on the master shape you edited will include the revised custom properties. You can save your changes by doing one of the following:

- If you edited a custom stencil, right-click the title bar, choose Save As, and then specify a file name and location for the stencil.

- If you edited a document stencil, choose File, Save to save the changes with the drawing file.

- Whenever you change a custom stencil the Save icon appears in the right side of its title bar. Just click the icon to save your changes.

Using Custom Property Sets

You can edit the properties for any individual shape, or you can take advantage of Visio's custom property set. This feature provides a quick way to define and work with a group of custom properties, and then apply them wholesale to a group of shapes. To create a custom property set, you define a name for the set and then add the properties you want to include. Then you can apply your property set to selected shapes on the drawing page, the document stencil, or any open custom stencil. When you create custom properties in this way, it's easy to edit labels and formats for the entire set.

Custom property sets become especially useful when you import objects to use as shapes or draw shapes from scratch. The imported and from-scratch shapes won't have the same custom properties as other shapes in the drawing. For example, in a floor plan, shapes can be used to track facilities and equipment information through their custom properties. If you convert a CAD symbol library to Visio shapes, the converted shapes don't have custom properties. However, you can quickly add the entire set of facilities and equipment properties to the converted shapes.

You can apply only one custom property set to a shape or custom stencil master shape. When you apply a custom property set to a shape that already has a set, Visio applies the new property set and removes the previous one. If you apply a custom property set to a shape that has custom properties, but not a custom property set, the original properties are retained and the new set of properties is added.

Inside Out

Inside custom property sets

Technically, a custom property set definition is stored as an XML string in a user-defined cell (_CPM_SetDefns) in the document. This matters to you only if you're developing your own shapes or creating programs to automate shapes and drawings with custom properties.

Defining a Set of Custom Properties

To define a custom property set or edit its definition, you use the Edit Custom Property Set add-on, which lets you do the following:

- Create a new custom property set for a document.
- Rename an existing custom property set.
- Delete an entire custom property set or a property within a set.
- Add a new custom property to an existing set.
- Use existing custom properties in a shape to create a set.

The definition of a custom property set includes the names of the set as well as names (labels) for each custom property in the set and its data type, format, value, and prompt, as Figure 6-11 shows. A custom property set is saved with a document. If you open a custom stencil file and create a custom property set, the set is saved with the stencil, and you can then apply it to master shapes on the stencil. If you define a custom property set in a drawing, you can apply the set to shapes on the drawing page or master shapes on the drawing's document stencil.

Figure 6-11. With the Edit Custom Property Set add-on, you can create a new custom property set and define its properties as well as add and remove individual custom properties.

You can also change the definition of an existing custom property set to rename or delete a set, or work with individual custom properties in a set. For example, you can edit property labels so that the labels you want appear in the Custom Properties window, or add and remove individual custom properties that are included in a set.

Chapter 6

Tip If you're creating a drawing based on a Process Engineering template (included only with Visio Professional), you can define custom property sets in the Component Model Properties dialog box.

Defining a New Set Based on Existing Custom Properties

An easy way to create a custom property set is to copy the custom properties defined for an existing shape, and then create a set from those properties. You can also copy the custom properties that are included in an existing set to create a new custom property set and revise its definition as you want. When you copy custom properties, you avoid starting from scratch and can take advantage of existing definitions. For example, if you're working with Visio shapes that include a custom property set, you can create a new set based on the existing one and then revise the property labels so that the names you want appear in the Custom Properties window. That way, you don't alter the original shapes or their definitions, but you can customize at will.

To create a new custom property set based on a shape with properties, follow these steps:

1. Select a shape for which custom properties have already been defined—either a shape on the drawing page or a master shape from a custom stencil you've opened for editing.

2. Select Tools, Custom Property Sets.

3 Click Add.

In the Add Custom Property Set dialog box, the option Create A New Set From The Shape Selected In Visio is selected.

4 In the Name box, type a name for the custom property set as you want it to appear in the Apply Custom Property Set dialog box.

5 Click OK.

In the Custom Property Sets box, the new set is listed. Select it, and its properties, taken from the selected shape, are listed under Custom Properties at the bottom of the dialog box.

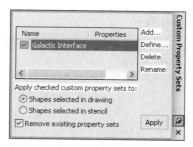

6 You can close the box.

A new custom property set is created and stored with the document. To apply the set to other shapes, see the sections that follow.

To create a new custom property set based on the definition of an existing set, follow these steps:

1 Choose Tools, Custom Property Sets.

2 In the Custom Property Sets dialog box, click Add.

3   In the Name box, type a name for the new set.

4   Select Create A New Set From An Existing Set.

5   In the Custom Property Set box, select the custom property set that you want to copy, and then click OK.

    Visio adds the new custom property set and its property definitions to the active document.

6   Click the the set and then choose Define to edit the custom properties you copied from the existing set, or choose whether to apply the set to selected shapes in the drawing or stencil, and then click Apply.

Defining a New Set and Its Properties

You can create a custom property set from scratch and define each custom property that you want to include in the set. If you're working with stencils and documents that do not contain custom properties, such as a new stencil that you've created, this is the best way to add custom properties. You create a set, define each property in the set, and then apply the set to your shapes as described later in this chapter.

To create a new custom property set and define its properties, follow these steps:

1   Open the document in which you want to save the custom property set.

    You can open either a drawing or custom stencil file. If you plan to apply the set to master shapes, open the custom stencil for editing (right-click its title bar, and then click Edit).

2   Make sure nothing is selected, and then select Tools, Custom Property Sets.

3   Click Add.

4 In the Name box, type a name for the custom property set.

5 Click OK.

The new set is listed in the Edit Custom Property Sets dialog box. In the Custom Properties box, no properties are listed.

6 Click Define.

The Define Custom Properties dialog box appears and lists Property1 as the default, initial custom property.

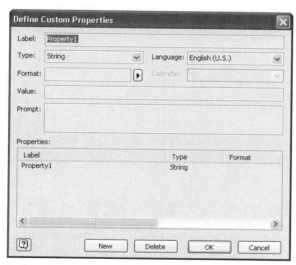

7 Define the new property by typing or selecting the values you want for Label, Type, Format, Value, and Prompt.

For details about these options, see Table 6-2. If you're not certain which Type option to select, select String.

8 When you've defined the property, do one of the following:

■ Click New to define another custom property for the set.

■ Click OK to close the Define Custom Properties dialog box.

9 In the Edit Custom Property Sets dialog box, click OK.

A new custom property set is created and stored with the document. To apply the set to other shapes, see the sections that follow.

Editing Custom Property Sets

You can edit the definition of a custom property set. Specifically, you can change the name of the set itself and you can edit the custom properties in the set. When you revise an existing set, the changes are saved in the active document, which can be a drawing or custom stencil file. If you apply the set to a master shape of a custom stencil, all instances of the document's shapes are updated. To edit a custom property set, follow these steps:

1 In a document that contains custom property sets, choose Tools, Custom Property Sets.

2 In the Custom Property Sets box, select the set you want to edit.

3 If you want to rename the set, click Rename, type a new name in the Name box, and then click OK.

4 If you want to edit, add, or remove custom properties in the set, click Define.

The Define Custom Properties dialog box appears and lists the definition for the first custom property, which is selected in the Properties list at the bottom of the dialog box.

> **Note** Any changes you make are immediately applied to the selected custom property.

5 In the Properties box, select a custom property, and then revise its definition by typing or selecting the values you want in the Label, Type, Format, Value, and Prompt boxes. For details about these options, see Table 6-2.

6 When you've defined the property, do one of the following:

■ Select a new property to edit in the Properties box.

■ Click New to define a new custom property.

■ Click OK to close the Define Custom Properties dialog box.

Visio adds the properties to the shape, which you can see in the Custom Properties window.

Applying a Custom Property Set to Shapes

You can assign a custom property set to specified shapes in a drawing. It's probably more often the case that you'd apply custom property sets to master shapes, but sometimes you just need to update shapes on the drawing page. For example, if you use the drawing tools to create new shapes in a diagram, you can apply the custom property set used by other shapes to the new shapes. Selecting Tools, Custom Property Set lists all the custom property sets defined for the active document—that is, your drawing file. You choose the custom property set you want, select whether you want to apply the custom property set to the shapes selected in the drawing or the shapes selected in the stencil, click Apply, and then Visio adds the set of properties to the selected shape.

Before you can apply custom property sets, you need to make sure that your document contains custom property sets. If the active document does not include a set, you'll see <Sample, Description, ID> listed in the Custom Property Sets Window. Occasionally, you might find a Visio shape that includes custom properties that were defined the old-fashioned way—without the custom property set feature. You can use the Custom Property Sets window to define a new custom property set and then apply it using the procedure that follows.

> **Caution**   In previous versions of Visio only one set of custom properties could be applied to a shape. Now, however, you can add a custom property set to a shape, in addition to previous properties. If you wish to replace the existing property set, click Remove Existing Property Sets in the Custom Property Sets dialog box.

To add a custom property set to selected shapes, follow these steps:

1   Select a shape or set of shapes in a drawing, and then select Tools, Custom Property Set.

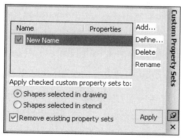

2   In the Custom Property Set list, select the name of the set you want.

3   Make sure that the Shapes Selected In Drawing option is selected.

   If this option is unavailable, no shapes are selected on the page. Click the shape to which you wish to apply the property set.

4   Click OK to add the set of custom properties to the selected shapes.

Troubleshooting

After editing property names in a set, the changes do not appear in the Custom Properties window for selected shapes

When you use the Edit Custom Property Set command, you can make changes to an existing set of properties, but Visio does not apply those changes to existing shapes, even if they are assigned to the set you edited. You must use the Apply Custom Property Set command to update the shapes with the edited set.

Applying Custom Property Sets to Master Shapes on a Custom Stencil

If you've created your own shapes, or want to revise Visio master shapes to use a particular set of custom properties, you can apply a custom property set to all or selected master shapes on a custom stencil. You can use the Custom Property Sets command to add sets of properties to the master shapes you select in an open custom stencil file. The stencil file can be any of the following:

- A Visio custom stencil that you've opened for editing (right-click the title bar, and then choose Edit). You may save your changes as a new stencil file so that you retain the original stencil. You might need it if your changes to the shapes' properties have unexpected consequences.

- A stencil that you've created (choose File, Shapes, My Shapes, and then open your .VSS file)

- The document stencil for your drawing (choose File, Shapes, Document Stencil). All the shapes in your drawing will be updated with the changes made to the master shapes on the document stencil.

To add a custom property set to selected master shapes, follow these steps.

1. Do one of the following to open a stencil containing the master shapes you want:
   - To apply the set to an existing custom stencil file, open the stencil, right-click its title bar, and then select Edit.
   - To apply the set to the drawing's document stencil, choose File, Shapes, Document Stencil.

2. Choose Tools, Custom Property Set.

   In the Apply Custom Property Set dialog box, select the Shapes Selected In Stencil option.

Chapter 6

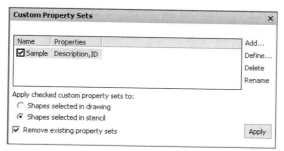

3   Select the shapes you wish to apply the property set to on the document stencil.

4   In the Custom Property Set dialog box, click Apply.

Visio applies the custom property set to the selected master shapes. Depending on the number of shapes you select, you might see a progress indicator as Visio applies the set to all the shapes. The next time you drag a master shape from the stencil, the shape on the page will include the set of custom properties.

Deleting Custom Properties

You can delete individual custom properties from shapes and master shapes on a custom stencil. You can also delete custom property sets, although all you delete is the definition for the set. If you apply a custom property set to shapes, and then delete the set, the shapes retain their custom properties. However, the document no longer knows that the properties came from a set.

To delete a custom property set, follow these steps:

1   In a document that contains custom property sets, choose Tools, Custom Property Sets.

2   In the Custom Property Sets list, select the set you want to delete, and then click Delete.

3   Click Apply.

Visio removes the custom property set from the active document. Shapes that include custom properties from the deleted set are not changed—they retain their custom properties.

It's wise not to delete built-in custom properties that come with many of the Visio shapes. These properties might be required by the solution to accommodate the shape's "smart" behavior. For example, organization chart shapes include a number of invisible custom properties that don't appear in the Custom Properties window, but might appear in the Define Custom Properties dialog box, which means that you can delete them. However, the organization chart engine uses these properties to track document and layout options, so you do not want to delete them.

To delete an individual custom property from a shape or master shape, follow these steps:

1   Select a shape on the drawing page, a master shape on the document stencil, or a master shape on a Visio custom stencil.

> **Tip**   To open a master shape for editing so that you can select it, right-click a custom stencil's title bar, and then choose Edit. On the stencil, double-click a master shape to open it in a drawing window. If necessary, select the master shape.

2   If the Custom Properties window is not open, select View, Custom Properties Window.

3   Right-click in the Custom Properties window, and then select Define Properties.

4   In the Properties box, select the property you want to delete, and then click Delete.

Visio deletes the custom property from the selected shape. You don't get a warning first, but you can undo the operation after you've closed the dialog boxes.

5   Click OK.

> **Note**   To restore the deleted property, press Ctrl+Z or choose Edit, Undo.

6   If you edited a master shape, click Close Window in the master drawing window. Make sure to click the correct button. Don't click the Visio window's Close button.

Visio displays a message asking whether you want to update the master.

7   Click Yes.

If you edited a document stencil, all the shapes in the drawing that are based on the master shape you edited will no longer include the deleted custom property.

8   To save your changes to the stencil, do one of the following:

- If you edited a Visio custom stencil, right-click the title bar, choose Save As, and then specify a file name and location for the stencil.

- If you edited a document stencil, choose File, Save to save the changes with the drawing file.

Creating Reports

If shapes have custom property fields in which you have entered data, you can generate a report that includes selected properties and values. Visio includes a number of predefined reports that you can use for specific types of information, such as asset reports, or you can create your own report and define its contents. What a report looks like depends on what you put in it and how you want to save it. Visio can save a report as an external file in XML format (with the file extension .VRD) or as a table shape on the drawing page that's linked to the information.

> **Note** In earlier versions of Visio, you could use the Property Reporting Wizard to create inventory and asset reports. This wizard is no longer included in Visio. It has been replaced by the Reports command on the Tools menu.

To set up a new report or run an existing one, you use the Report command on the Tools menu. The Report tool lists existing reports that you can run or modify, as Figure 6-12 shows, or you can define your own reports. Because the Report tool is meant to be a design tool, its contents vary depending on whether anyone has created new reports for you to run. Visio 2003 Standard and Visio 2003 Professional come with different built-in reports for specific diagram types. For example, Visio Professional includes a report called the Door Schedule, which a builder or architect might run to show all the door specifications in a floor plan. You can even customize any of the built-in reports to tailor the report to your needs.

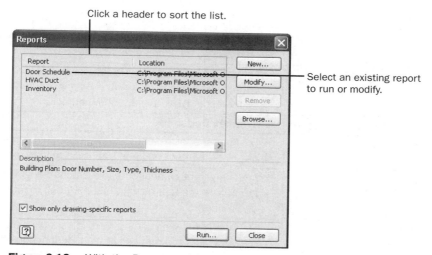

Figure 6-12. With the Report tool, you can create new reports based on the custom property data in your drawing, or you can run one of the existing reports.

> **Note** By default, the Report tool lists any report definitions (*.vrd) stored in the \Samples\ Visio Extras folder as well as any of the Visio drawing paths.

Running a Report

Many Visio solutions include predefined reports that you can run to evaluate the data stored with a drawing. For example, a flowchart report tabulates cost, duration, and resources associated with the shapes in a flowchart. A door schedule lists all door specifications for a building plan. Table 6-3 lists the predefined reports that are included with different templates. To run a report, you use the Report command on the Tools menu, and then specify the output format you want.

Chapter 6

Visio can create the report's contents as a table shape on the drawing page, or it can save your report as an external Microsoft Excel, HTML, or XML file.

Table 6-3. Built-In Report Definitions

Visio Standard Report	What It Does
Flowchart Report	For flowchart shapes, lists the text displayed on flowchart shapes as well as the values of the resources, cost, and duration of custom properties sorted by shape.
Gantt Chart Report	For each resource in a Gantt chart shape, lists the task name, start date, end date, duration, user-defined number, and percent complete.
Organization Chart Report	For each department, lists the employee name, title, and telephone number.
Shape Inventory	For all the shapes in any diagram, lists the text displayed on shapes, and each shape's height, width, and location on the page (as x and y coordinates).
Asset Report	For shapes in a floor plan, space plan, or office layout, shows who owns an asset (the BelongsTo field), as well as the asset type, name, and manufacturer.

Visio Professional Report	What It Does
Door Schedule	For door shapes in a floor plan, space plan, or office layout, lists the door number, size, type, and thickness.
Equipment List	For equipment components in a process engineering diagram, lists the tag, description, material, manufacturer, and model.
Instrument List	For instrumentation components in a process engineering diagram, lists the tag, description, connection size, service, manufacturer, and model.
Pipeline List	For pipeline components in a process engineering diagram, lists the tag, description, line size, schedule, design pressure, and design temperature.
Space Report	For shapes in a space plan, lists the department, room number, use, and area.
Valve List	For valve components in a process engineering diagram, lists the tag, description, line size, valve class, manufacturer, and model.
Window Schedule	For window shapes in a floor plan, space plan, or office layout, lists the window number, size, and type.

To run a report, follow these steps:

1. Choose Tools, Reports.

The Report dialog box appears and displays all the predefined reports in the Report Definition list. Different reports will appear depending on whether you have Visio Standard or Visio Professional.

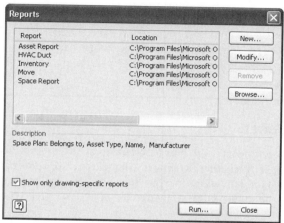

2 Under Report Definition, select the report you wish to compile, and then click Run.

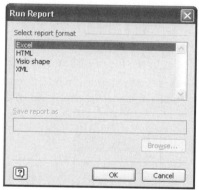

3 In the Select Report Format box, select an output format.

If you choose Microsoft Excel (File), HTML, or XML, specify a name for the report file that Visio creates in the folder you want. If you choose Microsoft Excel (Shape) or Visio Table Shape, choose whether to link shapes to the report definition or save a copy of it with the shapes.

4 In the Run Report dialog box, click OK.

Visio displays a progress indicator as it generates the report. Visio displays the report when it is created.

If the output is a table shape, Visio creates the shape and adds it with the custom property information to the current page.

5 In the Report dialog box, click OK or choose another report to run.

Troubleshooting

When running a report, Visio displays a message that no shapes had the selected properties or satisfied the report selection criteria

Visio displays an error message and cancels the report if the shapes in your diagram do not contain custom properties, or contain different custom properties than specified in the report definition. To see which properties are specified by a report, select the report name and then choose Modify in the Report dialog box.

Defining a Custom Report

You can define a new report from scratch or based on an existing report definition. In the report definition, you specify whether the report will include all or some of the custom properties stored with your shapes. In addition, you can set up your report to run for all the shapes on a page or all the shapes in the drawing file.

To create a new report definition, choose Tools, Reports, and then click New, or select an existing report definition and click Modify. When you create a new report or modify an existing one, the Report Definition Wizard walks you through the steps. Visio stores your report definition as a .VRD file in the location you specify and adds it to the list in the Report dialog box.

To define a new report, follow these steps:

1   Specify whether to report on all shapes in the file or just on the page.

2   Select the properties you want to include in the report. In addition to custom properties, your report can include other internal properties that Visio tracks for shapes, as Figure 6-13 shows.

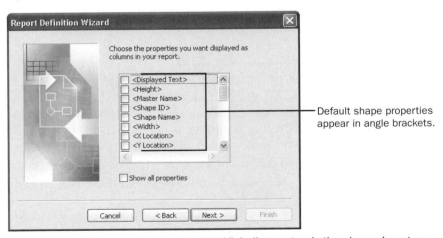

Default shape properties appear in angle brackets.

Figure 6-13.   When you set up a report, Visio lists not only the shapes' custom property fields, but also default shape properties and internal properties used by the solution called user-defined properties, which appear in the ShapeSheet's User-Defined Cells section.

3 Specify how to filter the data for your report. The Report tool reviews all the custom properties, including hidden properties created for the solution and user-defined properties in the ShapeSheet. You probably don't want all this information in your report, so you can select just the properties you do want.

4 Choose how to format the report. You can group, sort, and specify output formats for the custom property fields and their values.

5 Choose whether to save the report definition as part of the current drawing file or as a report file (.VRD) that can be run from other Visio drawing files. When you save a report definition with your drawing, you can run the report whenever you open the drawing.

> **Note** These steps create the report definition—Visio does not run the report. You can do that next or run it later using different data.

Selecting Report Contents

Defining a report starts with the decision about which shapes and properties to include. The Report Definition Wizard includes a Limit Selection option that lets you filter properties according to criteria you define, as Figure 6-14 shows. You can choose to include any of the following in a report:

- Shapes on a particular layer
- Shapes that include a particular custom property
- Shapes that include a custom property with a particular value
- Shapes that include a particular user-defined cell value
- For network diagrams in Visio Professional, device shapes that result from the Auto-Discovery command

Choose from custom properties, default shape properties (which appear
in angle brackets), and user-defined properties from the ShapeSheet.

Select a condition operator. The property's data
format determines the operators that appear.

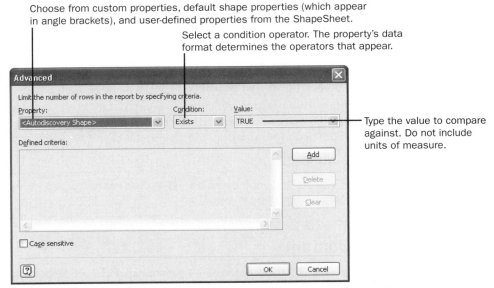

Type the value to compare
against. Do not include
units of measure.

Figure 6-14. You can specify quite precisely the set of shapes and properties to report on
by defining criteria in the Advanced dialog box. When you run a report, Visio includes only the
shapes with properties that meet the criteria in the finished report.

In the Limit Selection dialog box, you use a generic query language to specify the criteria for
shapes to include in your report. If you've used any of the typical spreadsheet or database
query operations, the options here should look familiar. You select a property that you want
to use in a comparison, specify an operator (such as =, <>, >, <, >=, or <=), and then type a
value to compare against. Depending on the property and condition operator, the value can
be true or false or a number. For strings, the comparison criteria are case sensitive or case
insensitive. For example, you can filter your report so that it looks only at shapes where the
Height property is greater than 2 inches.

Formatting a Custom Report

After you've selected the shapes and properties you want to include, you can specify how to
organize the information in your report. The Report Definition Wizard includes options for
specifying how to group, sort, and format data, as Figure 6-15 shows. Visio can group the
output by master name or by custom property, and then show totals and subtotals for each
property as well as other standard calculations (count, total, average, median, minimum,
maximum).

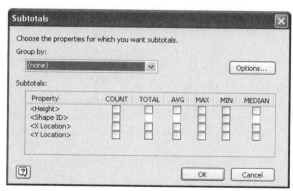

Figure 6-15. In the Report Definition Wizard, you can choose how to organize the contents of your report.

Performing Calculations on Report Contents

To group subsets of data and calculate new values from the data in the individual groups, as shown in Figure 6-16, use the options (listed in Table 6-4 on the next page) in the Subtotals dialog box, which appears when you click Subtotals.

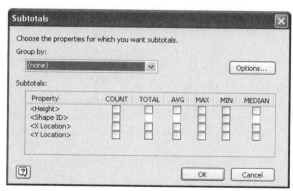

Figure 6-16. You can perform calculations on groups of data.

Chapter 6

Table 6-4. Options in the Subtotals Dialog Box

Option	What It Does
Group By	Lists all properties. If you select a custom property, report values are grouped according to the values of the selected property. In technical terms, this option is the equivalent of a GROUP BY clause in SQL.
Options	Displays the Options dialog box, where you can choose to show all values for the group, not repeat identical values, show only subtotals with a group, and show grand totals.
Property	Lists the properties you've selected to appear as columns in your report. For each property, you can select a calculation. If the calculation is not valid for the type of data represented by the property value, the option's check box is displayed in gray.
Count	Calculates the number of objects with a particular value for the property.
Total	Calculates the sum of the list of property values.
Avg	Calculates the average (arithmetic mean) of the property values.
Max	Calculates the largest number from the list of property values.
Min	Calculates the smallest number from the list of property values.
Median	Calculates the median of the property values. The median is the number in the middle of a set of numbers; that is, half the numbers have values that are greater than the median, and half have values that are less.

Sorting Report Contents

When you sort a report, you determine the order in which properties are listed in the rows and columns of the final output. To sort a report, click Sort in the Report Definition Wizard. In the Sort dialog box, you sort the following:

1 In the Column Order list, choose the order in which you want the property names to appear across the top of the report.

2 In the Row Order options, choose the order in which property values are listed in the body of the report. You can sort a report based on the contents of one or more columns. For example, if your report contains employee information, you can sort based on the hiring date and on the employee names to show who was hired when, as Figure 6-17 shows.

Hiring Report				
Name	*Title*	*Reports To*	*Date of Hire*	*Phone Ext.*
Steve Alboucq	Vice President		1995	0029
Karan Khanna	Sales Manager	Alboucq	1996	0657
Ido Ben-Sachar	Office Manager	Ramirez	1997	4568
Deanna Daum	N.A. Sales	Khanna	1997	2785
Erik Gavriluk	AsiaPac Sales	Khanna	1998	0657
Kaarin Dolliver	S.A. Sales	Khanna	1998	4698
Prasanna Samarawickrama	Sales Associate	Daum	1998	0781
Aaron Con	Admin. Assistant	Chai	1999	5468
Simi Nikore	Brand Marketing	Alboucq	1999	4987
Leonard Zuvela	Sales Associate	Daum	1999	0098
Sean Chai	Channel Manager	Daum	2000	0129
Jolie Lenehan	Product Manager	Khanna	2000	5123
Francisco Ramirez	European Sales	Khanna	2000	2783
Derik Stenerson	Graphic Designer	Nikore	2000	2781
Florian Voss	P.R. Lead	Nikore	2000	5379

Figure 6-17. This report is sorted in chronological order by date of hire. For each date, employees are sorted in alphabetical order.

Tip If you need to sort by more than three columns, sort by the least important columns first.

Table 6-5 lists the options in the Sort dialog box.

Note When you create subtotals in a report, the property you specify in the Group By option does not appear in the Sort dialog box as an option.

Table 6-5. Options in the Sort Dialog Box

Option	What It Does
Column Order	Lists the properties you've selected to appear in the report. When you run a report, the properties are listed in columns from left to right in the order they appear in this box. You can select a property and then use the Move Up and Move Down buttons to adjust its order.
Move Up	Moves a property selected in the Column Order box one position higher in the list.
Move Down	Moves a property selected in the Column Order box one position lower in the list.
Sort By	Sorts rows in the selected order (ascending or descending) based on the value of the selected custom property,
Ascending	Sorts values for the property in the Sort By box in ascending (1 to 9, A to Z) order.
Descending	Sorts values for the property in the Sort By box in descending (9 to 1, Z to A) order.
Then By	Sorts rows in the selected order (ascending or descending) based on the value of the selected custom property.

Chapter 6

Specifying Numeric Precision for Values

For numeric output, you can specify the level of precision as the number of values to the right of the decimal and whether to include units of measure. In the Report Definition Wizard, click Format to display the Format dialog box, which allows you to define the way that the data values are displayed, as Figure 6-18 shows. Table 6-6 lists the options in the Format dialog box.

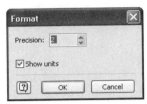

Figure 6-18. For custom property values that specify dimensions, you can specify the precision and display units of measure.

Table 6-6. Options in the Format Dialog Box

Option	What It Does
Precision	Applies to numbers only. Enter a value from 0 to 14.
Show Units	Specifies whether to display units of measure in the final report.

Saving a Report Definition

The final step in creating a report definition is to name the report and indicate where to save it. The Report Definition Wizard provides options for you to save your settings with the current drawing file or as a separate file that can be opened from within other Visio drawings, as Figure 6-19 shows.

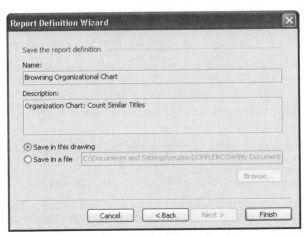

Figure 6-19. You can specify a name and description that appear in the Report dialog box for your new report definition.

Saving a report definition is a two-step process: First, click Finish in the Report Definition Wizard, and then click OK in the Report dialog box. If you click Cancel, Visio will warn you that your report definition will be lost. Table 6-7 lists the options in the Report Definition Wizard for saving your report.

Table 6-7. Options for Saving the Report Definition

Option	What It Does
Name	Identifies the report definition. The name you type here appears in the Report dialog box.
Description	Provides identifying information about the report that appears in the Description box of the Report dialog box. The text you type here can act as a prompt, which is particularly useful if others will be running the report, but it's optional.
Save In This Drawing	Specifies to save the report definition in the drawing file. When you choose this option, you can run the report whenever you open the drawing. If you select Save In A File, this option is not available.
Save In A File	Specifies to save the report definition as an external report file (.VRD) that can be run from other Visio drawing files. Type a file path and name in the box, or click Browse to specify the path. If you select Save In This Drawing, this option is not available.
Browse	Opens the Report Wizard dialog box, which provides the standard options for saving a file. By default, Visio supplies the name Report_1.vrd for report files and saves them in the My Documents folder. You can type a new name and specify a different folder to save it in. Visio saves report files in .VRD format only. If you select Save In This Drawing, this button is not available.

When you save a report definition, it is listed in the Report dialog box. To see whether your report definition provides the expected output, you need to run the report. Creating a report definition does not automatically run a report. To do that, select the report name in the list of report definitions, and then click Run.

Chapter 7

Using Visio Diagrams with Other Programs

Perhaps that report you're creating in Microsoft Word or the e-mail message you're composing would be clearer if you included a Microsoft Office Visio 2003 flowchart of the process. Maybe you want to display your organization chart on a Microsoft PowerPoint slide. In most organizations, people create and share information in a number of different applications, and Visio is one of many desktop programs. Visio is designed to work with other applications. Diagrams and shapes can be displayed in other documents in a variety of ways, and information from other applications can be displayed in Visio as well.

As a part of the Microsoft Office System, Visio provides many of the same tools as Word 2003, Microsoft Office Excel 2003, and PowerPoint 2003 for sharing information. For example, you can use object linking and embedding (OLE) to place information from one application in another. You can also save Visio diagrams in alternative file formats, including Web-compatible graphics formats like GIF and JPEG, and e-mail Visio drawings right from your Visio toolbar. Just as you can use Visio data in different ways in other applications, you can pull all kinds of graphic or text information into Visio drawings.

This chapter provides the ins and outs of getting data in and out of Visio.

Working with OLE

OLE provides the easiest way to place Visio shapes or diagrams into Word, Excel, PowerPoint, and other applications that support the Windows Clipboard and OLE. When you use OLE to place Visio shapes or diagrams, you maintain a connection with Visio, so you can edit the shapes or diagrams using Visio tools and features. OLE is just a broad name for the technology that allows you to use information from one application in another. All the Office System applications support OLE, which means that you can insert and edit Office documents within Visio, or add Visio diagrams to Office documents, as Figure 7-1 shows. Although OLE has been around for a while, you might not be familiar with the term. If you've ever copied and pasted information from one program into another, or used the Paste Special command in an Office application, you've probably taken advantage of OLE.

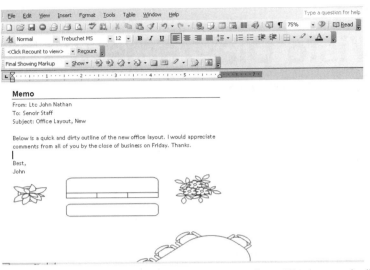

Figure 7-1. With OLE, you can embellish an ordinary Word memo by linking or embedding a Visio diagram in the document.

OLE boils down to linking and embedding, both of which support editing in place. Which technique should you use? It depends on the number of documents that will include the Visio information and how frequently you expect to revise the information.

- *Link* a saved Visio diagram when you want to use it in one or more other documents.   When you update the original Visio file, the diagram will be updated in every document that contains it. Likewise, when you update the diagram within another document, the original and any other linked diagrams will also be updated.

- *Embed* an existing Visio shape or drawing in another document when you want to be able to edit the Visio information without leaving the application's document.   This is probably the most common way to place Visio information into another program—pasting Visio shapes into an Office document automatically embeds them.

- Create a Visio diagram *in place* when you don't want to switch between different application windows.   You can start Visio from within another application to add and edit shapes—and if you're working in an Office document, plenty of Visio tools are available to use. Your shapes are saved with the application's document, not as a separate Visio drawing file.

One benefit of linking instead of embedding is that the document in which you use the Visio data stores only a reference to the Visio data. This keeps your document file size smaller and more manageable. However, applications keep track of links using the file name and location of each linked file—the link will be broken if you change the file name of the original diagram or move the files.

The main advantage of embedding is that you can maintain separate versions of a Visio diagram for different purposes. An embedded shape or diagram isn't linked to the original Visio drawing file, so you can make changes there that don't affect any of the embedded copies. In addition, an embedded diagram is available even if the original file is not. For example, you can print a Word document that contains an embedded Visio diagram from any computer, whether or not Visio is installed and the original Visio diagram file is on the computer. Of course, because the entire Visio diagram must be embedded in the document, the document's file size can increase dramatically.

You can also embed, link, and import objects created in other programs into Visio. The basic principles are the same. For details, see "Embedding and Linking Microsoft Office Documents in Visio," page 222.

 Visio Has a Viewer!

Visio now has a viewer that enables people who do not have Visio installed on their computer to view Visio drawings. The Visio Viewer is an ActiveX control that allows users to open and view Visio drawings. When a Visio drawing is opened with the viewer it is displayed in a Microsoft Internet Explorer (version 5.0 or later) window. You can download the viewer at the Microsoft Download Center.

There are, however, several other ways you can share Visio diagrams with users who don't have Visio. You can export the diagram in a graphic format that can be placed into another application. For example, you can export a Visio diagram as a bitmap that can be inserted into a Word document or other application. You can also save the diagram as a Portable Document Format (PDF) file that can be viewed in Adobe Acrobat Reader or save the diagram as an HTML file that can be viewed in any Web browser. For details about these options, see the corresponding topics later in this chapter.

 Inside Out

Import your text from Word

Visio does many things well, but it probably wouldn't be your first choice for word processing. For text-based documents, you'll save yourself some headaches if you create the diagrams in Visio, the words in another program, and then bring them all together using OLE. You can embed Visio diagrams in your word processor document or embed the text from your document in Visio.

Linking a Diagram to a Microsoft Office Document

When you link a Visio diagram to a document in an Office System application, the document file stores a reference to the original diagram. If you edit the diagram—either in Visio or within the document—the diagram changes in both places. And if you've linked the diagram to more than one document, each of those documents will be updated. Because each of these documents is linked to a single Visio diagram, your document stays smaller, which means you can work in the document more quickly and it takes up less space on your hard disk.

However, any time you need to use the Office document that contains the link, the original Visio diagram must be available.

A linked file is tracked and updated based on its file name and location. Let's say you link a Visio diagram to a PowerPoint slide. The next time you open that PowerPoint presentation, it searches for the Visio drawing file referenced by the link and displays the latest version. If you change the name of the Visio diagram file, or move it to a different folder after you link it, the link will be broken and the diagram won't appear in PowerPoint. If you link a diagram to an Office document, it's simplest to store the Visio diagram in the same folder as the Office document; if you need to move the document to another computer, make sure you move both the document and the linked diagram file. For example, if you created a presentation on your laptop computer, and then want to run the presentation from a different computer, copy both the presentation file and the linked Visio drawing file to the new computer. Before you can link a Visio diagram, you must save the file.

> **Note**   To display a linked Visio diagram in a document, your computer must have the applications used to create both the document and the Visio diagram. This limitation makes documents with links less portable. To send a document that contains links to another person, you must include all the files referenced by the links, and the recipient must also have all the applications used to create the documents and files. However, it doesn't matter which version of Visio the recipient has—both Visio 2003 Standard and Visio 2003 Professional can open diagrams created in the other version. Do not use object linking if you need to print the document from a computer that doesn't have Visio installed; embed the diagram instead.

To link to a Visio diagram from another application, follow these steps:

1   In Visio, select the shapes or diagram on the Visio drawing page, and then choose Edit, Copy. Or, to include the entire drawing in the document, make sure nothing is selected on the Visio drawing page, and choose Edit, Copy Drawing.

2   Open the document in which you want the data to appear. (For example, open PowerPoint, and then display the slide in which you want the Visio diagram to appear.)

3   Choose Edit, Paste Special to display the Paste Special dialog box.

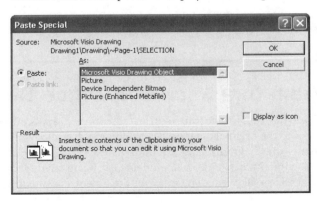

> **Note** Don't use the Paste command or the keyboard shortcut (Ctrl+V), because you won't be able to create a link.

4   Select Microsoft Visio Drawing Object, and then select the Paste Link option.

You can paste only one page at a time, so if you want to paste multiple drawing pages from Visio, you'll need to repeat this process for each page.

5   Click OK to paste the copied object.

Editing a Linked Diagram

After you link a Visio diagram to another document, you can continue to work on the diagram. The document containing the link will reflect your changes.

To edit a linked Visio diagram, open the diagram in Visio, make any changes you want, and then save the file with the same file name in the same folder. You can also edit the linked diagram from within the document it's linked to. To do this, double-click the diagram in the document. Essentially, you've just used a shortcut to start Visio and open the drawing; otherwise, you work in Visio exactly as you would if you had opened the application separately.

Updating a Linked Diagram

In most OLE client applications, linked objects are updated automatically each time you open the document. When you open the document, the application searches for each file referenced in a link and updates the appearance of the document to match the current version of the linked diagram. If the application can't find the file, it will prompt you to locate it. Even when a linked object is set to update automatically, you can manually update the link at any time to reflect changes you've made in the diagram.

If you expect to edit your original Visio diagram frequently and won't always have access to it from the linked document, you might want to set the object to manual linking, rather than to automatic. That way, you won't receive prompts to locate the file every time you open the document. If you do set a link for manual updating, make sure you actually update the link before you print or publish it so that changes you've made to the diagram are reflected in the document.

To update a link manually in most OLE-compatible applications, follow these steps:

1   Select the linked Visio object in the document, and then choose Edit, Links to display the Links dialog box.

Depending on the application you're working in, the dialog box might not exactly match the illustration that follows. If you don't see this command in your application, refer to its documentation for links management commands.

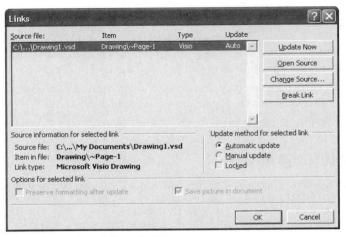

2 Select Manual, and then click OK.

3 To update the link manually, choose Edit, Links.

4 Select the Visio source file, and then click Update Now.

> **Tip** You can manually update a link at any time whether you've chosen the automatic or manual update method.

Embedding a Diagram in a Microsoft Office Document

You can embed Visio shapes or diagrams into Office documents. Embedding has some convenient advantages:

- Embedded shapes or diagrams are stored in the document in their entirety, but you can edit them using Visio tools without switching to Visio or leaving the document.

- The embedded document is stored separately from any other Visio diagram, so changes you make won't affect the original diagram file.

- Because embedded diagrams are stored in the document, they travel with the document, so you can view and print them accurately when you open the document on a computer that doesn't have Visio installed.

The primary disadvantage of embedding is file size. Because all the Visio shape data is stored in the document, its file size can increase dramatically when you embed a Visio image.

You might not be aware that Visio shapes are automatically embedded in an Office document every time you copy from Visio and paste in Office. You can also drag shapes from Visio to a document in Word, Excel, PowerPoint, or other OLE-compliant applications. Just make sure both applications are open and visible and that neither window is maximized, so you can see them both at once. Hold down the Ctrl key while you drag the shape you want from the Visio drawing into the other document.

> **Note** Dragging shapes from a Visio diagram into a document in another application moves the shapes to the other document and deletes them from the Visio diagram. To drag a copy of the shape, press the Ctrl key as you drag. The pointer displays a plus sign to indicate that you are copying the shape, not moving it. If you accidentally move the object and delete it from the Visio diagram, choose Edit, Undo from the Visio menu to recover it.

If you want to ensure that you don't disturb your original Visio diagram, a safer option for embedding shapes and diagrams is to copy and paste them. First select the shapes you want to embed. Then copy the shapes to the Clipboard using your favorite method of copying: press Ctrl+C, choose Edit, Copy, or click the Copy button on the Standard toolbar. Next, switch to the document in which you want to embed the shapes (for example, press Alt+Tab to switch between open programs in Windows), and press Ctrl+V or choose Edit, Paste. The shapes appear as part of your document. In an Office document or in any other application that supports OLE, the shapes are embedded, so you can edit them from within the document.

> **Tip** If you paste shapes into an application that doesn't support OLE, the shapes are pasted as a graphic that you can't edit.

Embedding an Entire Visio Diagram

You can embed an entire Visio diagram in another document if you use the Copy Drawing command, as Figure 7-2 shows. If you have a multiple-page Visio diagram, you can copy only one page at a time. You can then embed that page and repeat for each page in the diagram.

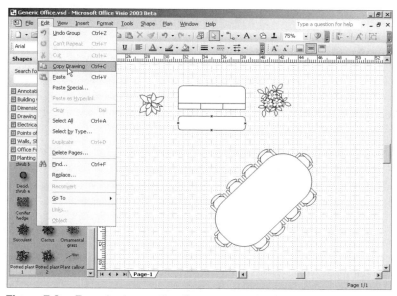

Figure 7-2. To embed an entire diagram, use the Copy Drawing command to copy each page, and then paste in the desired document.

Inside Out

Don't worry about losing your layer settings in embedded drawings

In some earlier versions of Visio, when you embedded a Visio drawing that included layers, your layer settings were ignored in the embedded copy. For the most part, this limitation only affected hidden layers, which would unexpectedly appear in the embedded diagram. Fortunately, Visio 2002 and Visio 2003 don't include this restriction. Hidden layers remain hidden, even if you embed your diagram.

To embed an entire page of a Visio diagram, follow these steps:

1 In Visio, display the page you want to copy and embed.

Copy Drawing

2 Make sure nothing is selected, and click Copy Drawing on the Standard toolbar or choose Edit, Copy Drawing.

Visio copies everything in the diagram, including shapes on other pages and backgrounds. Stencils aren't copied, nor are other parts of the Visio window that aren't part of your diagram, such as the Pan & Zoom window.

3 Switch to the document into which you want to embed the diagram.

Tip Press Alt+Tab to switch between applications.

4 Place the cursor where you want to insert the diagram, and then press Ctrl+V or choose Edit, Paste to paste it into your document.

Troubleshooting

You receive an error when you edit a linked or embedded diagram

The error message you receive might vary, depending on the application you're using and the problem it encounters. Most likely, though, either the application cannot find the original Visio diagram (in the case of a linked diagram) or your computer can't start Visio. Verify the following:

- **Is Visio installed on the computer you're using?** Make sure that the computer has enough memory to run both applications.

- **If Visio is running, is it displaying a dialog box?** If Visio is awaiting your instructions, it cannot respond to the call made by the other application.

- **Is a copy of the diagram open in Visio?** You can have only one copy of the diagram open at a time.

- **Has a linked file been moved or renamed?** If you're working with a linked diagram, verify the name and location of the original diagram file. If it has been renamed or moved, you can update the link in the document. To do this, choose Edit, Links in the open document containing the link, and then choose Change Source. (The command name may vary in non-Office applications.)

Using Visio Shapes in Other Programs

If you're working in another program, such as Word or PowerPoint, you can quickly add Visio shapes to your document using the same drag-and-drop technique you use in Visio. Although you can always drag shapes from a Visio drawing page or stencil to another application, there's a great shortcut for using shapes without opening Visio. You might find it more efficient to open only a stencil, as Figure 7-3 shows. The stencil takes up less screen real estate than the full Visio application, so it's easier to see what you're doing.

Chapter 7

Figure 7-3. A quick way to add Visio shapes to another document is to open only a Visio stencil file (.VSS) using Windows Explorer. Then, you can drag the shapes you want into the document.

The trick is to open a Visio stencil file directly from Windows Explorer when Visio isn't running. In Windows Explorer, double-click on the Visio stencil that contains the shapes you want to use. If Visio is running, you'll see the entire application window, which isn't the desired result in this case. You want to see just the stencil window. When you add a shape to the other application's document, the application adds it as an embedded object. You can then double-click the shape to edit it with Visio drawing tools.

The location of the stencil file depends on how you installed Visio. If you accepted the default destination folders during installation, you'll find stencil files in C:\Program Files\Microsoft Office\Visio11\1033\<*filename*>. For example, to open the Basic Shapes stencil, navigate to C:\Program Files\Microsoft Office\Visio11\1033\Basic_u.vss.

Inside Out

.VSS and .VST files

The 1033 folder includes stencil files (.VSS) and template files (.VST). If you open a template file, the entire Visio window opens. If Windows Explorer doesn't display file extensions, you can see whether the file is a template or stencil file by looking in the Type column next to the file, which displays either "Microsoft Visio Stencil" or "Microsoft Visio Template." You can also hover the mouse over a file's icon to display a ScreenTip that shows the file type and other information.

Creating a Visio Diagram Within Another Application

Suppose you're working on a report or presentation and you realize that you can make your point more clearly with a quick timeline or flowchart. You can bring an existing Visio diagram into your document, or create a brand new one, without ever leaving your report or presentation. In fact, any application that supports the current Windows OLE standard allows you to work with Visio in place. This means you can edit Visio shapes within the other application's window, as Figure 7-4 shows.

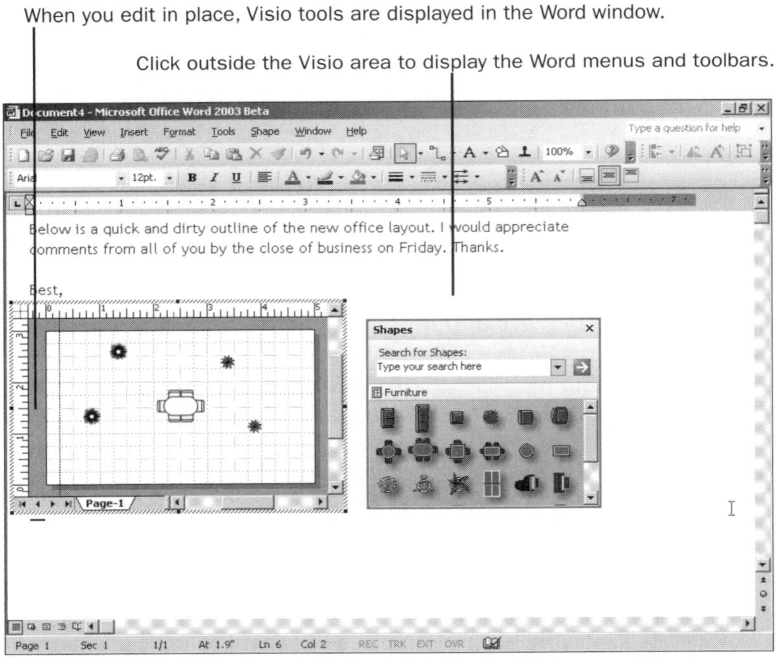

When you edit in place, Visio tools are displayed in the Word window.

Click outside the Visio area to display the Word menus and toolbars.

Figure 7-4. When you edit a Visio diagram in place, you can use the Visio tools to create a diagram within your application window.

> **Tip** **Check your application for linking and embedding support**
>
> To find out whether an application supports the latest OLE standard, open the application, and search for an Insert Object command. (You can usually find this command on the Insert menu but it might be located elsewhere.) Check the application's documentation or online Help files as well.

Not all applications support in-place editing. Sometimes, when you edit an embedded or linked Visio diagram, the Visio program window opens instead. The instructions provided here apply to the Office System applications, but the process is similar in any application that supports in-place editing.To create a Visio drawing in place in an Office document, follow these steps:

1 In your Office document, place the cursor where you'd like the diagram to appear, and then choose Insert, Object.

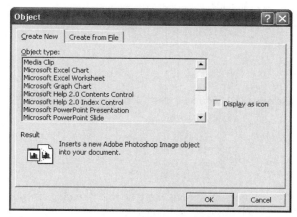

2 Select Microsoft Visio Drawing from the Object Type list, and then click OK.

The Choose Drawing Type window opens just as if you had started Visio to create a new diagram.

3 Select a template for the type of diagram you want to create, and then click OK.

A Visio drawing page opens with a set of stencils, and the Visio toolbars and menus replace the original application toolbars and menus. If the Visio program window opens instead, your application doesn't support in-place editing, but you can still create and embed a Visio diagram.

4 Create the Visio diagram, working as you ordinarily would in Visio—that is, add shapes, connections, text, and so on.

5 To return to the original application, click somewhere in the document outside the Visio diagram.

The original toolbars and menus appear. If your application doesn't support in-place editing, and you've been working in the Visio program window, choose File, Exit to return to the original application.

> **Tip** To move an embedded Visio diagram around on the page, select it, and then drag it by the selection border. Drag a handle on the selection border to resize the embedded diagram.

Editing an Embedded Diagram

To make changes to an embedded Visio diagram—whether you pasted, dragged, or created it in place—double-click the embedded object. For example, if you paste a single Visio shape into an Excel document, you can double-click the shape to open it for editing, as Figure 7-5 shows. If you're working in an Office program of recent vintage, the Visio toolbars and menus temporarily replace the application's tools. For other programs, Visio starts in a new window that displays the embedded diagram or shape.

When you edit an embedded shape, the
Visio drawing page and rulers appear.

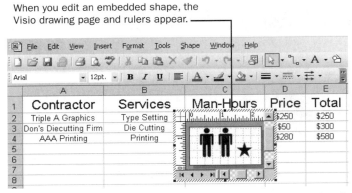

Figure 7-5. Whether you've embedded one shape or an entire diagram, you can edit it within the document that contains the embedded data by double-clicking the Visio image.

If you embed an entire drawing page or diagram and then edit it, Visio also opens any stencils that were open with the original drawing, as Figure 7-6 shows. To open an additional stencil, use the Shapes button on the Standard toolbar or choose File, Shapes and navigate to the stencil you want to open.

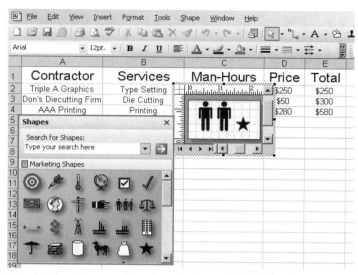

Figure 7-6.   You can open stencils from within the Visio editing window when you're working on an embedded diagram.

Tip   **Enlarge the window when editing in place**
When you edit an embedded object, you can gain working space and resize the drawing in the same way. Point to a handle on the in-place selection border. The pointer displays a two-headed arrow. Now you can drag to change the size of the Visio diagram that is displayed.

When you edit an embedded shape or diagram, you can insert new pages, display the Drawing Explorer or Pan & Zoom window, reorder pages, and more. When you're done making changes, you can return control to the other application in one of two ways:

- If you're editing in place, click the document page outside of the Visio window. The application's toolbars and menus are restored.

- If you're editing in a Visio program window, choose File, Exit And Return To <*name of your document*>.

Make sure to save the document after you make changes to the embedded object. An embedded diagram exists only in the Office document, so if you don't save it, you could lose all your changes.

Tip   **Insert a hyperlink to an embedded diagram**
When working in the Office System, you can also insert a hyperlink to an embedded diagram. Right-click on the diagram and choose Hyperlink. This displays the Insert Hyperlink dialog box. Choose the type of link you wish to insert, browse to its location, and click OK.

Inside Out

Save an embedded diagram as a Visio file

There's a way to save an embedded diagram as a separate Visio file as long as you're working on a computer that has Visio installed. For example, if you embed a diagram in a Word document and don't save the original Visio drawing file, you can save the embedded object. To do so, select the embedded Visio object, and then choose Edit, Visio Object, Open. This opens Visio with the embedded diagram displayed on a drawing page. Choose File, Save Copy As, and then name the file and choose a location for it.

Sizing an Embedded Visio Diagram

When you copy an entire Visio drawing page and then embed or link it, the size of the Visio object in the new document is based on the page size specified for the original Visio page. Sometimes this can create a large area of white around the Visio object; at other times, the embedded Visio shapes might appear crowded. You can size an embedded object by dragging a handle on the thick selection border, but sometimes that isn't enough. You can also adjust the spacing within Visio. Select the embedded or linked Visio diagram, and then choose Edit, Visio Object, Open or Open Link. Then do one of the following:

- To reduce the amount of white space around an embedded or linked diagram, choose File, Page Setup, and then click the Page Size tab. Select the SizeTo Fit Drawing Contents option, and then click OK to close the Page Setup dialog box. Choose File, Exit And Return To <name of your document>.

Fill Color

- To increase the space that appears around shapes, click the Rectangle tool on the Standard toolbar. Draw a rectangle that defines the size of the area you want. To move the rectangle to the back of the drawing, select it, and then choose Shape, Order, Send To Back. If you want, select the rectangle, click the drop-down arrow on the Fill Color button on the Formatting toolbar, and choose No Fill. You can also set its line style to No Line, making the rectangle completely transparent.

> **Tip** To return control to the other application, click anywhere outside the Visio drawing window.

Pasting Without Embedding

If you don't expect to edit a diagram or shapes that you're displaying in another document, you can keep your file size smaller by pasting without embedding. You won't be able to double-click the diagram and have instant access to all the Visio tools, but you also won't clutter your file with all the information that a document includes to support OLE. You can use the Picture or Picture (Enhanced Metafile) options in the Paste Special dialog box to paste Visio shapes into an Office document in a way that takes up less space, as Figure 7-7 shows.

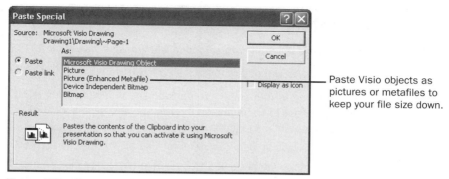

Paste Visio objects as pictures or metafiles to keep your file size down.

Figure 7-7. To paste Visio shapes into another document without embedding them, choose Edit, Paste Special to display these options.

In Visio, you can copy the shapes you want. To copy an entire page, choose Edit, Copy Drawing. In the Office document, position the cursor where you want to insert the diagram or shapes, and then choose Edit, Paste Special. Select either Picture or Picture (Enhanced Metafile), and then click OK.

> **Tip** The Paste Special command works in Visio, too, and is a great way to paste text from Word when you don't want to retain its formatting. Paste it as Unformatted Text.

Exporting Shapes and Diagrams

If you plan to use shapes as a Web graphic, or if you want to distribute a diagram to someone who doesn't have Visio or the Visio Viewer, you can export the contents of a drawing file as a graphic file. Visio can save files in many different formats, including JPEG, GIF, PNG, TIFF, WMF, EMF, and several less common formats. You can also save your Visio diagram as an HTML file.

Which format should you use? It depends, of course, on how you plan to use the diagram. If you want to include shapes as Web graphics, save them as GIF, JPEG, or PNG files. If the shapes are to be used in a document that will be professionally printed, save them as TIFF files. For use in other Windows applications, save them as WMF or EMF files. A general guideline is to consider whether you'll need to edit the shapes after exporting them. If you export shapes as a graphic in bitmap format (which includes BMP, TIFF, and JPEG files), the graphic cannot be edited easily in other nonimage editing applications. If you export shapes in a vector graphic format, such as WMF and EMF, you probably can edit them in other applications.

When you export in a graphic format, Visio converts objects on the drawing page into the graphic format. The resulting image might not look exactly the same when you import it into another application, because the importing application probably also goes through a conversion process to bring the image in.

Troubleshooting

You need to share a Visio diagram with someone who doesn't have Visio

You can share your diagram with others if you take a few extra steps:

- You can publish the diagram on an internal Web site or distribute an HTML file. You can use the Save As Web command on the File menu to save a Visio diagram as an HTML file or a Web-compatible graphic file.
- For details, see "Exporting Visio Diagrams for Use on the Web," page 153.
- You can use one of the methods described in this chapter to include the Visio diagram in a document in another application. For example, if your diagram's audience has Word, you can export the Visio diagram as a graphic file, insert it in a Word document, and then distribute the document.
- If people in your organization use Adobe Acrobat, you can create a PDF file of the diagram as described in this chapter. That way, others can view it in Adobe Acrobat Reader, a freely available viewer.
- As described earlier in the chapter, your co-workers can now view Visio documents even if they don't have Visio installed on their computers. They need only download the Visio Viewer from the Microsoft Download Center.
- In Visio 2003 you can also share your documents in a Document Workspace site. This is a Microsoft Windows Sharepoint Services site centered on your document. Eligible co-workers can view and edit your drawing from the site. See Chapter 8, "Saving and Printing Your Work," for more information.

Exporting a Shape as a Graphic

You can export a single shape, or multiple shapes, as a graphic that can be inserted or imported into another application. The Save As Type option of the Save As dialog box, shown in Figure 7-8, lists all the formats that Visio can export as.

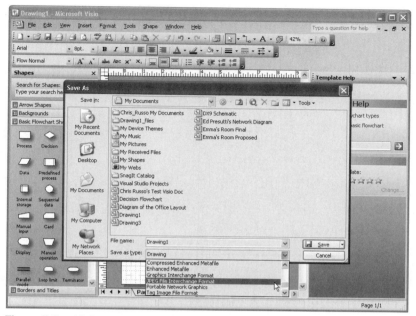

Figure 7-8. Visio can save a shape or diagram in many different formats.

To export a shape or multiple shapes as a graphic, follow these steps:

1   Select the shapes you want to export. Or, to export an entire page, display the page you want.

2   Select File, Save As.

3   In the File Name box, type a name for the file.

4   Click the Save As Type drop-down list arrow to display a list of file formats, and then select the format you want.

5   Click Save.

For many file formats, one of the following format-specific dialog boxes appears with additional options:

●   When you save your diagram as a JPEG image, you can choose operation type, format (RGB color, VCC color, Grayscale, or YCC color), background color, quality, transformation, resolution, and size for the image. You can also specify whether it will be a baseline JPEG or a progressive image.

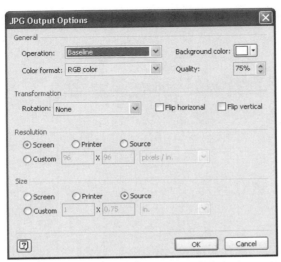

- The GIF Output Options dialog box provides options for color reduction, background color, transparency, transformation, resolution, and size. You can also specify whether you want the GIF image to be interlaced.

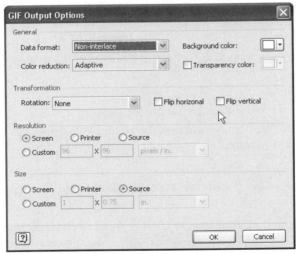

- The options for exporting a PNG file are the same as they are for a GIF file, but you can also choose a color format.

- When you export a TIFF image, you can choose data compression method, TIFF color format, background color, transformation, resolution, and size.

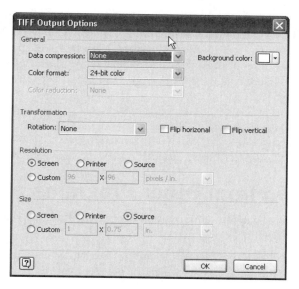

Troubleshooting

Some shapes don't appear when exported to other formats

If the Visio shape that you're trying to export is actually a metafile, as is the case with Visio Network Equipment shapes, the shape might not appear in the exported file. One way to tell whether a shape is a metafile is to select the shape and then choose Format, Special. You'll see Type: Metafile if the shape is a metafile. Then, you can ungroup the metafile, which converts it to separate Visio shapes. You might need to use the Ungroup command (Shape, Grouping, Ungroup) more than once until all parts are ungrouped and converted. You can then export the resulting shapes.

Exporting a Diagram in PDF Format

If you need to distribute a Visio drawing to people who don't have Visio, consider saving your diagram in PDF format. That way, you can hand someone a Visio file they can look at right away in Adobe Acrobat Reader, a free and widely available viewer. (You can download it from the Adobe Web site.)

A PDF file is a great way to save your diagram in a format others can read without compromising the integrity of the image. There's no option for saving in PDF directly from Visio, because you need Adobe Acrobat Distiller to create a high-quality PDF file. But if you have the full version of Adobe Acrobat, or an Adobe product that includes Acrobat Distiller (such as Adobe PageMaker), you can create a PDF file that can be viewed and printed by anyone who has the free Adobe Acrobat Reader, whether they're using a Windows, Macintosh, or UNIX operating system.

To create a PDF file from a Visio diagram, you must have a PostScript printer driver installed. You can install one through the Windows Add Printer utility, and you can install the driver without actually owning the device. Once Distiller is installed, it appears in the printer folder and can be treated just like any other printer. To produce the PDF file, simply print to Distiller, which then posts a file save dialog for the name of the PDF file. Printing to a file is unnecessary.

> **Tip** Another option for distributing your Visio drawings is to save them as Web pages. For details, see "Exporting Visio Diagrams for Use on the Web," page 153.

Importing Information from Other Programs

Just as there are many ways to display Visio information in other applications, there are several methods for bringing data in. Which method should you use?

- If you think you'll need to edit the original file later, OLE is a good choice, but your computer must include the application in which the file was created.
- If you want to include an image but don't plan to do anything more than resize or rotate it, export the image from another program in a graphic format that Visio can import. Graphic files that you import without OLE take up less space in the Visio drawing file.

Embedding and Linking Microsoft Office Documents in Visio

Earlier in the chapter, you learned how to use OLE to insert Visio diagrams into other documents. To insert other documents or objects into Visio diagrams, you use the same techniques.

If you add a link to another document from within a diagram, Visio stores a reference to that document file in the diagram, and it automatically updates the link every time you open the diagram. You can edit the original document either by double-clicking the linked file in the Visio diagram or by editing the original in its native application. Either way, both will be updated at the same time. Of course, you can only use the linked data if the other application is installed on your computer and if the linked file keeps the same name and remains in the same location.

If you embed a document in a Visio diagram, you don't need to worry about the location of the original, and you don't need to have the document's native application installed. If you do have access to the native application, though, you can edit the embedded object from within the Visio diagram. Double-clicking it will give you full editing capabilities. When you edit an embedded object, it has no effect on the original document. However, because the entire object is included in the drawing file, rather than just a reference, the drawing's file size will be much larger.

To link to a document in Visio, follow these steps:

1 In Visio, choose Insert, Object.

2 In the Insert Object dialog box, select the Create From File option, and then locate the file to which you want to link.

3 Select Link To File.

4 Click OK to return to the Visio diagram.

To edit the object, double-click it to display the toolbars from its native application. When you're done editing the object, click anywhere in the drawing outside the object window; the Visio controls reappear.

To embed a document in Visio, follow these steps:

1 In Visio, choose Insert, Object.

2 In the Insert Object dialog box, select the Create From File option, and then locate the file you want to link to.

3 Click OK to return to the Visio diagram.

> **Tip** If you want to create a new document, select Create New instead, and then select the drawing type. A drawing window for the other application appears, where you can create your object.

Troubleshooting

An imported image doesn't appear correctly in an embedded diagram

If you embed or export a Visio diagram that includes an inserted enhanced metafile picture, the image might appear as a crossed-out box. This happens when you save the Visio drawing file in Windows Metafile Format (WMF) or when you embed the Visio diagram into an application that supports only WMF files. You can safely embed enhanced metafiles (which Visio creates when you rotate a metafile) in applications that support this file format, including Visio and Office. As long as you don't need to rotate the inserted picture, your Visio drawing file will be compatible with more applications if you import graphics as WMF files instead of picture (enhanced metafile) files.

Importing Graphics

You can import a picture or graphic file that was created in another application even if you don't have that application. For example, you can import a corporate logo that appears on the page with an organization chart. Visio can import most of the standard graphic file formats, so there's almost certainly a format that Visio and the graphics application have in common.

Inside Out

How Visio imports an image

When you export a file from another application, the file's data is translated and saved to a separate file in a different format. When you import the file into a Visio drawing, the file is translated again. Because an image is changed slightly each time it's translated, the picture you import into your Visio drawing might not look exactly the way it does in the original application.

There are two ways to import graphic files:

- If you *open* the file, Visio creates a drawing with the bitmap or metafile graphic on it.
- If you *insert* the file, Visio imports the bitmap or metafile graphic into the drawing that's currently open.

Files you open are larger than files you insert, so if you need to keep your drawing file small, insert the data.

To insert a picture or graphic file, choose Insert, Picture, From File. The Insert Picture dialog box can display small previews, or *thumbnails*, of your files' contents, as Figure 7-9 shows. To insert a file, double-click a thumbnail or file name. Depending on the format of the file, you might see another dialog box that includes importing options. Visio uses the same filters to open and insert pictures and graphic files, so the same dialog boxes appear for both procedures.

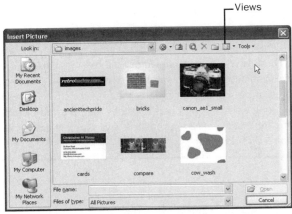

Figure 7-9. The View Thumbnails option makes it easier to find the picture you want but slower to scroll through many picture files.

Tip If you don't see the file you want to open, make sure the appropriate file type appears in the Files Of Type box.

Troubleshooting

Quality is poor with an imported graphic file

There could be a couple of reasons for this, depending on the type of graphic you're importing. Try the following procedures:

- With some vector-based graphics lines might appear jagged in the Visio drawing. You might get better results with these file formats if you open (File, Open) them, which places the image in its native format into Visio. By contrast, inserting (Insert, Picture) converts the images to metafiles.

- When you import a bitmap or raster graphic (.JPG, .GIF, .BMP, .TIF) into Visio, the graphic can become fuzzy or indistinct, particularly if you resize it. Although bitmaps always look better at 100 percent size, the new smoothing technology (called *anti-aliasing*) in Visio might have softened the edges too much. However, you can turn this feature off for graphics (and also for text, which is a separate option). Choose Tools, Options. On the View tab, clear the Higher Quality Shape Display check box.

When you import a graphic in a bitmap format, it comes into your Visio drawing as a single picture that you can edit a little—you can resize it, move it around on the page, crop it, or move it to a different layer. Bitmap graphics include files with the following extensions: .BMP, .DIB, .GIF, .JPG, .PCT, .PNG, and .TIF.

Vector graphic formats, however, give you a little more control. Most vector graphics are converted to metafiles as they are imported. Visio can import the following vector formats: .DWG, .DXF, .EMF, .IGS, .SVG, .SVGC, and .WMF. You can move a vector graphic around on the page, just as you can move a bitmap picture. You might also be able to convert it to Visio shapes, which creates a new shape for every separate component that makes up the metafile. To do this, select the metafile, and then choose Shape, Grouping, Ungroup (or press Shift+Ctrl+U). You might need to do this more than once to ungroup everything.

Note When you ungroup a metafile graphic, you might get dozens or hundreds of components. For example, you'll see all the paths or each band of a gradient fill. Additionally, text might appear as outlines.

Using Filter Options When Importing

The Filter Options dialog box gives you some control over the conversion of a picture or graphic file as Visio imports it. Most of the filters provide color translation options (which are the only options for bitmap files). The color translation options are the same as those available in Visio export filters. Table 7-1 lists what each does. Filters for some other vector formats include additional options that determine how the converted graphic appears, as Table 7-2 shows.

Table 7-1. Color Translation Options When Importing Bitmaps

Option	Result
Normal	Visio attempts to match the colors of the original image.
Inverse	Visio reverses the colors of the image. Black becomes white, dark blue becomes light yellow, and so on.
Inverse Grays Only	Visio retains the image's original colors but reverses their black, gray, and white values so that dark blue becomes light blue, light red becomes dark red, and so on.
Gray Scale	Visio converts all colors of an object to their gray values.
Inverse Gray Scale	Visio applies both Gray Scale and Inverse options, as in a photographic negative.

Table 7-2. Color Translation Options When Importing Vector Formats

Option	Result
Retain Gradients	Visio re-creates the gradients in the original image. If you don't select this option, Visio fills the object containing the gradient with the last color of the gradient.
Retain Background	Visio preserves the background color of the original image. To do this, Visio creates a background rectangle in that color and overlays the image.
Emulate Line Styles	Visio draws thick or patterned lines as polygons rather than as simple lines to ensure that they match the line styles of the original file.

Editing Imported Graphics

You can improve an imported picture's appearance by adjusting its contrast, brightness, and other values. Using the Picture command on the Format menu, you can work with color editing tools that might be familiar to you if you use other picture editing programs. As Figure 7-10 shows, you can adjust the levels of several properties and get immediate feedback—the preview shows the effect of an option. For example, if an imported picture looks dark on your computer screen, adjust the brightness (the gamma option). To make the edges in the picture stand out, increase the sharpness.

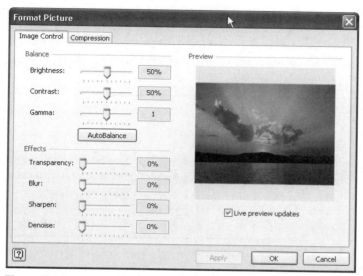

Figure 7-10. Adjust contrast, brightness, midtones, and other options with the Format Picture command.

Troubleshooting

An imported graphic cannot be edited in Visio as expected

There are several possibilities when this occurs:

- If the imported graphic is a metafile and you're trying to group or ungroup it, the problem could be that the metafile is rotated. The Convert To Group and Ungroup commands are unpredictable when used with a rotated metafile, and it can take a long time to see any results.

- If you want to crop a metafile and encounter resistance, make sure the Visio drawing page and the metafile are both upright. You can tell whether a metafile is upright by looking at the handles that appear when you crop it. If they're gray, the metafile isn't upright. If you can't select the cropping tool at all, the page isn't upright. If you want to rotate as well as crop a metafile, first crop it, and then rotate it.

- If you rotate a metafile in Visio and the quality is poor, your best option might be to rotate the picture in its original application before exporting it for use in Visio. When you rotate a metafile in Visio, it's converted to a picture in enhanced metafile format. If your diagram includes several on one page, they might not all appear in Microsoft Windows 98, but the data isn't lost.

Inserting Pictures from a Scanner or Digital Camera

Another way to bring information into Visio is to insert it directly from your scanner or digital camera. If you have set up the hardware and installed the software for either a TWAIN-compliant or WIA-compliant digital camera or scanner, you can use it to insert pictures into Visio. Choose Insert, Picture, From Scanner Or Camera to display the Insert

Microsoft Office Visio 2003 Inside Out

Picture From Scanner Or Camera dialog box. Use the Web Quality or Print Quality option for quick results. These options specify default settings for images you'll display on the screen or Web (choose Web Quality) or use in a printed diagram (choose Print Quality).To adjust settings yourself, or if you're using a digital camera, click Custom Insert. Visio embeds the image as a picture that can't be edited.

Inside Out

TWAIN and WIA interfaces

A TWAIN or WIA interface allows a scanner or digital camera to be controlled by another program, such as Visio, so that the hardware device's output can be used directly by the program. TWAIN stands for Technology (or Tool) Without An Interesting Name—evidently, its inventors were stumped. WIA stands for Windows Image Acquisition and was originally developed for Microsoft Windows Me.

Tip Using the Microsoft Clip Organizer

When you scan pictures, Visio adds them to the Microsoft Clip Organizer so that you can reuse them. To display the Clip Organizer, choose Insert, Picture, Clip Art. To prevent Visio from adding your scanned images, in the Insert Picture From Scanner Or Camera dialog box, clear the Add Pictures To Media Gallery option.

Troubleshooting

The Insert Picture From Scanner Or Camera command won't work

Is your digital camera or scanner turned on and connected to the port where its card is installed? It's always wise to check connections. If that's not the problem, you can try some standard hardware and software diagnostics:

- **Check the cables** Make sure the cables are fully inserted and not kinked, bent, dusty, or damaged.
- **Check the software** Make sure the camera or scanner software is installed in Control Panel (Add/Remove Programs).
- **Check the hardware** See if Windows can detect the device. In Control Panel, double-click System. In Microsoft Windows XP, click Control Panel, Printers And Other Hardware, and Scanners And Cameras. In Microsoft Windows 2000, click the Hardware tab, and then click Device Manager. In Windows 98, click the Device Manager tab. Then double-click a component associated with the camera or scanner to see its Device Status. If it indicates anything other than that the device is operating properly, you might need to install or reinstall your camera or scanner software.
- **Reinstall the software** Remove the camera or scanner software using Add/Remove Programs, restart Windows, and then reinstall the software.
- **Check device compatibility** Make sure your device and its card are compatible with each other and that their drivers are compatible with your operating system.

Other Methods for Using Data from Other Applications in Visio

Although linking, embedding, and importing graphics are the most common methods for bringing pictures, text, and other data into Visio diagrams, there are a few other ways you can import information:

- **Import clip art**   If you have the Office System and you installed the Microsoft Media Gallery, you can import clip art into your Visio drawing by choosing Insert, Picture, Clip Art.

- **Embed a graph**   If you have the Office System and you installed Microsoft Graph, you can use it to create a graph in a diagram. In Visio, choose Insert, Microsoft Graph. The Microsoft Graph menus and tools are displayed in Visio. When you're finished creating the graph, click in the drawing window outside the graph to return to the default Visio menus.

- **Drag**   You can drag objects onto your Visio drawing page if you have another application open at the same time. When you drag an object from another application, it's copied into your Visio drawing.

Chapter 8

Saving and Printing Your Work

What do you do with a drawing or diagram when you're finished working on it? Save and print it, usually. Microsoft Office Visio 2003 saves and prints like other Microsoft Office System applications. Saving can be as simple as pressing Ctrl+S, and printing is as easy as pressing Ctrl+P. However, Visio provides more complex saving options that are useful when you need to perform tasks such as distributing your work to others. For instance, you can save your drawing file with protections that prevent others from changing it.

When you want to share your work with others, you can distribute drawing files using e-mail or print copies. Visio's printing options are different from other Office applications because your drawing or diagram can be any size, so it might not fit on your printer's paper. The sections on printing in this chapter help you figure out how to get drawings and diagrams of all sizes to print the way you want.

Saving a Diagram

Save often.

That's obvious but sound advice, regardless of the software you're using. It's particularly good counsel if you use Visio for long periods of time or if you typically have several programs open while you work. Save your changes frequently using any of the following methods:

- Press Ctrl+S.
- Click the Save button on the Standard toolbar.
- Choose File, Save.

Save

The first time you save a diagram, regardless of the method you use, the Save As dialog box appears so that you can specify a name and location for the drawing file, as Figure 8-1 shows. After you specify this information, press Ctrl+S to save incremental changes to the diagram.

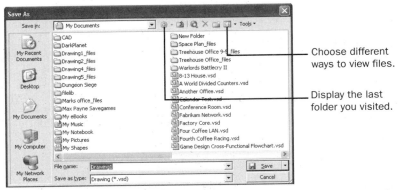

Figure 8-1. You can save files in different locations and formats in the Save As dialog box. Place the pointer over the buttons in the Save As dialog box to display a ScreenTip.

You might wonder exactly what is saved. Unless you specify otherwise, Visio saves any changes you've made to shapes, pages, and their properties (such as size and styles). Visio also saves a drawing's *workspace*, which saves the position of all the open windows in the file, such as the Custom Properties, and the Size & Position, Pan & Zoom, and Drawing Explorer windows. The next time you open the file, the stencil, drawing page, and other windows will look the same as when you last saved the file.

However, there are less obvious options that you can use when saving Visio files. You can do the following:

- Save information about the drawing file by specifying properties with the File, Properties command.
- Save a file as read-only to prevent others from editing it.
- Save a Visio drawing file by using the default (.vsd) format or as an XML (.vdx) document.

> For details about Visio and XML, see "Visio and XML File Formats," page 616.

- Save a drawing file as a stencil or template simply by using the Save As command and specifying Stencil (.vss) or Template (.vst) in the Save As Type list.

> For details, see "Mastering Visio Documents," page 609.

- Save a drawing file in Web (HTML) or graphic format.

> For details, see "Exporting Visio Diagrams for Use on the Web," page 153, and see "Exporting Shapes and Diagrams," page 217.

- Share your work as part of a presentation or by linking or embedding a diagram in another application.

> For details, see "Using Visio Shapes and Diagrams in Presentations," page 345, and "Working with OLE," page 203.

Document Workspaces

Document Workspaces are Microsoft Windows SharePoint sites that let you make your drawings available for coworkers to read and modify. To go into detail about SharePoint services and sites would take another book, but suffice to say you can share your document by e-mailing it as a shared attachment or by utilizing the Shared Workspace task pane.

To e-mail a document as a shared attachment follow this procedure:

1 Open the drawing that you wish to share.

2 Click the Mail Recipient button on the Standard toolbar.

3 Fill in the e-mail as you normally do.

4 Click Attachment Options, and select Shared Attachments.

5 Type in the address of the document workspace. The address must be a valid SharePoint location.

6 Click Send to send the e-mail.

Mail Recipient

The recipients receive a copy of the drawing that is also held in the document workspace. The drawing in the workspace is automatically updated when other recipients upload their changes.

You can also share your drawings using the Shared Workspace task pane. To do so, follow these steps:

1 Select View, Task Pane to display the Visio task pane.

2 Select Shared Workspace from the task pane's drop-down menu.

3 Type in the document workspace name, and the location of the workspace. The address must be a valid SharePoint location.

4 Click Create.

Chapter 8

Including File Properties with a Diagram

After you have saved a file, you can right-click the file to display the Properties dialog box. This box helps you customize and identify your file.

The Properties dialog box contains so many options, who has time to fill them all in? However, if you supply some or all of the requested information, it can help you identify your drawing or diagram later without having to open it, because other dialog boxes can read a file's properties and display the information to you. For example, when you select a file in the Open dialog box, you can click the Tools button, and then choose Properties to view the file information, as Figure 8-2 shows.

Figure 8-2. If you enter file properties in Visio, the information can help you differentiate among Visio diagrams when you're looking for a particular drawing file.

To enter properties for an open drawing file, follow these steps:

1 Choose File, Properties.

2 On the Summary tab of the Properties dialog box, enter the information you want to save with the diagram.

   Most of the boxes allow you to type up to 63 characters. The Description box accepts up to 191 characters. The Hyperlink Base box accepts up to 259 characters.

3 Click OK.

Chapter 8

Saving a Preview of a Diagram

Another way to locate a particular Visio file is to save a preview of the drawing. You can then display it in the Open dialog box. To save a preview, choose File, Properties, and then choose Save Preview Picture on the Summary tab. The preview is a handy way to find one Visio diagram when you have a lot of them; however, the preview image does add to the file size of the diagram. To see a file's preview in the Open dialog box, click Views, and then click Preview.

If you're using an older version of the Windows operating system, you can take advantage of the Quick View tool to preview Visio diagrams. Quick View is available in Microsoft Windows 98, Microsoft Windows 95, or Microsoft Windows NT 4, but not in Microsoft Windows 2000. The preview image appears when you right-click a Visio file in Windows Explorer and then click Quick View.

Changing Where Diagrams Are Saved

When you save a drawing file, Visio initially displays the My Documents or Personal (if you have Windows NT) folder to save it in. This folder is also the first place Visio looks when you open an existing drawing file. Whenever you use the Save As command to save a drawing file, you can specify a different location in the Save In box, the same way you do in other Office applications. If you always save your work in a different location, it might make more sense to change the default *file path* Visio uses to locate and save files. For example, if you set D:\Work\ Visio as the default file path, when you use the Save As command, that folder is displayed in the Save In box.

To save your work to a different location, follow these steps:

1 Choose File, Save As, and then click the drop-down arrow in the Save In list to display a list of available drives and folders.

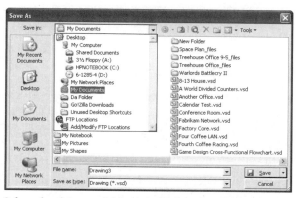

2 Select the drive or folder in which you want to save your file.

A list of existing files and folders in that location is displayed.

3 To save your drawing file in a subfolder, double-click it.

4   Make sure the file name appears the way you want, and then click Save.

To change the default location (file path) for saving drawing files, follow these steps:

1   Choose Tools, Options, click the Advanced tab, and then click File Paths.

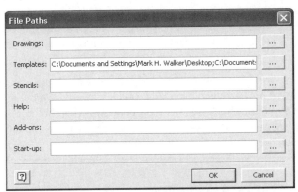

2   In the Drawings box, select the existing text, and then type the file path you want; for example, **D:\Work\Visio**, or click the button to the right of the box and browse to the location that you wish to use.

If you don't want to replace the existing path but add to it, type a semicolon (;) after the existing path, and then type your file path.

3   Click OK.

The next time you choose the Save As command, the new default appears as the initial location in the Save In list.

Tip   **Specify multiple default file paths**

You can specify more than one default file path, which is more useful for locating add-ons, filters, and help files than opening or saving drawing files. To do this, type a semicolon between file paths; for example: C:\My Documents;D:\Work\Visio. Do not add a space after the semicolon.

Saving to a Document Management System

If you work with a document management system (DMS) that supports the Open Document Management Architecture (ODMA) standard, you can store Visio drawings and diagrams with it. Many organizations that work on collaborative projects use these systems to track documents that must be accessed and modified by many people across a network. A DMS tracks revisions, monitors document access, and facilitates version control.

If Visio detects the presence of an ODMA 1.5–compliant system on your computer, you can choose File, Save or Save As to save your drawing file, and the DMS Save dialog box appears instead of the Save dialog box. If the DMS Save dialog box does not appear, you might need to register Visio with your DMS. Refer to the documentation that came with your DMS.

Chapter 8

Protecting a Visio Document

 In Visio 2003, you can save your file to a SharePoint shared workspace that permits more than one person at a time to open the same Visio file. The first person to open the drawing file has write access, which means that only he or she can save changes to the original file. When a second person opens the same file, Visio displays a message, as Figure 8-3 shows. The second person can still edit the file but must save the changed drawing as a copy using a different file name.

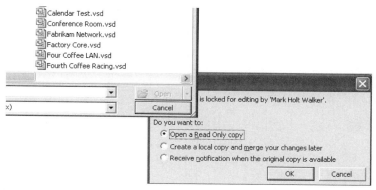

Figure 8-3. If you open a file that someone else has opened, Visio asks whether you want to open a read-only copy.

Visio provides two other ways that you can share your drawing file with others while protecting the original work:

- **Save as read-only** You can save drawings and diagrams as read-only files, which means that no one can have write access to the file.
- **Lock shapes** You can build protection into your drawing or diagram by locking shapes that you don't want others to change.

The sections that follow provide more details.

Saving Read-Only Diagrams

One way you can protect a Visio file (drawing, stencil, or template) is to save a read-only version. Typically, a drawing file is saved as a *read-write* file, meaning that the next time you open it, you can both see (read) and make changes to (write) the file. When you save a diagram that you plan to distribute to others, you can save the file as read-only to protect it from changes. When you open a read-only file, you can edit shapes and make other changes, but that changed file must be saved under a different name. If you try to save your changes to the original file, an error message appears, as Figure 8-4 shows.

Figure 8-4. If a message like this appears when you try to save a diagram, the drawing file has been saved as a read-only file. The original file can't be edited unless you reset the file's read-only status in your file manager.

To save a file as a read-only file, follow these steps:

1 Choose File, Save As.

2 In the Save As dialog box, specify a file name and location, and then click the drop-down list arrow on the Save button to display additional options.

3 Select the Read Only option, and then click Save.

Visio saves the drawing file as a noneditable, read-only file.

You can get around read-only protection, though. In a file manager, you can reset the read-only status. For example, in Windows Explorer, right-click the name of the read-only file, choose Properties, and then clear the Read-Only check box on the General tab.

Locking a Diagram Against Changes

If you want to be able to save changes to a diagram but still provide protection for its contents, you can set protection locks. A *protection lock* disables a particular action, such as resizing a shape. You can't lock an entire diagram against editing, but you can prevent shapes on the drawing page from being deleted, selected, or moved.

Chapter 8

To set protection locks for a diagram, follow these steps:

1 Select the shapes you want to protect, and then choose Format, Protection.

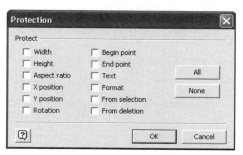

2 In the Protection dialog box, click All to set all the locks, or select only the check boxes you want.

3 Click OK.

Visio sets the locks, which means that you won't be able to take any of the actions that you've locked, nor will anyone else, until the locks are removed (by clearing the check boxes you selected in the Protection dialog box).

Inside Out

Locking layers

If you want to distribute your drawing or diagram for others to review, you can use the layers feature to protect parts of the drawing that you don't want others to change. For example, you can assign specific shapes to a layer, and then lock that layer against changes. For details, see "Controlling Shapes with Layers," page 460.

Sending Diagrams in E-Mail

Like other Office products, Visio lets you quickly send a drawing or diagram to another person via e-mail as an attachment. To open the attachment, your recipient must have Visio 2000 or later or download the Visio viewer from Microsoft at *http://go.microsoft.com/fwlink/ ?linkid=13116&clcid=0x409*. Visio works with any e-mail program that supports the Messaging Application Programming Interface (MAPI) protocol, which includes Microsoft Outlook, Microsoft Outlook Express, and Microsoft Exchange Client. Visio is heavily tested for compatibility with these e-mail programs, because they're the ones that Microsoft employees use. If your e-mail program is MAPI-compatible, you'll see the Mapi32.dll file in the Windows System folder.

Note An e-mail program must be installed on your computer for the Mail Recipient and Routing Recipient commands to work.

To include a drawing file in an e-mail message, follow these steps:

1 While the drawing file is open, select File, Send To, Mail Recipient (as Attachment) or click the Mail Recipient button on the Standard toolbar.

Visio starts your e-mail program (if necessary) and displays a new message to which the drawing file is attached.

2 Complete the message as you normally would—type an address and any other text.

3 Click Send or equivalent.

To view a Visio file sent by e-mail, open the e-mail message, and then double-click the Visio icon or file name.

Note To open a Visio drawing received through e-mail, you must have Visio 2000 or later or the Microsoft Visio Viewer.

Routing Documents

A great way to solicit feedback on a diagram or drawing is to route it as an e-mail attachment to a list of reviewers. To do this, you create a routing slip that specifies how and to whom the drawing file is sent. You can send a file to one person at a time, in a particular order, so that each person reads the comments of reviewers who received the file before them, or you can send it to all the reviewers simultaneously, so that everyone can review a copy at the same time. You can even track the drawing file's progress as each recipient sends it to the next one. When the last reviewer has seen the drawing file, it can be returned to you automatically.

You can route a drawing to a group e-mail alias, but then everyone in the group will receive a copy of the drawing file to review. If you want to route the drawing file to one person at a time, you must specify each person's e-mail address rather than use a group alias.

To send a drawing with a routing slip, follow these steps:

1 Open the drawing you want to send, and then choose File, Send To, Routing Recipient. If the Choose Profiles box appears, select the profile you want to use, and then click OK.

Saving and Printing Your Work

2 Click Address to open the Address Book or your post office address list, and then select the recipient names for routing. When you've finished adding to the recipient list, click OK.

3 To route the drawing file to the recipients in a specific order, select a name, and then click the Move arrows to move the name up or down in the list.

4 In the Subject box, type the subject line as it will appear in the e-mail message.

5 In the Message Text box, type any information that you want to appear in the body of the e-mail message.

6 To specify how the drawing file is routed, select One After Another or All At Once.

If you select One After Another, the first person on the list will receive the drawing file for review, and then must route it to the next person. If you click All At Once, everyone receives a copy of the drawing file.

7 If you want to receive notification when a reviewer routes the drawing to the next person, select theTrack Status check box.

8 If you want the drawing to be sent to you automatically after it's been sent to everyone on the routing slip, select the Return When Done check box.

9 Click Route to send the file.

Tip   Route a Visio diagram to the next recipient

If you receive a routed drawing and want to route it to the next person, choose File, Next Routing Recipient. If you want to route the drawing to someone who isn't on the list, choose File, Other Routing Recipient, and then follow steps 2 through 7 of the preceding list.

Sending Diagrams to Microsoft Exchange

Visio can save a diagram in a Microsoft Exchange public folder as an embedded object. This technique allows you or another user to open the diagram as an embedded object from within Microsoft Exchange. You must have permission to use public folders, and you must use Microsoft Exchange Server. If your computer doesn't use Exchange Server, nothing will happen when you choose the Exchange Folder command.

To send a drawing directly to an Exchange folder, follow these steps:

1 Display the drawing you want to send, and then choose File, Send To, Exchange Folder.

2 In the folder list, select the folder in which you want to post the drawing.

3 Click OK.

Printing Diagrams of Any Size

Most of the time, you can print a Visio diagram or drawing by choosing File, Print, and then clicking OK in the Print dialog box, shown in Figure 8-5. Most Visio templates are set up so that the drawing page and printed page sizes are the same, so you don't have to change page settings to get the printed drawing you expect. Visio adjusts your diagram's colors to match your printer's capabilities. If your diagram uses color and you don't have a color printer, your output is displayed in shades of gray.

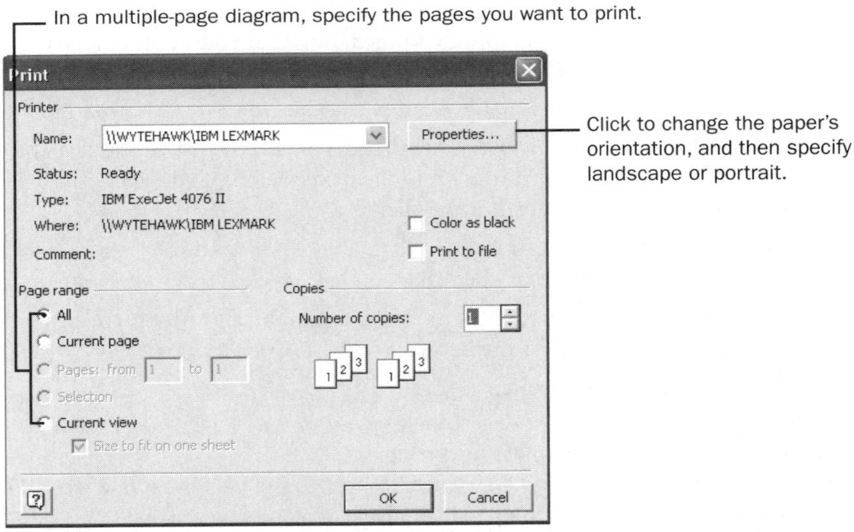

In a multiple-page diagram, specify the pages you want to print.

Click to change the paper's orientation, and then specify landscape or portrait.

Figure 8-5. In the Print dialog box, you can specify page ranges and other options.

To print a drawing, do one of the following:

Print

● Click the Print button on the Standard toolbar.

● Press Ctrl+P.

● Choose File, Print.

Printing in Visio frequently gives people headaches, primarily because the page you see can vary in size from the paper in your printer. How do you get one to fit the other? You might have to adjust settings when you print if you change the size, orientation, or scale of the *drawing page*—the page you see in Visio. It's not difficult if you remember that *drawing page* means the area you draw on in Visio, which might not be the same size and shape as the *printed page*, because it depends on the size of the paper in your printer.

> **Note** An object must be on the drawing page to be printed. Shapes and objects outside the drawing page on the *pasteboard* (the gray area) won't be printed.

Most templates in Visio Standard assume that you're using a typical office printer and standard, letter-sized paper. If you're in the United States, letter-sized is 8.5 by 11 inches. Everywhere else, it's A4 paper. Some Visio Professional templates (notably those in the Building Plan folder) assume that you're working with larger architectural or engineering drawings that will be printed with a plotter using standard ANSI sizes (A through E).

The rest of this section explains how to adjust printing options to suit your paper and drawing sizes.

Inside Out

The printer paper size option

To easily match the size of your drawing page and the size of the printer paper use the Same As Printer Paper Size option. Choose File, Page Setup, click the Page Size tab, and then select this option. Although there are exceptions for technical drawings and diagrams, most business diagrams benefit from this setting.

Troubleshooting

The Print command causes a page orientation error

If the Visio drawing page is oriented differently from the printed page (for example, one is landscape and the other portrait), you will receive an error message.

Landscape orientation means the page is wider than it is tall. Portrait orientation is the opposite. If you change the orientation of your drawing, you need to change the orientation of your printer's paper as well, unless you specifically want the drawing to print on several pages. You can do one of two things:

- Click OK to continue printing. The parts of the drawing that don't fit on one page will print on separate pages.

- Click Cancel, and then set the drawing page and printer paper orientation so that they match. To do this, choose File, Page Setup. On the Page Size tab, notice the setting under Page Orientation. Is the drawing page portrait or landscape? Then click the Print Setup tab, and make sure that the Paper Orientation option matches the orientation on the Page Size tab.

Printing Tiled Drawings and Diagrams

If the size of your drawing or diagram is larger than the size of your printer's paper, Visio will *tile* the drawing, which means that the drawing file's contents are printed on as many pages as it requires. Think of ceramic tiles—if you wanted to display a wall-sized image on standard-sized square tiles, you would break up portions of the image to fit on many tiles. Each printer page is a tile that your drawing or diagram must fit on. If you're using a typical office printer with letter-sized or A4 paper, and your drawing is larger than that, your drawing will be tiled. Visio previews a tiled page in the Page Setup dialog box, as Figure 8-6 shows.

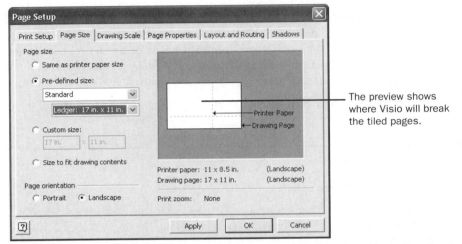

The preview shows where Visio will break the tiled pages.

Figure 8-6. If the drawing page is too large to fit on a printed page, Visio tiles the drawing page along the dotted lines, as shown in the Page Setup dialog box.

When Visio tiles a drawing or diagram, the shapes and objects that overlap the page breaks can end up being printed twice—that is, on the two pages that share the page break. To avoid this, specify a larger size of paper to print on. Not all printers support this option, though. Another option is to reduce the size of your diagram when you print it so that it fits on the page as described later. However, if you can't print on a larger size of paper, and page reduction isn't an option, you can at least adjust the contents of the drawing page to minimize overlapping areas when you print.

To see where pages will tile when you print, choose View, Page Breaks, as Figure 8-7 shows.

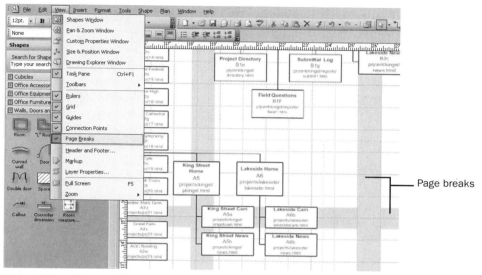

Figure 8-7. Choose View, Page Breaks to display gray lines on the drawing page that show how the page will be tiled to fit on the printed page.

The visible page breaks show where shapes and objects overlap page edges. For example, in Figure 8-7, several boxes in the Web site map fall into the gray area, indicating that they overlap the page edges and will be cut off or duplicated when printed. The thickness of the gray lines is determined by the margins that are set for the printed page. One way to control what prints where is to make sure that no shapes touch the margins. That way, you avoid the problem of duplicate shapes when you print. You can also increase the width of the page breaks to see more easily where shapes might overlap when printed.

Controlling How Tiled Pages Break

You can change where page breaks occur in a tiled drawing or diagram and also the number of page breaks used. By changing the printed page margins, you can effectively define the area in which a large drawing will print when Visio tiles the pages.

To change the printed page margins, follow these steps:

1 Choose File, Page Setup, and then click the Print Setup tab.

2 Near the Paper Orientation area, click Setup to open the Print Setup dialog box.

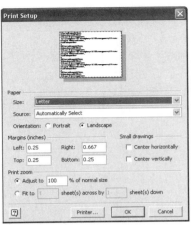

3   In the Margins boxes, type larger numbers for Left, Right, Top, or Bottom to specify the area in which you want your diagram to print. The larger the margins, the greater the overlap.

4   Click OK in the Print Setup dialog box, and then click OK in the Page Setup dialog box.

The width of the page breaks changes based on your margin settings. If page breaks aren't visible, choose View, Page Breaks.

5   To print the drawing file, press Ctrl+P, and then click OK in the Print dialog box.

Note   Visio does not crop a drawing to fit within the margins you set.

Reducing a Tiled Diagram to Fit the Page

If you don't want your diagram or drawing to be tiled across several printed pages, you can shrink the drawing to fit when you print. The dialog boxes refer to this option as print zoom, which means that the drawing page is reduced by a percentage that you can specify.

To fit a drawing page to the printed page, follow these steps:

1   Choose File, Page Setup, and then click the Print Setup tab.

2   In the Print Zoom area, click Adjust To, and then select or type the percentage of reduction you want.

The preview picture shows how the drawing page will fit on the printed page.

3   Click OK in the Print Setup dialog box, and then click OK in the Page Setup dialog box.

4   To print the drawing file, press Ctrl+P, and then click OK in the Print dialog box.

Troubleshooting

Your drawing prints on multiple pages, and you want it to fit on one page

To keep a drawing on a single page, try one or more of these methods:

- **If your printer can use different sizes of paper, specify larger paper**   For example, print on legal-sized paper instead of letter-sized. To do this, click Properties in the Print dialog box, and then choose a paper size option.

- **Shrink the drawing when you print**   This is like using a copy machine to create a copy at a reduced size, such as 75 percent. The size of the original drawing or diagram doesn't change. To do this, choose File, Page Setup, and then click the Print Setup tab. You can either click Adjust To and then specify a percentage, or click Fit To and then specify 1 Sheet Across By 1 Sheet Down.

- **Change the drawing page orientation to see if your drawing fits**   For example, if your drawing is too wide to fit on the page, use landscape orientation, where the page is wider than it is tall. To do this, choose File, Page Setup, and click the Page Size tab. Click Custom Size, and then click an option under Page Orientation. Click the Print Setup tab, and then make sure that the Paper Orientation option matches the Page Orientation you just selected.

- **Apply a drawing scale that reduces all the shapes on the drawing page**   You tend to get better results when you specify a drawing scale before you begin using shapes. Applying a drawing scale later can cause shape and text alignment to get out of whack. However, if all else fails, it's worth a try. (You can undo the results if necessary.) Choose File, Page Setup, click the Drawing Scale tab, and then choose a predefined or custom scale. For example, try a custom scale of 1 in. or 1 cm to 1.5 in., or 1.5 cm for a business diagram. For details, see "Working with a Drawing Scale," page 422.

Fitting a Tiled Diagram on a Specified Number of Pages

Another way to control how a tiled drawing is printed is to specify the number of printed pages to fit the drawing on. When you do this, Visio ensures that your drawing or diagram will fit—even if it must be reduced in size. For example, if your large organization chart needs to fit on one page across and two pages down, Visio might have to reduce the chart to fit on one page across, but only the printed output is reduced. Your diagram isn't scaled or zoomed in any way.

To specify the number of pages for a tiled drawing, follow these steps:

1   Choose File, Page Setup, and then click the Print Setup tab.

2   In the Print Zoom area, select the FitTo option, and then type the number of sheets across and down in the boxes.

    For best results, specify a number of pages that corresponds to the proportions of the drawing. For example, in a wide drawing, make sure the Across value is bigger than the Down value.

Chapter 8

3   Click OK in the Print Setup dialog box, and then click OK in the Page Setup dialog box.

4   To print the drawing file, press Ctrl+P, and then click OK in the Print dialog box.

 Troubleshooting

Enlarging a drawing causes unnecessary blank printed pages

Depending on how you resize the contents of your drawing page, you might find that when you print a large drawing or diagram, several extra pages are printed as well—and some of them might be blank. Even when your file's contents print on one page, this can happen, and the extra pages can be a nuisance. Extra pages indicate that the drawing page size is larger than your printer's paper, and Visio is tiling your drawing across several pages. Although they are blank, those pages are a part of your drawing page.

To avoid this problem, do one of the following:

- Resize the drawing page so that it encompasses the page's contents only. To do this, choose File, Page Setup, and then click the Page Size tab. Select the Size To Fit Drawing Contents option, and then click OK. Your drawing page still might not match your printed page, but this solution should reduce the number of extra pages printed.

- Specify a smaller drawing page size. If you have extra white space around your drawing, you can remove it by choosing a standard page size that's smaller—but still large enough for your diagram's contents. Follow the technique just described, but select Same As Printer Paper Size or a predefined size, depending on the paper size options your printer supports.

Centering a Diagram Before Printing

A quick way to fine-tune a drawing's placement is to center it on the drawing page before you print. Choose Shape, Center Drawing. This is all you need to do if the drawing page and printer paper are the same size.

There's another option for odd-sized diagrams that you intend to print on a standard-sized printer page. Let's say you're creating a very small diagram—something as small as a business card. You might find it easier to work in Visio if you size the drawing page to fit the contents of your small diagram alone, as Figure 8-8 shows. When you print it, though, you can make sure the small image prints where you want it on the printer paper.

Figure 8-8. You can size the drawing page to fit its contents alone, which can make it easier to work with small drawings like this business card.

To center all your drawing or diagram on the drawing page, follow these steps:

1 Choose File, Page Setup, and then click the Page Size tab.

2 Select the Size To Fit Drawing Contents option.

In the preview area, the size of the drawing page is updated. If the drawing page is now smaller than the printed page, you can adjust where the image will print. If the drawing page is now larger than the printed page, see the previous section for tips about working with tiled diagrams.

3 Click the Print Setup tab, and then click Setup.

4 Select the Center Horizontally or Center Vertically check boxes (or both), and then click OK.

5 In the Page Setup dialog box, click OK.

Visio changes the drawing page size so that it tightly encompasses your diagram, without any surrounding white space. On the screen, it looks like you zoomed in on the drawing, which is why this setting is useful for working with small objects. In fact, Visio shape designers use this setting when they are designing individual master shapes to make it easier to edit the shape before saving it on a stencil.

The Size To Fit Drawing Contents option also makes adjusting page margins easier. With it, you can print a small drawing exactly where you want it on a sheet of paper, as Figure 8-9 shows.

Click to set margins or to center the
drawing page on the printer paper.

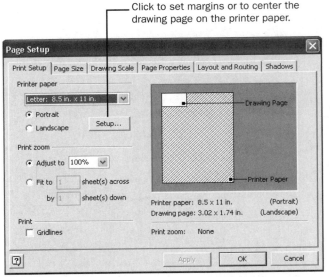

Figure 8-9. You can control where a small drawing prints on regular-sized printer paper. By
default, Visio prints small drawings in the top left corner, as the preview here shows.

To specify where on the page a small drawing prints, follow these steps:

1 Choose File, Page Setup, and click the Print Setup tab.

2 Click Setup.

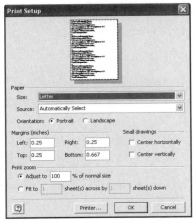

3 Enter the size of the margins you want in the Left, Right, Top, and Bottom boxes.

To preview the effect of the settings, click OK in the Print Setup dialog box. If the
results aren't what you expected, click Setup again and adjust the values in the Margins
boxes.

Chapter 8

4 Click OK in the Print Setup dialog box, and then click OK in the Page Setup dialog box.

When you're ready to print, Visio will use the margins you specified to adjust the position of the small diagram on your printer's paper.

Troubleshooting

Text in the drawing looks different than it did in previous versions of Visio

The printer fonts found in much earlier versions of Visio are not supported by current versions. If you open a drawing file created in one of these earlier versions, a Windows font is substituted. Try changing the font in your drawing to any available TrueType, OpenType, or PostScript font. Visio distinguishes between these fonts in the Text dialog box. The logo to the left of the font name tells you what type of font it is.

Printing Multiple-Page Drawings

The thing to know about multiple-page drawings is that you can specify a different size and orientation for every page in your drawing file, but Visio will print the entire document using one set of printer settings. The Print Setup options apply to the entire drawing file. For example, one page in your drawing file can use portrait orientation, and the next page can use landscape orientation. When you print, you must specify one paper orientation. What are your options? Either make sure that all your drawing pages are the same size and orientation, or else print each page separately and reset the printer settings for each page before you print it.

The Page Setup dialog box is the place to specify any of these options (File, Page Setup). When your drawing file includes multiple pages, the options on the Page Setup tab refer to the page that's currently displayed. The options on the Print Setup tab tell you what the printer is set to do for the entire drawing file.

Printing Selected Shapes or Pages

If you don't want to print your entire drawing, you can print only the pages you specify, only the page currently displayed, or only the background of a single page. You can also define shapes or layers as nonprinting so that they show up on the screen but not on the printed page.

To print only the pages you specify, follow these steps:

1 Choose File, Print.

2 Under Page Range, select the Pages option, and then type the page number range in the From and To boxes.

> **Note** The Pages options are unavailable for diagrams with only one page.

3 Choose other options you want, and then click Print.

Printing Selected Shapes

You can select the shapes on the drawing page that you want to print. Visio will print only the selected shapes and nothing else. To print selected shapes, follow these steps:

1 Select the shapes that you want to print.

> **Tip** Select multiple shapes
> To select multiple shapes, Shift+click the shapes you want, choose Area Select or Multiple Select from the Pointer Tool drop-down menu, or select the Lasso pointer from the Pointer Tool drop-down menu and draw a lasso around the shapes.

2 Choose File, Print.
3 In the Print dialog box under Page Range, select Selection.
4 Choose other options you want, and then click Print.

Troubleshooting

Text in the drawing file won't display in a transparent color

You can't make text formatted with a PostScript font transparent. Format your text with a TrueType or OpenType font instead.

Setting Shapes to Not Print

You can prevent a shape or several shapes from printing when you print a diagram. To specify that a shape is nonprinting, follow these steps:

1 Select a shape, or select multiple shapes, and then choose Format, Behavior.

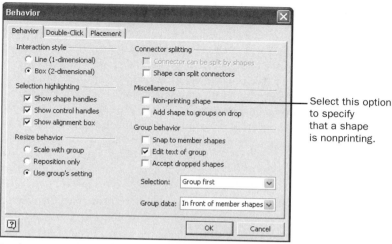

Select this option
to specify
that a shape
is nonprinting.

2 Under Miscellaneous, select the Non-Printing Shape check box.

3 Click OK.

Inside Out

Using nonprinting layers

Using layers in a Visio diagram gives you more control when you print, which is a great reason to use them. For example, you can assign shapes containing annotations or other details to a separate layer and set that layer to be nonprinting. Then when you print your diagram, only the parts of the drawing you want appear, without all the clutter. To make a layer nonprinting, select View, Layer Properties, and clear the check mark for the layer in the Print column. For details, see "Using Layers to Protect, Hide, and Organize Shapes," page 467.

Troubleshooting

Some shapes don't appear in the printed drawing

The printer driver might have translated the color of the shape's line and fill as white. On the File menu, choose Print, and then select the Color As Black check box.

The lines and fills of all shapes are converted to black before sending them to the printer, so shapes are visible in the printed drawing. This is helpful if you can't determine which shapes are missing from the printed drawing.

The shape might be set as a nonprinting shape, or it might be on a nonprinting layer. Select the shape, and then on the Format menu, choose Behavior. If a check mark appears for Non-Printing Shape, clear it. To find out what layer a shape is on, select the shape, and then choose Format, Layer. To make sure the layer prints, choose View, Layer Properties. Make sure that the Print column is selected for that layer.

Printing Foreground and Background Pages

If your diagram or drawing includes both foreground and background pages, you can choose to print the background separately. Many architectural and engineering drawings display a border or title block on a background page. Typically, when you print a drawing page, Visio prints the foreground page, its background, and any background layers. If you want to review the contents of the background only, you can display a background page, and then print only that page. Or perhaps you're using an ornate background from the Backgrounds stencil, and you don't want it to show up in the printed output. You can print only a background, but to print a foreground page without its background, you must temporarily unassign the background.

To print only a background page, follow these steps:

1 Display the background page that you want to print, and then choose File, Print.

> **Note** To identify a background page, display the page, choose File, Page Setup, and then click the Page Properties tab. The Background option is selected if the page is a background page.

2 Under Page Range, select Current Page.
3 Click OK.

Visio prints the background page you displayed and any backgrounds assigned to that page.

To print only a foreground page without its background, follow these steps:

1 Display the foreground page, and then choose File, Page Setup.
2 Click the Page Properties tab.
3 In the Background box, select None, and then click OK.
4 To print the page, choose File, Print, specify the settings you want, and then click OK.

To restore the background, follow steps 1 and 2, and then in the Background box, select the name of the background page.

Printing a Diagram to a File

You can print a drawing to a file, such as a PostScript file that you might submit to a commercial printer. Printing to a file lets you prepare a version of your drawing file that you want to print and save it in printable format. You can then continue to work on your drawing or diagram and print it later. For this procedure to work, a printer driver must be installed for the printer or output device that you intend as the file's ultimate destination.

To print a diagram to a file, follow these steps:

1 Choose File, Print.

2 In the Name list, select the printer that will be used to print the file. For example, click a PostScript printer.

3 Select the Print To File check box, and then click OK.

4 In the Print To File dialog box, select the folder in which you want to store the file, type a file name, and then click OK.

The PostScript file can't be opened in Visio or any other Office program. A printer file is intended to be sent directly to a printer port, which you can do in Microsoft MS-DOS by using the Copy command. For example, the following MS-DOS command sends the printer file called Form.prn that's stored in the C:\My Documents folder to the printer connected to port LPT1:

```
copy C:\Mydocu~1\form.prn lpt1 /b.
```

In MS-DOS, long file names (longer than eight characters) are truncated, and a tilde (~) is substituted. The /b switch sends the file in binary format.

Troubleshooting

Saving a file causes it to print

In the past, Visio had a known problem with certain printers. When you saved your drawing file, the diagram automatically printed. Visio must communicate with the printer driver to share font and page settings, but sometimes that communication is misinterpreted as a command to print. Some users find that assigning a different version of a printer driver to their printer is a successful solution. For more details, either search the Internet for Visio user groups or check the Microsoft Knowledge Base for the most up-to-date information.

Past versions of Visio (2000 and earlier) required a manual entry in the Windows Registry to change a printer driver setting, but Visio 2003 no longer requires this repair.

Previewing Before You Print

You can prevent most unexpected printing results by previewing the printed drawing before you print it. You can use the Print Preview command on the File menu to do this or use the preview images that appear in the Page Setup dialog box. The following sections help you troubleshoot the most common problems that users encounter when printing Visio drawings and diagrams.

Using the Print Preview Window

Most Office applications have a preview window that you can use to see what a document looks like when printed. The Print Preview window in Visio works pretty much like all the others and can help you diagnose drawing page and printed page conflicts before you send your diagram to the printer.

Print Preview

To preview a drawing or diagram, choose File, Print Preview, or click the Print Preview button on the Standard toolbar.

When Visio displays your drawing page in the preview window, the margins that are set for your printer appear as gray lines. If your drawing page is larger than the printer paper, the gray lines show you the page breaks, as Figure 8-10 shows.

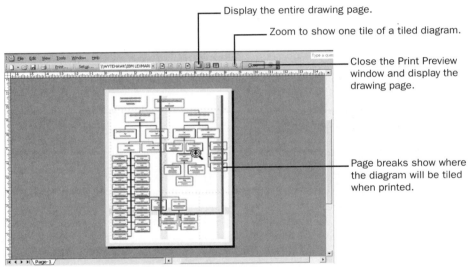

Display the entire drawing page.

Zoom to show one tile of a tiled diagram.

Close the Print Preview window and display the drawing page.

Page breaks show where the diagram will be tiled when printed.

Figure 8-10. This diagram is larger than the specified printer paper, so gray lines appear to indicate how Visio will tile the printed diagram.

You can't edit shapes in the Print Preview window, but you can display the window alongside the drawing page to see the effect of changes you make there. This technique can be useful for large diagrams that tile across several pages. To display the window in this manner, select Window, Tile. Then you can move shapes on the drawing page to make sure they don't fall into the margin area on the printed page.

The page and paper settings available in the Print Preview window are the same as those available when you're working on the drawing page. To change these settings, click the Setup button on the Print Preview window's toolbar to display the Page Setup dialog box.

Inside Out

Using a slide show to preview your print job

You can preview Visio diagrams like a slide show by displaying them in full-screen view. This view hides the toolbars, title bars, status bar, menus, scrollbars, and stencils so that the drawing page takes up the entire screen. To do this, choose View, Full Screen. To exit full-screen view, press the Esc key. For details, see "Delivering a Slide Show in Visio," page 362.

Previewing with the Print Setup Command

You can predict printing and page size conflicts with the Print Setup and Page Setup tabs in the Page Setup dialog box (File, Page Setup). Visio shows you whether your drawing page will fit on the paper specified for your printer. When you display this tab, you want to make sure that the drawing page and the printer paper match, as they do in Figure 8-11. When the preview shows you something different, as Figures 8-12, 8-13, and 8-14 show, you might want to adjust either the page setup or the print setup options.

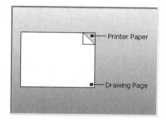

Figure 8-11. This preview shows that your drawing page and printer paper match in size and orientation.

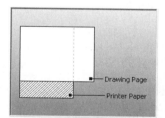

Figure 8-12. This preview shows that the drawing page and printer paper do not have the same orientation. You need to set the Paper Orientation option on the Print Setup tab to match the Page Orientation option on the Page Size tab.

Chapter 8

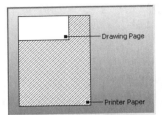

Figure 8-13. This preview shows a drawing page that is much smaller than the printer paper. To control where the diagram is printed, you can center the drawing page on the printed page or adjust page margins, or you can enlarge the drawing to fit the printer paper.

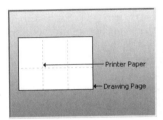

Figure 8-14. This preview shows a drawing page that will tile across several printed pages. To clearly see where the pages will break, display the diagram, and then choose View, Page Breaks.

Troubleshooting

Printed text looks different from text on the screen

Visio 2003 includes type display functionality that makes text and lines look crisp on the screen, so your printed output should resemble the screen more closely. However, text might print in the wrong font or look rough when there is a conflict with the printer driver. Here are some things to try:

- If your drawing file contains TrueType fonts, you can download them to the printer as a bitmap font, which might resemble your diagram more exactly. This option is available for some printers in the Advanced Options dialog box for the printer driver. For example, choose File, Print, and then click Properties. Look for an Advanced button, Advanced tab, or Fonts tab that contains TrueType options, such as Download As Soft Font or Download TrueType Fonts As Bitmap Soft Fonts.

- If your printer supports font substitution, try turning it off.

- Verify that you have the latest printer driver for your printer. Check the Web site of the printer manufacturer or call your printer vendor for verification.

- If the printer driver is set to emulate another printer, try turning off emulation.

Part 2

Inside Business Diagrams

Creating Flowcharts

There are many industry buzzwords for processes that result in flowcharts: change management, continuous improvement, business process re-engineering, and breakthrough or Hoshin planning, just to name a few. Whether your organization is involved in documenting standards and processes, or whether you're looking for a way to organize information visually for a presentation slide, Visio includes a variety of useful tools for organizing, connecting, and formatting data, processes, procedures, and other information.

People often think of Microsoft Office Visio 2003 primarily as a flowcharting tool. As the size of this book attests, Visio can be used for more than flowcharts. However, it's especially well suited to the task of connecting information visually, which is a common feature of the flowchart templates that Visio includes. This chapter describes how to create the most common styles of flowcharts in Visio, but the same techniques apply to just about any connected diagram.

Understanding Flowcharts in Visio

What is a flowchart? In Visio terms, it's any of several templates stored in the Flowcharts folder that you can use to create a connected diagram. Most flowcharts (also called flow sheets or flow diagrams) include text and lines that imply a process or order, but such a simple explanation doesn't adequately express the variety of diagrams that you can create, as Figure 9-1 shows. A flowchart can schematically represent items in a structure, steps in a process, or a chronology. For example, you can use a flowchart to depict the sequence of operations in an accounting system, departmental interdependencies in a new process, or the steps that contributed to the fall of the Roman Empire. To Visio, they're all types of information that a connected diagram, or flowchart, can convey.

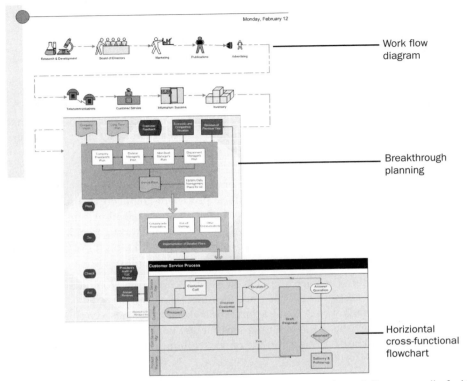

Figure 9-1. You can use a flowchart template to create a variety of diagrams, all of which organize information in a sequence or hierarchy.

Choosing a Flowchart Template

Visio includes several flowchart templates, each designed for a different purpose. Which one should you use?

- **Basic Flowchart** Use this template if you're documenting a process from beginning to end, or organizing information hierarchically.

- **Cause And Effect Diagram** Use this template to create fishbone diagrams that illustrate all the factors that result in a particular goal or problem.

- **Cross-Functional Flowchart** Use this template to show the interrelationship between different areas of your organization as they relate to a process.

- **Audit Diagram** Use this template to document accounting or bookkeeping practices.

- **Total Quality Management Diagram** This template creates documentation for Total Quality Management (TQM) initiatives. TQM diagrams provide a way to document policies and processes as part of an ongoing organizational effort toward improving and controlling quality.

- **Work Flow Diagram** Use this template to depict high-level task management. For example, you can diagram an ideal work flow that minimizes material handling costs, uses space and labor efficiently, and eliminates bottlenecks.

To start a new flowchart based on one of these templates, choose File, New, Flowchart, and then select the type of diagram you want to create.

Note The Mind Mapping flowchart available in Visio 2002 has been improved, expanded, renamed, and moved to the new Brainstorming template.

The rest of this chapter describes how to create flowcharts using the Basic Flowchart, Cause And Effect, and Cross-Functional Flowchart templates. All the other flowchart types are created using similar techniques. For help getting started with other flowcharts, refer to Visio Help.

Tip Display flowchart help

To display a help topic about a specific flowchart type, choose Help, Microsoft Visio Help, and then click the Table Of Contents tab. (If it isn't visible, click Show.) On the Table Of Contents tab, expand Creating Drawings, expand Flowchart, and then expand the topics for the type of flowchart you want to create.

Additional Flowcharts and Process Diagrams in Visio Professional

An entire industry has arisen to support business and data modeling, which encompass a variety of theories and methodologies for streamlining business and engineering practices. Visio Professional provides additional flowchart templates for the following:

- For structured analysis and design using the techniques of Gane and Sarson as well as Yourdon and DeMarco, use the Data Flow Diagram template (shown in Figure 9-2). To model data flows using the Gane-Sarson DFD notation, use the Data Flow Model Diagram template in the Software folder. For details, see "Using the Data Flow Model Diagram Template," page 583.

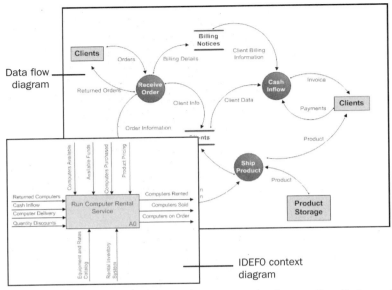

Data flow diagram

IDEF0 context diagram

Figure 9-2. Visio Professional includes templates for creating diagrams based on business and process modeling methodologies.

- To create charts based on the CCITT Specification and Description Language (SDL), use the SDL Diagram template. SDL is a symbol set used to specify event-driven systems. Because it can represent concurrent, real-time processes, it is widely used to represent telecommunication systems and design data communication protocols. CCITT is the International Telegraph and Telephone Consultative Committee.

- For process modeling and functional analysis based on the IDEF0 methodology, use the IDEF0 Diagram template (also shown in Figure 9-2). The IDEF0 notation is used to create function models, a graphical depiction of systems and process decomposition based on the Structured Analysis and Design Technique (SADT).

Note that although the methodologies underlying the data flow, SDL, and IDEF0 shapes impose rules for their use, Visio doesn't check for errors with these diagram types.

Creating a Basic Flowchart

The template name is Basic, but the diagrams you can create with it don't have to be. In general, the Basic Flowchart template is useful for showing items or steps in a process. When should you create a flowchart?

- To capture a bird's-eye view of an entire process.
- To identify the critical points, bottlenecks, or problem areas in a process.
- To see how each step in a process is related to another.

- To document the ideal flow of a process from start to finish.
- To design a new work process.

Basic flowchart shapes are designed to work with the automatic layout tools in Visio. The quickest way to create a flowchart in Visio is to drag shapes onto the page, type your text, and then with a single command have Visio connect them. Otherwise, you can quickly connect shapes as you add them, and then use the multitude of layout styles to refine the results, as Figure 9-3 shows. Visio can even number shapes as you add them to the page.

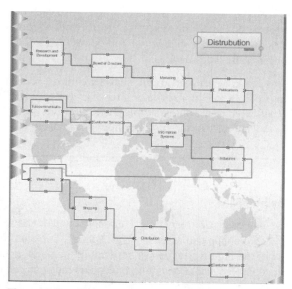

Figure 9-3. Even simple flowcharts look polished when you add a background and title and apply a color scheme.

In general, you can add and connect flowchart shapes in any of the following ways:

Connector tool

- Use the Connector tool to drag shapes onto the page and connect them shape-to-shape as you add them, a technique described in greater detail in the next section.

- Drag shapes onto the page, arrange them as you like, and then use the Connector tool to connect them shape-to-shape or point-to-point.

- Add all the shapes you need to the page without connecting them. Select the shapes in order from start to finish, and then choose Shape, Connect Shapes to let Visio connect them shape-to-shape for you. This technique works best for linear flowcharts that don't include decision loops.

> **Note** When you add shapes to a flowchart, create shape-to-shape connections for the greatest flexibility in rearranging shapes. Visio always creates shape-to-shape connections when you use the Connect Shapes command or if you press the Ctrl key while using the Connector tool. For details, see "Adding Connectors to Your Diagrams," page 63.

Starting a New Flowchart

You can quickly create a basic flowchart with steps that are connected to each other. When you start a new diagram with the Basic Flowchart template, Visio creates a letter-sized page (8.5 × 11 inches) in portrait orientation (taller than wide) and opens the Basic Flowchart Shapes, Backgrounds, and Borders And Titles stencils.

Is there a "correct" flowchart shape to use for a diagram? That depends on your audience. If you aren't sure which shape to use for a step, pause the pointer over a master shape in the stencil to display a ScreenTip that explains the shape's typical use. However, you can use any shape for any purpose, as long as it's clear to your audience how you're using it.

 Inside Out

Use the generic Flowchart Shapes shape

If you aren't sure what shape you'll need, use the generic Flowchart Shapes shape on the Basic Flowchart Shapes stencil. This shape can represent the Process, Decision, Document, or Data shape. To configure the shape after you've added it to the page, right-click the shape, and then choose Process, Decision, Document, or Data. In fact, you can quickly construct an entire flowchart using only this shape, and then figure out which step needs to be represented by which type of shape.

To number shapes automatically as you add them, see "Numbering Flowchart Shapes Automatically," page 268.

Follow these steps to create a new flowchart:

1 Choose File, New, Flowchart, Basic Flowchart.

> **Tip** To create an audit, TQM, or work flow diagram, open the Audit Diagram, TQM Diagram, or Work Flow Diagram template instead of the Basic Flowchart template. The steps that follow apply to those templates also.

2 Click the Connector tool on the Standard toolbar. The pointer changes to a connector with arrows.

3 Drag the first flowchart shape from the stencil onto the drawing page.

4 With the first shape still selected, drag the second shape in your flowchart onto the drawing page to connect the two shapes in order.

Pointer Tool

5 Repeat the process to add and connect shapes. When you're done connecting shapes, press the Esc key or click the Pointer tool on the Standard toolbar to release the Connector tool.

6 Select a shape, and then type the appropriate text for it. When you're done typing, press the Esc key, or click outside the shape. Repeat for each shape.

Aligning Flowchart Shapes

When you start a diagram with the Basic Flowchart Shapes template, Visio turns on the *dynamic grid*, a type of visual feedback that shows you where to place shapes. As you drag a shape on the page, dotted lines show you how to align the shape horizontally and vertically with respect to other shapes on the page, as Figure 9-4 shows. The dynamic grid is part of the snap-and-glue behavior in Visio diagrams that helps you position shapes. You can turn it on and off with the Snap & Glue command on the Tools menu. You can also align shapes by selecting the shapes you wish to align, selecting Shape, Align Shapes, and choosing the desired alignment.

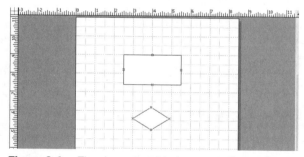

Figure 9-4. The dynamic grid shows you the perfect alignment as you drag shapes on the drawing page.

For details about using the dynamic grid and other alignment tools, see "Positioning Shapes Precisely," page 436.

Adding and Removing Flowchart Shapes

What if you have already connected the shapes in your flowchart and need to add or remove a step in the process? Disconnecting and reconnecting flowchart shapes can be messy, but the dynamic grid can help you realign the shapes. Use the Pointer tool to select a connector. You can then delete it or redirect it to connect to a new shape. To add a shape to the process, drag a connector by its endpoint to the middle of the new shape. Visio highlights the entire shape in red to indicate shape-to-shape glue. If a point on the shape turns red (indicating point-to-point glue), drag closer to the shape's center.

> **Tip** To quickly zoom in, press Ctrl+Shift+click with the mouse.

Troubleshooting

Connectors go haywire when using the Lay Out Shapes command with a flowchart

When you consider how many details Visio tracks to support the automated layout feature, perhaps you won't be surprised if things go awry. Just remember that you can press Ctrl+Z to reverse the results of the Lay Out Shapes command and restore the last layout. The problem is most likely that your diagram includes a combination of shapes with point-to-point and shape-to-shape connections, which affects where Visio can place connectors when it lays out shapes. You'll get the best results with the Lay Out Shapes command when you use shape-to-shape connections for all flowchart shapes and connect shapes in the order of the steps they represent. For details, see "Adding Connectors to Your Diagrams," page 63.

Numbering Flowchart Shapes Automatically

You can number shapes in a flowchart to make it easier to track documentation associated with a process or to indicate a sequence of steps. Visio can number shapes as you drop them on the page or at any time after they're on the page. You can number all shapes at once, or selected shapes, with the Number Shapes command on the Tools menu, (Tools, Add-Ons, Visio Extras, Number Shapes) as Figure 9-5 shows.

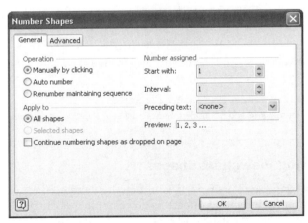

Figure 9-5. You can use the Number Shapes command to number flowchart shapes sequentially as you add them or after you add them.

By default, Visio numbers shapes from left to right and top to bottom in the diagram. However, you can choose a different order, including back to front, which is based on the shape's stacking order (the order you added them to the page), or the order in which you select them. You can also display a numbering tool on the screen, which lets you number shapes manually as you work.

Follow these steps to number flowchart shapes:

1 If you want to number only specific shapes, select them in order.

2 Choose Tools, Add-Ons, Visio Extras, Number Shapes to display the General tab of the Number Shapes dialog box.

3 Choose the shape numbering options you want:

- Under Operation, choose to number shapes manually with the Manually By Clicking option or Auto Number option. The option you select here determines the options that are available on the Advanced tab. You can also choose to renumber your shapes maintaining the chosen sequence.

- Under Number Assigned, choose the numbering style you want to use. Use the Preview box to verify that the numbers look the way you want.

- Under Apply To, choose whether to apply the options to the selected shapes or all shapes in the drawing.

- If you want the numbering sequence to include shapes you add to the page later, select the Continue Numbering Shapes As Dropped On Page check box.

4 Click the Advanced tab, and then choose the following options:

- Under Place Number, indicate where the numbers should be placed with respect to the shape's existing text.

- Under Auto Numbering Sequence, select the order in which shapes are to be numbered. This option isn't available when you number shapes manually. If you have chosen to renumber the shapes in your drawing, select your renumbering options.

- Under the Apply To options select the layers to which you wish the options to apply.

5 When you have selected the options you want, click OK.

Tip Turn shape numbering on and off
You can switch automatic shape numbering on and off by choosing Shape, Actions, Number Shape On Drop. This command is available only after you've used the Number Shapes command and when no shapes are selected.

Numbering Shapes in a Specific Order

To control the order in which shapes are numbered, you can specify manual numbering. Choose Tools, Add-Ons, Visio Extras, Number Shapes, and then select the Manually By Clicking option. Visio displays the Manual Numbering dialog box, as Figure 9-6 shows, which stays on the screen as you work. To number shapes manually, click each shape on the page in the desired order. To end the manual numbering process, click Close.

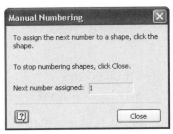

Figure 9-6. You can control the order in which shapes are numbered when you number them manually.

Creating a Cross-Functional Flowchart

Cross-functional flowcharts portray relationships, interactions, and work flows for an organization or process. They're particularly useful for portraying two characteristics at once:

- The steps in a specific process
- How the departments or functions involved in the process interact

In a cross-functional flowchart, *functional bands* show where processes cross functions, as Figure 9-7 shows. For example, a review process might involve several departments. In a cross-functional flowchart, you show this by placing the process shape on the border of two bands or resizing it to span multiple bands. When you start a cross-functional flowchart, Visio prompts you for the number and orientation of the bands, and then adds the bands to the page so that you can drag flowchart shapes into them. Once you add a shape to a functional band, Visio considers the shape and band a unit. If you move or delete a functional band, the shapes it contains go with it.

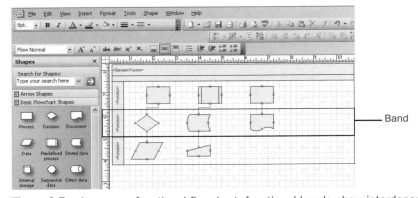

Figure 9-7. In a cross-functional flowchart, functional bands show interdependencies in a process. You can orient the diagram horizontally (as shown here) or vertically.

Follow these steps to create a cross-functional flowchart:

1   Choose File, New, Flowchart, Cross-Functional Flowchart.

Visio prompts you for information about the flowchart's orientation and number of bands.

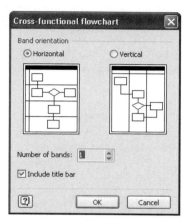

2   Select Horizontal or Vertical, and then type a number from 1 to 5 in the Number Of Bands box. Indicate whether you want to add a title bar above the bands, and then click OK.

> **Note**   You can add or delete bands later, but you can't change from one orientation to another after you've started the diagram.

Visio adds the specified number of bands to the page and opens the Cross-Functional Flowchart Shapes and Basic Flowchart Shapes stencils.

3   To label a functional band, select the band, and then type.

> **Tip**   Although you can't change the orientation of the bands, you can change the orientation of their labels. Right-click the flowchart title, and then choose Display All Band Labels Vertically (or Horizontally).

4   Drag flowchart shapes onto the page and connect them as you would in a basic flowchart. Click the Connector tool before you drag shapes to the page to connect them automatically with dynamic glue.

5   To indicate that a step or function crosses functional bands, drag a selection handle on the shape to stretch it to span the desired functions.

Adding Functional Bands

You can add functional bands as you work on a cross-functional flowchart. Although the initial dialog box allows you to set up only five bands, in practice you can add as many as will fit. Visio sets up a letter-sized page that accommodates five bands, but you can increase the page size to fit additional bands. To add a band to the diagram, drag a Functional Band shape from the Cross-Functional Flowchart Shapes stencil to the approximate position in the flowchart, as Figure 9-8 shows. Visio snaps the band into position and rearranges the other functional bands on the page. If you add a band between two bands that share a shape (that is, the shape stretches over the first two bands), the shape stretches to span all three bands. To add a label to the new band, select the band, and then type.

Caution When you delete a functional band, you also delete any shapes in that band. Visio doesn't warn you. However, you can use the Undo command (or press Ctrl+Z) to retrieve the band and its shapes. To delete a functional band, click its label, and then press Delete.

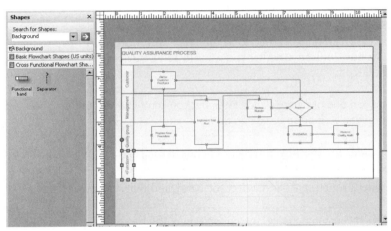

Figure 9-8. To add a functional band, drag it onto the flowchart. When you release the mouse button, Visio automatically realigns the bands.

Editing and Reordering Functional Bands

When you move a functional band, all the shapes in the band move, too. If you have connected the flowchart shapes, Visio reroutes the connectors and resizes shapes that span bands to maintain the appropriate cross-functional relationship, as Figure 9-9 shows. However, the results might not be as tidy as you would like. You can clean up a connector by dragging its control handle (the green x that appears midline when the shape is selected). Table 9-1 lists techniques for editing cross-functional flowcharts.

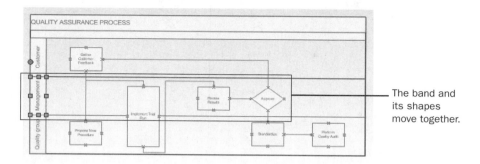

The band and
its shapes
move together.

Figure 9-9. You can rearrange bands in a cross-functional flowchart even if you've added and connected flowchart shapes. Visio resizes shapes that span functional bands.

Table 9-1. Editing Cross-Functional Flowcharts

Task	Technique
Move a band in a cross-functional flowchart	Click its label and drag it to the new location. Its shapes move with it, even if they're overlapping other bands.
Change the width of a functional band	Click its label and drag a selection handle until it's the width you want. If the chart is horizontal, drag a bottom or top selection handle; if it's vertical, drag a side selection handle.
Change the length of all functional bands	Click the flowchart title or border to display selection handles. Drag a side, top, or bottom handle until the bands are the length you want.

Moving Shapes to a New Band

Bands aren't barriers to shapes—that is, you can move a shape to another band just by dragging it there. If the shape is connected to other shapes, it remains connected to them. To extend a shape across multiple bands, drag it onto the boundary of two bands, or resize it to span as many bands as you want, as Figure 9-10 shows. If you move or resize a band, a shape that spans multiple bands will adjust to remain inside each of those bands.

Chapter 9

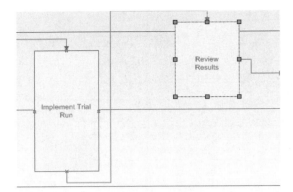

Figure 9-10. To show that a step spans multiple functions, use the Pointer tool to drag a selection handle and resize the shape.

Adding a Separator to a Flowchart

Separator shapes add borders between subprocesses or phases, as Figure 9-11 shows. For example, you could add a separator between the design and test phases of a new product development process. If you are creating a vertical cross-functional flowchart, separator shapes are horizontal; if you are creating a horizontal flowchart, they're vertical. Separator shapes are smart—when you move one, all the flowchart shapes that follow it also move, so that the phase contains the same steps as before.

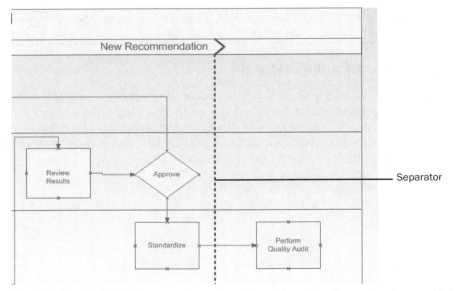

Figure 9-11. To indicate a new phase in a process, use the Separator shape, which automatically sizes to fit the flowchart.

Follow these steps to add a separator shape to a flowchart:

1 Drag a Separator shape from the Cross-Functional Flowchart Shapes stencil to where the phase begins.

2 To name a phase, select the separator and type a label.

3 To format the separator right-click it and select Format, Line.

> **Warning** It can be difficult to click on the separator (they're thin!), and if you miss you can get some unexpected formatting results. Zoom your drawing to 200% to make the line easier to see and click.

> **Tip** By default, separators appear as dashed lines. To change the line format, right-click the shape, and then choose Format, Line.

Showing Cause and Effect

With the Cause And Effect template, you can diagram the variables that lead to a particular outcome. Cause and effect diagrams are also called *fishbone diagrams*, after their skeletal appearance, or Ishikawa diagrams, after their inventor, Dr. Kaoru Ishikawa, a quality control statistician. They represent a different paradigm from a flowchart, in which one step leads to another. A fishbone diagram shows input from numerous sources, as Figure 9-12 shows, which makes it a great tool for the following:

- To study a problem or issue and determine its root cause.
- To show that success will require efforts from several departments.
- To identify areas for data collection.
- To show why a process isn't running smoothly or producing the desired results.

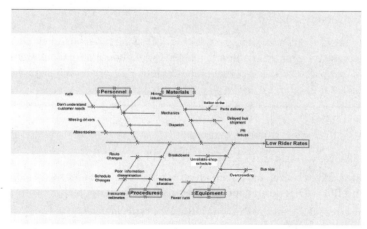

Figure 9-12. You can create a fishbone diagram with the Cause And Effect template.

Chapter 9

Creating a Fishbone Diagram

When you open the Cause And Effect Diagram template, Visio creates a page that includes a blank fishbone diagram: an effect shape (the spine) and four category boxes, as Figure 9-13 shows. You can add, remove, or reposition the category boxes, and you can add as many cause shapes as you need.

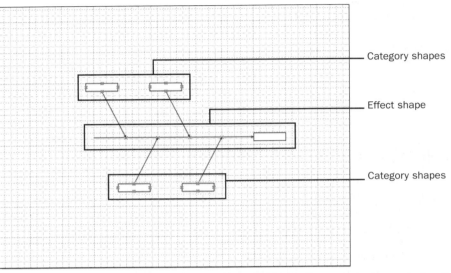

Figure 9-13. Visio sets up the bare bones of a fishbone diagram when you start a diagram with the Cause And Effect template.

Inside Out

Categories of a fishbone diagram

Visio creates a fishbone diagram with space for four categories, because fishbone methodology suggests these categories: materials, machines, methods, and manpower (the four M's); provisions, people, place, and procedures (the four P's); or surroundings, suppliers, systems, and skills (the four S's).

Follow these steps to create a fishbone diagram:

1   Choose File, New, Business Process, Cause And Effect Diagram.

Visio creates a letter-sized page with an effect and four category shapes and opens the Cause And Effect Diagram Shapes, Borders And Titles, and Backgrounds stencils.

2   Select the effect shape in the drawing, and then type its label.

This text should describe the effect, problem, or objective whose causes you're illustrating.

3   Select a category box, and then type a name for the category of causes it represents.

4   To add a category, drag a Category 1 or Category 2 shape to the effect shape so that the category's arrowhead touches the effect line (the spine).

5   To delete a category you don't need, select a category shape, and then press Delete.

6   Drag a Primary Cause 1 or Primary Cause 2 shape from the stencil to a category shape. Place the arrowhead on the category line to glue the shapes.

Align Left

Tip   If your text doesn't fit, try realigning the paragraph. Visio centers the text by default, but depending on the direction in which the shape points, you can choose Align Left or Align Right from the Formatting toolbar to move text closer to the line.

Align Right

7   Drag a Secondary Cause shape from the stencil to a primary cause shape in the diagram.

Tip   The only difference between the different primary and secondary cause shapes on the stencil is the direction of the line and placement of the text. The shapes are numbered only to differentiate them, not to imply any sequence or hierarchy.

8   To label a primary or secondary cause, select the shape, and then type.

Editing Text

Fishbone diagrams can quickly become crowded or cluttered. Actually, this is a good sign. Because each bone or rib represents a related idea, a diagram with many branches explores that many more possibilities. However, to make the diagram easier to read, be judicious with the label wording. Use text to state problems or issues, not solutions.

If long labels overlap other shapes, try one of the following:

- Click Align Left or Align Right on the Formatting toolbar to move the text closer to its line.

Text tool

- Add line breaks. Select the Text tool, click in the text, and then press Ctrl+Enter.

Effect, category, and cause shapes are all examples of 1-D shapes. For details about working with text on 1-D shapes, see "Adding Text to Lines and Connectors," page 93.

Chapter 9

Moving Cause and Effect Shapes

To move cause and category shapes in your diagram, drag the line by its middle, rather than its endpoints, to move the entire shape without changing the line's angle. When you drag a shape that has other shapes glued to it, the shape you drag moves, and the connected shapes stretch to remain attached. To move an entire branch, select all the shapes, as Figure 9-14 shows. To lengthen or shorten lines, drag an endpoint.

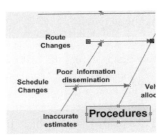

Figure 9-14. To move crowded shapes, select a primary cause shape and all the secondary cause shapes, and then drag. If you drag only the primary cause shape, secondary cause shapes stretch to remain attached.

Note Visio 2003 does not include the Import Flowchart Data Wizard. You can, however, open flowcharts created with the wizard in earlier versions of Visio.

Creating Multiple-Page Flowcharts

Sometimes it's easier to communicate information if you provide an overview of a process on one page and more detailed portions of the process on additional pages.
In Visio, you can link flowchart pages to each other to keep drawings uncluttered without sacrificing continuity.

Continuing a Flowchart on Another Page

Whether you need to continue a complex process or link to additional information, you can use the on-page and off-page reference shapes to indicate a continuation in your flowchart. Both shapes provide a visual cue to your audience that the diagram is continued. The on-page reference is only a visual cue. It works like a cross-reference in a document to direct your attention to another part of the page where a process is continued. The off-page reference shape inserts a new page and sets up links between pages.

To create an off-page reference, drag the Off-Page Reference shape from the Basic Flowchart Shapes stencil onto the drawing page. Visio prompts you to specify a page to link to, as Figure 9-15 shows. When you click OK, Visio inserts a page with an identical off-page reference shape and links the two shapes. To navigate from one page to the other, double-click the off-page reference.

Creating Flowcharts

Tip Locating an off-page shape

If the Basic Flowchart Shapes stencil is not already open (for example, your diagram is based on the Cause And Effect Diagram or another template), you can quickly locate the off-page reference shape by clicking the Shapes button on the toolbar, and then selecting Flowchart, Basic Flowchart Shapes.

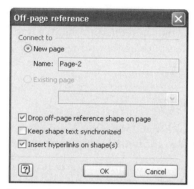

Figure 9-15. To show the continuation of a process, use an off-page reference shape as both a visual cue and a quick way to insert a new page with hyperlinks.

To label a page reference shape, select the shape, and then type. You can use the label to indicate that the shape links to a more detailed process or to tell readers where they've come from. To change the look of the off-page reference shape, right-click the shape, and then select an option, as Figure 9-16 shows.

Figure 9-16. You can right-click an off-page reference shape to configure it as an outgoing or incoming symbol, a circle, or an arrow.

Tip To insert a page without using the off-page reference shape, choose New Page from the Insert menu.

Enlarging a Page to Fit a Large Flowchart

To enlarge the drawing page so that more of your flowchart fits, choose File, Page Setup. On the Page Size tab, choose the size you want. If you select Size To Fit Drawing Contents, Visio automatically creates a page large enough for everything to fit, but the result is probably a nonstandard page size that might be difficult to print. Paper size isn't an issue if you're distributing the flowchart electronically, but if you plan to print the diagram, try to change the paper size to a printable size large enough for your entire diagram.

If your drawing won't fit on one printable page, you can reduce it to fit, tile it to multiple pages, or split the diagram into multiple flowcharts. For help printing large files, see "Printing Diagrams of Any Size," page 242.

Formatting a Flowchart Quickly

You can add the final polish to your flowchart quickly and without a lot of effort. Figure 9-17 provides an example of a simple flowchart that was formatted using some of these methods:

- **Add a background**   Drag a background shape from the Backgrounds stencil onto your drawing. When Visio prompts you to create a background page, click Yes. For details, see "Adding Backgrounds and Borders," page 62.

- **Add a border or title**   Add a border or title shape to give your flowchart a more professional look. Drag the shape you want from the Borders And Titles stencil, and then type. For details, see "Adding a Title Block to a Diagram," page 134.

- **Format shapes with styles**   Use styles to change text, fill, and line formatting quickly and consistently. For example, you can change the definition of the Flow-Normal style to quickly reformat all the text in a diagram. To do this, choose Format, Define Styles, and then select Flow-Normal and specify new options. For details, see "Creating and Editing Styles," page 688.

- **Apply a color scheme**   Quickly assign fill, line, and text colors to each shape in your drawing. Choose Tools, Add-Ons, Visio Extras, Color Schemes. Select a color scheme, click Apply to preview it, and click OK to accept it.

 Troubleshooting

After adding a background to a flowchart, text on the connectors appears with an obvious box behind it

To make text on a line more readable, Visio adds a solid color behind the text block, but you can easily turn this off. Select the connectors that include text, and then choose Format, Text. On the Text Block tab, select None for Text Background, and then click OK.

Chapter 9

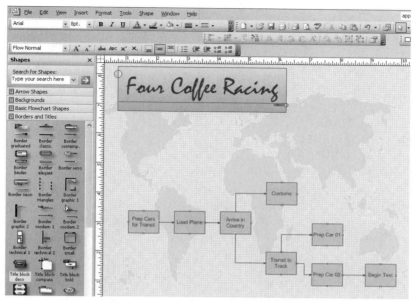

Figure 9-17. A flowchart with the Title Block Deco shape (Mistral Font) from the Borders And Titles stencil, the Background World shape from the Backgrounds stencil, and a color scheme.

Chapter 9

Visualizing an Organization

Keeping track of who reports to whom and what responsibilities each employee has can be difficult, especially in a growing company. Organization charts provide a graphical view of those relationships, and the Organization Chart template and wizard in Microsoft Office Visio 2003 make it easy to keep the chart up to date. To get the most use out of your chart, you can also store data about each employee, such as the date of hire, e-mail address, or responsibilities. You can print reports, display the information on the organization chart itself, and even export it to a spreadsheet or database file for use by other departments.

The way you work with organization charts in Visio is different from other similar-looking diagrams, such as flowcharts. This chapter tells you what you need to create and import organization charts efficiently and successfully.

Understanding Organization Charts in Visio

Organization charts are a special type of flowchart that displays a hierarchy. You could create an organization chart with the flowchart shapes or by drawing rectangles and the lines between them, but with the Organization Chart template in Visio, you can take advantage of several very efficient features:

- **Use the drop-on-top feature**   To create a chart, you simply drag an employee shape on top of a manager shape to create a reporting relationship and the connector between the shapes.

- **Let Visio arrange shapes for you**   You can rearrange branches of a chart and adjust spacing without dragging shapes. Just choose from a variety of layout styles, and then let Visio arrange it for you.

- **Keep employee information in sync**   Visio keeps track of employees in your chart. You can move a department or section to a new page and keep the information in sync with other pages that include the same employees.

- **Use the Organization Chart Wizard**   If your organizational information is stored in a database, you can use the Organization Chart Wizard to import the employee data and automatically generate a chart.

Although an up-to-date organization chart is useful in itself, Visio also stores information about an employee as *custom properties* of a shape. For example, an employee shape can include custom properties for name, department, telephone number, e-mail address, and other information, as Figure 10-1 shows. As with custom property data in other Visio drawings, you can use the data to generate reports, export spreadsheets or database files, or simply store the data with the chart.

Custom properties for the selected employee

Automated layout options

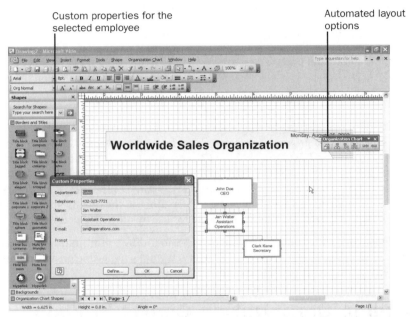

Figure 10-1. You can use a diagram to track information about employees as custom properties, which you can create or import.

Inside Out

PowerPoint's organization chart tool

Microsoft Office PowerPoint 2003 also includes an organization chart tool. If you want a quick, professional-looking chart for a presentation and don't have many employees, use the tools in PowerPoint. However, if you want a reusable organization chart and the ability to revise easily, the Visio Organization Chart template is more versatile.

Using the Organization Chart Tools

The Organization Chart template provides tools that aren't available with any other Visio solution. When you start a drawing with the Organization Chart template, Visio adds the Organization Chart toolbar, as Figure 10-2 shows. This toolbar is your clue *not* to rearrange shapes manually—Visio will do it for you. To adjust the layout and position of a department, select the department's top-level shape, such as a manager, and then click a button on the toolbar. Use the new Auto-Arrange Shapes button to adjust the spacing and layout of the entire chart. If you close the Organization Chart toolbar, you can reopen it by choosing View, Toolbars, Organization Chart, or by right-clicking any toolbar and then selecting Organization Chart.

Adjust the overall layout with Auto-Arrange Shapes.

Click to display layout options.

Move departments in the chart.

Figure 10-2.   Quickly rearrange departments or the entire chart with these Organization Chart toolbar buttons.

The Organization Chart menu repeats the layout options on the toolbar and includes additional layout styles in the Arrange Subordinates command. Other commands help you use the chart to locate people as well as import, export, and compare organizational data, as Figure 10-3 shows.

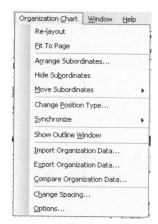

Organization Chart | Window | Help
- Re-layout
- Fit To Page
- Arrange Subordinates...
- Hide Subordinates
- Move Subordinates ▶
- Change Position Type...
- Synchronize ▶
- Show Outline Window
- Import Organization Data...
- Export Organization Data...
- Compare Organization Data...
- Change Spacing...
- Options...

Figure 10-3.   The Organization Chart menu contains commands specifically designed for working with organizational data.

Inside Out

Changes to the Organization Chart toolbar

The Organization Chart toolbar in Visio 2003 looks a little different than the toolbars in Visio 2000 and earlier versions. Since Visio 2002 it includes fewer horizontal, vertical, and side-by-side layout options. This change makes it easier to distinguish one option from another in the small toolbar buttons. To see all the options, choose Organization Chart, Arrange Subordinates.

Converting Earlier Visio Organization Charts

If you created an organization chart in Visio 2002 or 2000 you can open it in Visio 2003 to work with all of the organization chart tools. Just select the chart as you would any other. Visio 2003 will display a menu that asks if you would like to convert the chart as Figure 10-4 shows. Charts constructed in versions of Visio earlier than 2000 cannot be converted into Visio 2003 unless they are first opened in either Visio 2000 or 2002 and saved in that format.

Converting creates a new Visio drawing file. Your original organization chart isn't changed.

Note If you don't know which version of Visio was used to create an organization chart, try converting it. The converter tells you if the drawing file does not need to be converted.

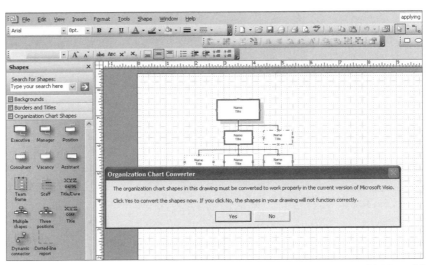

Figure 10-4. You must convert organization charts created in Visio 2000 or 2002 to work with the tools in Visio 2003.

Note Visio no longer includes the MultiStaff shape. If your Visio 2000 organization chart includes the MultiStaff shape, each position is converted to a Staff shape when you open the organization chart in Visio 2003.

Creating an Organization Chart Manually

Although it's easier to import employee data for complex organization charts, you might want to create an organization chart manually for a small organization or if the employee data doesn't already exist in a database or spreadsheet. When you create an organization chart manually, you drag shapes from the stencil onto the page, starting with the top position in the hierarchical order (usually a CEO, president, or executive director). To specify the reporting structure, you drop a shape directly on top of another, as Figure 10-5 shows.

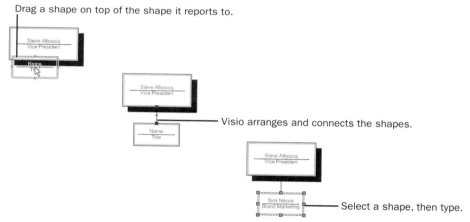

Figure 10-5. Unlike flowcharts and other Visio diagrams, organization charts build connections for you when you drag a shape on top of another shape.

The Organization Chart Shapes stencil includes shapes with names that imply specific positions; however, you don't have to use the shapes as they are named. For example, you can use the executive shape for every employee in the chart. The shape names do provide information that Visio can use in reports and to manage reporting relationships, so most people use the shapes as named, but it's not necessary.

Note If you want a particular look for a type of shape, you can apply a design theme to your chart. For details about themes, see "Formatting an Organization Chart," page 303.

Follow these steps to create a new organization chart:

1 Choose File, New, Organization Chart, Organization Chart.

2 Drag the Executive shape from the Organization Chart Shapes stencil onto the drawing page.

Chapter 10

The first time you create an organization chart, Visio displays a message box that shows you how to connect shapes automatically. Click OK.

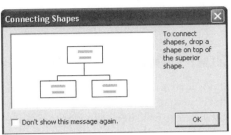

3 With the shape selected, type the employee's name, press Enter, and then type the employee's title.

Tip To switch from typing text to using the Pointer tool, press Esc or click in the page.

4 Drag a Manager shape from the stencil onto the executive shape, and then release the mouse. Visio arranges the shapes and adds a connector between them to create a reporting relationship.

Tip You can insert an employee's picture into his or her shape. Right-click the shape and choose Insert Picture. Browse to the picture's location and select it.

5 With the manager shape selected, type a name, press Enter, and then type the manager's title.

6 Continue dragging shapes from the stencil onto the shape in the chart they report to. Drop Position shapes on top of Manager shapes. Add Assistant, Vacancy, and Consultant shapes as appropriate. Label the shapes as you have done previously.

Visio lays out subordinates horizontally as you add shapes.

Tip To quickly add several shapes at once, use the Three Positions or Multiple Shapes shape.

7 If shapes overlap one another, click the Re-layout button on the Organization Chart toolbar. You can also select Organization Chart, Fit To Page, to alter the shape's layout.

Re-layout

8   To change the layout for a group or department, select the top-level shape in the group, such as a manager, and then click a layout option on the Organization Chart toolbar.

Vertical Layout

For example, to change the layout for only the sales manager and the people who report directly to him or her, click the sales manager shape, click the Vertical Layout button on the Organization Chart toolbar, and then click the layout you want. Visio arranges the manager and all subordinate shapes automatically.

The Organization Chart Shapes stencil now includes the Dotted Line connector to display a dotted line relationship in the organization. Just drag it onto the page and connect it to the appropriate shapes.

Once the basic chart is in place with employee names and titles, you can format and work with the information in a variety of ways. For example, you can change the size and appearance of shapes, format text in the shapes, and change the displayed text, as described later in this chapter.

For details about tracking employee data with an organization chart you create manually, see "Entering Data in Shapes," page 174.

Inside Out

Other uses for the Organization Chart template

Because the Organization Chart template lets you drop shapes on others to create hierarchical arrangements, you might want to use it for more than just creating organization charts. The drop-on-top functionality comes in handy for quickly prototyping Web sites or creating other hierarchical diagrams.

Importing Organizational Data to Create a Chart

Most companies store employee data electronically in a human resources database. You can save time by using the Organization Chart Wizard to import your employee information and generate an organization chart, as Figure 10-6 shows. Visio can import from any ODBC-compliant data source (Microsoft SQL Server, for example), Microsoft Exchange Server, Microsoft Office Excel 2003, and text files. You can also use the wizard to set up an Excel or text file with employee information, and then import it.

Chapter 10

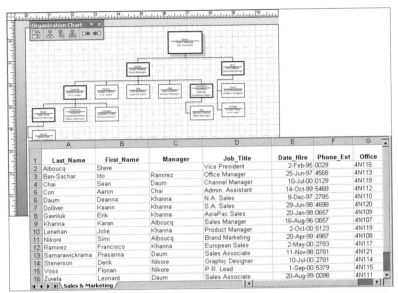

Figure 10-6. The Organization Chart Wizard can generate a multiple-page chart from a variety of data sources, including Excel.

To import employee data, the wizard requires that a data source include at least an employee name and the name of the employee's manager. Specifically, the wizard looks for a Name and requires a Reports To field in your data source so it can create the right type of connection to your other shapes. For the employee at the top of a hierarchy, such as a CEO or president, leave the manager or Reports To field blank. If the data source also includes a Department, Title, and Telephone field with those names, Visio imports the data into the shapes' built-in custom properties. If your fields have different names, you can import the data anyway, but you might end up with duplicate fields in the Custom Properties window. If your data source includes other organizational data, such as office location or date of hire, you can import it as well. Visio adds this information as new custom properties.

Importing Data from an Existing File

You can start a new diagram with the Organization Chart Wizard, or start the wizard from within an existing diagram. In either case, the wizard walks you through the process of selecting an existing data source, mapping its fields to shapes and custom properties in Visio, and then choosing the number of pages to generate. The key to success with the wizard is knowing how the columns in your data file relate to the data you want in your organization chart. Because an organization chart is dependent on reporting relationships, your data file must include a column that shows each employee's manager.

Connecting to the Organization Chart Wizard Using Automation

If you use enterprise planning software, such as PeopleSoft or SAP/R3, you might find it easier to create a macro or executable file that generates an organization chart without stepping through the Organization Chart Wizard. For details about this method of working, see the topic in Visio Help called "Run the Organization Chart Wizard from the Command Line."

Step 1: Identify the Data Source

When you start the Organization Chart Wizard, you can choose whether to start from an existing data source or create a new one, as Figure 10-7 shows.

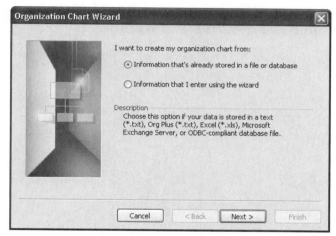

Figure 10-7. On the first screen of the Organization Chart Wizard, you can choose whether to import information from a data source or to create a file that can be imported.

Follow these steps to start a diagram and start the Organization Chart Wizard:

1 Start Visio, and in the Choose Drawing Type window, choose Organization Chart, Organization Chart Wizard.

Note In an existing organization chart diagram, choose Organization Chart, Import Organization Data. In a drawing file based on a different template, choose Tools, Add-Ons, Organization Chart, Organization Chart Wizard.

2 On the first screen, select Information That's Already Stored In A File Or Database, and then click Next.

Chapter 10

3   On the next screen, select the type of file you're importing, and then click Next. The options vary depending on the type of file you're importing.

4   Follow the instructions to locate the file, directory, or data source, and then click Next to continue with the wizard.

Step 2: Map Data to the Organization Chart

On the next screen of the Organization Chart Wizard, you map the columns from your data source to the columns the wizard expects, as Figure 10-8 shows. The wizard requires only the Name and Reports To fields, which it uses to lay out the chart. In the Name box, select the field in your data source that contains the complete employee name. If your data source provides two or more fields for the name (for example, First Name and Last Name fields), select the field for last name, and then in the First Name box, select the field for first name. In the Reports To box, select the field in your data source that contains the manager name. Click Next to continue.

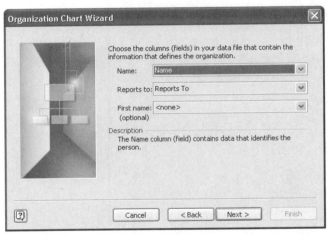

Figure 10-8.   The wizard assumes that your data source provides the full employee name in a single field. If not, use both the Name and First Name lists on this screen.

Step 3: Specify the Information to Display

When the wizard creates the organization chart, it labels each shape with data from the fields you select on the next screen of the Organization Chart Wizard, as Figure 10-9 shows. To choose shape labels, select a field in the Data File Columns list, and then click Add. The Displayed Fields list lists the fields in the order in which they will be displayed, and the wizard previews the results. If the previewed shape doesn't look the way you want, you can do the following:

●   To remove a field from the display, select the field in the Displayed Fields list, and then click Remove.

292

- To change the order in which fields appear, select a field in the Displayed Fields list, and then click Up or Down.

Click Next to continue.

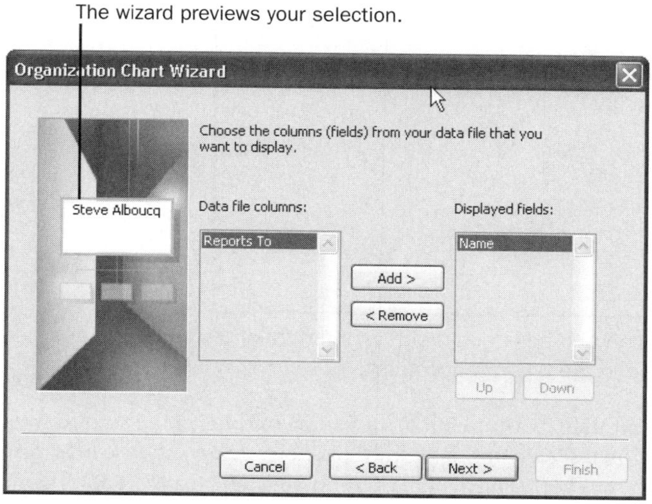

The wizard previews your selection.

Figure 10-9. On this screen, you can choose the text that appears on shapes.

Step 4: Specify Custom Property Fields

One of the benefits of a Visio organization chart is the data behind the drawing. You can import as many additional data fields as you like as custom properties on the next screen of the wizard, as Figure 10-10 shows. In the Data File Columns list, select a field from your data source, and then click Add to add it to the organization chart as a custom property. The Custom Property Fields list shows all the properties that the wizard will add to employee shapes in the organization chart. When you've completed the list, click Next.

> **Tip** To see the properties associated with an employee, display the Custom Properties window (View, Custom Properties Window) or right-click a shape and select View, Custom Properties Window. When you select a shape, its properties are displayed.

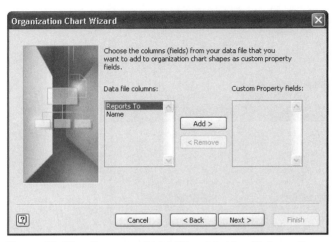

Figure 10-10. You can add additional fields of information as custom properties that Visio stores for each shape in the organization chart.

If you selected the An ODBC-Compliant Data Source option on the second wizard screen, you will see an additional screen at this point that allows you to choose how you want the data to be stored with the chart. The benefit of importing data to create an organization chart is that the data you maintain about employees can be stored as custom properties for the shapes in the organization chart. You can either copy the values from the data source cells into the custom property fields for shapes, or you can create dynamic links between the source data and the chart shapes. Linking data allows you to keep the chart up to date with any changes you make to the database. Select the Copy Database Records To Shapes option to copy data, or select the Link Database Records To Shapes option to link data, and then click Next. For details, see "Linking Shapes and Databases," page 721.

Step 5: Choose Layout Options for Large Organization Charts

An organization of more than 20 or 30 employees is probably too large to fit on a single letter-sized page. On the next screen of the wizard, you can decide how you want your chart to be divided across pages, as Figure 10-11 shows. If you want to control exactly which groups appear on pages of a multiple-page chart, choose the first option. Otherwise, let Visio do the work and select the second option, in which case the wizard will divide the chart only if it doesn't fit on a single page.

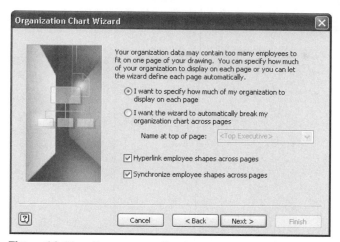

Figure 10-11. You can specify where to break a large organization chart across pages or let the wizard do it for you.

> **Tip** You might want to divide your organization chart into multiple pages even if it all fits on one page. For example, select the I Want To Specify... option if you want to include only high-level employees on one page and more detail on successive pages.

You can choose to display the same employee on more than one page by *synchronizing* employee shapes and optionally creating links between the synchronized copies. For example, a manager can appear on a top-level page and also on a detail page that includes the employees who report directly to him or her. When you import your organizational data, you can choose the following options on this wizard screen:

- **Hyperlink Employee Shapes Across Pages** Select this check box to create links between shapes that represent the same employee on different pages.
- **Synchronize Employee Shapes Across Pages** Select this check box to synchronize shapes that represent the same employee on different pages. If the shapes are synchronized, changes you make to the text and custom properties for the shape on one page affect the data for that shape on other pages.

Step 6: Choose Where to Break Pages

If you select the I Want To Specify... option, when you click Next, the wizard provides the options shown in Figure 10-12. Initially, the wizard shows only one page that lists the highest ranking employee in the data file. When you add a page, you select the top-ranking employee to display on that page and up to eight subordinate levels.

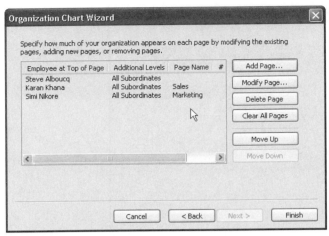

Figure 10-12. On this screen, the wizard shows you the top-level employee on each page of a multiple-page organization chart.

Tip To get a better view of your data, you can resize a column in the preview area of the wizard. The headings (Page Number, Employee At Top Of Page, and so on) work like column headings in Excel.

To add a page and specify what goes on it, click Add Page to display the options shown in Figure 10-13. In the Name At Top Of Page list, select the name of the top-level employee you want to appear on the page. In the Number Of Additional Levels list, specify how many of that employee's subordinates should appear. To include only employees who report directly, choose 1; to include those employees as well as the people who report directly to them, choose 2; and so on. You can also type a page name that will appear on the page tab at the bottom of the drawing window. Click OK to add the page. Add as many pages as you want, and then click Finish to create the organization chart.

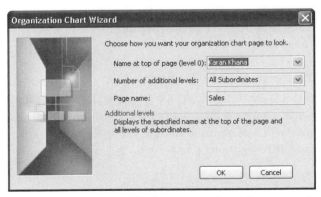

Figure 10-13. To specify where pages break in an organization chart, identify the top-level employee that you want to appear on the new page.

Importing Data from a New File You Create

If you don't already have a data file, you can use the wizard to create an importable file or work directly with the sample files that Visio provides. Sometimes it's just easier to enter data in a spreadsheet or text file rather than type names in shapes. If you use the wizard to create a text or Excel file, the wizard opens the appropriate sample file, where you can type your names over the sample data. The wizard stays open while you work. When you exit the sample file, the wizard continues and imports the data.

To use the wizard to create the file, follow these steps:

1 Choose File, New, Organization Chart, Organization Chart Wizard.

> **Note** If you have already opened the Organization Chart template, choose Organization Chart, Import Organization Data to start the wizard.

2 On the first screen, select the Information That I Enter Using The Wizard option and click Next.

3 Follow the instructions on the screen to create the file and then import it.

Troubleshooting

The organization chart looks too crowded or the spaces between the shapes are uneven

- **Change the shape spacing** Choose Organization Chart, Change Spacing. Choose the Custom option to specify exactly how much space should be between shapes.

- **Change the size of the shapes** Choose Organization Chart, Options, and then type values in the Width and Height boxes to specify the size you want to use for all shapes in the chart.

- **Break the organization chart into multiple pages** See "Working with Multiple-Page Organization Charts," page 299.

Working with an Organization Chart

In many organizations, reporting relationships change frequently—because of promotions, special projects, or changes in resource allocations. Visio helps you keep your chart up to date by making it easy to find, arrange, and update employee information. For example, when an employee is promoted, you can change the shape used to represent that employee in the organization chart. Table 10-1 summarizes the ways you can work with employee shapes in an organization chart.

Table 10-1. Finding and Updating Organization Chart Information

Task	Technique
Locate an employee	Ensure no shape is selected, press Ctrl+F or choose Edit, Find. Type the name of the person or any other text string, select the search options you want, and then click Find Next.
Change the type of shape used for an employee	Right-click the shape, and then choose Change Position Type. Select the new position type, and then click OK.
Change the order in which an employee is displayed under a manager	Select an employee shape, and then click one of the Move buttons on the Organization Chart toolbar.
Change a reporting relationship	Drag an employee shape onto the new manager's shape. Visio reconnects the affected shape.
Remove an employee and all custom property information stored with the employee shape	Select the employee shape, and then press Delete. If the same employee appears on more than one page (that is, you've created synchronized copies), delete the shape from each page.
Adjust a group's layout after a shape is moved or deleted	Select the top-level shape in the group, such as the manager. On the Organization Chart toolbar, click Horizontal Layout, Vertical Layout, or Side-By-Side Layout, and then click the style you want.
Adjust the spacing between selected shapes or all shapes	Choose Organization Chart, Change Spacing. Select the options you want, and then click OK.

Troubleshooting

The automatic layout options have no effect on the organization chart

In theory, you should never have to drag shapes to position them in an organization chart. You can adjust the layout with an automated option from the Organization Chart toolbar, but when you add shapes to an organization chart, Visio doesn't move shapes on the page out of the way. If groups overlap, you can select a manager shape, and then choose a layout option from the toolbar to rearrange the manager and subordinate shapes.

If you manually rearrange shapes, you can inadvertently break the automated layouts, so that the toolbar options and Organization Chart menu commands have no effect or work improperly. If you inherit an organization chart from someone else and the automated layout options don't work, the last author might have inadvertently disabled the automated layout options by manually positioning shapes. When this happens, your only recourse is to adjust the spacing by dragging shapes into position, and that's a drag.

> **Note** Your chart spacing might become uneven when you move shapes around. For a tidier chart, click the Auto-Arrange Shapes button on the Organization Chart toolbar.

Working with Multiple-Page Organization Charts

Visio can help you organize the information in an organization chart with many employees. You can create *synchronized copies* of employee shapes on different pages of a multiple-page diagram. If you imported employee data, the Organization Chart Wizard might have done this for you and even linked the synchronized shapes, as Figure 10-14 shows. For example, you can display the sales manager and other top-level managers on the first page of your diagram, and hide the employees who report directly to them—what Visio calls the *subordinate shapes*. Then, you can use the Create Synchronized Copies command to copy a manager and his or her subordinates to a new page.

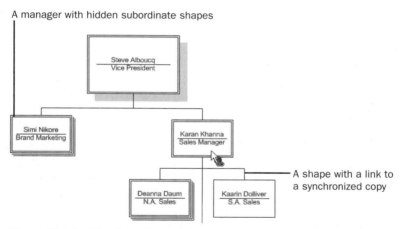

Figure 10-14. The Organization Chart Wizard can add hyperlinks between synchronized copies of shapes. To navigate, right-click a linked shape, and then choose the name of the hyperlink.

When you add text or edit the custom properties of a synchronized shape on one page, Visio updates all copies of the shape in the diagram. However, adding, deleting, or moving a shape doesn't affect the synchronized copies.

Follow these steps to copy a group or department to a new page:

1. Select the shape at the highest level of the group you want to copy, and then choose Organization Chart, Synchronize, Create Synchronized Copy. Right-clicking the shape and selecting Create Synchronized Copy accomplishes the same thing.

2   Choose New Page. If you want to display only the manager or top-level shape on the current page and show the employees who report directly to him or her on the detail page, select the Hide Subordinates On Original Page check box.

3   Click OK to add a new page that contains the group.

4   To link the copies of the shape, select the shape on one page, and then choose Insert, Hyperlinks. Next to the Sub-Address box, click Browse, choose the page that contains the copy, and then click OK. Click OK in the Hyperlinks dialog box to add the link.

Visio adds a hyperlink command to the shortcut menu for the synchronized shapes. When you right-click the shape, the name of the page you linked it to appears as the name of the link.

Inside Out

Panning and Zooming with Hyperlinks

When you click a hyperlink, Visio can pan to a specific shape and zoom in. To specify this behavior when you add a hyperlink to synchronized copies, use the Shape and Zoom options in the Hyperlink dialog box. For Shape, type the Shape ID, which is the unique name Visio assigns to each shape in a diagram. To see a shape's ID, select a shape, and then choose Format, Special. The ID is *Sheet.n*, where *n* is a number.

Comparing Charts and Creating Reports

You can use your diagram to track changes in an organization. Visio can compare two organization charts and list the ways in which they differ. If you imported organizational data, you can even compare changes to custom properties, such as job title or manager. You can also create reports based on the custom properties stored in your diagram. Visio includes a built-in organization chart report, and you can create your own reports of the particular information you want to see.

Comparing and Updating Versions of an Organization Chart

You can see changes between two versions of an organization chart with the Compare Organization Data dialog box, shown in Figure 10-15. The Compare Organization Data command is most useful if you used the Organization Chart Wizard to import employee information. You can even compare specific imported fields. For example, if you imported location information, you can compare the Office fields in the two organization charts to see who's moved. When you compare two organization charts, you can either create a report that shows you the differences, or you can automatically update the older chart with the information in the newer chart.

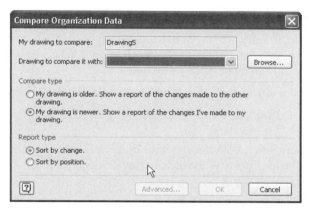

Figure 10-15. Use the Compare Organization Data dialog box to compare the employee information in two versions of an organization chart.

To compare versions of an organization chart and report on the changes, follow these steps:

1. Open the newer organization chart, and then choose Organization Chart, Compare Organization Data.

   In the My Drawing To Compare list, the name of the open drawing file is displayed.

2. In the Drawing To Compare It With list, select the drawing file that contains the older organization chart or click Browse to locate the file.

3. Select My Drawing Is Newer, and then click OK.

Visio opens the older organization chart, compares the contents of the two drawing files, and then displays an HTML report that shows the differences, as Figure 10-16 shows. You may save the report as an HTML text file to print or review later. Just select File, Save As. You'll need to name it and specify a place for the file to be saved. If the open file is older and you would like to update it to include the new data, click Update Drawing.

> **Note** If you only want to compare some of the data in the charts, click Advanced in the Compare Organization Data dialog box, and select the fields containing data you want to compare.

Chapter 10

301

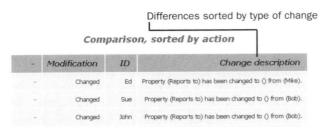

Figure 10-16. Visio 2003 can compare two versions of an organization chart.

Updating an Organization Chart

Visio can update an older organization chart to match the changes you have made to a new version. Only the text data is updated, not the layout information. That is, the position, size, or other attributes of the shapes aren't updated.

Follow these steps to compare versions of an organization chart and update the older version:

1 Open the older organization chart, and then choose Organization Chart, Compare Organization Data.

2 In the Drawing To Compare It With list, select the drawing file that contains the newer organization chart or click Browse to navigate to the file's location.

3 Select My Drawing Is Older, and then click OK.

   Visio displays the Comparison Report dialog box that lists every change that will be made to the older organization chart.

4 Click Update Drawing.

5 In the message box that appears, click Yes.

   Visio makes the changes and updates the organization chart. When it's finished, it displays the Comparison Report again to show you the changes that have been made.

Creating Reports About an Organization

Visio includes a built-in report that lists the names, departments, titles, and telephone numbers of employees in your organization chart. The report uses the default custom properties that Visio stores with each organization chart shape. If you entered data for these fields in the Custom Properties window, you can create a report like the one in Figure 10-17. To create such a report, choose Tools, Report; select Organization Chart Report; and then click Run. Select a format for the report and type a name, and then click OK. Visio includes all the data from the custom property fields in your organization chart to create the report in the format you requested.

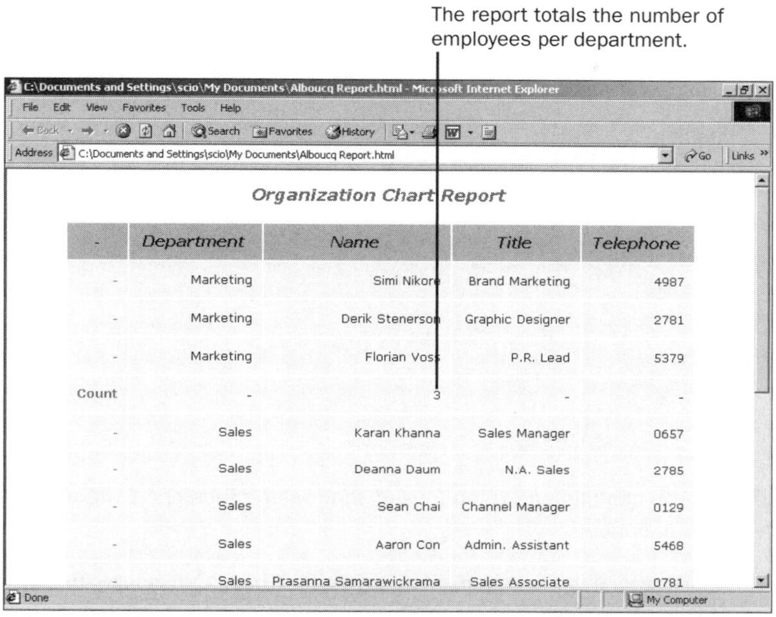

The report totals the number of
employees per department.

Figure 10-17. You can quickly create a report that lists information for all the employees in your organization.

If you imported employee information, your organization chart might contain additional fields that you would like to include in a report. The built-in report uses the default Name, Title, Department, and Telephone properties. If you have custom properties with different names, or additional properties you would like to include, you can modify the organization report or create a new report based on the existing one.

For details about creating and editing reports, see "Creating Reports," page 190.

Formatting an Organization Chart

With other diagram types, you can format shapes and text by using the commands on the Format, Tools, and Shape menus. With an organization chart, you use the Organization Chart, Options command to customize the look of shapes and text and maintain a consistent look for your diagram. You can apply a *design theme*, which is a set of shape borders and text styles that apply to the entire diagram.You can also change the size of employee shapes and choose and format the text used for shape labels, as Figure 10-18 shows.

Chapter 10

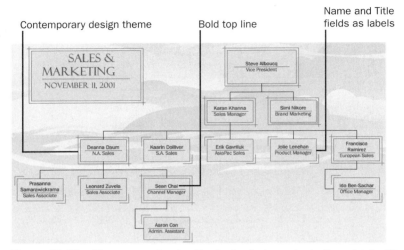

Contemporary design theme   Bold top line   Name and Title fields as labels

Figure 10-18. You can customize the look of your organization chart with design themes and text formatting options.

To open the Options dialog box, choose Organization Chart, Options to display the Options dialog box, as Figure 10-19 shows. Table 10-2 summarizes the formatting options that you can use in this dialog box.

> **Tip** To apply settings in the Options dialog box to all newly created organization charts, select the Use These Option Settings For New Organization Charts check box.

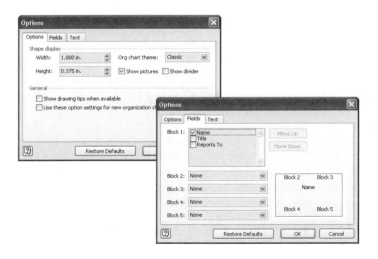

Figure 10-19. Use the Options command on the Organization Chart menu to specify shape and text settings for your diagram. Use the Set Display Fields command to choose the text that appears on shapes.

Table 10-2. Formatting Organization Chart Text and Shapes

Task	Technique
Change the design theme of an organization chart	In the Organization Chart Theme box, select a theme.
Resize employee shapes uniformly	In the Width and Height boxes, use the arrow buttons to increase or decrease the displayed size, or type a size and units.
Change the format of all employee names	Under Text Display, select a font for all text labels of shapes in the Text Font list. To format the first line displayed on shapes differently (such as italic or bold), choose an option in the Top Line Style list.
Display different text on shapes	Click the Fields tab, select a custom property for each of the five blocks, or select none (for blocks 2 through 5). To remove a field, deselect it in the appropriate block.
Hide the line that Visio displays between the top and bottom lines of text in shapes	Clear the Show Divider check box.
Clear or display pictures.	Select or clear the Show Pictures check box.

Chapter 10

Displaying Relationships and Processes in Block Diagrams

Microsoft Office Visio 2003 includes block diagram templates that were originally designed as a way for business professionals to create quick and easy presentation graphics. Today they're one of the most popular templates because of their versatility. Whether you want to illustrate a proposal, presentation, report, or any business-related communication, block diagrams are a great way to represent complex concepts and processes simply. With only basic shapes, such as triangles, squares, circles, ellipses, and arrows, you can convey data structure, hierarchy, signal flow, and data flow.

The block diagram templates are best suited to meet the needs of the drawing generalist—that is, anyone who creates a wide variety of drawings, such as managers, marketing professionals, project managers, engineers, technical writers, and trainers. If you are a business professional who communicates ideas and concepts to others, you're in the right place. This chapter provides the details you need to create block diagrams in Visio.

Choosing a Block Diagram

The block diagram templates are among the best examples of what separates Visio from the competition. Block diagrams refer to the diagrams you can create with any of the templates in the Block Diagram folder: Basic Diagram, Block Diagram, and Block Diagram With Perspective. Using only the fundamental drag-and-drop technique and common text and formatting tools, you can create functional and attractive diagrams, as Figure 11-1 shows.

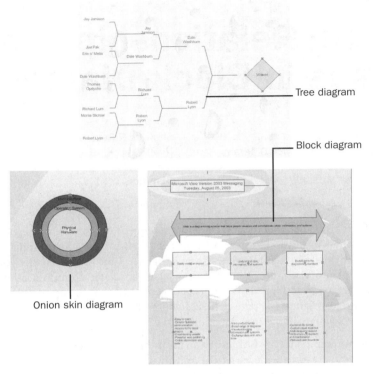

Tree diagram

Block diagram

Onion skin diagram

Figure 11-1. With block diagram shapes, you can capture layered concepts and hierarchies in an easy-to-understand format.

The truth is, each time Visio has been updated, most of the effort has gone into expanding the shape capabilities of other templates and developing wizards and macros that automate the drawing process. Automating block diagrams has never been deemed a high priority, probably because they're already so easy to use. Marketing surveys show that many people use block diagrams, and they use them to create an amazing variety of diagrams. And if it ain't broke, well…. Regardless of the reason, block diagram shapes haven't changed much since the first version of Visio and consequently remain easy to use—as well as versatile.

With a block diagram template, you can create four general types of diagrams, as Table 11-1 shows.

Table 11-1. **General Block Diagram Types**

Diagram Type	Uses	Description
Block	Reports, presentation graphics, proposal visuals; display brainstorming results, planning, product prototyping, process flow	Basic diagrams that communicate business relationships and processes using block shapes, such as boxes, diamonds, circles, and arrows
Tree	Hierarchical charts; display system integration, data structure, data flow, tournaments	Hierarchical diagrams, such as family trees or tournament plans, using branching tree shapes
Onion	Reports, presentation graphics, proposal visuals, slide shows; display component relationships	Concentric relationship diagrams in which each consecutive layer is dependent on the inner layer, and all layers are dependent on the core
3-D Block	Presentation graphics, slide shows, marketing reports, financial reports, hierarchical charts	Perspective diagrams that convey information more dramatically, such as presentation graphics, using 3-D blocks and arrows

Using the Block Diagram Templates

If you're new to block diagrams, you might wonder how to begin. The Choose Drawing Type window contains template descriptions when you point to a template; however, the descriptions for the block diagrams are nearly identical. Which one should you use? In some ways, it doesn't really matter. You can start with the Block Diagram template, which contains the most commonly used shapes, and then open other stencils as you need them. Visio includes the following block diagram templates:

- **Basic Diagram** Opens a letter-sized drawing page and the Basic Shapes, Borders And Titles, and Backgrounds stencils.

- **Block Diagram** Opens a letter-sized drawing page and the Blocks, Blocks Raised, Borders And Titles, and Backgrounds stencils.

Shapes

- **Block Diagram With Perspective** Opens a letter-sized drawing page oriented toward a vanishing point on the page. Also opens the Blocks With Perspective, Borders And Titles, and Backgrounds stencils.

> **Tip** To add a stencil, click Shapes on the Standard toolbar, and then select a stencil.

Chapter 11

Starting a Block Diagram

You can assemble most block diagrams in the same way using the basic steps outlined next. If you would rather jump right into creating a particular type of block diagram, skip ahead to the section in this chapter that describes how to create a hierarchical, tree, onion, or 3-D diagram.

In general, follow these steps to create a block diagram:

1 Decide whether you want to create a block, raised block, or perspective block diagram, and then choose File, New, Block Diagram, and select the appropriate template.

2 Decide which shape or shapes to use to represent the main idea you want to communicate.

Note Most of the procedures in this chapter refer to the Blocks and Blocks With Perspective stencils. For details about using the Borders And Titles and Backgrounds stencils that open with the Block Diagram templates, see "Quickly Formatting Shapes and Diagrams," page 54.

3 Drag shapes from the Blocks stencil or other stencils onto the drawing page.

4 Size, align, and format shapes as desired.

5 Format the page with borders, title blocks, a background, or a color scheme.

6 Save the drawing file.

Showing Hierarchies with Block Diagram Shapes

In a block diagram, you can graphically represent many types of systems. The components of the system are represented by blocks, which are often labeled, as shown in Figure 11-2. You can add arrows to show the direction in which a process flows or to depict system inputs and outputs. Most people create block diagrams with the goal of including them within a presentation, report, Web site, or other document. Manufacturers of equipment, such as electronic and computer equipment, often create block diagrams and add links from each component to another page that describes the component in detail.

For details about linking Visio pages, see "Linking Visio Shapes and Pages," page 146.

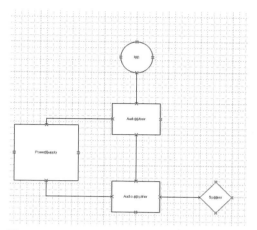

Figure 11-2.   This block diagram represents an audio system.

Creating Block Diagrams

When you create a block diagram, you start by dragging out the shapes you want to create, and then you go back and type the text. Finally, you arrange the shapes where you want them on the drawing page. Visio contains a number of alignment tools that can help you position the shapes. For example, display the Action toolbar (choose View, Toolbars, Action) to put the alignment and other useful tools close at hand.

Follow these steps to create a block diagram:

Connector tool

1   Choose File, New, Block Diagram, Block Diagram.

2   From the Blocks stencil, drag shapes onto the drawing page.

> **Tip**   Select the Connector Tool before you drag a shape so that the shape automatically connects to the previous shape you dropped.

3   To add text to a shape, select the shape, and then type. Visio automatically zooms in so you can read the text more easily.

4   To change the order of overlapping shapes, select a shape, and then choose Shape, Order, Bring Forward or Send Backward.

5   To nudge a shape a tiny amount in any direction, select the shape, and then press an arrow key.

6   To add arrows to your drawing, drag shapes from the Blocks or Blocks Raised stencil.

> **Tip**   To add shapes, such as triangles, squares, and other geometric shapes, open the Basic Shapes stencil by choosing File, Stencils, Block Diagram, Basic Shapes.

Chapter 11

7   To align shapes more precisely, use the Align Shapes and Distribute Shapes tools on the Action toolbar.

For details about aligning shapes, see "Positioning Shapes Precisely," page 436.

Modifying Block Diagram Shapes

With block diagram shapes, you can safely use the generic Visio editing techniques described elsewhere in this book. For example:

● Drag a green selection handle to resize a shape.

● Use the Pencil tool to add vertices and reshape shapes.

● Glue 1-D arrows to 2-D blocks at the blue connection points.

A few shapes include shortcut menu options and control handles that you use for reshaping and editing. As Figure 11-3 shows, a control handle is the yellow, diamond-shaped handle that appears when you select a shape. You can drag a control handle to change the shape's appearance. Table 11-2 includes the names of common block diagram shapes with descriptions of how you modify them.

Figure 11-3.   Drag the yellow control handles to change the shape's appearance.

Table 11-2. **Shortcuts for Editing Block Shapes**

Shape Name	Editing Shortcut
3-D Box	Use the control handles to adjust depth and orientation of the shape's shadow.
Arrow Box	Use the control handles to adjust the size and position of the arrow with respect to the rectangle.
1-D Single, 2-D Single	Right-click the shape, and then choose Open Tail to remove the ending line.
1-D Single Open, 2-D Single Open	Right-click the shape, and then choose Close Tail to add an ending line.
Curved Arrow	Use the control handles to adjust the curvature and arrowhead location.

There are many ways to modify block diagram shapes. The best advice is to play around, have fun, and realize that whatever you do to a shape can be undone when you choose Edit, Undo (or press Ctrl+Z).

Creating Tree Diagrams

Tree diagrams show hierarchical relationships, which cover everything from hardware connections to tournament playoffs, as Figure 11-4 shows. Use a tree diagram for the following:

- To show the relationship between a central idea and its subsidiary concepts
- To show the connection between one component and others within a process or system
- To indicate descendants and ancestors
- To represent taxonomy

Figure 11-4. With a tree diagram, you can document many types of hierarchical structures.

Starting a New Tree Diagram

To create a tree diagram, begin by dragging as many boxes as there are components in your tree structure. Then, drag a tree shape and connect the branch ends to the connection points of the boxes. Finally, position your boxes on the page. If you glue the boxes to the tree structure, they stay attached as you rearrange shapes.

Follow these steps to create a tree diagram:

1. Choose File, New, Block Diagram, Block Diagram.
2. Drag box shapes or other shapes from the Blocks stencil onto the drawing page to represent the components in your structure.
3. Drag one of the four tree shapes from the Blocks stencil onto the drawing page (Double Tree Sloped, Double Tree Square, Multi-Tree Sloped, or Multi-Tree Square).

> **Tip** If you want two branches, use a Double-Tree shape. If you want more than two branches, use a Multi-Tree shape.

4. Drag a control handle on the branch of a tree shape to a connection point on a block shape. The endpoints turn red when they are connected.

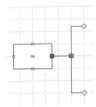

> **Tip** **Rotate a tree shape with keyboard commands**
> If a tree shape doesn't point in the right direction, select the shape, and then press Ctrl+H
> to flip the shape horizontally or Ctrl+L to rotate it 90 degrees to the left. By the same token,
> Ctrl+R rotates the shape 90 degrees to the right, and Ctrl+J makes the shape jump. Just
> kidding... Ctrl+J flips the shape vertically.

5 To add branches to a Multi-Tree shape, drag the control handle on the trunk away
from the shape to create up to six more branches. Drag the control handle at the end
of a branch (horizontally or vertically) to change the branch length or position.

6 Drag arrows and other shapes to emphasize your main idea.

7 To add text to a shape, select the shape, and then type.

8 To move a main branch up or down the tree trunk, select the tree shape, and then
press an arrow key.

Modifying Tree Diagram Shapes

The tree shapes on the Blocks stencil look pretty simple but include some clever behavior. For
example, when you select a tree shape that's glued to box shapes on the drawing page, you can
use the arrow keys to move the branches without moving the entire structure. Table 11-3
describes other shortcuts for working with tree shapes.

Table 11-3. Shortcuts for Editing Tree Shapes

Task	Editing Shortcut
Adjust the position of a branch	Drag the control handle on the end of a tree shape to a new position.
Move the trunk of a tree shape	If the tree is glued to other shapes, select the tree, and then press an arrow key.
Add up to six branches to a Multi-Tree	Drag the control handle on the trunk of a Multi-Tree shape away from the shape.
Adjust the distance between branches in a connected tree structure	Drag the box to which the tree is connected to a new location.
Remove a branch from a tree shape	Drag the control handle for the branch you want to remove until it's directly over the trunk or another branch, and then release the mouse button.

Troubleshooting

When moving a tree branch, the entire tree structure moves instead

Tree shapes, as specialized as they are, can be challenging to modify. Your best option when shapes move unexpectedly is to immediately press Ctrl+Z to reverse the effect. If you have performed several actions since the inadvertent move, press Ctrl+Z several times to back up and undo them all. For better success when moving branches, zoom to the tree shape before dragging it (or its control handle) to a new position. To zoom in quickly, press Shift+Ctrl+click with the mouse.

Showing Relationships in an Onion Diagram

An onion (or onion skin) diagram uses concentric circles to represent layered systems. Each component is a ring that builds on a single, core component, as Figure 11-5 shows. All the shapes you need to create an onion diagram are located on the Blocks stencil, which opens with the Block Diagram template.

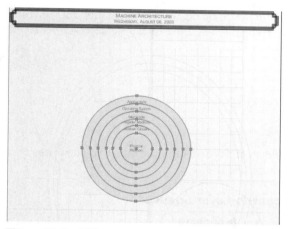

Figure 11-5. This onion diagram depicts the layered nature of computer architecture.

Creating Onion Diagrams

To create an onion diagram, start with the outer concept and work your way in. Use a concentric layer shape of the appropriate size to represent each new concept or layer. The concentric layer shapes fit together tightly. As long as you have no more than four layers in your diagram and don't need to resize shapes, the diagram is easy to create. To represent five or more layers, you must manually resize the largest concentric layer shape to fit.

Follow these steps to create an onion diagram:

1   Choose File, New, Block Diagram, Block Diagram.

2 Drag the Concentric Layer 1 shape from the Blocks stencil to the drawing page to form the outer layer of the onion.

3 Drag the Concentric Layer 2 shape inside the outer layer until it snaps into place.

4 Drag the Concentric Layer 3 and Concentric Center shapes until you have up to four layers in place.

5 To add text to each layer, select a layer, and then type.

6 To add more layers, drag the Concentric Layer 1 shape onto the drawing page, and then drag a corner selection handle until the shape is wider than the outer layer.

> **Tip** If your diagram includes five or more layers, you can nudge the outer layers into place. Select the shape, and then press an arrow key to move the shape by tiny increments.

Revising Shapes in an Onion Diagram

Perhaps the biggest challenge when working with layer shapes is getting the text to fit. Visio doesn't support text on a curve, so long lines of text can extend beyond a layer's borders. To enlarge a layer so that more text fits, drag a corner selection handle, as Figure 11-6 shows. You'll have to enlarge each layer in the onion diagram a similar amount, and then realign the shapes. Start with the outside layer, and then resize each inner layer. Other techniques for revising shapes are summarized in Table 11-4.

Figure 11-6. To change the radius of a concentric layer, drag a selection handle to resize the layer as needed.

Table 11-4. Revising Concentric Layer Shapes

Task	Technique
Align onion layers	Select all the layer shapes, and then choose Shape, Align Shapes. Choose a center alignment option, and then click OK.
Change the thickness of a concentric layer	Drag the control handle on the shape's inside rim to the thickness you want. If you don't know which control handle to use, pause the pointer over a control handle to display a ScreenTip.
Move the text label on a layer	Drag the control handle in the middle of the layer. If you have trouble dragging the handle, disable snapping—Choose Tools, Snap & Glue, clear the Snap check box, and then click OK.

Troubleshooting

Text doesn't fit in an onion layer

If you want to add more text than fits within the curves of an onion layer, you have a couple of options. Although curved text isn't one of those options, you can try the following:

● Choose a narrower font, such as Arial Narrow.

● Use callouts to display the text alongside the diagram and point to the appropriate layer. The Callouts stencil in the Visio Extras folder contains shapes you can use.

Dividing a Layer into Sections

Although onion diagrams are not complex, you can represent complex ideas by segmenting a layer. The partial layer shapes (Partial Layer 1, Partial Layer 2, and so on) on the Blocks stencil are designed to fit on top of the concentric layer shapes, as Figure 11-7 shows. You can use them to represent subcomponents of a larger system.

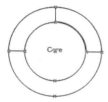

Figure 11-7.   Two Partial Layer 2 shapes suggest partitions or components on top of a Concentric Layer 2 shape.

Note   Make sure the Snap option is enabled for this procedure. To do so, choose Tools, Snap & Glue, select the Snap check box, and then click OK.

Follow these steps to divide a layer into sections:

1   Drag a partial layer shape from the Blocks stencil onto the layer you want to divide.

   If the partial layer shape is equal in size to the concentric layer you want to divide, the shape snaps into place. The endpoints turn red when they are connected.

2   To size the partial layer to match a concentric layer, drag an endpoint.

3   Adjust the orientation or position of the partial layer as necessary. Do any of the following:

   ■ To change its orientation, select the shape, choose Shape, Rotate Or Flip, and then select the command you want.

   ■ To adjust its thickness, drag the inner control handle left or right.

■ To increase or decrease the size of the section, drag the outer control handle left or right.

4 Select the partial layer, and then type the text you want.

Showing Concepts with 3-D Block Diagrams

Because 3-D block diagrams are eye-catching, they're commonly used to emphasize key concepts in a presentation or report. Figure 11-8 provides an example. You can use 3-D block diagrams to organize ideas in a variety of manners, from a simple chronology or hierarchy to a complex object model. When you open the Block Diagrams With Perspective template, the drawing page includes a *vanishing point* in the lower right corner. The vanishing point is a locked shape that sets the 3-D orientation of the perspective block shapes. You can move the vanishing point to change the direction of shape shadows and perspective lines on the page. Although working with 3-D representation might be a bit rough at first, in very little time you can create a basic 3-D perspective diagram that looks as though you spent hours creating it.

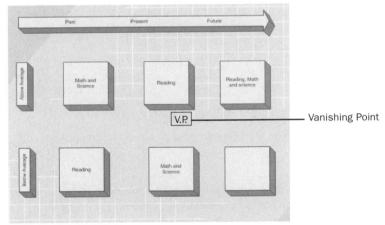

Figure 11-8. A 3-D block diagram is a handsome way of depicting relationships and associations.

> **Note** Only shapes from the Blocks With Perspective stencil adjust to the vanishing point. Shapes from the Blocks Raised stencil look very similar but don't adjust their perspective to the vanishing point.

Creating 3-D Block Diagrams

To create a 3-D block diagram, first decide what shape or shapes to use to represent the main idea you want to communicate. Then, add text to the shapes. Finally, play with the diagram's perspective, and add color to the shapes for emphasis.

Follow these steps to create a 3-D block diagram:

1 Choose File, New, Block Diagram, Block Diagram With Perspective.

2 Drag a 3-D perspective shape from the Blocks With Perspective stencil onto the drawing page.

Visio adjusts the depth of the shape and its shadow to accommodate the vanishing point.

3 Select the shape, and then type the text you want.

4 To change the diagram's perspective, make sure no shapes are selected, and then drag the V.P. shape to a new position on or off the drawing page.

All perspective shapes are redirected toward the vanishing point.

Changing the Diagram's Perspective

Perspective shapes respond to the position of the V.P. shape on the page, yet you can adjust individual shapes to make them more or less prominent. When you move the V.P. shape, Visio reorients all the shapes. If a shape doesn't respond, it might not be designed to work with the vanishing point, or it might have become disconnected. To determine whether a shape is connected to the vanishing point, select the shape. If the shape's control handle is glued to the V.P. shape and displayed in red, it's connected to the vanishing point, as Figure 11-9 shows. Table 11-5 summarizes techniques for working with perspective shapes and the vanishing point.

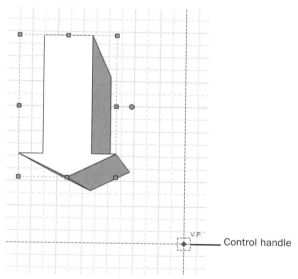

Figure 11-9. Perspective shapes must be connected to the vanishing point (V.P. shape).

Table 11-5. Adjusting 3-D Perspective

Task	Technique
Change the perspective for a specific shape	Select the shape, and then drag the red control handle on the V.P. shape to a new position. The control handle turns yellow, showing that the shape is no longer connected to the vanishing point.
Associate a shape with the vanishing point	Select the shape and drag its control handle to the connection point of the V.P. shape. The shape's control handle turns red to show that it's connected.
Change the depth of a 3-D shape	Right-click the shape, choose Set Depth, and then select a percentage, as Figure 11-10 shows. The greater the percentage, the deeper the shadow.

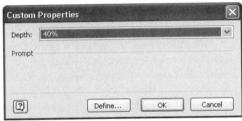

Figure 11-10. You can change the shadow depth for a single shape to make it appear more or less prominently.

Inside Out

Add some perspective

If you want to get fancy with perspective, add a second Vanishing Point shape from the Blocks With Perspective stencil to the drawing page, and then manually associate shapes with the new point. When you add one or more vanishing points, existing shapes continue to be associated with the original vanishing point. Any additional shapes you drag onto the page will also be associated with the original vanishing point. You must connect shapes to the new vanishing point as described in Table 11-5.

Hiding the Vanishing Point

You can hide the V.P. shape on the drawing page while you work and when you print. The shape is assigned to a layer so that you can control its visibility, color, and other attributes. To hide the V.P. shape, choose View, Layer Properties. (See Figure 11-11.) In the Vanishing Point row, clear the check mark in the Visible column to hide the shape. Clear the check mark in the Print column to prevent the shape from printing.

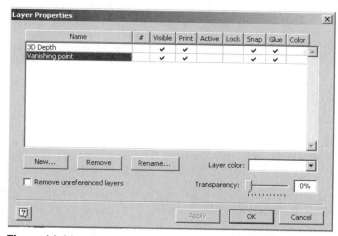

Figure 11-11.   You can change attributes of the Vanishing Point layer to affect the V.P. shape on the drawing page.

Adjusting the Shadow Color

Using a shape's shortcut menu, you can make changes to the shape's shadow color. Visio provides three options, as Figure 11-12 shows:

- **Automatic Shadow**   This is the default. Visio sets the shadow color automatically based on the shape's fill color. You cannot change the color.
- **Manual Shadow**   You can change the shape's shadow color. Use the Fill or Shadow commands on the Format menu.
- **Color Scheme Shadow**   Visio changes the shadow color of all shapes based on a color scheme that you apply (choose Shape, Actions, Color Scheme Shadow).

Figure 11-12.   Right-click the shape to change the depth and color of its shadow.

Chapter 11

Tracking Projects and Schedules

To assess project status at a glance, you can create any of several project schedule diagrams in Microsoft Office Visio 2003. Scheduling is perhaps the most crucial aspect of the project management process, and Visio can help you plan and document tasks with simple-to-use shapes. Coordinating multiple tasks and resources over a period of time is daunting enough without the struggle many complicated project scheduling tools put you through. Of course, some projects demand a highly sophisticated scheduling tool, but for everyday use, Visio provides enough power to track tasks, dates, and dependencies, and the resulting diagrams are well suited for display on a Web site or presentation slide.

This chapter tells you how to use the vastly improved project scheduling templates in this version of Visio to create timelines, calendars, Program Evaluation and Review Technique (PERT) charts, and Gantt charts. It also covers how to import information from Microsoft Outlook.

Project Scheduling in Visio

Most people need a scheduling tool at one time or another. Whether you want to clarify project milestones or track task dependencies, Visio includes a template to meet your needs. For example, you can create timelines and Gantt charts that double as attractive illustrations in status reports, in slide shows, on your intranet site, or in other documentation, as Figure 12-1 shows.

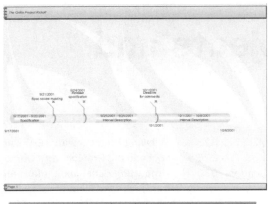

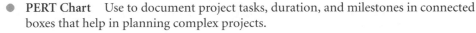

Figure 12-1. You can use Visio to create timelines and Gantt charts like these, as well as monthly calendars and PERT charts.

Visio's strength is in providing easy-to-use tools for high-level scheduling tasks. You can use Visio to coordinate dozens of resources and track hundreds of tasks, but the project scheduling templates are really designed for smaller scale projects. You can create the following four types of project scheduling diagrams in Visio:

- **Timeline** Use to document high-level project milestones. A timeline displays start and finish dates and milestones for projects at a glance.

- **Gantt Chart** Use to provide a hierarchical view of the entire lifetime of a project. A Gantt chart can show how much of a task has been completed and helps you track a project's progress.

- **Calendar** Use to create all-purpose monthly or yearly calendars.

   You can import Outlook scheduling information into your Visio 2003 calendar.

- **PERT Chart** Use to document project tasks, duration, and milestones in connected boxes that help in planning complex projects.

Using Visio with Microsoft Project

If you use Microsoft Project or work with people who do, consider Visio a companion product. You can easily import .MPX files into Visio to generate timelines and Gantt charts. However, Visio is simply not in the same project management league as Project—nor is it meant to be. Some people register for weeklong courses to learn how to use Project's powerful scheduling tools. With Visio, you can assemble a diagram in a couple of hours, if that, to track tasks and milestones. However, you don't have access to the type of reporting and advanced tracking features that Project offers.

324

Chapter 12

Instead, Visio provides the best means to create attractive and simplified visual representations of a complex Project schedule. In addition, you can use Visio to develop high-level schedules that can be shared with Project users. When you save a Visio timeline or Gantt chart diagram in XML format, the data can be imported for additional analysis in Project. To make Visio easier to use with Project, the Visio designers even renamed some commands to match Project. For example, Promote Task and Demote Task in the Gantt Chart template are now Outdent and Indent.

> **Note** The XML file format replaces the MPX format for exchanging project scheduling files used in Microsoft Visio 2000. Microsoft Project 2000 and later versions do not support the MPX format.

Creating a Project Timeline

Timelines show the life span of a project or process in a linear format that includes tasks, milestones, and intervals, as Figure 12-2 shows. A timeline can help you visualize a sequence of events or the high-level tasks associated with a complex project. Whether you're trying to keep track of hiring processes, development timelines, product release schedules, or project cycles, a Visio timeline can clarify critical milestones.

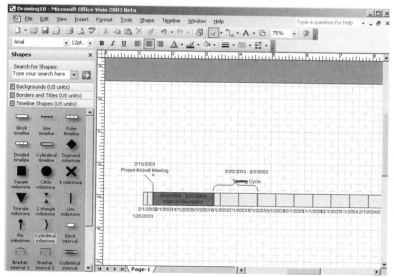

Figure 12-2. A timeline clarifies project milestones.

To create a timeline in Visio, you start with the Timeline template in the Project Schedules folder. You can enter starting and ending dates to generate an initial timeline, and then use the shapes on the Timeline stencil to provide details. Or you can import existing schedule information from a text, Microsoft Excel, or Project file.

Chapter 12

Creating a Timeline from Scratch

When you start a diagram with the Timeline template, Visio opens a letter-sized, landscape-oriented drawing page and the Timeline Shapes, Backgrounds, and Borders And Titles stencils. Visio includes six styles of timeline shapes for you to choose from, which differ only in their look on the page: Block Timeline, 1-D Timeline, Ruler Timeline, Divided Timeline, and Cylindrical Timeline. When you drag a timeline shape from the stencil, Visio prompts you to set start and end dates, specify a time scale, and choose formatting options in the Configure Timeline dialog box, shown in Figure 12-3. When you click OK, Visio adds the timeline to the drawing page.

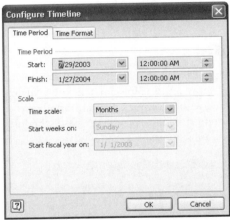

Figure 12-3. When you drag a timeline shape onto the drawing page, the Configure Timeline dialog box appears. If you don't specify starting and ending dates, Visio uses today's date and a six-month duration.

After the basic timeline is in place, you can add milestone shapes for the events or tasks you want to track. Visio can even update milestone dates as you move milestone shapes along the timeline.

Follow these steps to create a timeline:

1   Choose File, New, Project Schedule, Timeline.

2   From the Timeline Shapes stencil, drag one of the timeline shapes (Block Timeline, 1-D Timeline, Ruler Timeline, Divided Timeline, or Cylindrical Timeline).

3   In the Configure Timeline dialog box, choose a start date and finish date, select units for the time scale, and set formatting options for the date and time scale. Click OK to create the timeline.

4   If you don't like the results, right-click the timeline, and then choose Configure Timeline to specify different dates or formats.

> **Tip** To update dates automatically on marker, milestone, and interval shapes when you move them on the timeline, select the Automatically Update Dates When Markers Are Moved check box on the Time Format tab.

Showing Project Milestones

To document important tasks, events, and hand-offs, you can add milestone shapes to your timeline. The Timeline Shapes stencil includes several styles of milestones. Milestone shapes snap into place on timeline shapes. A few, such as the Cylindrical Milestone, are intended for use with a specific style of timeline shape. Even so, the milestone shapes differ only in their look, so you can use the one that looks best to you. Like the timeline shapes, milestone shapes prompt you for date information when you add them to the drawing page.

> **Tip** Because timelines tend to be wide, you might find it convenient to dock the stencils on the top or bottom of the drawing window rather than on the side.

Follow these steps to add project milestones:

1   From the Timeline Shapes stencil, drag a milestone shape onto the timeline shape.

    Even if you drop a milestone on the drawing page away from the timeline, Visio snaps the milestone to the timeline shape, displays the Configure Milestone dialog box, and sets the milestone date based on the shape's position on the timeline.

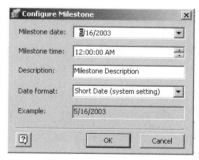

2   If the Milestone Date setting in the Configure Milestone dialog box isn't correct, type a new date in the box, or click the drop-down arrow to display a calendar and locate the date you want.

3   In the Date Format box, choose the format you want to use for milestone dates, and then click OK to update the milestone shape.

4   Type a description in the Milestone Description box.

5   To adjust text position, drag the top (yellow) control handle.

> **Tip** To quickly reorient a milestone so that its text and callout appear under the timeline, select the milestone shape, and then press Ctrl+J.

Chapter 12

327

6   To change the look of the milestone after you've dropped it on the timeline, right-click the shape, choose Set Milestone Type, and select from one of the nine shapes in the Milestone Shape list of the Custom Properties dialog box.

Troubleshooting

After typing a milestone or interval description, the date disappeared

If you accidentally type over the milestone or interval dates when you add the description text, you can restore them. Right-click the shape, and then choose Show Date (for milestone shape) or Show Dates (for interval shapes).

NEW FEATURE! If you have more than one timeline or interval on a page, you can synchronize them. To do so select an interval and then choose Timeline, Synchronize Milestone, or Synchronize Interval. Choose the format you would like to use and click OK. A dotted line links the two shapes, symbolizing their connection. If you change the information on one, it will change the information on its linked cousin. You can also start from scratch by dragging a synchronized milestone or interval onto your drawing, choosing the format, and clicking OK.

Adding an Interval to a Timeline

Intervals show the starting and ending dates of a task or process, as Figure 12-4 shows. The interval shapes on the Timeline Shapes stencil aren't quite as smart as the milestone shapes—after you have added an interval to the timeline, you can't change its look as you can with milestones.

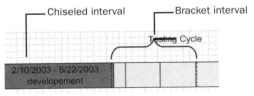

Figure 12-4.   Interval shapes snap onto a timeline to show ongoing tasks.

Depending on the size of your timeline, an interval shape can obscure markers or milestones. Remember stacking order? You can change a shape's stacking order so that it appears on top or in back with the Order commands on the Shape menu.

Follow these steps to add an interval to a timeline:

1   Drag an interval shape from the Timeline Shapes stencil onto the timeline, which opens the Configure Interval dialog box.

Chapter 12

Like milestone shapes, interval shapes snap to the timeline even if you drop them elsewhere on the page.

2 In the Configure Interval dialog box, choose the interval start date, finish date, and date format, and then click OK.

3 Type a new description in the Interval Description box.

4 If you're using a bracket interval shape, you can adjust the height of the bracket by dragging the control handle up or down.

Tip You can add a marker or display elapsed time on a timeline to see how much progress you've made. The Today Marker and Elapsed Time shapes on the Timeline Shapes stencil use your computer's date setting to establish the current date.

Creating a Vertical Timeline

New in Visio 2003, you can create a vertical timeline. This comes in handy when printing in portrait format. It allows you to place a much longer timeline on the same size sheet of paper.

Follow these steps to create a vertical timeline:

1 Drag the timeline shape onto the page, or select a previously created timeline.

2 Choose Shape, Rotate Or Flip, and then select what you want to do with the shape.

3 You can also select the shape with the pointer tool and then drag the endpoint to reposition the timeline to any angle.

Expanded Timeline

Sometimes you'll need to zoom in on a specific section of a project timeline. Perhaps there is a lot going on in a short period of time or perhaps what is going on is very important. Whatever the reason, you can now use Visio 2003 to do the zooming, as Figure 12-5 shows. The expanded timeline shape allows you to expand a section of your timeline.

Chapter 12

329

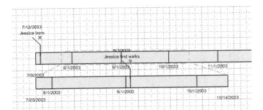

Figure 12-5. You can use expanded timelines to show greater detail.

Follow these steps to add an expanded timeline shape:

1 Drag the shape onto the page from the Timeline Shapes stencil.

2 Select the time period, scale, and format from the Configure Timeline dialog box.

3 Click OK.

> **Tip** You can even expand an expanded timeline. Just drop another expanded timeline shape below it. Fill out the Configure Timeline dialog box, and you are on your way.

Creating a Gantt Chart from a Timeline

To capture a different view of your project, you can create a Gantt chart based on the dates in a Visio timeline. Choose Tools, Add-Ons, Project Schedule, Export Project Data Wizard. The wizard uses the milestone and interval dates in a timeline to specify starting and ending dates. You can then add the additional project information that a Gantt chart can display.

> For details about Gantt charts, see "Scheduling Projects with Gantt Charts," page 336.

> **Note** The wizard does not link the Gantt chart to the timeline. Changes you make to one diagram won't update the information in the other.

Creating Monthly and Yearly Calendars

The Calendar template has been a favorite of many users since the early Visio days, probably because it's so well designed and easy to use. Visio does most of the work for you. When you drag a calendar shape on the page, Visio prompts you for the date, as Figure 12-6 shows. Depending on the shape you use, you can display one month or an annual calendar on a single page.

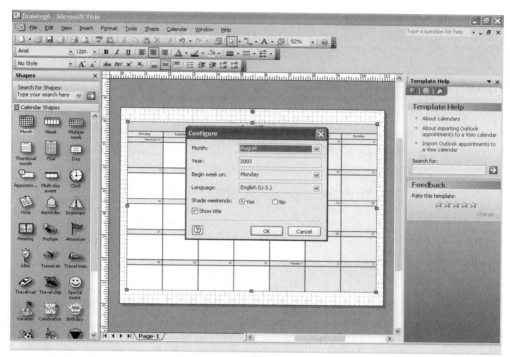

Figure 12-6. When you use a calendar shape, Visio prompts you for date and formatting information.

Creating a Monthly Calendar

Follow these steps to create a monthly calendar:

1 Choose File, New, Project Schedule, Calendar.

2 Drag the Large Month shape from the Calendar Shapes stencil onto the drawing page. The calendar snaps into place, regardless of where you drop the shape.

3 In the Custom Properties dialog box, specify date and formatting options. When you click OK, Visio creates the calendar based on your choices.

> **Tip** If you want to change an option you have selected—for example, you don't want the default shaded weekends—right-click the calendar, and then choose Properties to display the Custom Properties dialog box.

4 To add text to a specific day, click a date square, and then type.

5 To highlight important dates or events, drag the Arrow, Timeline, or one of the label shapes to a date, and then type the text you want.

Chapter 12

6   To show the previous or next month in a miniature calendar, drag a Small Month shape onto a blank day at the start or end of the month. In the Custom Properties dialog box, specify the month you want, and then click OK.

Creating a Yearly Calendar

Follow these steps to create a yearly calendar on one page:

1   Choose File, New, Project Schedule, Calendar.

2   Drag the Yearly Calendar shape from the Calendar Shapes stencil onto the drawing page to display the Custom Properties dialog box.

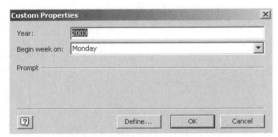

3   To specify a year other than the current one, type the year in the Year box. To change the day used as the first day of the week to Monday, select Monday from the Begin Week On drop-down list. Click OK to create the calendar.

> **Tip**   **Change calendar page orientation**
> If you're using the Calendar template to create a yearly calendar, the default landscape orientation for the drawing page might not be appropriate, because the yearly shape is taller than it is wide. To change the page orientation, choose File, Page Setup. On the Print Setup tab, click Portrait, and then click OK.

Modifying the Look of Your Calendar

The simplicity of the calendars has its downside. Because Visio creates the calendar for you, it assumes certain formatting properties, such as shading, line, and text formatting. In addition, Visio locks calendar shapes to prevent them from being moved or deleted as you add text, as Figure 12-7 shows. Despite the locks, you can change the look of your calendar by specifying different text, line, and fill formats. The formatting task goes more smoothly when you recognize that Visio creates a calendar as a group, which allows you to subselect calendar shapes and edit them individually. For example, the default look for the days of the week for the Large Month shape is white text on a black background. If you would like something less stark, you can subselect the weekday shape, and then specify different text, line, and fill options.

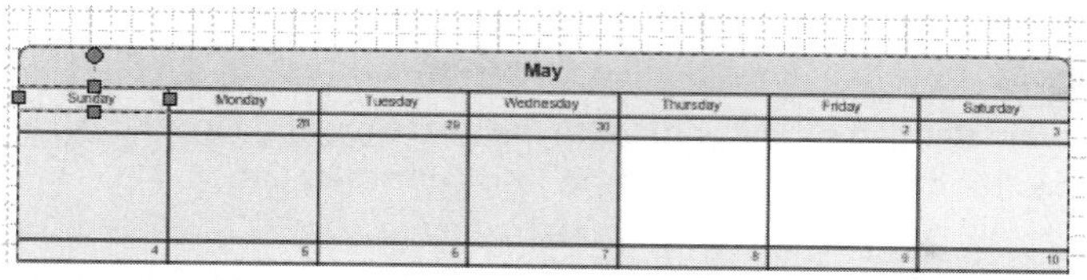

Figure 12-7. Visio locks shapes to keep them from moving, but you can still change their format.

The advantage of groups is that they're easy to resize. To change the size of a calendar, drag a corner selection handle to the desired size.

For details about editing groups, see "Working with Groups," page 668.

Troubleshooting

When you try to subselect a calendar shape to format it, an error message appears

Text tool

Individual days in a monthly calendar are locked against text editing. If you select the date numbers in a monthly calendar with the Text tool, a warning message appears telling you that shape protection or layer properties prevent the command's execution. You can, however, edit the styles applied to locked calendar shapes to change their text formatting. For example, to change the font used to format the calendar day numbers, choose Format, Define Styles. In the Name box, choose Calendar Normal. Click Text, choose the font you want, and then click OK to close all the dialog boxes.

For details about editing styles, see "Editing Existing Styles," page 691.

Note You can apply a color scheme to quickly change the look of a calendar. However, if you have manually formatted calendar shapes, those shapes won't adopt the color scheme. To apply a color scheme, choose Tools, Color Schemes.

Importing Data from Microsoft Outlook

Many people keep track of their appointments and tasks using Microsoft Outlook. It would be time consuming and wasteful to reenter the data into Visio. The good news is that you don't need to! You can import your scheduling data right from Outlook into your Visio 2003 calendar by following these steps:

1 Select the calendar into which you wish to import data.
2 Choose Calendar, Import Outlook Data Wizard.

Chapter 12

333

3 In the Import Outlook Data Wizard, choose whether you want to import data into the selected calendar or into a new calendar that you will create.

4 Select the parameter dates, review them in the next box, and click Finish when you are ready for Visio to import the information into your calendar.

> **Tip** You can also ask Visio to create a new calendar and import your Outlook data. To do so select New Calendar in step 3 and fill in the subsequent dialog boxes. Visio creates a brand new calendar with your Outlook data positioned on it.

Viewing Projects with PERT Charts

PERT refers to the Program Evaluation and Review Technique, a project management method originally developed in the 1950s by the U.S. Navy. A PERT chart is a diagram that reveals task, duration, and dependency information. Because of their ability to represent extensive detail, PERT charts continue to be popular today, particularly in manufacturing environments. With the PERT Chart template in Visio, you can create the style of chart variously called a network, subproject, or logic diagram. Visio doesn't add a time scale or provide any automated tools for grouping or marking critical path tasks. Instead, you use drag-and-drop PERT shapes and connectors to assemble a diagram, and then type in the details, as Figure 12-8 shows.

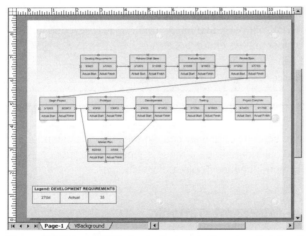

Figure 12-8. A PERT chart shows start and end dates for project tasks in a connected diagram.

The PERT Chart template in Visio comes equipped with a deceptively small number of shapes, but you don't need many to create even complex diagrams. However, you might need time. Visio doesn't include wizards or other tools for automating the chart assembly process. You must type all the duration and task information you want to manage in a PERT shape, which represents one *node*—that is, a task, event, or activity associated with a project. Visio offers two styles of PERT shape, which differ only in the information they display, as Figure 12-9 shows. Both are groups. To connect each node to its successor, you use connectors from the stencil or toolbar.

Figure 12-9. You can choose from two task styles by using either the PERT 1 (left) or PERT 2 (right) shape on the PERT Chart Shapes stencil.

Typically, a PERT chart ends at a major review point, such as the end of the analysis stage or a funding review cycle. You can insert pages and then create additional PERT charts to represent the components of an entire project.

Follow these steps to create a PERT chart:

1 Choose File, New, Project Schedule, PERT Chart.
2 Drag a PERT 1 or PERT 2 shape from the PERT Chart Shapes stencil onto the drawing page to create the first node.
3 With the shape selected, type the task name.
4 To add other task data, such as the scheduled start and finish dates, subselect a box in the PERT shape, and then type.

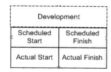

Tip   To delete text and leave the box empty, subselect the text box, and then press the Spacebar.

---

5 To add nodes for tasks in your project, drag PERT 1 and PERT 2 shapes onto the page.

Connector tool

6 To connect the nodes with arrows, click the Connector tool on the Standard toolbar, and then drag from the connection point on the first node shape to a connection point on the next shape.

Tip   Drawing with the Connector tool has exactly the same effect as using the Dynamic Connector shape on the PERT Chart Shapes stencil. Most people find it faster to use the Connector tool than the shape.

---

7 Drag a Legend shape from the PERT Chart Shapes stencil onto the drawing page.
8 With the legend selected, type a title for the PERT chart.
9 To add additional data to the legend, subselect a box, and then type.

Chapter 12

Inside Out

Formatting lines

Project managers commonly indicate slack time between the end of one task and the start of another with a dotted line between tasks. Similarly, a thick line represents a critical path. To format lines in Visio, select a connector line shape, and then click the Line Pattern or Line Weight tool on the Formatting toolbar. Or choose Format, Line.

Scheduling Projects with Gantt Charts

The Gantt chart was originated by Charles Gantt in 1917, and its clarity and hierarchical format have helped project managers ever since. Essentially a horizontal bar chart, a Gantt chart focuses on the sequence of tasks necessary for completing a project. The Gantt Chart template in Visio includes horizontal task bar shapes that are updated for you based on the duration of a task and its start time, as Figure 12-10 shows. The template also adds a floating toolbar and the Gantt Chart menu to the Visio window. Most of the work you do to refine your chart involves these two tools.

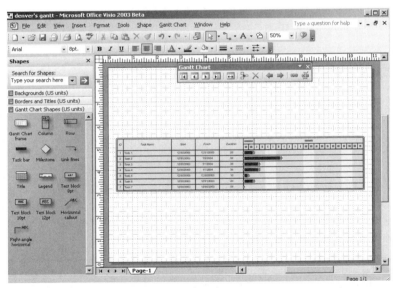

Figure 12-10. For small-scale projects or high-level task management, you can create Gantt charts in Visio that show dependent tasks and milestones.

Note Because Gantt charts are usually wider than they are tall, you might want to dock the stencils below the drawing page while you work.

Creating a Gantt Chart

When you start a diagram with the Gantt Chart template, Visio immediately prompts you for information with the Gantt Chart Options dialog box, shown in Figure 12-11. You can choose from a number of options for customizing the information that appears in the chart. For example, you can add markers to show the estimated and actual start and end dates. On a task bar, you can display the name of the person assigned to the task or other information. For ongoing projects, you can display a progress line to indicate actual start and completion dates. Although you use the Gantt Chart Options dialog box to set up your chart, you can also add rows, columns, and tasks as you work. A primary design goal was to provide consistency with Project, so command names and toolbar buttons in Visio match those in Project.

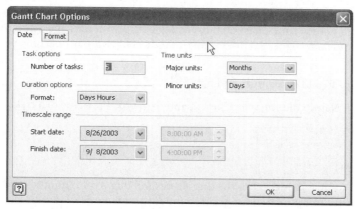

Figure 12-11. In the Gantt Chart Options dialog box, you specify the initial settings you want. Later, you can choose different options by choosing Options from the Gantt Chart menu.

Although Gantt charts can become quite complex, it's best to include no more than 15 tasks in one chart so that your chart remains manageable. You can create subtasks to represent more than 15 tasks in one chart or insert pages and use the Gantt Chart Frame shape to show additional project information.

Follow these steps to create a new Gantt chart:

1 Choose File, New, Project Schedule, Gantt Chart.
2 On the Date tab, type the number of tasks you want to start with, the units of time, duration format, and date range for the chart.
3 Click the Format tab, and then choose options for the appearance of the task bars, milestones, and summary bars.

Note   The options on the Format tab affect the look of all Gantt charts on a drawing page.

4 Click OK. Visio creates the Gantt chart on the drawing page.

Chapter 12

If the results aren't what you expected, you can change date and format options by choosing Gantt Chart, Options.

> **Tip** To move a Gantt chart on the page, drag its thick outer border. You might need to zoom in first.

Adding Task Names and Dates

After you have set up a Gantt chart, the next step is to replace the default task names and add dates. Visio requires only a duration value. Based on that number and the start date you specified in the Gantt Chart Options dialog box, Visio updates the start and finish dates for a task. When you specify duration, you can type just a number, which Visio interprets using the units you selected in the Gantt Chart Options dialog box, or you can type a number and any unit of time that Visio recognizes. For example, to indicate a two-day duration, you can type **2d** or **48h**.

Follow these steps to add task names and dates:

1 In the Task Name column, select Task 1, and then type the name of a task.

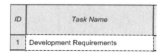

2 In the Duration column, select the first shape, and then type a number and a unit of time. Type **m** for minutes, **h** for hours, **d** for days, or **w** for weeks.

> **Tip** To switch from the insertion point (which appears when you type) to the Pointer tool, press the Esc key or click outside the shape you're typing in.

3 Repeat this procedure to add task names and durations in each row.

4 To indicate that a task represents a milestone, type **0** for the duration.

Inside Out

Change the chart's calendar

Although you never have to type a date in the Start or Finish column, you can. Visio changes the length of the task bar and the duration value to match the new dates. However, if you change the date in the Start column of the first task, Visio doesn't change the calendar displayed above the task bars. To change the chart's calendar, choose Gantt Chart, Options, and specify a new date in the Start Date list.

Editing Tasks

To add, remove, and reorder tasks in your Gantt chart, you can use the commands on the Gantt Chart menu or the shapes' shortcut menus, as Table 12-1 describes.

Table 12-1. Editing Tasks

Task	Technique
Add tasks to the end of a chart	Select the thick, outer border on the Gantt chart to display its selection handles. Drag the center selection handle at the bottom of the frame to fill the space with new task rows.
Insert a new task in the middle of a chart	Right-click the task name that will follow the new task, and then choose New Task. Or drag the Row shape from the Gantt Chart Shapes stencil into approximate position.
Delete a task	Right-click a task name, and then choose Delete Task.
Reorder tasks	Drag a task row to the desired position. It's easiest to drag by the ID, but you can drag the task name or other column.
Edit an existing task name	Double-click in a Task Name shape. This feature places the insertion point inside the text box so you can type.
Change the row height	Select a shape in the row, and then drag the top or bottom selection handle.

Adding Subtasks

Indent

When you need to show that a task involves several related steps, you can insert a subtask. Visio indents subtasks to show that they are subordinate to a main task and then displays the parent task in bold and adds *summary bars* to the parent task bar, as Figure 12-12 shows. To add and edit a subtask, follow the steps described in Table 12-1 for adding and editing tasks, then select the subtask, and click Indent on the Gantt Chart toolbar.

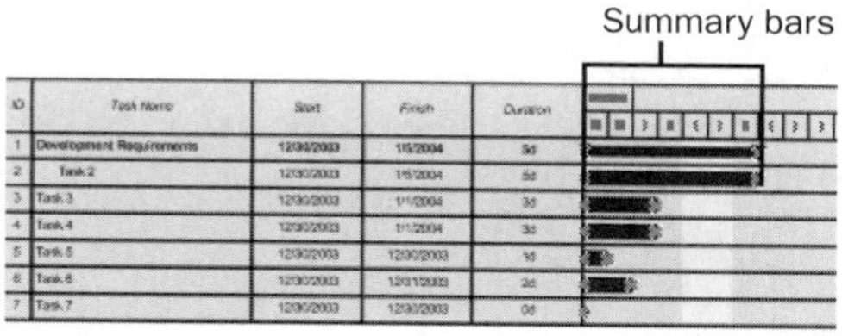

Summary bars

Figure 12-12. Subtasks are indented below a parent task, which appears in bold. Its summary bar displays black triangles on each end.

Tip You can convert milestones into tasks and vice versa. You can either type a new duration or drag a green handle on the shape to change its duration. Use a duration of 0 to indicate a milestone.

Chapter 12

339

Adding Task Bar Labels

You can display the value of any column as a label on the task bar shapes. For example, you can display the task duration, as Figure 12-13 shows. Visio displays labels on all the task bar shapes on the drawing page. You can't selectively add labels to tasks.

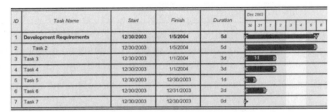

Figure 12-13. You can add labels to task bar shapes to display project information, such as duration.

Follow these steps to add a task bar label:

1 Choose Gantt Chart, Options, and then click the Format tab.

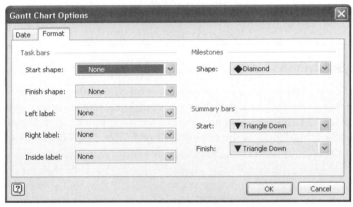

2 In the Left Label, Right Label, or Inside Label lists, select the name of a column heading that appears in your Gantt chart.

3 Click OK.

Linking Tasks to Show Dependencies

Linked tasks are the heart of a Gantt chart. As you adjust dates for a linked task, all subsequent tasks change to reflect the new information. Linked tasks appear connected in the chart with a blue link line, as Figure 12-14 shows. You can link tasks in a number of ways—by using the Gantt Chart menu, the shapes' shortcut menus, the Gantt Chart toolbar, or by modifying task bar and milestone shapes directly. The shapes include yellow control handles

Chapter 12

that you can drag to link to another task bar or milestone shape. However, it's easier to use the Gantt Chart toolbar.

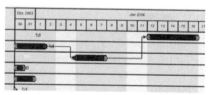

Figure 12-14. To link tasks, you can select the task bar shapes, task names, dates, or durations and then use the Link Tasks button on the Gantt Chart toolbar.

Follow these steps to link tasks:

1 Select the starting task or milestone, and then select the subsequent tasks *in order*.

> **Tip** Press Shift+click to select multiple shapes.

Link Tasks

2 Click the Link Tasks button on the Gantt Chart toolbar.

Unlink Tasks

3 To unlink two tasks, select both of them and click the Unlink Tasks button on the Gantt Chart toolbar. Or select the link line between two tasks and press Delete.

Troubleshooting

Visio doesn't align simultaneous tasks correctly

It's a little tricky to represent simultaneous tasks in a Gantt chart. Your best option is to link in the correct order using the Link Tasks button on the Gantt Chart toolbar. For example, if tasks 2 and 3 occur simultaneously, link tasks like this: select task 1 and 2, and then click Link Tasks. Select tasks 1 and 3, and then click Link Tasks. Now repeat, linking tasks 2 and 4, and then tasks 3 and 4. You usually end up with overlapping connectors, as shown in Figure 12-15.

Figure 12-15. Linked simultaneous tasks show overlapping tasks.

Customizing Columns in a Gantt Chart

To customize the project information that your Gantt chart tracks, you can add, delete, and reorder columns and edit the column header text. When you add a column (choose Gantt Chart, Insert Column), the Insert Column dialog box appears, as Figure 12-16 shows. You can choose from an assortment of standard column types, such as % Complete, as well as oddly named columns, such as User Defined Number and User Defined Text. The user-defined columns are just that—columns designed to support a particular data type, such as a number, text, or date, that you can use for any purpose. To see a complete list of the data types associated with each column type, click the Help button in the Insert Column dialog box.

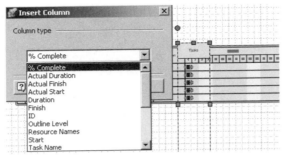

Figure 12-16.   You can choose from 21 standard and custom column types to insert in your Gantt chart.

Help

If you're accustomed to adding and editing columns in Excel, you'll find that Visio works a little differently. For details, see Table 12-2.

Table 12-2. Adding and Editing Columns

Task	Technique
Add a column	Right-click an existing column, and then choose Insert Column. Select a column type, and then click OK. Visio inserts the column to the left of the selection.
Delete a column	Right-click a column, and then choose Hide Column.
Move a column	Drag a column by its name to a new position.
Rename a column	Click the Text tool on the Standard toolbar, select the column text, and then type.
Change the column width	Select a cell and move the left or right green selection handle.

Note   To restore a hidden column, right-click an existing column, choose Insert Column, and then choose the hidden column in the Column Type box.

Troubleshooting

An error appears when you select a task bar shape

If you select a task bar shape with the Text tool, Visio displays the following message:

 Shape protection and/or layer properties prevent complete execution of this command.

Task bars are locked against text editing; however, you can insert up to three labels that display the values from the chart's columns. For details, see "Adding Task Bar Labels," page 340.

Exporting a Visio Gantt Chart to Use in Project

When you need the detailed tracking features of Project, you can export a Visio Gantt chart in a format that Project can import.

Follow these steps to export a Visio Gantt chart:

1 Select the tasks you want to export, or drag a selection rectangle around the entire Gantt chart, and then choose Gantt Chart, Export.

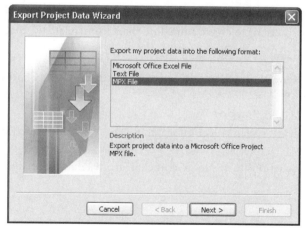

2 Select MPX File, and then click Next.

3 Type a name for the new file, and then click Next. Or click Browse to specify a location and file name, click Save, and then click Next.

4 Click Finish. Visio displays a message when the project export is successful.

Chapter 12

343

Importing Scheduling Information

With the Import Project Data Wizard, you can import tasks and milestones from another data source to create a Gantt chart. The wizard accepts information from text (.TXT or .CSV), Excel (.XLS), and Project (.MPX and .MPP) files. With text and Excel files, your file must contain the task number, task name, start date, and either finish date or duration.

Inside Out

Clean up a timeline

If you use the Import Project Data Wizard to create a timeline, the result can include a lot of overlapping text. Milestones are displayed in text callouts above the timeline. Expect to do some clean-up work on your diagram. Typically, this involves dragging the control handle on a text callout to a new, out-of-the-way position.

Follow these steps to import a Visio timeline:

1   Choose File, New, Project Schedule, Timeline.

2   Choose Tools, Add-Ons, Project Schedule, Import Project Data Wizard.

3   On the first wizard screen, select Information That's Already Stored In A File, and then click Next.

4   Follow the instructions to create a timeline chart from a data file that you specify.

Follow these steps to import a Visio Gantt chart:

1   Choose File, New, Project Schedule, Gantt Chart. In the Gantt Chart Options dialog box, click Cancel.

2   Choose Gantt Chart, Import.

3   On the first wizard screen, select Information That's Already Stored In A File, and then click Next.

4   Follow the instructions to create a Gantt chart from a data file that you specify.

Chapter 13

Adding Impact to Microsoft PowerPoint Presentations

Creating Microsoft PowerPoint presentations, you'll discover that using Microsoft Office Visio 2003 shapes and diagrams as slide illustrations offers some great benefits. Slides with visuals—including charts, diagrams, and conceptual illustrations—have more impact with your audience. Moreover, research has proven that an audience can remember information more easily when it is presented in a visual form. PowerPoint's drawing tools work well for quick, one-use-only slide art. However, if you want to invest a little more time in your slide graphics, take advantage of the shapes and tools in Visio to create just the image you want.

The other chapters in this book describe in detail how to create those images. This chapter provides tips for formatting Visio diagrams for display on the big screen and tells you how to get that shape or diagram into PowerPoint with minimum fuss.

Using Visio Shapes and Diagrams in Presentations

You're giving a presentation to the team and need to unveil the schedule for a new project. Could you do it using only bullet points? Certainly. But if you've read those books about how to create winning presentations, you know that a picture carries more weight with your audience than a slide full of text, as the slides in Figure 13-1 show.

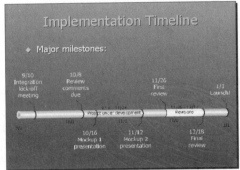

Figure 13-1. Two looks at the same slide: Before Visio, the slide used only text to convey its message. After replacing bullets with a Visio timeline, the slide's purpose is much clearer.

In the past, many Office customers used PowerPoint as their primary diagramming tool mostly because it was already on their desktop and included reasonably simple drawing tools. However, you can create so many more kinds of diagrams in Visio than PowerPoint, and revise them far more easily, that it's well worthwhile to use Visio as the diagramming extension to your PowerPoint presentation. Plus, the diagrams you create in Visio can be saved separately from the presentation and used for other purposes.

Methods for Adding Shapes and Diagrams to Slides

The process for getting your Visio diagram into PowerPoint doesn't have to be any more complex than copying and pasting. However, there are a couple of different ways you can copy in Visio depending on what you want to do, and there are a couple of different ways to paste in PowerPoint, depending on how you want to use the item you copied.

Here's a summary of the techniques you can use to display Visio shapes and diagrams in PowerPoint slides:

- **Copy shapes** If you have a shape or several shapes in Visio that you want to use on a slide, select the shapes, press Ctrl+C to copy them, and then in PowerPoint press Ctrl+V to paste them.

- **Copy a drawing**   If you want to use an entire, one-page Visio diagram on a slide, use the Copy Drawing command on the Edit menu in Visio, and then paste it on a slide.

- **Edit in place**   If you just need a quick Visio diagram to use one time only on a slide, you can open Visio from within PowerPoint to do what's called *in-place editing*.

- **Link or embed**   If you want to create a Visio diagram as a separate file so that you can revise it more easily or use it in other documents besides the presentation, create your diagram, and then *link* or *embed* a copy of it on a slide.

> For details about linking, embedding, and in-place editing, see Chapter 7, "Using Visio Diagrams with Other Programs."

Formatting Visio Diagrams for PowerPoint Slides

Text that looks fine in a Visio diagram can be too small to read on a PowerPoint slide. Frankly, this can be irritating when you want that flowchart or diagram to occupy a prominent and readable position in your presentation. The default text size for most Visio drawing types is 8 to 12 points, which is readable when printed or when you're sitting right in front of the computer monitor. When copied onto a slide and projected onto a larger screen, however, the text can get lost.

A guideline for slide text that will be projected onto a large screen is to use 24-point type. In a Visio diagram that uses shapes formatted for 8- to 12-point type, you will probably have to fuss a bit with both the shape size and the text format if you really want to make sure that the diagram's text can be read in a big room.

Inside Out

Judging text readability

To determine whether the text in your diagram will be readable in a projected presentation, step back from your computer monitor a distance of about eight times the width of the diagram. For example, for a diagram that's 8 inches wide, step back about 5 feet (8 inches times 8, or 64 inches).

Formatting Visio Text for Slides

The simplest way to increase the font size of text in a diagram is to select the text or shapes you want to resize, and then enter a larger font size in the Font Size list on the Format Text toolbar.

Tip   Type a Font Size on the toolbar
You might find it faster to type directly in the Font Size box on the Format Text toolbar than to use the arrow buttons to scroll the size up and down. For example, to set text to 24 points, select the text or a shape with text you want to change, type **24** in the Font Size box, and then press Enter.

If the text becomes too large to fit in the shape (which, for example, typically happens when you set text in a flowchart shape to 24 points), you can do one or both of the following:

Text Block tool

● Use the Text Block tool to move the position of the text without resizing the shape.

● Drag a selection handle on the shape to resize it to fit the text.

As discussed in other chapters about specific diagram types, some shapes require other methods for resizing text or include protection locks that prevent you from resizing or reformatting them. Refer to the chapter about your diagram type for more information about working with those shapes.

Quickly Copying Text Formats

Format Painter

If your diagram contains one shape with text that's formatted the way you want, you can copy that shape's format to any other shape. To do this, select the formatted shape, click the Format Painter button on the Standard toolbar, and then click the shape to which you want to apply the same format. To undo the results, press Ctrl+Z.

For details, see "Formatting Text," page 110.

Using Styles to Format Text

If you're working in a Visio template using styles to format the text, you can quickly format all the text to which a particular style has been applied by redefining the style. This technique is somewhat advanced, primarily because most people don't use styles much in Visio. However, it's a good method for ensuring consistency, particularly in a diagram with many shapes.

For example, in a flowchart, text in most of the basic flowchart shapes is formatted with the Flow Normal style, which is displayed in the Styles list on the Formatting toolbar when you select a shape, as Figure 13-2 shows. You can choose Format, Define Styles, choose Flow Normal in the Styles list, and then click the Text button to define a different format for the style, such as 12-point type. When you apply the change, all text formatted with the Flow Normal style will appear in 12-point type.

Figure 13-2.   If you select a shape that is formatted with a style, the style's name appears in the Styles list on the Formatting toolbar. Editing styles is a quick way to reformat shapes.

For details about working with styles in Visio, see "Understanding Text, Line, and Fill Styles," page 681.

Adjusting Visio Text Colors for PowerPoint

Besides making the text bigger, you can make Visio text more distinct by using a text color that contrasts sharply with the background. For presentations projected onto a large screen in a darkened room, light text on a dark background tends to be most readable. The dark background absorbs the light emitted by the projector, and the contrast with the light-colored foreground elements, such as your text, makes the slide more readable. If the Visio text is in a shape, make sure the text color and shape fill color contrast. If the Visio text is on a transparent background, so that the slide's background shows through when you add the Visio diagram to PowerPoint, you might have to change the text color in Visio for readability.

You can use one of the techniques mentioned earlier to format text with a different color (for example, use the Format Painter button or redefine the text style). You can also experiment with different colors in your diagram by applying a color scheme. White or yellow text is usually quite readable against a slide's dark background, but not very readable on a white drawing page in Visio. Light gray text on a white page in Visio is readable and also looks good against many of the dark backgrounds in PowerPoint.

To apply a color scheme to a diagram, right-click the drawing page, and then choose Color Schemes to open the Color Schemes dialog box, as Figure 13-3 shows. Choose one of the schemes in the dialog box, and then click OK. If you don't like the results, press Ctrl+Z to undo them.

> **Note** If you don't see the Color Schemes command, and it doesn't appear on the Shape, Action menu, select Tools, Add-Ons, Visio Extras, Color Schemes. For details, see "Working with Color Schemes," page 59.

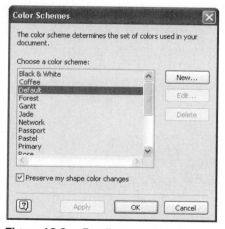

Figure 13-3. For diagram types that support the use of color schemes, you can quickly format shapes by choosing Tools, Add-Ons, Visio Extras, Color Schemes.

Applying PowerPoint Colors to a Visio Diagram

If you create a Visio diagram from within PowerPoint, Visio can create a color scheme based on the PowerPoint slide. This technique works only for the Visio diagram types that support the use of color schemes, which includes most of the business-oriented templates in Visio Standard 2003 and Visio Professional 2003.

For a list of diagram types that support color schemes, see "Working with Color Schemes," page 59.

Troubleshooting

You need text in Visio to be a specific color that doesn't show up well on a slide

What if you really don't want to change the text color in Visio? Try one of the following formatting ideas:

- **Apply a background** In a diagram without a background, adding a background shape from the Backgrounds stencil can make text stand out more. You can also create a background page manually (choose Insert, Page) and then apply it to the foreground.

- **Draw a box behind shapes** You can draw a box, and then fill it with solid color and move it behind the areas you want to set off. To move the box behind everything else, select it, and then choose Shape, Order, Send To Back.

- **Use solid color behind the text** If you don't want a background, and the text is too dark to be easily read when you add the diagram to a slide, you can add an opaque background that will only appear behind the text box. To do this, select the shapes containing the text, and choose Format, Text. Click the Text Block tab, as shown in Figure 13-4. Under Text Background, select Solid Color, choose a contrasting color, and then click OK.

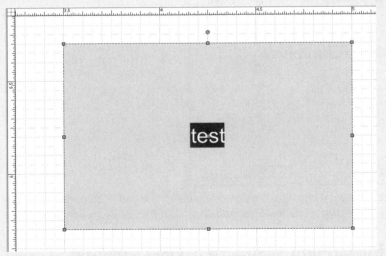

Figure 13-4.   In the Text dialogue box (Format, Text), you can apply a solid block of color that will appear behind the shape's text. Make sure to apply a color that's different than the font's color.

With this technique, you work in the PowerPoint slide and use the Insert, Object command to open a Visio window within PowerPoint, where you can create a diagram. Because the diagram is an inserted object, you can display the slide at any time and double-click the diagram to edit it with the Visio drawing tools. The flip side of this technique is that the diagram is saved as an embedded object within with the presentation. It doesn't exist as a separate .VSD file unless you explicitly save a copy of it while you're in Visio by using the Save As command.

Follow these steps to create a Visio diagram with a slide's color scheme:

1   In PowerPoint, display the slide to which you want to add a Visio diagram, and then choose Insert, Object.

2   Make sure the Create New option is selected. In the Object Type list, select Microsoft Visio Drawing, and then click OK.

3   Choose the drawing type you want, and then click OK.

   Visio displays a message asking whether you want to apply the PowerPoint color scheme to your diagram.

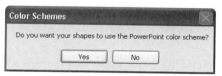

4   Click Yes.

5   Create the diagram as usual. To return to the PowerPoint slide, click anywhere on the slide outside of the diagram.

For details about embedded Visio objects, see the next section, "Pasting and Embedding a Diagram on a Slide."

Pasting and Embedding a Diagram on a Slide

When you embed a Visio diagram in PowerPoint, you add an editable copy of the diagram to a slide. You can then edit in place, which means that you can open a Visio drawing window from within PowerPoint. The original Visio drawing file, however, doesn't reflect any changes you make. An advantage of working this way is that unlike the diagram linking method, this technique doesn't include any links to update or break. You don't have to worry about moving or renaming the original drawing file. If you want to revise the diagram specifically for the purposes of the presentation without affecting the original—for example, modifying colors for projection—embedding is what you want to do.

Inside Out

Pasting from Visio into PowerPoint

When you copy from Visio and paste in PowerPoint using the Paste command or Ctrl+V, you're in fact embedding a Visio object on a slide. Double-click the embedded object to edit it.

The drawback to embedding is that it increases the file size of your presentation by storing potentially large Visio objects in the presentation file.

Embed when:

- You want to be able to revise the diagram as it appears on the slide, but don't need to put those changes in the original Visio file.
- You want to edit your diagram within PowerPoint without having to switch between programs.
- You don't want to track a separate Visio drawing file along with your PowerPoint file, and presentation file size is not an issue.
- You want to create an animated build of your Visio diagram in PowerPoint.
- You want to use only some shapes from a diagram on your slide, and you want to be able to edit those shapes.

Embedding Shapes or Diagrams on a Slide

You can embed selected shapes or the contents of an entire drawing page. The simplest way to embed shapes is to select the ones you want in Visio, press Ctrl+C to copy them, and then display a slide in PowerPoint and press Ctrl+V to paste them. You can also drag shapes from Visio to PowerPoint, but you'll remove the shapes from Visio altogether unless you press Ctrl while dragging. Pressing the Ctrl key as you drag always drags a copy of a Visio shape.

Follow these steps to embed an entire Visio page on a PowerPoint slide:

1   In Visio, display the diagram you want to embed. If the diagram has multiple pages, display the page that you want to embed.

2   Make sure nothing is selected, and then choose Edit, Copy Drawing.

3   In PowerPoint, display the slide to which you want to add the diagram, and then press Ctrl+V (or click the Paste button on the Standard toolbar, or choose Edit, Paste).

PowerPoint pastes the diagram as an embedded object that you can edit by double-clicking it.

Editing an Embedded Diagram in Place

To edit an embedded diagram in PowerPoint, double-click it. A Visio drawing window opens, as Figure 13-5 shows, and a special set of Visio menus and toolbars (technically called the in-place editing controls) temporarily replaces most of the PowerPoint menus and tools. If your original Visio file had stencils, they open as well. You can even add shapes by dragging from one of the open stencils or by opening the stencil you need. After you finish editing, click on the slide outside the Visio drawing window to return control to PowerPoint.

Figure 13-5. When you embed a Visio diagram on a slide, you can double-click the diagram to open it in place for editing.

Linking and Embedding Multiple-Page Diagrams

When you have a multiple-page Visio diagram that you want to use in a PowerPoint presentation, you must copy it one page at a time. Only the page displayed at the time you choose the Copy Drawing command appears on the slide when you paste. You can use the Paste button or command in PowerPoint to paste each page as an embedded object, or the Paste Special command to paste each page as a linked object.

Linking Visio and PowerPoint

When you link your diagram to a slide, you keep the original Visio drawing file and create a copy of it in PowerPoint that's linked to the original. You can then make changes to the original drawing file and update the copy on the slide to reflect the changes.

Link when:

- You're going to change your source diagram frequently.
- You want your presentation to include the latest version.
- You need to limit the size of your presentation file. (The actual drawing is stored in the Visio source file. Only a copy is displayed within your presentation.)

> **Note** A link is a reference to a file saved in a specific location on a disk. You must save the drawing you want to link by choosing File, Save.

Linking a Diagram to a Slide

When a diagram is linked, you have to manage two files: the Visio drawing file and the PowerPoint presentation file. Because you link to a diagram file in a specific location, you have to keep the two files together.

Follow these steps to link a Visio diagram to a PowerPoint slide:

1. Open the diagram you want to use in the presentation. If the diagram has more than one page, display the page you want to appear on the slide.

2. If you haven't done so already, save the diagram (click the Save button on the Standard toolbar, or press Ctrl+S).

> **Tip** The link that PowerPoint creates is really just a reference to the Visio drawing file, so you need to give that file a name before proceeding.

3. Make sure nothing on the drawing is selected, and then choose Edit, Copy Drawing.

4. Keep Visio open, and start PowerPoint. If PowerPoint is already open, press Alt+Tab to switch to it.

> **Note** The Visio application must remain open for PowerPoint to paste and link the diagram.

5. Display the slide where you want the Visio diagram to appear, and then choose Edit, Paste Special.

6. Select Paste Link, as Figure 13-6 shows.

7. Click OK to paste and link the diagram.

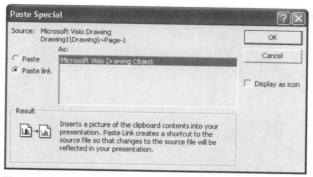

Figure 13-6. When you paste a drawing as a link, you ensure that the most up-to-date version of the drawing is used in the presentation.

Editing and Updating Linked Diagrams

Every time you open a presentation file containing linked objects, including Visio diagrams, PowerPoint prompts you to update the links so that the slides display the latest version of your Visio diagrams, as Figure 13-7 shows. You can also manually update a linked diagram at any time, such as when you're switching back and forth between PowerPoint and Visio to refine a presentation.

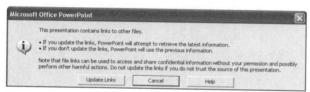

Figure 13-7. When you open a presentation containing linked objects such as Visio diagrams, you'll see a message similar to this one. Click Update Links to update the linked objects with the latest versions.

When you're working on a PowerPoint slide that contains a linked Visio diagram, you can right-click the diagram to display a shortcut menu that contains commands for working with the linked diagram, as Figure 13-8 shows. Depending on the version of PowerPoint you are using, the command names vary slightly, as follows:

- Linked Visio Object, Edit (or Edit VISIO Link)
- Linked Visio Object, Open (Open VISIO Link)
- Update Link

Use the Edit or Open command to open a Visio drawing window with the diagram, where you can edit it. Save your changes in Visio, and then return to PowerPoint and use the Update Link command to see the changes immediately.

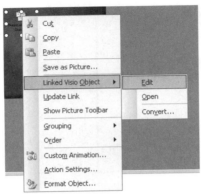

Figure 13-8. You can right-click a linked slide to display commands for editing the link.

To see all the linked diagrams in a presentation, use the Links command on the Edit menu. The Links dialog box lists all the linked objects (including Visio diagrams and other objects) and displays the status of the link. To update any of the links that are listed, select the one you want, and then click Update Now.

Troubleshooting

The message to update links gets in the way of the presentation

If you don't want PowerPoint to automatically update a link every time you open the presentation file, you can specify a manual link. If you don't want to see the update message when you start PowerPoint, you can specify that a link is manual. You'll still be able to update the link, but you control when. To do this, choose Edit, Links in PowerPoint. In the Links dialog box, select a link, and then select Manual as the Update option. Click Close. When you want to update the link, return to the Links dialog box in PowerPoint and choose Update Now.

Repairing Links When Files Are Moved or Renamed

If PowerPoint can't find a Visio diagram that is linked to a slide, you'll see a message the next time you update the links that says that the links were unavailable, as Figure 13-9 shows. Even so, the last version of the diagram that you linked to the slide still appears—the diagram doesn't disappear from the slide, but it might be out of date. If you moved or renamed the original Visio drawing file, you can tell PowerPoint how to redirect the link so that you can update the diagram.

Figure 13-9. If PowerPoint can't find a file that is linked to a slide, this message is displayed.

Follow these steps to reconnect a linked diagram:

1 In PowerPoint, select Edit, Links.

The Links dialog box appears and lists all linked objects in the presentation. If Unavailable appears in the Update column it means the link for that object is broken, as Figure 13-10 shows.

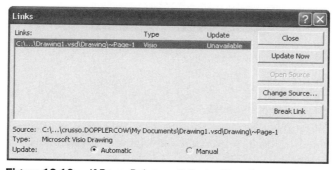

Figure 13-10. If PowerPoint can't find a file referenced by a link, the file is listed as Unavailable.

2 Click the linked object you want to reconnect, and then click Change Source.

3 In the Change Source dialog box, locate the moved or renamed file, and then click OK.

4 In the Links dialog box, click Update Now to update the diagram.

5 Click OK.

Converting Linked Diagrams to Pictures

You can deliberately break a link between a slide and a Visio diagram to convert shapes to pictures that you can edit in PowerPoint using its drawing tools (see Figure 13-11). It's best to do this only after you no longer need the diagram in the slide to match the original Visio file. In addition, a useful side-effect of breaking links is that you no longer see the Unavailable message as PowerPoint searches for linked files. If you need the Visio drawing only for the purposes of the presentation, you might find it faster to edit shapes this way.

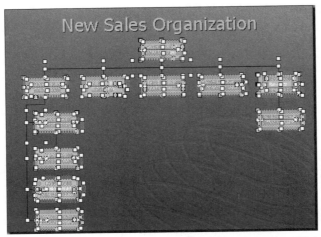

Figure 13-11. You can convert each shape in a linked Visio diagram to pictures that can be edited with the PowerPoint drawing tools.

Follow these steps to break a link:

1 In PowerPoint, choose Edit, Links.

2 In the Links dialog box, select the link you want to break, and then click Break Link. PowerPoint discards the reference to the original Visio file, which is no longer listed in the dialog box.

3 Click Close to convert the diagram to a metafile picture.

4 Display the slide containing the picture. Right-click the image, click Grouping, and then click Ungroup. A message appears, asking whether you want to convert the picture to a Microsoft Office drawing.

5 Click Yes. The shapes and text are converted to pictures.

Animating and Building Visio Diagrams in PowerPoint

You can use the PowerPoint build features to animate Visio shapes on your slides. Builds are particularly handy for introducing complex ideas. If you illustrate the concept in Visio, you can display it, one element at a time, in your presentation. PowerPoint offers two types of builds that you can use with Visio diagrams, *animated builds* and *sequential slide builds*.

In an animated build, you copy elements of a Visio drawing individually, paste or embed them on a slide, and then animate each element in PowerPoint to build the drawing, as Figure 13-12 shows. You can even control the way different parts of a drawing appear on a slide, allowing elements to enter the slide from different directions. This technique adds a sense of motion and direction to otherwise static shapes, which you can use to convey a message of change or to introduce visual concepts gradually. (A build can also function as gratuitous razzle-dazzle to keep the audience awake.)

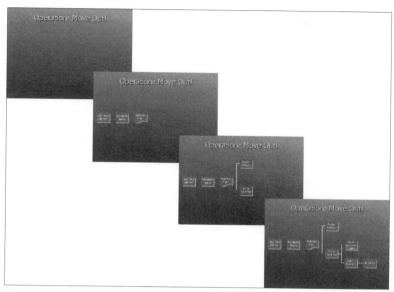

Figure 13-12. An animated build displays elements one at a time on a slide.

In a sequential slide build, you paste the entire drawing on one slide, ungroup it, then copy and paste parts of the drawing onto successive slides. By moving through consecutive slides, you build the entire drawing sequentially over successive slides without having to animate the elements.

With either technique, the Visio shapes and diagrams you use in a build cannot be linked objects. You can paste or embed them (the same thing, really), but you can't maintain a link between a diagram used for builds and its original Visio file.

Creating Diagrams for PowerPoint Animation

When you want to animate a Visio shape on a PowerPoint slide, it's pretty straightforward: Copy the shape, paste it on the slide, and then use PowerPoint's animation tools to make it dance. When you want to animate a larger diagram so that shapes in the diagram appear on the slide at different times or with special effects, the technique is somewhat more complicated. You copy each element in the diagram that you want to animate separately. It's a little easier on the PowerPoint end if you copy the Visio sections in the order in which you want to animate them, but it isn't necessary.

For example, suppose you have a flowchart of a new process that you want to present to your group. Rather than overwhelm your colleagues with the complexity of the process all at once, you want to bring sections of the flowchart onto your slide in a step-by-step fashion as you explain them. To do this, you copy all the shapes in your flowchart that make up step 1, as Figure 13-13 shows. In PowerPoint, you paste the shapes and then repeat for each set of shapes that represent a step. After all the Visio steps appear on the slide, you use the Slide Show, Custom Animation command (in Microsoft PowerPoint 97 and later versions) to set the effects you want, as Figure 13-14 shows.

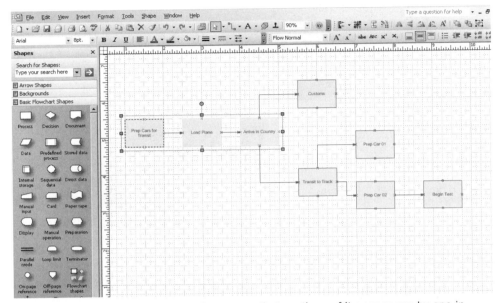

Figure 13-13. To animate a Visio diagram so that sections of it appear one by one in PowerPoint, copy and paste each section you want to animate separately.

Using PowerPoint Clip Art and Images in Visio

If you work a lot in PowerPoint, you might find that you can't live without a particular PowerPoint shape or clip art graphic. You can copy PowerPoint clip art and shapes and then paste them onto the Visio drawing page. If the pasted object doesn't behave as you expect, it might have been converted to a different type of object. For example, PowerPoint titles and bullet points are pasted into Visio as pictures (in metafile format), not text.

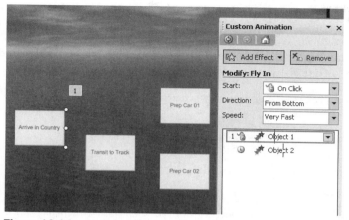

Figure 13-14. In PowerPoint, each section you paste appears in the Custom Animation dialog box as a separate Visio object that you can animate.

Note When you paste shapes on a slide for animation, they become embedded objects that you can edit—even after you've animated them. Just double-click the shape or section to open a Visio window for editing.

Showing Visio Diagrams Sequentially in Slides

You can display a Visio diagram, or parts of it, as part of a series of sequential slides. The idea is that as you display each slide in a series, a new part of the diagram appears until the entire diagram is displayed. When you can animate sections of a diagram separately on one slide, why use this technique? There are a couple of reasons. When you're printing handouts of your presentation and you want the diagram to appear incrementally in both the slide show and in the handouts, you need to set it up this way. An animated diagram appears in its entirety on handouts. Also, if you want to describe each diagram section with a new title or bullet points when it appears, you have to use a sequential build.

The easiest way to distribute a Visio diagram over several slides is to copy the entire diagram in Visio (Edit, Copy Drawing), paste it on a slide using Ctrl + V or the Paste button on the Standard toolbar, and then ungroup it (Draw, Ungroup in PowerPoint). Then select a portion of the ungrouped diagram, copy it (Ctrl+C), and paste the copy onto a different slide. The key to this technique is that the pasted section appears on the new slide in the same location it occupied on the original slide. In a slide show, the sections of your diagram reappear in the correct locations as the diagram is built. The drawback to using this technique is that when you ungroup the Visio diagram in PowerPoint, the diagram is converted to a picture—a different type of object—that you can no longer edit with Visio. However, you can edit the ungrouped objects with the PowerPoint drawing tools.

Delivering a Slide Show in Visio

If you don't have PowerPoint or don't want to use it, you can deliver a slide show in Visio. The Full Screen view in Visio displays the drawing page alone without the toolbars and menu in a similar fashion to Slide Show view in PowerPoint, as Figure 13-15 shows.

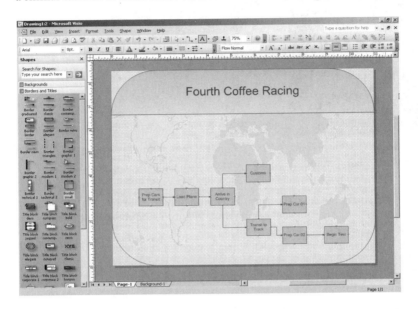

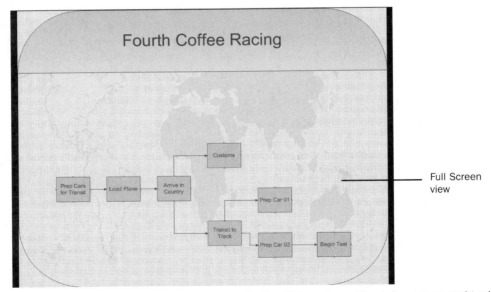

Figure 13-15. In Full Screen view, you can display Visio pages without the menus and toolbars, as you would in a slide show.

You can navigate from one page in the drawing file to the next using the keyboard shortcuts, just as you can display one slide after another in PowerPoint.

Of course, it's easier to create a presentation using a tool designed specifically for that purpose—PowerPoint includes many handy features, such as outlines and the slide sorter, that Visio doesn't have. However, it's possible to set up a Visio file with multiple pages, one for each slide, and deliver it on the screen as you would a PowerPoint presentation.

> **Tip** Press F5 to display a drawing page in Full Screen view.

Follow these general steps to create a presentation in Visio:

1   To set up the pages in the drawing file to look like slides, choose File, Page Setup, and then specify letter-sized, landscape-oriented pages. Click OK.

2   To design a background for the slides, choose Insert, New Page, and under Page Properties, select Background as the Type. Click OK. On the background page, add one of the designs from the Backgrounds stencil or add other shapes and graphics that you want to appear on all the slides.

3   To add a foreground page for each slide in the presentation, choose Insert, New Page, and under Page Properties, select Foreground as the Type, and in the Background list, select the name of the background page you created in step 2.

4   Add text and shapes to each page (slide).

5   To deliver the presentation, choose View, Full Screen or press F5. See Table 13-1 for page navigation techniques.

6   To return to the normal view in Visio, which includes toolbars and menus, press F5 again, the Esc key, or right-click a page, and then click Close.

> **Note** Full Screen view is for display only. You can't make changes or edit the shapes.

Table 13-1. Navigating Between Pages in Full-Screen View

Page to Display	Techniques
Next page	Click the screen Press the Right Arrow key Press the Page Down key Press the N key
Previous page	Right-click the screen and choose Previous Page Press the Left Arrow key Press the Page Up key Press the P key
Specific page anywhere in the drawing file	Right-click the screen, choose Go To, and then select the page name

Chapter 13

Inside Out

Change the Full Screen view background

The background in Full Screen view doesn't have to be black. Even though Visio displays your page like a slide on a black background, you can specify a different color. To customize the background color, choose Tools, Options, and then click the View tab. Under Color Settings, change the color setting for Full Screen Background. Presto!

Part 3
Inside Network Diagrams

Chapter 14

Creating Network Diagrams

If the monster in your closet is a jumble of network cable and blinking equipment, perhaps it's time to bring the beast down to size in a Microsoft Office Visio 2003 diagram. Among the earliest adopters of the Visio application were IT professionals and network administrators who discovered how easy it could be to create a picture of their network. Shapes that represent network devices snap together to show you what you have or to demonstrate the system you would like. With Visio, you can create network diagrams that provide necessary documentation for training, proposals, troubleshooting, planning, and so on. Network diagrams easily integrate with documents that you create in other programs, such as budget and asset worksheets you create in Microsoft Office Excel 2003 or presentations you deliver in Microsoft Office PowerPoint 2003.

Use the new and improved basic network diagram to make sharp diagrams that show how different pieces of equipment can be installed. These new shapes look better and you can choose from 22 predefined definitions to generate reports of your shapes. The detailed network diagram template has shapes included for documenting the physical and local topology of your network. Not only do the shapes perform better, but they are better looking, too.

Keep in mind that Visio Standard includes basic network equipment shapes. Visio Professional expands the equipment collection and provides additional shapes for diagramming local area networks (LANs) and wide area networks (WANs) as well as additional templates for detailing a directory services schema. Shapes from either version of Visio can be data-driven—that is, linked to your spreadsheet or database of asset information—so that your diagram provides an accurate and up-to-date picture of your network. This chapter describes how to use Visio to create logical and physical network diagrams and directory services diagrams.

Starting a Network Diagram

The tools in Visio Standard and Visio Professional work best for creating high-level logical designs for presentations and proposals. These high-level network diagrams need to be accurate, but you typically don't need to show specific network equipment in detail, as Figure 14-1 shows. Both Visio Standard and Visio Professional include shapes for diagramming a small-sized or medium-sized network; Visio Professional simply includes more shapes.

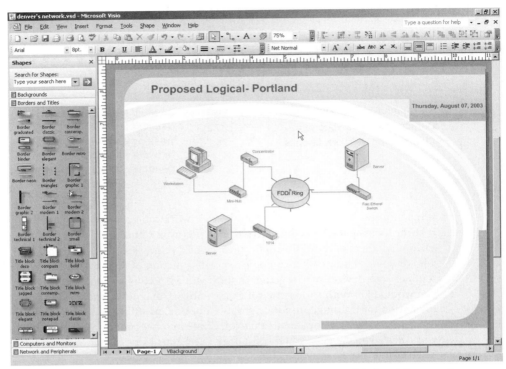

Figure 14-1. A high-level logical network diagram provides a useful visual for reports, proposals, and presentations.

The bit about diagramming a "small-sized to medium-sized network" is important. What you're doing is dragging Visio shapes that look like network equipment onto the drawing page, one by one. One network specialist in a Visio focus group complained that Visio wasn't much better than using pen and paper. That's an extreme view, but it represents a valid point for people in charge of large networks. You'll probably want a more automated tool if you want to show every hub, router, and workstation on your network. That tool used to be Visio 2000 Enterprise Edition, which included the AutoDiscovery And Layout tool. Although that product is no longer supported, its automated tools are still available as add-ins.

What if you need more detailed documentation for troubleshooting or asset management? Your network diagrams can include this type of information, such as a device's model, tracking number, and network address. Network shapes include built-in *custom properties*, which you can use as data entry fields to store detailed attributes with each shape. In turn, the data you enter helps you troubleshoot problem areas, generate cost estimates and other reports, and perform quick inventories.

Choosing a Network Template

To start a new network diagram of any type, it's best to start with a template, which opens up the stencils containing the shapes you'll need and sets up the drawing page for you. Depend-

Creating Network Diagrams

ing on the Visio product version you have, you might not have much of a choice when it comes to choosing a network template. Visio Standard includes only one (Basic Network). Visio Professional includes several more, as well as all the shapes that are in Visio Standard.

Visio Standard Network Tools

If you have Visio Standard, you have the Basic Network template, which is useful for diagramming a simple network. Figure 14-2 shows a simple network diagram in Visio Professional. When you start a network diagram with this template, Visio opens an unscaled, letter-sized drawing page and the following stencils:

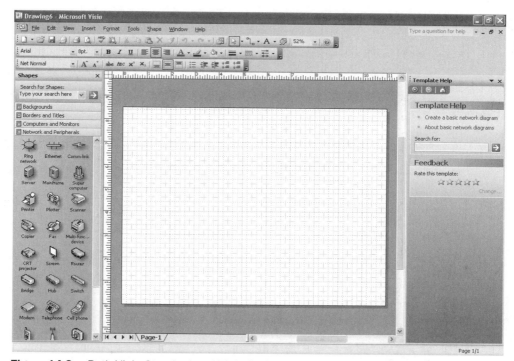

Figure 14-2. Both Visio Standard and Visio Professional include the Basic Network template, which was used to diagram this e-commerce server.

- **Computers And Monitors**   As the name implies, this stencil includes PCs, iMacs, tablet computers, and monitors.

- **Network And Peripherals**   This stencil includes everything from network connection shapes, such as the Ring Network shape, to servers, bridges, and hubs. It also contains mainframes, network controllers, cell phones, modems, firewalls, and even a legend.

- **Borders And Titles**   This stencil contains a set of ornamental page borders and title shapes for identifying your diagram.

● **Backgrounds**   This stencil contains decorative images for formatting the background of your diagram. The Background World and Background Expedition shapes are useful images for WANs.

There is no longer a 3D Shapes stencil. All of these Visio 2003 shapes are three-dimensional.

Visio Professional Network Tools

If you have Visio Professional, in addition to the Basic Network template, you also have the Detailed Network Diagram template, shown in Figure 14-3. Use this template to diagram the following:

● Logical networks that represent the equipment in a network and their interconnections.

● Physical networks that show physical connections between network equipment, or site-specific layouts, such as a server room.

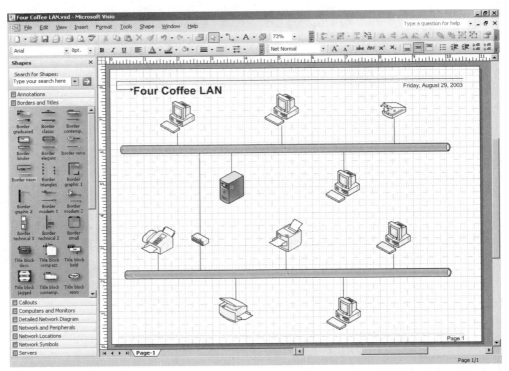

Figure 14-3.   With Visio Professional, you can use the Detailed Network Diagram template to assemble a network diagram quickly.

Visio Professional also includes the Microsoft Active Directory, LDAP (Lightweight Directory Access Protocol) Directory, Novell Directory Services, and Rack Diagram templates. We'll discuss those later in this chapter.

The Detailed Network Diagram template opens the following stencils:

- **Borders And Titles**   This stencil contains typical borders and titles.
- **Annotations**   This stencil includes several annotation shapes that can be used to label equipment or functions. Also included are column, break line, and direction shapes.
- **Callouts**   This stencil provides various callouts to label shapes and place notes within the diagram.
- **Computers And Monitors**   As the name implies, this stencil contains computers and monitors.
- **Network And Peripherals**   This stencil contains a wider variety of devices, such as hubs, bridges, routers, and servers.
- **Servers**   This stencil contains a variety of servers.
- **Detailed Network Diagram**   This stencil contains shapes such as the A/B switchbox, external hard drive, radio tower, repeater, and smart card reader.
- **Network Locations**   This stencil contains shapes representing buildings, such as house, university building, and government building.
- **Network Symbols**   This stencil contains shapes representing ISDN switches, small hubs, terminal servers, and many other network symbols.

> **Note**   Visio Professional includes network templates for creating a directory diagram of Active Directory, Novell Directory Services, and LDAP Directory. For details about using these templates, see "Creating a Directory Diagram," page 390.

Setting Up a New Network Diagram

To set up a new network diagram, follow these steps:

1 Choose File, New, Network, and then choose the name of the template you want. Visio opens a letter-sized, blank drawing page and the appropriate stencils.

2 If you want to change the size or orientation of the page, choose File, Page Setup, click the Page Size tab, and then specify the page settings you want.

3 If you plan to print your network diagram, click the Print Setup tab, and make sure that the page size that you set on the Page Size tab will work with your printer.

> **Note**   For details about how page size and printer settings interact, see "Printing Diagrams of Any Size," page 242.

4 If you started your diagram with the Detailed Network Diagram template, click the Drawing Scale tab, and then change the Custom Scale setting if you want.

5 Click OK to close the Page Setup dialog box.

6 If you want to customize the grid that's displayed on the drawing page, choose Tools, Ruler & Grid. In the Grid area, specify the settings you want, and then click OK.

For details about grid settings, see "Controlling Grid Spacing and Origin," page 434.

Now that you have verified that the template created the size and style of page you want, you can start adding shapes to your diagram. Start with the physical topology shapes if you're creating a logical diagram. For a WAN, start with the background image you want to use, such as a map, an imported graphic or clip art, or a shape from the Backgrounds stencil.

After you have connected all the network equipment that you want to represent in your diagram, you have several options, which are covered later in this chapter:

- Assign shapes to layers to view or print categories of shapes.
- Edit the network shapes.
- Import or add data to shapes, and then generate reports.
- Link shapes to other drawing pages, other files, or World Wide Web locations.

Defining Network Topology

The place to start when diagramming a network is with the physical topology. Both Visio Standard and Visio Professional include shapes for linear (straight) bus, star, star-wired (token ring), dual ring (FDDI), and linear bus Ethernet topologies. The topology shapes all work in a similar manner. You drop them on the drawing page first. Then you add the nodes you want to display and drag them into approximate position around the topology shape. To connect them, drag a yellow control handle from the topology shape and glue it to a blue connection point on another shape, as Figure 14-4 shows. The handle turns red when it's glued.

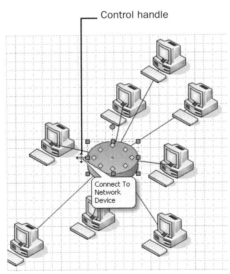

Control handle

Connect To Network Device

Figure 14-4. To connect nodes to a network, drag a yellow control handle from the topology shape to a connection point on the node. When you point to a control handle, the pointer changes to a four-way arrow to show that you can drag it.

Topology shapes are located on the Network And Peripherals stencil.

> **Tip** To quickly open a stencil, click the Shapes button on the Standard toolbar, choose Network, and then select the name of the stencil you want.

Attaching Nodes and Devices

Network shapes are designed to connect and stay connected as you drag them around the drawing page. They stay connected because glue keeps them that way. It's possible (and quite common) to drag connecting lines without gluing them. Usually, they look fine on the page and print as expected. However, it doesn't take any longer to glue shapes, and it certainly makes them easier to rearrange later. For example, when you move a workstation shape that's glued to a topology shape, the connecting line moves as well—and stays connected. Figure 14-5 shows how to glue shapes together.

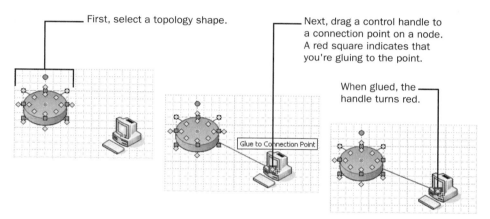

First, select a topology shape.

Next, drag a control handle to a connection point on a node. A red square indicates that you're gluing to the point.

When glued, the handle turns red.

Glue to Connection Point

Figure 14-5. Visio tells you when you're gluing shapes; a red square around a point shows that the line will be glued to the point. In addition, a ScreenTip appears when you position the mouse over a point that you can glue to.

What if you want to attach more than eight nodes to a topology shape? All the topology shapes include eight control handles. The quick and dirty way to get more connections is to drag a second topology shape on top of the first one, and then use the second shape to connect more nodes. You should do this only after you have connected the first topology shape to its devices. A downside of this method is that your diagram now includes two shapes that in reality represent only one bus or ring, and if you generate reports based on the diagram, you could get inaccurate results.

Inside Out

Adding connection points

You can add connection points to shapes and then draw lines between the points. To add a connection point, select the Connection Point tool on the Standard toolbar, press the Ctrl key, and then click to add a point. It helps to zoom in as you do this.

Drawing Network Connections

Line tool

There are a couple of different ways to represent connections, such as the coaxial or fiber-optic cable between devices in a network. You can always draw them using the Line tool or Pencil tool on the Drawing toolbar, which is a quick way to represent network connections. To draw connections, click the tool you want on the Standard toolbar, and then draw from a connection point on one shape to a connection point on another. If you connect shapes this way, you won't be able to represent the connections in any reports that you create for the diagram, unless you add custom properties to the lines.

Pencil tool

Visio also includes several shapes that you can use to connect network nodes, as Figure 14-6 shows. The shapes are designed to provide different routing behaviors and other attributes that you don't get by drawing connections with the Line tool.

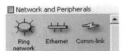

Figure 14-6. You can connect devices in a network using these and other connector shapes, which appear on the Network And Peripherals stencil.

Here are some of your connecting options when designing a network:

- **Use the Dynamic Connector** This shape is useful if you're showing a multitude of devices and want Visio to lay them out automatically for you. It appears on several stencils including the Basic Flowchart Shapes and Object Relational stencils. This shape has the same effect as using the Connector tool. After you connect shapes with the Dynamic Connector, use the Lay Out Shapes command on the Shape menu for automatic layout and routing. The best advice for using the Lay Out Shapes command is to remember that the results can be undone by pressing Ctrl+Z. Then you can try different settings to see which provides the best results.

For details, see "Laying Out Shapes Automatically," page 70.

Tip The Dynamic Connector shape does not include custom properties, so if you're creating reports based on your diagram's contents, connections created with this tool won't be included.

- **Use the Connector tool**   In a large network, it might be quickest to start with the nodes, and then connect them with the Connector tool on the Standard toolbar. You can also select the Connector tool and then drag shapes from stencils onto the drawing page. The shapes will be added with connections between them.

- **Use connector shapes**   Other connector shapes that are available on the Connector stencil (Line Connector and Line-Curve Connector) work with the Lay Out Shapes command.

- **Use the Comm-Link shape**   The Comm-Link shape uses the common lightning bolt notation for indicating a link to a satellite, microwave tower, the Internet, and so on. It includes custom properties for tracking manufacturer, asset number, and more.

If you're using the Connector tool, the Dynamic Connector shape, or one of the line connector shapes to draw lines between network shapes, you might want to review the information about connections and glue in Chapter 3, "Connecting Shapes." This is particularly good advice if you're hoping to take advantage of the Lay Out Shapes command, which is powerful but can have unpredictable results.

For details about connector shapes, see "Adding Connectors to Your Diagrams," page 63.

Using Layers to Represent Different Networks

When you start a diagram with the Basic Network Diagram template, Visio sets up a drawing page automatically that includes layers you can use to organize shapes. You might not think this is particularly useful, but if, for example, you want to see alternative views of your network based on manufacturer, you can work with layers to do so. By default, Visio creates several manufacturer-specific layers as well as the Network and Connector layers.

As you drag shapes from the network stencils onto the page, they are added to the Network or Connector layer. You can choose to add shapes to the manufacturer-specific layers, and you can create new layers. Layers, however, are stored with a drawing page, not with a shape. If you insert a new page, it does not include the manufacturer layers. It might include the Network or Connector layer, however, which is added to the page when you add a shape that's assigned to that layer. Confusing? Perhaps, but the bottom line is that layers are useful for hiding and showing parts of a network or for selectively printing shapes by manufacturer.

To see the layers that are already included with your network diagram, choose View, Layer Properties. The Layer Properties dialog box lists the layers that have been created for the current page, as Figure 14-7 shows.

Chapter 14

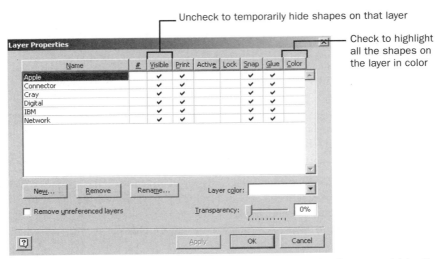

Uncheck to temporarily hide shapes on that layer

Check to highlight all the shapes on the layer in color

Figure 14-7. Visio assigns network shapes to layers by manufacturer, which allows you to work selectively with all the shapes assigned to a particular manufacturer.

For details about all the ways you can work with layers, see "Controlling Shapes with Layers," page 460.

The sections that follow summarize key information for working with layers in network diagrams.

Assigning a Network Shape to a Layer

To take advantage of the organizational possibilities that layers provide, shapes in a diagram must be assigned to a layer. Most network shapes are already assigned to either the Network or Connector layer. These assignments are maintained when you select a new layer assignment. That is, a shape can be assigned to more than one layer.

Follow these steps to assign a shape to a layer:

1 Select a shape, and then choose Format, Layer.

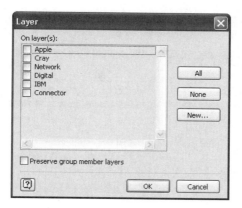

2 In the On Layer(s) box, select the layer you want to assign the shape to. If you want to create a new layer for a manufacturer that isn't listed, click New, type the manufacturer name, and then click OK. Visio assigns the shape to the layer you selected.

3 Click OK.

Viewing Shapes by Layer

You can view a list of the diagram's layers and the shapes assigned to each in the Drawing Explorer window. When you assign shapes to manufacturer layers, the Drawing Explorer provides a quick equipment list. Follow these steps to view a list of the diagram's layers:

1 Choose View, Drawing Explorer Window.

2 Double-click the Foreground Pages folder to see all the pages in your diagram.

3 Double-click the page you're currently working on (or Page-1 if you haven't added or renamed any pages).

4 Double-click the Layers folder.

If nothing happens, your drawing contains no layers. Otherwise, Visio lists all the layers on the page, as Figure 14-8 shows. If you expand a layer, you can see all the shapes assigned to it.

Chapter 14

To see a list of equipment shapes
by manufacturer, expand a layer

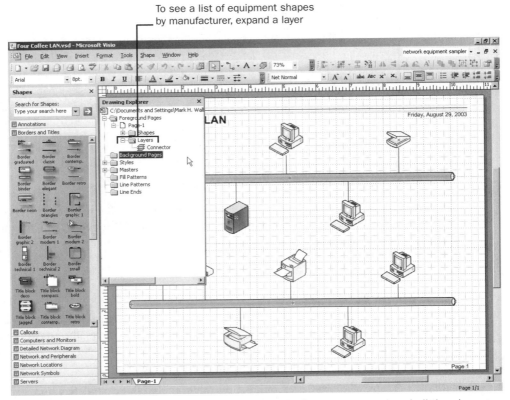

Figure 14-8. The Drawing Explorer window lists all the layers on a page and all the shapes assigned to a particular layer.

> **Tip** Right-click a layer in the Drawing Explorer window to display a shortcut menu with options that allow you to make them Visible, Active, or even delete the layer.

Numbering the Shapes in a Network Diagram

You can keep track of equipment in a network diagram by assigning numbers to shapes. Visio can automatically number shapes, as Figure 14-9 shows, and provide you with options for the style of the number. You can also specify numbering options before you add shapes to the drawing page. That way, they'll be numbered automatically as you add them.

> **Tip** You can switch automatic shape numbering on and off by choosing Shape, Actions, Number Shape On Drop. This command is available only after you have used the Number Shapes command and if no shapes are selected.

Creating Network Diagrams

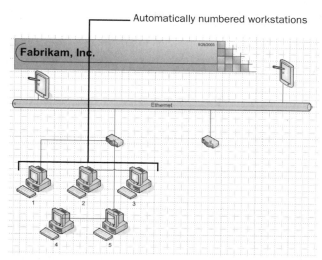

Figure 14-9. You can automatically number devices, nodes, or other shapes in your network diagram.

The Number Shapes command gives you several numbering options. You can do any of the following:

- Number all the shapes in the network diagram sequentially.
- Select a set of shapes, and then have Visio number them sequentially.
- Display a numbering tool on the screen, which lets you add and number shapes in your network diagram as you work.
- Specify a numbering style that automatically numbers each new shape you add to the diagram.

Visio numbers the shapes in the order you specify. If you don't specify an order, shapes are numbered from left to right and top to bottom. You can choose a different order, however, including back to front, which is based on the shape's stacking order (the order in which you dropped them on the page), or the order in which you select them.

To number shapes, follow these steps:

1. Select the shapes you want to number, or cancel all selections to number all the shapes on the page.

2. Choose Tools, Add-Ons, Visio Extras, Number Shapes to display the Number Shapes dialog box, as Figure 14-10 shows.

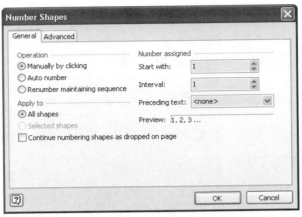

Figure 14-10. With the Number Shapes command, you can number devices sequentially as you add them or after you add them.

3 Choose the shape numbering options you want:

- Under Operation, choose whether to number shapes manually or automatically. The option you choose here determines the options that are available on the Advanced tab.

- Under Number Assigned, choose the numbering style you want to use. Use the Preview box to verify that the numbers look the way you want.

- If you want the numbering sequence to include shapes you add to the page later, select the Continue Numbering Shapes As Dropped On Page check box.

4 Click the Advanced tab, and then choose the following options:

- Under Place Number, indicate where the numbers should be placed with respect to the shape's existing text.

- Under Auto Numbering Sequence, select the order in which shapes are to be numbered. This option isn't available when you number shapes manually.

- Under Apply To Options, indicate whether to number shapes according to their layer assignment.

Tip For a description of each option, click the Help button in the Number Shapes dialog box.

Help

5 Click OK to number the shapes.

Tip To number shapes on other pages of a multiple-page network diagram, display the page, and then repeat the procedure. Shape numbering can be applied to only one page at a time.

The Network And Peripherals stencil contains a nifty new shape called a Legend, which keeps track of every shape that you have placed on the page and even keeps an inventory of how many of the shapes the page contains.

Customizing Network Shapes

In a network diagram of any complexity, you'll probably find that you need to move text around or revise a shape to represent a unique device. Most of the network shapes are actually groups, which means they might not always work the way you expect them to.

The sections that follow describe common editing techniques that work for network shapes. In addition, you can add titles to the page using the shapes from the Borders And Titles stencil.

For details about shape labels, see "Using Visio Shapes to Display Text," page 130.

Editing Label Text

To change the text that appears in a label, you can select the shape, and then type. In past versions of Visio some network shapes didn't work that way, but now all Visio network shapes do.

Text tool

If you're having difficulty typing a label, try clicking the Text tool on the Standard toolbar, and then clicking carefully in the text block you want to edit. Because the equipment shapes are groups, and each shape in a group can have its own text block, the "click and type" rule doesn't always apply—text can sometimes end up in the wrong place.

For details about text in groups, see "Adding and Editing Text in Groups," page 96.

Tip If you have entered custom property data for network shapes, you can display the value of any property as the label text for a network shape. To do this, see "Displaying Values in a Custom Callout," page 132.

 Troubleshooting

When typing to replace a label on a network shape, Visio creates a new label instead of overwriting the existing one

Most network equipment shapes are groups, which means that each shape in the group can have a text block and the group can have a text block. When you try to type a label, sometimes the text appears in a second label and doesn't overwrite the existing text as you expected. It can be easier to find the text block you want to overwrite when you click a group using the Text tool rather than the Pointer tool. You can also open a group in the group window by selecting the shape and then clicking Edit, Open Group or, if the shape has a name, Open <Shape Name>.

Chapter 14

Repositioning Labels

What if you want to move the label? The intention of the network shapes is to make this easy, but in practice, the shortcut is sometimes tricky to use. Shapes include a yellow control handle that you can drag to move the shape's text block, or label, as Figure 14-11 shows. Sometimes the handle seems sticky, and the label lurches farther than you intended. It can help to zoom in very closely, but it might just be quicker to use the manual method of moving a text block: click the Text Block tool on the Standard toolbar (it's located under the Text tool), and then drag the label exactly where you want it.

> **Tip** Use Shift+Ctrl+click to quickly zoom in on a drawing page.

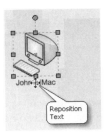

Figure 14-11. Pause the pointer over a control handle to display a ScreenTip about the handle's purpose. Labels on network shapes are designed so that moving the control handle repositions the label.

Adding a Background Behind Text

Connectors in a network diagram can run right through your labels. Sometimes it's impractical to move the labels out of the way, but you can make the text more readable by placing a solid-color background behind it. There are a couple of ways to do this, but this technique is probably quickest:

1 Select a shape with a label, and then choose Format, Text.

2 Click the Text Block tab in the Text dialog box.

3 In the Text Background section, select Solid Color, and then choose a color from the list box.

4 Click OK to fill the area behind the shape's text with the solid color you selected. If you type more text, the area of solid color is adjusted to fit.

Editing Network Equipment Shapes

Regardless of the number of equipment shapes in Visio, there never seem to be enough. You can customize any network shape to simulate a device that isn't included. Most of the network shapes are groups. If you open the shape in the group window, you can then use the Format, Special command to identify its type as Figure 14-12 shows. To edit the shape ungroup it so that you can work with its constituent parts. When you're done editing, you can regroup all the parts again.

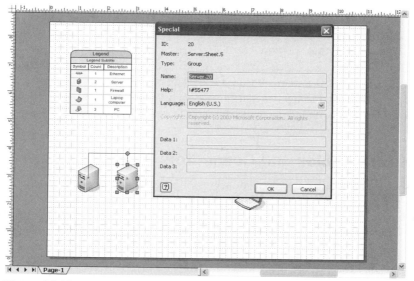

Figure 14-12. The Special dialog box (Format, Special) indicates which shapes are groups.

For details about editing groups, including locked shapes within a group, see "Working with Groups," page 668.

Troubleshooting

A connector line shows through text even though the text background is solid

If you used the technique in the previous section, "Adding a Background Behind Text," to add a solid-color background to a label, but the connector line still shows through, the problem might be with the shape's stacking order. The label needs to be on top of the connector. If the connector is on top, its line will continue to show. To adjust stacking order, select a shape, and then choose Shape, Order, Bring Forward. If necessary, repeat until the line no longer appears.

Now you're ready to edit your shape, but where should you do it? If you edit a shape on the drawing page, you're changing just that shape. If you want to make the same change to a dozen shapes, you don't want to edit them one by one. Here are some options:

- **Edit a master shape on the document stencil** If your diagram includes copies of a shape, and you want to change them all, you can edit the master shape on the document stencil. When you save your changes, every shape in your drawing that is an instance of that master will be updated. To display the document stencil, choose File,

383

Shapes, Show Document Stencil. Right-click the shape on the document stencil that you want to change, and then choose Edit Master.

● **Save an edited shape as new master shape**   You can revise one shape, and then save it as a master on a stencil that you have created. That way, you can reuse the master to create copies of the shape in your diagram. To save the shape as a master, drag the shape onto a stencil that you have created.

> **Tip**   You can make a custom stencil by selecting File, Shapes, and then selecting New Stencil. You can add a shape to a stencil that you have previously created by selecting File, Shapes, My Shapes, and then choosing a stencil.

Editing Network Cables and Connectors

Methods for changing the look of connectors in a network diagram vary depending on the shape you use. All of the assorted connector shapes, including lines you draw with one of the drawing tools, are instances of what's called a *1-D shape* in Visio. Among other things, this means that any topic in this book about 1-D shapes applies to network connectors as well. You can work with 1-D shapes or connectors as follows:

● To label a connector, select the connector, and then type.

> For details about how text works on labels, see "Adding Text to Lines and Connectors," page 93.

Line Pattern tool

Line Color tool

● You can apply a line pattern to a network connector to show connections as dashed or dotted lines. Select a pattern from the Line Pattern tool to format your connector.

● You can change the connector color as you would any other line. Select the shape, and then choose a line color with the Line Color tool.

Creating Multiple-Page Network Diagrams

When you want to show alternative views of a network, or different sections or domains, you can create your diagram on multiple pages. You can link shapes in pages as well to indicate that additional information is contained elsewhere in the drawing. There aren't any special techniques to creating multiple-page network diagrams; the general information about Visio pages applies.

One thing to know is that each page can have a different size and drawing scale, which is sometimes useful. For example, you can include a building plan on one page, such as an imported architectural drawing that shows where network cable should go. You can then insert pages to show network details, such as the workstation layout in a lab. The detail page can use a different drawing scale than the building plan page.

For details about working with drawing scales, see "Setting Up Measurements in a Diagram," page 421.

Tip You can share network diagrams by pasting them into any Office document or e-mail message. You can also save any network diagram as a Web page (choose File, Save As Web Page) and post it on an intranet or the Internet.

 You can also click the Mail Recipient button on the Standard toolbar to mail your network diagram as an e-mail attachment. That really isn't new, but each e-mail you instigate in this manner includes a link to the Visio viewer. That is new.

Resizing the Page to Fit a Large Network Diagram

You can print large, wall-sized diagrams of an entire network or a diagram of a single rack. If your network runs off the drawing page as you add nodes and connectors, you can adjust the page size or move portions of the network onto a new page.

The size of the drawing page is a function of the page setup options, which you can change by choosing File, Page Setup. It's important to size the page correctly regardless of whether you want to print your diagram or paste it into another document. You can quickly resize the drawing page to fit your drawing, which is particularly useful if you plan to use your diagram on a presentation slide or in another document. To do this, click the Page Size tab, and then select the SizeTo Fit Drawing Contents option, as Figure 14-13 shows. Visio resizes the drawing page so that it tightly encompasses all of your network. You will probably end up with a nonstandard page size that might not fit on your printer's paper, but the preview image in the Page Setup dialog box will show you if that's the case. You can also choose a larger standard size in the Pre-Defined Size list. To make sure that you'll be able to print your larger drawing, click the Print Setup tab, and adjust the paper size.

For details about printing, see "Printing Diagrams of Any Size," page 242.

 Inside Out

Continuing a diagram

To continue a diagram on another page, you can use the Cut, Copy, and Paste commands to move elements. Visio doesn't offer an automated method for continuing a network diagram, but you can add a hyperlink from one page to another, as described in the next section.

Chapter 14

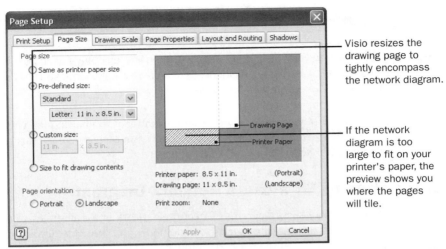

Visio resizes the drawing page to tightly encompass the network diagram.

If the network diagram is too large to fit on your printer's paper, the preview shows you where the pages will tile.

Figure 14-13. Resizing the drawing page to just fit its contents gives you more drawing space for a large diagram or eliminates extra white space for small diagrams that you plan to paste into another document.

Adding Hyperlinks to Multiple-Page Diagrams

To show details, alternative views, or provide navigation in a large document, you can add hyperlinks to shapes or to the drawing page. For example, you can link shapes on a high-level diagram to a detail page so that you can jump quickly to details about specific devices. Hyperlinks help you connect information on different pages, but they also work well as navigation controls when your goal is to publish a network diagram on an intranet or other Web site. If you add hyperlinks to your network diagram, and then save it as a Web page, Visio retains the hyperlinks.

When you insert a hyperlink, you specify its destination as one of the following:

- Another page in your network diagram
- Another Visio diagram
- A document other than a Visio diagram, such as a report or spreadsheet
- A Web site

Visio includes several hyperlink navigation shapes on the Borders And Titles stencil, which are handy because they look like links (an example is shown in Figure 14-14). Alternatively, you can add a hyperlink directly to a shape as a shortcut option that appears when you right-click the shape.

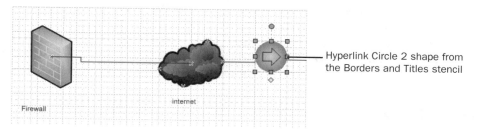

Figure 14-14. You can link to details on another page, in another document, or on the Web by adding a hyperlink.

For details about hyperlinks, see "Linking Visio Shapes and Pages," page 146.

Tracking and Reporting on Network Equipment

To add detail to a high-level network diagram, you can add data to the equipment shapes. This means either typing or importing information such as manufacturer, product name, description, and model number, and storing it with the shapes in your diagram. Network shapes include built-in data fields called custom properties that you can use to track asset and equipment information with your network diagram, as Figure 14-15 shows.

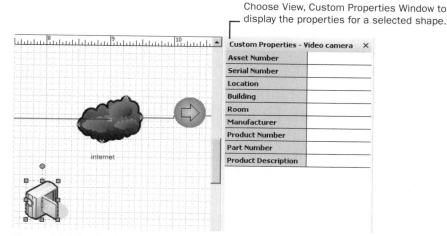

Figure 14-15. Basic network equipment shapes include built-in custom properties that you can use to store more detailed information about the devices in a network diagram.

Chapter 14

Microsoft Office Visio 2003 Inside Out

You can use the predefined custom properties that Visio includes with shapes or create your own. After you have added custom property data to a diagram, the information can be used to generate reports based on your diagram's contents. You can also export the information to a spreadsheet or database and even set up a link between an existing spreadsheet or database of equipment information and the custom properties in your network diagram's shapes.

Associating Serial Numbers and Other Data with Network Shapes

To enter and manage the data stored in network shapes, you work in the Custom Properties window, which displays data for a selected shape. The easiest way to work with the Custom Properties window is to dock it on the screen while you work in your diagram. To display it, choose View, Custom Properties Window. When you select a shape in your diagram, its properties and values appear in the Custom Properties window. To add data to shapes, select a shape, and then type the information you want in the appropriate fields of the Custom Properties window.

Tip Right-click a shape, and then choose Properties to display the shape's custom properties.

For details about creating your own properties, see "Defining Custom Properties," page 175.

In a large network diagram, typing manufacturer names and model numbers would quickly become tedious. Visio can automate the process, but it requires some effort. You can link the custom property fields to records in a database and then share data between the two sources.

For details about linking a database to your diagram, see Chapter 24, "Connecting Diagrams and Databases."

Generating Reports from Network Data

 Visio now includes three useful reports that you can use with networks. They are the Network Device, Network Equipment, and PC Reports. You can access them by selecting Tools, Reports. These reports will be displayed if you are working on a network report. You can generate reports based on the custom property data that's stored with your network shapes. A report can include any set of custom properties that you select. For example, you can use the Report tool to define a new report called Your Equipment (or whatever) that includes the manufacturer, model, product name, and description for each network equipment shape in your diagram, for example.

To determine the properties to include in your report, you save a new report definition. Then you can select the report from the list and run it to produce an HTML or XML document, a table in Visio, or an Excel spreadsheet. The Report tool scans the values of the custom properties that are specified by the report definition and then produces a report, as Figure 14-16 shows. Your report can include information from only one page of a multiple-page network diagram or all shapes on all pages.

For details about defining reports, see "Creating Reports," page 190.

	A	B	C	D
	Arial ▾ 10 ▾ **B** *I* <u>U</u>			$
	A3 ▾	*fx* N5540		
1				
2	**Building**	**Room**	**Displayed Text**	**Network Na**
3	N5540		Operations	
4	N5540		PR	
5	N5540	76	Admin	
6	N5541		Scanner	
7	N5541	17	Operations	
8	N5542	Ops	Admin	

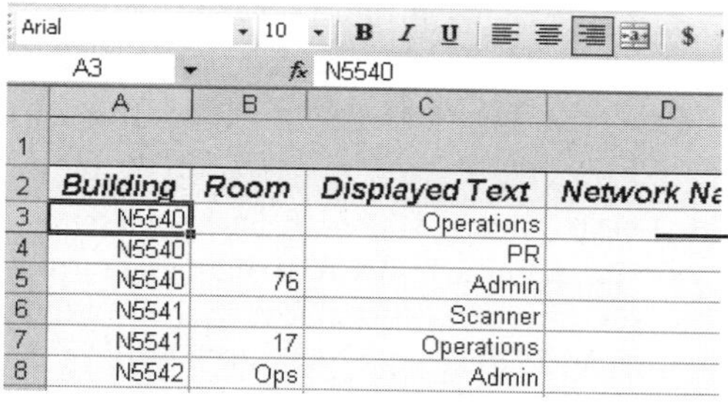

The custom property values for each shape in your diagram appear in the report

Figure 14-16. You can generate a report as an Excel spreadsheet or another format, including HTML or XML. The information in a report varies depending on the report definition, which you can customize.

Troubleshooting

You can't find the Property Reporting Wizard used to create network reports in Visio 2000

If you used Microsoft Office Visio 2000 or an earlier version, you might have used the Property Reporting Wizard to create reports based on your network diagrams. This wizard wasn't included in Visio 2002 or Visio 2003. A more functional Report tool has replaced it, which you can start by choosing Tools, Report.

For details, see "Creating Reports," page 190.

About the Visio 2000 Network Wizards

If you have upgraded to Visio 2003 from Visio 2000 or an earlier version, you might wonder where the Network Database Wizard and Network Diagram Wizard have gone. These wizards aren't included in this version, and Microsoft doesn't plan to support them. However, new tools and add-ins, network shapes, and presumably better support are planned for the Visio Network Center. For details, choose Help, Visio Network Solutions.

In Visio 2003, the database connectivity tools have been consolidated in the Export To Database command on the Tools menu. In addition, the Link To Database command (Tools, Add-Ons, Visio Extras) can establish two-way links between shapes' custom properties and database records.

For details about these tools, see "Linking Shapes and Databases," page 721.

Creating a Directory Diagram

Visio Professional includes templates for diagramming directory services structures from any LDAP-compliant source as well as templates specifically for working with Novell Directory Services (NDS) and Active Directory. Visio Professional provides a way to prototype new directories or plan network resources by dragging and dropping shapes. You can design a service and even set policies and permissions for network objects, but you do it all manually.

Whether you're diagramming generic LDAP objects, Microsoft Exchange servers, or NDS trees in Visio Professional, you use a similar approach. Because these diagrams maintain a model of your directory structure, the way you work with shapes in them differs somewhat from the way you manage shapes in other Visio diagram types (see Figure 14-17). The following guidelines apply:

- To add objects or classes to the drawing page, you can drag a shape from a stencil just as you would when working with other stencils.

- Shapes must be connected in the correct order to preserve the directory hierarchy. Like subordinate shapes in organization charts, directory services' child shapes can be dropped on top of parent shapes to form a hierarchical connection automatically.

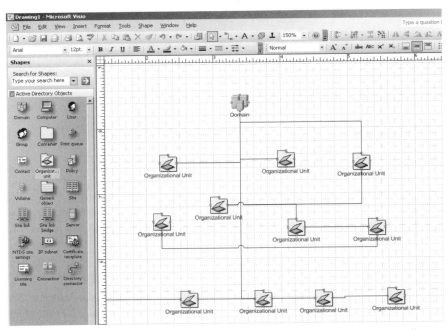

Figure 14-17. When you start a drawing with one of the directory services diagram templates, Visio provides numerous shapes for diagramming a directory.

Starting a Directory Diagram

Visio Professional includes three templates for diagramming directory structures, as Table 14-1 shows. To start a new diagram, choose File, New, Network, and then choose a template for the type of directory diagram you want to create. Note that Visio no longer includes the Directory Services menu and Directory Navigator.

Table 14-1. Directory Services Diagram Types

Template	Shapes
Active Directory	Active Directory Objects, Active Directory Sites And Services, and Exchange Objects
LDAP Directory	LDAP Objects
Novell Directory Services	NDS Additional Objects, NDS Objects, NDS Partitions, NDS GroupWise, and NDS ZENworks

Using Shapes to Add Objects and Classes

When you're first starting a directory diagram, perhaps the quickest way to populate your directory structure is by dragging shapes onto the page. Once the shapes are in place you can connect them with the Connector tool. Of course you can also first select the Connector tool, and then drag the shapes on the page in the order in which you wish to connect them.

Visio provides a unique name for each new object, which you can change by clicking the shape and typing a new name, as Figure 14-18 shows.

Figure 14-18. Click the object as you would any other and enter the name.

For details about connecting and gluing shapes, see "Adding Connectors to Your Diagrams," page 63.

Chapter 15

Planning and Mapping Web Sites

Most Web sites include hundreds of links to content such as Active Server Pages (ASPs), JavaScript, and countless graphic files. The sheer volume of links and content can make it difficult to manage a Web site and keep it up to date. However, if you have Microsoft Office Visio 2003 Professional, you also have a powerful visual tool for analyzing Web site content. Whether your site is served by an intranet, the Internet, or a network staging area, you can automatically diagram every page, link, and piece of content and even control the level of detail.

In Visio 2003 this version of the Web Site Map template maps more detail than in the past and offers a greater level of control with support for additional Hypertext Markup Language (HTML) tags, Java, Microsoft Office FrontPage 2003, Active Server Pages scripts (ASPs), and more. Visio provides information about every link it encounters, including its target address and whether that target was available. As a troubleshooting tool for locating broken links, Visio excels. Enhancements to the template include new, more compact layout options, editable shape text, and new shapes for representing current and upcoming technologies. With the new interactive discovery feature, you can map protected Web site areas if you have access rights. In short, this chapter shows you how to generate a Web site map with the contents you want and how to work with the results in Visio.

Understanding the Web Site Map Template

When you start a drawing based on the Web Site Map template, Visio adds shapes and tools for automatically creating a diagram of a Web site. The template adds the Generate Site Map command, which runs a *crawler* (sometimes called a *spider* or *bot*)—that is, a type of program that retrieves a Web document and follows all the links in it. Visio's site map crawler looks specifically for HTML pages on the Internet, an intranet, or in local folders such as a test or staging site. Through this process, Visio discovers all the pages, documents, graphic and media files, program files, and other information on a Web site and then creates a hierarchical model of what it found.

Visio not only generates a site map, it also creates a *model* of your site. Like other model-based templates in Visio Professional, this one offers alternative views of your information and changes the way you work with shapes. In other words, the shapes on the page aren't the most important part of what's stored in the drawing file. The diagram on the page shows one view of the model, which might or might not include every link and piece of content. The List and Filter windows show the complete model with everything that Visio discovered when it crawled through your site, as Figure 15-1 shows.

Displays every linked file on your site

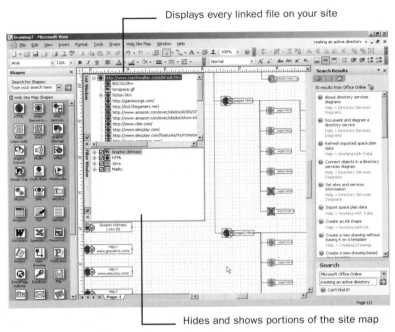

Hides and shows portions of the site map

Figure 15-1. You can choose which options you want to see in the site map by selecting them in the Filter window. The List window displays all your content in a tree view.

Viewing a Site Map

Visio provides information about your Web site in the way it displays shapes in a site map. Shapes include symbols and colors that indicate broken and duplicate links as well as other information. Table 15-1 shows you what each symbol means.

Table 15-1. **Web Site Map Symbols**

Symbol	What It Means
	A plus (+) sign on a shape's bottom edge indicates a link that you can expand.
	A minus (–) sign on a shape indicates an expanded link.
	No symbol on a shape indicates a link that cannot be expanded.
	A red X on a shape indicates a broken link.
	A dimmed shape indicates a duplicate link.

Troubleshooting

Some shapes in the site map appear dimmed

If a shape in your site map represents a duplicate link, the shape appears dimmed on the page. As an alternative to dimmed shapes, you can have Visio hide duplicate links as collapsed items. That way, the links are included with the model of your site, but they don't appear in the diagram unless you expand a shape's links. To control this option, when you generate a site map, click Settings in the Generate Site Map dialog box. On the Advanced tab, select the Display Duplicate Links As Expandable option.

Collapsing and Expanding Site Maps

When Visio initially generates a site map diagram, it displays every link that it discovered. As a result, site maps are typically very wide. To make the site's structure more apparent, you can collapse and expand branches, or subtrees, of your site as follows:

- **Collapsing a subtree** Right-click a shape that displays a minus (–) sign on the bottom edge, and then choose Collapse *<Address>*.
- **Expanding a subtree** Right-click a shape that displays a plus (+) sign on the bottom edge, and then choose Expand *<Address>*, as Figure 15-2 shows.

Chapter 15

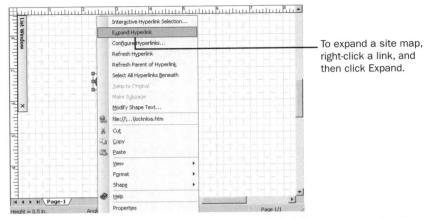

To expand a site map, right-click a link, and then click Expand.

Figure 15-2. If a page includes links to another level of site content, the shape that represents the page includes the Expand command on its shortcut menu.

Viewing a Web Site Model

You can choose how much of your site map you want to see on the drawing page. However, the entire model—all the links that Visio mapped—always appears in the List and Filter windows, as Figure 15-3 shows.

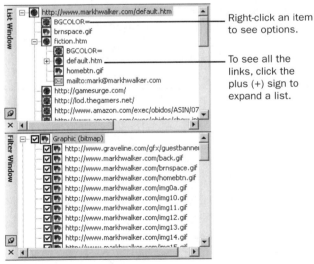

Right-click an item to see options.

To see all the links, click the plus (+) sign to expand a list.

Figure 15-3. The List and Filter windows display all the content referenced by the links that Visio found when it created the site map.

The Filter window provides a way to view categories of content in a site map. For example, you can temporarily hide all graphic shapes from the site map by clearing the check mark beside the Graphic option, so that you don't have to look at every bullet and logo graphic on your site and can more easily see the page hierarchy or other elements. The List window also lets you expand and collapse hierarchical branches of content.

The Web Site Map template opens these windows by default when you start a new drawing. You can also open a window by choosing Web Site Map, Windows, and then choosing a window to display. Visio docks these windows on the left side of the drawing page, but you can drag them to a new position—for example, with the stencils.

When you work in the List or Filter window, you affect the model of your site map, whereas working on the drawing page with shapes doesn't necessarily change the model. For example, if you delete a shape on the drawing page, the link that the shape represented still appears in the List and Filter windows—that is, it's still part of the model—and you can drag it back into the diagram. To delete a link from your model, delete it from the List or Filter window by right-clicking the link, and then choosing Delete. You can map different parts of your site on different pages of a drawing file by dragging a link from the List or Filter window onto a new drawing page. Visio maps that portion of the site and adds all the links below the one you dragged onto the page.

> **Tip** **Display one branch of a Web site**
> You can use the List window to quickly display a branch or subtree of your site. For example, you can insert a new page and then drag an item from the List window onto the page. Visio diagrams that branch of your site.

Determining What Is Mapped

When you generate a site map, Visio follows the trail of links contained in HTML and other pages based on file extensions, common communication protocols, and attributes to HTML tags or elements. However, when you generate a site map, you can do the following:

- Specify the number of levels of a site to map as well as the number of links on a level to follow.
- Disable links to types of content that you don't want to include.
- Add a file extension, protocol, or HTML attribute to the list so that Visio examines links to other types of content.
- Change the shape used to represent a type of link.

A Web site is typically structured with one home page that contains links to branching pages. A *level* represents one layer of the site's hierarchy or navigation. For example, a link on the home page might take you to a page on the first level of the site. A link on that page could send you to a page at the second level, and so on, as Figure 15-4 shows. For every level of a site, you can choose the maximum number of links that Visio will follow before proceeding to map the next level.

By default, a site map includes links to files with any of the extensions shown in Table 15-2.

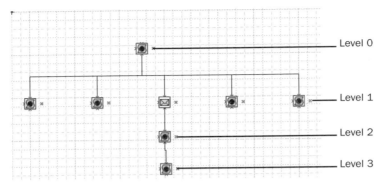

Figure 15-4. Visio regards the navigational structure or hierarchy of a Web site as its levels and can map a site containing up to 25 levels.

Table 15-2. File Extensions That Are Mapped by Default

Site Content	File Extension
Active Server Page	.asp, .asa, .cdx
Archive	.zip, .cab, .z, .gz, .tgz, .uu, .uue, .hqx, .lha, .lzh, .sit, .sea
Audio	.wav, .snd, .au, .aif, .aifc, .aiff, .mp2, .mp3, .mid, .rmi, .midi, .wma, .ra, .ram
Document	.doc, .xls, .ppt, .mdb, .pub, .prj, .vsd, .rtf, .pdf, .txt
FrontPage file	.fpweb, .fphtml
Generic	*other* (*.*)
Graphic	.img, .jpg, .jpeg, .gif, .bmp, .png, .art, .jpe
HTML	.htm, .html, .shtm, .shtml, .stm, .htw, .mht, .mhtml, .jhtml, .php, .php3
Image map	.map
Java and JavaScript	.class, .js, .java
Multimedia	.swf, .dcr, .swl, .wrl, .wm, .rm
Plug-in	.ocx, .dll
Program	.exe, .bin
Script	.cgi, .vbs, .cfm
Template	.css, .asx, .htx, .htt
Video	.avi, .mov, .qt, .mpg, .mpeg, .mpe, .wmv, .m1v, .mpv2, .mp2v, .mpa, .asf
XML	.xml, .xsl, .dtd, .osd, .cdf

Troubleshooting

The List and Filter windows don't display a type of link that the Web site includes

When you use the Generate Site Map command, Visio crawls your site by following the links with the file extensions, protocols, and attributes that are specified in the Web Site Map Settings dialog box. What you see in the List and Filter windows reflects those settings. For example, if you were expecting to see links to executable (.exe) files, but the Program option was disabled when you generated the site map, you won't see any links to files of that type in Visio. The only way to add links to that file type is to generate a new site map. To do that, choose Web Site Map, Generate Site Map, and then click Settings to specify the file extensions to include.

For details about modifying map settings, see "Changing Site Mapping Settings," page 402.

Creating a Site Map

The Web Site Map template includes all the tools you need to analyze a Web site and create a diagram of it. When you start a new drawing with the Web Site Map template, Visio also starts the Generate Site Map command. If you specify an address or file location and then click OK, Visio proceeds to search your site and create a diagram. That's really all you need to do. The rest of the topics in this section discuss your options when generating a site.

An unusual outcome of the site mapping process is that Visio automatically sizes the drawing page to fit the width of the site map, as Figure 15-5 shows. The template initially creates a letter-sized drawing page, but after a site map has been generated, the page might be a non-standard size. In this way, Visio ensures that no content falls off the page, but if you want to print the diagram on a particular size of printer paper, you might need to make adjustments.

For details about adjusting page size when printing a Web site map, see "Printing Diagrams of Any Size," page 242.

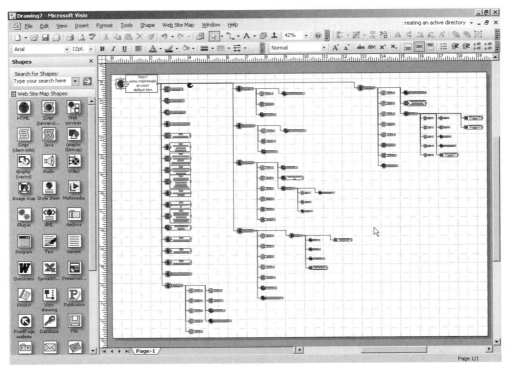

Figure 15-5. The rulers indicate that Visio resized the drawing page to fit this site map.

> **Note** To work properly, the Web Site Map Shapes stencil needs to be open, because Visio uses the shapes on this stencil to create your site map. If the stencil isn't already open, Visio opens it. If Visio can't find this stencil for some reason, you'll get an error message, and the site map won't be generated.

Adding a Site Map to Another Diagram

You can add a site map to any Visio diagram, no matter which template was used to create it. For example, suppose you have a timeline that shows your Web site launch schedule, and you want to include a site map. Unlike previous versions of Visio, you cannot choose the Generate Site Map command from a special location. You must first create the site map in a separate document as described earlier.

Once you have created a site map, follow these steps to add it to an existing diagram:

1 Right-click the page with the site map and choose Copy Drawing.

2 Switch to the diagram to which you wish to add the site map and select Insert, New Page.

3 Click the new page and select Insert, Object, and then select Microsoft Visio Drawing.

Planning and Mapping Web Sites

4   Choose Create From File, and Link To File. Browse to where the drawing is located, select it, and click OK. Visio inserts the drawing.

5   If the site map is larger than the page select File, Page Setup. On the Page Size tab, choose Size To Fit Drawing Contents and click OK.

Choosing a Web Site to Map

When you choose the Generate Site Map command on the Web menu, the first step is to specify an address, as shown in Figure 15-6. In fact, an address is the only piece of information Visio needs to map a Web site; every other option merely helps you narrow the scope of Visio's mapping process.

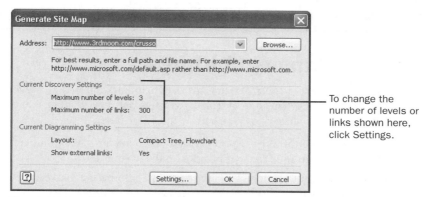

To change the number of levels or links shown here, click Settings.

Figure 15-6.   Choose Web, Generate Site Map to display this dialog box. Although you can configure many options by clicking Settings, all you really need to specify is an address.

As long as the address you specify is valid, Visio doesn't care whether it represents an Internet site, local test or staging site, File Transfer Protocol (FTP) site, or other location of HTML files. The Browse button helps you locate folders that contain content you want to map. Otherwise, type a URL in the Address box, such as *http://www.microsoft.com/default.htm* or *http://officeupdate.microsoft.com/default.htm*. It helps to specify a starting file, such as default.htm or index.htm, but you don't have to. When you click OK, Visio starts searching the site and its subdirectories down as many levels as specified under Current Discovery Settings.

Follow these steps to start a new Web site diagram and create a site map:

1   Choose File, New, Web Diagram, Web Site Map to start a new drawing and open the Generate Site Map dialog box.

2   In the Address box, type a URL and starting page for the Web site you want to map or click Browse to locate HTML files on a local or network drive.

3   Click OK to start diagramming the site.

The speed with which Visio can map a Web site depends on the speed of your computer, the speed of your network connection, and the number of levels and links you specified.

Chapter 15

401

Although this version of the site mapping add-in is considerably faster than in previous versions of Visio, you might have to wait a few minutes to map a very large site.

Troubleshooting

The site map doesn't display all the levels that were specified in the Generate Site Map dialog box

Your levels might be present but collapsed. Shapes that include links to additional levels in the site are displayed with a plus (+) sign. You can expand the shape to see its links by right-clicking the shape, and then choosing Expand *<Address>*. For a large site, it's easiest to create a subpage first, and then expand the shape. For details, see "Formatting a Site Map Across Multiple Pages," page 412.

Changing Site Mapping Settings

You can exert a great deal of control over Visio's site mapping capabilities. Maybe you just need a list of graphics, or you need to find links to out-of-date pages. When you click Settings in the Generate Site Map dialog box, you can do the following:

- Change the number of levels in your site that Visio analyzes, the number of links per level, and the layout used for the site map on the Layout tab.

- Choose the content to include and the shapes used in the site map on the Extensions, Protocols, and Attributes tabs.

- Specify the scope of the site search and provide proxy authentication on the Advanced tab.

To best use the options in the Web Site Map Settings dialog box you need a working knowledge of HTML and Web site structure. Knowing which attributes to tell a crawler to examine and which to ignore requires a certain amount of experience with HTML source code. For example, if you're trying to determine how many graphics are used on a site, you can disable Audio on the Extensions tab so that Visio doesn't include .wav files in your site map. Although you can also filter the view of your site map after it's generated and temporarily hide particular types of content from view, the Web Site Map Settings dialog box gives you more control over items you don't need to see in the first place. In addition, by disabling options, Visio can generate a site map more quickly, and you're less likely to end up with an unmanageably huge diagram.

Note Visio lets you delete options from the Web Site Map Settings dialog box. On the Extensions, Protocols, and Attributes tabs, select an item, and then click Remove. Visio prompts you to confirm the action. For example, if you add a custom extension, protocol, or attribute, you can later delete it when you no longer want to include it in a site map.

Choosing a Layout for a Site Map

On the Layout tab, shown in Figure 15-7, you can choose how much of a site to *discover*, Visio's term for searching the hierarchy of folders and links on a site. You can map up to 12 levels with a maximum number of 5000 links in the layout. You have these options:

- **Maximum Number Of Levels and Maximum Number Of Links**   Determine how "deep" into the Web site your search will go.

- **Complete Current Level After Maximum Number Of Links Have Been Discovered.**   This option continues searching a level even after the maximum number of links has been found.

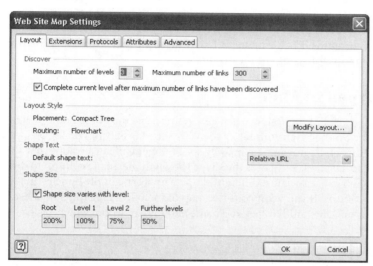

Figure 15-7.   You can specify how much of a Web site to analyze and how to lay out the results on the Layout tab of the Web Site Map Settings dialog box.

In the Layout Style section, you can also specify the type of layout you want to use when the site map is created on the drawing page. The options you choose here (repeated in the Generate Site Map dialog box) reflect the built-in layout and routing behavior that Visio supports for all connected diagram types, which you can change before or after the site map is generated. To display options, click Modify Layout. The Circular and Flowchart styles tend to be most useful, but you can always modify any layout style on the drawing page by dragging shapes or choosing the Shape, Lay Out Shapes command.

Chapter 15

403

Troubleshooting

The Web site's navigational hierarchy is not preserved in the site map that Visio creates

Unless your Web site's navigation is static—that is, not dynamically created as the page is displayed—it won't show up correctly in the site map diagram that Visio creates. Visio finds all the links on your page regardless of how your menu is structured, and all links within the file are displayed. For example, if you use dynamic HTML–based cascading menus (as many portions of the Microsoft Web site do), the organization of your site map won't match the organization of your site's menu. The hierarchy of your menu is not preserved.

The Shape Text section provides the shape text display options. You can choose to display the relative URL, absolute URL, file name, HTML title, or no text. Finally, the Shape Size section displays the options for sizing the located links.

Choosing File Types to Map

Visio decides which links to follow when generating a site map based on the file extension of a site's content. On the Extensions tab of the Web Site Map Settings dialog box, you can select the elements to include in your site map by specifying the file extensions that Visio searches for, as Figure 15-8 shows. Visio uses the shape shown in the Shape column to display links in the site map. You can associate a different shape with a type of file by selecting a name and then clicking Modify. If you want your site map to include a file type that doesn't appear on the Extensions tab, click Add to specify a name and file extension, which Visio adds to the list.

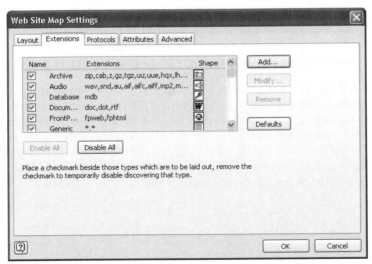

Figure 15-8. In the Web Site Map Settings dialog box, the Extensions tab lets you choose links to specific file types based on their file extension.

Chapter 15

> **Note** You can clear HTML if you want to create a list of only graphics, ASPs, or some other site content. Visio still searches the site's hypertext to locate content and links, but HTML pages aren't included in the site map.

Including Link Protocols

When Visio crawls a site, it can search the syntax of a link to see if it includes a particular communication protocol, such as MailTo, as Figure 15-9 shows. You can select the protocols to include and define new ones on the Protocols tab of the Web Site Map Settings dialog box, shown in Figure 15-10. For example, a link that generates an e-mail message or displays a MailTo site doesn't have a file associated with it, but you might still want to include information about the link in your site map.

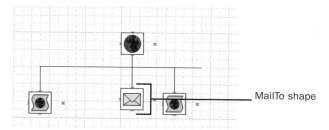

MailTo shape

Figure 15-9. This site includes a link that specifies the MailTo protocol, which Visio displays with the MailTo shape.

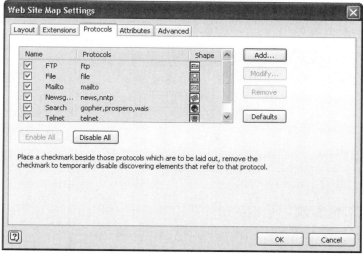

Figure 15-10. You can instruct Visio to include links that reference a particular protocol on the Protocols tab of the Web Site Map Settings dialog box.

Visio supports the following protocols, not all of which are listed on the Protocols tab: HTTP, HTTPS, File, FTP, GOPHER, MailTo, NEWS, NNTP, PROSPERO, TELNET, and WAIS. If a protocol you follow isn't included, click Add to add it to the list. In the Shape column of the Protocols tab, Visio displays the shape it will use in your site map if it finds a link that uses the selected protocol. You can assign a different shape to a protocol by selecting an option in the Name column, and then clicking Modify.

Inside Out

HTTP

Even though Hypertext Transfer Protocol (HTTP) doesn't appear as an option on the Protocols tab, Visio searches links that rely on this protocol. If it didn't, you wouldn't get much of a site map.

Specifying HTML Attributes

For a finer level of control, you can specify the attributes of HTML elements or tags that you want to include in a site map on the Attributes tab, as Figure 15-11 shows. For example, Visio can examine the BACKGROUND attribute of the <BODY> tag to look for additional graphic files that are used as backgrounds. Visio can map just about any combination of linkable elements and attributes that are supported by HTML, including extensions that are specific to Microsoft Internet Explorer and Netscape Navigator. When you select an option on this tab, Visio searches for and displays any files referenced by the attribute. When you clear a check box, Visio ignores links to content referenced by that attribute.

Add an attribute that is not already listed. ⎯⎯

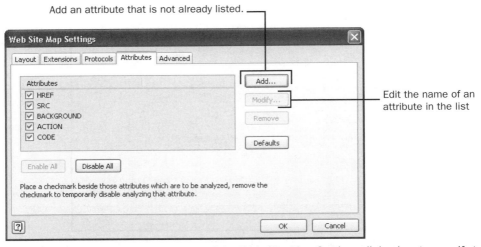

Edit the name of an attribute in the list

Figure 15-11. Use the Attributes tab of the Web Site Map Settings dialog box to specify tag or element attributes that include links.

> **Note** Because the HREF attribute is the basis for a site map, you cannot modify it. Visio requires this attribute to search for links.

Table 15-3 lists the attributes that Visio supports and the elements or tags that use the attributes.

Table 15-3. HTML Attributes You Can Map

Attributes	Elements or Tags
ACTION	<FORM>
BACKGROUND	<BODY>
CODE	<APPLET>
HREF	<A>, <AREA>, <BASE>, <LINK>
SRC	<BGSOUND>, <DYNSRC>, <EMBED> (Netscape 2), <FRAME>, <IFRAME>, <IMG>, <INPUT>, <SCRIPT>

Narrowing the Scope of Site Mapping

You can specify criteria that limit the areas that Visio searches when you generate a site map on the Advanced tab, as Figure 15-12 shows.

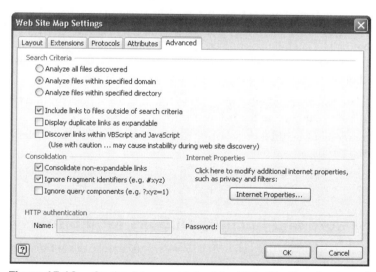

Figure 15-12. On the Advanced tab of the Web Site Map Settings dialog box, you can specify scope and proxy authentication.

The first three options narrow the scope of the search in different ways:

- **Analyze All Files Discovered**   Visio does not limit the scope of the search.
- **Analyze Files Within Specified Domain**   Visio searches all servers within a common domain. For example, if you specify *http://www.microsoft.com* as the address to map, Visio searches all domains in microsoft.com only.
- **Analyze Files Within Specified Directory**   Visio searches only the user-specified directory and the folder beneath it.

Within the search area, you can specify the links to include with the following check boxes:

- **Include Links To Files Outside Of Search Criteria**   Select this check box to display one level of any link that falls outside of the specified search criteria. If you selected Analyze All Files Discovered, this check box isn't relevant, because everything will be in the search criteria. If you select this check box, the Generate Site Map dialog box displays Show External Links: Yes.
- **Display Duplicate Links As Expandable**   Select this check box to include duplicate links, which Visio lists as collapsed items that you can expand. Otherwise, Visio includes the links and displays them as dimmed items.
- **Discover Links Within VBScript And JavaScript**   Select this check box to locate links within scripts.

Caution   If you select the Discover Links Within VBScript And JavaScript check box, Visio might cause Internet Explorer to crash. For details, see the sidebar, "Locating Links Within VBScript or JavaScript," later in this chapter.

You can also choose from the following consolidation options:

- **Consolidate Non-Expandable Links**   Selecting this check box consolidates the links within the site that have no tier below them.
- **Ignore Fragment Identifiers**   Selecting this check box causes Visio to ignore identifiers of Web site page fragments.
- **Ignore Query Components**   Selecting this check box causes Visio to ignore components that are written to generate a query.

Specifying a Password and Security Options for a Site

To provide authentication for protected Web servers, you can use the options on the Advanced tab of the Web Site Map Settings dialog box. When you're mapping a password-protected Web site, you can enter your authentication information in the Name and Password boxes. Visio remembers your password throughout your current working session with the Web Site Map template but doesn't store it after you close the drawing file.

Note   Although you can enter HTTP authentication, you can't specify a password for a Microsoft Windows NT–protected shared resource, which is stored on the network level.

Locating Links Within VBScript or JavaScript

On the Advanced tab of the Web Site Map Settings dialog box, you have the option to include links in your site map that are embedded within VBScript or JavaScript code. Typically, scripts are hidden within comment tags to avoid confusing older browsers. However, if you select this option, Visio can search within HTML-embedded scripts for links. The problem is that Internet Explorer can crash, because it wasn't designed to support this type of search. For details about the issue, see Knowledge Base article Q266343.

You can also modify security settings that have been established for your browser on the Advanced tab. If you click Internet Properties, the Internet Properties dialog box opens, where you can change Content or Security filters before continuing with the site mapping process.

Customizing Web Site Shapes

When you generate a site map, you can select the shapes you want to represent the elements and links that Visio finds as well as the extensions and protocols that will be included. You can specify different shapes for any extension or protocol.

Adding Shapes to a Web Site Map

The quickest way to create a new Web site shape is to drag an existing one from the stencil onto the drawing page and then edit it. The Web site shapes are groups for which subselection behavior has been disabled. If you want to edit one of these shapes, it's easiest to open the group by selecting the shape and then choosing Edit, Open <*Shape Name*>. For example, to edit the Graphic shape, select the shape, and then choose Edit, Open Graphic. Visio opens a drawing page for the group, as Figure 15-13 shows, so you can more easily select and edit the shapes that make up the group. When you have made the changes you want, close the window for the group's drawing page.

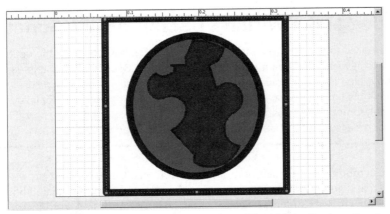

Figure 15-13. When you open a group for editing, Visio displays the group on its own drawing page.

Tip Edit text for Web site shapes

To change the text in a shape's label, right-click the shape, choose Configure Hyperlink, type new text in the Description box, and then click OK.

For details about editing groups, see "Working with Groups," page 668.

Adding Web Site Shapes to the Model

You can drag shapes from the Web Site Map Shapes stencil to your site map to prototype new sections of your site or to provide details that Visio did not include. These shapes won't appear in the List and Filter windows, because they aren't part of the model that Visio generated. However, you can add shapes to the model simply by specifying an address in the Hyperlinks dialog box, as Figure 15-14 shows.

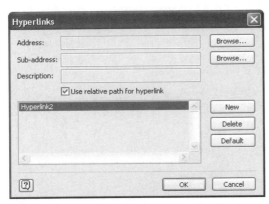

Figure 15-14. To add a new shape to the model of your map, right-click the shape, choose Configure Hyperlinks, and then specify an address.

Follow these steps to add a shape to the Web site model:

1 Right-click a shape, and then choose Configure Hyperlinks.

2 In the Address box, type a URL or file path that includes the name of the link, such as **demo.htm**. If you want, specify a specific page or anchor in the Sub-Address box. To add a label to the shape other than the address, type in the Description box. Click OK.

Connector tool

3 To connect thae shape to other shapes in your site map, click the Connector tool on the Standard toolbar, and then draw a line from the originating link to the new shape.

Locating a Shape in a Site Map

You can use the List and Filter windows to locate shapes in a diagram. When you right-click an item in either window, you can choose Show On Page to select the shape that represents the item, as Figure 15-15 shows.

> **Tip** Double-click an item in the List or Filter window to select the shape associated with it, and pan the site map to the selected shape.

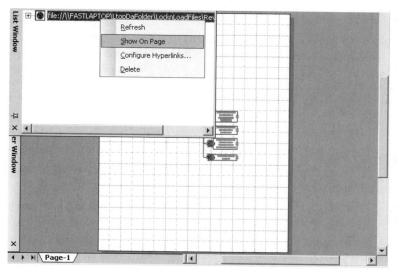

Figure 15-15. Right-click an item in the List window to locate the shape in the site map that represents that item. The same right-click technique works in the Filter window, too.

Modifying Web Site Maps

In addition to using the List and Filter windows to provide alternative views of your site content, you can change the view of the site map on the drawing page. Visio provides several options. You can do any of the following:

● Change the layout to another style, such as radial or circular.

● Focus the site map on one page and its links with a page-centric view.

● Move entire sections, or subtrees, of your site to a new page.

To change the overall layout of your site map, you use the Lay Out Shapes command on the Shape menu. This is the same command you would use to change the layout for any connected diagram, including flowcharts or network diagrams. The best advice for using the layout options is to remember that you can always undo the results. Try an option, click OK, and if you don't like what you see, press Ctrl+Z (or choose Edit, Undo) to restore the previous layout.

> For details, see "Laying Out Shapes Automatically," page 70.

Viewing One Page and Its Links

You can place one page at the center of your site map and examine all the links associated with that page. Visio provides a page-centric view of a site map that displays links for a selected page or item. To display a page-centric view, choose a shape in your site map, and then choose Web Site Map, View, Page Centric. Visio displays the links to and from the selected item, as Figure 15-16 shows.

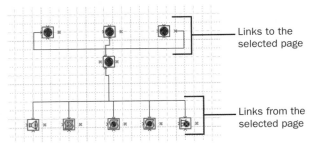

Figure 15-16. In a page-centric view of the Visio section of the Microsoft Office Web site, you can see the links to and from the Visio page.

Formatting a Site Map Across Multiple Pages

You can easily make your site map more manageable by moving branches to new pages. When you use the Make SubPage command, Visio automatically moves a selected shape and all of its links to a new page and then inserts an off-page connector shape that links to the new page as Figure 15-17 shows. On the new page, Visio inserts another off-page connector to return you to the home page. When you move a shape to a subpage, Visio creates a copy of the shape on the new page and moves its links. In the List and Filter windows, the site model is maintained—Visio recognizes that only one link is being represented on multiple pages.

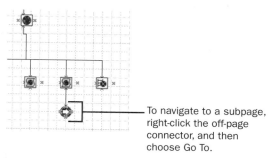

To navigate to a subpage, right-click the off-page connector, and then choose Go To.

Figure 15-17. To move a section of your site map to a new page, right-click a shape, and then choose Make Subpage.

To move a shape to a new page, right-click the shape, and then click Make Subpage. Double-click an off-page connector to move between pages.

> **Tip** Show more detail in a site map
>
> When you add subpages to a site map, you have more room for detail. You can expand a level or section of your site map to display more links. To do this, right-click a shape with links (a shape displaying a plus [+] sign), and then choose Expand <Address>. For example, to display the links associated with the demo.htm page, right-click the shape for the demo.htm page, and then choose Expand Demo.htm.

Troubleshooting Web Sites

Visio shows you broken links in your site map by displaying a red X on shapes that represent a broken link. Even better, Visio stores the reason for the broken link as a custom property of the shape. You can right-click a shape in the site map and then choose Properties to display information about the link, including errors associated with broken links (as Figure 15-18 shows). Visio can't fix the error for you—you have to do that using your Web development tool. However, after you have repaired the problem on the site, you can update your site map by right-clicking the broken link shape, and then choosing Refresh Hyperlink <Address>.

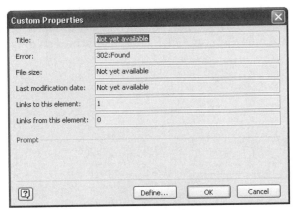

Figure 15-18. Visio displays a red X on shapes that represent broken links. In the Custom Properties dialog box, the Error field reveals the type of error that Visio uncovered when mapping the site.

Visio can help you troubleshoot a site in other ways as well. You can generate reports that provide information about links or shapes in your site map, and you can compare different versions of a site map. The sections that follow tell you how.

Reporting on a Site's Problems

Visio can create reports about the contents of your site map and the errors that were found when the site map was generated. Reports are based on the underlying model that Visio created when it generated your site map, not just the shapes that appear on the drawing page. Both of the following reports list broken links and other errors; they differ in how they organize the information:

- When you choose Web Site Map, Reports, Web Site Map Links With Errors, Visio creates a list of all the broken links that were found when it mapped your site.
- When you choose Web, Reports, Web Site Map All Links, Visio lists all links.
- When you choose Web Site Map, Reports, Inventory, Visio lists every link and piece of content by its file type.

Visio creates reports as HTML, Excel, Visio shape, or XML documents that open in your browser, as Figure 15-19 shows. To save a report, choose File, Save As, and then type a new name and location.

For details about customizing reports based on the shapes in your site map, see "Creating Reports," page 190.

Chapter 15

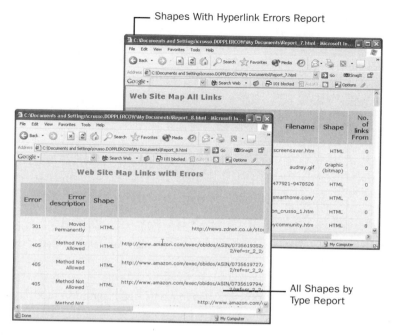

Figure 15-19. When you create a report, you can see all your broken links at a glance or review a list of links by file type.

Comparing Versions of a Site

If you have saved a site map diagram that you created earlier for a site that you're mapping again, you can compare the two versions of the site. Visio includes a report specifically for listing modifications to a Web site based on a site map saved in a separate drawing file. Visio compares the links stored in the site's two models and looks for files that are unique to each version. For each modification, the report lists the type of change, the hyperlink address and shape associated with it, and any errors, as Figure 15-20 shows.

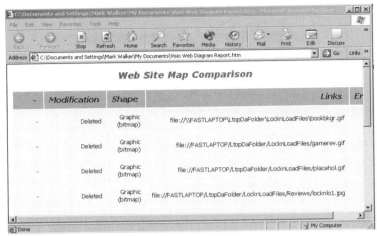

Figure 15-20. When you compare two versions of a site map, Visio creates an HTML page that lists all the modifications.

> **Tip** You can compare a Visio 2003 site map to a site map diagram created in Visio 2000 or 2002.

Follow these steps to compare site maps:

1 Display the more recent site map in Visio, and then choose Web Site Map, Compare To Previous Document.

2 Locate and select the drawing file (.vsd) that contains the earlier version of the site map, and then click Open.

   Visio compares the two files and generates an HTML document, which is automatically opened in your browser.

3 To save the report, choose File, Save in your browser.

NEW FEATURE! Conceptual Web Sites

Visio 2003 not only lets you map your Web site, but also allows you to conceptualize a new one. With the Visio 2003 Conceptual Web Site template, you can build the roadmap for complex Web sites with little more than a handful of clicks and a couple of drags. Note that this tool doesn't actually build a Web site, but rather maps the site that you will build with your favorite Web development tool.

Here are the basic steps of conceptualizing a new Web site:

1 Choose New, Web Diagram, Conceptual Web Site.

2 This opens a blank page and three stencils: Callouts, Web Site Map Shapes, and Conceptual Web Shapes.

3 Drag the shapes on your page to create the Web site. Note that you can click the Connector tool to connect shapes as you drag them onto the page.

Tip You can open the Conceptual Web Site stencil when working on a Web site diagram built from an actual site. Click on the Shapes button on the Standard toolbar, select Open Stencil, browse to the stencil's location, and select it.

Chapter 15

Part 4

Inside Scaled Drawings

Measuring and Dimensioning with Precision

You take great care to make your drawings accurate, because people and projects depend on it. Yet with all the other tasks that go into detailed technical drawings such as architectural or facilities management plans, you can't spend all your time measuring shapes. Of course, guesswork doesn't save you any time in the long run, because accuracy matters.

In fact, when accuracy matters, it *really* matters, as indicated by this man's remark, recently overheard in a café. "On the drawing that I'm working on," he told a friend, "they have actually drawn the crack in the door. Now that's accuracy!" He was almost certainly using a computer-aided design (CAD) program. Microsoft Office Visio 2003 will never replace full-fledged CAD systems. Even the comparison is unfair. However, one Visio manager, a former architect, drafted extremely thorough and accurate plans for his house in Visio, a task not for the faint of heart, but entirely within the realm of possibility. Even if your diagramming goals aren't as elaborate, you can still get the level of precision you need.

This chapter tells you how to set up scaled drawings, position shapes precisely, display measurements, and work with the many drawing aids that can help you draw and position shapes with precision. Even if you're not drawing to scale and just want to align and distribute shapes perfectly, this chapter can tell you how.

Setting Up Measurements in a Diagram

What's especially nice about Visio is that it can do much of the measuring and dimensioning work for you. Tools such as the dynamic grid and shape extension lines make it quick to position shapes exactly, and smart dimension line shapes attach to shapes such as walls and automatically display measurements. In addition, if you start a diagram using one of Visio's built-in templates, issues of drawing scale and measurement are already taken care of. For example, the Office Layout template sets up the diagram so that 1/2 inch (in.) on the drawing page represents 1 foot (ft.) in the real world, a standard architectural drawing scale (see Figure 16-1). You can print the drawing page on ordinary, letter-sized paper, but when you view it on the screen, the rulers show that it represents an area of 22 ft. by 17 ft. That's the beauty of a drawing scale. It allows you to accurately represent real-world objects in a manageable size.

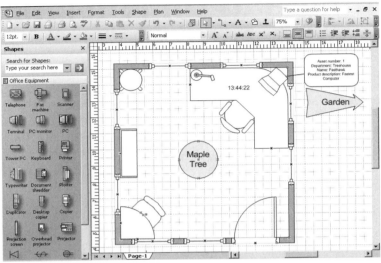

Figure 16-1. When you draw to scale, Visio displays the real-world size of objects in the rulers.

The sections that follow tell you how to set up a new drawing scale if you're drawing from scratch or just want to change the scale Visio supplies. You can choose the units of measure you want to work with as well. Whenever you're drawing to scale, the rulers and grid become important tools for positioning shapes precisely. Later sections tell you how to customize their settings to suit your working style.

Working with a Drawing Scale

If you have worked with measured drawings before (and you have if you've ever used a map), you understand why a drawing scale is necessary. In an architectural or landscape drawing, you might need to represent an area of thousands of feet on a manageable sheet of paper; for a map, you might even be drawing an area of thousands of miles. Conversely, if you're detailing an intricate item for manufacturing (such as a special screw), the drawing of the object might need to be many sizes larger than the object itself. You can do this using a drawing scale, which is simply the ratio of the size of the drawn object to the size of the actual object. For example, floor plans often have a drawing scale of 1/3 in. = 1 ft., where 1/3 in. of paper is equal to 1 ft. of real-life surface area. Similarly, a technical drawing of a bolt or a machined part might require a drawing scale of 10:1, where 10 millimeters (mm) on the page represents 1 mm of actual bolt. Visio drawings can use very different drawing scales, as Figure 16-2 shows.

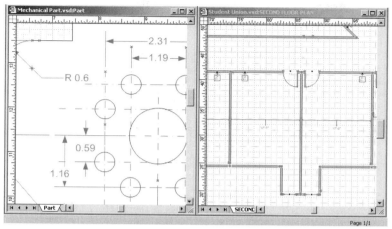

Figure 16-2. In this mechanical part drawing, 1 in. on the page represents 2 in. in real life, and in the floor plan drawing, 3/16 in. on the page represents 1 ft.

Most Visio solutions automatically set the drawing scale to one that is common for the type of drawing. For example, when you open a new Space Plan drawing, the drawing scale defaults to 1/8 in. = 1 ft. Drawings that represent concepts (organization charts, flowcharts, data flow diagrams, and so on) rather than real-world objects use a drawing scale of 1:1 (or no scale).

You can change a diagram's drawing scale at any time. You can even specify a different drawing scale for each page, making it easier to provide both detailed and overview information in the same drawing.

Setting a Page's Drawing Scale

If you're creating a new drawing without using a Visio solution, your only option is to set the drawing scale yourself. To avoid any unfortunate surprises, it's best to specify a drawing scale before you begin drawing.

To specify the drawing scale for a page, choose File, Page Setup, and then click the Drawing Scale tab, shown in Figure 16-3. You can select a predefined scale or specify your own. The predefined scales include common architectural, metric, and engineering scales.

Chapter 16

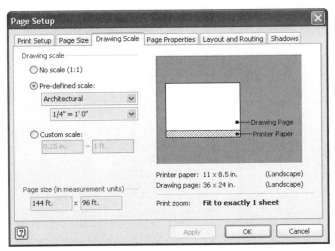

Figure 16-3. You can change drawing scale options in the Page Setup dialog box (choose File, Page Setup).

When you specify a drawing scale, the Page Size fields at the bottom of the Drawing Scale window display how many of the drawing units will fit on the page. For example, if you set a drawing scale of 1 mm = 1 m on a letter-sized page (215.9 mm wide by 279.4 mm long), these fields will show that the page can represent an area that is 215.9 m wide by 279.4 m long.

Caution Be sure to double check your units of measurement to avoid strange results.

Inside Out

Inserting a new page

When you insert a new page in a diagram, you can specify a different drawing scale. If you don't, the new page inherits the drawing scale of the current page. When you choose Insert, New Page, the Page Setup dialog box appears, which lets you determine the drawing scale and other settings that might differ from previous pages.

Displaying the Drawing Scale

You create a drawing to communicate, but other people can't understand your drawing if they don't know what drawing scale you've used. The easiest way to provide this information is to use the Drawing Scale shape, which is included only with Visio Professional (see Figure 16-4). This shape displays the drawing scale you have selected on the diagram.

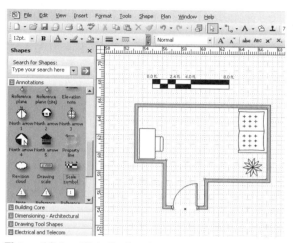

Figure 16-4. Visio Professional includes the Drawing Scale and Scale Symbol shapes, which automatically display a drawing's scale. Visio Standard doesn't include these shapes.

The Drawing Scale and Scale Symbol shapes are in the Annotations stencil. This stencil is automatically opened with many solutions, such as a floor plan, but if it isn't already available, you can open the stencil by choosing File, Shapes, Visio Extras, Annotations. To display either shape on the drawing page, just drag the desired shape from the Annotations stencil onto the drawing page.

You can change the way the drawing scale is displayed to use the most appropriate form for your audience. To specify how the drawing scale is written, right-click the Drawing Scale shape, and then choose Architectural, Civil, Mechanical, or Metric. For example, in a drawing scale where 1 mm on the page equals 1 m in real life, each of the scale styles would look like this:

- **Architectural**   1/64 in. = 1 ft.
- **Civil**   1 in. = 25.4 m
- **Mechanical**   1/1000:1
- **Metric**   1:1000

Système Internationale d'Unites (SI) Shape

If you're using metric units in the drawing with Visio Professional, you can add the symbol for Système Internationale d'Unites (SI). The SI Symbol shape is located on the Title Blocks stencil (choose File, Shapes, Visio Extras, Title Blocks). This symbol appears as solid block letters, but you can display it as hollow letters with the word "metric" below, as Figure 16-5 shows. Right-click the shape, and then choose Hollow "Metric" SI Symbol from the shortcut menu.

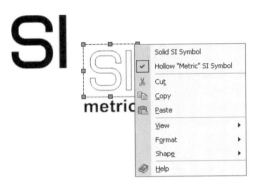

Figure 16-5. The SI Symbol indicates that the drawing uses metric units. To change its appearance, right-click the shape, and then choose an option. This shape is available only in Visio Professional.

For details about other title block shapes and ways to customize them, see "Adding a Title Block to a Diagram," page 134.

Using Shapes in Scaled Drawings

Visio shapes are designed to size correctly in scaled drawings. For example, when you drop a chair shape on a page, the chair appears to be the correct size with respect to the other furniture, whether the drawing scale is 1/4 in. to 1 ft. or 1 ft. to 10 ft., as Figure 16-6 shows. In both drawings, the chair is 3 ft. wide, but it takes up more space on the screen at the bigger scale (1/4 in. to 1 ft.). What if you drop that chair onto a page set to 1 inch to 1 mile? Will the chair look tiny on the page? As it turns out, Visio ignores the drawing scale in this case, because it doesn't make sense to display a chair at real-world size at such a scale. The chair looks the same as it does when dropped on an unscaled (1:1) drawing page.

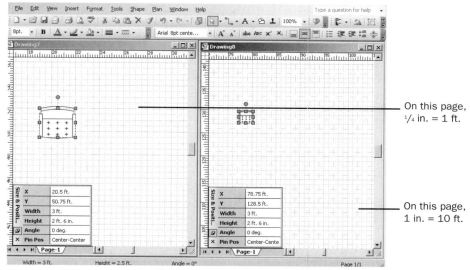

Figure 16-6. In real-world terms, a chair is 3 ft. wide regardless of the drawing scale, as the Width box of the Size & Position window indicates. However, the chair's apparent size on the page differs according to the scale, even though both pages are zoomed to 100 percent.

If a shape is designed to be used in a drawing of a particular scale, you can still use it in a drawing of a different scale. Usually you don't even have to think about whether the shape will work or not—Visio takes care of it. However, you sometimes see peculiar behavior if the shape's scale is dramatically different from the page's scale, or if the shape wasn't designed with drawing scales in mind. For example, some of the shapes on the Borders And Titles stencil "break" if you drop them on a page with a very big or very small drawing scale. "Dramatically different" turns out to be a factor of eight. Visio displays the shape correctly as long as its scale is within eight times the page's scale, as in the example on the left in Figure 16-6, where the drawing scale is 1/4 in. = 1 ft. But in the example on the right, where the drawing scale is 1 in. to 10 ft., the shape is *anti-scaled*. That is, Visio ignores the shape's scale and displays it at the size at which it was drawn.

Choosing the Units of Measure for the Drawing

The measurement units you see on the ruler and in the dimensions that Visio reports reflect the real-life size of the objects. For example, if you're drawing a floor plan, you're probably measuring the space in feet and inches. The rulers, then, display feet and inches, and any dimensions Visio reports are also measured in feet and inches.

When you use a predefined drawing scale, the measurement unit is automatically set. Architectural and Civil Engineering drawing scales use feet and inches, Metric drawing scales use meters, and Mechanical Engineering scales use inches. If you created a custom drawing scale, the unit of measure you typed in the drawing scale automatically appears in the Measurement Units field on the Page Properties tab. However, whether you're using default or custom

427

measurement units, you can change the units without changing the drawing scale. Just as each page can have a different drawing scale, each page can use a different unit of measurement, as Figure 16-7 shows.

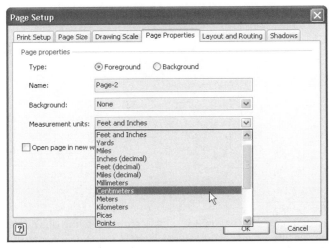

Figure 16-7. When you insert a page, you can specify a unit of measurement that differs from other pages in the drawing file.

Inside Out

Spatial and temporal units

Visio offers both spatial (such as yards or meters) and temporal (such as weeks or years) measurement options. Yes, *temporal* units. For example, you might want 1 in. to equal 1 week in a timeline. Hence, by combining the two measurements you can graphically depict the time allocated to a project on a timeline.

Follow these steps to set measurement units for a page:

1 Choose File, Page Setup, and then click the Page Properties tab.

2 In the Measurement Units list, select the units you want to use.

3 Click OK.

Tip When you use the Insert, New Page command to add pages to a diagram, you can specify unique measurement units for that page on the Page Properties tab.

Setting Default Units for the Drawing File

You can specify the default measurement units that Visio uses for the drawing file so that dialog box options are displayed with the units you want. The default units are automatically reflected in all new pages and objects in the drawing. To do this, you set the drawing's regional settings by choosing Tools, Options, and then clicking the Units tab, as Figure 16-8 shows. The options under Default Units let you specify the units for the page, text, angles, and duration. Table 16-1 explains each option.

Figure 16-8. The default units of measurement that Visio uses for a drawing are a regional setting.

Table 16-1. Options for Specifying Default Measurement Units

Option	Description
Current Page	Unit of measure for a page's dimensions, margins, drawing size, and drawing scale. The units you choose determine whether new, blank drawings open with metric or U.S. units.
Text	Unit of measure for indents, line spacing, and other text measurements. This unit of measure doesn't affect type size. The default unit for type size is points (1 point = 1/72 in.). You can enter type size in another unit of measure (for example, 1 ft. or 12 in.), but you can't change the default.
Angle	Unit of measure for the angle of rotation.
Duration	Unit of measure for elapsed time.

Customizing the Rulers

When you drag shapes, guides, or guide points on the drawing page, faint lines appear on the rulers that show the shape's position so that you can move the shape with precision (see Figure 16-9). Each drawing has both horizontal and vertical rulers, and you can fine-tune your rulers to provide more or less precision.

Chapter 16

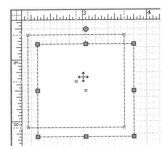

Figure 16-9. As you drag a shape, its position is shown on the rulers, which display the units of measure specified with the Page Setup command.

Specifying Measurement Units in Visio Dialog Boxes

In any Visio dialog box in which you enter a measurement, such as font size or line width, you can use any unit of measure that Visio recognizes. Consider the units that appear in a field to be merely suggestions; you can type any unit that Visio supports. For example, you can specify a custom width for a line. In the Custom Line Weight box, you can type **1"** or **1 inch** or **72 pt.** or **2.5 cm** and get the same result. If the field in a dialog box suggests a value—0 in. for paragraph indentation, for example—you can select the field's contents and type a different unit, such as **12 pt.**

Visio accepts units of measure in the English (U.S.) and metric systems, and you can specify angles in radians; decimal degrees or degrees; or degrees, minutes, and seconds. You can also use standard typographical measurements such as picas, points, ciceros, and didots. You can spell out the unit names or use the standard abbreviations.

The *ruler subdivisions* are the tick marks that reflect the drawing's units of measure and provide a reference for you as you position guides or shapes on the page. They also determine how far an object moves when you nudge it with an arrow key. The ruler's *zero point* shows where the horizontal and vertical rulers both measure 0 units; it is located in the lower left corner of the drawing page unless you move it.

Ruler subdivisions also provide points that shapes can snap to. You can set shapes to snap to ruler subdivisions rather than the grid, for example. You can also determine how easily shapes snap to the ruler subdivision. This kind of snap stickiness is called *snap strength*, and Visio measures it in pixels. The weaker the snap strength, the closer a shape needs to be to a ruler subdivision before it snaps to it.

Table 16-2 summarizes techniques for customizing rulers in a diagram. The sections that follow explain ruler options in more detail.

Table 16-2. **Techniques for Customizing Rulers**

Task	Technique
Set units of measure for rulers	Choose File, Page Setup, and then click the Page Properties tab. In the Measurement Units box, choose the units you want to use.
Set ruler increments	Choose Tools, Ruler & Grid, and then choose Horizontal and Vertical values for Subdivisions.
Change the ruler's zero point	Ctrl+drag from the ruler intersection, or Ctrl+drag from a ruler.
Return the zero point to its default position	Ctrl+double-click the ruler intersection.

Inside Out

Ruler subdivisions and nudge

Ruler subdivisions affect *nudge*, that nifty trick of using your keyboard's arrow keys to move shapes. Each time you nudge a shape using an arrow key, it moves to the next tick mark on the ruler. If you want to nudge a smaller or larger amount, you can change the ruler subdivisions (or just zoom in).

Caution   Ensure that NumLock is *not* enabled on your keyboard when attempting to nudge a shape. If it is, the shape won't nudge.

Setting Ruler Subdivisions

You can set the ruler subdivisions on the horizontal and vertical rulers separately. To change the level of detail on a ruler, choose Tools, Ruler & Grid, and then choose one of the following options for the subdivisions:

- *Fine* spacing provides the most detail, displaying the greatest number of ticks per unit.
- *Coarse* displays the smallest number of ticks.
- *Normal* falls in between.

The number of subdivisions you'll see between units varies depending on the view you're using, but the distance between the subdivisions on the screen remains constant. That is, as you zoom in, you'll see more marks between 20 and 30 ft., for example, but the space between each of the marks on the screen is similar to the space between the marks at a different view, as Figure 16-10 shows.

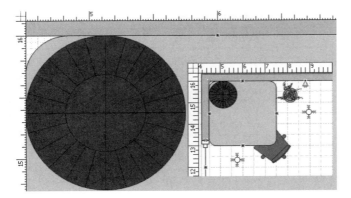

Figure 16-10. For each office layout, the drawing scale is the same and the ruler subdivisions are set to Fine.

Changing the Zero Point

In many measured drawings, it's common to move the zero point. For example, in a floor plan, you might want the zero point to align with a wall, as Figure 16-11 shows. You can set a separate zero point for each ruler, or you can reset both. For greatest precision, it's probably faster to type a value for each zero point to reset them rather than using the Ctrl+drag technique mentioned in Table 16-2.

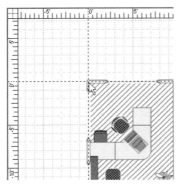

Figure 16-11. Hold the Ctrl key, and drag from the ruler intersection to quickly set the zero point for both rulers.

To type values for the zero points, choose Tools, Ruler & Grid, and then type a value for either the horizontal or vertical Ruler Zero option, as Figure 16-12 shows. Unlike many page layout applications (such as Adobe PageMaker or Quark XPress), in which the zero point is located in the top left corner, Visio places the default zero point in the lower left corner of the drawing page. By default, the horizontal ruler measures zero from the left edge of the page, and the vertical ruler measures zero from the bottom edge of the page.

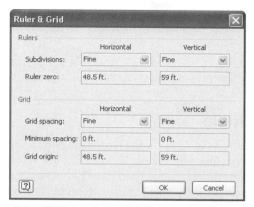

Figure 16-12. For more precision, type exact values in the Ruler Zero boxes to move the zero point.

Note The zero point specifies the center of rotation if you rotate your page or a guide on the page.

If you change the Ruler Zero value for the horizontal ruler to a positive number (for example, 3 in.), the zero point shifts to the right. If you change the value to a negative number (for example, –3 in.), the zero point shifts to the left. Likewise, if you change the value for the vertical ruler to a positive number, the zero point shifts up; if you change it to a negative number, the zero point shifts down. As you would expect, the ruler measurements are marked with positive and negative numbers on either side of the zero point.

Tip To reset the zero point to its default position, double-click in the upper left corner, where the blue lines cross at the ruler intersection.

Snapping Shapes to Ruler Subdivisions

When you're aligning shapes in a measured drawing, you might find it more useful to have shapes snap to the increments you've set on the ruler, rather than to the grid. You can also adjust the snap strength setting to accommodate different magnifications. For example, if you're zoomed in very close and set a strong snap strength, you can place shapes more precisely.

To snap shapes to ruler subdivisions, follow these steps:

1 Choose Tools, Snap & Glue.

2 In the Currently Active area, make sure Snap is selected.

3 Under Snap To, select the Ruler Subdivisions check box.

You might want to clear the Grid check box as well.

Chapter 16

433

4   Click the Advanced tab, and then move the Rulers slider to adjust the snap strength. Alternatively, you can type a value in the Pixels box, rather than use the slider.

5   Click OK.

For details about snapping to other objects, see "Snapping Shapes for Automatic Alignment," page 436.

Controlling Grid Spacing and Origin

It's hard to miss the grid in Visio: it's the set of nonprinting dotted lines on the drawing page that looks like graph paper. You can hide the grid (choose View, Grid), but any diagram you start with a Visio template displays the grid, which is a powerful alignment tool. To accommodate different drawing scales and diagram types, the grid is adjustable. You can control the grid's spacing and set a fixed distance between the lines, and you can shift the grid's point of origin. These options are available when you choose Tools, Ruler & Grid.

Grid spacing in Visio varies depending on the magnification, unless you specify otherwise. The term for this is *variable grid*, where the grid lines change depending on the zoom level. By contrast, a *fixed grid* doesn't change as you zoom the view, which is a more useful option in many measured drawings. In a fixed grid, grid lines that are 1/4 in. apart stay that way at any magnification.

Note   Because grid settings are part of the properties of a drawing page, you can have different settings for every page in a drawing.

Changing Variable Grid Spacing

Even though the grid spacing changes with the zoom level in a variable grid, you can still control how finely spaced the lines are, as Figure 16-13 shows. You can also choose different values for the horizontal and vertical grid lines. To see your options, choose Tools, Ruler & Grid.

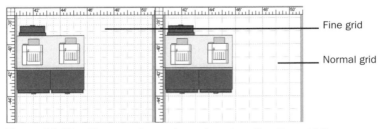

Figure 16-13.   You can change how close together the grid lines appear. Here, both drawing pages are zoomed to 100 percent, but one grid uses normal spacing and the other fine spacing.

The Grid Spacing values that apply to variable grids are Fine, Normal, and Coarse. With each, you'll see similar spacing between lines on your screen no matter what view you've zoomed in or out to. You can set the Minimum Spacing value to define the minimum value for the space between the lines, at any view. For example, if you choose Fine (which causes grid lines to be closer together) with a minimum space of 1 ft. in a scaled drawing, no matter how far you zoom out, the lines cannot be closer than a foot together.

Setting a Fixed Grid

When you need the grid to show you fixed spacing at any magnification, specify a fixed grid as follows:

1 Choose Tools, Ruler & Grid.

2 In the Grid Spacing boxes, select Fixed for both Horizontal and Vertical.

3 In the Minimum Spacing boxes, type a measurement for the line spacing.

   If you want an uneven grid, type different spacing values for Horizontal and Vertical.

4 Click OK.

When you specify Fixed for Grid Spacing, the Minimum Spacing boxes really represent the maximum value for the distance between grid lines. That distance doesn't change as you change zoom levels, so the space your computer screen displays between grid lines will be different in each view.

Setting the Grid Origin

The grid origin is the point from which the grid is measured. In a variable grid, you probably don't care about the grid origin, but in a fixed grid, you might want the grid lines to start at a specific measurement, which can be different for the horizontal and vertical lines, as Figure 16-14 shows. The grid always originates in relation to the ruler's zero point.

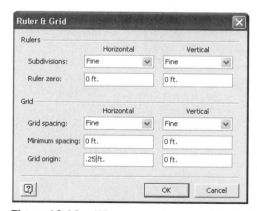

Figure 16-14.   When you enter a positive horizontal value in the Grid Origin box, the grid originates to the right of the zero point.

Chapter 16

By default, the grid origin is at the zero point, which by default is the lower left corner of the drawing page. To change the grid origin, choose Tools, Ruler & Grid, and type a starting measurement in the Grid Origin boxes.

For example, if you type **.25 in.** for the horizontal grid origin, the first horizontal grid line is drawn 1/4 in. from the ruler's zero point. The rest of the grid lines are spaced accordingly from that point.

Positioning Shapes Precisely

Visio offers several aids to guide you in aligning shapes precisely. Many of these tools let you work quickly as Visio does the difficult work for you. Snapping shapes to other shapes or guides ensures proper positioning. The dynamic grid provides a cheat sheet—in effect, it suggests the best positions for shapes in relation to others already on the page. Shape extension lines show you where to draw with respect to shape geometry, tangent points, or isometric points on shapes.

Snapping Shapes for Automatic Alignment

Snapping is one of those Visio behaviors that you don't often think about. It just works. You move a shape, and Visio seems to tug it into the correct position. Snapping works like magnetic attraction. It pulls a shape to a grid, guide, or another shape, making it easier to position and align shapes. For example, you can snap desk shapes to wall shapes, or snap valves to grid lines so that it's easier to draw pipelines between them. Visio even tells you when you're snapping to something, as Figure 16-15 shows.

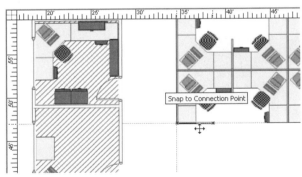

Figure 16-15. When snap is enabled, Visio alerts you to opportunities to snap a shape to guides or other shapes.

Snapping can become very irritating, however, when you're trying to draw precisely and the vertex keeps getting pulled in the wrong direction. At such times, you can quickly disable snapping, choose different snapping targets, or loosen the snap attraction. Snap strength is the stickiness of that attraction. Visio measures snap strength in pixels—the greater the number of pixels, the stronger the snap strength, because objects will attract other objects from farther away. Unfortunately, you can only specify one snap strength for all snap-to objects.

Chapter 16

> **Tip** **Disabaling snapping for categories of shapes**
> In diagrams with many shapes, such as a building plan, you can disable snapping for entire categories of shapes by assigning them to a layer. Layers in Visio are abstract, but definitely worth the effort. For details, see "Controlling Shapes with Layers," page 460.

Toggle Snap

It's easy to use the Snap & Glue toolbar if you want to quickly change snap settings, as Figure 16-16 shows. If it's not visible, choose View, Toolbars, Snap & Glue. For example, to quickly toggle snapping on and off, click the Snap button on the Snap & Glue toolbar.

Highlighted buttons indicate settings that are enabled.

Figure 16-16.   The Snap & Glue toolbar helps you change snap settings quickly.

For aligning shapes, the most useful options are to snap to ruler subdivisions, grids, and guides. Snapping to shapes is useful when you want to position a shape at an exact point on another shape without knowing the point's coordinates. For example, you can snap a line to a quadrant on a circle. Snapping to geometric points is similar to using object snaps in CAD software. Table 16-3 lists the objects you can snap to when you use the Snap & Glue command.

Table 16-3. Objects That Shapes Can Snap To

Object	Description
Ruler subdivisions	The tick marks on the ruler.
Grid	The grid, which appears as nonprinting lines on the page.
Alignment box	The dotted green box that appears around a shape when you move it.
Shape extensions	Any of the lines selected on the Advanced tab of the Snap & Glue dialog box that are used to show alignment. For details, see "Drawing Accurate Geometry with Shape Extension Lines," page 651.
Shape geometry	The visible edges of the shape. This option is more useful for gluing than for snapping alone.
Guides	Ruler guides and guide points. For details, see "Aligning and Moving Shapes with Guides," page 443.
Shape intersections	The point where two shapes intersect, where shape extensions and shapes intersect, or where shape edges are perpendicular to the grid.
Shape handles	The green selection handles that appear when you select a shape with the pointer.
Shape vertices	The green diamonds that show line segments when you select a shape with the Pencil tool. For details, see "Understanding Shape Geometry," page 637.
Connection points	The blue Xs to which connectors can be glued. For details, see "Adding Connection Points to Shapes," page 77.

Chapter 16

Follow these steps to choose the objects that shapes snap to:

1 Choose Tools, Snap & Glue.

2 Under Currently Active, make sure Snap is selected.

3 In the Snap To list, select the objects you want to snap to.

4 If you want to adjust snap strength, click the Advanced tab, and then use the sliders to adjust snap strength for the rulers, grid, guides, and points (connection points, vertices, and shape handles).

5 Click OK.

Changes you make in the Snap & Glue dialog box will not affect objects you've already placed, so you can change these settings as you work on different kinds of shapes.

> **Tip** Snap and glue often work hand in hand to help pull shapes into position and then keep them there. For details about glue, see "Controlling Connections with Glue," page 80.

Using the Dynamic Grid to Center Shapes

If you want to quickly center shapes with respect to other shapes on the drawing page, the dynamic grid makes your task easier. Don't confuse the dynamic grid with those nonprinting lines you see on the drawing page. Instead of measuring space on the page, the dynamic grid shows you the most desirable location for the center of a shape, based on where you've placed previous shapes. For example, if you have one shape on the page and the dynamic grid is activated, when you drag a new shape near the first, dotted lines show the center point of the first shape, as Figure 16-17 shows.

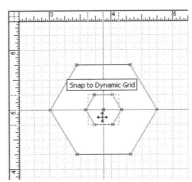

Figure 16-17.   When you drag a shape onto the dynamic grid, dotted lines show you where to drop it to align it with the shapes near it.

Snap to Dynamic Grid

To turn on the dynamic grid, choose Tools, Snap & Glue, and then click the General tab. Under Currently Active, select Dynamic Grid, and then click OK.

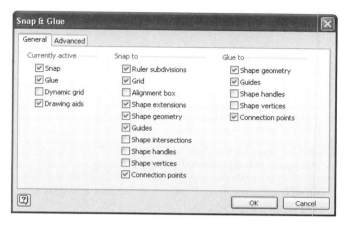

> **Tip** To quickly enable and disable the Dynamic Grid, make sure the Snap & Glue toolbar is displayed (choose View, Toolbars), and then click the Snap To Dynamic Grid button.

Entering Coordinates for Shape Position

You can enter coordinates to move a shape to a specific point on the page with the Size & Position window. To display this window, choose View, Size & Position Window. When you select the shape, its dimensions and location are displayed in the Size & Position window. Depending on the type of shape, different fields can appear. The position of a 1-D shape is described in terms of the position of the line's begin and end points. A 2-D shape's position is described in terms of the shape's *pin*, or center of rotation.

You can think of the horizontal ruler on the drawing page as the x-axis and the vertical ruler as the y-axis of Visio's coordinate plane. The horizontal position of a shape on the drawing page is its x-coordinate. A shape's vertical position is its y-coordinate. Together, these values are referred to as the *page coordinates* of the shape's position—that is, the shape's position relative to the page's axes. That position is measured in the drawing scale established for the page, which you see as the ruler's units.

A 2-D shape's position is given by the x- and y-coordinates of its pin, which marks its center of rotation. If you select a shape with the Rotation tool, its pin is the green circle in the middle. By the way, a shape doesn't have to rotate around its center. You can drag the pin with the Rotation tool to put it wherever you want. However, the Size & Position window always records the shape's position as its pin's position in the X and Y boxes, as Figure 16-18 shows.

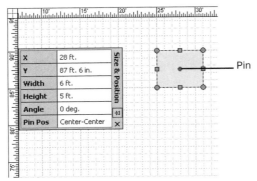

Figure 16-18. The position of a 2-D shape's pin, or center of rotation, appears in the X and Y boxes in the units of measure defined for the drawing page.

The Pin Pos box tells you where the pin is with respect to the shape's *alignment box*, the rectangle that appears around shapes when you move them. The pin position is displayed as the vertical and horizontal position. For example, Center-Center means the pin is centered vertically and horizontally with respect to the shape's alignment box. When you choose an option in the Pin Pos box, such as Top-Left or Bottom-Right, the *shape* moves so that the pin is located in the selected position.

> **Tip** If you have Visio Professional, you can also use the Move Shape add-in to move shapes. It provides a few more options than the Size & Position window. For details, see "Moving Shapes with the Move Shapes Add-In," page 441.

Displaying 1-D Shapes in the Size & Position Window

For 1-D shapes, the Size & Position window displays the x- and y-coordinates of the begin point and the endpoint for a total of four values, as Figure 16-19 shows. The begin point is the line's origin and is indicated by an X in the selection handle. The endpoint is marked with a plus (+) sign in the selection handle.

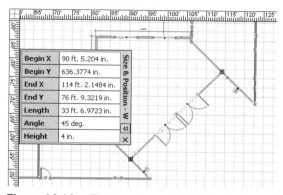

Figure 16-19. The position of this 1-D wall shape is displayed as two sets of coordinate points that locate the shape's begin point and endpoint.

Entering Values to Move Shapes

When you type new coordinates for a shape's position in the Size & Position window, the new values take effect as soon as you press the Enter key. Table 16-4 describes the effect of changing the x- and y-coordinates for 2-D and 1-D shapes.

Table 16-4. Options for Moving Shapes with the Size & Position Window

Size & Position Field	Effect of Entering a New Value
X	Changes the horizontal position of a 2-D shape as measured from its pin
Y	Changes the vertical position of a 2-D shape as measured from its pin
Begin X	Changes the horizontal position of a 1-D shape's begin point
Begin Y	Changes the vertical position of a 1-D shape's begin point
End X	Changes the horizontal position of a 1-D shape's endpoint
End Y	Changes the vertical position of a 1-D shape's endpoint

Moving Shapes with the Move Shapes Add-In

In addition to the Size & Position window, Visio Professional includes a different tool for moving shapes: the Move Shapes add-in, shown in Figure 16-20. (Visio Standard does not include this tool.) Its main advantage over the Size & Position window is that you can specify the distance as a function of the shape's current position, rather than using page coordinates (the X and Y boxes). In addition, you can move a copy of a shape rather than the original, and you can specify the distance to move in polar coordinates, which moves a shape along an angle.

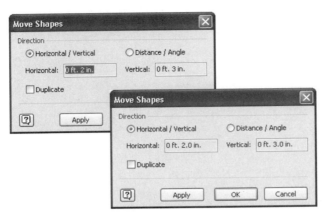

Figure 16-20. You can move shapes by specifying linear or polar coordinates with the Move Shapes add-in.

Follow these steps to use the Move Shapes add-in to move a shape:

1 Select a shape, and then choose Tools, Add-Ons, Visio Extras, Move Shapes.

2 To specify the new position using polar coordinates, select the Distance/Angle option, and then specify the following:

   ■ In the Distance box, type the radial distance you want to move the shape.

   ■ In the Angle box, type a number for the angle along which you want to move the shape.

   Angles are measured positively in a counterclockwise direction with respect to the shape's alignment box. For example, to move the shape up the page, type **90 degrees**; to move it to the left, type **180 degrees**; and to move it straight down, type **270 degrees**.

3 To specify the new position using linear coordinates, select Horizontal/Vertical, and enter the horizontal and vertical distances you want the shape to move.

4 To check the settings you've entered in the Move Shapes dialog box, click Apply, and then see where the shape moves.

   After you click OK, the next time you open the Move Shapes dialog box, the values are reset, so you won't have a record of the settings you used, which might be a problem if the shape moved in an unexpected direction.

5 Click OK. If the shape didn't move as expected, press Ctrl+Z to undo the results.

Chapter 16

Inside Out

Local coordinates

In Visio terms, the Move Shapes add-in moves a shape with respect to the shape's *local coordinates*, which are just the shape's width and height irrespective of its position on the page. For example, if you rotate a shape, its local x-axis (its width) is no longer parallel to the x-axis on the page. You can't do this in the Size & Position window.

Aligning and Moving Shapes with Guides

Guides help you align objects and position them with precision, as Figure 16-21 shows. You can drag guide lines and guide points from the Visio rulers and drop them anywhere on the page. You can also format shapes as guides to create curved guides.

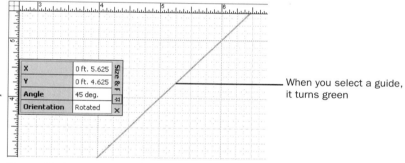

When you select a guide, it turns green

Figure 16-21. Using the Size & Position window, you can rotate a guide and pinpoint its exact location on the page.

Guides can be helpful reference points, providing a visible (and, by default, nonprinting) line along which to position shapes. When you glue shapes to a guide line or guide point, you can then drag the guide to move those shapes, retaining their relationship to each other and to the guide. To create a straight guide line, point to a ruler, and then drag a guide onto the page.

As you drag a guide, you'll see a blue line on the screen and a dotted line on the ruler that shows the guide's position. When you release the mouse button, the guide remains selected and is highlighted in green. If you click elsewhere to cancel the selection, the guide is displayed as a blue dotted line.

Tip You can assign guides to layers, which is a useful way to visually connect information on different layers of your drawing. For details about layers, see "Assigning Shapes to Layers," page 464.

Chapter 16

Creating Nonlinear Guide Shapes

You can create a guide from any Visio shape, including arcs, splines, and ellipses. By applying a guide style to the shape, Visio changes the formatting of the shape so that it looks and behaves like a guide, as Figure 16-22 shows. Technically, the guide shape remains a shape—it includes selection handles and an alignment box, but you can disable their display.

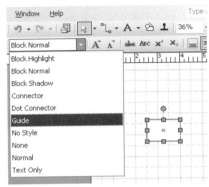

Figure 16-22. You can create a guide in any shape by drawing a shape and then applying the Guide style.

To create a nonlinear guide shape, select a shape that you want to use as a guide. In the Style list box on the Formatting toolbar, select the Guide style. Visio formats the shape as a guide. You can also use the Style command on the Format menu, and then select Guide in the Line Style box.

Disabling a Guide Shape's Selection Handles

If you want to turn off the display of the selection handles and alignment box for your guide shape, you can—but do so after you've moved the guide shape into place. If you turn off the display of selection handles, the guide shape definitely looks more like a guide, but you won't be able to tell when you have selected it, which makes it difficult (but not impossible) to move or copy.

Follow these steps to turn off the selection handles and alignment box for a guide shape:

1   Select the guide shape, and then choose Window, Show ShapeSheet.

    The ShapeSheet window opens and displays the guide shape's properties.

2   Scroll down until the Miscellaneous section is visible.

3   Click in the NoObjHandles cell, and type **TRUE** to make selection handles invisible.

4   Click in the NoAlignBox cell and type **TRUE** to make the shape's alignment box invisible.

5   To close the ShapeSheet window, click its Close button.

Chapter 16

Troubleshooting

A shape won't snap or glue to a guide or guide point

You can snap and glue shapes to a guide point only if Snap and Glue are both enabled and the Guides option is checked in both the Snap To and Glue To sections of the Snap & Glue dialog box.

Moving and Rotating Guides

Although you can just drag a rectilinear guide from the ruler, sometimes you need to position a guide more precisely or to place an angled guide line in your drawing. The Size & Position window gives you this flexibility. When you select a guide, its position is displayed in the Size & Position window. To select a guide, click it. Table 16-5 describes how to use the Size & Position window to move and rotate guides.

Table 16-5. Techniques for Moving and Rotating Guides Using the Size & Position Window

Task	Technique
Change a horizontal guide's position on the drawing page	Type a different X value, and then press Enter. (The Y value shows you where the pointer was when you selected the guide.)
Change a vertical guide's position	Type a new Y value, and then press Enter. (The X value shows you where the pointer was when you selected the guide.)
Rotate a guide	Type an angle in the Angle box.
Quickly unrotate a guide	Click in the Orientation box, click the arrow, and then choose Horizontal or Vertical.

Hiding Guides

Guides

To hide guides, choose View, Guides, or click Guides on the View toolbar. You can easily hide guides temporarily to unclutter your screen and bring them back into view when you need them. Objects you've snapped or glued to guides retain their positions when you hide guides, but you can't snap or glue additional shapes to guides while they're hidden.

Tip If you need a printable guide, or any type of reference line that you can format, you can create an *infinite line*. For details, see "Creating Infinite Lines," page 648.

Using the ShapeSheet to Move Guides

You can specify values for a guide's position and angle in its ShapeSheet window. Select a guide and then choose Window, Show ShapeSheet to display the ShapeSheet. This fact is primarily of interest to people who want to programmatically create a diagram and align shapes

Chapter 16

with guides. The same fields you used in the Size & Position window are available here, in addition to many other controls.

> **Note** For details about editing ShapeSheet cells, see "Using the ShapeSheet Window," page 735.

Moving Shapes and Guides Together

In many desktop layout applications, guide lines serve as reference points only. In Visio you can also glue shapes to a guide, so when you move the guide, the shapes move right along with it, as Figure 16-23 shows. This technique is invaluable when you need to adjust a set of shapes to change their relationship with a different set of shapes but don't want to change their relationship with each other.

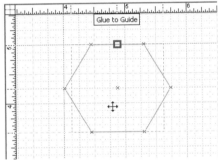

Figure 16-23. When you glue shapes to a guide, you can drag the guide on the page to reposition all the shapes glued to that guide.

You can glue shapes to an existing guide, create a new guide specifically for that purpose, or let Visio create a guide for you automatically. To glue shapes to a guide, both Snap and Glue must be enabled. Choose Tools, Snap & Glue, and make sure both the Snap and Glue options are checked in the Currently Active list. Then, make sure the Guides option is checked in both the Snap To and Glue To lists, and click OK.

> **Tip** If the Snap & Glue toolbar is visible, you can click the Snap and Glue buttons, and then click the Guides button to enable them all.

Spacing Shapes on a Guide

If you want to control the spacing of the shapes on the guide, glue each one manually. That is, move each shape toward the guide until you see red shape handles, which indicate that the shape is glued to the guide. After you've glued all the shapes, you can drag the guide anywhere on the page and all the shapes will move with it. As you move the guide, a dotted line in the ruler shows you its position.

Chapter 16

Distributing Shapes on a Guide

If you want shapes to be evenly distributed or perfectly aligned along a guide line, let Visio do it for you. For example, Visio can create a guide for each shape you select, as Figure 16-24 shows. Then, when you move one guide, the other shapes move, too, to maintain their alignment or distribution.

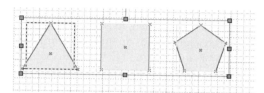

Figure 16-24. Visio can align shapes evenly and glue them to guides so that moving the guide moves the shapes and maintains their alignment.

Follow these steps to automatically create aligned or distributed guides and glue shapes to them:

1 Select the shapes you want to glue to a guide.

Tip To select multiple shapes, press the Shift key as you click, or drag a selection rectangle around the shapes you want.

2 Choose Shape, Align Shapes or choose Shape, Distribute Shapes.

3 Click the alignment or distribution option you want, and then select the Create Guide And Glue Shapes To It check box. Click OK. If you just wish to align your shapes, you can click on the Align Or Distribute Shapes button on the Action toolbar.

When you click OK, Visio creates a guide and glues the shapes to it in the relationship you have specified. Here are the results:

● If you used the Distribute Shapes command, when you move the outermost guides in the set, Visio moves the other shapes in the set so that they retain consistent distribution. Although you can see all the guides, you can move only the outermost ones.

● If you used the Align Shapes command, Visio creates one guide and automatically glues the selected shapes to it in the alignment style you selected.

For details about the Align Shapes and Distribute Shapes commands, see "Aligning Shapes to Each Other," page 449.

Tip Locking shapes into position

Gluing a shape to a guide isn't the same as locking its position. You can still move the shape anywhere else on the page. To lock a shape's position, select the shape, and then choose Format, Protection. Select the X Position and Y Position check boxes, and then click OK.

Setting a Reference with Guide Points

In addition to guide lines, you can use the rulers to create guide points, which have the same snap and glue properties as guides. However, guide points exist at only one point, instead of applying to an entire set of points on a vertical or horizontal line.

To create a guide point, drag your mouse from the blue crossbar at the intersection of the rulers to the point where you want the guide point. The guide point looks like a circle with two blue lines crossed through it, as Figure 16-25 shows. Then, to align a shape with a guide point, drag the shape to the guide point, and align a point on the shape with the guide point. If glue is enabled, it's easier to see when the shape is aligned to the guide point.

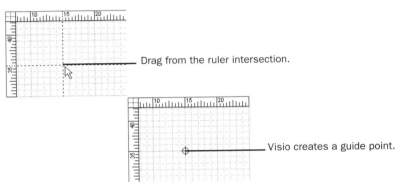

Drag from the ruler intersection.

Visio creates a guide point.

Figure 16-25. To align shapes to a specific point on the page, create a guide point.

Moving a Guide Point

You can use the Size & Position window to position a guide point, as Figure 16-26 shows. When the guide point is selected, the Size & Position window displays the point's location on the page in the X and Y boxes. Together, these values represent the page coordinates for the point. To move the guide point to a precise location, type new values into the X and Y fields.

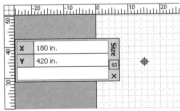

Figure 16-26. For precise position, type new X and Y values for a selected guide point in the Size & Position window (choose View, Size & Position Window).

> **Tip** If you want to keep the Size & Position window handy, but don't want to surrender screen real estate to it, click the AutoHide button.

Printing Guides

Visio considers guides to be nonprintable objects, but you can change this if you're willing to edit a guide's ShapeSheet. The ability to print a guide is a shape property that's stored in the Miscellaneous section of the ShapeSheet window. If you change the setting, when you next print your drawing, the guides print along with the drawing.

To set a guide or guide point to print, follow these steps:

1 Click to select a guide, and then choose Window, Show ShapeSheet.

The ShapeSheet window opens and displays the guide's properties.

2 Scroll down until the Miscellaneous section is visible.

Miscellaneous					
NoObjHandles	FALSE	HideText	FALSE	ObjType	0
NoCtlHandles	FALSE	UpdateAlignBox	FALSE	IsDropSource	FALSE
NoAlignBox	FALSE	DynFeedback	0	Comment	""
NonPrinting	TRUE	NoLiveDynamics	FALSE	DropOnPageScale	100%
LangID	1033	Calendar	0	LocalizeMerge	FALSE

3 Click in the NonPrinting cell, and type **FALSE** to set a guide to print.

> **Tip** When you click in a ShapeSheet cell that contains a value of TRUE or FALSE, Visio displays a drop-down list box, where you can select the value you want instead of typing.

4 To close the ShapeSheet window, click its Close button.

Aligning Shapes to Each Other

Just as you can align shapes to guides and grid lines, you can align them to each other. In fact, Visio makes it easy to align shapes to other shapes automatically along their tops, bottoms, sides, or middles. You can also *distribute* shapes so that they're equidistant from each other.

Adjusting Shape Alignment

With the Align Shapes options, you can align shapes along their bottom edges, top edges, center points, right edges, or left edges. If you display the Action toolbar (choose View, Toolbars, Action), you can quickly change shape alignment with the Align Shapes button, which includes the drop-down options shown in Figure 16-27.

Figure 16-27. You can display the Action toolbar to provide quick access to alignment options.

> **Tip** If you click the drop-down arrow for the Align Shapes button, the alignment options are displayed. If you click the button (not its arrow), the Align Shapes dialog box appears.

The only trick, if you can call it that, to aligning shapes is that Visio must align shapes to a reference point, which is the first shape you select. If you select multiple shapes by dragging a selection rectangle around a group of shapes, the reference shape used for alignment is the shape at the front of the stacking order. You can always tell which shape the others will be aligned to by its green selection handles. Note, though, that if you have selected more than 25 shapes, the reference shape will not appear with green selection handles.

Follow these steps to align shapes:

1   Select a shape that's correctly positioned. Green selection handles appear around the shape. Visio uses this as the reference shape.

2   Hold the Shift key, and click (or drag) to select the other shapes you want to align to the first. A thick, magenta box surrounds the first shape, and a thinner magenta box surrounds the second.

3   Click the Align Shapes button, and then choose the option you want.

4   Click OK to align the shapes.

Using the Align Shapes Command

If you're using the Align Shapes command on the Shapes menu rather than the Align Shapes button on the Action toolbar, you might find it a little easier to predict the effect of the alignment options because they're labeled, as Figure 16-28 shows.

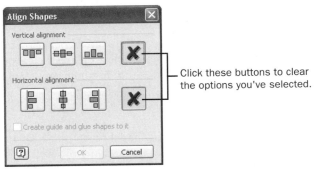

Figure 16-28.   You can see the alignment options more easily in the Align Shapes dialog box.

In the Align Shapes dialog box, the Up/Down Alignment options align the shapes by their top edges, bottom edges, or vertical centers. The Left/Right Alignment options align shapes by their left edges, right edges, or horizontal centers. Only in the dialog box can you select both an Up/Down Alignment option and a Left/Right Alignment option and apply them simultaneously. The result is that all of the shapes you selected will be positioned on top of each other, which can be handy if you want to merge or group them.

Adjusting Shape Distribution

One way to arrange shapes evenly on a page is to use the Distribute Shapes command. It evens out the horizontal or vertical spacing between three or more selected shapes. For example, you can adjust spacing between flowchart shapes, as Figure 16-29 shows, or draw a series of lines, and then use this command to create evenly spaced stripes. You can distribute shapes evenly according to their sides, tops, bottoms, or centers, but you can't specify the distance between the shapes; Visio calculates the distribution according to the positions of the shapes on the page.

Distribute Shapes button

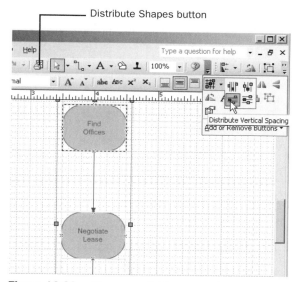

Figure 16-29. You can quickly space shapes evenly with the Distribute Shapes button on the Action toolbar or with the command on the Shapes menu.

Here's how the Distribute Shapes command works: first, select the shapes you want to distribute. (As always, use the Shift key to select multiple objects.) You can select the shapes in any order; unlike the shape alignment options, the shape distribution options aren't affected by the order of selection. Then choose Shapes, Distribute Shapes. In the Distribute Shapes dialog box, choose a distribution option, as Figure 16-30 shows, and then click OK.

Chapter 16

451

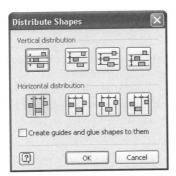

Figure 16-30. Use the Distribute Shapes dialog box to create even spacing between shapes.

Tip   Move evenly spaced shapes
You can use the check box at the bottom of the Distribute Shapes dialog box to add guides to which the distributed shapes are glued. Then you can drag the outermost guides to move the shapes without disrupting the even spacing.

Even with the visual feedback that the dialog box provides, the results aren't always apparent. All the options vary in how the spacing between shapes is measured. Table 16-6 shows how the options in the Distribute Shapes dialog box provide even spacing between objects.

Table 16-6. Options for Distributing Shapes

Option	Description
	Distributes equal amounts of space between the left and right edges of shapes
	Distributes the shapes so that there is equal spacing between the left edges of the shapes
	Distributes the centers of shapes evenly
	Distributes the shapes so that their right edges are uniformly spaced
	Distributes equal amounts of space between the bottom and top edges of the shapes
	Distributes the shapes so that their top edges are evenly spaced

Table 16-6. Options for Distributing Shapes

Option	Description
	Distributes the centers of shapes evenly
	Distributes the shapes so that their bottom edges are uniformly spaced

> **Tip** **Arrange shapes evenly**
>
> Use the Distribute Shapes button on the Action toolbar to quickly apply the most common distribution options. If you click the drop-down arrow for the Distribute Shapes button, a palette of options appears. However, the palette doesn't offer as many distribution options as the dialog box. To see all the options, click the Distribute Shapes button (not its arrow) to display the Distribute Shapes dialog box.

Troubleshooting

The Distribute Shapes command doesn't arrange shapes precisely enough

The Distribute Shapes command measures the distance between the first two shapes you select and places the same amount of space between all other selected shapes. If you need more control over the way shapes are distributed, try one of the following techniques:

- Drag out guides at precise intervals, and then glue shapes to them.
- Use the Offset command to create shapes that are offset from one another at a distance you specify. For details, see "Creating and Offsetting Lines with Shape Operations," page 665.

Calculating and Displaying Dimensions

Often, it's not enough that your shapes are precisely the right size. To communicate clearly with your audience, and to provide accessible reference points, you might need to show the dimensions of shapes in a drawing, especially if you're creating engineering or architectural drawings. You can display the dimensions using dimension lines or geometry fields. Using either of these methods, Visio calculates and displays shape dimensions, updating the information when you resize or otherwise change a shape. In addition, Visio Professional includes a handy tool that calculates the total area and total perimeter of any shape for you.

Using Dimension Lines to Show Size

Visio includes dimension lines for displaying linear, angular, and radial dimensions. You can quickly add dimensions to a drawing when you use a dimension line shape and connect it to points on a shape that you want to measure, as Figure 16-31 shows. Depending on the product edition you have, you can choose from several different dimensioning shapes. Visio Professional includes more built-in dimension line shapes than Visio Standard, because Professional supports more measured drawing types. In Visio Standard, the only measured drawing is the Office Layout diagram.

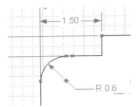

Figure 16-31. This mechanical-parts drawing uses horizontal and arc radius dimension line shapes that automatically display the dimensions of the shapes to which they're glued.

Many of the dimensioning shapes on the different Visio Professional stencils have the same name and behavior. However, shapes from each stencil display the dimension lines differently as follows:

- **Dimensioning—Architectural stencil** Shapes from this stencil display the dimension value above the dimension line and use a slash for line ends on linear dimensions.
- **Dimensioning—Engineering stencil** Shapes from this stencil display the dimension value in the middle of the dimension line and use an arrowhead for line ends on linear dimensions.

To open a dimensioning stencil, choose File, Shapes, Visio Extras, and then either Dimensioning—Architectural or Dimensioning—Engineering. You can also click the Shapes button on the Standard toolbar, select Visio Extras, and then either Dimensioning—Architectural or Dimensioning—Engineering.

Adding a Dimension Line

Some shapes display dimension lines automatically, such as room shapes. However, you can easily add a dimension line shape to any drawing to measure outside or inside dimensions (as in a building), baselines, diameter and radius, and angles. Figure 16-32 shows dimension lines around the walls of a room.

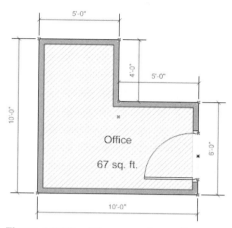

Figure 16-32.   When you glue a dimension line to a wall, the dimensions are updated as you size the wall.

If the stencils you're working with don't already include a dimension line shape, you can open one of the following stencils:

- If you have Visio Standard, choose File, Stencils, Building Plans, and then select the Walls, Doors And Windows stencil. Use the Controller Dimension shape.

- If you have Visio Professional, choose File, Shapes, Visio Extras, and then choose the Dimensioning—Architectural or Annotations stencil.

Most of the dimension line shapes work in approximately the same way to calculate and display linear and angled dimensions. You can glue one of these dimension line shapes to the shape you're measuring so that, when you resize the shape, its new dimensions are calculated and displayed automatically.

Follow these steps to add a dimension line shape to a drawing:

1   Drag a dimension line shape from one of the dimensioning stencils onto the page.

2   Drag an endpoint on the dimension line until it is glued to the selection handles of the shape that you want to measure. The handle turns red when it is glued to the shape.

Warning   If glue has been disabled, the handle won't turn red. To reactivate glue, choose Tools, Snap & Glue, select the Glue check box under Currently Active, and then click OK.

3   Repeat for each endpoint on the dimension line.

Controlling the Way Dimensions Are Displayed

Visio's dimension line shapes display the measurement units you have set for the drawing page. However, you can set a unit of measure for a dimension line that differs from the one set for the page as follows:

1   Right-click a dimension line shape, and choose Precision & Units.

The Custom Properties dialog box appears, as shown in Figure 16-33.

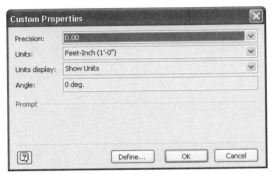

Figure 16-33.   You can specify the units of measure and the degree of precision displayed by a dimension line.

2   Click the drop-down arrow for the Precision list, and select the style of display you want to use.

3   Click the drop-down arrow for the Units list, and select the units you want to use.

4   In the Units Display list, choose whether to display units or not.

5   In the Angle box, type a value to rotate the dimension line.

For example, type **35 deg.** to rotate the line by that amount.

6   Click OK.

Displaying Custom Measurements

You could say that all Visio shapes "know" how big they are. Width and height are among the many properties that Visio records for every object. In addition, many shapes include custom properties. For example, a desk shape in an office layout can have the property Manufacturer, and the valve shape in a piping diagram can have the property Design Pressure. You display these properties automatically in a custom callout shape. Like dimension line shapes, custom callouts have control handles that you can drag to attach the line to a shape. Once glued to a shape, the custom callout can "read" that shape's custom properties. You can choose which properties will appear on the callout line.

For example, in an office layout, you could use custom callout shapes to display inventory properties for furniture in the drawing, as Figure 16-34 shows. After you set up one custom callout to display the information you want, you can copy the callout and glue it to other shapes that contain the same property.

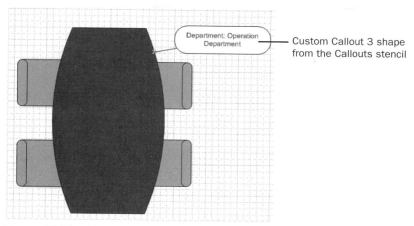

Custom Callout 3 shape
from the Callouts stencil

Figure 16-34. You can use a custom callout shape to display any custom property for a shape, not just dimensions. Here, the callout displays the Department property for the table shape.

Displaying Width, Height, or Angle on Shapes

A shape can display its own dimension when you add a geometry field to its text block. For example, you can add a text field to a sofa shape that displays the shape's width, making it easier to move in a floor plan, as Figure 16-35 shows. A geometry field is one of several dynamic fields that you can add to a shape. Geometry fields can display the width, height, or angle of a shape. Visio automatically calculates and updates values whenever you resize or rotate the shape.

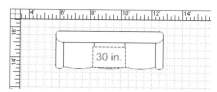

Figure 16-35. By adding a geometry field to a shape like this sofa, you can display the shape's dimensions.

You can format the geometry field to display the level of precision you need. The dimensions are displayed using the drawing's units of measure, so in a scaled drawing, shape width and height reflect real-world dimensions. If you display shape angle, you can display the value in radians or degrees.

Chapter 16

Inside Out

Using the degree symbol

If you display the angle in degrees, you can add the degree symbol instead of displaying the label "deg." To do this, choose General under Format, and then click OK. With the text pointer still in the shape, make sure NumLock is on, and then press Alt+0176.

To insert a geometry field into the text of a shape, follow these steps:

Text tool

1 Click the Text tool, and then click the shape. If the shape already has text, position the insertion point where you want the field to appear.

2 Choose Insert, Field, and then in the Category list, click Geometry.

Geometry fields appear in the Field list.

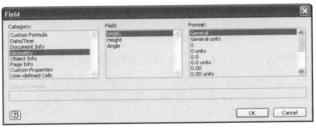

3 Select the field you want to display.

In the Format list, options appear for formatting the field's value. For example, if you select Width, choose 0.000 units to display the width to three decimal places with the drawing's units of measure (such as 5.398 in.).

4 Click OK.

Note You can insert more than one geometry field into a text block, just as you can include other text fields and text that you type. However, you can insert only one field at a time.

For details about using callouts and text fields, see "Annotating Diagrams with Callout Shapes," page 130, and "Creating Text Fields to Display Information," page 141.

Calculating Perimeter and Area

Only Visio Professional includes the tool for calculating perimeter and area automatically—Visio Standard does not. Visio Professional can calculate the total perimeter and area of any closed shape, including shapes from a stencil or those you draw. For example, you can calculate the area of a room for which you want to order carpeting, or the perimeter of an entire building for security equipment planning. The Shape Area And Perimeter dialog box works something like the Size & Position window. It displays the total area and total perimeter for the shape or shapes you have selected, as Figure 16-36 shows. By default, the measurement is displayed in inches (perimeter) and square inches (area), but you can select other units of measure.

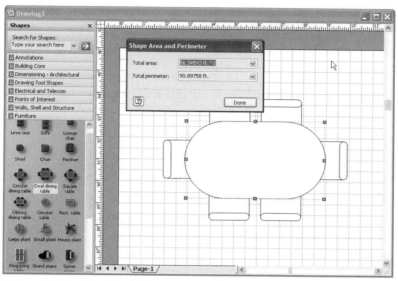

Figure 16-36.   The Shape Area And Perimeter dialog box displays values for selected shapes.

To display this dialog box, choose Tools, Add-Ons, Visio Extras, Shape Area And Perimeter. To select the measurement unit you prefer, choose an option in theTotal Area and Total Perimeter lists.

You don't have to select shapes before opening the Shape Area And Perimeter dialog box, nor do you have to reopen it each time you want to calculate the area and perimeter of a different shape. Like the Size & Position window, the Shape Area And Perimeter dialog box displays the area and perimeter for shapes as you select them. If you select multiple shapes, the Total Area and Total Perimeter values reflect all the shapes combined.

> **Note**   The Shape Area And Perimeter dialog box does not report the area for open shapes—that is, shapes without a seamless border or boundary. For open shapes, it displays only the perimeter. You also cannot measure the area or perimeter for an imported ("foreign") object.

Measuring Multiple Shapes

Pencil tool

Line tool

If you want to measure the perimeter and area of a drawing that contains multiple shapes, you don't have to measure each separate shape, and then add them up. Instead, use the Pencil or Line tool to trace the boundary of all the shapes, and then find the area and perimeter of the simple boundary shape. Choose Tools, Add-Ons, Visio Extras, Shape Area And Perimeter.

What if you want to measure the perimeter or area of multiple, separate areas? For example, in a floor plan, you might need to calculate the area of several, nonadjoining rooms so that you can order the same flooring for all of them. In this case, you can select all of the objects and then choose Tools, Add-Ons, Visio Extras, Shape Area And Perimeter. The dialog box calculates the totals for the selected shapes.

Measuring Area with Empty Space

In architectural drawings and floor plans, you frequently need to know the total area of a space without including an empty space contained within it, such as a stairwell. Here's a tricky way to do this using Visio's drawing tools instead of your calculator:

1 Click the Line tool, draw a shape around the floor perimeter, and then draw a shape around the stairwell.

2 Select both shapes, and then choose Shape, Operations, Combine.

   The Combine command creates a hole in the floor shape equal in size to the stairwell shape.

3 Choose Tools, Add-Ons, Visio Extras, Shape Area And Perimeter.

   The Total Area and Total Perimeter values reflect the total floor area minus the hole.

Controlling Shapes with Layers

Layers are essential in multiple-page drawings or diagrams that contain many shapes. Layers help you organize related shapes on a drawing page so that you can work with and view shapes according to their layer assignment. For example, you can create a detailed drawing that includes electrical outlets, computer networking details, furniture layouts, and more, and then use layers to display selected information. When you want to rearrange the furniture, you can hide electrical outlets and computer networking details. When you're most interested in your drawing's electrical outlets, you can hide everything else. Not only does this help you see the big picture electrically, but it keeps you from rearranging other objects accidentally, such as furniture, when you're positioning those outlets. You can hide, lock, print, count, snap, or glue shapes based on their layer assignment.

About Layers

Layers might not be what you think they are based on your experience with other layout or design programs. Visio layers are not stacking order. Layers don't control which shapes appear in front and in back. Layers don't really work like stacks of transparencies. They're more of a concept for grouping or cataloging shapes. Technically, a *layer* is a named category to which you can assign shapes. For example, you can create a Furniture layer in a floor plan. The layer doesn't do or mean anything unless you assign a shape to it. Let's say you assign all the desks and chairs to your Furniture layer, but not the walls and cubicle panels. Now the layer becomes useful. For example, you can hide all the shapes on the Furniture layer to make it easier to work with just the walls.

Besides hiding and showing shapes, layers can be used to protect your work. You can lock a layer so that none of the shapes assigned to it can be edited. Unlike other applications, Visio lets you assign a shape to more than one layer. Those cubicle panels can belong to both a Walls layer and a Moveable Furniture layer. Because layers are the property of a drawing page, in a multiple-page drawing, the layers you create for one page don't appear on any other pages—but if you need them to, see "Using Layers in Multiple-Page Diagrams," page 469.

Using Shapes with Preassigned Layers

You don't have to create layers to take advantage of them. When you start a diagram with a Visio template, you might find that your drawing already includes layers. Many Visio masters are already assigned to layers, so when you drop them onto the page, the layer is added as well. For example, when you open the Office Layout template, the masters are already assigned to layers. As you drop instances of the masters, the layers are created automatically. A room shape is assigned to the Spaces layer; its dimension lines are assigned to the Dimensions layer; and the outline of the space is assigned to the Building Envelope layer. The Layer box on the Format Shapes toolbar displays the layer to which a selected shape is assigned, as Figure 16-37 shows. If the shape is assigned to more than one layer, Multiple Layers is displayed in the Layer box.

Figure 16-37. In an office layout diagram, the Format Shapes toolbar displays the layers to which selected furniture shapes are assigned—in this case, the Movable Furnishings layer.

Follow these steps to select all the shapes on a layer:

1   Choose Edit, Select By Type.
2   In the Select By area, choose the Layer option.

Chapter 16

3   In the Layer list, select the layer that contains the shapes you want. To select more than one layer, press Ctrl+click. To select shapes that aren't assigned to any layer, choose No Layer.

4   Click OK.

Visio selects the shapes assigned to the layer.

Layers for CAD Users

Layers in Visio differ from layers or levels in CAD programs in some key ways. Think of layers as an organizing principle rather than stacked sheets of paper or Mylar sheets on a drafting table. Because they're used to organize, Visio layers don't affect which shapes appear in front or in back. They can offer different views of a diagram inasmuch as you can hide and show shapes according to the layer they're assigned to. Here are several basic truths about Visio layers that often surprise CAD users:

- A shape can be assigned to more than one layer.
- A shape can belong to no layer.
- A Visio drawing can have no layers.
- You can't group layers. (Some CAD programs offer group layer management, where several layers can be given a group name.)

Viewing Layers in a Diagram in the Drawing Explorer

You can see all the pages in your diagram, including all the shapes and layers on each page, in the Drawing Explorer window. To display it, choose View, Drawing Explorer Window. To see details about pages and layers, double-click the Foreground Pages folder, and then double-click the page you're currently working on (or Page-1 if you haven't added or renamed any pages). Double-click the Layers folder. If nothing happens, your drawing contains no layers. Otherwise, Visio lists all the layers on the page. If you expand a layer, you can see all the shapes assigned to it, as Figure 16-38 shows.

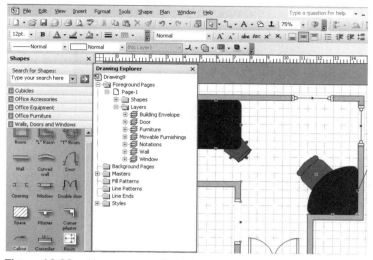

Figure 16-38. You can see all the layers on a page—as well as all the shapes assigned to that layer—in the Drawing Explorer window.

In the Drawing Explorer window, you can quickly make a layer visible or active: right-click the layer, and then select the option you want. You can also delete layers with this method (which does *not* delete the shapes on the layer). When you make a layer active, each shape you subsequently add to the diagram is assigned to that layer automatically.

Creating Layers in a Diagram

You can create your own layers to add to the ones Visio supplies or add layers to a drawing that doesn't include them already. When you create a new layer, it is added to the current page only, not to other pages in your diagram. You can define new layers as you insert new pages into a diagram. Or, you can just copy shapes with layer assignments from one page to the new page—when you paste the shape, any layers it's assigned to are added to the new page. Visio is smart enough to know if the page already has a layer with the same name and adds the shape to the existing layer.

Follow these steps to create a new layer:

Layer Properties

1 Choose View, Layer Properties. Or click the Layer Properties button on the View toolbar.

Chapter 16

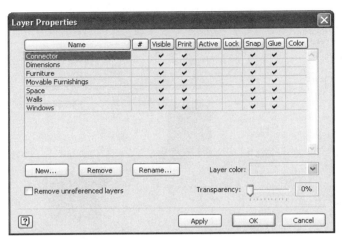

2 Click New to open the New Layer dialog box.

3 In the Layer Name box, type a name for the new layer, and then click OK.

4 In the Layer Properties dialog box, select the options you want for the new layer, and then click OK.

For example, if you select Active, all shapes you subsequently add to the diagram are assigned to the new layer automatically (until you designate a different active layer.)

Inside Out

Deleting empty layers

The Remove Unreferenced Layers check box in the Layer Properties dialog box is a quick way to delete layers to which no shapes are assigned. This option is primarily intended to help you clean up your drawing files.

Assigning Shapes to Layers

Of course, layers are only useful if some shapes have been assigned to them. You can assign a shape to more than one layer, or you can leave a shape unassigned. To assign an individual shape to a layer or layers, follow these steps:

1 Select a shape, and then choose Format, Layer.

2 Click the layers you want to assign to the shape. Press the Ctrl key as you click to select multiple layers.

3 Click OK.

If the Format Shapes toolbar is visible, you can select a shape, and then select a layer from the drop-down list in the Layer box.

> **Note** You can't add shapes to a locked layer. A layer is locked when you select the Lock option in the Layer Properties dialog box (choose View, Layer Properties).

Assigning Visio Masters to Different Layers

Many master shapes are already assigned to layers, but you can change those assignments. This is worth doing if you frequently use shapes from a Visio stencil that are preassigned to layers you don't use. For example, if you find yourself creating the same new layer every time you start a new office layout, consider adding your shape to a custom stencil. Let's say you always assign panel shapes to a Cubicle layer. You can save your edited panel shape on a custom stencil, effectively creating a new master panel shape with your Cubicle layer. Every time you add that shape to a drawing page in the future, the Cubicle layer is added to the page.

As an alternative, you can edit one of the existing masters to reassign its layers. To do this, right-click a stencil title bar, choose Edit, and then edit any of the master shapes. You can then save your changes as a new stencil or with the original stencil. Note that in Visio 2003, you can only edit stencils that you have created (custom stencils). You cannot edit the stencils that ship with the software. To create a custom stencil, click the Shapes button on the Standard toolbar, and then select New Stencil. On the other hand, you can also choose Files, Shapes, New Stencil.

When you edit a master shape, Visio opens a master drawing page and displays all the commands that apply, including Format, Layers (where you can assign the master to a new layer) and View, Layer Properties (where you can rename an existing layer). Editing masters is just like editing shapes once you're working in the master drawing window.

For details about how to open stencils and edit masters, see "Creating a New Stencil," page 625.

Assigning Groups to Layers

To assign a group to a layer, first group the shapes and then choose Format, Layer and select the layer to which you want to assign the group. All of the group members are assigned to the new layer, and their previous layer assignments are canceled. If you want the individual shapes to retain their current layer assignments, select the Preserve Group Member Layers check box in the Layer dialog box. For example, you might group a prep cart and a microwave oven and then assign the group to the Kitchen layer but also want the prep cart to remain on the Furniture layer and the microwave on the Appliances layer.

Working with Active Layers

If you add a shape that doesn't already have a predefined layer assignment to a page, the shape is assigned to the *active layer* automatically. By making a layer active, you can quickly add shapes to a diagram and assign them to a layer all at once.

Tip **Make a layer active**
If you keep the Drawing Explorer window open (choose View, Drawing Explorer Window) when you're working in a drawing with layers, you can quickly select the active layer by right-clicking a layer in the Drawing Explorer window, and then choosing Active.

To specify the active layer, choose View, Layer Properties, and then click in the Active column of each layer that you want to make active, as Figure 16-39 shows.

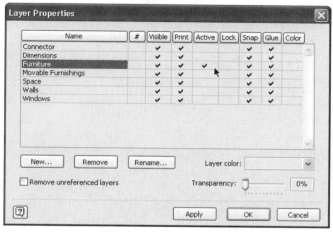

Figure 16-39. Click in a layer's Active column to make it the active layer. More than one layer can be active at a time. You can't make a locked layer the active layer.

Inside Out

Working with the active layer

When you're working with active layers, remember to reset the active layer as you work so that new shapes are added to the appropriate layer. For example, before adding electrical outlet shapes to a drawing of an office layout, make the Power/Comm layer active.

Don't bother to specify an active layer if you're only using Visio master shapes, such as those on the Walls, Doors And Windows stencil. They're already assigned to the correct layer anyway. If you don't specify an active layer, new shapes are not assigned to any layer unless you're using a master shape with a built-in layer assignment.

Using Layers to Protect, Hide, and Organize Shapes

After you have assigned shapes to a layer, you can work with them as a group. You can lock them against editing, hide them temporarily from view, set entire layers to not print, and determine whether other shapes can snap or be glued to them. For example, while you're adding furniture to an office layout, you might want to disable snapping for all the shapes on the Power/Comm layer so that desks don't snap to electrical outlets. Then, you can disable printing for all the shapes on the Furniture layer to print a copy of the diagram that shows only the walls and wiring.

Chapter 16

To specify options for each layer, you must work in the Layer Properties dialog box, as shown in Figure 16-40. You can open the Layer Properties dialog box in several different ways, depending on which windows and toolbars are available:

- Choose View, Layer Properties.
- Click the Layer Properties button on the View toolbar.
- Right-click the Layers folder in the Drawing Explorer window, and then choose Layer Properties.

Tip To count the number of shapes assigned to a specific layer, click the # button to the right of the Name column.

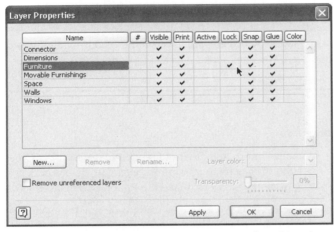

Figure 16-40. To work with all the shapes assigned to a layer, choose View, Layer Properties, and then click in a column to enable an action, such as Snap, for a layer.

Table 16-7 describes the options that are available for shapes assigned to layers.

Table 16-7. Options for Layer Properties

Option	Description
Visible	When checked, all the shapes assigned to the layer are displayed. Clear to temporarily hide shapes.
Print	When checked, shapes assigned to the layer appear when you print the page. When cleared, shapes assigned to the layer don't print, a useful technique when you want to print different parts of a drawing for different audiences. If a shape is assigned to multiple layers, you must cancel the Print option for every layer the shape is assigned to for the behavior to work.
Active	When checked, makes the layer the active layer. For details, see the previous section, "Working with Active Layers."

468

Table 16-7. **Options for Layer Properties**

Option	Description
Lock	When checked, shapes assigned to the layer cannot be selected, moved, or edited, and the layer cannot be set as Active. You cannot add shapes to a locked layer.
Snap	When checked, you can snap shapes to the shapes assigned to the layer. When cleared, the shapes assigned to the layer cannot be the target of snapping, although the shapes themselves still snap. If a shape is assigned to multiple layers, you must cancel the Snap option for every layer the shape is assigned to for the behavior to work.
Glue	When checked, you can glue shapes to the shapes assigned to the layer. When cleared, the shapes assigned to the layer cannot receive connections (that is, other shapes cannot be glued to them), but any connectors on the layer can still connect and glue to other shapes. If a shape is assigned to multiple layers, you must cancel the Glue option for every layer the shape is assigned to for the behavior to work.
Color	When checked, the Layer Color list box appears in the Layer Properties dialog box, and all shapes assigned to the layer are highlighted in the selected color. Each layer for which this option is selected can be displayed in a different color. The color temporarily overrides the shape's original color. If a shape is assigned to multiple layers, it always appears in its original color unless you specify the same color for each layer to which the shape is assigned.

 Inside Out

Nonprinting or locked layers

If your drawing includes nonprinting or locked layers, enable the Color option for those layers, and then choose a color (for example, gray for nonprinting layers and red for locked layers). That way, you'll have a visual reminder on the page that the shapes have special attributes.

Using Layers in Multiple-Page Diagrams

In many diagram types with multiple pages, a repeating element can appear on all pages. Maybe it's something as simple as a corporate logo or title block. You can place such elements on a background page and then assign that background to every foreground page on which you want it to appear. In technical drawings, you can get even fancier with background pages and use them to organize, hide, and reveal elements on multiple-page diagrams. To do this, you assign background shapes to layers. Because a background can be shared by more than one page, so, too, can its layers—this is a critical point, because layers can't be used on more than one page.

Chapter 16

For example, in an office layout where the same room outline is used on multiple pages, you can put the walls and moveable panels on the background, and then use different foreground pages to display furniture layouts, electrical wiring, network cabling, and so on. If you assign the wall shapes to one layer on the background and the panels to another, you can hide the moveable panels on all the pages that display the background whenever you need to see only structural elements.

You can also use background layers as a way to protect information that shouldn't be modified, such as the project's permit number or a company logo. To do this, create a new layer (for example, the Permanent layer), assign these shapes to the layer, and then lock the layer with the Layer Properties command on the View menu. You can then pass the file to others without risk.

Chapter 17

Using CAD Drawings in Visio

You're designing a sound system or a conference room layout or some ductwork—something that you know Microsoft Office Visio 2003 can do—and you want to include an existing CAD drawing from the architect or engineer. Why start from scratch? Visio does a good job of importing CAD drawings as background images that you can annotate with Visio shapes. You can even convert CAD objects to Visio shapes when you want to edit more extensively. In addition, you can convert Visio drawings to CAD-readable format. Visio includes filters and converters for both Autodesk AutoCAD DWG and DFX formats, IntelliCAD DWG format, and Bentley MicroStation DGN format. In Visio 2003 the improved DWG converter assures that the drawings converted to Visio have higher fidelity than the original CAD files, allowing you to work with even more accuracy than before.

In case you are new to the concept, let us explain. CAD refers to a variety of specialized drawing programs capable of producing highly detailed, accurate drawings, such as for machined parts or construction. Obviously, Visio's strengths differ from those of a CAD program. Whether you know much about CAD programs or not, this chapter provides the information you need to help you get the best results when you're working with CAD files in Visio drawings.

How Visio Works with CAD Programs

Experienced CAD users might come to Visio with expectations that Visio can't meet. Visio was never intended to be a substitute for high-end drafting and design tools. However, many people work with drafters, engineers, and architects and simply want the benefit of working with their drawings—without taking a CAD class first. That's where Visio can help. Visio provides several methods of bringing CAD files into a Visio document or using Visio diagrams in a CAD program. You can do the following:

- *Import* a CAD drawing for display only. Visio online Help refers to this as "inserting" a CAD drawing. Visio displays a copy of the CAD drawing as an OLE embedded object that you can use as a background page, reference layer, or detailed insert, but you can't edit its contents.

- *Convert* a CAD drawing, which converts the original objects to fully editable Visio shapes.

- *Export* a Visio diagram as a DWG, DXF, or DGN file. In a multiple-page Visio diagram, you must export each page separately.

Most of the time, when you need to display a CAD drawing in Visio, your best option is to insert it as a display-only object rather than convert it, as Figure 17-1 shows. You can use the display-only CAD image as a background layer so that you can enter comments or drag Visio shapes on top of it, or you can insert the CAD drawing onto the page and crop it to provide detail for a portion of your Visio drawing.

Warning CAD drawings are often large files and importing them into a drawing may make Visio respond sluggishly on slower computers.

Shapes snap to the underlying geometry of the CAD drawing

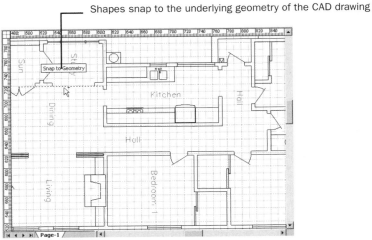

Figure 17-1. An inserted CAD floor plan provides an accurate backdrop for electrical, HVAC, network, or other shapes, which you can drop on top.

For details about background pages in Visio, see "Using Background Pages," page 51.

For occasions when you really need to edit the geometry of a CAD object within Visio, you can convert a drawing. For example, maybe you have a legacy CAD file that you need to revise, but no access to the program used to create it. By converting the CAD objects to Visio shapes, you gain full control of the file. You can also convert in the other direction—converting a Visio diagram into a CAD-readable format. However, no one at Microsoft recommends round-tripping Visio and CAD files. Consider the two conversion features to be one-way only.

Note The ability to insert CAD drawings in Visio files is included with both Visio Standard and Visio Professional.

Chapter 17

Using Visio for CAD Users

If you're used to working in a CAD program, you'll notice that Visio products use a different approach to drawing. For starters, Visio uses a drawing page instead of model space, and you create shapes with masters rather than blocks. Several other tasks you perform in CAD programs are also accomplished differently in Visio as the following sections describe.

Model Space Versus the Drawing Page

In CAD programs, you create a model in the coordinate system referred to as *model space*. If you display a model in a view port, the coordinate system is transformed to *paper space*, so you can print or plot the diagram.

In Visio, however, you begin and end your work on the drawing page. In CAD terms, you can think of the Visio drawing page as a single, two-dimensional view port into model space. Visio shapes are vectors for which dimensions are measured as width and height. A shape's location is its position on the plane represented by the drawing page. The coordinates on the drawing page are measured in units that correspond with the real-world measurement units of the object or space you're representing, as Figure 17-2 shows. For example, if you're drawing a floor plan, the Visio ruler might show that the drawing page is 100 feet (ft.) wide, but in reality, the drawing page prints on a standard paper size, such as D-size plotter paper.

The rulers measure feet and inches to convey the size of the floor plan.

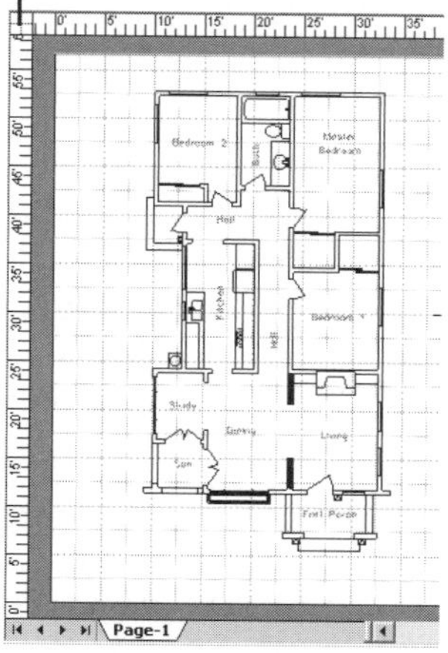

Figure 17-2. On the Visio drawing page, coordinates are measured in units that correspond with the actual size of the represented objects.

The last view in which a CAD drawing was saved before you bring it into Visio affects how it looks and what you can do with it in Visio. In general, you'll get better results if the CAD drawing is saved in model space. This is especially true if you're converting the drawing and its contents to shapes. Visio can convert all the objects and text from the specified layers of a drawing saved in model space. If the drawing was saved in paper space, Visio converts objects and text quite literally as they appear—but at least they're converted. For example, if an object or text in paper space appears to be clipped at the edge of the view port, the clipping is converted to Visio lines, rather than the whole object represented by the clipped portion.

In addition, if a CAD drawing was last saved in paper space, you won't be able to change its drawing scale when you insert or convert it.

World Coordinates Versus Drawing Units

In CAD programs, you draw in the real-world units of the world coordinate system. In Visio, you draw in *drawing units*, which can be any units you specify. In addition, you usually specify a drawing scale in Visio before you start to draw. A drawing scale is the ratio of space on the page to real-world measurement units. In a floor plan, for example, it's impractical (to say the least) to print a page that is 40 ft. wide. But if you specify a drawing scale of 1/4 in. = 1 ft., you can represent a building that's 40 ft. wide on standard letter-sized paper.

> **Note** For details about drawing scales and units of measure in Visio, see "Setting Up Measurements in a Diagram," page 421.

When you insert or convert a CAD drawing, Visio sets a custom drawing scale that ensures the CAD drawing will fit on the Visio drawing page. If the CAD drawing is large, and the Visio drawing page is small, the result is a new drawing scale that forces the CAD drawing to fit—which might not be the ideal drawing scale for your purpose. You can, however, control the drawing scale and the page size either when you insert or convert the drawing, or later after it's in Visio.

Visio Equivalents for CAD Commands

If you're used to working in a CAD program, you might find Visio terminology confusing. Some of the commands common to CAD programs aren't available in Visio at all; others are a little different and might even be easier to use in Visio. Table 17-1 summarizes commands and tasks that are commonly available in CAD programs and the equivalent functionality in Visio.

Table 17-1. Visio Equivalents for CAD Operations

Task in a CAD Program	Technique in Visio
Set the drawing scale	Choose File, Page Setup, click the Drawing Scale tab, and then select a scale. In Visio, set the drawing scale before you begin to work. For details, see "Setting Up Measurements in a Diagram," page 421.
Move an object	Select a shape with the Pointer tool and drag it. Or choose View, Size & Position Window to open a window in which you can specify a new shape position.

Table 17-1. Visio Equivalents for CAD Operations

Task in a CAD Program	Technique in Visio
Move an object a specific distance	Use the Size & Position window. If you have Visio Professional, you can use the Move Shapes add-in (choose Tools, Add-Ons, Visio Extras, Move Shapes). For details, see "Moving Shapes with the Move Shapes Add-In," page 441.
Copy an object	Select a shape, and then hold the Ctrl key while you drag a copy to a new location. Or use the standard Windows shortcuts—Ctrl+C and Ctrl+V—to copy and paste objects.
Create a block or a cell	Use the Visio drawing tools to create a shape, and then drag the shape to a stencil to create a master shape.
Pan and zoom a drawing	Choose View, Pan & Zoom Window to open a window in which you can adjust the view of a drawing.
Use operations such as Union, Fragment, and Join to create objects	Choose Shape, Operations, and then choose an action. For details, see "Merging Shapes to Create New Ones," page 660.
Add a hatch pattern to an object	Select a shape, and then choose Format, Fill. You can set the color, pattern, and pattern color for the hatch. You can also create your own patterns. See "Creating Your Own Line and Fill Patterns," page 693.
Use entity snaps or object snaps	Choose Tools, Snap & Glue, and select the Shape Extensions option. On the Advanced tab, select the shape extensions you want to use.

Drawings with Externally Referenced or Image Files

If you import or convert a CAD drawing that includes xref commands, Visio looks for the referenced files and displays a message if it can't find them. You can avoid seeing the warning message about externally referenced files in one of two ways: either create the same folder hierarchy on your computer, or place all externally referenced files in the same folder as the Visio drawing.

In addition, if you import a DWG file that includes embedded image files, Visio can display them—but not until you convert the CAD drawing. The image files won't appear when you import the file, but if you convert the drawing to Visio shapes, any image files included will appear.

Chapter 17

Importing CAD Drawings in Visio

The easiest way to work with a CAD drawing in Visio is to import it as a display-only object rather than convert it to Visio shapes. After importing a CAD file, you can drag Visio shapes onto it, add annotations or text for comments, rescale it, crop and pan it, and hide and show its layers or levels. However, you can't edit the CAD drawing itself. For example, when you want to review and annotate a CAD file without changing the original, import it in Visio, mark changes, and then save the results in Visio or CAD format.

Typically, CAD files are imported for the following reasons:

- An architectural drawing of a floor plan already exists, and you want to use it as a background for adding office furniture, network shapes, electrical outlets, or other building services.

- You want to review a CAD drawing in Visio without changing the original so that you can make notes or additions and then send your comments back to the drawing's author.

- You want to provide additional detail for some part of a manufacturing diagram or electrical schematic by using an existing CAD drawing as a detail image or callout. You can rescale, move, and crop the inserted drawing to position it just where it's most needed on the page.

Although the imported CAD drawing is display-only—which means that you can't change its geometry—Visio does recognize that geometry. So shapes you add will snap to the lines in the CAD drawing, making quick work of aligning objects.

You can use either of the following commands to import a CAD drawing in much the same way you open or import other graphic file formats:

- Choose File, Open to create a new file containing the CAD image, and set the drawing scale of the Visio page to match the scale of the CAD drawing.

- Choose Insert, CAD Drawing to add the image to the existing page.

With either command, Visio displays the CAD Drawing Properties dialog box, which provides unique features for imported CAD objects, as Figure 17-3 shows. Within this dialog box, you can change the drawing scale and units of the imported drawing, hide layers or levels, and protect the drawing from accidental changes after it's inserted.

> **Note** Visio will only import DWG and DXF files. If you wish to import other CAD drawings you must first convert them to either DWG or DXF format.

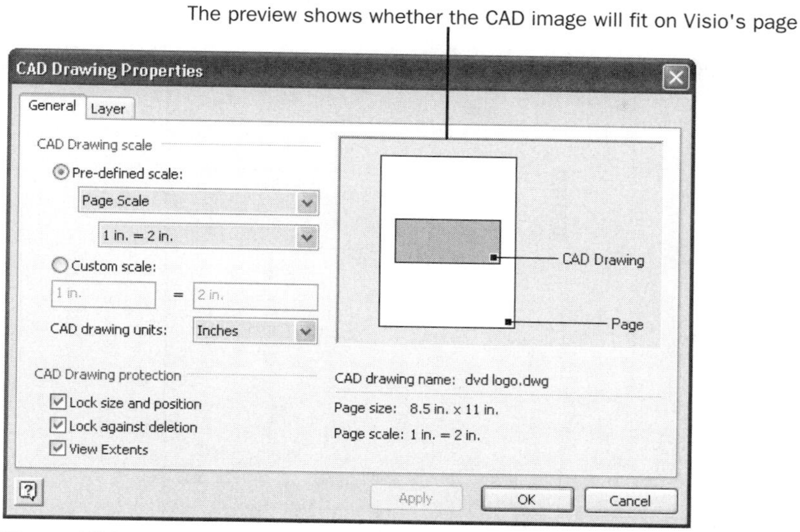

The preview shows whether the CAD image will fit on Visio's page

Figure 17-3. When you import a CAD file (choose File, Open or choose Insert, CAD Drawing), Visio displays this dialog box, where you choose the options you want.

> **Tip** Displaying the CAD Drawing Properties box
> To display the CAD Drawing Properties dialog box for a drawing you've already inserted, right-click the CAD drawing and choose <File Type> Object, Properties. For example, choose CAD Drawing Object, Properties or MicroStation DGN File Object, Properties.

Importing Layers and Levels

Although a CAD drawing might comprise several layers or levels, the entire image is assigned to one Visio layer, named CAD Drawing. However, you can choose which of the original CAD layers or levels is visible and, depending on the file type, choose other options as well.

In the CAD Drawing Properties dialog box, the Layer tab appears when you import DWG and DXF files. The tab gives you the ability to hide layers or levels in the imported CAD drawing file by selecting the Visible option, as Figure 17-4 shows. You can also change the color and line weight applied to objects on each layer. You can change these options when you import the file or afterward.To display these options again, right-click the imported drawing, choose CAD Drawing Object, and then choose Properties. On the Layer tab, click a color or line in the dialog box to edit it.

Choose the levels you want to import from DGN files.

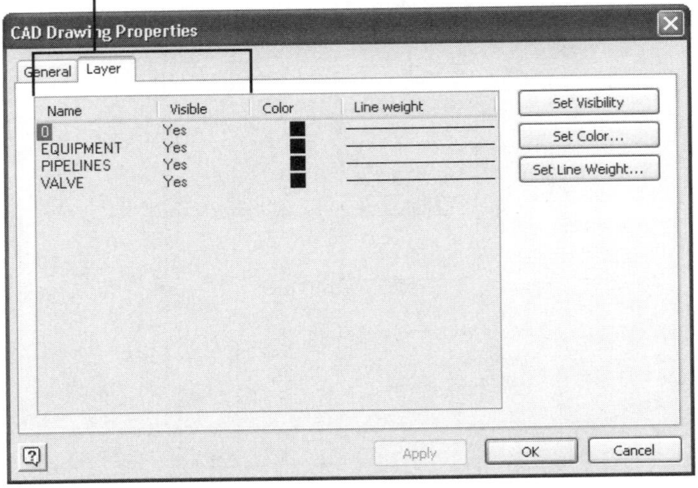

CAD Drawing Properties

General | Layer

Name	Visible	Color	Line weight
0	Yes		
EQUIPMENT	Yes	■	
PIPELINES	Yes	■	
VALVE	Yes	■	

Set Visibility
Set Color...
Set Line Weight...

Apply | OK | Cancel

Figure 17-4. When you import a CAD drawing, you can hide layers or levels by clearing the Visible option, which makes the drawing display faster in Visio.

For details about how Visio uses layers, see "Controlling Shapes with Layers," page 460.

Troubleshooting

The CAD file does not import as expected in Visio

How well Visio imports a CAD drawing depends in part on how the drawing was saved in the CAD program. For example, Visio displays the CAD drawing as it was last saved in the CAD application. If that view was 200 percent, you might not see much of your drawing in Visio. Additionally, Visio can't display proxy objects, which are proprietary objects defined by AutoCAD programming code, so if your drawing contains proxy objects, much of the Visio page could be blank.

To avoid these and similar problems, ask your CAD program operator to make the following adjustments to the CAD drawing before providing it to you:

- Use the Purge All and Audit commands to clean up the drawing.
- Use the ChProp command to select all entities and set the color to BYLAYER. (This ensures you'll be able to change layer colors in the CAD Drawing Properties dialog box in Visio.)
- Set Tilemode = 1 to put the drawing in model space.
- Use the Zoom Extents command to set the view appropriately.
- Save the drawing as an R14 DWG file, or, if the file contains proxy objects, save it as an R12 DXF file.

Importing a CAD File

By importing, you add a CAD drawing to a Visio drawing file as a display-only background on top of which you can add shapes or review comments, as Figure 17-5 shows.

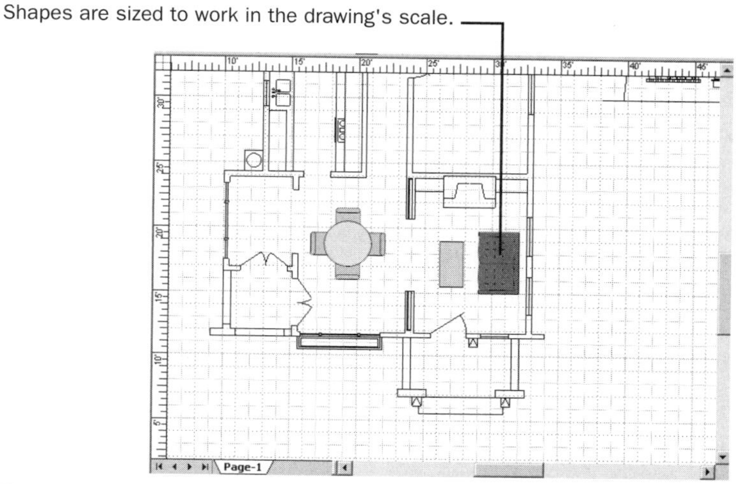

Shapes are sized to work in the drawing's scale. ———

Figure 17-5. When you import a CAD drawing as a background layer, you can use Visio shapes and text to annotate it.

> **Warning** CAD drawings are often large files and importing them into a drawing may make Visio respond sluggishly on slower computers.

To import a CAD drawing, follow these steps:

1 Do one of the following:

- To start a new Visio drawing with the CAD drawing, choose File, Open.
- To insert the CAD drawing into an existing file, open the Visio drawing file you want, and then choose Insert, CAD Drawing.

2 In the Files Of Type list of the Open dialog box, select AutoCAD Drawing (DWG Pr DXF File). Locate and select the CAD file you want, and then click Open.

3 To choose a drawing scale, do one of the following:

- If you plan to drag Visio shapes on top of the CAD image, select the Pre-Defined Scale option, and then click the PageScale tab to set the Visio drawing scale to match that of the CAD drawing. Click OK.
- If you won't be adding Visio shapes to the CAD drawing, you can reduce or enlarge the CAD drawing as you import it. In the CAD Drawing Scale area, select the scale you want to use, which does not need to match the scale of the Visio drawing page.

4   If you want to be able to reposition or resize the imported drawing, clear the Lock Position and Lock Cropping check boxes.

> **Tip**   If the CAD drawing shown in the preview area looks like it isn't centered on the page, clear the Lock Position check box. You'll want to be able to drag the inserted drawing into position on the page, after which you can lock its position.

5   If you want to hide some of the layers or levels in the CAD drawing, click the Layer tab, and then clear the Visible option for those layers.

6   Click OK. If the CAD Drawing dialog box appears, you can continue by clicking OK.

> For details about adjusting the page size and drawing scale, see "Changing the Scale of an Imported CAD Drawing," page 484.

Troubleshooting

After importing a DWG file, the drawing scale cannot be changed

If the DWG file was saved in paper space, you won't be able to set its drawing scale. Ask the drawing's author to save the CAD drawing in model space instead, and then import it again.

Snapping to Objects in the CAD Drawing

If you have inserted a DWG file, you can snap shapes to its geometry just as you could snap them to other shapes in the Visio drawing. This is pretty impressive, because you haven't actually converted the CAD objects to Visio shapes. Although shapes in previous versions of Visio could snap to the underlying geometry of imported CAD drawings, snap support is more accurate in this version. You can also snap to endpoints and midpoints in DWG files, as Figure 17-6 shows. However, if you have difficulty snapping the shape where you want it, drag a guide from one of the rulers and snap to the guide instead.

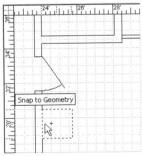

Figure 17-6.   ScreenTips show you where to place shapes to snap to the underlying geometry of an imported DWG file.

For details about working with guides and setting snap options, see "Positioning Shapes Precisely," page 436.

Troubleshooting

When you add Visio shapes to an inserted CAD drawing, they're the wrong size

If the drawing scale of the CAD drawing you import doesn't match the drawing scale of the page, you'll have trouble adding Visio shapes to the drawing. Even if you don't plan to place shapes on the page, you'll prevent a great deal of confusion if the CAD drawing scale and Visio drawing scale match. The Page Scale option in the CAD Drawing Properties dialog box is included for this purpose.

Locking and Unlocking a CAD Drawing

When you import a CAD drawing, you can use the Lock Position check box in the CAD Drawing Properties dialog box as a measure of protection. When checked, this option ensures that the CAD drawing isn't accidentally repositioned as you work with objects on the Visio drawing page. However, if you need to reposition the CAD drawing in Visio, you can remove this lock. To do this, right-click the CAD drawing in Visio, and choose <*File Type*> Object, Properties. In the CAD Drawing Properties dialog box, clear the Lock Position check box, and then click OK.

Visio offers other protections against inadvertent change. For example, you can lock the layer to which Visio assigns the imported drawing. Locking any Visio layer prevents you from accidentally selecting, moving, or resizing the shapes on that layer while you are working on other things. If you lock the background layer that contains a CAD drawing, you can be certain that you won't inadvertently move the drawing. If you import a DWG file, you can still snap shapes to its objects even if the background layer is locked.

Locking the background layer is superfluous if you've selected the Lock Position and Lock Cropping options in the CAD Drawing Properties dialog box. However, if you also lock the background layer, you prevent the drawing from moving when you pan with the Crop tool. To lock the background layer, right-click the CAD drawing, and then choose View, Layer Properties. Place a check mark in the Lock column for the CAD Drawing layer, and then click OK.

For details about Visio's layer and locking behavior, see "Controlling Shapes with Layers," page 460.

Chapter 17

Troubleshooting

The imported drawing can't be selected or right-clicked

If you can't select the CAD drawing or right-click the drawing to display its shortcut menu, the CAD Drawing layer might be locked. A locked layer cannot be edited. To restore editing capabilities, choose View, Layer Properties, and then clear the Lock column for CAD Drawing.

Modifying Inserted CAD Drawings

When you import a CAD drawing, you can modify it in certain ways, even though the image is for display only. You can drag Visio shapes onto it, rescale it, crop and pan it, and hide and show layers and levels within it.

Tip   View CAD file information in Visio

Visio stores the file name and timestamp of an inserted CAD drawing as custom properties for the inserted object. To display these properties, right-click an inserted drawing, and select View, Custom Properties Window. The Custom Properties window displays the full file name and path as well as the date and time when the CAD drawing was last updated.

Positioning an Imported CAD Drawing

After you have imported a CAD drawing, you can move it on the page and also move the image within its border. The tool you use determines what happens:

Pointer tool

Crop tool

- Use the Pointer tool on the Standard toolbar to drag the entire drawing to a new position.

- Use the Crop tool to move the portion of the drawing that's visible within its border. This is called *panning* the drawing and is shown in Figure 17-7. The pointer displays a hand icon when you pan a drawing. Select the crop tool by choosing Shape, Action, Crop Tool, or by right-clicking the CAD drawing and selecting Crop Tool.

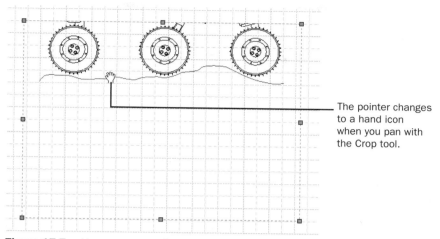

The pointer changes to a hand icon when you pan with the Crop tool.

Figure 17-7. You can pan an imported CAD drawing to adjust the visible portion within the border.

Visio always stores the entire imported drawing on the page. By panning, you choose an area within the whole to display. After you have positioned the CAD drawing the way you want it, you probably want to lock its position. To do this, right-click the drawing, choose *<File Type>* Object, Properties, and then select the Lock Position check box. If you want, select the Lock Cropping check box as well for added security. Then click OK to close the dialog box.

> **Note** Even if you select the Lock Cropping check box, you can still pan the CAD image with the Crop tool. To prevent this from happening, lock the CAD drawing layer as described in "Locking and Unlocking a CAD Drawing," page 481.

Sizing an Imported CAD Drawing

After you import a CAD drawing, you can enlarge or reduce it in a couple of ways, depending on the effect you want. You can:

- **Crop the drawing** When you *crop* a drawing, you change the size of the area in which the CAD drawing appears, as Figure 17-8 shows. To do this, right-click the CAD drawing and select the Crop Tool, and then drag the green selection handles on the drawing border to move its edges inward, obscuring part of the drawing. Cropped objects always have rectangular drawing borders.

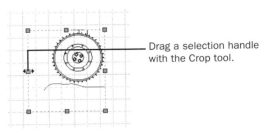

Drag a selection handle
with the Crop tool.

Figure 17-8. You can crop an imported CAD drawing to reduce the visible portion.

- **Resize the drawing** Use the Pointer tool to resize the drawing by dragging a corner selection handle if it's not important to preserve the drawing scale of the CAD image.

- **Change the scale** Enlarge or reduce the drawing by changing its drawing scale as the following sections describe. This is the best option when you're using Visio shapes on top of the drawing and you need the imported drawing to occupy more or less space on the drawing page.

Changing the Scale of an Imported CAD Drawing

When you first import a CAD drawing, Visio automatically sets a custom drawing scale that ensures the drawing will fit on the page. This behavior results in the nonstandard drawing scales that you see in the CAD Drawing Properties box when you import. For example, Visio might establish a drawing scale of 1 in. = 300 in. for a large building plan—an odd scale, but one that ensures the image will fit on standard, letter-sized paper. If the Visio page is set to architectural, D-size paper, Visio imports the building using a scale of 1 in. = 70 in. The preview area in the CAD Drawing Properties dialog box reflects Visio's bias for making drawings fit on paper, as Figure 17-9 shows.

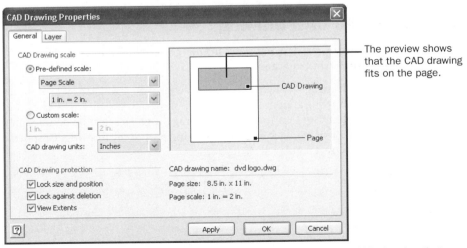

The preview shows
that the CAD drawing
fits on the page.

Figure 17-9. By default, Visio establishes a scale for an imported CAD drawing that ensures the entire image will fit on the page.

Changing the Drawing Scale

You can adjust the CAD drawing scale in the CAD Drawing Properties dialog box when you import the file or display this dialog box afterward by right-clicking the imported drawing, and then choosing <*File Type*> Object, Properties. The drawing scale for the CAD drawing is displayed on the General tab of the CAD Drawing Properties dialog box, whereas the drawing scale for the Visio page is shown on the Drawing Scale tab of the Page Setup dialog box, as Figure 17-10 shows.

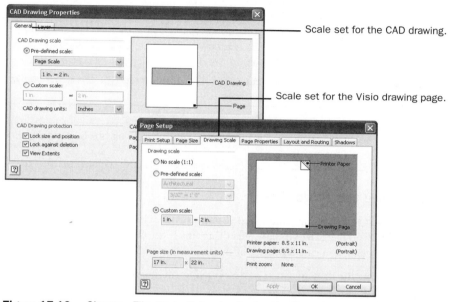

Figure 17-10.   Choose, File, Page Setup to display the Page Setup dialog box, where you can set the page drawing scale.

Table 17-2 describes the drawing scale options that are available in the CAD Drawing Properties dialog box.

Table 17-2. Drawing Scale Options

Task	Option
Choose a standard drawing scale for the CAD drawing	Select Pre-Defined Scale, and then choose Architectural, Civil Engineering, Metric, or Mechanical Engineering. In the drawing scale list box, select a scale. You can safely choose one of these drawing scales if you plan to add only annotation shapes, text blocks, or other unscaled shapes.
Match the CAD drawing's scale to the drawing scale of the Visio drawing page	Select Pre-Defined Scale, and then choose Page Scale. For example, if the Visio page is set to 1/32 in. = 1 ft., choosing Page Scale sets the CAD drawing's scale to 1/32 in. = 1 ft. as well. This option is the easiest way to ensure good results when you add scaled Visio shapes, such as office furniture or network shapes, to the drawing.
Specify a drawing scale for the CAD drawing	Select Custom Scale, and then type the scale you want to use in the boxes.

Tip You can also display the CAD Drawing Properties dialog box by choosing Edit, CAD Drawing Object, Properties.

Adjusting the Page Size

If you adjust the drawing scale when you import or while you work, you might also need to adjust the Visio page size so that everything fits. If the CAD drawing is larger or smaller than your Visio page, you can do either of the following:

- Change the drawing scale as described in the previous section.
- Change the drawing page size.

To change the size of the drawing page, choose File, Page Setup, and then click the Page Size tab. It's quickest to select Size To Fit Drawing Contents, which gives you a sense of just how big the CAD object is. However, this setting most likely results in an odd-sized page that might not fit on your printer's paper.

For details about page size and printing, see "Printing Diagrams of Any Size," page 242.

Troubleshooting

The inserted CAD drawing can't be repositioned or rotated on the page

When you insert a CAD drawing, Visio automatically locks it to prevent you from moving, stretching, or rotating the image. The assumption is that you want to use the CAD image as a background on top of which you'll add shapes, so naturally you don't want the background to move. You might, however, have other plans. To move the inserted image on the drawing page, right-click it, select <*File Type*> Object, and then choose Properties. Clear the Lock Position check box, and then click OK. This allows you to drag the inserted CAD image to a new location. However, you still can't resize or rotate it. To clear the aspect ratio and rotation locks that prevent you from these actions, select the CAD image, and then choose Format, Protection. Clear the check boxes for any locks you want to remove.

Converting CAD Drawings into Visio Format

You can make many changes to inserted CAD drawings without converting them. However, you cannot delete, resize, or modify the objects in a drawing unless you convert them to Visio shapes. If you have an existing library of CAD symbols that you want to use in Visio diagrams, you probably want to convert them into reusable master shapes. Because a typical CAD drawing can include hundreds or thousands of objects, it's best to convert selectively. Visio lets you convert objects in a CAD drawing that you've already imported on the basis of their layers or levels. You can also convert several CAD drawings and all their layers at once.

Converting a CAD drawing brings to light the very different natures of the DWG/DXF file formats and the Visio file format. As one Visio product planner put it, "CAD is just a bag of vectors." When you convert a CAD drawing, *each vector* is converted to a shape, as Figure 17-11 shows. For example, the four lines that make up a rectangular room in a CAD drawing might become four Visio shapes—one for each wall. By contrast, a room shape from the Walls, Doors And Windows stencil is just one shape no matter how many lines it contains. In addition, the speed with which Visio can redraw the display is based on the number of shapes in a drawing, so more shapes means slower performance.

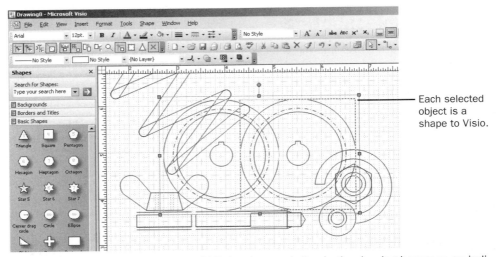

Each selected object is a shape to Visio.

Figure 17-11. When you convert a CAD drawing, each line in the drawing becomes an individual Visio shape that you can select.

Converting an Imported CAD Drawing

After you import a display-only CAD drawing, you can quickly convert it to Visio shapes with the Convert Wizard. In the wizard, you choose the CAD layer or level that contains the objects you want to convert. The three-step conversion process can take a few minutes, depending on the complexity of the CAD drawing, the number of layers or levels you're converting, and the speed of your machine. After conversion, the objects in the CAD drawing will appear as an outline. You can then group, edit, or add them to a stencil. In short, you can do anything with them that you can do with any other Visio shape.

Inside Out

Changes in the CAD converters

Visio products have included CAD converters for several versions. If you're used to using earlier versions of the converter, you might notice that the streamlined version (introduced with Visio 2000) provides fewer options in the interface. However, many of the options that are no longer in the converter interface itself are still available through the CAD Drawing Properties dialog box and the converter template.

Step 1: Select the Layers to Convert

Follow these steps to convert CAD objects to Visio format:

1   Import a CAD drawing as described earlier.

2   Right-click the CAD drawing, and then select *<File Type>* Object, Convert to start the Convert Wizard, as Figure 17-12 shows.

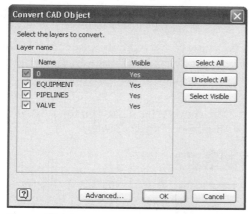

Figure 17-12.   The Convert Wizard steps you through the options when converting an imported CAD drawing to Visio shapes.

3   Click Unselect All, and then select the layers or levels containing the CAD objects you want to convert. To select multiple layers or levels, hold down the Ctrl key while clicking.

4   When you've selected all the layers, you can click OK to convert the layers or, for additional options, click Advanced.

Inside Out

Converting selectively

For performance reasons, it's in your best interest to convert only the layers of a CAD drawing that contain objects you really want to edit. Visio not only displays unconverted (that is, display-only) CAD drawings faster, but also displays them more clearly.

Chapter 17

489

Step 2: Hiding or Deleting CAD Layers

For this step, click Advanced. The options presented determine how much of the original imported CAD drawing to retain (see Figure 17-13). The wizard's language is a little counter-intuitive, but these are your options:

- **Delete Selected DWG Layers** Visio converts the objects on the selected layers to shapes but removes the original layers from the imported CAD drawing. That way, you'll still see the unconverted layers as a display-only object. (This option isn't available for DGN files.)

- **Hide Selected DWG Layers** Visio converts the objects on the selected layers to shapes and retains the original layers, but hides them. That way, the converted shapes won't duplicate portions of the CAD drawing, but the original display-only drawing remains intact.

- **Delete All DWG Layers** Visio converts the objects on the selected layers to shapes, but removes the imported, display-only CAD drawing.

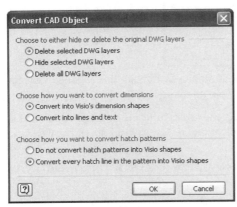

Figure 17-13.   The Convert Wizard can retain all, some, or none of the original layers of the CAD drawing as a display-only object. The wizard can also convert dimension lines into intelligent Visio dimension shapes. Hatch patterns can be converted to not-so-intelligent Visio lines.

Step 3: Converting Dimensions and Hatch Patterns

You can choose how to convert dimensions and hatch patterns in Step 3 of the Convert Wizard, as Figure 17-13 shows. You have the following options:

- **Convert Into Visio's Dimension Shapes** Displays dimensions that are automatically updated when you resize the shapes they're associated with. The converted dimension lines lose the font and line style they had in the CAD drawing.

- **Convert Into Lines And Text** Preserves the CAD formatting of dimension lines, which will appear as static annotations that are not automatically updated.

- **Do Not Convert Hatch Patterns Into Visio Shapes** Preserves the CAD formatting of hatch patterns, which you can't edit in Visio.
- **Convert Every Hatch Line In The Pattern Into Visio Shapes** The wizard converts each vector in a hatch pattern into a separate Visio line shape that you can edit.

Converting Multiple CAD Drawings

You can convert more than one CAD drawing at a time with the Convert CAD Drawings add-in, as Figure 17-14 shows. Although this method is efficient when you have several drawings to convert, you don't have as much control as you do when you convert drawings individually. Each CAD drawing is converted into a separate Visio file, and every layer or level in each CAD drawing is converted. To start this add-in, chooseTools, Add-Ons, Visio Extras, Convert CAD Drawings. Select the drawing you want (use Shift+click to select multiple drawings), and then click Open. The conversion might take a few minutes. When the process is finished, the converted files are opened in Visio.

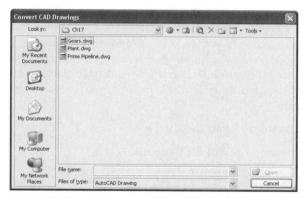

Figure 17-14. You can select multiple CAD drawings to convert at once with the Convert CAD Drawings add-in.

Note Before you start, make sure all of the CAD files you want to convert are located in the same folder. Bulk conversion works only for files in one folder.

 Troubleshooting

Converted CAD objects become ungrouped

The Visio CAD converter might not recognize every object or block as you expect it to. That is, you might find that some objects that appear obvious to you have been converted into smaller components, such as separate line segments. To group the components into a single shape, select all of the component's objects, and then select Shape, Grouping, Group. (Press Shift+click to select multiple shapes.)

Chapter 17

Customizing the CAD Conversion Process

Hidden away in the Solutions folder, Visio provides two templates specifically for the purpose of converting CAD files. You can control the way CAD drawings are converted into Visio drawings by editing the converter template that Visio uses when it performs the conversion. The converter template is a Visio file that contains default settings for converted CAD drawings. You can edit the converter template to control the following:

- **Line and font conversion**   CAD line styles and fonts are converted to Visio line styles and fonts that have the same name. So, to preserve your font styles, you could create a Visio text style that uses the blueprint font you use in your CAD drawings.

- **Drawing scale conversion**   The default drawing scale in the template also determines the drawing scale Visio uses for CAD drawings when you use File, Open.

- **Measurement unit conversion**   Visio interprets one CAD drawing unit as one Visio measurement unit. By default, the measurement unit is set to either inches or millimeters. The measurement units you use determine how big the converted CAD drawing is. The measurement unit also applies to CAD drawings you open by choosing File, Open.

- **Symbol-to-shape conversion**   If symbols you use in your CAD drawings have already been converted and added to a stencil, the converter can create instances of these masters instead of converting each block. This can save you considerable time during the conversion process. These stencils are available to the converter even when you don't have the template open.

To edit the CAD converter template, follow these steps:

1 In Visio, choose File, Open to display the Open dialog box.

2 In the Files Of Type box, select Template (*.vst, *.vtx).

3 Locate and select the template for DWG or DWX files, at Program Files\Microsoft Office\Visio11\1033\ _dwgcnv_u.vst (U.S. Units).

4 Click the drop-down arrow on the Open button, and then select Original or Copy.

5 In the opened conversion template, you can make changes as follows:

- To modify a style, choose Format, Define Styles. Select a style to modify, and then make changes and click OK.

- To create a new style, choose Format, Define Styles. Type a name for the new style, select the options you want, and click OK.

- To set the page size and the drawing scale, choose File, Page Setup. On the Page Size tab, specify a page size and orientation. On the Drawing Scale tab, specify a drawing scale. Click OK.

- To set the measurement units, choose File, Page Setup. On the Page Properties tab, select a measurement unit and click OK.

For details about changing a page's units of measure, see "Choosing the Units of Measure for the Drawing," page 427.

■ To add a stencil containing converted symbol libraries, choose File, Shapes, Open Stencil. In the Open Stencil dialog box, select the stencil file (with a .vss extension) that contains the converted symbol library, and click Open. (For information about converting symbol libraries into stencils, see the following section.)

6 To save your changes, press Ctrl+S or choose File, Save, and then close the template.

Inside Out

Using template files

Why are the converters part of an obscure template tucked away in an obscure folder? The purpose of the templates is simply to load the add-in program that does the conversion. In the same way, the Organization Chart template loads the add-in that converts data from Microsoft Exchange files into organization charts. A lot of task-specific behavior in Visio is stored in template files, which is why you're usually better off starting from a template when you're creating a specific type of diagram in Visio rather than starting from a blank diagram.

Converting Symbol Libraries into Stencils

If you use symbol libraries in your DWG or DGN drawings, you can convert them into Visio stencils for use in your Visio drawings. You can also add the converted stencils to the converter template, so that the converter can create instances of the stencil shapes in drawings you convert, rather than having to convert each block in the drawing separately. A symbol library comprises DWG or DGN files that contain blocks or cells—collections of objects grouped together to form one object, such as a piece of furniture. When you convert a symbol library, Visio converts each block or cell into a Visio master, and it places all the masters on the same stencil. Each master is named for the block or cell from which it originated.

When you convert blocks or cells that include multiple visible attributes, Visio creates shapes with multiple text fields to display the text as well as attribute values. For example, when an AutoCAD block is converted to create a Visio master shape, all text in block attributes is converted to custom properties of the master shape. When you drag a block master shape onto the page, Visio displays the value of the custom properties as text shapes.

Inside Out

Using blocks and master shapes

If you've used the Autodesk AutoCAD program, you're familiar with blocks. The equivalent in Visio is a master shape. The difference is that you scale each block as you insert it, because the blocks themselves are usually less than full scale. However, Visio master shapes are already drawn full scale. Therefore, the master shapes that Visio creates from converted AutoCAD blocks might result in shapes that are smaller than the shape instances already in the drawing. You might need to resize these shapes.

Chapter 17

493

Follow these steps to convert a symbol library into a Visio stencil:

1 Choose Tools, Add-Ons, Visio Extras, Convert CAD Library.

2 In the Convert CAD Library dialog box, select the file or files you want to convert.

3 Click Open. Each block or cell in the original file is converted to a master, and all the masters are placed on the document stencil.

4 To save the stencil, select File, Save. In the Files Of Type box, select Stencil (*.vss). Specify a file name and location, and then click Save.

5 Close the Visio stencil file. When you want to use the converted block or cell master shapes, open the stencil you created.

Adjusting How Converted Shapes Overlap

When you convert CAD objects to Visio shapes, a *stacking order* is applied to them. This means that shapes can appear to be on top of other shapes. If the top shape is transparent, the bottom shape shows through. To adjust which shape appears where in Visio, you can change the shapes' stacking order using the commands on the Shape, Order menu (choose Bring To Front, Send To Back, Bring Forward, or Send Backward).

For details about stacking order, see "Using Stacking Order," page 45.

Troubleshooting

Converted CAD objects are no longer solid

If a converted CAD object appears transparent in Visio and you want it to look solid, try selecting the object, and then applying a fill color, such as white. If that doesn't work, you can edit the object's ShapeSheet so that the shape can be filled, but it's a weird process.

For details, see "Drawing Closed Shapes, " page 645.

Converting Visio Diagrams into CAD Format

If you work with engineers, architects, or others who use a CAD drawing program, you might need to convert a Visio drawing into CAD format for them to review. Visio exports one page of a drawing into CAD format without affecting the original Visio drawing. If the Visio drawing file includes multiple pages, you must convert each one separately. You can convert a drawing page to Autodesk AutoCAD DWG or DXF format using the Save As command on the File menu, as Figure 17-15 shows. Choose the file format from the Save As Type list, type a name for the new file, and click Save. Repeat the process for each page you want to export.

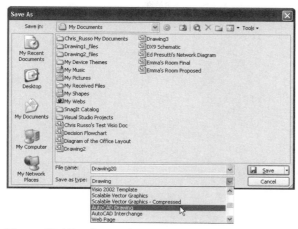

Figure 17-15. Converting a Visio drawing file to CAD format is as simple as saving it in the format you want.

Note As with any conversion process, some data might be lost each time you convert the file. For example, if you convert CAD dimension lines into Visio format, the dimension lines are no longer formatted with their fonts, line styles, and fills. Data integrity usually remains acceptable when you convert CAD files to Visio drawings or when you export Visio drawings to CAD files. However, when you round-trip files or convert them multiple times, the integrity of your files suffers.

Chapter 17

Laying Out Floor and Site Plans

Whether you're trying to make the setup of your manufacturing plant more efficient or just documenting the office seating chart, Microsoft Office Visio 2003 is a great tool for floor and site plans. Visio Standard includes a limited number of shapes specifically designed for creating office layouts, but you can, in fact, create a building shell for any purpose using its wall shapes. Visio Professional includes many more shapes for depicting home plans, manufacturing plants, office space, and all the related building services, such as heating and cooling systems, plumbing lines, and electrical layouts.

The shapes and templates for creating building plans were designed for simplicity. Anyone can create an accurate, to-scale floor plan if he or she measures and draws carefully. At the same time, if you have a background in architecture, construction, or engineering, you're more likely to know how to design a *good* plan. If you don't have that background, you'll need to look elsewhere to fill in the gaps, but with this chapter you will learn how to take advantage of the tools that Visio offers.

 Visio 2003 includes a new Space Plan Startup Wizard that makes it a snap to get up and running, and even easier to import data. Once you are finished, you can design custom Visio smart tags to assist your co-workers in using the plan. We'll cover the Space Plan Startup Wizard in Chapter 26, "Managing Facilities with Space Plans."

> **Note** Some of the techniques, shapes, and commands described in this chapter are available only in Visio Professional. A note appears when this is the case.

Starting with a Basic Floor Plan

Whether you're designing the interior or exterior of a home, plant, or office building, you start by creating a floor plan. It's important to start any type of floor plan with the appropriate template. In Visio Standard, that's the Office Layout template; in Visio Professional, that's any of the building plan templates.

When you start a new drawing with an Office Layout or building plan template, Visio opens with the stencils you need to define interior and exterior spaces and walls, as well as special tools and commands that aren't found in other templates.

Visio Standard includes only one template for floor plans, the Office Layout template in the Building Plan template folder. This template is also included in Visio Professional, which has many more templates in the Building Plan folder for drawing the following types of plans:

- *Floor plans* for designing any type of building shell and interiors.
- *Home plans* for designing kitchens and bathrooms, planning furniture layouts, creating remodeling and landscaping plans, and so on.
- *Plant layouts* for designing manufacturing plants, warehouses, and other buildings used in the process of manufacturing and distributing goods.
- *Reflected ceiling plans* for designing the layout of ceiling tile, lighting panels, heating, ventilation, and air conditioning (HVAC) grills, and diffusers for commercial buildings.
- *Site plans* for designing commercial or home sites and landscaping plans.

When you start a drawing based on one of these templates, Visio adds the Plan menu to the menu bar, which contains commands for working with walls and other shapes, as Figure 18-1 shows. You can then add the windows, doorways, and other permanent structures in a building. The shapes you use for your particular plan will vary, but the general steps are the same: start with a floor plan, and then add shapes to provide the detail you need.

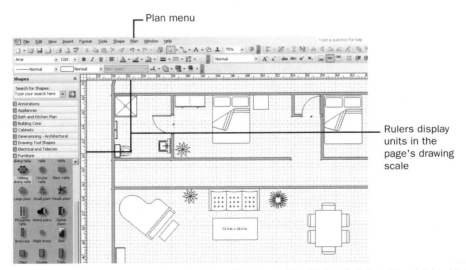

Figure 18-1. When you start a drawing with a template in the Building Plan folder, Visio Professional opens stencils with an assortment of architectural shapes and adds the Plan menu to the menu bar.

There are several ways to create a floor plan in Visio:

- **Use the Pencil tool to draw lines**   This is the least automated technique, but if you want to approximate a sketch on paper with a pencil, you can.

- **Draw with wall shapes**   This technique saves you a few steps but is still labor-intensive, because you must drag one wall at a time onto the page to create a building shell and its rooms.

- **Draw with space shapes or the Rectangle tool**   You can design a floor plan by using shapes that show you square footage or by drawing rectangles to represent areas. Then you can convert the shapes to walls. This technique is probably quicker than just using wall shapes, but you need to know about (and locate) the Convert To Walls command.

- **Draw with room shapes**   If you can conceptualize your floor plan as a series of rooms rather than walls, you can use the room shapes to quickly put a floor plan together. This technique might be the most efficient, because you simply specify the room's dimensions and you're done.

If you're creating a floor plan from scratch, you can start by drawing a building shell using room or wall shapes. If you're still in the planning stage, though, you might want to start by using space shapes to mock up a floor plan, which you can rearrange and resize easily before creating a building shell. On the other hand, if you have an existing floor plan that was created in Visio or with a computer-aided design (CAD) program, you can add shapes on top to define furniture layouts, electrical schematics, and so on.

The sections that follow provide details about starting a floor plan from scratch or with an existing drawing. If you want to plan your space first, the following sections describe how to work with the space shapes.

Starting with the Office Layout Template

If you have Visio Standard and want to start any type of floor plan, you can use the Office Layout template. Although it's intended to show office space, this template is the best choice for any type of scaled drawing that includes walls, because it's the only template in Visio Standard that includes wall shapes. Because Visio Professional includes a greater variety of building plan templates, the Office Layout template might not be the best way to start. (See the sidebar "Office Layout in Visio Professional," page 501.)

When you start a drawing with the Office Layout template, it opens a letter-sized drawing page set to a drawing scale of 1/2 inch (in.) to 1 foot (ft.). (These page size and drawing scale settings differ from the other building plan templates in Visio Professional.) The following stencils are opened as well:

- **Walls, Doors And Windows**   This stencil contains shapes for adding entire rooms as well as individual walls and the standard architectural wall openings.

- **Office Furniture**   This stencil includes shapes for desks, chairs, and tables.

- **Office Equipment**   This stencil contains shapes for computers, copy machines, printers, and other peripheral devices, plus a few electrical and telecommunication symbols.

Chapter 18

- **Office Accessories**   This stencil includes plant, lamp, and other shapes.
- **Cubicles**   This stencil comes with a variety of workstation configurations as well as moveable panels.

There are a couple of ways to lay out the walls in an office plan. The simplest method is probably to start with a room shape and then adjust its size and shape to suit your space. You can add individual walls as necessary. Another method is to start with space shapes, and then convert them to walls. If none of the room shapes are configured the way you want, it might be faster to create your layout with space shapes instead, even though that method involves the extra wall conversion step.

To start an office layout and draw the walls, follow these steps:

1   Choose File, New, Building Plan, Office Layout.

> **Tip**   If you have just started Visio 2003 select Building Plan and then choose the type of layout you would like from the options displayed.

Visio opens a new, scaled drawing page where 1/2 in. = 1 ft. The page size is 8.5 by 11 in., which allows for a space of 22 ft. by 17 ft.

2   Choose File, Page Setup. On the Page Size tab, verify that the drawing uses the size settings you want, and make any changes. Then click the Drawing Scale tab, verify that the scale is the one you want, and make any changes. Click OK.

> For details about setting up page size and drawing scale, see "Setting Up Measurements in a Diagram," page 421.

3   Add rooms or walls using one of the following techniques, or a combination of the two:

- Drag the Room, "L" Room, or "T" Room shape from the Walls, Doors And Windows stencil onto the drawing page. Drag selection handles to resize the room, or use the yellow, diamond-shaped control handles to move walls.

  The wall's dimensions are displayed when the room shape is selected.

> For details about working with room shapes, see "Designing Space with Room Shapes," page 520.

- Drag the Space shape from the Walls, Doors And Windows stencil onto the drawing page. Drag selection handles to resize the shape. To create odd-shaped rooms, overlap several space shapes, select them all, right-click, and select Union. To convert space shapes to walls, right-click the shape, and then select Convert To Walls. When you use the Convert To Walls command, you can specify which wall shape to use as well as display options, such as whether to display dimension lines or add guides to the wall shapes. After you convert a space shape to walls, the original space shape is deleted unless you specify otherwise. If you plan to track space in a drawing apart from other structures or want to display square footage in rooms, you can retain the space shape after conversion.

The wall's dimensions are displayed when the shape is selected.

> For details about working with space shapes, see "Using Space Shapes to Start a Floor Plan," page 512.

> **Tip** When you pause the pointer over a control handle, a ScreenTip appears that describes the handle's purpose.

4. To add individual walls, drag the Wall shape from the Walls, Doors And Windows stencil, and position it inside the room. To connect walls, drag an endpoint of one wall to another wall. The endpoints turn red when the walls are glued. Wall corners are joined automatically.

5. To add a guide to any wall, right-click a wall, and then choose Add A Guide.

   Visio displays a guide on the wall and glues the wall shape to the guide. To move the wall, you can drag the guide.

Office Layout in Visio Professional

Visio Professional includes the same Office Layout template that's in Visio Standard. If you have Visio Professional, you can use the Office Layout template to lay out office space, but you're probably better off starting with the Floor Plan template, which uses a standard architectural page size and includes a larger variety of building core shapes. Then you can open the Office Equipment, Office Furniture, Office Accessories, and Cubicles stencils to fill in the details.

In addition, the Office Layout template opens the Walls, Doors And Windows stencil, whereas the Floor Plan template opens the Walls, Shell And Structure stencil. The former stencil contains only a subset of the shapes on the latter. Visio Professional is designed for technical professionals, so it includes more shapes for walls, doors, and building core elements.

Starting a Building Shell in Visio Professional

Before you can create rooms and include details in a building plan, you have to draw the skeleton, or shell of the building. The building shell comprises exterior walls, columns, interior walls, and structural features such as stairways and elevators, as Figure 18-2 shows. The Visio Professional building plan templates provide the shapes you need to draw a building shell for home and commercial spaces and sites.

Chapter 18

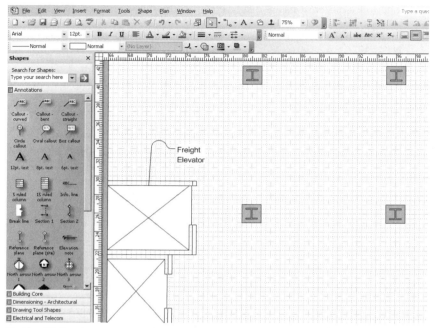

Figure 18-2. You can quickly create a simple building shell in Visio Professional by adding walls and other structural elements.

If you're drawing the building shell for an existing building, first measure the building and its major structural features. If you're planning a new building, note the exterior dimensions and the planned location of structures such as staircases, elevators, and columns. Visio includes shapes for walls, windows, columns, and other structural and building core elements.

Tip If you have a CAD drawing of your building you may import it to Visio. See Chapter 17, "Using CAD Drawings in Visio."

When you're ready to start drawing, you can choose from one of several templates, as Table 18-1 shows. Each sets up an appropriate drawing scale on an American National Standards Institute (ANSI) standard page of 36 by 24 in. and opens stencils with the shapes you need. The stencils are designed to be used in any of the building plan templates, and the page settings are customizable. So it turns out that it doesn't necessarily matter which building plan template you start with—you can always adjust the page size, drawing scale, and open any stencils you want access to. The important thing is to start with one of the templates, because they all include specialized macros that add the Plan menu to the menu bar and other commands that you need to work with the wall and space shapes.

Table 18-1. **Building Plan Templates for Drawing Floor Plans**

Template	Drawing Scale	Stencils
Floor Plan	1/4 in. = 1 ft.	Annotations Building Core Dimensioning—Architectural Drawing Tool Shapes Electrical And Telecom Points Of Interest Walls, Shell And Structure
Home Plan	1/4 in. = 1 ft.	Annotations Appliances Bath And Kitchen Plan Building Core Cabinets Dimensioning—Architectural Drawing Tool Shapes Electrical And Telecom Furniture Garden Accessories Walls, Shell And Structure
Plant Layout	1/4 in. = 1 ft.	Annotations Building Core Dimensioning—Architectural Drawing Tool Shapes Electrical And Telecom Shop Floor—Machines And Equipment Shop Floor—Storage And Distribution Vehicles Walls, Shell And Structure

Table 18-1. **Building Plan Templates for Drawing Floor Plans**

Template	Drawing Scale	Stencils
Reflected Ceiling Plan	1/4 in. = 1 ft.	Annotations Building Core Drawing Tool Shapes Electrical And Telecom Registers, Grills And Diffusers Walls, Shell And Structure
Site Plan	1 in. = 10 ft.	Annotations Dimensioning—Architectural Drawing Tool Shapes Garden Accessories Irrigation Parking And Roads Planting Points Of Interest Site Accessories Sport Fields And Recreation Vehicles

All the building plan shapes include intelligence in the form of custom properties that you can use to define shape specifications. For example, you can specify the width of walls and beams and the height of doors and column walls. Some properties affect the appearance of the shape. For example, you can specify whether a wall is exterior or interior in the wall's Custom Properties window, which changes the thickness of the wall shape on the drawing page. Other properties are included for tracking information in the drawing, such as model number and manufacturer. The data you enter becomes especially valuable when you use it to automate the creation of parts lists and reports.

Follow these steps to start a building plan:

1   Choose File, New, Building Plan, and then choose the template for the type of building plan you're creating. (For example, select Floor Plan, Home Plan, Plant Layout, or Site Plan.)

2   Choose File, Page Setup. On the Page Size tab, verify that the drawing uses the size settings you want, and make any changes. Then click the Drawing Scale tab, and verify that the scale is the one you want, and make any changes. Click OK.

> For details about setting up page size and drawing scale, see "Setting Up Measurements in a Diagram," page 421.

3   Drag guides from the horizontal and vertical rulers onto the page to indicate the outer edges of the building.

> For details about using guides and setting up page size and drawing scale, see "Aligning and Moving Shapes with Guides," page 443.

4 To make sure that gluing is enabled for the drawing, select Tools, Snap & Glue. Under Currently Active, verify that the Glue check box is selected. Under Glue To, verify that the Shape Geometry check box is selected.

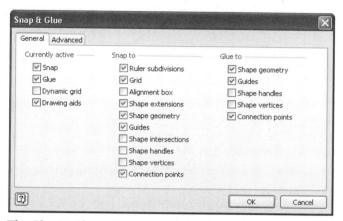

The Glue To Shape Geometry option is required for wall shapes to connect together.

5 Add the exterior walls using any of the following methods or a combination:

- Drag space shapes from the Walls, Shell And Structure stencil onto the page. Drag selection handles to resize the shape. Create odd-shaped exteriors by overlapping several space shapes, and then select them all, right-click, and select Union. To convert space shapes to walls, right-click the shape, select Convert To Walls, and then specify exterior walls and the settings you want.

> For details about working with space shapes, see "Using Space Shapes to Start a Floor Plan," page 512.

- Drag Exterior Wall shapes from the Walls, Shell And Structure stencil onto the page. To adjust a wall's position or orientation, drag an endpoint of the wall shape and glue it to the intersection of a horizontal and vertical guide. Make sure that the wall's handles face the interior of the shell. Repeat for the wall's other endpoint.

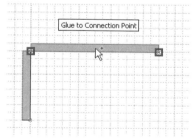

As you glue the endpoints of the walls to the guide intersections, Visio glues each wall segment to the next and smoothes the corners where they join.

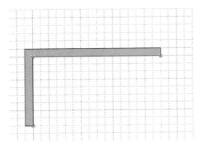

6 If a guide or a wall's selection handles appear on the exterior of the building rather than the interior, right-click the wall, and then select Flip Wall On Reference Line.

7 From the Walls, Shell And Structure stencil, drag column, beam, pilaster, and other structural shapes onto your drawing.

8 From the Building Core stencil, drag elevator, stair, and other building shapes onto your drawing.

9 To configure structural or building core shapes, right-click a shape, and then select Properties.

The Custom Properties dialog box appears with specifications for the shape. For example, you can enter width and number of treads for a Stair shape, and cab width and manufacturer for an Elevator shape.

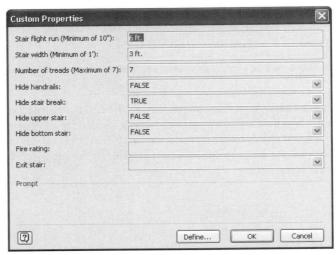

You can also edit the shape ScreenTip that appears when you pause the mouse pointer over the shape. This might come in handy if you want to specifically identify a piece of the building, for example the freight elevator, when you hover the mouse over it. To do so follow these steps:

1 Select the shape.

2 Choose Insert, Edit Screen Shape Tip.

3 Type a new tip in the Screen Shape Tip window.

4 Click OK.

Tip **Pan and zoom large drawings**

To pan around in a large plan, you can open the Pan & Zoom window (choose View, Pan & Zoom Window). Or use the keyboard/mouse shortcut, Ctrl+Shift+drag using the right mouse button, to pan a drawing.

Moving a Building Shell to the Background

If you want to use your building shell in a drawing that represents a multiple-floor building or as a backdrop for other designs, you can place the shell on a background page. Then, you can add other shapes on top of the building shell by placing them on foreground pages that are assigned to the building shell background. That way you can use one building shell page for every floor in a building or to show different plans, such as a heating and ventilation system on one page, furniture layouts on another, and the electrical system on another. Everything on the background appears on the foreground, but you can't select any background objects while you're working on the foreground page. That way, you protect the building shell from inadvertent changes as you work on your design.

You can move a building shell you created in Visio or one inserted from a CAD drawing to the background. The technique is simple: you display the page containing the shell, and then designate it as a background page. When you insert new foreground pages in the same drawing file, you assign the building shell background to them.

Solution Migration: Visio Technical Versus Visio Professional

If you have been a loyal user of Visio's architectural, construction, and building shapes over the years and product versions, you might notice that these shapes have moved around a lot starting with Microsoft Office Visio Professional 2002. Visio Professional 2003 contains all the shapes (and then some) that were part of the Building Architecture and Building Services solutions of Visio 2000 Technical Edition. Before the 2000 Edition, Microsoft Visio Technical 5 included something called AEC solutions, which included the shapes from which many of today's versions evolved.

Why all the change in stencil and template names and locations? In part, the product designers wanted to make these shapes and templates more visible to the people who use them. And a variety of people do use them, which might be part of the problem. Because so many industries create and work with architectural, engineering, and construction blueprints and schematics, there isn't any one name for the set of tools. So whether they're called building plans or building architecture solutions or AEC templates, you're getting the same thing—templates that open a scaled drawing page and stencils with appropriate shapes.

Chapter 18

To move the building shell page to a background page, follow these steps:

1 Display the page containing the building shell, and then choose File, Page Setup. Click the Page Properties tab.

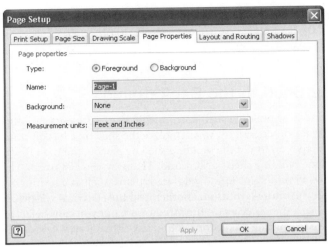

2 For Type, select Background.

3 In the Name box, type a name for the background page. For example, type **Building Shell**.

4 Click OK. Visio displays the background page's name on the page tab.

5 To display the building shell background on another page, do one of the following:

- If the page doesn't exist, choose Insert, New Page.
- If the page already exists, display the page; choose File, Page Setup, and then click the Page Properties tab.

6 For Type, select Foreground.

7 Click the drop-down arrow in the Background list to display the list of background pages, select Building Shell, and then click OK.

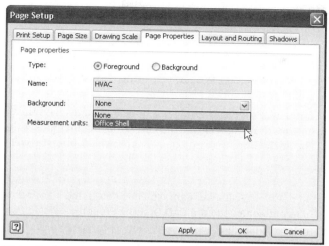

Visio displays the foreground page with the building shell background.

> **Tip** A background page can have a background. For example, you can create a title block on a background page and then assign the title block background to every foreground and background page in the drawing so that it appears on all pages.

Starting from an Existing Floor Plan

If you already have a building shell in the form of an existing CAD drawing or Visio drawing file, you can use it in a new floor, home, office, plant, or site layout. The way you use the existing building shell depends on its file format as follows:

- **Use a CAD drawing**   If the existing floor plan is a CAD drawing, you can insert it into a Visio drawing. Your best bet is to insert it on a background page and then assign foreground pages to that background so that you can see the drawing while you add other shapes.

- **Use a Visio drawing**   If the existing floor plan is a Visio drawing, you can copy it and then paste the drawing into your drawing. You can paste the floor plan on a background page so that it appears on every foreground page or use its built-in layers to lock the shapes in the floor plan against editing.

Using a Floor Plan from a CAD Drawing

Follow these steps to start a new floor plan and insert a CAD drawing:

1   Choose File, New, Building Plan, and then choose the template you want to use.

2   Choose File, Page Setup. On the Page Size tab, verify that the drawing uses the size settings you want, and make any changes. Then click the Drawing Scale tab, and verify that the scale is the one you want, and make any changes. Click OK.

For details about setting up page size and drawing scale, see "Setting Up Measurements in a Diagram," page 421.

3 Click Insert, CAD Drawing.

4 Under Files Of Type, select AutoCAD Drawing (*.dwg, *.dxf). Locate and select the CAD file, and then click Open.

   The CAD Drawing Properties dialog box appears and displays the General tab. Visio chooses a custom drawing scale for the CAD drawing that makes the drawing fit on the page. The Lock Cropping and Lock Position check boxes are selected.

5 Click OK.

Note If you don't get the results you want, you can delete the inserted image and then start over using different settings in the CAD Drawing Properties dialog box. For details about your options, see "Importing CAD Drawings in Visio," page 476.

6 To use the inserted drawing as a background, choose File, Page Setup, and click the Page Properties tab. For Type, select Background, and then click OK.

For details about background pages and adding foreground pages that use the background, see "Moving a Building Shell to the Background," page 507.

Copying an Existing Visio Floor Plan

When you want to use parts of an existing Visio drawing (or the whole thing) in a new drawing, it can be as easy as copying from one drawing and pasting into the other. You will need to consider whether the two drawings use the same or a similar drawing scale, however. Scaled shapes, such as furniture, walls, and so on, are designed to work in different drawing scales. When Visio pastes scaled shapes, it converts them to the new page's drawing scale. Usually there's no problem pasting from one drawing scale to another unless the drawings use dramatically different scales (that is, more than eight times larger or smaller).

Follow these steps to copy an existing Visio floor plan drawing into a new drawing:

1 Choose File, New, Building Plan, and then choose the template you want to use.

2 Choose File, Page Setup. On the Page Size tab, verify that the drawing uses the size settings you want, and make any changes. Then click the Drawing Scale tab, and verify that the scale is the one you want, and make any changes. Click OK.

For details about setting up page size and drawing scale, see "Setting Up Measurements in a Diagram," page 421.

3 Choose File, Open, and then locate and select the existing Visio drawing containing the floor plan you want to use. Click OK to open the drawing in a new window.

4　In the existing floor plan drawing, select the shapes you want to use, and then select Edit, Copy. Or choose Edit, Copy Drawing to copy everything on the page. You can also select the shapes and copy them by pressing Ctrl+C.

5　Choose Window, and then choose the name of the new drawing file.

6　To paste the shapes on the current page, select Edit, Paste, or by press Ctrl+V.

> For details about background pages and adding foreground pages that use the background, see "Moving a Building Shell to the Background," page 507.

Troubleshooting

Copied shapes look out of proportion when pasted into a scaled drawing

If you copy shapes from one drawing and then paste them into a scaled drawing, such as a floor plan, the shapes might look too large or too small in some cases. The problem could be that the drawing scales of the two Visio drawings are out of range. To change the new drawing's scale to match the existing one, choose File, Page Setup, click the Drawing Scale tab, and then select a new drawing scale.

> For details about drawing scale issues, see "Working with a Drawing Scale," page 422.

> **Tip**　Locking layers to protect a drawing
> You can lock the layers of the existing Visio drawing. By doing so, you can create a new drawing on top of the existing drawing without accidentally changing the existing one. For details, see "Using Layers to Protect, Hide, and Organize Shapes," page 467

Opening a Floor Plan Created in Visio 2000

When you open a home plan, office layout, or other architectural or building plan drawing that was created in Visio 2000, Visio 2003 prompts you to convert the shapes.

When you click Yes, Visio updates the shape, property, and macro names to match those used by Visio 2003. When the process is complete, your shapes look the same but will work with the new space plan features in Visio Professional. Click No if you don't plan to make changes to the drawing or to save it in Visio 2003 format.

Chapter 18

511

Using Space Shapes to Start a Floor Plan

If you're documenting an existing floor plan, you already know where the rooms go. However, if you're designing a new space, you probably want to start with some conceptual designs that you can refine before committing to wall placement. You can use one of the space shapes to approximate room locations, which you can easily rearrange as you experiment with your design.

Space shapes have two distinct purposes:

- You can rough out the areas you want with space shapes, and then convert the shapes to walls to create a building shell and rooms, as Figure 18-3 shows.

- You can use space shapes as they are to designate space within existing rooms, such as in an office. This specialized use is associated with space plan drawings, in which space shapes can track facilities information. Space plan drawings are described in detail in Chapter 26, "Managing Facilities with Space Plans."

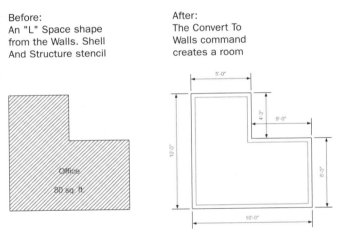

Before:
An "L" Space shape from the Walls. Shell And Structure stencil

After:
The Convert To Walls command creates a room

Figure 18-3. You can easily convert a space shape into walls and even add dimension lines, as shown here, guides, and other options.

The Visio 2003 Space Plan Wizard makes creating and designating spaces much easier. We'll cover this new feature in Chapter 26.

You can also draw a rough space plan using the drawing tools. As long as you start your drawing using a template from the Building Plan folder, Visio includes the command to convert shapes you draw into walls.

Chapter 18

512

Tracking Assets and Other Data in a Space Plan

In Visio Professional, space shapes can be used for tracking people and assets in a floor plan. When you want to use space shapes in this way, you don't convert the space shapes into walls. Instead, you drag space shapes into an existing building plan to designate offices. The space shapes automatically size themselves to fit an office created by using Visio wall, door, and window shapes.

To convert any plan—floor, home, plant, or office—into a space plan for tracking assets, moving employees, and managing facilities information, choose Tools, Add-Ons, Building Plan, Enable Space Plan. Visio displays the Category Explorer window and adds commands to the Plan menu for working with data.

For details about creating this type of space plan, see Chapter 26, "Managing Facilities with Space Plans."

Designing Space in a Building Plan

Depending on which product edition you have, you can designate space in a building plan in one of the following ways:

- Drag space shapes onto the drawing page.
- Draw lines, arcs (with the Pencil tool), and rectangles to represent rooms or the outline of the floor plan, and then convert the shapes to space and walls.

Either way, Visio automatically creates walls based on the perimeters defined by your spaces.

Using Space Shapes

To start a new building plan and define spaces using space shapes, follow these steps:

1. Choose File, New, Building Plan, and then choose the template you want.

Tip You can also start from an existing floor plan. Make sure the Walls, Doors And Windows or the Walls, Shell And Structure stencil is open.

2. If you're starting a new drawing, choose File, Page Setup. On the Page Size tab, verify that the drawing uses the size settings you want, and make any changes. Then click the Drawing Scale tab, and verify that the scale is the one you want, and make any changes. Click OK.

For details about setting up page size and drawing scale, see "Setting Up Measurements in a Diagram," page 421.

Chapter 18

3 Drag the Space, "L" Space, or "T" Space shape onto the drawing page.

In Visio Standard, the Space shape is on the Walls, Doors And Windows stencil. In Visio Professional, the space shapes are on the Walls, Shell And Structure stencil.

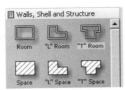

The size of the area is displayed on the shape.

Note To define space within an existing structure, drop the space shape away from the existing walls, and then move it into position. Otherwise, if you drop the shape onto a building shell or other walls, the space is automatically sized to fill the area.

4 To adjust the size of the space, drag a handle on the space shape.

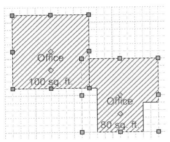

5 To create a uniquely shaped area, overlap multiple space shapes.

6 To combine multiple, contiguous space shapes into one space, select all the shapes, right-click, and then select Union from the shortcut menu.

Visio combines the area of all the spaces into one space shape. You might need to adjust the position of the shape's text.

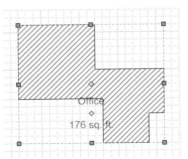

7 To change where the text appears on the space shape, drag the yellow control handle.

If you want to convert the space shapes to walls, or add walls to them, see "Converting Space Shapes into Walls," page 518.

> **Tip** You can change the formatting of a space shape. By default, space shapes appear with diagonal green lines. To change the background fill of an individual shape, right-click the shape and choose Format, Fill from the shortcut menu.

Creating Space with the Drawing Tools

Drawings created with one of the building plan templates include the added ability to convert shapes you draw into walls. You can specify whether to add dimension lines or guides to walls. If you're creating a floor plan that will be used as part of a facilities or space plan, you can create a space shape within the walls you've drawn when you convert the original geometry.

To start a new building plan and define spaces by drawing, follow these steps:

1 Choose File, New, Building Plan, and then choose the template for the type of building plan you're creating.

You can also start from an existing floor plan as long as it was created using a template from the Building Plan folder, which adds the Plan menu to Visio's menu bar.

2 If you're starting a new drawing, choose File, Page Setup. On the Page Size tab, verify that the drawing uses the size settings you want, and make any changes. Then click the Drawing Scale tab, and verify that the scale is the one you want, and make any changes. Click OK.

> For details about setting up page size and drawing scale, see "Setting Up Measurements in a Diagram," page 421.

Line tool

3 Click the Drawing Tools button on the Standard toolbar to display the drawing tools and then select a drawing tool, such as the Line tool or the Rectangle tool. Then draw overlapping boxes to form an area in the shape you want.

> **Tip** To create areas with curved walls, use the Arc or Pencil tool.

4 To create a single shape that represents the space, select the shapes, choose Shape, Operations, and then choose one of the following commands:

- Choose Union to combine the areas of all the shapes.
- Choose Subtract to take the first shape you select and subtract subsequently selected shapes from that area.
- Choose Intersect to create a new shape from the areas that overlap in your selected shapes.
- Choose Combine to combine the shapes and omit their overlapping areas.

Chapter 18

515

■ Choose Fragment to break the shapes into smaller shapes defined by their intersection.

For details about combining, subtracting, and intersecting shapes, see "Merging Shapes to Create New Ones," page 660.

5 To convert the shape to walls or walls plus space, select the shape, and then choose Plan, Convert To Walls.

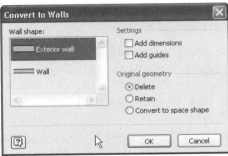

6 In the Wall Shape box, select the type of shape you want to use for walls.

The list includes wall shapes from all the stencils you have open.

7 If you want to display dimension lines on the room's perimeter, select the Add Dimensions check box.

8 If you want to display guides with the walls, which makes the walls easier to reposition, select the Add Guides check box.

9 If you want to fill the area within the walls with a space shape, select Convert To Space Shape, and then click OK. Visio converts the shape to walls using the options you selected.

10 To adjust the position of a wall, drag a guide to which the wall is attached. As you drag, the walls glued to the guide are resized. If you did not add guides, drag a wall or one of its endpoints to a new position. If you created a space shape, it does not change size. You can right-click it, and then select Auto Size to make it match the new area.

Customizing Space Shapes

You can change the look of a space shape, including its format, labels, and units of measure. By default, Visio space shapes display diagonal green lines with a centered label identifying the space and its square footage. Space shapes that you draw typically have white fill and no label. You can manually format individual space shapes to change their fill pattern and color. The labels and measurement units that appear on space shapes are properties that Visio stores with the page, so if you choose different options, all space shapes on the page reflect the change.

To change the fill for a shape, right-click the shape, select Format, Fill, and then specify new options in the Fill dialog box. You can use different colors and patterns in space shapes to designate different areas in a floor plan, as Figure 18-4 shows. If you later convert the space to walls, the fill pattern and color are discarded.

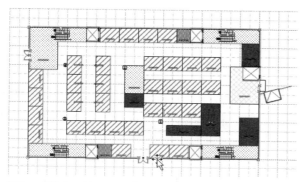

Figure 18-4. You can change a space shape's fill to indicate how the space will be used. In this drawing, different fills are used for offices, conference rooms, and public areas.

Follow these steps to change labels and units for all space shapes on a page:

1 Open a floor plan drawing, choose Plan, Set Display Options, and then click the Spaces tab.

   The Spaces tab displays options for changing labels and measurement units.

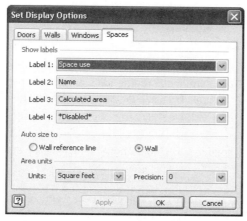

2 Under Show Labels, select from among the available options to display a field on the space shape.

   In Visio 2003 you can display up to four labels for each space. In each label window shown in the Set Display Options window, on the Space tab, you can choose to display one of the following in each subwindow: Space Use, Calculated Area, Name, Space ID, Shape Class, Subshape Type, Shape Type, Department, Phone Number, Occupancy, Capacity, Space Height, Base Elevation, or Zones.

The values for most of these areas are entered in the space's custom properties. To view the custom properties, right-click the space shape and select Properties. Some values, such as Calculated Area, are automatically calculated, whereas others, such as Shape Class, Subshape Type, and Shape Type are displayed on demand.

3 In the Units list, select the measurement units in which you want to display the area.

> **Tip**   The units for the shapes don't need to match the measurement units used by the drawing page.

To display the space shape based on the endpoints of the wall shapes rather than the interior of walls, select theWall Reference Line option.

4 Click OK to update all the space shapes on the page with the new settings.

5 If your drawing has multiple pages and you want to use the same settings throughout the drawing, click a page tab to display a page, and then repeat steps 1 through 4.

Converting Space Shapes into Walls

When you're ready to commit to the design of your space plan, you can convert space shapes to rooms, as Figure 18-5 shows. To do this, you use the Convert To Walls command, which is available on the Plan menu or when you right-click shapes.

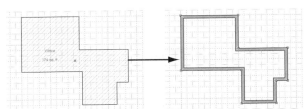

Figure 18-5.   The Convert To Walls command creates walls around the perimeter of a space shape or shapes you draw. You can specify to add dimension lines and guides automatically as well.

> **Note**   The Convert To Walls command is available when you right-click a space shape. The command is also available on the Plan menu.

When you use the Convert To Walls command, you can specify which wall shape to use as well as display options, such as whether to display dimension lines or add guides to the wall shapes. After you convert a space shape to walls, the original space shape is deleted unless you specify otherwise. If you plan to track space in a drawing apart from other structures or want to display square footage in rooms, you can retain the space shape after conversion. The space shape sizes separately from the room or building it's in.

Tip If you are going to use your building plan with the Space Plan template, keep the original space shape when you use the Convert To Walls command.

To convert the space shapes into walls, follow these steps:

1 Right-click a space shape, and then choose Convert To Walls.

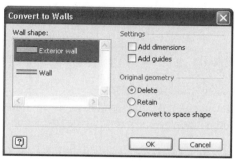

2 In the Wall Shape box, select the type of shape you want to use for walls.

The list includes wall shapes from all the stencils you have open.

3 If you want to display dimension lines on the room's perimeter, select the Add Dimensions check box.

4 If you want to display guides with the walls, which makes it easier to reposition walls, select the Add Guides check box.

5 If you want to keep the original space shape after conversion, select the Retain option.

When you start with a space shape, the Retain and Convert To Space Shape options have the same effect.

6 Click OK to convert the space using the options you selected.

7 To adjust the position of a wall, drag a guide to which the wall is attached.

As you drag, the walls glued to the guide are resized. If you retained the space shape, it doesn't change size. To update the space shape to match the new area, right-click the shape, and then choose Auto Size.

Tip You can also create rectangles, squares, and trapezoids drawn with the Line tool into walls.

Chapter 18

519

Adding Interior Walls and Cubicles

You can define interior rooms manually by dragging wall shapes into a building shell. The more automated method of defining rooms is to use room shapes, which define a space with four or more walls automatically. You can use room and space shapes together to display both square footage and dimensions in a building plan. For office designs, you can add prebuilt workstations with movable panel walls to show employee cubicles, which are available on the Cubicles stencil, as Figure 18-6 shows.

Figure 18-6. Visio Professional includes the Cubicles stencil, which features a variety of workstation and panel configurations that you can use to model the modern, movable office.

Inside Out

Calculating shape area and perimeter

Visio Professional can calculate the perimeter and area of any closed shape, which is a useful bit of information if you need to know the area of a room or the perimeter of an entire building for security equipment planning. To calculate these quantities, select Tools, Add-Ons, Visio Extras, Shape Area And Perimeter.

Designing Space with Room Shapes

Room shapes are a quick way to add four or more noncurving walls to a floor plan at once. When you select a room shape, Visio selects the entire room and displays the dimensions for all the walls, as Figure 18-7 shows. By contrast, if you add four wall shapes to a drawing to form a room, you can select each wall individually.

Drag to resize the entire room shape. ────────────

Drag to move the wall within the room. ────────────

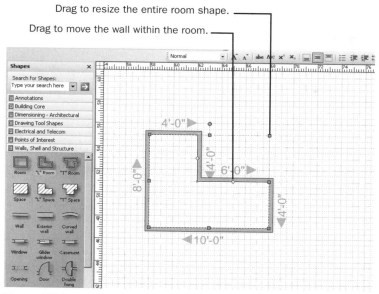

Figure 18-7. The "L" Room shape creates a room with six joined walls, which you can reposition. When you select a room shape, the walls' dimensions are displayed.

When you drag a room shape onto the drawing page, Visio automatically adds joined walls with dimensions that appear only when the shape is selected. A room shape is actually a group, but you cannot subselect shapes in the group, such as individual walls. Control handles let you reposition the walls of the room. Because it's a group, a room is easy to move on the drawing page—you can drag the entire room without worrying about its walls stretching out of shape. You can also add abutting walls to a room shape by gluing the walls' endpoints to connection points on the room.

> **Tip** If you aren't sure how big your rooms will be or where you want them, use space shapes to rough out a floor plan. You can always convert them to rooms later.

To create a room, follow these steps:

1 Drag the Room, "L" Room, or "T" Room shape onto the drawing page.

In Visio Standard, these shapes are on the Walls, Doors And Windows stencil. In Visio Professional, they're on the Walls, Shell And Structure stencil.

2 To set the room's size, select the shape, and then select Shape, Action, Properties.

Chapter 18

521

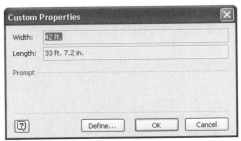

3   Type values in the Width and Length boxes, and then click OK.

    Visio adjusts the size of the room. You can also drag a selection handle to size a room.

4   To move a wall, drag a control handle to the position you want. (When you point to
    the correct control handle, its ScreenTip will display "Reposition Walls.")

Adding Interior Walls

You can define interior layouts by gluing wall shapes to other wall and room shapes. It's easiest to add walls to a plan by gluing them to guides, as Figure 18-8 shows. The selection handles on a wall shape designate its interior edge, so it's important to orient a wall shape
correctly when adding it to a drawing. This behavior differs from that in Visio 2000. If you
glue a wall "backward," you can use the Flip Wall On Reference Line command on the shape's
shortcut menu to correct the wall's orientation.

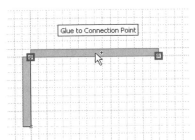

Figure 18-8.   When selected, double-line walls display selection handles on their interior
wall.

By default, walls look like double lines filled with gray, but you can display walls as single lines
instead or as double lines with a reference line. Visio Professional also includes an Exterior
Wall shape, which is thicker than the Wall shape. However, even if you're working with the
Visio Standard Wall shape, you can convert an exterior wall to an interior one and vice versa
by changing the setting in the Exterior Wall field in the Custom Properties window.

When you glue wall shapes together, Visio joins their corners and T-joints so that walls are
displayed correctly, as Figure 18-9 shows. Walls are smart in other ways as well. For example,
you can quickly add a guide to any wall to help with alignment; when you select a wall shape,
its dimensions are displayed.

Chapter 18

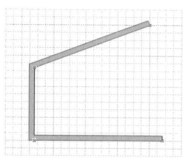

Figure 18-9. When you add individual wall shapes to a page, Visio joins their corners.

Follow these steps to add interior walls:

1   Drag the Wall shape from the stencil and position it inside the exterior structure. Repeat this process for all interior walls. In Visio Standard, theWall shape is on the Walls, Doors And Windows stencil. In Visio Professional, the Wall shape is also on the Walls, Shell And Structure stencil.

2   To connect walls, drag an endpoint of one wall to another wall until the points turn red, indicating that the walls are glued.

3   To add a guide and glue the wall shape to it, right-click a wall, and then choose Add A Guide.

> **Tip**   To move the wall, drag the guide.

4   If the guide or the wall's selection handles appear on the exterior of a room rather than its interior, right-click the wall shape, and then select Flip Wall On Reference Line.

Troubleshooting

Walls don't connect correctly

For wall shapes to join properly, both snap and glue must be turned on. To see these settings, choose Tools, Snap & Glue. Under Currently Active, make sure that the Snap and Glue check boxes are selected. In both the Snap To and Glue To lists, make sure that the Shape Geometry and Connection Points options are selected.

Customizing the Appearance of Wall Shapes

Walls are displayed as double lines with gray fill by default, but you can customize all the walls on a page to show single lines or double lines with a reference line, as Figure 18-10 shows. Display options for walls are a property of the drawing page, so when you choose an option, all the wall shapes (but not exterior wall shapes) on the current page are affected, but not shapes on other pages.

Chapter 18

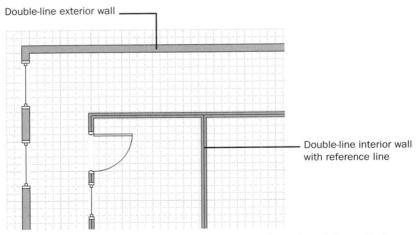

Double-line exterior wall

Double-line interior wall
with reference line

Figure 18-10. When you set the display options for walls, all the wall shapes on a page adopt the style. Exterior wall shapes are not affected.

To change how all walls on a page are displayed, follow these steps:

1 In a floor plan drawing, choose Plan, Set Display Options, and then click the Walls tab in the Set Display Options dialog box.

Note This command is not available in Visio Standard.

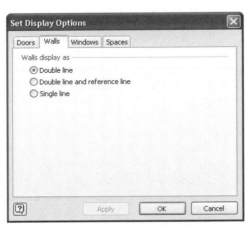

2 Choose an option, and then click OK to display all the wall shapes on the page with the new settings.

3 If your drawing has multiple pages and you want to use the same settings throughout the drawing, click the page tab near the bottom of the Visio window to display a page, and then repeat steps 1 and 2.

Creating a Ceiling Grid

If you're using a floor plan to design what goes overhead, you need to show ceiling tiles and lighting panels and perhaps HVAC grills and diffusers. The Reflected Ceiling Plan template opens a combination of stencils for designing a ceiling grid, as Figure 18-11 shows. However, you can add the same information to any floor plan by opening just two stencils:

- Electrical And Telecom
- Registers, Grills And Diffusers

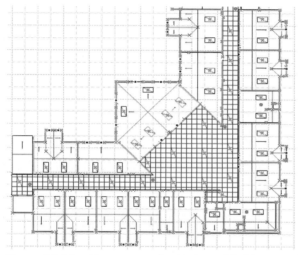

Figure 18-11. You can use the Reflected Ceiling Plan template to show a ceiling grid like this one, but you can also add ceiling tiles to any floor plan.

Visio doesn't really have an automated way of creating a ceiling grid, which is why it doesn't matter whether you use the Reflected Ceiling Plan template or not. You can easily start with any of the building plan templates to create a building shell and interior walls, and then add the ceiling grid. The basic technique goes like this: use the Line or Rectangle tool from the Standard toolbar to draw a ceiling grid.

You can save time by using the Array Shapes command to create multiple copies of ceiling panel shapes at regular, orthogonal intervals. In this case, draw one ceiling tile or a portion of the grid, select the shapes, and then chooseTools, Add-Ons, Visio Extras, Array Shapes to display the Array Shapes dialog box as Figure 18-12 shows.

Chapter 18

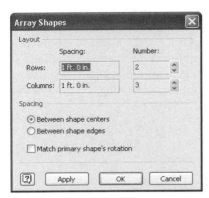

Figure 18-12. The Array Shapes command in Visio Professional helps you create an evenly spaced grid of shapes, such as for a tiled ceiling.

The Layout options reflect the drawing scale and measurement units of the floor plan. Set Spacing to 0 to draw a grid. Or specify the distance between the edges of the tiles, and then select the Between Shape Edges option.

You can then add lighting panels, grills, diffusers, and other HVAC shapes to your ceiling plan. Drag lighting shapes from the Electrical And Telecom stencil and air device shapes from the Register, Grills And Diffusers stencil onto your drawing.

For details about HVAC shapes, see "Adding Building Services," page 532.

Adding Doors, Windows, and Openings

Integral to any floor plan are the doors, windows, and other openings in a wall surface. When you add a shape that represents an opening in a wall, such as a door or window, the shape automatically rotates to align with the wall, glues itself in place and adjusts its thickness to match the wall. In addition, when you move the wall, the openings move with it. Visio also makes it easy to reverse the direction from which a door or window opens. The shapes include a command to flip the orientation on a shortcut menu.

You can choose from among several door and window shapes that represent standard architectural types. Visio Professional includes more shapes than Visio Standard, but all the shapes can be configured to represent different varieties of doors and windows. For example, you can use the Window Type field to specify louver, picture, pivot, single-hung, and transom windows. The Door Type field lets you specify single- and double-hung doors, as Figure 18-13 shows. Other custom property fields let you specify door and window width, height, and other information that you can later use to generate parts lists or reports.

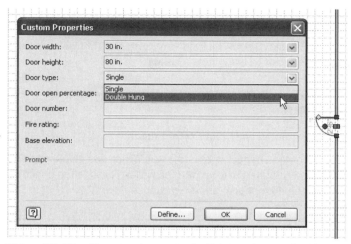

Figure 18-13. You can change a single-hung door to double-hung in the Custom Properties window. To see a shape's properties, right-click the shape, and then select Properties. Or choose View, Custom Properties Window to keep the window open while you work.

Follow these steps to add a door, window, or other opening shape to a wall:

1. Drag a door, window, or opening shape from the stencil onto a wall. When you release the mouse button, the door or window snaps into place and acquires the wall's thickness.

   In Visio Standard, the wall opening shapes are on the Walls, Doors And Windows stencil. In Visio Professional, these shapes are also on the Walls, Shell And Structure stencil.

2. To reverse the direction of the opening or door swing, right-click the shape, and then choose Reverse Left/Right Opening or Reverse In/Out Opening.

3. To adjust the position of a door or window, drag it along the wall.

4. To change the width of a window or door, open the Custom Properties window. Or right-click the shape, and then choose Properties.

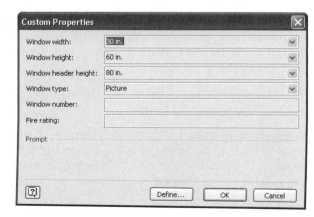

Chapter 18

5   Click in the Door Width or Window Width field, and then select a size from the drop-down list.

6   To specify other options, click in the field you want, and then select an option or type the information you want to use.

Troubleshooting

Doors are not oriented correctly, and I can't rotate them

If you need to rotate one of the shapes, drag it to a wall. When you glue these shapes to a wall, the shape automatically rotates to align with the wall. To change the direction in which a door opens, right-click the door shape, and then choose Reverse Left/Right Opening or Reverse In/Out Opening.

Inside Out

Tracking hardware specifications

Visio shapes include a number of fields that might not seem relevant to you. Many fields are provided for your convenience in tracking hardware specifications with building plans. You don't have to fill out information about the manufacturer or fire rating, for example, if you don't plan to generate reports from the drawing. However, if you are tracking specifications with a building plan and have a spreadsheet or database of equipment information, you can import that data into the shape's custom property fields.

> For details about linking custom property fields to a database, see Chapter 24, "Connecting Diagrams and Databases."

Choosing Doors and Windows Defaults

In Visio Professional, door and window shapes have additional display options that affect the appearance of all the shapes on the page. You can specify the components to display, such as the header and frame, with the Set Display Options command. You choose whether to display the following:

● For doors: frames, headers, swings, thresholds, stops, panels, and closed panels.

● For windows: headers, sills, sashes, and frames.

Because these display options are properties of the drawing page, when you choose one, all the shapes on the page use the setting. So, for example, you can choose to show the swing for all doors or no doors, but you can't selectively show the door swing for some door shapes and not others on a page. In a multiple-page drawing, you need to set the display options for each page separately.

You can also specify the default configuration used by doors and windows on the page, as Figure 18-14 shows. For example, if you know that all the windows you're installing have a frame width of 3 in., you can specify that information as a property that's stored with the drawing. Then you can create a report (a door schedule or window schedule) that includes the defaults you have specified.

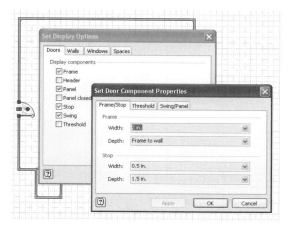

Figure 18-14. The Set Display Options dialog box controls the appearance of all the shapes on a page. The Properties button in this dialog box opens the Set Component Properties dialog box, where you can set default specifications that are used in reports.

Follow these steps to enter door and window specifications:

1 Right-click any door or window shape, and then choose Set Display Options. Or choose the Set Display Options command from the Plan menu.

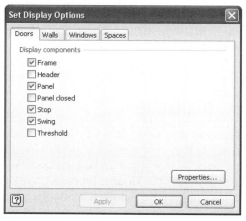

2 Click the Doors tab, and then select the check boxes for the options you want to show on all the door shapes.

3 Click Properties to display the Set Door Component Properties dialog box.

4   If you plan to create a door schedule based on the component specifications for the doors in the drawing, click a tab, specify the options you want, and then click OK.

5   In the Set Display Options dialog box, click the Windows tab.

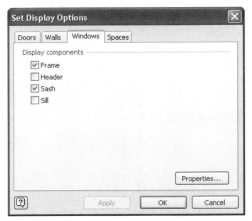

6   Select the check boxes for the options you want to show on all window shapes, and then click OK.

7   If your drawing has multiple pages and you want to use the same settings throughout the drawing, click each of the page tabs near the bottom of the Visio window to display a page, and then repeat steps 1 through 6.

Tip   **Creating a blank building plan**

In fact you can drag a window or door on your drawing, set all the options that you like, delete the window or door and the options remain set. This is important because you can set these options, delete any shape on the drawing, and then save the drawing with a generic name such as "blank building plan." Whenever you want to draw a building plan open your drawing with your preferred settings, draw your floor plan, and then save it under a different name. In essence you have created a complete template and drawing space with your preferred settings.

Creating a Door and Window Schedule

In Visio Professional, you can create an automated door schedule or window schedule based on the configuration information you have specified in a building plan drawing. This information is stored as the custom properties of window and door shapes. A door schedule includes information from the Number, Width, Height, Type, and Panel Thickness fields. A window schedule includes information from the Number, Width, Height, and Type fields. However, a schedule can list any custom property, such as fire rating. In addition, if you need to specify particular parameters in a door schedule that aren't already included as custom properties for door shapes, you can add the properties.

For details, see "Defining Custom Properties," page 175.

The door and window schedules are types of reports that you can display on a Visio drawing page in a table shape, as Figure 18-15 shows. You can also save reports as a separate file in Hypertext Markup Language (HTML) or Extensible Markup Language (XML) format, which can be opened in a browser.

Window Schedule			
Number	Width	Height	Type
d72	30 in.	60 in.	Picture
d73	30 in.	60 in.	Louver
d74	30 in.	60 in.	Picture
d75	30 in.	60 in.	Transom
d75	4.25 ft.	60 in.	Picture
d76	30 in.	60 in.	Picture

Figure 18-15.   A very simple door schedule with the default fields saved on the drawing page as a table shape.

You can easily create a door or window schedule by dragging the Door Schedule or Window Schedule shape onto a page, as Figure 18-16 shows. Visio uses the existing definition for the Door Schedule or Window Schedule report to add a table shape to the page containing columns of information.

If you want to show different fields in the schedule or save it as an external file, you must use the Report command.

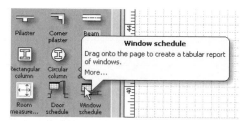

Figure 18-16.   To quickly add a door or window schedule to the drawing page, you can drag one of the schedule shapes from the Walls, Shell And Structure stencil, which adds a table shape to the page.

Follow these steps to create a door or window schedule:

1 Choose Tools, Reports.

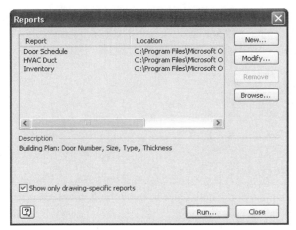

2 In the Report Definition column, select Door Schedule or Window Schedule, and then click Run to display the Run Report dialog box.

3 Choose a format for the report, type a file name and path, and then click OK.

4 When done, Visio displays the report.

Rather than create a door or window schedule with the default fields, you can modify the report or create a new one that includes the information you want. In the Report dialog box, click New to display the Report Definition Wizard, where you can choose the properties you want to display in the columns of your schedule.

For details about creating and modifying reports, see "Creating Reports," page 190.

Adding Building Services

After you've created a floor plan for a home, office, or industrial site, you can add services for the facility, as Figure 18-17 shows. Visio Professional provides the shapes and tools you need to create plans for HVAC, plumbing, electrical, and security systems. If you have Visio Standard, the Office Layout template includes a few electrical shapes, but for the most part, the sections that follow apply only to Visio Professional.

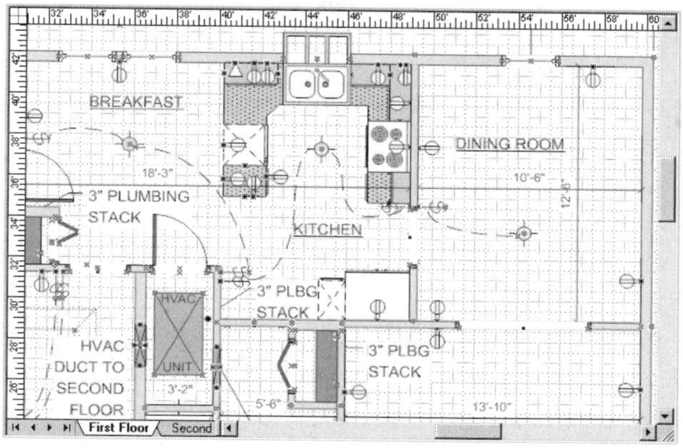

Figure 18-17. This home plan includes ductwork, plumbing, and electrical information.

It's beyond the scope of this book to describe best practices for designing these systems—the assumption is that you know more than the author about building architecture and services. However, the sections that follow can help you work most efficiently with the shapes. The key strategies to remember when working with these shapes are the following:

- Right-click shapes to display a shortcut menu that might contain shape options.
- Use the Custom Properties window to set shape specifications.
- Use the drawing's layers to organize different elements in your plan. All the building plan shapes are already assigned to layers.

The following sections tell you more specifically about how to use these techniques to customize your drawing, whether it's a floor plan you've created in Visio or a CAD drawing you've imported.

If you're planning services for an office, plant, or even a home, chances are good that you'll need to include a computer network. There are many different ways of configuring a network and just as many ways to diagram them. Both Visio Standard and Visio Professional include network shapes that you can add to a floor plan. For details, see Chapter 14, "Creating Network Diagrams."

Troubleshooting

When you add shapes to a floor plan, you accidentally move walls and other structural shapes

Before you begin to add services or network shapes to a floor plan, lock the layers that make up the floor plan so that you don't move a wall accidentally, for example, when you're positioning an electrical outlet. There are two ways to lock layers depending on the type of floor plan you have:

- If you created the floor plan in Visio, choose View, Layer Properties, and then check the Lock column for any layer you want to protect.

- To lock a CAD drawing you've imported, right-click the drawing, and then choose <*File Type*> Object, Properties. For example, choose CAD Drawing Object, Properties. In the CAD Drawing Properties dialog box, select the Lock Position check box.

Adding HVAC Services to a Plan

Your floor plan can show the equipment and controls for what one company charmingly calls "indoor comfort systems," as Figure 18-18 shows. Visio includes shapes for designing the cooling, heating, and ventilating equipment and controls, from temperature sensors to water chillers. The Building Plan solutions folder includes two HVAC templates, one for creating control logic schematics and the other for ductwork and equipment.

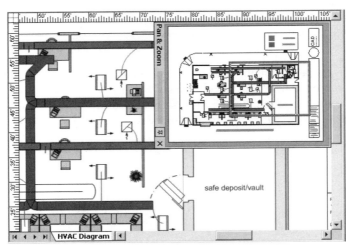

Figure 18-18. The return and supply ducts in this plan are color coded to indicate their use. The Pan & Zoom window makes it easy to see the entire drawing while you work closely on one segment.

The HVAC Control Logic Diagram template opens a scaled drawing page and the following stencils:

- **HVAC Controls**   This stencil provides a variety of sensors.
- **HVAC Controls Equipment**   This stencil includes shapes for ducts, fans, filters, pumps, and so on.
- **Annotations**   This stencil includes callout shapes for labeling the schematic.

The HVAC Plan template opens a scaled drawing page and these stencils:

- **HVAC Equipment**   This stencil includes shapes for pumps, condensers, and fans.
- **HVAC Ductwork**   This stencil contains a variety of duct shapes.
- **Registers, Grills And Diffusers**   This stencil includes standard inlet, outlet, and diffuser shapes.
- **Drawing Tool Shapes**   This stencil comes with geometric shapes for creating other objects.
- **Walls, Shell And Structure**   This stencil includes the basic tools for designing multiroom buildings.
- **Building Core**   This stencil includes the shapes needed to flesh out the basic interior of a building. Included are stairs, elevators, ramps, and so on.
- **Annotations**   This stencil includes callout shapes for labeling the schematic.

The way you start working with these shapes depends on whether you want to add HVAC information to an existing floor plan or design from scratch. You have the following options:

Shapes

- To insert HVAC information in a floor plan you created in Visio, open the floor plan, and then use the Shapes button on the Standard toolbar to open the HVAC stencils you need.
- To add HVAC information to a floor plan created in a CAD program, start in Visio by choosing File, New, Building Plan, and then select one of the two HVAC templates. Then insert the CAD drawing (choose Insert, CAD Drawing).

> For details, see "Using a Floor Plan from a CAD Drawing," page 509, or refer to Chapter 17, "Using CAD Drawings in Visio."

- To start a new HVAC diagram from scratch, start Visio, choose File, New, Building Plan, and then choose the HVAC template you want.

You might find it most convenient when using HVAC shapes to keep the Custom Properties window docked on the drawing page. To display it, select View, Custom Properties Window. When you select a shape on the page, its configuration properties appear in this window. All of the built-in Visio control and equipment shapes include custom property fields. You can set specifications for shapes in this window, such as sensor type or voltage limits. You can also use any of the HVAC shapes to track other information as well, such as part number, manufacturer, model identifier or tag number, and so on. When you enter values for these properties, you can then generate reports or parts lists automatically (choose Tools, Report).

Chapter 18

The shapes on the HVAC Controls Equipment template conform to the relevant standards for graphic symbols of the American Society of Heating, Refrigerating, and Air Conditioning Engineers, Inc. (ASHRAE). The primary concern of ASHRAE is to set American standards. If you're designing plans for buildings outside of the United States, the standards vary.

Inserting Control Logic Schematics

You can design control logic schematics that show the equipment, wiring, and sensors used to control an HVAC system. Visio packs a lot of features in a few shapes. Don't be deceived if you don't see the exact control symbol you're looking for. Many of the shapes have a switchable configuration that you specify in the in the Custom Properties window (or a shape's Properties dialog box). For example, if the Custom Properties window is open, you can select a pressure sensor shape, and then select the type of control from the Type list as Figure 18-19 shows.

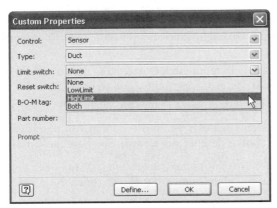

Figure 18-19. You can customize many HVAC shapes in the Custom Properties window. Click in a field to display a drop-down list.

> **Tip** To determine whether a shape property can be customized, click in a field of the Custom Properties window. A drop-down list of options appears for some properties, including Control, Type, Limit Switch, and Reset Switch.

If you're working in an existing floor plan, follow these steps to open the stencils you need to insert control logic symbols:

1 Click the drop-down arrow on the Shapes button on the Standard toolbar to display the list of drawing types.

2 Choose Building Plan, HVAC Controls.

3 Repeat to open the HVAC Controls Equipment stencil.

4 If you plan to annotate the diagram, click the Shapes button's drop-down arrow, and select Visio Extras, Annotations to open the Annotations stencil.

The HVAC shapes are designed to connect and stay glued, as Figure 18-20 shows. When you drag the endpoint of a shape near the connection point on another shape, a red square appears around the point where it will be glued, and Visio displays a ScreenTip that says Glue To Connection Point.

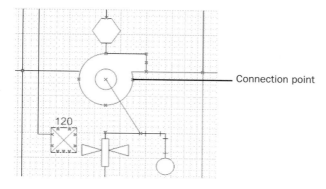

— Connection point

Figure 18-20. Connection points on a shape show where you can connect valves, pipes, and lines.

Labeling HVAC Shapes

HVAC schematics often include text in the form of shape labels and instructions. In some cases, you can label a shape by selecting it and then typing. Other shapes are locked to prevent this, because they are labeled automatically when configured in certain ways. For example, when you specify a load voltage for a magnetic starter in the Custom Properties window, the voltage is displayed on the shape. To reposition a label, drag its control handle (the yellow diamond).

One cool thing you can do with the HVAC shapes (or any shapes that include custom properties) is to label the shape with a property value automatically, such as the part number or bill of material tag. To do this, you can insert a text field that displays the custom property (choose Insert, Field), or you can use a custom callout shape.

For details about labels, see "Using Visio Shapes to Display Text," page 130.

Adding Ductwork

You can design single-line and double-line HVAC plans that show the location and configuration of ductwork and piping. Visio consolidates the ductwork shapes on one stencil, HVAC Ductwork. (Longtime users probably remember that Visio 2000 stored duct shapes on two different stencils depending on whether the ducts were rectangular or circular.) You can configure any duct shape in Visio to be either rectangular or circular in the Custom Properties window.

Chapter 18

When you add ductwork to a floor plan, your task is made simpler by some pretty smart shapes. For example, the duct shape is designed to look like a line while you drag it on the page, which makes it easier to position precisely. In addition, control equipment shapes are designed to work together. Dampers, sensors, and other shapes can be dropped on ducts, where they snap and rotate into place. That frees you to concentrate on more important tasks, such as how to design your system for optimum indoor air quality.

To configure ducts, diffusers, and other equipment shapes, right-click a shape, and then choose Properties. The Custom Properties window lists relevant options. For example, to show how a grille diffuser is used, you can click in the Air Flow Type of its Custom Properties window to choose from Supply and Return. To open the Custom Properties window, choose View, Custom Properties Window.

> **Tip**   **Drag a shape to an exact position**
> When you drag a shape such as the Duct shape from the stencil onto the drawing page, watch the status bar at the bottom of the Visio window. The duct's position on the page is given as the x-coordinate and the y-coordinate of the two ends of the duct.

For other shape configuration options, right-click a shape and see whether it has any commands on its shortcut menu. For example, you can specify whether a return diffuser is hidden, and you can add fins to or remove the plate from a pipe coil.

HVAC Shapes and Layers

When you add ductwork to an existing floor plan, the shapes are assigned to the HVAC layer, as Figure 18-21 shows. That way, you can lock other drawing layers to prevent them from changing while you add the HVAC equipment, and you can view the floor plan without the HVAC equipment. HVAC shapes can be assigned to more than one layer. For example, you can assign the Starter shape to an HVAC layer as well as the Flow Equipment, Notations, Piping, Power/Comm, and Valve layers. That gives you a lot of flexibility to work with the different information in a floor plan. You can do the following:

- To see which layers a shape is assigned to or add it to a new layer, select the shape, and then choose Format, Layers.
- To work with layers in a drawing, choose View, Layer Properties. For details, see "Using Layers to Protect, Hide, and Organize Shapes," page 467.

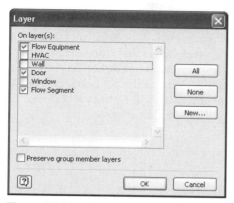

Figure 18-21. Visio duct shapes are preassigned to the HVAC layer, as the Layer dialog box shows.

Drawing the Plumbing Layout

A floor plan can include the layout of pipes, valves, and fittings with shapes from the Plumbing And Piping Plan template. You can also use this template to show drainage in a site plan or to design water supply systems, wastewater disposal systems, and other schematics that show water lines, pipes, and valves. When you start a drawing with the Plumbing And Piping Plan template, Visio sets up a scaled drawing page and opens the following stencils:

- **Pipes And Valves—Pipes 1 and 2**   These two stencils contain shapes that represent a variety of pipelines and devices used with pipelines. The pipelines are 1-D shapes that you can resize and rotate by dragging an endpoint.

- **Pipes And Valves—Valves 1 and 2**   These two stencils contain standard valve symbols. The blue connection points on valve shapes are designed to be glued to the endpoints on pipeline shapes.

- **Plumbing**   This stencil includes standard plumbing shapes from the boiler down to the towel bar.

- **Drawing Tool Shapes**   This stencil comes with geometric shapes for creating other objects.

- **Walls, Shell And Structure**   This stencil includes the basic tools for designing multi-room buildings.

- **Annotations**   This stencil includes callout shapes for labeling the schematic.

To show plumbing or piping information in an existing floor plan, open the floor plan first, and then open these stencils, which are stored in the Building Plan folder. When you want to start a design from scratch, open the Plumbing And Piping Plan template in the Building Plan folder.

Chapter 18

539

Adding Plumbing Equipment

When you add plumbing equipment and fixtures to a floor plan, you can show a cutaway view of how piping moves through the walls with shapes that represent a side perspective. Or you can show the customary top-down view of fixtures in a floor plan. Some shapes also include shortcut commands that you can use to change their appearance. For example, a boiler can be displayed with flat, curved, or angled ends, as Figure 18-22 shows. To determine whether a shape has shortcut commands, right-click the shape.

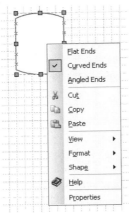

Figure 18-22.   Right-click a shape to see its shortcut menu with commands for configuring the shape's appearance.

Other shapes include custom properties that affect how they're displayed, although none of the shapes on the Plumbing stencil do this. So even if you don't see a particular symbol on a stencil, Visio might include a configurable shape that looks the way you want. For example, you can change the In-Line Valve shape on the Pipes And Valves—Valves 1 stencil to be displayed as an in-line, three-way, or four-way valve, as Figure 18-23 shows. To find out whether a shape can be customized, display its Custom Properties window or right-click the shape, and then select Properties to display its Custom Properties dialog box.

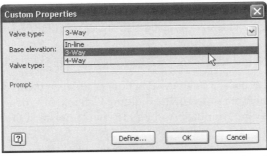

Figure 18-23.   You can change the configuration for some shapes in the Custom Properties window. This in-line valve can morph to a 3-way or 4-way valve.

Inside Out

Rotating fixtures

When you use the drawing tools to create fixtures such as a T-joint, you might need to rotate them, but only 90-degree orientations are valid. If you're drawing pipes or other representational lines with the Line tool, you can snap lines to specific angles with shape extension lines. To turn on shape extension lines, choose Tools, Snap & Glue. On the General tab, select Drawing Aids. On the Advanced tab, scroll down the list, and then select Isometric Angle Lines. In the Isometric Angles box, type the angle measure (in degrees) of the angle you want the line to snap to.

The isometric angle lines were originally developed for diagrams where pipes run horizontally and vertically. When it doesn't make sense to rotate shapes at other angles, you can use shape extension lines to show you how to constrain lines to a valid angle when you draw them.

Using Layers with Piping Shapes

All the plumbing, piping, and valve shapes are assigned to layers, which gives you added flexibility when adding shapes to an existing floor plan. For example, the Power Signal shape is assigned to both the Valve layer and the Flow Controller layer. The Heating/Cooling Coil shape is assigned to the Plumbing and the Flow Equipment layers. You can work with shapes selectively based on their layer assignments.

For details about working with layers, see "Using Layers to Protect, Hide, and Organize Shapes," page 467.

Tip   To keep pipes together after you've laid them out on the drawing page, you can group them: select the shapes you want, and then press Shift+Ctrl+G.

Adding Electrical and Telecommunication Services

The Electrical And Telecom stencil provides the shapes you need to show the location of lighting, outlets, service panels, and so on in a home, office, or manufacturing plant, as Figure 18-24 shows. When you're working in a floor plan, you can open this stencil by clicking the drop-down arrow on the Shapes button on the Standard toolbar, and then selecting Building Plan, Electrical And Telecom.

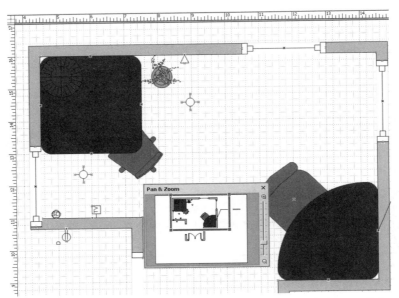

Figure 18-24.   This floor plan shows the placement of switches, outlets, smoke detectors, ceiling lights, and doorbell chimes with shapes from the Electrical And Telecom stencil.

You can use the Electrical And Telecom Plan template to create a diagram from scratch. This template opens the Electrical And Telecom stencil as well as the Drawing Tools, Walls, Shell And Structure, and Annotations stencils.To start a new electrical plan, choose File, New, Building Plan, Electrical And Telecom Plan.

Configuring Electrical and Telecommunication Shapes

There are more symbols that you can display than there are shapes—several shapes include custom properties that you can set to show different types of outlets, switches, and so forth. For example, the Switches shape can represent single pole, three-way, four-way, timer, or weatherproof switches. The Socket Outlets shape can represent standard, dedicated, or split-wire outlets. To find out whether a shape has configurable properties, right-click a shape, and then select Properties to display the Custom Properties dialog box.

To configure a shape, right-click the shape to display a shortcut menu with options. For example, you can right-click a service panel and specify whether to display it as an inset or surface panel.

Some of the lighting shapes provide built-in options. For example, with the Troffer Floures shape, you can choose the number of lamps (1 to 4) as well as the length (4 ft. or 8 ft.).

Inside Out

No more prompts

If you used the electrical and telecommunication shapes in Visio 2000, you'll notice that Visio 2003 doesn't prompt you for information when you drag a shape from the stencil onto the drawing page. This change represents a philosophical shift among the product designers—they now think such prompts are intrusive.

Connecting and Positioning Electrical Shapes

Outlets and switches are designed to connect to wall shapes in a floor plan, but they aren't smart enough to rotate themselves into position. If the shape is oriented differently than the wall you want to attach it to, you can rotate it manually around its rotation point. If you want to reverse the shape's orientation, there's a shortcut: right-click the outlet or switch, and then choose Flip Orientation.

> **Tip** To quickly rotate a shape 90 degrees to the left, press Ctrl+L. To rotate a shape 90 degrees to the right, press Ctrl+R.

Freeform tool

If you want to show connection wires between the switches in a floor plan, you'll need to draw them; Visio doesn't have an automated method. Use the Freeform tool on the Drawing toolbar. Freeform lines are a little tricky to draw—it's best to drag very slowly when using this tool. To connect lines, click the Freeform tool, and then drag from a connection point on the shape where the connection wire starts to the connection point on the shape where the wire ends.

> **Note** For more electrical and electronic symbols, see the templates and stencils in the Electrical Engineering folder. For shapes that represent telecommunication devices (such as cell phones and pagers), see the Network And Peripherals stencil in the Network folder.

Adding Security Systems

You can add video surveillance and other cool security devices to your floor plans with shapes from the Security And Access Plan template. Visio includes shapes for surveillance cameras, intercom systems, alarms, and other devices, as Figure 18-25 shows. You can start a security and access plan on a blank page or as a layer in an existing floor plan. To design a security system from scratch, you can open the Security And Access Plan template, which opens a scaled drawing page and the following stencils:

- **Alarm And Access Control** This stencil includes shapes for various card readers, keypads, and other access devices.
- **Initiation And Annunciation** This stencil contains shapes for designing digital- and microprocessor-controlled intercom paging and alarm systems.

Chapter 18

- **Video Surveillance**   This stencil includes shapes for motion detectors, sensors, cameras, and switches.
- **Annotations**   This stencil includes callout shapes for labeling the schematic.

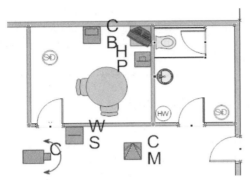

Figure 18-25.   This partial floor plan shows a camera (C), ceiling-mounted microwave motion detector (CM), wall-mounted smart card–type card reader (WS), ceiling-mounted burglar alarm (CB), and hidden panic button (HP) shapes. Looks like a tough nut to crack.

Adding Security System Shapes

To add security systems to an existing floor plan, you can start in one of two ways:

- To insert security systems in a floor plan you created in Visio, open the floor plan, and then use the Shapes button on the Standard toolbar to open the stencils you need in the Building Plan folder.
- To add security systems to a floor plan created in a CAD program, start in Visio by selecting File, New, Building Plan, Security And Access Plan. Then insert the CAD drawing (Insert, CAD Drawing). For details, see "Using a Floor Plan from a CAD Drawing," page 509, or refer to Chapter 17, "Using CAD Drawings in Visio."

Configuring Security System Shapes

You can configure some security devices by setting properties in the Custom Properties window. For example, you can specify how a device is mounted—on the ceiling, rack, desk, wall, and so on—by choosing an option, as Figure 18-26 shows. The shape's label changes to reflect the type of mount. To view a shape's custom properties, open the Custom Properties window or right-click the shape, choose Properties, and make the changes in the Custom Properties dialog box.

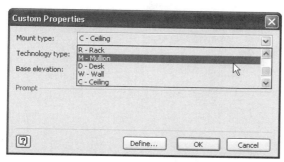

Figure 18-26. To see the configurable properties for security and alarm shapes, anchor the Custom Properties window on the drawing page. This shape includes options for the type of mount and base elevation.

Security and alarm shapes are assigned to layers. When you add these shapes to a floor plan, Visio adds the Security, Surveillance, and Video Surveillance layers to the drawing depending on the shapes used. You can take advantage of layers to selectively show and print shapes in a drawing.

For details about working with layers, see "Using Layers to Protect, Hide, and Organize Shapes," page 467.

Creating Site and Landscaping Plans

Site plans fall into two broad categories depending on whether they depict a commercial location or a home. A commercial or architectural site plan might show landscaping, irrigation, driveways, on- and off-street parking, and other traffic management features. A site plan for a home or garden typically includes plants, fences, irrigation lines, swimming pool, sport fields, and so on. In either case, a typical site plan represents a space considerably larger than a floor plan.

Note Visio Standard does not include site planning and landscaping shapes.

You can start a new site plan with the Site Plan template, or start with an existing floor plan to combine interior and exterior views. Figure 18-27 shows a simple site plan.

Chapter 18

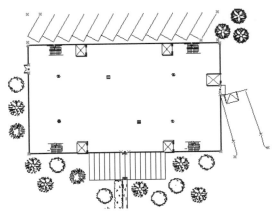

Figure 18-27. This simple site plan includes parking spaces and landscaping.

In general, you start a site plan by measuring the property and noting the distance between landmarks. If you have the legal description of the property, you can use that to determine the property's dimensions. In Visio, you use these measurements to add buildings and other structures to the site plan. If you're working with an existing floor plan, the main building already exists. If you only want to represent a shell of the floor plan, drag exterior wall shapes from the Walls, Shell And Structure stencil to draw the structures. To open this stencil, choose File, Shapes, Building Plan, Walls, Shell And Structure.

To start a new site plan, follow these steps:

1 Choose File, New, Building Plan, Site Plan.

   Visio opens a new, scaled drawing page where 1 in. = 10 ft. The page size is the ANSI standard 36 in. by 24 in.

> **Note** If you want to add a site plan to an existing floor plan, open the floor plan drawing in Visio, and then open the following stencils: Garden Accessories, Irrigation, Parking And Roads, Planting, Site Accessories, Sport Fields And Recreation, and Vehicles.

2 Choose File, Page Setup. On the Page Size tab, verify that the drawing uses the size settings you want, and make any changes. Then click the Drawing Scale tab, and verify that the scale is the one you want, and make any changes. Click OK.

> For details about setting up page size and drawing scale, see "Setting Up Measurements in a Diagram," page 421.

3 To incorporate buildings into your site plan, do one of the following:

   ■ Use the Line or Rectangle tool to draw outlines of buildings.

   ■ Copy and paste an existing Visio floor plan drawing into the drawing. For details, see "Copying an Existing Visio Floor Plan," page 510. Use Visio's drawing tools to draw a boundary for the property.

4   Add landscaping features, parking lots, sport fields, and plants using the shapes from the stencils included in the template. See the following sections for details.

Adding Landscaping Details

The Planting stencil includes shapes for plants and a unique annotation shape, Plant Callout, which you can use to label plants. Other landscaping features, such as fences, trash cans, and stone paths are on the Garden Accessories and Site Accessories stencils. Irrigation equipment shapes are, appropriately enough, on the Irrigation stencil.

Note   Landscape shapes are available only in Visio Professional.

Follow these steps to add landscaping elements to a site plan:

1   From the Garden Accessories stencil, drag fence shapes and gate shapes onto a drawing page.

2   From the Sport Fields And Recreation stencil, position large recreational equipment, such as a pool or a swing set, by dragging a shape onto a drawing page.

3   From the Garden Accessories stencil, add patios and walkways by dragging shapes onto the drawing page.

4   From the Irrigation stencil, add irrigation equipment by dragging shapes onto the drawing page.

5   Add plants by dragging shapes from the Planting stencil onto the drawing page. Use the Plant Callout shape to label plants. You can record the plant's common name and foliage type as custom properties.

6   To enter custom property values for plants, right-click a plant shape, and then select Properties to open the Custom Properties dialog box for the plant. Then click in a field, and type a name.

Note   To create and arrange multiple copies of shapes in orderly rows and columns, such as paving stones, try the Array Shapes command (choose Tools, Add-Ons, Visio Extras, Array Shapes).

Adding Roads to a Site Plan

Using shapes on the Parking And Roads stencil, you can identify driveways leading to the property, as well as parking lots, sidewalk ramps, and roadway islands. Footpath shapes and an additional driveway shape are on the Garden Accessories stencil. You can also use shapes from the Vehicles stencil to ensure you have enough space in your parking lot or garage for vehicles of different sizes. The Vehicles stencil includes shapes to show the turnaround space for buses, semitrailers, and trucks.

Chapter 18

> **Note** Although there are sidewalk ramp shapes on the Parking And Roads stencil, there are no sidewalk shapes on any stencil. You can draw sidewalks using the Line and Rectangle tools on the Drawing toolbar.

To add roads and parking stalls, follow these steps:

1 From the horizontal and vertical rulers, drag guides and position them on the page to mark the locations of the site perimeter, stalls, and roads in the drawing.

2 From the Parking And Roads stencil, drag curbs and driveways onto the drawing page. Use lines to connect the curbs and driveways.

3 From the Parking And Roads stencil, drag parking strips, stalls, and islands and position them on the drawing page. Glue their endpoints to guides.

4 To reposition parking stalls, drag the guide to which they are glued.

> **Tip** To keep the alignment of a shape from changing while you move the shape, press the Shift key.

5 From the Vehicles, Site Accessories, and Planting stencils, position vehicles, parking accessories, and landscape shapes around the parking strips and stalls. Glue their endpoints to guides.

> **Tip** Use shapes from the Annotations and Dimensioning—Architectural stencils to add labels or dimension lines to your site plan.

Adding Recreation Equipment to a Site Plan

The Sport Fields And Recreation Equipment stencil includes shapes for swimming pools, children's playground equipment, baseball diamonds, and other specialized sports fields. Fencing and footpath shapes are on the Garden Accessories stencil; outdoor furniture, bike racks, and barbecue shapes are on the Site Accessories stencil.

Adding Dimensions to Floor and Site Plans

In a floor plan or a site plan, you often need to refer to the specific measurements of furniture, walls, paths, or other objects. Although shape dimensions appear in the Size & Position window while you work in Visio, you can easily add dimension lines that display measurements dynamically as you reposition and size shapes. Table 18-2 summarizes shapes and techniques you can use to display measurements.

Table 18-2. Techniques for Adding Dimensions to Plans

Type of Dimension	Technique
Add dimension line shapes that calculate and display linear and angular dimensions	See the shapes on the Dimensioning—Architectural stencil in the Visio Extras folder. For details, see "Calculating and Displaying Dimensions," page 453.
Display the dimensions of a shape within the shape itself	Add a geometry field to the shape's text block with the Field command on the Insert menu. For details, see "Displaying Custom Measurements," page 456.
Label a room and display its dimensions	Drag the Room Measurements shape (see Figure 18-28) from the Walls, Doors And Windows or Walls, Shell And Structure stencil into a room.

Figure 18-28. When you drop the Room Measurements shape in a room, it sizes to fit the space and displays the word "Room" with the dimensions below. You can change the font of the measurements using the Text tool, and you can delete or edit the word "Room."

In addition to dimensions, building plans frequently include other annotations and text information. Useful techniques are described elsewhere in this book:

- You can point out relevant features and highlight information with callout shapes. For details, see "Annotating Diagrams with Callout Shapes," page 130.

- You can create custom callouts that automatically display information from the Custom Properties window. Because all the building plan shapes have a variety of built-in properties, you can design automated annotations. For details, see "Displaying Values in a Custom Callout," page 132.

- For details about working with the shapes on the Title Block stencil, see "Adding a Title Block to a Diagram," page 134.

Chapter 18

Part 5

Inside Database and Software Diagrams

Diagramming and Documenting Databases

Given the complexity of database management systems (DBMSs), visual documentation is an effective means of promoting communication between technical experts and their clients. With Microsoft Office Visio 2003 Professional, you can take a snapshot of your database and its code to create a concise and accurate *database model diagram*—that is, a diagram that models a physical database schema. Visio Professional reverse engineers client/server databases from Microsoft, Oracle, and others, as well as desktop databases such as Microsoft Access, and provides several views of your database schema. Using shapes that represent Relational, IDEF1X, or Crow's Feet notation, you can diagram relational or object-relational databases and easily keep the diagram up to date as modifications are made to the database.

The Database Model Diagram template is the place to start. With it, you can describe all or part of a database schema and even create a model that is independent of its implementation on any particular DBMS. This chapter assumes that you are already familiar with database concepts and architecture and describes the unique database modeling tools that you can use in Visio Professional.

> **Note** The templates and shapes described in this chapter are included only with Visio Professional.

Modeling Relational and Object-Relational Databases

Whether you've inherited the company's e-commerce back end and want to document it, or you simply need to understand the legacy purchasing system, an accurate database model diagram can help. Although Visio can reverse engineer a database and create a diagram based on the schema, the result is more than a series of connected shapes. Visio creates a *model* that represents the logical and physical structure of a database, including tables or entities, columns or attributes, and relationships. Visio supports notation for primary keys, foreign keys, alternate keys, and indexes, as well as referential integrity and IDEF1X cardinality constraints. To view and edit this information, you work in several special-purpose anchored windows as well as the drawing page, as Figure 19-1 shows.

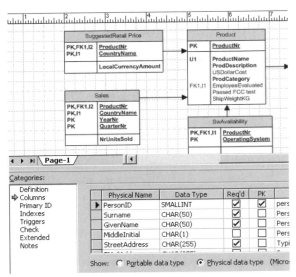

Figure 19-1. You can reverse engineer a database to extract tables, views, code, and other database elements and create a database model diagram.

The Database Model Diagram template is an application unto itself. As with other drawing types, you can drag shapes to add objects to your database model. However, the template adds the Database menu and other tools specifically for working with your database model diagram. Because of these additions, the way you create and modify database diagrams isn't always the same way that you work with other Visio drawings.

Starting a New Database Model Diagram

Most people use the Database Model Diagram template to reverse engineer a database that already exists. However, you can also use the template to prototype new designs.

Follow these steps to start a new database model diagram and set modeling options:

1 Choose File, New, Database, Database Model Diagram.
2 To set the modeling options you want to use, choose Database, Options, Document.

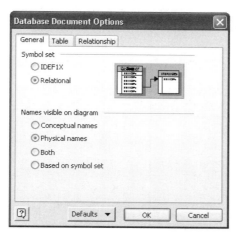

3 Under Symbol Set, select IDEF1X or Relational, and then specify the name options you want to display.

4 Click the Table tab, and then choose the attributes you want to have displayed in table shapes, primary key order, data type display, and whether to display IDEF1X optionality.

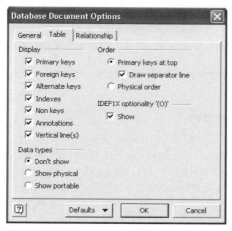

5 Click the Relationship tab, and then choose whether to display relationships. If you do, specify the relationship notation you want to use (such as Crow's Feet), whether to display cardinality and referential integrity, and how to display the relationship verb phrase and name (role text).

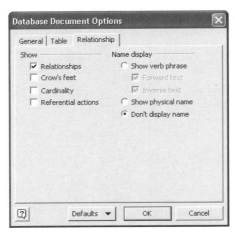

6 Click OK to apply the settings to the drawing file.

Tip Import a Database Model Diagram

If you have an existing database diagram from PLATINUM ERwin or VisioModeler that you would like to edit in Visio, you can import it. Visio Professional can import ERX files from ER*win* 2.6, 3, and 3.52 (although Visio doesn't import stored procedures, custom triggers, or ER*win* displays). You can import models from VisioModeler 2 or later. To import a model, choose Database, Import.

Troubleshooting

The Database menu is no longer visible

Solution-specific menus can disappear when Visio encounters an unexpected error from an external source. If the Database menu no longer appears between the Shape and Window menus, choose Tools, Options. On the Security tab, select Enable Automation Events, and then click OK. Save changes to any open diagrams, and then exit Visio. Restart Visio, and then open your database model or start a new diagram with the Database Model Diagram template.

Viewing Tables and Other Model Elements

You can add shapes to the drawing page to provide one view of a database model. Visio stores another view of your model in the Tables And Views window, which lists the names of tables and views extracted from a database, as Figure 19-2 shows. To display this window, choose Database, View, Tables And Views. Whether or not the diagram shows every table and view in your model, the Tables And Views window does. You can drag elements from the window onto your diagram, where you can view them along with any associated relationships.

Figure 19-2. The Tables And Views window is an anchored window that you can float or dock in a convenient location as you work on your database model diagram.

> **Note** You can view the tables related to a particular table without viewing the entire model diagram.

Getting Feedback from the Output Window

When you start a new diagram with the Database Model Diagram template, the Output window appears below the drawing page. This window displays progress and status information when you reverse engineer a database, as Figure 19-3 shows. You can verify that the database schema was extracted as specified and view a summary at the bottom of the window of the number of tables and other items, including code, that were extracted from your database.

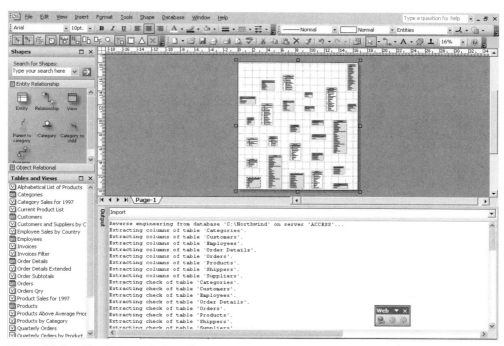

Figure 19-3. The Output window shows you every step Visio takes when reverse engineering a database.

Visio validates your model when you reverse engineer a database. Messages about conflicting names, data types, or other errors appear in the Output window. You can copy the messages and paste them into Notepad or another text editor to keep them on hand for troubleshooting. Right-click in the Output window, and then choose Copy Message or Copy All Messages.

Inside Out

Output window options

At the top of the Output window is a list box with two options: Import and Info. In Visio Professional, the Info option isn't used and is provided solely for compatibility with the advanced forward engineering and model validation features in Microsoft Visual Studio .NET Enterprise Edition.

Viewing Database Code

If your database includes code, such as check clauses or stored procedures, Visio can extract it when you reverse engineer a database. The Code window lists all code for a particular database platform, as Figure 19-4 shows. You can view, edit, and delete stored procedures, functions, triggers, check clauses, view definitions, and even raw data definition language (DDL) code, each of which is represented by a different icon in the Code window.

Figure 19-4. You can view, edit, and delete the code associated with your database model diagram.

To display the Code window, choose Database, View, Code. The Code window lists two types of code:

- *Global code* refers to any stored procedure, function, view definition, or raw DDL code that's not associated with a specific table.

Window Properties

Insert Code Skeleton

- *Local code* refers to triggers or check clauses for a specific table or column in your database model diagram.

To display any code module, select it, and then click Edit to open the Code Editor. The Code Editor is a full-featured editor. You can specify keyword colors, assign keyboard shortcuts, and more with the Window Properties button on the Code Editor toolbar. For example, you can indent lines automatically as you enter code in accordance with language-specific scoping rules. Use the Insert Code Skeleton button to do just that—insert a blank code skeleton for the type of code you have specified.

Setting Modeling Preferences

You can set preferences for the way shapes look and behave in a database model diagram. For example, you can specify whether deleting a shape from the diagram deletes the object from the model. When you choose Database, Options, Modeling, you specify the default settings that are stored with the Database Model Diagram template and remain in effect until you specify otherwise. As Figure 19-5 shows, the Logical Diagram tab includes the following options:

- **When Removing An Object From The Diagram**   Specifies whether to remove a deleted object from the drawing page only, retaining it in the Tables And Views window, or remove it from the drawing file (and model) altogether.

- **Show Relationships After Adding Table To Diagram**   Shows relationships on the current page between a newly added table and any other tables on the page.

- **Show Relationships After Adding Type To Diagram**   Shows relationships between a newly added type in the diagram and any other types on the page.

- **Sync Conceptual And Physical Names In New Tables And Columns When Typing**   Specifies that typing a name in one field creates the name in the other field automatically when you change database properties.

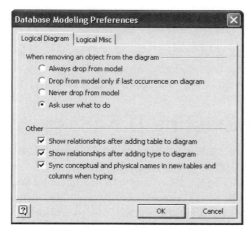

Figure 19-5.   With the options on the Logical Diagram tab, you can customize the behavior of the shapes that represent your database model.

On the Logical Misc tab, you can control the way names and relationships appear in the diagram so that shapes reflect your preferred modeling style, as Figure 19-6 shows. You can set the following properties:

- **FK Propagation**   Specifies the behavior when a relationship shape is connected between a parent and child table. If Propagate On Add is selected, Visio creates a foreign key relationship when you connect a relationship shape. If Propagate On Delete is selected, Visio removes the foreign key from the model when you delete a relationship shape.

- **Name Conflict Resolution**   Specifies the behavior when you add a foreign key to a table that contains a column of the same name.

- **Default Name Prefixes**   Specifies the prefix that is added to the suffix under Default Name Suffixes to form the default conceptual name for objects added to a model.

- **Default Name Suffixes**   Specifies the suffix that is added to the prefix under Default Name Prefixes to form the default conceptual name for objects added to a model.

- **FK Name Generation Option**   Specifies how to construct the default foreign key name that appears in a model. Suffix refers to the value of the Foreign Key box under Default Name Suffixes.

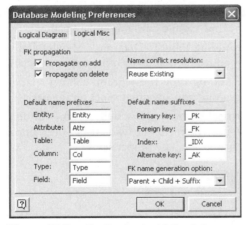

Figure 19-6.   On the Logical Misc tab, you can choose how foreign keys are propagated and how to build default names and resolve name conflicts.

Reverse Engineering an Existing Database

Visio Professional makes it easy to extract information from a DBMS and add it to the drawing page. The Reverse Engineer Wizard walks you through the steps required to connect to a data source, specify a data source name (DSN), connect to a target database, and select the objects to *extract* from the database. Visio can create a diagram automatically based on the objects you extracted, or you can create the diagram yourself. The wizard analyzes and validates the schema before adding it to the database model diagram in Visio.

The information that the wizard can extract depends on your target DBMS. If the DBMS doesn't make all of the schema definition available, the wizard displays options for the available items and dims other options. After you finish using the wizard, its status is displayed in the Output window and the extracted schema is displayed in the Tables And Views window, Code window, and the drawing page if you choose.

Setting Up a Data Source

You can use the Reverse Engineer Wizard to connect to a target DBMS, but it's quicker to configure a default driver first. To connect to and extract information from a database, Visio uses built-in database drivers that are enhanced to work specifically with the Database Model Diagram template. Visio includes built-in drivers for the following DBMSs:

- IBM DB2 Universal Database
- INFORMIX OnLine/SE Server
- Microsoft Access
- Microsoft SQL Server
- Oracle Server
- Sybase Adaptive Service Enterprise

In addition, a generic object linking and embedding (OLE) DB Provider and Open Database Connectivity (ODBC) driver are included. If you are developing a database for a DBMS other than the ones listed here, you can use the generic ODBC driver with a vendor-supplied 32-bit ODBC driver to connect to your DBMS.

Using the Drivers command, you can configure a driver in advance to specify default data type properties and a default data type to use when creating columns, as Figure 19-7 shows.

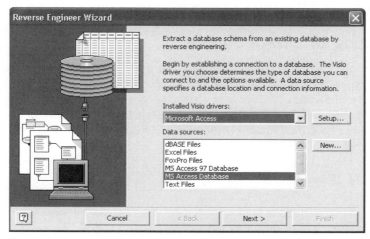

Figure 19-7. You can set up and select a database driver before using the Reverse Engineer Wizard.

Follow these steps to specify a default database driver:

1 Choose Database, Options, Drivers.

2 In the Default Driver For Visio box, select the driver you want to use.

3 To associate a vendor-specific driver with the selected Visio driver, click Setup, specify the settings you want, and then click OK.

4 Click the Default Mapping tab.

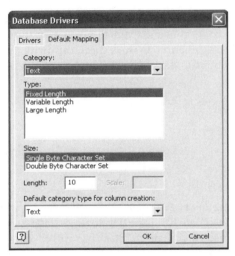

5 Under Default Category Type For Column Creation, choose the default category type, and then for each category type, set the default data Category, Type, Size, Length, and Precision or Scale.

6 Click OK.

Step 1: Connecting to a Data Source

When you start the Reverse Engineer Wizard, you can create a data source for a particular database. A data source includes the data you want to access and crucial information for accessing that data, such as the name of the database, the server on which it resides, and network information. Visio refers to a data source by its DSN and lists default DSNs on the first screen of the wizard, as Figure 19-8 shows. You can create, edit, and manage DSNs within Visio.

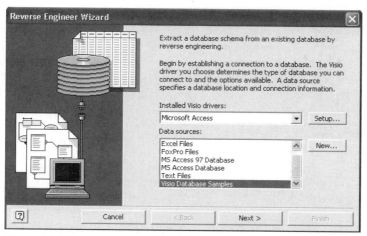

Figure 19-8. You can connect to a database by specifying a Visio driver and then an associated data source.

Follow these steps to start the wizard and connect to a data source:

1 Choose Database, Reverse Engineer.

2 In the Installed Visio Drivers list, the driver you set up in the previous section is selected.

3 If you want to set up a new driver, click Setup, associate the selected Visio driver with a vendor-supplied driver, and then click OK.

4 In the Data Sources list, select the data source that points to your database. Or click New to create a new File DSN, User DSN, or System DSN. When you are finished, click OK to add the new DSN to the Data Sources list.

5 In the wizard, click Next to proceed. The Connect Data Source dialog box appears. Enter a valid user name in the User box and password in the Password box. Then click OK. If the database is not password-protected, just click OK.

6 If a Select Database, Select Workbook, or any other dialog box opens for you to select a file, locate the file you want to reverse engineer and click OK.

Step 2: Extracting Database Objects

On the next screen of the Reverse Engineer Wizard, you can choose the schema information to extract, as Figure 19-9 shows. Select the objects you want, and clear the check boxes for the objects you don't want to include in your database model. To proceed, click Next.

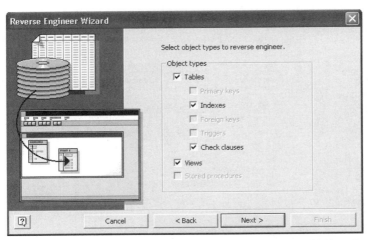

Figure 19-9. You can select from the options that your DBMS makes available to Visio. An Access database does not support triggers and stored procedures, so those options appear dimmed.

Step 3: Selecting Tables and Views

Visio lists the tables and views that your target database contains on the next screen of the Reverse Engineer Wizard, as Figure 19-10 shows. For convenience, you can click Select All, and then clear the check boxes for any tables you don't want to include. The tables you select here will be included in the model that Visio preserves, but don't necessarily have to appear in the diagram—which is an option on the next screen of the wizard. Click Next to continue.

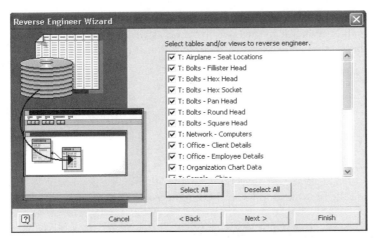

Figure 19-10. You can choose the tables and views you want to include in the model that Visio creates.

Step 4: Creating a Diagram

If you want Visio to generate a diagram based on the objects you've extracted from the database, you can select the Yes, Add The Shapes To The Current Page option on the next screen of the wizard, as Figure 19-11 shows. If you select the No, I Will Add The Shapes Later option, Visio still extracts the selected information from the database and adds it to the model that's stored with the diagram. However, no shapes for the tables, views, and relationships are added to the drawing page. Instead, the objects are listed in the Tables And Views window. To continue, click Next.

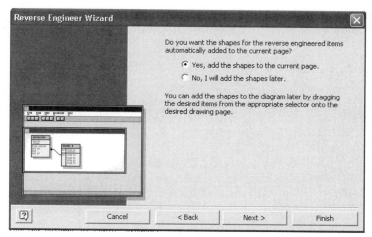

Figure 19-11. You can choose whether Visio diagrams the tables and views that the wizard extracts or adds them to the model without adding them to the drawing page.

Step 5: Finishing the Wizard

On the last screen of the wizard, you can review the options you've selected. Click Back to change your selections on any of the screens, or click Finish to extract the selected information and add it to the model in the Visio drawing file. Visio creates a database diagram if you selected that option. Otherwise, choose Database, View, Tables And Views to see the tables and views extracted from the target database. Review the contents of the Output window for information about the reverse engineering process.

Tip **Display related tables**
To quickly display related tables on the drawing page, drag a table from the Tables And Views window onto the page. Right-click the shape, and then choose Show Related Tables. Visio adds all the tables in your model that have a relationship to the first table and connects them.

Updating a Database Model Diagram

To keep your model in sync as changes are made to the physical database, you can use the Refresh Model command on the Database menu. This command starts a wizard that looks and works much like the Reverse Engineer Wizard. With the Refresh Model Wizard, you connect to your target DBMS, and then the wizard compares your database model diagram to the current physical schema. If the wizard detects any differences, you can choose to update the diagram to match the database, or ignore the difference on the screen shown in Figure 19-12.

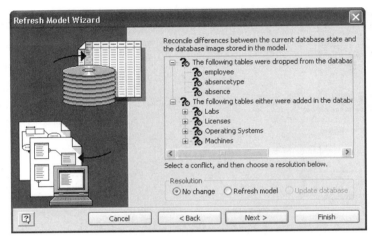

Figure 19-12. If your diagram no longer matches the target database, the wizard lists each difference.

To run the wizard, choose Database, Refresh Model. To resolve a conflict, select an item from the list displayed by the Refresh Model Wizard, and then choose the No Change option to ignore the conflict or the Refresh Model option to update your diagram.

Note In Visio Professional, the Update Database option in the Refresh Model Wizard always appears dimmed. This option is provided for compatibility with Visual Studio .NET Enterprise Edition.

Modifying a Database Model

Visio Professional provides extensive options for working with the tables, columns, views, and relationships in a database model diagram. You can define and edit settings for data types, referential integrity, indexes, and extended attributes, and see your changes reflected in the shapes on the page.

Visio displays detailed information about the database shapes in the Database Properties window, as Figure 19-13 shows. To display this window, right-click a shape, and then choose Database Properties.

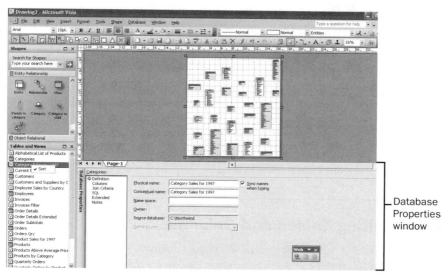

Database
Properties
window

Figure 19-13.   For convenience while editing the diagram, drag the Database Properties window by its title bar into the Output window to merge the windows at the bottom of the screen.

The Database Properties window makes it easy to refine the tables in your database model. In the Categories list, you can select an item to work with its properties. Table 19-1 summarizes the options available for each category.

Table 19-1. **Categories in the Database Properties Window**

Category	Description
Definition	Use this category to specify physical and conceptual names for the table and choose whether to synchronize the names. You can specify a namespace value for the table to distinguish it from similarly named tables in the model. Definition also displays information reported by the host DBMS about the database owner and the path of the source database. The defining type field is available only when a table is empty; it lists all composite data types, so you can create a typed table.
Columns	Use this category to add, remove, edit, and change the order of columns in a table. You can identify a column as a primary key or foreign key and specify whether physical or portable data types are displayed.
Primary ID	Use this category to edit, define, or delete primary keys from a list of available columns and to choose whether to create an index on primary keys.
Indexes	Use this category to create, edit, define, rename, delete, or set extended attributes for indexes. Use this tab to specify the type of index you create for a particular column.

Table 19-1. **Categories in the Database Properties Window**

Category	Description
Triggers	Use this category to add, edit, or remove the code for triggers that are included with your model. When you click Add or Edit, the Code Editor opens so that you can create or edit a trigger.
Check	Use this category to add, edit, or remove the code for check clauses that are included with your model. When you click Add or Edit, the Code Editor opens so that you can create or edit a check clause.
Extended	Use this category to set DBMS-specific extended attributes for use with the Visio database drivers.
Notes	Use this category to add notes about a table.

Adding and Editing Tables and Columns

Visio represents a table in your database model diagram with the Entity shape. When you want to add a new table to the diagram, you can drag a shape from either the Entity Relationship or Object Relational stencil depending on the modeling methodology you want to use. Visio makes changes to the appearance of the Entity shape based on the modeling and display options you have specified. For example, if you specify IDEF1X, Visio displays the relationship between parent and child tables, as Figure 19-14 shows.

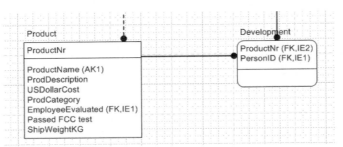

Figure 19-14. If you're using IDEF1X notation, Visio displays dependent tables with rounded corners.

> **Note** There is no graphical notation for independent and dependent tables if your model uses Relational notation. In that case, primary, alternate, and foreign keys are visible on the table.

When you specify Relational notation for your database model diagram, the Entity shape has a shaded box at the top that contains the table's conceptual name, as Figure 19-15 shows.

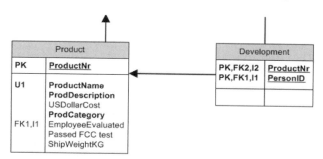

Figure 19-15. If you're using Relational notation, you can display primary keys, foreign keys, and indexes on the table.

> **Tip** To change the modeling notation, choose Database, Options, Document. Under Symbol Set, select the notation you want to use, and then click OK.

Follow these steps to add and name a new table:

1   Drag an Entity shape from the Entity Relationship or Object Relational stencil onto the drawing page.

2   If the Database Properties window is not visible, right-click the new table, and then choose Database Properties.

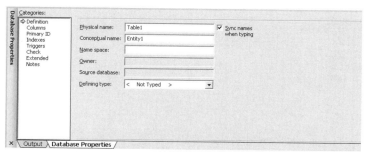

3   Type a name in the Physical Name box. Visio updates the Conceptual Name box if the Sync Names When Typing check box is selected (the default); otherwise, you must type a value for Conceptual Name.

> **Tip** To display the Database Properties window, double-click a table shape.

Adding Columns to a Table

You can add columns to an existing table or define columns for a new shape in the Database Properties window. When you add a column to a table, you can define it as the primary key. If you're using Relational notation, primary, alternate, and foreign keys are visible on the table, as Figure 19-16 shows. Visio automatically creates unique indexes on primary keys. Other columns can be assigned a nonunique index called the *inversion key.*

CompanyOffice	
PK	**OfficeLoc**
U1	**StreetAddress**
	IsHeadquarters
FK1,I1,U1	**Countryname**
U1	PostCode
U1	StateCode
U1	CityName

Figure 19-16. OfficeLoc is the primary key (PK); StreetAddress, IsHeadquarters, and Countryname are required values and appear in bold. PostCode, StateCode, and CityName are unique indexed columns (U1).

Before you start adding columns, you might want to define a default naming convention. Visio generates default names for columns, primary keys, foreign keys, and other attributes based on a prefix and suffix specified in the Database Modeling Preferences dialog box. For example, if you add a new column to the Orders table, Visio provides the name OrdersCol1. To specify default names, choose Database, Options, Modeling, and then change the settings on the Logical Misc tab.

Follow these steps to add a column and define its properties:

1   Right-click the table to which you want to add a column, and then choose Database Properties.

2   In the Categories box, choose Columns, and then click Add.

3   To create a primary key, place a check mark in the PK column.

4   To define the column's attributes, click Edit.

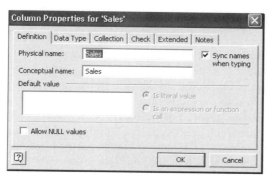

5 In the Column Properties dialog box, click the tab that contains the information you want to define and make your changes.

Table 19-2 describes the options available in the Column Properties dialog box. Visio updates the database model diagram to reflect your choices.

Table 19-2. Options in the Column Properties Dialog Box

Tab	Options
Definition	On this tab you can type in the Physical Name box to specify the column's name as it appears in the database or in the Conceptual Name box to specify the name as it appears in the database model. If you want to specify a default column value, type in the Default Value box, and then choose the Is Literal Value or Is An Expression Or Function Call option. Select the Allow NULL Values check box to make the column optional rather than mandatory.
Data Type	On this tab you can choose whether to display Portable or Physical Data Types and assign Data Types to columns.
Collection	On this tab you can specify whether the column in an object-relational model is a single value or contains a collection of information. Collections can be sets, lists, or multiple values.
Check	On this tab you can edit, add, or remove check clauses for a column. When you click Add or Edit, the Code Editor opens so that you can create or edit a check clause.
Extended	On this tab you can set DBMS-specific extended attributes for use with the Visio database drivers.
Notes	On this tab you can add notes about a column.

Tip Choose Primary ID in the Database Properties window to define a primary key and customize its physical name and key type.

Categorizing Subtypes of Tables

When you have a large number of tables of the same type, or attributes that are repeated for several entities, you can define a *category*, which Visio represents with the Category shape, as Figure 19-17 shows. The Parent To Category and Category To Child connectors create one-to-one relationships between parent and child tables in the category. The parent table includes all the common attributes, or columns, for the category, including the *discriminator*, the value of which identifies the categories of the subtypes. Attributes unique to a category are assigned to the appropriate child, or subtype. Each subtype inherits the primary key of the parent automatically. Visio can represent *complete* categories, in which all subtypes are included, or *incomplete* categories, which include only some subtypes.

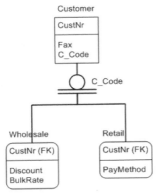

Figure 19-17. This complete category uses the C_Code column as the category discriminator.

Follow these steps to define a category:

1 Drag a Category shape to your database model.

2 Choose the Connector tool from the Standard toolbar, and then click the Parent To Category shape on either the Entity Relationship or Object Relational stencil.

3 Drag from the parent table to the Category shape.

4 With the Connector tool still selected, click the Category To Child shape, and then drag from the Category shape to the child table.

5 Repeat step 4 for each child table.

6 Right-click the Category connector shape, and then choose Database Properties.

7 If the category represents a complete category, select the Category Is Complete check box. An incomplete shape displays a single line below the circle. A complete shape displays a double line below the circle.

8 To specify a category discriminator, choose This Attribute, and then select the column you want to use.

Specifying Data Types

Each column in a table must be assigned a data type, and Visio provides advanced options for defining and assigning data types. You can use *portable data types* so that your model remains independent of the implementation requirements for any particular DBMS. However, if you're documenting a specific database, you can use the *physical data types* specified by the target DBMS. When you reverse engineer a database, Visio displays physical data types by default. To see all the built-in physical data types available in your model, choose Database, View, Types to display the Types window.

The Types window also lists *user-defined* data types. If you're working with portable data types, you can define your own types to provide consistent and reusable definitions for columns in your model.

> **Note**   To display data types on shapes in a database model diagram, choose Database, Options, Document. On the Table tab, choose Show Portable or Show Physical under Data Types.

Setting a Column's Data Type

When you assign a physical data type to a column, you must be familiar with the requirements of your DBMS. When you work with portable data types, you can use the default specifications or create a user-defined data type.

Follow these steps to specify the data type for a column:

1   Right-click the table containing the column you want to edit, and then choose Database Properties.

2   In the Categories box, select Columns.

3   For Show, select either Portable Data Type or Physical Data Type. Visio updates the Data Type column according to your selection.

4   Select a Column, and then click Edit.

5   In the Column Properties dialog box, click the Data Type tab. Visio displays either the mapped physical data type or the portable data type. To switch between two views, select either the Show Portable Data Type or Show Physical Data Type option at the bottom of the Column Properties dialog box.

6   To map the column to a different data type, click Edit, specify the options you want, and then click OK.

7   When you've specified the data type options you want, click OK.

> **Tip**   You can also change the data type by selecting Columns in the Database Properties window, left-clicking in the Data Type column, and selecting a data type from the drop-down list.

Inside Out

Integration with Visual Studio .NET

Although Visio Professional is used primarily to document existing databases through reverse engineering, it includes advanced features for creating platform-independent models and working with database code. The designers of the Database Model Diagram template intend the diagrams to be compatible with the model generation features in Visual Studio .NET Enterprise Edition. For example, if you plan to implement a model on more than one type of DBMS, you can define portable data types. In Visio Professional, you can't do much else with the portable data types. However, by optimizing your database model diagram in Visio Professional, you can then import it in Visual Studio .NET and work with the database generation features.

Creating User-Defined Data Types

When you define your own data types, you control the way Visio represents portable data types in your model. You create your own data types by using the User Defined Types command to define the type attributes, such as category (numeric, text, logical, and so on), type, and size.

Follow these steps to create a user-defined data type:

1. Choose Database, User Defined Types.
2. Click Add, and then type a name in the Data Type Name box.
3. To base your new data type on an existing one, select the Copy From check box, and then select the name of an existing user-defined data type.
4. Click OK to return to the User Defined Types dialog box.
5. Specify the category, type, and size in the appropriate box, and, if desired, type notes about the data type in the Description box.
6. Click OK.

Troubleshooting

Visio does not create the foreign key when you connect parent and child tables

Unless you change the default behavior, Visio creates a foreign key relationship when you connect a relationship line between two tables. In the child table, Visio adds a new column in and identifies a foreign key relationship between the two tables. When a foreign key is not automatically propagated, ask yourself the following questions:

- **Has the default foreign key behavior been reset?** On the Logical Misc tab of the Database Modeling Preferences dialog box, the Propagate On Add check box must be selected for Visio to create a foreign key relationship. Choose Database, Options, Modeling, and then verify that this check box is selected.

- **Is the relationship shape glued to both tables?** When you select a relationship connector, both endpoints appear red if the shape is properly glued to the two tables. If an endpoint is green, drag it slightly away from the table, and then press the Ctrl key as you drag it back to the table. A red border appears around the table shape to indicate that the shapes are connected (with shape-to-shape glue).

Specifying Relationships and Cardinality

Visio represents the parent–child relationships between tables in your database model diagram with the Relationship connector. You can control the way tables interact with one another—specifically, the way a child table inherits from a parent—by adding relationships and editing their properties. Relationship properties include direction, referential integrity, and cardinality, all of which can be displayed in your database model diagram depending on the notation you're using. For example, in Relational notation, an arrow signals the direction of the relationship and points to the parent table. In IDEF1X notation, a dot specifies the child table, as Figure 19-18 shows.

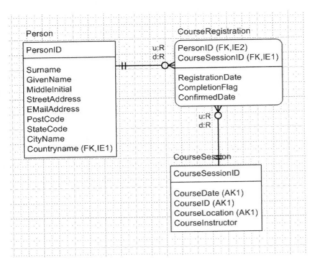

Figure 19-18. Relationship connectors indicate parent–child relationships between tables.

Connector tool

You can use the Relationship shape from either the Entity Relationship or Object Relational stencil to add a relationship that defines a foreign key relationship between tables. However, the Connector tool on the Standard toolbar does the same thing, and it's a little easier to use.

To add a relationship and specify its properties, follow these steps:

1 Click the Connector tool on the Standard toolbar, and then drag from the parent table to the child table. Visio adds any primary key in the parent table to the child table as a foreign key.

2 Right-click the new relationship connector, and then choose Database Properties.

3 In the Categories box, select the category that contains the information you want to edit, and then make your changes. See Table 19-3 for details.

Table 19-3. Categories for Specifying Relationship Properties

Category	Options
Definition	Use this category to create associations between columns in the parent and child tables and to enter role names for foreign keys.
Name	Use this category to type an optional phrase in the Verb Phrase box to describe the parent's role and in the Inverse Phrase box for the child's role. In the Physical Name box, you can type a name based on the requirements of the target DBMS. In the Notes box, you can add notes describing the relationship.
Miscellaneous	Use this category to choose the type of cardinality, whether the relationship is identifying or nonidentifying, and whether the relationship is optional.
Referential Action	Use this category to choose options that determine the effect on the child table when information in the parent table is updated or deleted.

Displaying Role Text on Relationships

To make your database model diagram easier to read, you can add role text to relationships. A *role* is the part played by an object in a relationship. To describe the role played by a parent table, you define a *verb phrase*. An *inverse phrase* describes the role in reverse, as played by a child table. Typical role phrases include *is a*, *is of*, or *has a*, as in *Person is of Country*, where the Person table and Country table have a foreign key relationship. Role text is displayed on the relationship connector, as Figure 19-19 shows.

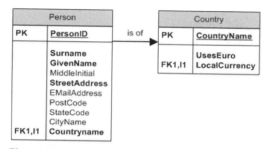

Figure 19-19. You can display the verb phrase, inverse phrase, or both on a relationship. The inverse phrase "is of" appears here.

Follow these steps to define and display role text:

1. Right-click the new relationship connector, and then choose Database Properties.

2. In the Categories box, select Name.

3. Type the phrases you want to display in the Verb Phrase and Inverse Phrase boxes.

4. Choose Database, Options, Document.

5. On the Relationship tab, select Show Verb Phrase. If you want to display only the verb phrase, select the ForwardText check box. If you want to display only the inverse phrase, select the InverseText check box.

6. Click OK.

Text Block tool

Tip If the connector line obscures the role text, click the Text Block tool on the Standard toolbar, and then use it to drag the text out of the way.

Role Text and Object Role Modeling

The Verb and Inverse Verb Phrase options for relationships in Visio Professional are designed to work with conceptual models created with the Object Role Modeling (ORM) method. In ORM, you can design and query database applications using English-like language. The resulting models are simpler for nontechnical audiences to understand. Visio Professional includes a stand-alone ORM template, but you can't use it to exchange data with the Database Model Diagram template.

You can, however, use Visual Studio .NET Enterprise Edition to define business rules in an ORM diagram and then upload the model into a relational or object-relational database model diagram, which in turn can be used to generate a script in DDL or a physical database schema. The ORM functionality in Visual Studio is based on a tool known as VisioModeler, now freely available as an unsupported product from Microsoft Corporation. To download VisioModeler (a 25-MB download), go to *http://www.microsoft.com/downloads/ search.asp?*. For more information about ORM, visit *http://www.orm.net*, a site maintained by Dr. Terry Halpin, who formalized the ORM notation.

Displaying Referential Integrity and Cardinality

When you define a parent–child relationship between tables, you can specify *referential integrity* as well, which determines how changes to the parent table affect the child. You can display an annotation on the relationship connector to indicate referential integrity. In addition, you can indicate the *cardinality* of a relationship in IDEF1X notation. For example, in Figure 19-19, Crow's Feet notation is used for the relationships and shows that the cardinality of the parent-to-child relationship is one to zero or more for both relationships.

Note To display Crow's Feet notation, choose Database, Options, Document, click the Relationship tab, and then select the Crow's Feet check box.

To display referential integrity or cardinality, choose Database, Options, Document to display the Database Document Options dialog box. On the Relationship tab, select the check boxes for Referential Integrity and/or Cardinality, and then click OK.

Note The Cardinality option is available only when you use the IDEF1X notation, which you can specify on the General tab of the Database Document Options dialog box.

Defining an Index

You can view and edit the indexes on columns that you reverse engineered and define new indexes for columns you plan to search frequently in your DBMS. The Database Properties window displays the attributes of an index, as Figure 19-20 shows.

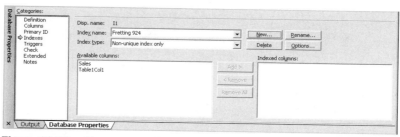

Figure 19-20. You can see the properties of an indexed column when you select Indexes in the Database Properties window.

To add an index, click New, type a name, and then click OK. In the Available Columns box, select the names of the columns that you want to include in this index, and then click Add. The Disp. Name area displays the index notation as it will appear in your database model diagram. Table 19-4 summarizes the properties you can specify for an index.

Table 19-4. Index Properties

Option	Description
Index Type	Choose whether the index is unique or nonunique or represents a constraint in this list box.
Asc	Select this option to set the sort order to ascending.
Options	Use this button to set driver-specific extended attributes for the index. Not all databases support extended attributes.

Note You can set extended attributes for a table, column, or relationship. Extended attributes are specific to a target DBMS.

Chapter 20

Diagramming Software Systems

Common sense dictates that the time you spend to plan your software projects before implementation is paid back down the road in a system that is easier to maintain. Microsoft Office Visio 2003 becomes an important tool in your development kit when you use it to visualize architectures, interfaces, data structures, and more before you write a line of code. Whether you create formal object models, diagram data flows, or prototype user interfaces, Visio includes the templates and shapes you need, representing a variety of methodologies and notations. In addition, with the advanced Unified Modeling Language (UML) tools, you can model the entire software development life cycle and even reverse engineer source code to quickly diagram classes and properties.

This chapter describes the types of software diagrams you can create and focuses primarily on the UML Model Diagram template.

Note The templates and shapes described in this chapter are included only with Visio Professional.

Deciding Which Software Solution to Use

When you use Visio to document a software system, the template and shapes you use depend on the task you want to perform, the type of diagram you want to create, and the notation you want to use. Visio includes two general types of software templates: static diagrams and dynamic models. For creating static software diagrams, Visio provides six templates with a simple drag-and-drop approach to software modeling. Some shapes conform to the notation used by a particular modeling methodology, but Visio doesn't check for compliance or semantic correctness. You can use the following templates to document software systems:

Warning Although Visio will diagram your software systems, it will not troubleshoot them. To ensure the best model, proof your system before importing it to Visio.

- **COM And OLE**   Use this template to create diagrams of Component Object Model (COM) and OLE interfaces for object-oriented programming and diagrams of public, exposed interfaces. Drag shapes such as COM Objects, Vtables, Process Boundaries, and Data Stores onto the drawing page and connect them with Interface and Reference shapes to create a diagram.

- **Enterprise Application**   Use this template to illustrate the requirements of large-scale business application architecture. Create logical models that identify business objects, services, and interfaces and physical models that show the physical architecture for your application. Drag shapes that represent PCs, mainframes, laptops, and architecture layers, and connect architecture shapes with Interface or Communication Link shapes.

- **Jackson**   Use this template to create diagrams that conform to the methodology developed by Michael Jackson for structured design and structured programming. With the Jackson method, you systematically map the structure of a problem to a program structure using diagrams that reveal data sequences, repetition, hierarchy, and alternatives. Drag Procedure and Process shapes onto the drawing page and connect them with Tree Connector and Logical Connector shapes to create your diagram.

- **Program Structure**   Use this template to document program architecture, including data flows, function calls, and memory management. Create structural diagrams, memory diagrams, and flowcharts using shapes that represent memory objects (stacks, arrays, pointers, and data blocks) and language constructs (functions, subroutines, and calls).

- **ROOM**   Use this template to create diagrams that conform to the Real-Time Object-Oriented Modeling (ROOM) method, which tailors object-oriented concepts to real-time systems. Create structure diagrams that represent system components and their relationships as well as behavior diagrams (ROOMcharts) that model a system's response to events.

- **Windows XP User Interface**   Use this template for creating prototypes of Microsoft Windows XP user interfaces. Use shapes to represent wizards, tabbed dialog boxes, toolbars, dialog boxes, and other user interface components.

In addition, Visio Professional includes two templates that are complete software modeling environments, the Data Flow Model Diagram and UML Model Diagram templates.

Note, however, that the Data Flow Model Diagram Model Explorer has been removed from the Data Flow Model Diagram template, but still resides in the UML Model Diagram template. The following section introduces the Data Flow Model Diagram template. The rest of this chapter details the UML Model Diagram template.

Inside Out

Enterprise Application and Window User Interface templates

The Enterprise Application and Windows User Interface templates are designed to work together to provide a complete picture of your system architecture and user interface. When you start a diagram with one template, you can add shapes from the other. To open a stencil, click the drop-down arrow on the Shapes button on the Standard toolbar, open the Software folder, and then select the stencil you want.

Using the Data Flow Model Diagram Template

Whether you're familiar with the formal Gane-Sarson notation or not, the Data Flow Model Diagram template in Visio provides a model-based, top-down approach to data flow diagrams (DFDs). With a DFD, you don't model processes, you discover the data in the processes by depicting information flow and the transformations that are applied as data moves from input to output. Chris Gane and Trish Sarson wrote one of the classic books on structured analysis and design (*Structured Systems Analysis: Tools and Techniques*, IST, Inc., New York: 1977), and their DFD notation is represented in the shapes of the Gane-Sarson stencil.

To open the Data Flow Model Diagram solution, choose File, New, Software, Data Flow Model Diagram. Visio Professional opens, the Gane-Sarson stencil and a drawing page, as Figure 20-1 shows.

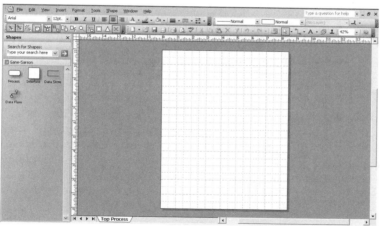

Figure 20-1. Visio displays the process, interface, data store, and data flow. The title is from the Borders And Titles stencil.

Drag Process, Interface, and Data Store shapes onto the drawing page to build your model.

For details about data flow diagrams, refer to Visio Help. Choose Help, Microsoft Visio Help, and then display the Contents tab. Expand Creating Drawings, expand Software, and then expand Data Flow Model Diagram.

> **Tip** To prevent syntax errors, connect shapes with glue—you'll see a red handle or border when shapes are connected properly.

Modeling Software Systems Using UML

UML specifies, constructs, visualizes, and documents a software system. Many teams are adopting UML for its life cycle approach to modeling software development and ability to represent everything from analyzing requirements and use cases to system implementation. Like blueprints, UML diagrams help teams visualize a system's architecture at each step in the development process, which typically includes the following phases:

- **Analyze use cases**   To describe the interactions between external actors and your system, you can create a *use case diagram* that depicts system requirements and the terminology used in the domain area.

- **Analyze the domain**   To provide a conceptual understanding of the objects and relationships in the real world that your system represents, you can create *conceptual* (also called *object*) *static structure diagrams* and *sequence diagrams.* To understand the life cycle of an object, you can create *activity* and *statechart diagrams* as well.

- **Define design requirements**   To develop a programming solution that meets the use case and domain requirements, you can create *collaboration diagrams* to determine how objects will communicate and *class static structure diagrams* to define the classes that you will implement in the software.

- **Plan the implementation**   To describe the physical and component structure of the development environment, you can create *component diagrams* and *deployment diagrams.*

With Visio, you can create the eight UML diagram types associated with each phase. Each diagram provides a different view of the software system. For example, use case diagrams show the software system from a user's perspective, whereas class structure diagrams translate user requirements into software classes and relationships. Most people linger in the design requirements phase and create class structure diagrams, which Visio can even create for you based on existing Visual C++ or Visual Basic code.

Inside Out

More about UML

UML is an extensive (and extensible) notation, and this chapter only brushes the surface of the topic of software modeling. To learn more about UML, search the Microsoft Developer Network (*http://msdn.microsoft.com*), which includes chapters from the book *Instant UML*. You can also download the complete notation specification, *UML Notation Guide Version 1.1*, in PDF format from *http://www.rational.com*.

Using the Model Explorer

A Visio drawing file represents one software system and can include many models and diagrams for the system. Visio displays the system model in the Model Explorer, a window that gives you a comprehensive picture of a software system and its *elements*—that is, the building blocks in each model, such as classes, use cases, and components. Elements are grouped into *packages*, which simply provide organization much as a file folder organizes documents. Each diagram within a package represents a *view* of the model. The current system model appears at the top of the Model Explorer window with the following default placeholders, as Figure 20-2 shows:

Figure 20-2. The Model Explorer contains all the elements of your model, whereas the drawing page contains assorted views.

- **Static Model**   Represents all the packages, elements, and views of one system model.
- **Top Package**   Represents the highest level of package in the model and contains all the static model elements and views.
- **Static Structure-1**   Represents a diagram and corresponds to a drawing page of the same name as the icon. By default, Visio inserts a static structure diagram in a new static model. To display the drawing page for a diagram, double-click the icon.

- **Data Types**   Represents all other model abstractions that are not elements. By default, a new model includes a package that contains the common Visual C++, IDL, and Visual Basic data types. You can delete the data type package and you can choose whether a new system model will include C++, IDL, or Visual Basic data types by default. You can also create packages that include your own data types.

 Visio 2003 also includes the fairly new data type, C#.

> **Tip**   To rename any item in the model, right-click a name in Model Explorer, choose Rename, and then type a new name.

You use the Model Explorer to create blank pages for UML diagrams. Then, you drag shapes from the UML stencils onto the drawing page to create the UML diagram. As you drag shapes onto the drawing page, Visio adds UML elements to the Model Explorer. In this way, you build the model as you create a diagram. Once you've created several UML diagrams, you can navigate between the diagrams by double-clicking a diagram in the Model Explorer or clicking a page tab at the bottom of the drawing window.

Troubleshooting

The UML menu is no longer visible

Solution-specific menus can disappear when Visio encounters an unexpected error from an outside source. If the UML menu disappears, choose Tools, Options, Security, select Enable Automation Events, and click OK. Save changes to any open diagrams, and then exit Visio. Restart Visio and then open your UML file.

About UML

UML was invented by Grady Booch, Jim Rumbaugh, and Ivar Jacobson, who are well known in object-oriented modeling circles for their pioneering work. UML combines the best notational tools from each of its authors' own methodologies: Booch, OMT (Object Modeling Technique, from Rumbaugh), and OOSE (Object-Oriented Software Engineering, from Jacobson). A language, not a methodology, UML provides a notation for documenting the software development cycle, but it does not prescribe any particular process. Similarly, the diagram types in Visio roughly correspond to the phases a development process might follow without recommending any particular process.

Defining Packages

In the Model Explorer, you can create packages to divide large diagrams and models into manageable subsets. The top package for the model serves as the container for all the elements, packages, and diagrams you create as part of the model. Each element can be owned by only one package, and one package can be nested in another. To see all the packages in a system model, choose UML, Packages, as Figure 20-3 shows.

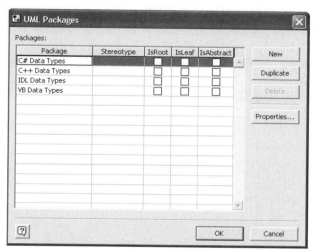

Figure 20-3. Specify commonly used values (Stereotype, IsRoot, IsLeaf, IsAbstract) in the UML Packages dialog box, or select a package, and then click Properties to see all package settings.

Table 20-1 describes how to use the Model Explorer to create packages and add elements to system models.

Table 20-1. Techniques for Working with Packages in the Model Explorer

Task	Technique
Create a new package in the model	Right-click an existing package, and then choose New, Package.
Add a package to a diagram	Display a diagram drawing page. Drag the Package shape from the UML Static Structure, UML Use Case, UML Component, or UML Deployment stencil onto the drawing page.
Add elements to a package	Right-click a package, choose New, and then choose the type of element.
Represent package contents in a diagram	Right-click a package, choose New, and then choose the type of diagram you want to include in the package. Visio displays the appropriate stencil and a blank drawing page. Drag shapes representing the elements you want to include in the package onto the drawing page.

Adding and Deleting Elements

As you drag shapes from the stencils onto the drawing page, Visio adds UML elements to the Model Explorer. However, you can add elements to your model without adding them to a diagram by right-clicking a package, and then choosing New. When you add an element in this fashion, it does not appear in a diagram, but you can drag the element from the Model Explorer to a drawing page to add an element shape to a diagram.

You can also delete elements from your model. When you delete an element from the Model Explorer, Visio also deletes it from all UML diagrams.

Caution When you delete a shape from a diagram, Visio deletes only the representation of the element. The corresponding element remains a part of the model and is displayed in the Model Explorer.

To quickly change the properties of an element, such as its name, attributes, or operations, double-click the element, change the properties in the UML Properties dialog box, and then click OK.

Troubleshooting

The Model Explorer is no longer visible

The view might have changed. In the Model Explorer window, you can view other property and documentation information. To change views in the window, right-click a tab at the bottom of the window. You can also select a view by choosing UML, View.

Customizing UML Shapes

The UML Model Diagram template includes all the shapes you need to create static structure, use case, collaboration, sequence, component, deployment, activity, and statechart diagrams. Shapes represent the UML notation and behave in ways that are consistent with UML semantics. For example, the Class shape has three compartments for name, attributes, and operations, and the shape expands automatically as you add values.

To change the values on shapes, right-click a shape, and then choose Shape Display Options, as Figure 20-4 shows. After you select the values you want to display, you can choose whether to apply the changes to shapes other than the one you selected to keep your model consistent. To change all the shapes of the same element type on the current drawing page, select the first of the two check boxes near the bottom of the dialog box (Apply To The Same Selected UML Shapes ...). To change all the shapes of the same element type that you add to the page, select the other check box (Apply To Subsequently Dropped UML Shapes ...).

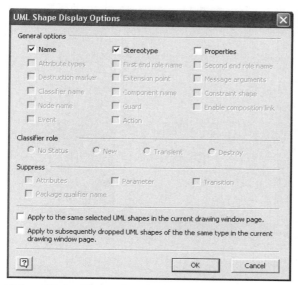

Figure 20-4. The options in the UML Shape Display Options dialog box vary depending on the selected shape. Here, you can choose the values to display on a Class shape.

Creating a New UML Model

When you start a new diagram with the UML Model Diagram template, Visio displays the Model Explorer window, opens UML stencils for each diagram type, and adds the UML menu, as Figure 20-5 shows.

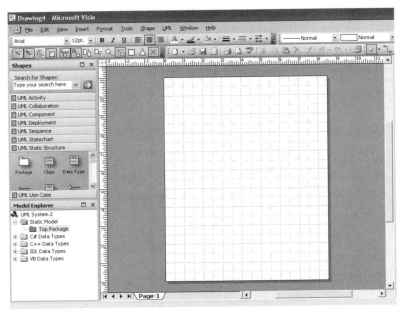

Figure 20-5. A new static model contains only one top package and the default data types.

Follow these steps to create a model for your system:

1. Choose File, New, Software, UML Model Diagram.

2. Choose UML, Models.

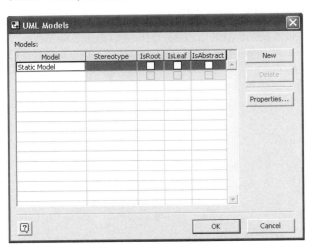

3. Click a cell in the Model column, type the name of your model, and then click OK. In the Model Explorer window, Visio adds the new model and a package.

4 To set the properties for a model, in the Model Explorer, right-click the model, and then choose Properties.

5 Select a category, change the properties as appropriate, and then click OK.

6 If you want to add an element to the model that doesn't appear in a diagram, in the Model Explorer, right-click a package or class, choose New, and then select the element you want to add.

> **Tip Add a diagram to the model**
> To add a diagram to the model, right-click a package, class, or use case in the Model Explorer, choose New, and then choose the type of UML diagram you want to add. Or right-click the drawing page for an existing static structure, use case, collaboration, sequence, deployment, or component diagram, and then choose Insert UML Diagram on the shortcut menu.

Creating a Use Case Diagram

Use case diagrams portray an interaction between a user and a system and represent one image of a system's functionality, which is triggered by user actions. You usually create use case diagrams in the early stages of development and refine them in later stages. A use case diagram typically depicts an overarching set of events that complete a process rather than an individual step or transaction. The use case diagram consists of the users (actor shapes), the system (the System Boundary shape), and the use cases themselves, as Figure 20-6 shows.

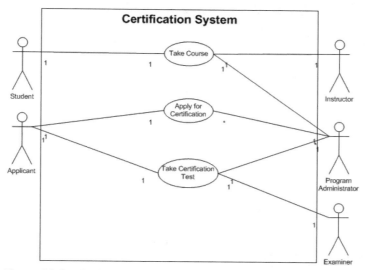

Figure 20-6.   In this use case diagram, the connectors represent relationships, which show where the actors participate in a use case in the deployment diagram.

The relationships among actors and use cases are represented by one of the following connectors:

- **Communicates**   Use this shape between actor and use case shapes to show that an actor participates in a use case.
- **Extends**   Use this shape between use case shapes to extend the behavior of a use case to another. For example, connect the Extends shape between use case A and use case B to show that an instance of B includes the behavior of A.
- **Uses**   Use this shape between use case shapes to show that the behavior of one use case uses the behavior of the other. For example, connect the Uses shape between use case A and use case B to show that an instance of A includes the behavior of B.

Follow these steps to create a use case diagram:

1   In the Model Explorer, right-click the package or subsystem in which you want to add a use case diagram, and then choose New, Use Case Diagram.

2   Drag the System Boundary shape from the UML Use Case stencil onto the drawing page.

3   Drag the Use Case shape from the stencil and place it inside the system boundary. Repeat for each use case.

4   Drag the Actor shape from the stencil and place it outside the system boundary. Repeat for each user or outside influence that interacts with the system.

5   Double-click a use case shape to display the UML Use Case Properties dialog box.

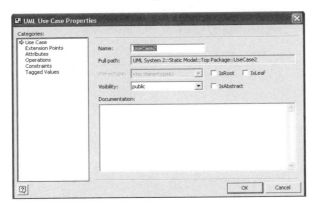

6   In the Name box, type a name, and then click OK.

> **Tip**   To hide the name of a use case shape, right-click the shape, choose Shape Display Options, uncheck Name, and then click OK.

7   Drag Communicates shapes from the stencil, and then connect them between use case and actor shapes.

8 Drag Uses and Extends shapes from the stencil, and then connect them between use case shapes.

9 To define element properties, double-click a shape to open its UML Properties dialog box, and then define the property values you want.

> **Note** The System Boundary shape does not have properties.

Creating a Static Structure Diagram

Class diagrams show the static structure of a model by describing the types of objects in a system and the relationships that exist among them. In a class diagram, you can specify attributes, associations, operations, methods, interfaces, and dependencies, as Figure 20-7 shows. If you create a class diagram with objects and no classes, the diagram is referred to as an object or conceptual static structure diagram. A conceptual diagram is a snapshot of a class diagram that shows instances of objects and data values and so is useful for providing examples of data structures. However, conceptual diagrams are not as common as class diagrams.

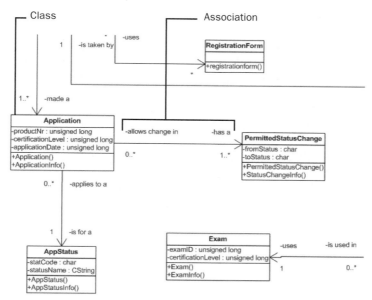

Figure 20-7. A class diagram is a static structure diagram that decomposes a software system into its parts—in this case, classes that represent fully defined software entities.

Follow these steps to create a static structure diagram:

1 In the Model Explorer, right-click the package or subsystem in which you want to add a static structure diagram, and then choose New, Static Structure Diagram.

2 Drag Class shapes onto the drawing page to represent the classes or objects you want to add to your class static structure diagram or conceptual model.

3 Double-click each shape to open its UML Properties dialog box, in which you can add a name, attributes, operations, and other property values. Then click OK.

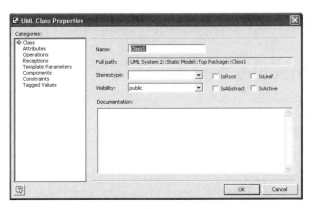

4 Right-click each class shape, and then choose Shape Display Options to select the properties to display on the shape.

Tip **Add an interface to a class**

To add an interface to a class, drag the Interface shape from the UML Static Structure stencil onto the drawing page, and then connect the end without the circle to a class. To change the appearance of the interface, right-click the shape, and then choose Show As Class-like Interface or Show As Lollipop Interface. When you connect an interface to a class, the operations in the interface are propagated to the class automatically.

---

5 Indicate relationships between the classes and objects using Association, Link, Dependency, Generalization, or Composition shapes.

6 Double-click each relationship shape to open its UML Association Properties dialog box, in which you can add association end adornments and other properties. Then click OK.

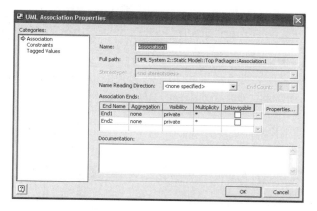

Creating a Sequence Diagram

Sequence diagrams show the actors or objects participating in an interaction and the events they generate arranged in a time sequence. As Figure 20-8 shows, the goal of the diagram is to express interactions. Because sequence diagrams show the explicit sequence of messages, they are well suited for representing real-time specifications and other complex scenarios.

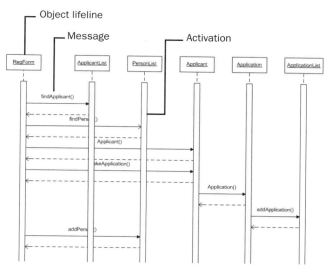

Figure 20-8. Sequence diagrams show an interaction. Objects' lifelines participate in the interaction and exchange messages.

Follow these steps to create a sequence diagram:

1 In the Model Explorer, right-click the package or subsystem in which you want to add a sequence diagram, and then choose New, Sequence Diagram.

Microsoft Office Visio 2003 Inside Out

2   For each object involved in an interaction, drag an Object Lifeline shape onto the drawing page. Use the control handle to adjust the length of a lifeline to correspond to the length of the objects' lives in the interaction.

> **Tip**   To add a destruction marker to a lifeline for objects that are destroyed, right-click a lifeline, choose Shape Display Options, select Destruction Marker, and then click OK.

3   Double-click an Object Lifeline shape to display the UML Classifier Role Properties dialog box.

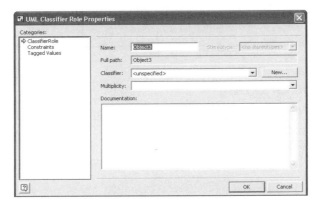

4   In the Classifier list, choose the classifier that the object represents. To create a new classifier, click New, define the classifier, and then click OK. In the UML Classifier Role Properties dialog box, click OK.

   The appearance of the lifeline shape is updated to reflect the classifier you chose.

5   To indicate when an object is performing an action, drag an Activation shape onto an object's lifeline. Glue the endpoints of the Activation shape to connection points on the Object Lifeline shape. Adjust the length of the activation rectangle to correspond to the object's period of activity.

6   Use Message shapes to indicate communication between objects.

7   Double-click a shape to open its UML Properties dialog box, in which you can add a name and other property values. Then click OK.

Creating an Activity Diagram

Activity diagrams portray the internal behavior of a method for a specific class or use case and represent a flow driven by internally generated actions. A type of statechart, an activity diagram shows all the states as action states, as Figure 20-9 shows. The flow of control is triggered by the completion of actions in the source state. Activity diagrams encourage you to notice and document parallel and concurrent activities. This makes them excellent tools for modeling work flow, analyzing use cases, and dealing with multithreaded applications.

Inside Out

Activity and statechart diagrams

An activity diagram is really just a variation of a state machine. When you want to show a flow that is driven by internally generated actions, create an activity diagram. When you want to represent a flow in response to external events, create a statechart diagram.

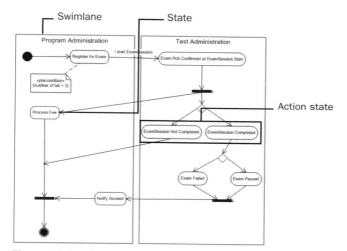

Figure 20-9. An activity diagram is attached to a class or to the implementation of an operation or a use case.

Follow these steps to create an activity diagram:

1 In the Model Explorer, right-click the package, subsystem, class, operation, or use case in which you want to create an activity diagram, and then choose New, Activity Diagram.

2 If you want to indicate responsibility in the activity diagram, drag a Swimlane shape from the UML Activity stencil onto the page for each class, person, or organizational unit you want to represent.

3 Drag an Action State or State shape onto the drawing page for each action or activity state you want to represent. Use the Initial State and Final State shapes to represent the object's state at the start and end of the activity.

4 Connect Control Flow shapes to State shapes to indicate the change from one state to another.

5 To represent a complex transition, drag the Transition (Fork) or Transition (Join) shape onto the drawing page.

Chapter 20

> **Tip** Use the Transition (Fork) shape to represent the forking of one action state into multiple parallel states. Use the Transition (Join) shape to represent the synchronization of multiple action states into one state.

6 If you want to replace transition strings with signal icons, use the Signal Send and Signal Receipt shapes to represent the signals.

7 Double-click a shape to open its UML Properties dialog box, in which you can add a name, transition string, guard condition, deferred event, and other property values. Then click OK.

Creating a Statechart Diagram

Statecharts show the sequence of states an object goes through during its life. A state machine, which is attached to a class or use case, is a graph of states and transitions that describes the response of an object to outside stimuli. A statechart diagram represents a state machine. By documenting events and transitions, a statechart diagram shows the sequence of states an object goes through during its life, as Figure 20-10 shows. In contrast, an activity diagram represents a flow driven by internally generated actions.

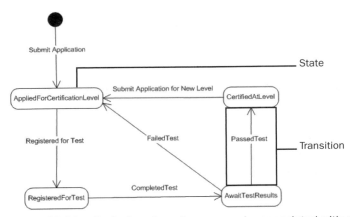

Figure 20-10. Each class in a diagram can be associated with a state machine, which you can represent with a statechart diagram.

Follow these steps to create a statechart diagram:

1 In the Model Explorer, right-click the class or use case that includes behavior you want to represent in a statechart, and then choose New, Statechart Diagram.

2 Drag State shapes from the UML Statechart stencil onto the drawing page to represent the sequence of states an object goes through.

3 Drag a Composite State shape onto the page to represent concurrent, mutually exclusive, or nested substates.

4 Connect states to other states using Transition shapes to indicate that an object in one state will enter the second state in response to an event.

> **Tip** To indicate that an object stays in the same state in response to an event, use the arc-shaped Transition shape. Connect both ends of the Transition shape to the same state shape.

5 Connect Transition shapes to Transition (Join) and Transition (Fork) shapes to represent the forking of one state into multiple states or the synchronization of multiple states into one state.

6 Use Shallow History or Deep History shapes to indicate that an object resumes a state it last held within a region.

7 Double-click each shape to open its UML Properties dialog box, in which you can add a name, actions, activities, events, and other property values. Then click OK.

Creating a Collaboration Diagram

You can create a collaboration diagram to describe the context in which certain behavior occurs, such as to clarify a use case or operation. A collaboration diagram shows an *interaction* among a group of objects—that is, their collaboration—as the connecting lines between classifier role shapes. Within an interaction, the objects collaborate by exchanging messages, which appear as the text above the association role connectors. The arrows on a connector point toward the recipient of the message as Figure 20-11 shows. Unlike a sequence diagram, a collaboration diagram does not imply sequence in the way messages are depicted, and so messages are numbered to show their sending order.

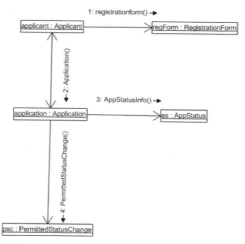

Figure 20-11. A collaboration diagram simultaneously shows an interaction and the relationships that facilitate the interaction.

Chapter 20

Follow these steps to create a collaboration diagram:

1 In the Model Explorer, right-click the package in which you want to add a collaboration diagram, and then choose New, Collaboration Diagram.

2 For each object role you want to represent in the collaboration, drag a Classifier Role shape from the UML Collaboration stencil onto the drawing page.

3 Double-click the Classifier Role shape to display the UML Classifier Role Properties dialog box.

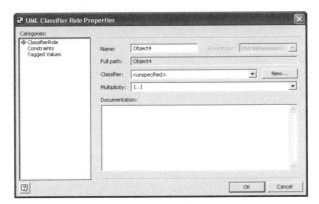

4 In the Name box, type a name for the classifier role. Define other properties as desired, and then click OK.

5 For each set of objects you want to represent, drag a Multi-Object shape onto the drawing page. To name the object, double-click the shape to display the UML Classifier Role Properties dialog box, and then type the name. Define other properties as desired, and then click OK.

6 To indicate links between the objects, connect Association Role shapes to the objects.

7 Double-click each Association Role shape to open the UML Association Role Properties dialog box, in which you can add a name, message flow, message label, multiplicity, and other property values. Then click OK.

Creating a Component Diagram

Component diagrams represent implementation decisions and show dependencies among *components*, such as source code files, binary code files, executable files, or dynamic-link libraries (DLLs), as Figure 20-12 shows. Typically, each component in a component diagram is documented in more detail in a use case or class diagram.

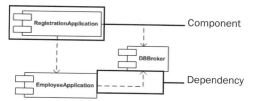

Figure 20-12. This component diagram shows the dependencies among applications.

Inside Out

Class specification and body

By default, each class has a specification that contains the class interface and a body that contains the implementation of the class. The Component shape represents the body. For example, in C++, a specification corresponds to a file with a .h suffix, and a body corresponds to a file with the .cpp suffix.

Follow these steps to create a component diagram:

1. In the Model Explorer, right-click the package or subsystem in which you want to add a component diagram, and then choose New, Component Diagram.

2. Drag a Component shape from the UML Component stencil onto the drawing page for each component you want to represent.

3. Where appropriate, drag an Interface shape onto the drawing page and glue the endpoint without the circle to a component shape.

4. Use Dependency shapes to indicate the relationships between components or between one component and another component's interface.

5. Double-click each shape to open its UML Properties dialog box, in which you can add a name, attributes, operations, and other property values. Then click OK.

Creating a Deployment Diagram

Like component diagrams, deployment diagrams represent system implementation. A deployment diagram symbolizes the structure of the run-time system and communicates the configuration and deployment of the hardware and software elements that make up an application. Deployment diagrams consist of nodes, components, and the relationships between them, as Figure 20-13 shows. A *node* is a run-time physical object that represents a processing resource, which can include both human resources and mechanical processing resources.

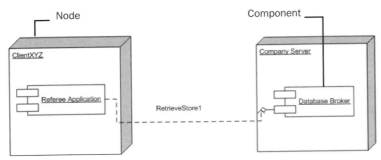

Figure 20-13. A single deployment diagram usually suffices to represent a system.

Follow these steps to create a deployment diagram:

1 In the Model Explorer, right-click the package or subsystem in which you want to add a deployment diagram, and then choose New, Deployment Diagram.

2 Drag a Node shape from the UML Deployment stencil onto the drawing page. Drag Component and Object shapes into the node. Drag a selection handle on the node to resize it. Repeat to add all the nodes you need.

3 Where appropriate, drag an Interface shape onto the drawing page and glue the end-point without the circle to a component shape.

4 Glue Communicates shapes between nodes to indicate the relationships between nodes.

5 Glue Dependency shapes between components and objects or between components and other components' interfaces.

> **Tip** To show which components can run on which nodes, define a «supports» stereotype for a dependency connector.

6 Double-click each shape to open its UML Properties dialog box, in which you can add a name, attributes, operations, and other property values. Then click OK.

Defining Common Model Properties

A common set of properties that can include stereotypes, tagged values, notes, constraints, dependencies, and type/instance and type/class dichotomies define a model element. You can define the characteristics of the properties associated with each element in the UML Properties dialog box, which lists the categories associated with each common property. When you double-click an element on the drawing page or in the Model Explorer, the UML Properties dialog box for the element appears with categories of properties that you can edit. For example, you can define constraints and tagged values for an attribute of a class, as Figure 20-14 shows.

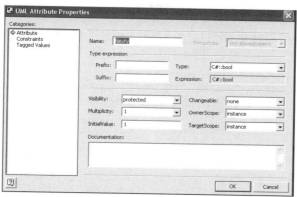

Figure 20-14. The UML Properties dialog box displays the attributes of the CourseRegistrationDate class.

Inside Out

Extending UML

Stereotypes, tagged values, and constraints allow you to extend UML. You can use stereotypes to create metamodel classes, tagged values to extend the attributes of the metamodel classes, and constraints to extend the metamodel semantics.

To open a UML Properties editor and add values to an element, double-click the icon that represents the element in the Model Explorer or the shape that represents the element in a diagram.

Reverse Engineering Source Code

Even if coding is underway, you can use UML diagrams to better understand a project. If you develop projects in Microsoft Visual C++ 6, Microsoft Visual Basic 6 (or newer versions of either), you can reverse engineer your projects' class definitions and generate UML static structure models in the Model Explorer. Visio includes the Microsoft Visio UML Add-In, which you can run from within Visual C++, and the Microsoft Visio UML Visual Basic Add-In, which you can run from within Visual Basic. Each add-in provides a toolbar similar to the one shown in Figure 20-15. With the toolbar buttons, you can open Visio and start a new diagram based on the UML Model Diagram template from within Visual C++ or Visual Basic as well as reverse engineer source code. After you reverse engineer a project, you can create a class diagram in Visio by dragging elements from the static structure model onto the drawing page.

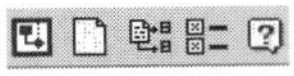

Figure 20-15. The UML add-in adds a toolbar to Visual C++ and Visual Basic. In Visual Basic, the Visio UML Options button does not appear.

Note The first time you install Visio, you must start it and exit it at least once before you can reverse engineer code. In addition, Microsoft Visual Studio Service Pack 3 must be installed to reverse engineer code.

Inside Out

Visual Studio .NET reverse engineering

Microsoft extends the reverse engineering capabilities of the UML Model Diagram template with Visual Studio .NET, which can reverse engineer code from Visual Basic 7, Visual C++ 7, and C#. In addition, Visual Studio .NET Enterprise Edition can generate code skeletons for Visual C++ 6 and later and Visual Basic 7.

Reverse Engineering Visual C++ 6 Source Code

When you reverse engineer a Visual C++ project, you must first customize Visual C++ with the Visio UML add-in. Your Visual C++ project must include a browse information file, which the Visio UML add-in uses to create a model in Visio. The Visio UML add-in can reverse engineer the following C++ language constructs: classes, user-defined types, enumerated types, member functions, member variables, and method parameters.

Follow these steps to customize Visual C++ code so you can reverse engineer it:

1　In Visual C++, choose Tools, Customize.

2　In the Customize dialog box, click the Add-Ins And Macro Files tab.

3　In the Add-Ins And Macro Files list, select Visio UML Add-In.

4　Click Close to add the floating Visio UML Add-In toolbar.

5　If you don't already have a browse information file for a project, open the project, and then choose Project, Settings.

6　In the Project Settings dialog box, choose the type of build configuration you want, click the C/C++ tab, and then select Generate Browse Info.

7　Click the Browse Info tab to specify the name and location of the browse information file, select Build Browse Info File, and then click OK.

Follow these steps to reverse engineer Visual C++ 6 source code:

1   Build the project in Visual C++.

> **Tip**   Make sure your project includes header files for your classes. If your project doesn't have a header file for a class, that class will not appear in the model that Visio reverse engineers.

Reverse Engineer UML Model

2   In Visual C++, click the Reverse Engineer UML Model button on the Visio UML Add-In toolbar.

> **Note**   If more than one project exists in the Visual C++ workspace, in the Select Project dialog box, select the project you want to reverse engineer, and then click OK. If more than one browse information file appears in the project hierarchy, in the Select Browse File dialog box, select the file you want to use, and then click OK.

Visio opens a blank static structure diagram drawing page and the Model Explorer, which is populated with elements that reflect the class definitions in the source code.

3   To create a static structure diagram, drag elements from the Model Explorer onto the blank static structure diagram drawing page.

Troubleshooting

Some elements of the C++ project were not reverse engineered correctly

Visio creates a model based on the contents of a browse information file, which can include errors. According to Microsoft, the browse information file application programming interface (API) has several known bugs that affect its ability to handle C++ templates. Because of this limitation, long parameter lists are not always reverse engineered, and class names and class method names are sometimes corrupted, which causes Visio to ignore them or sometimes add the corrupted name to the UML model. Visio creates a log file of errors detected during the reverse engineering process and saves the file in the system temporary folder with the name of the project; for example, C:\Winnt\Temp\Project.txt.

Reverse Engineering Visual Basic 6 Source Code

To reverse engineer Visual Basic source code, you must load the Microsoft Visio UML Visual Basic Add-In into Visual Basic. The add-in displays the Microsoft Visio UML Solution toolbar and adds the Microsoft Visio UML Solution menu to the Tools menu; both the toolbar and the menu will continue to appear every time you open Visual Basic. The UML add-in can reverse engineer the following Visual Basic language constructs: classes, modules, and forms;

functions and subroutines; parameters; constants; member variables; properties; events; and user-defined types.

Follow these steps to customize Visual Basic so you can reverse engineer Visual Basic 6 code:

1   In Visual Basic, choose Add-Ins, Add-In Manager.

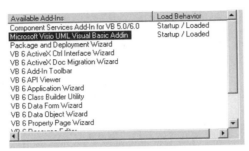

2   Select Microsoft Visio UML Visual Basic Addin. For Load Behavior, select the Loaded/ Unloaded and Load On Startup check boxes, and then click OK.

Note   You need to set up the add-in in the Add-In Manager only once.

3   Open the project that contains the source code you want to reverse engineer.

4   In Visual Basic, click the Reverse Engineer UML Model button on the Visio UML Solution toolbar.

Visio opens a blank static structure diagram drawing page and the Model Explorer, which is populated with elements that reflect the class definitions in the source code.

5   Drag elements from the Model Explorer onto the blank static structure diagram drawing page to create a static structure diagram.

Part 6

Inside the Visio Platform

Customizing Shapes and Solutions

If you think of Microsoft Office Visio 2003 as a visual toolbox rather than merely diagramming software, you'll begin to understand how flexible it can be. If you have a business problem that requires a graphical or visual answer, Visio might be able to help. Shapes, documents, and even the Visio user interface itself can be customized. Your custom solution can be as simple as a tweak to an existing shape that you save as a new master, or a more elaborate, interactive program that uses Microsoft Visual Basic for Applications 6.4 (VBA), which is built into Visio, or another programming language. Visio is a complete graphical development environment, or platform, that you can use to build visual solutions.

This book doesn't tell you how to program with Visio, which could easily take another thousand pages. This chapter does provide a place to start, however. With a deeper understanding of the Visio file format, you'll know how to create your own stencils and templates, which you can distribute to other users if you want. This chapter also introduces the VBA window and points you to additional resources for taking advantage of this development environment.

Mastering Visio Documents

Behind every shape, template, and solution in Visio is a file format that makes customization possible. If you want to create your own stencils, or customize templates for others or just yourself, you need to understand this fundamental fact of Visio life: All Visio files have the same format, and that format includes a drawing page and a stencil. That is, every drawing page has a stencil, and every stencil has a drawing page. The file name extension determines what you see when you open a file, which is why when you open a stencil (.vss) file, you typically don't see the drawing page, or when you open a blank drawing (.vsd) file, you don't see a stencil.

Here's a little experiment you can try to see how this works:

1 Start Visio.

2 If Visio is already running, save any changes, and close all open Visio documents.

3 Choose File, New, New Drawing.

   Visio opens a blank drawing page and no stencils.

4   Choose File, Shapes, New Stencil.

Visio opens a blank stencil, as Figure 21-1 shows.

Document stencil window   Drawing page window

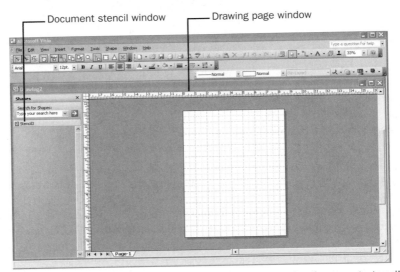

Figure 21-1. A Visio file includes a drawing page and a document stencil. The file name extension determines whether Visio opens both a drawing page window and a stencil window.

Why is this important? The fact that a Visio file has both a drawing page and a stencil has ramifications that can help you work with shapes more efficiently and keep file size down when you customize stencils and templates. Visio uses the document stencil to store copies of any masters added to that drawing file. Shapes on the drawing page are *instances* of the masters on the document stencil. One convenient side effect of the relationship between shapes on the page and masters on the document stencil is that you can edit masters on a document stencil, and the change will affect all the copies of the master in that drawing file.

If a Visio file always contains a drawing page and a stencil, why are there different types of files? You can open and save Visio files with the following file name extensions:

- Drawing (.vsd)
- Stencil (.vss)
- Template (.vst)

The Visio engine uses the file name extension to determine what to display on the screen when the document is opened—that is, which windows should be active. You can save a Visio file using any other Visio file name extension to change what appears when the file is opened. For example, you can save a drawing file (.vsd) as a template (.vst), which you can then open and work with as a template. The sections that follow describe what happens when you open each file type.

> **Note** Visio recognizes other file name extensions as well. A Visio report definition is saved as a file with the .vrd extension, but can be read only by the Reporting tool (Tools, Report). A .vdx, .vsx, or .vtx file is a Visio drawing, stencil, or template saved in XML format. For details, see "Visio and XML File Formats," page 616.

 Troubleshooting

The option to open a file as an original or copy, or as read-only, seems to be missing

In earlier versions of Visio, the Open dialog box included check boxes for opening a file as an original, copy, or read-only version. Those options still exist; they're just harder to find. In the Open dialog box, click the drop-down arrow on the Open button to display a menu. Choose the option you want, and then click the Open button again to open the selected file as specified.

Opening Drawing (.vsd) Files

In Microsoft Office–speak, a *document* is the generic term for a Microsoft Office Word 2003 file, or the thing you create when you press Ctrl+N. The equivalent generic term in Visio is *drawing file*, which has the .vsd file name extension. When you click the New button on the Standard toolbar, or press Ctrl+N in Visio, you create a drawing file. When you open an existing drawing file, Visio opens all the windows and files that were open when the file was last saved. Visio maintains an internal *workspace* list that saves this information. Typically, a drawing file displays only the drawing page window; its document stencil window is closed. To display the document stencil, choose File, Shapes, Show Document Stencil.

Each Visio drawing file always has at least one drawing page, a document stencil, and a workspace list. A drawing file's document stencil contains copies of any masters used on the drawing page. In addition, a drawing file always includes the five default Visio styles (Guide, No Style, None, Normal, and Text Only), a color palette, a default VBA project with an empty class module called ThisDocument, and a document sheet (that is, a ShapeSheet for the document) that can store user-defined data.

That is the minimum list of contents for a drawing file. You can customize the file's color palette and style lists, and those changes will be saved with the file, as will any VBA projects, with their own modules, class modules, and user forms.

Opening Files That Contain Macros

Although this book doesn't delve much into VBA, be aware that VBA projects are part of a drawing file. When you open a drawing file that includes VBA or other project code, as some of the sample files do, you'll see the message shown in Figure 21-2. This message is a safeguard feature of Visio. Despite the dire tone of the message, you probably want to click

Enable Macros if you know the source of the drawing file. The macros are most likely used to provide functionality within the drawing, such as adding a control, menu, or special command.

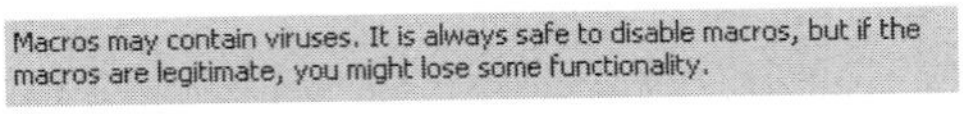

Macros may contain viruses. It is always safe to disable macros, but if the macros are legitimate, you might lose some functionality.

Figure 21-2.   When you open a drawing file that includes a VBA macro or other programming code, Visio displays this message to warn you about its contents. Usually the macros are needed to enable interactive features of the drawing.

You can prevent this message by lowering the security settings for Visio, which generally is not a good idea unless you have virus-scanning software installed on your computer. To do this, choose Tools, Macros, Security. On the Security Level tab of the Security dialog box, click the Low option, and then click OK.

Opening Stencil (.vss) Files

The philosophy of the Visio design team has changed somewhat since Visio 2002. In earlier versions of Visio, you could edit stencils and master shapes, but not so in Visio 2003. Actually, you can edit them, but the method is just a bit different.

A Visio file with the .vss extension is sometimes referred to as a *stand-alone stencil* to differentiate it from a document stencil. A stand-alone stencil can be opened by itself or with a template. It cannot, however, be edited.

To open a stencil, it's quickest to click the Shapes button on the Standard toolbar, browse through the templates, and then choose the stencil you wish to open.

Rather than edit the stencils included with Visio 2003, Visio allows you to make your own stencils composed of the shapes you most often employ in your drawings. Right-clicking a shape in any stencil displays the submenu displayed in Figure 21-3. From this menu you can save the shape to a previously constructed custom stencil (by either selecting a displayed stencil or clicking Add To Existing Stencil), save it to a new stencil (you'll be prompted to name the stencil), or just organize your previously created shapes. You can also select File, Shapes, New to open a new, blank, editable stencil. Note that you can no longer edit most Visio stencils or the master shapes that they contain. In fact, you can only edit the masters on a Document stencil or edit anything on a custom stencil that you have created.

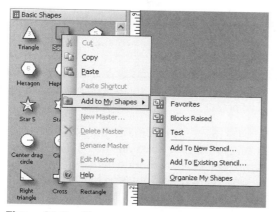

Figure 21-3. You can save a shape to one of your custom stencils by right-clicking it.

After you have edited a custom stencil, you can save it by right-clicking the title bar and choosing Save (if it has already been named) or Save As, if you are saving the stencil for the first time. If you choose Save As, Visio displays the Save As dialog box, shown in Figure 21-4. The Save drop-down menu in the lower right of the Save As dialog box allows you to save the file as a Read Only or Workspace file.

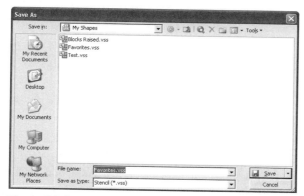

Figure 21-4. You can choose a name for your custom stencil in the Save As dialog box.

Saving and Opening Read-Only Stencils

Sometimes you cannot open a custom stencil for editing. Visio has two different ways of handling read-only custom stencils. You can drag a master onto a read-only custom stencil, and Visio prompts you to open the stencil for editing. This is the default Visio behavior for read-only stencils. However, stencils can be saved in such a way that they cannot be opened for editing. This type of read-only protection disables the editing option and displays a message if you try to open the stencil for editing, as Figure 21-5 shows.

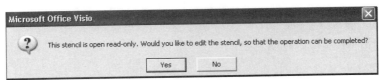

Figure 21-5. If a message like this appears when you try to open a stencil for editing, the stencil file has been saved as a read-only file.

Visio uses the Windows Read-Only flag to specify that the original stencil file cannot be edited. To set this flag, use the regular Save or Save As command on the File menu to save a stencil, but click the drop-down list arrow on the Save button in the dialog box, as Figure 21-6 shows. You'll see two options: Workspace and Read Only. Select Read Only, and then click Save to save the file as a noneditable, read-only file.

Click the arrow on the Save button to display options.

Figure 21-6. If you specify Read Only when you save a stencil file, the original stencil cannot be opened for editing until you clear the Read Only flag in Windows.

Once a file is flagged as read-only in this way, you can't edit the original file until you reset the Read Only flag. You can do this in Windows Explorer by locating the file, right-clicking the file name, and then choosing Properties. In the file's Properties dialog box, click the General tab, and then clear the Read-Only check box.

Note Remember, in Visio 2003 only custom stencils—in other words, user-created stencils—can be edited. Stencils that ship with Visio 2003 are permanently locked.

Inside Out

Workspace and Read Only options

In choosing to use the common dialog boxes of Office products, the Visio designers moved some options that used to be check boxes in the Save As dialog box of previous versions of Visio. That's why the Workspace and Read Only options are now tucked away under the Save button in the Save As dialog box.

Opening Template (.vst) Files

Many users are never even aware that they're opening a template when they start Visio and choose a drawing type. Despite the fact that templates have been a cornerstone of Visio functionality since the very first release, the word *template* seems to confuse people. Nonetheless, when you choose a drawing type on Visio's initial launch screen, you're really opening a template (.vst) file.

When you open a template, Visio's default behavior is to open an untitled *copy* of the template as a drawing file (.vsd) and open any other windows and files listed in the template's workspace. Just because most Visio templates have a blank drawing page doesn't mean that a template has to have a blank drawing page. For example, you can open a drawing, add a border and title block, and then save it as a template (.vst) file that can be opened to generate other drawings. A template can include more than one drawing page as well, although Visio's templates typically include only one page for ease of use. You can open an original template file to make changes to the template itself, such as adding stencils or setting default styles.

Follow these steps to open the original template file instead of the copy that Visio typically opens:

1. Choose File, Open. In the Files Of Type list, notice that All Visio Files appears, which means that you'll see template files as well as drawing and stencil files.

2. Locate a template (.vst) file.

   Visio installs its templates by default in the folders in C:\Program Files\Microsoft Office\Visio11\1033.

3. Select the file name, and then click the drop-down list arrow on the Open button to display a list of options.

4. Choose Original, and then click Open to open the original template file.

The tricky thing with templates is that you're usually opening at least two separate documents, and often more than two. Most templates include a Visio drawing file. That's the drawing page you see when you open the template. In addition, most templates include one or more stencil files. When you open a .vst file, Visio knows to open the drawing file's drawing page in a drawing window and the stencil file's document stencil in the stencil window. When you recall that both drawing and stencil files contain both a drawing page and a document stencil, you'll see that this makes sense.

Chapter 21

615

Templates also include a workspace list with information about the size and position of each open window, as well as the style definitions and colors that are available to users when they create diagrams. The drawing can have its own style definitions and color palette, as can the stencils, so if you're creating new templates, it's important to make sure that style and page settings work together across documents.

Visio and XML File Formats

Since the 2002 edition, Visio has supported Extensible Markup Language (XML) file formats. XML goes beyond HTML in describing file content and has quickly become a new standard for Web-based data. In Visio, the .vdx (drawing file), .vsx (stencil file), and .vtx (template file) extensions are the XML equivalents of .vsd, .vss, and .vst. You can export and import Visio files in XML format by using the standard Save As and Open commands on the File menu, as Figure 21-7 shows. In the Save As or Open dialog box, choose the appropriate XML format in the Save As Type or Files Of Type list.

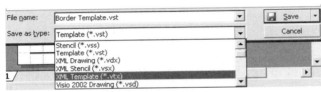

Figure 21-7. In the Save As dialog box, the XML file formats appear in the Save As Type list.

For most users, the XML interface is not particularly useful. "They'd best avoid it," is how a senior Visio programmer put it. Saving a drawing file in XML format expands the file size approximately eight times. So why is it there? XML is useful to organizations that want to incorporate the contents of Visio files into enterprise systems that exchange information in this format. For example, you can create a Visio flowchart that shows a business process, export the flowchart in XML format, and then share it with other businesses using the Microsoft BizTalk server. You can save drawings as well as customized stencils or templates in XML format.

Opening XML Files

When a Visio file is saved in XML format, you can open it in Visio and work with it in all the ways you can work with standard Visio drawing, stencil, and template files. Visio can open any file that contains well-formed XML code that complies with the Visio XML schema and the internal rules for Visio. You can also open the XML files that Visio creates in a text or code editor. Visio includes a tag for just about every Visio attribute, from line jump behavior to color definitions. If you're familiar with XML tags and Visio commands, you can easily recognize most of the tags that Visio creates.

Inside Out

XML interface documentation

Microsoft plans to document the XML interface in Visio, but the documentation was not available at the time this book was being written. Look for news of its release at the Visio Developer Center (*http://msdn.microsoft.com/visio*).

Making XML the Default File Format

You can make XML the default Visio drawing format. To do this, choose Tools, Options, and then click the Save tab, as Figure 21-8 shows. Select Visio XML Document from the Save Visio Files As list on the Save tab. In the same dialog box, you can specify whether you want Visio to display warnings and error messages when it opens XML files that contain information it cannot recognize or when it saves XML files that contain data other programs might not be able to read.

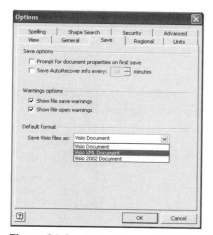

Figure 21-8. You can specify XML as the default file format for Visio documents by choosing Tools, Options.

Inside Out

Saving as HTML versus XML

If you want to use a Visio diagram as a Web page, it's better to save it as an HTML file than an XML file. If you post a Visio page in XML format on a Web site, visitors to the site can view the XML file only if they have Visio 2002 or Visio 2003 installed on their systems. In addition, if they can see the file, they can also edit it. You can offer viewers a large amount of data through the HTML file without risking the integrity of your drawing.

Chapter 21

Understanding Shapes and Masters

If you want to know what goes on behind the scenes when you work with Visio shapes, this section is for you. This information is useful primarily if you plan to create new shapes and save them for reuse as master shapes. Each master has an internal timestamp that records the date and time it was last updated. When you drag a master onto the drawing page, Visio uses its timestamp to determine whether to make a copy of the master on the document stencil. An instance or copy of the master appears on the drawing page, as Figure 21-9 shows. A drawing file always includes a document stencil that contains copies of the masters used in the drawing, even if the corresponding shapes are later deleted from the drawing page. An instance on the drawing page is linked to the copy of the master on the local stencil and inherits its behavior and appearance from that master. If you create a shape using the drawing tools, the shape is not linked to any master or the document stencil.

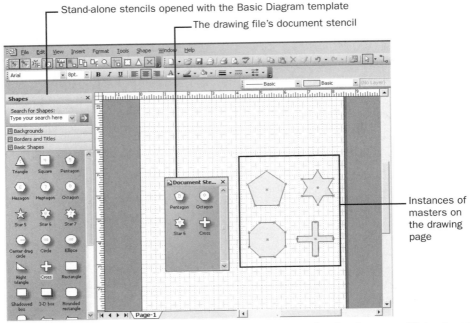

Figure 21-9. When you drag a shape from a stencil onto the drawing page, Visio places a copy of the master on the document stencil.

Inheritance is a weird fact of Visio life that keeps file management efficient and makes shapes reusable. Because of inheritance, you can quickly reformat all the instances of a master shape that you've already added to a drawing page by editing the copy of the master shape on the document stencil. You can also share shapes with other Visio users and know that the shape will look right on the other user's computer. Inheritance also explains why when you ungroup a shape created from a master, a dire-sounding message appears: "This action will sever the object's link to its master." This simply means that the shape on the page will no longer inherit from the master stored on the document stencil—that is, the shape is no longer an instance of the master. That severed master, however, remains on the document stencil. Only the link to the master has been removed.

To remove masters from a document stencil that are no longer linked to shapes on the page, you can display the document stencil and delete them manually. You can't tell by looking whether a master on the document stencil is linked to a shape instance on the drawing page, but if you try to delete a master that is still linked, you see the message shown in Figure 21-10. About the only time it's worth cleaning up a document stencil is if you're intending to save a drawing as a template and you want the drawing page and document stencil to be as small as possible in terms of file size.

Figure 21-10. You can clean up a document stencil by deleting unneeded masters. If a master is still linked to a shape on the page, Visio warns you.

Troubleshooting

The Find Shape tool does not locate master shapes that have been customized

If you create your own master shapes and want them to appear when you are searching for shapes, you must include keywords with the master shape. The keywords correspond to the search text users type in the Search For Shapes box in the Shapes window and are used by Visio to index shapes for searching. Keywords are an option in the Master Properties dialog box. For details, see "Editing Masters," page 621. Visio 2003, unlike previous versions of Visio, searches your entire hard drive and the Internet by default. Hence it will find a stencil or shape that contains the keyword you typed in the Search For Shapes box no matter what the stencil's file path is.

Tip Associate keywords with your custom stencils
You can also assign keywords to your custom stencils. Searching for shapes will also pull up these stencils. To do so, open the stencil for editing (right-click the stencil and select Edit Stencil), and then right-click the stencil and select Properties. Type the keyword that you wish to associate with the stencil in the Keywords box.

Saving Customized Shapes as Masters

In Visio 2003 you can drag any shape that you wish to save onto any open custom stencil, as Figure 21-11 shows. If the stencil is open as read-only, Visio asks you whether you want to open the stencil for editing, and if you click Yes, Visio creates a default master. That's the quickest way to create a master and save it on a stencil. You can then edit the master and its icon, as described in the next section. Note that in this instance a read-only stencil is a custom stencil that has not been opened for editing. If the file was previously saved as a read-only file, you can edit it only if you remove the read-only status by browsing to the file in Windows Explorer, displaying the file's properties, and clearing the Read-Only check box.

Drag a shape toward the open stencil
on which you want to create a master.

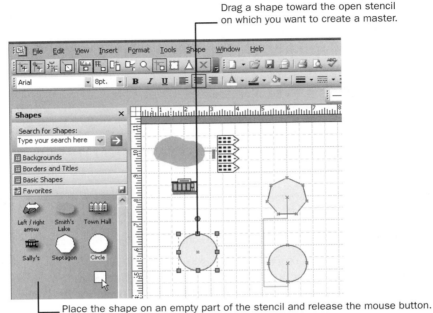

Place the shape on an empty part of the stencil and release the mouse button.

Figure 21-11. You can drag a shape onto any stencil to open the stencil for editing and save the shape as a master.

There are other ways to create a new master as well. You can do the following:

- Open a custom stencil for editing, add a new, blank master, and then create a shape. There might be an advantage to working this way; you get the same effect by creating your shape on the drawing page and then dragging it onto a stencil.

- Open a custom stencil for editing, edit an existing master, and then save your changes. This method is especially handy when you use a particular shape all the time and always edit it in the same way. You can instead go to the source and edit the master.

Tip You can create a master from an object that you have pasted or imported into the Visio application from another program.

Chapter 21

Editing Masters

As if Visio didn't have enough windows and panes already, the master drawing page window is the place where you can edit masters. To display this window, double-click a master on a custom stencil that's open for editing. Visio opens the master in its own drawing page, as Figure 21-12 shows. To close the window and save your changes, click the Close button in the master drawing window.

In the master drawing window, edit the master as you would any other Visio shape.

Use the menu and toolbar commands.

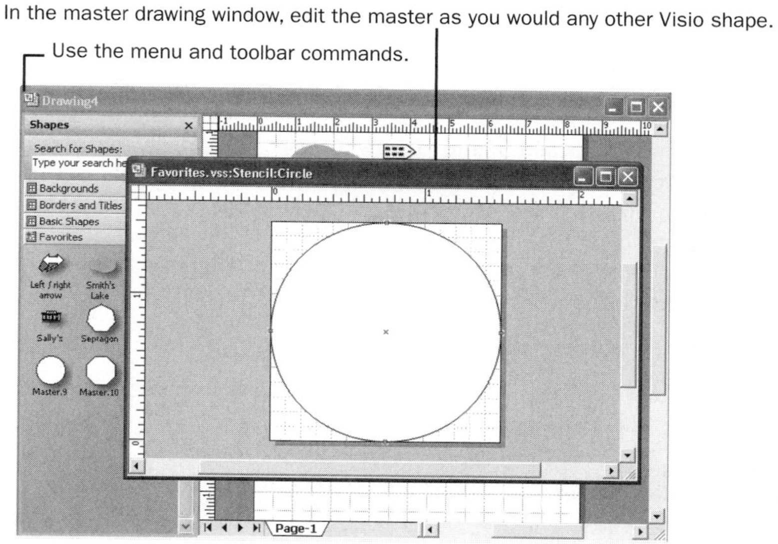

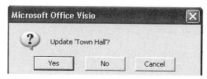

Figure 21-12. When you double-click a master, Visio opens the shape in the master drawing window. Often, the drawing page is sized to the shape.

In the master drawing window, you can edit the master as you would any other Visio shape. You can drag shapes from other stencils, draw or edit with the drawing tools, or paste an object from another application. The only difference is in how you save your changes: Click the Close button in the master drawing window. If you have made changes to the master, Visio prompts you with a message like the one shown in Figure 21-13. When you click Yes, Visio saves your changes and revises the master icon to match, if necessary (although you can disable this action).

Figure 21-13. When you click the Close button in the master drawing window, Visio prompts you to save your changes with this message.

Copyrighting Masters

The masters supplied by Microsoft Corporation are copyrighted. You are legally permitted to copy, modify, and reorganize them for your own use, and you can distribute drawings that contain them. However, you cannot legally sell or distribute original or modified Visio masters.

What you can do if you're in the business of creating and selling shapes is copyright your own. Shape copyrights are displayed in the Special dialog box (Format, Special). The Copyright field is a one-shot deal: Once you type your copyright information and click OK, you can't edit the field's value.

Visio creates an icon and default name for new masters, both of which you can change. For example, if you create a new master by dragging a shape onto a stencil, the master icon is a rectangle with a miniature image of the shape and a label "Master.*n*," where *n* is the number of shapes on the stencil. A master has properties that include its icon size, name, and prompt—the text that appears on the status bar when you point to a shape on a stencil. You can also specify how icons are displayed and aligned on a stencil.

To edit a master's properties, follow these steps:

1 On a custom stencil that's open for editing, right-click a master shape, and then choose Edit Master, Master Properties.

2 In the Name box, type the name of the master shape as you want it to appear on the stencil. Table 21-1 lists the other options that you can specify.

3 Click OK to close the Master Properties dialog box.

4 To save your changes, right-click the stencil's title bar, and then choose Save. Or if the stencil is open in a stand-alone window, choose File, Save.

Chapter 21

After you make a change to a custom stencil, the Save icon appears in the stencil title bar. Click the icon to save the changes.

Stencil icon

Tip The Master Properties command is available only when you right-click a master on a custom stencil that's open for editing. To edit a custom stencil, click the stencil's stencil icon (or right-click the title bar) and select Edit Stencil.

Table 21-1. Master Properties Dialog Box Options

Option	Description
Name	The master name that will appear with the master icon on the stencil. You can type up to 31 characters, but shorter is better. Visio truncates long names (exactly where depends on the screen resolution).
Prompt	The text that appears in the balloon when you point to a master shape on a stencil. Visio masters use this text to explain a shape's purpose, but anything you think is useful information can go here.
Icon Size	The size of the master icon on the stencil. The number in parentheses is the size in pixels. Normal is the setting Visio master shapes use.
Align Master Name	How the master name is aligned with respect to the master icon. Visio master shapes use the Center setting.
Keywords	Words that help users find shapes. Unless you're planning to distribute your stencil, you can probably ignore this. The Find Shapes command uses the words you type in this box to help users locate shapes. Separate each keyword with a comma. This field is not available if the master drawing page contains no shape.
Match Master By Name On Drop	An option that tells Visio whether to link the instance of a master to the master on the document stencil with the same name. Visio master shapes do not use this setting. If this check box is not selected, Visio uses the master's timestamp to determine whether the master needs to be copied to the document stencil.
Generate Icon Automatically From Shape Data	An option that tells Visio whether to re-create the master icon each time you save a change to the shape in the master drawing window.

Chapter 21

Designing and Displaying Master Icons

If you create and distribute master shapes on a custom stencil, well-designed, well-organized icons provide a nice touch. The master icon is a user's first clue about a shape's purpose. Although Visio creates and arranges master icons as you add new masters to a stencil, you'll probably want to refine both their look and location.

Creating Master Icons

There is a fine art to designing meaningful images in a space of 32 by 32 pixels, the default size of a master icon. If you want to design or edit the master icon on a stencil, you can work, pixel by pixel, in the icon editor. Visio typically creates an icon for you based on the appearance of the shape in the master drawing window. You can then refine the icon in the icon editor to change its shape and colors, as Figure 21-14 shows. Here's the trick: Select the Pencil tool and click the left mouse button to apply the Left Button Color to a pixel—likewise for the Right Button Color and the right mouse button. Select the colors on these buttons, and then left- and right-click with the Pencil tool to draw in the icon editor.

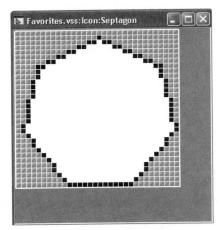

Figure 21-14.   You can design a master icon, pixel by pixel, in the icon editor, which includes basic tools for setting pixel color.

Icons can be larger than 32 by 32 pixels. Their size is set in the Master Properties dialog box, as explained in the previous section. The Icon Size you specify there determines the size of the area in the icon editor.

> **Note**   If you plan to design a unique master icon, make certain to clear the Generate Icon Automatically From Shape Data check box in the Master Properties dialog box as well. Otherwise, Visio will overwrite your icon every time you edit the master in the master drawing window.

Chapter 21

Follow these steps to edit a master icon in the icon editing window:

1. On a custom stencil that's open for editing, right-click a master, and then choose Edit Master, Edit Icon Image.

   Visio opens the icon editing window, displays the icon, and adds a toolbar with commands for editing the icon.

2. Use the tools to change the colors and shape of the icon.

   As you change the icon, your changes are reflected on the stencil. You might need to rearrange the windows to see both the stencil and icon editor windows.

3. After you've edited the icon, click the Close button to close the editing window. When Visio prompts you to save the changes to the stencil, click Yes.

4. If the results are disappointing, choose Edit, Undo Change Icon. Or press Ctrl+Z.

   You can also use the Undo command while you're working in the icon editor.

Displaying Master Icons on a Stencil

In addition to editing or designing a master icon, you can change the order in which master shapes appear on a stencil and choose whether a name and description are displayed with the icon. For example, you can display a description next to the master shape icon that indicates the shape's purpose. To change the order of the stencil's icons, simply drag the master shape icons into position. Visio snaps the icons into alignment and creates rows and columns based on the size of the stencil window.

You can also choose how much information Visio displays for all master shapes. By default, Visio displays the master icon and shape name. You can instead display only the icon, only the name, or both with a description as well. When you change the way Visio displays master shapes and icons, all stencils you subsequently open are affected.

Follow these steps to change how master shapes are displayed:

1. Close any drawing files that you have open.

2. Choose File, Shapes, and select a stencil file.

3. Right-click the stencil title bar, and then select View. Choose Icons And Names, Icons Only, Names Only, or Icons And Details. Visio changes the master shape display depending on the command you choose.

Creating a New Stencil

It's useful to create an entirely new stencil when you want to save shapes you create or consolidate masters from Visio stencils that you use frequently. To create a new, empty stencil file with write access, choose File, Shapes, New Stencil. If you already have a drawing file open, Visio opens the new stencil in a docked window that's open for editing. If nothing else is open in Visio when you create a new stencil, Visio displays the stencil in a stencil window and displays menus for working with stencils and masters, as Figure 21-15 shows.

Chapter 21

The Master menu includes commands that are also available when you right-click a master.

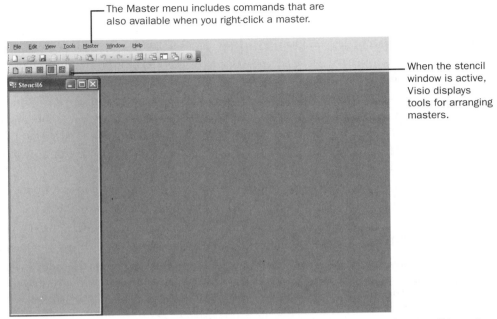

When the stencil window is active, Visio displays tools for arranging masters.

Figure 21-15. When you create a new, stand-alone stencil, Visio opens the stencil in a stencil window. The document's drawing page is closed.

There are a couple of advantages to starting a new stencil in a new window:

● Visio displays a toolbar with buttons for controlling the display of master icons in the stencil window.

● The new stencil document's drawing page is empty and its style lists include only the four default styles, so you're starting with the minimum file size.

Tip To display the stencil's drawing page, which provides a convenient work area while you add masters, choose Window, Show Drawing Page.

Adding Shapes to a New Stencil

You can open other stencils, and then drag masters onto your new stencil, or you can create and design masters from scratch in the stencil window. Table 21-2 summarizes techniques for working with stencils.

Table 21-2. Techniques for Working with Stencils

Task	Technique
Create a new, empty stencil	Choose File, Shapes, New Stencil.
Create a new stencil based on an existing stencil	Choose Open. In the Open dialog box, locate and select the stencil you want to use. Visio stencils are stored at C:\Program Files\Microsoft Office\Visio11\1033\. Click the Open button's drop-down arrow, choose Copy, and then click Open.
Add a master from one custom stencil to a different custom stencil	Open both stencils, and then drag the master from one stencil to another. Note that you can no longer add a shape to a stencil that ships with Visio 2003. You can make a copy of the stencil, as detailed earlier, and then add a master.
Save changes to a docked custom stencil that's open for editing	Right-click the stencil's title bar, and then click Save or Save As, or click the Save icon in the stencil's title bar.
Save changes to a custom stencil open in a stencil window	With the stencil window active (click its title bar), choose File, Save or Save As, or click the Save icon on the Standard toolbar.

Saving Changes to a New Stencil

To save your changes, do one of the following:

- If the new stencil is in a docked stencil pane, right-click the stencil's title bar, and then choose Save.

- If the new stencil is open in a stencil window, choose File, Save (or press Ctrl+S) or click the Save icon on the Standard toolbar.

To make sure that other users cannot open your stencil for editing, set the Read Only option in the Save As dialog box. For details, see "Saving and Opening Read-Only Stencils," page 613. The default location to which Visio 2003 saves stencil files is C:\Documents and Settings\<user>\My Documents\My Shapes, where <user> is the user login name used when starting Windows.

You can also set up a folder on your computer for your customized stencils and then direct Visio to that path. To set the default file paths that Visio searches for stencil files, choose Tools, Options, Advanced, and then click the File Paths tab. To add your path to the default shown in the Stencils box, click the button to the right of the box, browse to the location where you wish to save files, and then click Select. You'll return to the File Paths box. Click OK.

Chapter 21

Saving a Document Stencil as a New Stencil

If you've been working in a drawing and want to save the masters that have accumulated on its document stencil as a new, stand-alone stencil, it's easy. Basically, you save the drawing file as a stencil file. This can be a quick way to create a new stencil, but it can also result in a larger than normal file size. When you save a drawing file as a stencil file, Visio saves all the masters on the document stencil, but also saves any shapes you've left on the drawing page. When you next open the stencil file, it will open in the normal fashion—either docked or in a stand-alone window, depending on how you open it. The shapes left on the drawing page are still stored with the file and take up file space, but they're not visible because the stencil's drawing page is closed.

It's best to delete the shapes from the drawing page when you want to save a drawing file as a stencil. Then only the masters on the document stencil are saved, which is really all you need if you plan to use the document as a stencil.

Follow these steps to save a drawing file's document stencil as a new stencil:

1 Choose File, Shapes, Document Stencil to display the drawing file's document stencil if it is not already visible.

2 Make sure that the document stencil contains the masters you want. You can delete masters you don't need, edit the master properties to change the master names, and drag master icons to arrange them in the order you want.

3 To clean up the file before you save it, delete all the shapes from the drawing page.

> **Tip** A quick way to remove all shapes from the page is to choose Edit, Select All, and then press Delete.

4 Choose File, Save As.

5 In the Save As Type list, select Stencil. Type a file name and specify the location you want.

6 If you want to share your stencil with others but ensure that they can't edit it, click the Save button's drop-down list arrow, and choose Read Only.

> For details about read-only stencils, see "Saving and Opening Read-Only Stencils," page 613.

7 Click Save to display the Properties dialog box, in which you can type information about the file if you want. When you click OK, Visio saves the document as a stencil that you can open with other drawings.

> **Tip** You may also click the Shapes button on the Standard toolbar, and choose a new stencil. Drag the shapes you wish to save from the document stencil to the new stencil and save them.

Chapter 21

Customizing Templates

When you create or customize a template, you set up a reusable environment that includes one or more drawing pages, the page settings you require, and the stencils that you want to make available. The simplest way to create a template with custom settings is to open a drawing, choose the page settings and stencils you want, and then save everything as a template (.vst) file. It's no more complicated than that.

Most Visio templates open with a blank drawing page, but you can create a template that already includes shapes. For example, you can save a border and title block on the drawing page and then save the drawing as a template. Or you can add your company logo to a background page and then save the file as a template so that the logo will appear on each page of a diagram created with that template, as Figure 21-16 shows. People typically create their own templates when they want a convenient way of opening several frequently used stencils together, or when they want to save custom page settings and window positions.

Open the stencils you use most in a new drawing, and then save it as a template.

Save your template with shapes or pictures, such as a company logo.

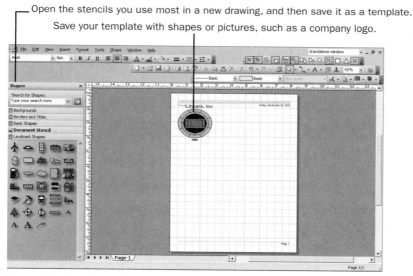

Figure 21-16. You can save the settings and shapes you use most as a reusable template.

You can save any Visio file as a template. When you save the file, you're also saving the file's page settings, print settings, style definitions, VBA macros, color palette, layers, window sizes and positions, and snap and glue options. Make sure to specify the options you want in your template, because those are the options that will appear as the defaults in any diagram based on that template.

The default location to which Visio installs template files is C:\Documents and Settings\ *<user>*\My Documents\My Shapes, where *<user>* is the user login name used when starting Windows. However, you can specify other paths with the Options command (choose Tools, Options Advanced, and then click the File Paths button). You can subsequently open the template by clicking File, Open and then browsing to the template's location. The user-created template will also show up in the Other folder on the Visio 2003 startup screen.

To create a template from a drawing file or an existing template, follow these steps:

1 Open a drawing (.vsd) file, or start a new drawing based on the template you want to modify.

2 Open the stencils you want to save with the template.

3 Insert pages, if you want, and specify the drawing page settings you want to use in all diagrams based on this template.

   For example, choose File, Page Setup to specify the page size and drawing scale.

4 If you want the template to include open windows automatically, display the windows you want.

   For example, choose View, Pan & Zoom Window to have the Pan & Zoom window open every time you start a drawing with the template.

5 When you've added the settings you want, choose File, Save As.

6 In the Save As Type list, select Template (*.vst).

7 Type a file name for your template and specify a location.

8 Click the Save button's drop-down arrow, and verify that the settings you want are selected.

   By default, Workspace is selected, which means that Visio saves the size and position of all the open windows with the file's other contents. The Read Only option isn't necessary unless you really don't want anyone to be able to open the original template file—an error will appear if you try to open the original version of a template saved as read-only.

9 Click Save to create the template file in the specified location.

Adding Stencils to a Template

Your template can include stencils that Visio opens in the default fashion: as docked windows in the Shapes area of the Visio window. However, if you prefer working with stencils in a different location, or with some stencils docked and others floating, you can do this in your template, as Figure 21-17 shows. When you're creating your template, all you have to do is arrange the stencils in the way you want them to open. As long as you save the template file and its workspace list (the default behavior when you save), the stencils will open as specified when you start a drawing based on your template.

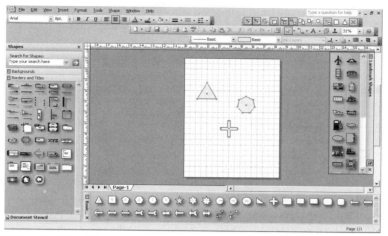

Figure 21-17. Visio saves the position and size of the open windows in your template as part of the file's workspace list.

If you're saving stencil and template files that are meant to work together, make sure that their styles and colors are compatible. Because stencils are separate Visio files that the template file opens, Visio's inheritance rules apply when shapes are dragged between files. Odd complications can arise if you've used a color theme or styles for your masters that are different from the settings in your template. Recall that the style and color settings are saved with the file, so for masters, that means the settings are saved with the stencil file. The template file can have different settings that can override those specified by the stencil.

For example, if a master shape is formatted with a custom style, that style is saved with the stencil file. If you include that stencil file in a template, but the template doesn't include the same style, Visio adds the style to the template when the master is added to the drawing page. No problem. But what if the template file also has a style of the same name? Perhaps the Normal style in the stencil file specifies 8-point Arial type and the Normal style in the template file specifies 12-point Arial type. When you add the shape, the style will inherit the characteristics of the style from the drawing page, which inherited the template's settings.

For details about how styles are inherited, see "Copying Styles and Color Schemes to Other Diagrams," page 692.

Creating Templates for Scaled Drawings

If you are creating a template for scaled drawings, such as a floor plan, the page scale is set by the template's drawing page. The scale at which the shape is drawn determines the master scale. It's possible to create master shapes at one drawing scale and save them with a template that specifies a different drawing scale. As long as the scales are fairly close (specifically, no more than eight times larger or smaller), you won't have a problem using the shapes on that page.

You specify the drawing scale for masters the same way you do for templates: Use the Page Setup command on the File menu, and then click the Drawing Scale tab. The difference is that if you're editing a master, you're probably working on the master drawing page. If you're specifying a template's settings, you're probably working on the template's drawing page.

> For details about drawing scales, see "Working with a Drawing Scale," page 422. Chapter 16, "Measuring and Dimensioning with Precision," also provides information about other options you might want to include in a scaled template, such as a variable grid, guide lines, and useful snap settings.

Protecting File Settings

To ensure that styles, shapes, backgrounds, and other settings you specify for a drawing, stencil, or template file are not changed, you can password-protect a Visio document. With the Protect Document command, you can supply a password to prevent others from changing any of the following elements:

- **Styles**   Users can apply styles but can't create or edit them.
- **Shapes**   Users can't select shapes. You must also select From Selection in the Protection dialog box (Format, Protection).
- **Preview**   Visio won't update the preview image for the file. This option applies primarily to templates, which display a preview in the Choose A Drawing window.
- **Backgrounds**   Users can't delete or edit background pages.
- **Master Shapes**   Users can drag masters from stencils but can't create, edit, or delete master shapes.

Follow these steps to specify a password and the document elements to protect:

1   Open the Visio document you want to protect, and then choose View, Drawing Explorer Window.

2   In the Drawing Explorer window, right-click the name of the document, and then choose Protect Document.

3   In the Password box, type a password, and then select the options you want to protect. Click OK.

Programming Solutions with VBA

What is Visual Basic for Applications 6.4 (VBA) doing in Visio? Think like a programmer for a minute. What if every action that you can do to shapes could be done automatically? What if there was a way to collect information from a drawing, such as through a form or an interactive control? What if the information in a drawing could be sent to another program for analysis automatically? With VBA, you can write a separate program called a *macro* that controls actions in Visio. You can actually automate Visio using any development tool that's capable of creating Microsoft Windows applications, but VBA is the tool that's built in. To display the VBA editor in Visio, choose Tools, Macros, Visual Basic Editor. The VBA editor appears, as Figure 21-18 shows.

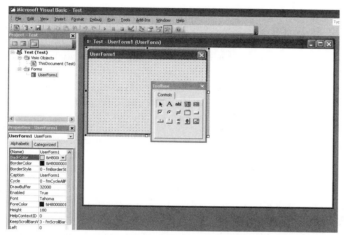

Figure 21-18.   In the VBA window, you can write a macro program to control an object in Visio.

If you're not a programmer, it might be a little hard to imagine what you can do in the VBA window. If you are a programmer, you might become frustrated by the lack of detail in this book about what you can do. The thing to know is that Visio has an open architecture, which means that Visio exposes its objects, such as windows, drawing pages, shapes, layers, menus, and toolbars, through a structured interface called the *object model*. Just about anything that Visio can do, you can do programmatically through the object model. In fact, the Visio programmers at Microsoft use the same tools that are available to you to create much of the automated behavior in many templates.

For example, one popular area of Visio customization is creating automated sales tools that can generate a purchase order or bill of materials from a Visio drawing. Custom shapes are linked to database information about the properties of the company's equipment. Sales personnel can then use the shapes to prototype configurations for prospective clients in Visio. VBA macros can scan the equipment in the drawing to create a bill of materials or purchase order on the spot.

Chapter 21

Inside Out

Enabling and disabling VBA

You can enable and disable VBA in Visio with the Options command, which also includes options for enabling Component Object Model (COM) add-ins and Automation events. Choose Tools, Options, and then click the Advanced tab to see the developer settings.

About Writing Add-Ins

The easiest way to create an add-in is to create a public procedure in a VBA module. VBA code is stored as part of the drawing file and runs in the same memory space as Visio. However, you can also create an add-in as an executable (.exe) file that can be launched from Visio or executed as a stand-alone program, and you can write the add-in using any programming language that supports COM. Executable files run in their own memory space. If you're a C++ programmer, you can also create an add-in as a Visio library (.vsl), a special type of dynamic-link library (DLL) that is loaded by Visio at run time. This is how most wizards in Visio are created—if you look in the Solutions folders, you'll see many files with the .vsl extension.

Visio includes a type library, a file that contains Automation descriptions of the objects, properties, methods, events, and constants that Visio exposes to Automation controllers. The Object Browser in the VBA window (View, Object Browser) displays the Visio Automation descriptions and includes code templates that you can copy.

Tip Use digital signatures with Visio
If you want to add a macro or add-in to a Visio document, you might want to investigate the digital signature support in Visio. You can digitally sign your VBA projects using a signature that can be obtained from any number of certification companies.

Getting More Information

There are so many guides for programming with VBA that this book doesn't try to tell you how to write code. However, if you want to find out more about what you can do with Visio, you can take advantage of the many Web-based resources that Microsoft makes available. The Microsoft Visio team also produces very thorough documentation for developers, some of which is delivered in reference form with the product, and the rest of which is available on the Web.

Here are some places to look for more information:

- In Visio, choose Help, Developer Reference to display the Visio Developer Reference. You'll find some conceptual information about using Automation with the Visio object model and a complete reference of the events, methods, objects, and properties that you can use.

Chapter 21

- In the VBA window, choose Help, Microsoft Visual Basic Help for help on using the editing tools in the VBA environment. This is generic Visual Basic help and doesn't tell you about any Visio-specific options.

- On the Web, go to *http://msdn.microsoft.com*, the technical site for developers, and type **Visio** in the Search box. The MSDN site includes the complete text of *Developing Microsoft Visio Solutions*, the definitive guide to the Visio development platform, as well as a wealth of resources and technical articles about Automation, Visual Basic, and more.

Chapter 21

Drawing and Editing to Create New Shapes

If you're like most people, you would prefer that Microsoft Office Visio 2003 contain all the shapes you want. At some point, however, you'll probably need to create a shape that Visio doesn't already have or revise a shape slightly (or extensively) to better suit a diagram. At these times, you'll need to take advantage of Visio's drawing tools. Whether you're a whiz with drawing tools or not, the good news is that you don't necessarily have to draw a shape from scratch even when you can't find the exact shape you want on an existing stencil. It's almost always faster to start with an existing shape and then modify it to suit your needs.

This chapter presents the pros and cons of various shape drawing and editing techniques and describes in detail all the drawing tools and techniques you can use. For shape developers and others who want to understand shapes inside out, this chapter also discusses shapes in terms of their geometry.

Understanding Shape Geometry

You can create most Visio diagrams successfully without a detailed understanding of how shapes work. However, if you want to create your own shapes or revise an existing shape, your task is easier if you know what you're dealing with. This section breaks shapes down into their geometric parts, explains shape vocabulary, and explains why shape geometry is useful to understand. If you remember your high school geometry, you have an advantage, but even if you don't know a vertex from a vortex, you'll learn some practical techniques for getting shapes to look and act the way you want.

Visio includes many terms for describing the vector-based geometry that underlies shapes. If you reduce any shape to its simplest, constituent parts—what's left after you remove the colors, styles, and other formatting attributes—you have *line segments* and *arc segments*. It's easiest to see them when you select shapes with the Pencil tool, as Figure 22-1 shows. Where these segments join, a diamond-shaped *vertex* appears. In the middle of a line segment, a *control point* appears, which looks like a circle with a dot in it. To reshape any shape, you can add, move, and delete vertices using the Pencil tool. You can also change the curvature of a line segment by dragging its control point.

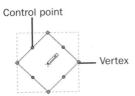

Control point

Vertex

Figure 22-1. When you select a shape with the Pencil tool, its vertices and control points are displayed so that you can control shape geometry.

Using the Drawing Tools

Visio tucks a number of drawing tools into drop-down toolbars. Often, you end up displaying them all before you find the tool you want. The last tool used becomes the one shown on the toolbar. Figure 22-2 shows the drawing tools. To access them, click the Drawing Tools button on the Standard toolbar or select View, Toolbars, Drawing.

Figure 22-2. To draw new shapes, use the drawing tools on the Standard toolbar.

Despite the number of drawing tools in Visio, you can really create only the following types of shape geometry, as Figure 22-3 shows:

- **Lines** To create lines, use either the Line or Pencil tool. The Rectangle tool merely draws four contiguous line segments (sometimes called *polygonal lines*).

- **Elliptical arcs** To create elliptical arcs, use the Arc tool or the Ellipse tool. A circle in Visio is really two contiguous elliptical arc segments (created by pressing Shift while using the Ellipse tool).

- **Circular arcs** To create circular arcs, use the Pencil tool. Because these arcs are a portion of a circle, they behave differently from elliptical arcs when stretched. Circular arcs bulge like a cloverleaf, whereas elliptical arcs resize smoothly.

- **Splines** To create a spline, use the Freeform tool or convert lines. Technically, Visio creates nonuniform rational B-splines (or NURBS for short), but you can also think of a spline as a curve that passes through specific points.

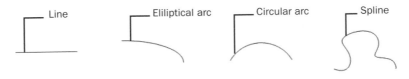

Line Eliliptical arc Circular arc Spline

Figure 22-3. All shapes are made up of line segments, arc segments, or splines.

Chapter 22

Editing Shapes with the Pencil Tool

To change the look of a shape—that is, to edit its geometry—use the Pencil tool. By selecting, moving, and deleting vertices and control points, you can radically alter shape geometry, turning squares into stars or triangles, flat lines into mountains or valleys, and so on.

To select a vertex, click the Pencil tool, and then select a shape to display its vertices. Click a vertex, which turns magenta to show it's selected.

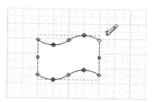

To move a shape vertex, click the Pencil tool, and then select a shape to display its vertices. Drag a vertex to reposition the line segment.

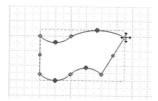

To add a vertex and reshape a shape, click the Pencil tool, and then select a shape to display its vertices. Hold the Ctrl key, and then click on a line segment where you want to add a vertex.

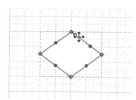

Drag the new vertex to reposition the line segment.

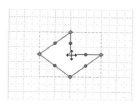

To delete a line segment, select a vertex on the line segment you want to remove.

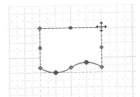

After you've selected the vertex, press Delete.

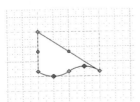

Identifying Shape Behavior

Just as vertices and line segments constitute basic shape geometry, lines and boxes represent the basic differences in shape *behavior*. Behavior means the way you interact with shapes on the page—that is, moving, sizing, and connecting them. When a shape behaves like a line, it can be stretched and rotated in one step by dragging an endpoint. For example, the Wall shape on the Office Layout Shapes stencil behaves like a line. 1-D shapes have this behavior. When a shape behaves like a box, it can have up to eight selection handles, including corner handles that you can use to resize the shape. 2-D shapes have this behavior.

Chapter 2, "Creating a Diagram," introduced the difference between 1-D and 2-D shapes. How much more do you need to know about 1-D and 2-D shapes? If you want to design your own shapes, you'll need to understand shape behavior, a fundamental Visio concept that helps you answer important questions: What kind of sizing behavior do you want your shape to have? Do you want your shape to connect to other shapes? If you create and revise shapes only as needed for different diagrams, it's still useful information, because 1-D and 2-D shapes look different when you select them and act quite differently when you use them.

Understanding 1-D Shape Behavior

A 1-D shape behaves like a line, but note that it doesn't necessarily have to look like a line, as Figure 22-4 shows. To identify a 1-D shape, select it, and then choose Format, Behavior. If Line (1-Dimensional) is selected under Interaction Style, it's a 1-D shape.

Chapter 22

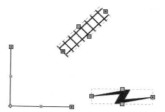

Figure 22-4. You can tell these are 1-D shapes, because each has a begin point and end-point.

Technically, any shape that has a begin point (the end with an x) and an endpoint (the end with a +), either of which can be glued to other shapes, is 1-D. Together, these two points form part of the built-in intelligence of 1-D shapes. If other shapes are connected to the line, the begin and endpoints can imply directionality. The begin and endpoints also determine where the arrows and other line end styles go when you apply them with the Format, Line command, as Figure 22-5 shows. Only 1-D shapes can have line ends.

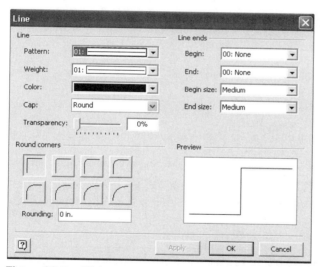

Figure 22-5. Visio applies the line end patterns to the begin point and endpoint when you select an option in the Begin and End lists of the Line dialog box.

Chapter 22

Inside Out

Visual feedback in Visio

During the design phase for the first version of Visio, the developers decided that Visio should provide feedback to users. Vertices, control points, selection handles, begin and endpoints—all those green, yellow, and red points you see when a shape is selected—are examples of visual feedback. They're meant only to help you more easily edit and work with shapes. Some users find the feedback visually distracting, but Visio provides for this possibility. You can turn off the display of some types of visual feedback by selecting an option on the Tools, Options, View menu.

Understanding 2-D Shape Behavior

A shape that has selection handles for changing width and height is a 2-D shape, as Figure 22-6 shows. To identify a 2-D shape, select it, and then choose Shape, Behavior. If Box (2-Dimensional) is selected under Interaction Style, it's a 2-D shape.

Figure 22-6. You can tell this is a 2-D shape because of the corner selection handles.

Visio includes two special types of 2-D shapes that can have confusing behavior:

- **Merged shape** The term *merged shape* refers to any shape created as a result of using a shape operation command, such as Combine or Join. These shapes are noteworthy, because they typically have complex geometry and resemble groups. However, they are 2-D shapes with unique formatting behavior.

For details about merged shapes, see "Merging Shapes to Create New Ones," page 660.

- **Group** A group is an object in its own right made up of other shapes. Each shape in the group can have independent attributes, as can the group.

For details about groups, see "Working with Groups," page 668.

Identifying Other Visio Objects

Shapes aren't the only objects in Visio with properties and behavior. Groups, imported graphics, guide lines, connection points, and even the drawing page are all objects in Visio. Like shapes, these other objects are represented in the ShapeSheet window. That means you can control them programmatically—a useful exercise when you want to automate diagrams.

Converting 2-D Shapes to 1-D Shapes

You can convert a 2-D shape to a 1-D shape when you want a shape to behave like a line. In fact, the easiest way to create a 1-D shape is often to draw a 2-D shape, and then convert it. The important thing to remember is to draw from left to right so that after you convert the shape to 1-D, its begin and endpoints behave correctly. For example, if you draw the outline of an arrow using lines, you'll create a 2-D shape. If you want the arrow to connect to other shapes or align more easily, you can convert it to 1-D, as Figure 22-7 shows. When you convert a shape to 1-D, its handles change to begin and endpoints, and the alignment box is updated.

Figure 22-7. You can use the Behavior command to convert a 2-D arrow to a 1-D arrow that can be glued to other shapes.

To convert a 2-D shape to a 1-D shape, first select the shape, and then choose Format, Behavior.

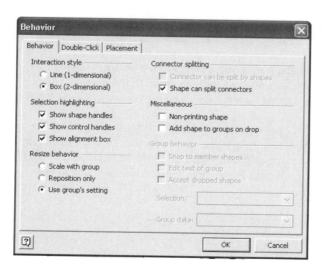

Next, under Interaction Style, select Line (1-Dimensional), and then click OK.

> **Tip**   **Reverse the begin and endpoints**
> After you convert a shape, make sure its begin point (x) is on the left or top and its endpoint (+) is on the right or bottom. If they're backward, you can switch them easily. Select the shape, and then choose Shape, Operations, Reverse Ends.

Converting a shape dramatically alters its ShapeSheet, which you need to know if you want to create SmartShapes formulas. After you convert a 2-D shape to a 1-D shape, the Alignment section is deleted, the 1-D Endpoints section is added, and new 1-D formulas are added to the Width, Angle, PinX, and PinY cells of the Shape Transform section.

Understanding Closed and Open Shapes

Shapes must be closed for fill patterns and colors to be applied. *Closed* means that the shape's line segments form a continuous path. The less precise way to think of this is that the line is sealed all the way around, so fill won't leak out. However, this analogy ultimately fails, as you'll see. Sometimes an entire shape is a closed path, such as a rectangle. Sometimes a shape contains multiple closed paths, such as a rectangle with polka dots. If you select the plain rectangle and click a fill color (let's say yellow), the entire rectangle turns yellow. If you select the polka-dotted rectangle, and then click the yellow fill, what happens? You might expect the dots to turn yellow, but perhaps you really want the rectangle around the dots to turn yellow, as Figure 22-8 shows. Either behavior can happen, depending on how the shape was designed, which is why you need to consider the closed paths in shapes that you create.

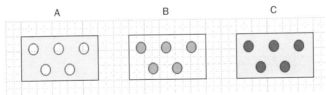

Figure 22-8.   In merged shape A (the Swiss cheese), the dots are open paths, and in merged shape B, the rectangle is an open path. In group C, the dots are a group, and they're grouped with the rectangle so that both the dots and the rectangle can be filled separately.

If the line segments in a shape are not continuous, the shape is *open*, which explains why you cannot fill certain shapes. For example, if you draw an arc, it's an open path, and you can't apply a fill color to it under normal circumstances. (However, you can edit the shape's geometry to accept fill. It's weird but true. For details, see the sidebar "How to Fill Open Shapes.")

Drawing Closed Shapes

When you're drawing 2-D shapes with the Pencil, Line, Arc, or Freeform tool, you must close the path if you want the shape to have a fill color or pattern. In practice, closing a path is tricky. If the last segment you draw doesn't overlap the first, the shape is open and can't be filled. You can use the Pencil tool to close an open shape or path in an existing shape.

How to Fill Open Shapes

You can fill just about any shape you want, including arcs, lines, and squiggles that don't look like their paths are closed. In the ShapeSheet window, you can define a shape to be closed even if it looks wide open.

Try it yourself: use the Pencil or Arc tool to draw a bowl-like curve. Select the curve, and then choose Window, Show ShapeSheet. Scroll down to the Geometry 1 section. (Click the heading to expand it if necessary.) In the cell labeled Geometry1.NoFill, the value is set to TRUE, meaning that it's true that you cannot fill this shape. Select the cell (not its label), type **FALSE**, and then press Enter. Now you can fill the shape. Close the ShapeSheet window, and then apply a fill color and see what happens.

Although it's possible to fill such shapes, does it make sense to do so? It's useful to know about the NoFill cell when you're working with shapes that have multiple closed paths, such as the rectangle with polka dots shown earlier in Figure 22-8. Such shapes can result from using a shape operation such as Combine to create a merged shape. Should the dots or the rectangle receive fill color? Maybe you want the entire shape, dots and all, to be filled. If so, you would want to know how to make the closed paths open. (Set their NoFill cell to TRUE.)

Tip When you draw a closed shape, Visio fills it with white fill color by default. If you can see the grid through your shape, you know it's not closed.

Follow these steps to close a shape:

1 Click the Pencil tool, and then select the shape to display its vertices.

2 To close a path, select a vertex, and then drag the vertex over the vertex of the first segment.

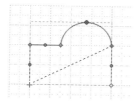

645

3 To draw a line that closes the open path, draw a line from the last vertex to the first.

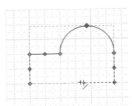

Troubleshooting

When closing a line segment, the line stretches instead

When you're dragging a vertex with the Pencil tool, it's easy to stretch the line accidentally instead of closing the path. The ending vertex must align exactly with the starting vertex to close a path. If the vertices don't line up exactly, Visio creates a new line segment instead, and the shape isn't closed. It's sometimes easier to repair the problem if the shape is not selected. Then click the Pencil tool and draw a line segment from one vertex to another. To make the task smoother, try the following:

- **Turn snapping on** Choose Tools, Snap & Glue. On the General tab, select the Snap check box. Under Snap To, make sure Grid is selected.

- **Align the shape's vertices to the grid** Use the arrow keys to nudge the shape into alignment with the grid.

- **Zoom in close** Press Shift+Ctrl+click with the mouse to zoom in.

Drawing Lines

To draw a straight line, you can use the Pencil tool or the Line tool. The Pencil tool responds to the direction of the mouse. If you drag in a curving motion, Visio draws an arc. If you drag in a straight line, Visio draws a line segment. (See Figure 22-9.) If you're like a lot of people, you try to drag in a straight line and end up with an arc anyway. Fortunately, you can convert arcs to lines and vice versa—or you can use the Line tool, which always creates a straight line.

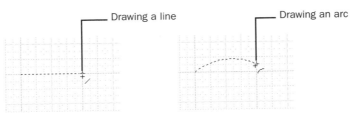

Figure 22-9. As you drag with the Pencil tool, the pointer provides useful feedback by changing to show whether you're creating an arc or a line.

To create consecutive line segments at once, drag with the Pencil or Line tool to draw the first line segment, and then lift your finger from the mouse button without moving the mouse. Then drag to draw the next line segment. If the lines are crooked, wait until you're done drawing the shape, and then use the Pencil tool to repair crooked line segments.

Converting Arcs to Lines

If you draw with the Pencil tool and end up creating an arc segment when you meant to draw a straight line segment, you can repair the problem without redrawing the entire shape. The technique is a little tricky only in that it requires you to work in the ShapeSheet window, but sometimes that's simpler than starting over. Here's how you do it:

1 Select the shape you want to revise, and then choose Window, Show ShapeSheet.

2 Scroll in the ShapeSheet window until you can see the Geometry 1 section. If necessary, arrange the drawing window and the ShapeSheet window so that you can see both the shape and the Geometry 1 section.

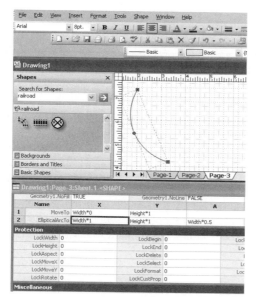

Depending on the shape, the Name column of the Geometry section contains a variable number of rows labeled MoveTo, LineTo, and EllipticalArcTo.

3 Click in the X column of the EllipticalArcTo row. On the drawing page, Visio highlights the vertex that corresponds to the point represented by the cell you have selected.

> **Tip** If the shape contains more than one EllipticalArcTo row, click in the X columns for each one until the vertex that starts the arc you want to change is selected on the drawing page.

Chapter 22

4 Right-click the cell in the X column of the EllipticalArcTo row, and then choose
   Change Row Type.

5 Choose LineTo, and then click OK.

6 Close the ShapeSheet window.

Troubleshooting

You can't select the vertex you want to change in the ShapeSheet window

If the shape you're editing is actually a merged shape or a group, you might have difficulty locating a vertex. If the ShapeSheet window includes multiple Geometry sections labeled Geometry 1, Geometry 2, and so on, the shape is a merged shape. Click each cell in the X column for all the Geometry sections until the corresponding vertex is selected on the drawing page, and then proceed to make the change you want.

If you select a group, you won't see a Geometry section at all in the ShapeSheet window, but if you scroll down, you'll see the Group Properties section. What you need to do is subselect the individual shape that contains the geometry you want to change, and then display its ShapeSheet window.

Creating Infinite Lines

In certain drawing types, it's useful to align shapes to a line that acts as a reference. In Visio, you can drag a guide line out from the rulers and align shapes to that, but the guide's blue line interrupts a drawing. For technical or architectural drawings, you can create a true construction line and format it to look the way you want. Visio refers to these as *infinite lines*. You can create them by drawing a regular line with the Line tool and then editing the ShapeSheet to convert it to an infinite line, as Figure 22-10 shows.

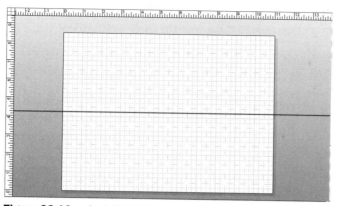

Figure 22-10. An infinite line extends indefinitely into space and is useful as a reference for dimensions or setouts in construction and architectural drawings.

Follow these steps to create an infinite line:

1 Use the Line tool to draw a line that extends in the direction you want. With the line selected, choose Window, Show ShapeSheet.

2 Scroll in the ShapeSheet window until you can see the Geometry 1 section.

The Name column contains MoveTo and LineTo rows.

3 Right-click the cell in the X column of the LineTo row, and then choose Change Row Type.

4 Select the InfiniteLine option, and then click OK. Visio converts the line to an infinite line, but retains the line's original begin and endpoints, which you can use to change the direction of the line.

5 Close the ShapeSheet window.

Drawing Angled Lines

When you need to position shapes along precise 45-degree lines, Visio includes a feature with the rather generic name of *drawing aids* that works like the dynamic grid. How drawing aids are displayed differs depending on which drawing tool you're using, but like the dynamic grid, they appear on screen as dotted lines that show you where to draw, as Figure 22-11 shows.

Figure 22-11. You can turn on drawing aids to display reference lines at 45-degree intervals.

Chapter 22

To make drawing aids visible, choose Tools, Snap & Glue, and then select the Drawing Aids check box. Depending on the drawing tool you use, you'll see the following:

Line tool

- If you select the Line tool, dotted extension lines appear at 45-degree increments as you draw. This makes it easy to draw lines at 0, 45, 90, 135, 180, 225, 270, or 315 degrees from a point.

- If you select the Rectangle or Ellipse tool, drawing aids show where you can end the shape along a 45-, 135-, 225-, or 315-degree line to create a circle or square.

> **Tip**   If the Snap & Glue toolbar is visible, you can enable and disable the drawing aids by clicking the Drawing Aids tool.

Drawing Tangent Lines on Curves

Together, the shape extension lines and the Line tool make it very easy to create lines that are perfectly tangent to one or two curves, as Figure 22-12 shows.

Figure 22-12.   When you display the curve interior tangent extension line, you can draw a line that is perfectly tangent with respect to two curves.

The following steps were provided by the Visio engineer who designed this feature, which he admits many users never discover, but it's cool, and it works. Here's how:

1   Choose Tools, Snap & Glue, and then make sure that Shape Extensions and Shape Geometry are selected in the Snap To column.

2   Click the Advanced tab, select Curve Interior Tangent in the Shape Extension Options list, and then click OK.

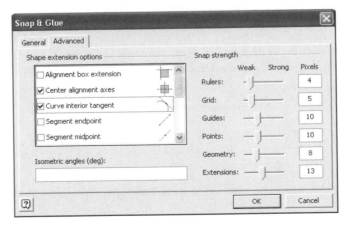

3   Click the Pencil, Ellipse, or Arc tool, and then draw the circle or curve you want.

4   Click the Line tool, and then point to the edge of the curve where you want the line to start. As you start to drag with the Line tool, an extension line appears to show you the line that is tangent with respect to the circle. Depending on the direction you drag, two lines can appear, one showing the tangent line and the other showing a perpendicular line.

5   Continue to drag on the tangent line until it turns red.

Red signifies "tangent mode." If the line doesn't turn red, try dragging slowly back and forth along the tangent line. Once you enter tangent mode, the line remains tangent to the circle as you drag. You can drag in tangent laps around the circle if you want.

6   To create a line that's tangent with respect to a second curve, drag the endpoint to the other curve until the line turns blue.

> **Tip**   To work with the first tangent point only, press the Ctrl key as you drag the line. Pressing Ctrl is also a good technique for creating a tangent line on a crowded drawing page.

Drawing Accurate Geometry with Shape Extension Lines

Just as the dynamic grid shows you options for aligning shapes, shape extension lines show you how to draw lines and arcs accurately with respect to other shapes, as Figure 22-13 shows. Displaying shape extension lines is similar to using object snaps in CAD programs. They appear on screen as dotted lines or snap points when you're using the Line, Arc, Freeform, Pencil, Ellipse, Rectangle, or Connection Point tools.

Chapter 22

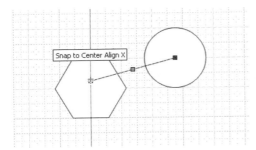

Figure 22-13. Shape extension lines show you where to snap to precise points on shape geometry.

You can choose to display different types of shape extension lines, which Visio identifies with ScreenTips as you're drawing. For example, you can draw a line that intersects another line at its exact midpoint, or you can ensure that the arc you're drawing begins and ends in exact relationship to existing shapes. Table 22-1 describes each type of shape extension line (except isometric angles, which are described shortly).

> **Tip   Turn off ScreenTips**
> ScreenTips are helpful, but they can also overcrowd your screen. To turn them off, choose Tools, Options, and then click the View tab. Clear the Other ScreenTips check box, and then click OK.

Table 22-1. Shape Extension Lines

Option	Description	Option	Description
Alignment Box Extension	Displays an extension line from the shape's alignment box so that you can align shapes by their edges	Curved Extension	Displays an extension line from an arc segment to form an ellipse or from the nearest point on a spline to extend the curve
Center Alignment Axes	Displays an extension line from the center of the shape's alignment box so that you can align shapes by their centers	Endpoint Perpendicular	Displays a perpendicular line from the nearest endpoint of a line or arc segment so that you can create two right angles with two lines

Table 22-1. Shape Extension Lines

Option	Description	Option	Description
Curve Interior Tangent	Displays an extension line that shows a curve's tangent at the midpoint of the arc segment so that you can create a tangent to the arc	Midpoint Perpendicular	Displays a perpendicular line from the midpoint of a line or arc segment so that you can create four right angles with two lines
Segment Endpoint	Highlights an endpoint of an arc or line segment so that you can connect a shape or line to a segment's endpoint	Horizontal Line At Endpoint	Displays a horizontal line (with respect to the screen) on the endpoint of a line or arc segment so that you can place a horizontal line on another line's endpoint
Segment Midpoint	Highlights a midpoint of an arc or line segment so that you can connect a shape or line to a segment's midpoint	Vertical Line At Endpoint	Displays a vertical line (with respect to the screen) on the endpoint of a line or arc segment so that you can place a vertical line on another line's endpoint
Linear Extension	Extends a line segment from the endpoint you're near so that you can see where the line would be continued	Ellipse Center Point	Highlights the center point of an ellipse so that you can connect lines to the center

Displaying Shape Extension Lines

Follow these steps to turn on shape extension lines:

1. Choose Tools, Snap & Glue.

2. Under Snap To, make sure the Shape Extensions option is selected. This option turns on any shape extensions you have selected on the Advanced tab.

3. Click the Advanced tab. In the Shape Extension Options list, select the type of extensions you want, and then click OK.

4. To display the shape extension lines, click a drawing tool, and then move the pointer toward or along a shape.

Chapter 22

Inside Out

Drawing aids vs. shape extension lines

There's some overlap in the function of drawing aids and shape extension lines, both of which appear as options in the Snap & Glue dialog box. Think of drawing aids as a simpler set of tools that show you how to draw tangent and perpendicular lines. Drawing aids do not include ScreenTips. Both drawing aids and shape extension lines use the same drawing engine.

Displaying and Controlling Isometric Alignment Tools

If you are drawing isometric diagrams (2-D drawings that represent 3-D objects), isometric extension lines can help you draw lines along isometric planes. As Figure 22-14 shows, these lines are simply a type of shape extension line, but they differ from the other types in that you can specify the angle of the line that appears when you draw. When you use a drawing tool, the isometric angle lines appear as dotted lines that extend from a vertex at an angle, or set of angles, that you specify.

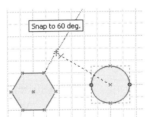

Figure 22-14. You can specify a series of isometric angles to provide snap-to points for an isometric drawing.

Follow these steps to display isometric shape extension lines:

1 Choose Tools, Snap & Glue, and then click the Advanced tab.

2 Scroll to the bottom of the Shape Extension Options list, and then select Isometric Angle Lines.

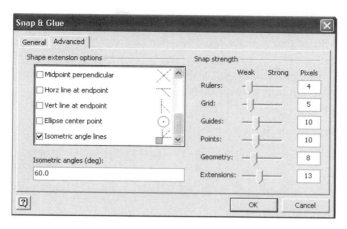

3   In the Isometric Angles (Deg) box, type the measures, in degrees, of the angles you want to use for isometric angles, separated by commas. You can specify up to 10 angles (in degrees) in this box. For example, type **30, 60, 150**.

4   Click OK.

Note   The value in the Isometric Angles (Deg) box is also used when you rotate a shape while holding down the Shift key. By default, Visio constrains the angle of rotation to 30, 45, and 60 degrees. However, if you've entered new values in the Isometric Angle field, Visio cycles through that list of angles.

Drawing Curves

Curves is shorthand for arcs and splines, distinct types of geometry that Visio can represent. If you just need to draw a wavy line or curved shape and don't care about its geometry, you can use the Pencil, Arc, or Freeform tool to do so. The fastest way to get the result you want is usually to sketch a curve quickly with one of the drawing tools, and then use the Pencil tool to edit its curvature. When you select an arc or spline with the Pencil tool, Visio displays the control point for each curve segment, which you can drag to change a line's curvature.

To change the curvature of an arc segment or spline, click the Pencil tool, and then select a shape to display its vertices and control points. Drag a control point to a new position.

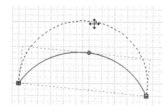

Chapter 22

Tip If you drag the control point to a position that removes the curvature between the two endpoints, the arc segment is converted to a line segment.

If the curve of an arc or spline doesn't lean quite the way you want, you can adjust its symmetry. An arc's control point has *eccentricity handles* that you can stretch and rotate to change the line's symmetry.

Follow these steps to adjust the symmetry of a curve:

1 Click the Pencil tool, and then select a shape to display its vertices and control points.

2 Click a control point to display its three handles. The two round handles are eccentricity handles, and the square shape can be used to alter the shape's size.

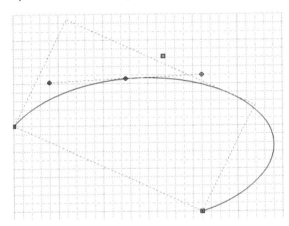

3 Drag an eccentricity handle around the control point to change the arc's angle of eccentricity (the way it leans). Drag an eccentricity handle out or in to change the arc's magnitude (the way it bulges).

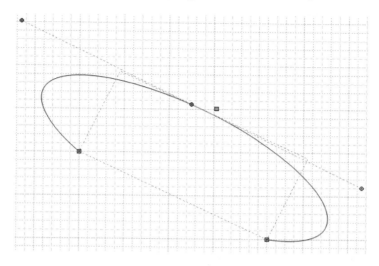

Chapter 22

 Troubleshooting

An arc's eccentricity handles don't show up

If the eccentricity handles don't appear when you select an arc segment with the Pencil tool, hold down the Ctrl key, and then drag the pointer slightly away from the control point.

Drawing Circular and Elliptical Arcs

You can create circular arcs or elliptical arcs. The Pencil tool always draws a circular arc, which is a segment of a whole circle. The Arc tool creates elliptical arcs, which are a quarter of an ellipse. Figure 22-15 shows the results of using these tools.

Tip   To create a circle, choose the Ellipse tool, and then press the Shift key as you drag.

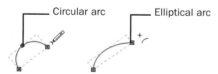

Figure 22-15.   Technically, the Pencil tool creates circular arc segments, and the Arc and Ellipse tools create elliptical arc segments.

Drawing Freeform Curves or Splines

If you don't care about the details of curve and surface geometry, consider using the Freeform tool as a fun method for drawing wavy lines called splines. Splines are a special type of curve that have unique properties that govern their behavior. This behavior affects the way you interact with splines on the drawing page. When you draw with the Freeform tool, Visio creates a NURBS, as Figure 22-16 shows. For longtime Visio users and those with a CAD background, this is significant, because the Freeform tool in older versions of Visio created only NUBSs (nonuniform B-splines). What's the difference? In a NURBS, all weights are equal, whereas in a NUBS, weights can be unequal.

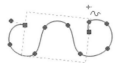

Figure 22-16. For best results with the Freeform tool, draw very slowly and keep in mind that you can always edit the results.

> **Tip**   For better results when using the Freeform tool, turn snapping off. Choose Tool, Snap & Glue, clear the Snap check box, and then click OK.

Adjusting the Freeform Tool

One way to adjust the results of the Freeform tool is to change the settings that control its actions. You can specify the precision with which the Freeform tool follows your mouse movements.

Follow these steps to adjust the Freeform tool:

1 Choose Tools, Options, and then click the Advanced tab.

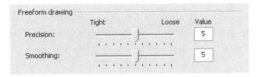

2 Under Freeform Drawing, move the Precision slider to control how tightly the Freeform tool follows your mouse actions to change from drawing a line to drawing a spline.

3 Move the Smoothing slider to affect the smoothness of the line created by your dragging actions.

4 Click OK.

Fitting a Curve to Specific Points

The Freeform tool isn't always easy to control. When your goal is precision, you might prefer to convert a polygonal line (that is, contiguous line segments) to a spline. For example, you can use the Line tool to draw a zigzag, and then convert it to a wave-like spline. In technical terms, Visio draws a spline exactly through a polygonal line's vertices. The original shape can be open or closed. If you convert a closed shape, such as a rectangle, the result is a *periodic* (seamless) spline.

Follow these steps to convert a shape to a nonperiodic spline:

1 Select the shape you want to convert.

2 Choose Shape, Operations, Fit Curve.

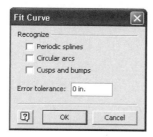

3 Clear the Periodic Splines check box. Make sure the default Error Tolerance is set to 0 in.

Tip To retain more of the original shape's angles, select the Cusps And Bumps check box.

4 Click OK to convert the shape.

Inside Out

Using error tolerance

An Error Tolerance setting of 0 converts a polygonal line to a spline that goes exactly through the vertices. When you enter a higher Error Tolerance number, you indicate a looser tolerance—that is, that you'll tolerate more error. The result is a simpler shape with fewer points that takes up less disk space.

Merging Shapes to Create New Ones

Sometimes the easiest—or only—way to create a shape is to draw several shapes and splice or merge them to get the geometry you want. Using the shape operation commands shown in Figure 22-17, you can build new shapes out of the geometry of existing shapes. *Shape operations* is a loose term for the commands on the Operations submenu of the Shape menu.

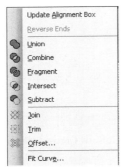

Figure 22-17. With the shape operation commands, you can create merged shapes.

In general, the shape operations work by merging the geometry of several shapes to create one new shape or by splitting out sections in cookie-cutter fashion to create several new shapes, as Figure 22-18 shows. Technically, these commands let you create *complex boundary paths*—shapes that are represented in the ShapeSheet window by multiple Geometry sections. Some shape operations apply only to 2-D shapes; others apply to lines.

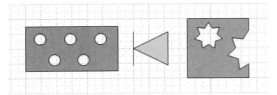

Figure 22-18. You could try to use the Pencil tool or Group command to create shapes with complex geometry like these, but the shape operation commands work faster and produce more compact shapes (in terms of disk space).

Chapter 22

> **Caution** If you are creating new shapes that include SmartShapes formulas, use the shape operation commands before you write any formulas in the ShapeSheet window. These commands work by creating a new shape and discarding the originals. Any formulas in the original shapes aren't preserved after you apply a shape operation command.

All of the commands discussed in the following sections are located on the Shape, Operations menu. These sections group the commands according to the type of shape they apply to. Commands for working with 2-D shapes are discussed first, followed by techniques for joining, trimming, and offsetting 1-D shapes (lines and arcs).

Merging 2-D Shapes with Shape Operations

When you can't create the exact shape you want using the drawing tools, you can select two or more 2-D shapes with parts of what you want and then merge shapes. The Combine, Fragment, Intersect, Subtract, and Union commands each operate on closed, 2-D shapes in a different way to produce a 2-D shape that can have both closed and open paths. Recall that a closed 2-D shape is a shape that behaves like a box and can have a fill pattern. For each command except Fragment, you select multiple shapes and choose a command to produce a single shape. Fragment produces multiple shapes. In all cases, the original shapes are discarded, so you might want to use the command on copies of your shapes, or just remember to use the Undo command if you don't get what you expected.

What's Constructive Solid Geometry Doing in a Nice Place Like Visio?

If you studied computer science, you might remember from your advanced graphics class that constructive solid geometry (CSG) is basically Boolean set operations applied to closed primitives. The three CSG operations are *union*, *intersection*, and *difference*. If you missed that class, its application to the Visio program might not be clear unless you realize that the architects of the Visio drawing engine did take the class. That's why you see the commands Union, Intersect, and Subtract on the Shape, Operations menu, and that's why the results of these commands are, in fact, logical. Sometimes these commands are referred to as the Boolean operation tools, hearkening back to their technical origins.

If you've worked in CAD programs or studied geometry, you might find that the results of the shape operation commands are predictable. For the rest of us, the shape operations provide a research opportunity—by experimenting, you will eventually find the command, or combination of commands, that gives you the result you want. It helps if you always did well on spatial relations tests. Otherwise, there's always the Undo command (Ctrl+Z).

Chapter 22

Note Selection order is very important when using these commands. The format of the first command you select will be applied to the resulting shape. For example, if you select a red shape and a green shape, in that order, and then click Intersect, the resulting shape will be red.

How the Combine Command Works

Use the Combine command when you want to create a shape, such as a picture frame or a window, that has filled and transparent (that is, closed and open) sections. The Combine command creates a new shape from two or more selected shapes. Where the shapes overlap, Visio makes the path transparent, creating holes in the new shape. The original shapes are deleted, and the new shape inherits the text and formatting of the first shape you selected.

To combine shapes, first select the first shape whose format you want to use in the resulting shape, and then press Shift+click to select the other shapes you want to merge.

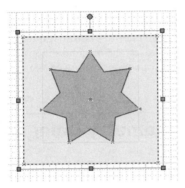

Next, choose Shape, Operations, Combine.

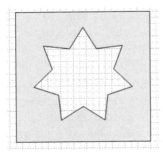

In ShapeSheet terms, the Combine command creates a new shape represented by a single ShapeSheet spreadsheet, which contains the Geometry rows from each of the original shapes.

> **Tip** If you don't get the results you want from the Combine command, try the Union or Join command.

How the Fragment Command Works

Sometimes the simplest way to create an irregular polygon or unusual shape is to use the Fragment command. When you select two or more shapes and fragment them, any overlapping areas become new 2-D shapes, and any areas enclosed by intersecting lines also become new 2-D shapes, as Figure 22-19 shows. Unlike the other shape operations discussed in this section, the Fragment command operates on 1-D shapes. For example, you can draw lines through a 2-D shape to show where you want to fragment the shape. The result of fragmenting the shapes will be multiple, small 2-D shapes formed from the areas defined by the intersecting lines. Or if you fragment three intersecting lines, you'll create a 2-D triangle from the enclosed area. None of the original shapes remain after you use the Fragment command.

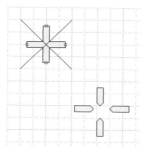

Figure 22-19. With the Fragment command, two lines and a cross shape become four new shapes, which you can pull apart.

To fragment shapes, select the first shape whose format you want to use in the resulting shape, and then press Shift+click to select the other shapes you want to merge. Next, choose Shape, Operations, Fragment.

> **Tip** If you don't get the result you want from the Fragment command, try the Trim command.

How the Intersect Command Works

To create a shape from the area enclosed by two or more overlapping shapes, use the Intersect command, which creates one new shape and deletes the originals. The resulting shape is defined by the geometry of the overlapping area. This command is often the easiest way to create irregular, curving shapes. If you select two or more shapes that don't overlap, their intersection is (in mathematical terms) an empty set, so the original shapes just disappear. Another way to think about how intersection works is that the resulting shape is a set of all the points that were common to the original shapes.

To intersect shapes, select the first shape whose format you want to use in the resulting shape, and then press Shift+click to select the other shapes you want to merge.

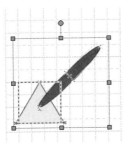

Next, choose Shape, Operations, Intersect.

How Subtract Works

To cut a shape out of another shape in cookie-cutter fashion, use the Subtract command, which creates a new shape from the geometry of the first shape you select minus the area where the second shape overlapped the first, as Figure 22-20 shows. Obviously, the order in which you select the shapes matters when you use the Subtract command. If you select more than two shapes when you use the Subtract command, Visio subtracts the shape geometry of the successive shapes from the first in the order in which you select them to create a single, new shape. All the original shapes are deleted.

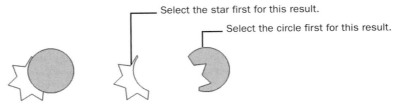

Select the star first for this result.

Select the circle first for this result.

Figure 22-20. The result of the Subtract command varies depending on selection order.

To subtract shapes, select the first shape whose format you want to use in the resulting shape, and then press Shift+click to select the other shapes you want to merge. Next, choose Shape, Operations, Subtract.

Chapter 22

How the Union Command Works

The effect of the Union command is easy to predict: it creates a new shape that encloses the entire area of the original shapes. If you select two or more overlapping shapes, the Union command creates a new shape from the total filled area of the original shapes. The original shapes are deleted.

To unite shapes, select the first shape whose format you want to use in the resulting shape, and then press Shift+click to select the other shapes you want to merge.

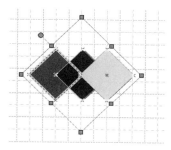

Next, choose Shape, Operations, Union.

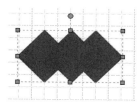

Tip   Using the Union command instead of grouping shapes

You can select shapes that don't overlap—the Union command creates a new shape that looks just like the originals, but with a single bounding box. However, you're probably better off using the Group command in cases such as this. Group behavior is more flexible.

Creating and Offsetting Lines with Shape Operations

When you want to combine and split apart lines, Visio includes the Join, Offset, and Trim commands, which might look familiar if you've ever worked with CAD software. Unlike the shape operations discussed earlier, these commands are designed specifically to operate on 1-D shapes. For example, you can draw a series of overlapping lines, and then use the Join command to create a 2-D grid shape.

How the Join Command Works

The Join command works a lot like the Combine command. Sometimes they're interchangeable. However, the Join command is specifically intended to merge selected 1-D line and arc segments into paths. The resulting shape is always a 2-D shape, even if it still looks like a line. Because the Join command is intended to operate on lines, it ignores fill color or patterns that are applied to the original shapes; the resulting shape has no fill, but inherits the text and line formats of the first shape you selected. The original shapes are deleted.

To join shapes, select the first shape whose format you want to use in the resulting shape, and then press Shift+click to select the other shapes you want to merge.

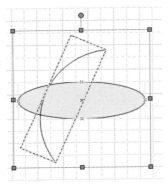

Next, choose Shape, Operations, Join.

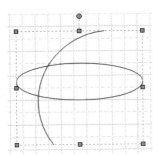

Chapter 22

Tip **Join and combine shapes**
Although the Join command is similar to the Combine command, you can see the difference when you use them on filled shapes. The Join command ignores fill color, so you won't get the cookie-cutter shape that the Combine command can produce.

How the Offset Command Works

The Offset command is the best way to quickly produce grids, concentric rings, and repeating patterns that must be exactly spaced. It creates a set of parallel lines and curves at a specified distance from either side of the original shape, as Figure 22-21 shows. You can use the command to offset line segments from an original 2-D shape, but it's designed to operate on 1-D shapes. Unlike the other shape operations, you can apply the Offset command to a single shape (which results in three offset shapes); the original shape is not deleted.

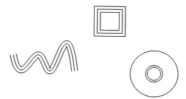

Figure 22-21.   With the Offset command, a single line becomes three lines offset by a specified distance.

To offset shapes, select a shape, and then choose Shape, Operations, Offset.

In the Offset Distance box, type the exact distance at which to offset the new lines, and then click OK.

Note   If you offset a filled shape, the resulting shapes will not be filled, but you can apply a fill color or pattern to them.

How the Trim Command Works

The Trim command splits two or more shapes where their lines intersect. This command is similar to the Fragment command. However, the Trim command analyzes the intersecting and overlapping lines of selected shapes, whereas Fragment looks at intersecting and overlapping shape areas. As with most other shape operations, the Trim command deletes the original shapes.

Chapter 22

Follow these steps to trim shapes:

1 Select the first shape whose format you want to use in the resulting shape, and then press Shift+click to select the other shapes you want to merge.

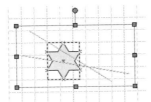

2 Choose Shape, Operations, Trim.

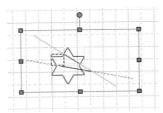

3 To see the new shapes more easily, drag them apart.

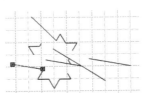

A noteworthy and counterintuitive side effect of the Trim command is that it produces only 2-D shapes. Even if the trimmed bits look like lines, Visio defines them as 2-D objects. You can trim filled shapes, but the resulting shapes won't be filled, although they do inherit the text and line styles of the first shape you select.

Working with Groups

When you want to be able to move several shapes together as a unit, the simplest thing to do is group them: select the shapes, and then press Shift+Ctrl+G. When you want to ungroup a group, press Shift+Ctrl+U (or use the commands on the Shape, Grouping menu). That might be all you need to know about groups. However, Visio groups are actually quite smart, meaning they have editing and behavior options that you can control. Moreover, many Visio shapes are groups, as Figure 22-22 shows, and these groups have been designed with special behavior that affects the way you select and format them. So if you want to know savvy techniques for revising existing groups, or all the ways to create and control your own groups, read on.

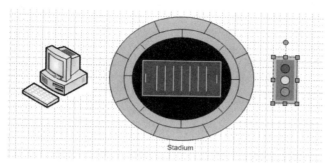

Figure 22-22. Many Visio master shapes are groups. These master shapes were made by grouping several differently formatted shapes to create a single, easy-to-use object.

Because a group is an object, it can include attributes that are independent of the shapes in the group. Accordingly, you might want to create a group in the following situations:

- **You want a single object with parts that are formatted differently**   In a group, each shape can have different styles and formats applied to it while still moving and sizing together as a group. For example, the Title Block Corporate 1 shape from the Borders And Titles stencil is a group with multiple text shapes. Because it is configured this way, the title can appear in a large font in one text box, the file details can appear in a smaller font in a different text box, and the whole title block can work as a single object.

- **You want to keep several shapes together**   A group unites shapes in your drawing while retaining the ability to work with each shape independently within the group. Shapes in a group can be subselected, and then moved, resized, or rotated.

- **You want an object with component parts that can be reconstituted if necessary**   You can always ungroup a group to restore its original shapes; however, the original shapes used during a shape operation such as the Combine command cannot be recovered.

> **Note**   You can create a group using more than just shapes. A group can be any combination of shapes, guides (the blue lines you drag out from the rulers), other groups, and objects from other programs.

There are also programmatic reasons for creating a group. When you group shapes, references to the group are inserted into each shape's ShapeSheet. You can define shape formulas for each shape as well as for the group, and you can make the shape and group formulas interdependent. For example, a shape formula can specify unique sizing behavior as a function of the group size. When you ungroup shapes, the group's ShapeSheet is discarded, which breaks any custom formulas that refer to the group.

Chapter 22

Inside Out

Group ShapeSheets

Technically, a group is a separate type of object in Visio. Each shape in a group is represented by a ShapeSheet, and the group is also represented by a ShapeSheet. The group's ShapeSheet stores attributes and behaviors of the group, but not of the shapes in it. For example, when a group is resized, its behavior is a property of the group, and the setting that controls sizing is stored in the Group Properties ShapeSheet section.

Troubleshooting

Visio displays a message when ungrouping

When you ungroup certain shapes that came from a Visio stencil, the following message appears:

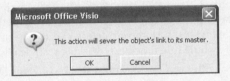

The explanation for this message is rather technical, but the short answer is to click OK if you're really sure you want to ungroup the object.

Here's the long answer: every time you drag a master shape from a stencil onto the drawing page, you create an instance of the master. The instance—that is, the shape you see on the drawing page—remains linked to its master and inherits formulas from the master. That way, if you have 100 instances of the same master in a diagram, which could easily happen in a diagram such as an organization chart, the formulas used to create that shape are stored in only one place, which makes for smaller file sizes. When you ungroup a group, you're destroying the object (the group) that is linked to the master. If that object no longer exists, Visio obviously can't link it to anything, and so the warning message appears.

Identifying Groups

It's easy to confuse groups and merged shapes, those complex shapes that result from using a shape operation command. To verify that a shape is really a group, select the shape, and then choose Format, Special. If you see Group in the Type field, it's a group, as Figure 22-23 shows.

Chapter 22

Figure 22-23. One sure way to identify a group is to use the Format, Special command and inspect the Type field.

Here are some other ways to tell whether an object is a group:

- Select the object, and then choose Format, Behavior. If the options under Group Behavior appear dimmed, the object is not a group.
- Select the object, and then press Shift+Ctrl+U (Ungroup command). If you can ungroup it, it was a group. (You can also ungroup certain types of imported objects, such as metafiles, to convert them to Visio shapes.)
- Select the object, and then choose Window, Show ShapeSheet. If it's a group, you'll see the Group Properties section when you scroll down.

Editing Shapes in a Group

You can subselect a shape in a group by double-clicking it, and then move or format the shape while retaining its group membership. When you subselect a shape, the selection handles have small Xs, as Figure 22-24 shows. If the shape is locked, gray boxes appear instead, and you might not be able to format or reposition the shape depending on the type of lock that's been set.

Chapter 22

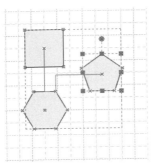

Figure 22-24. Depending on a group's behavior settings, you can subselect an individual shape that is a member of a group to edit or move it.

You can add a shape to or remove one from an existing group with a single command, so you don't have to ungroup and regroup. Table 22-2 summarizes how to edit shapes in a group.

Table 22-2. Techniques for Editing Shapes in a Group

Task	Technique
Edit shapes in a group	Select the group, and then click a shape in the group to subselect it. Format or move the subselected shape or its text.
Add a shape to a group	Select the shape and the group, and then choose Shape, Grouping, Add To Group.
Remove a shape from a group	Subselect the shape you want to remove from the group, and then choose Shape, Grouping, Remove From Group.

Subselecting Shapes in Locked Groups

What if you can't subselect a shape in a group? Some Visio groups are set to prevent subselection, but you can reset this option as follows:

1 Select the group, and then choose Format, Behavior.

2 In the Group Behavior area, check the setting in the Selection list. If Group Only appears, the group has been protected to prevent subselection.

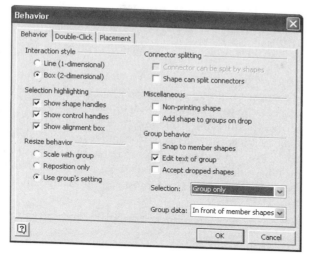

3 Change the Selection option to Group First or Members First, and then click OK.

> For details about the behavior options for groups, see "Controlling Shape Behavior in Groups," page 676.

Troubleshooting

When you subselect a shape in a group, you can't reposition the shape

Tucked into a group's ShapeSheet spreadsheet is an option that prevents you from moving the group's component shapes, or *children* as the option refers to them. The only way to reset this option is to edit the group's ShapeSheet settings as follows:

1 Select the group, and then choose Window, Show ShapeSheet.

2 Scroll down until you see the Group Properties section, which includes a cell labeled DontMoveChildren in the right column. If the value of this cell is TRUE, you've identi-fied the problem—the group is locked to prevent shapes from moving.

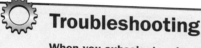

Group Properties					
SelectMode	1	IsTextEditTarget	TRUE	IsDropTarget	FALSE
DisplayMode	2	IsSnapTarget	FALSE	DontMoveChildren	TRUE

3 Click the DontMoveChildren cell (not the label), type **FALSE**, and then press Enter.

Editing Locked Groups

If you edit the groups that come with Visio stencils, you will probably encounter the message shown in Figure 22-25. Visio displays this message when a group is locked to prevent ungrouping.

Chapter 22

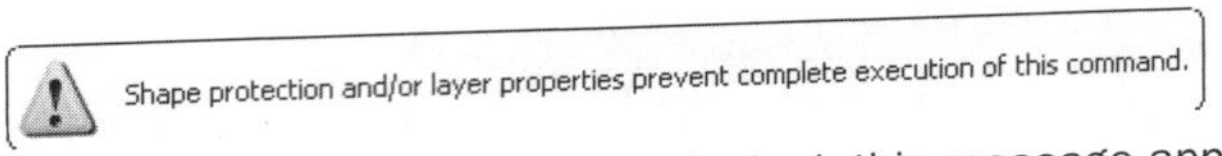

 Shape protection and/or layer properties prevent complete execution of this command.

Figure 22-25. When a group is locked, this message appears when you try to ungroup it.

Group behavior and protection options can be set to prohibit certain actions, but these protections are designed to make the group work the way you expect (or the way the shape designers think you expect it to work). Protection settings prevent you from accidentally resetting any SmartShapes formulas the group might include. For example, the 3-D Box shape on the Blocks stencil is a group with a control handle that lets you adjust the box's depth. The shape is locked so that you can't ungroup it, because doing so would remove the control handle's built-in behavior. This option to lock a group is found only in the ShapeSheet window, so to change the lock, you must edit the group's ShapeSheet settings.

 Inside Out

Unlocking with care

When unlocking groups, one caveat applies: groups are typically locked for a good reason. To be on the safe side, make a copy before you ungroup or unlock a protected group. If you're working with a group that came from a Visio stencil, remember that you can always restore the group from the stencil if there's a problem.

Follow these steps to unlock a locked group:

1 Select the group, and then choose Window, Show ShapeSheet.
2 Scroll down until you see the Protection section, which includes a cell labeled Lock-Group in the right column.
3 Click the LockGroup cell (not the label), type **0**, and then press Enter.

You have now changed the value of the LockGroup cell from 1 (or true, meaning that the group is locked) to 0 (or false, meaning that it's no longer locked). Now you can close the ShapeSheet window and ungroup the group by pressing Shift+Ctrl+U.

Editing Locked Shapes in a Group

Sometimes, a shape in a group will be locked against moving or resizing. When you subselect a locked shape in the group, gray selection handles appear around the shape, and you can't resize it. For example, the square in the simple grouping in Figure 22-26 is locked against resizing.

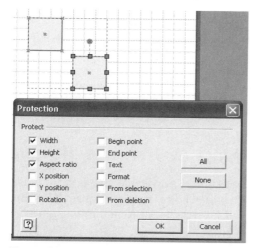

Figure 22-26. When you select a group and see solid gray handles, it's your clue that protection locks have been set. To change the locks, choose Format, Protection.

To unlock a shape in a group, select the group, and then click the shape to subselect it. Next, choose Format, Protection, and then clear the Width, Height, or other check boxes that you want to unlock. Click OK.

Editing in the Group Window

Sometimes it's easier to edit grouped shapes when you work in the group window, in which Visio displays a group as if it were an entire drawing of independent shapes, as Figure 22-27 shows. The shapes are not rotated in the group window even if the group is rotated on the drawing page, so you can more easily align shapes with the grid, guides, and rulers. You can select and edit the shapes individually in the group window by using the same menus and tools as in the drawing window. As you make changes in the group window, the group is updated immediately on the main drawing page.

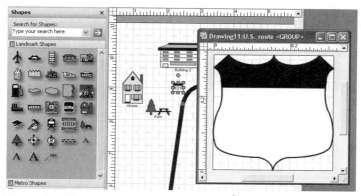

Figure 22-27. You can switch between the group window and the main drawing page by clicking the title bar of the window in which you want to work.

Chapter 22

675

Follow these steps to display a group in the group window:

1 Select a group, and then choose Edit, Open Group. If the group has a name, the command replaces Group with the group's name; for example, Open Interstate.

2 Select and edit the shapes as you would if you were working on the drawing page. As long as the group window is active, the commands apply to the shapes in that window.

3 Click the Close button for the group window to save your changes and return to the drawing window.

Repairing a Group's Alignment Box

For a group, the alignment box is the selection rectangle that usually surrounds the group tightly. If you reposition the shapes in a group, however, the alignment box's dimensions might not match the group. You can quickly reset its size to fit the group's new dimensions.

To reset an alignment box, select a group, then choose Shape, Operations, Update Alignment Box.

Inside Out

What the alignment box is for

The purpose of the alignment box is to make a shape easier to align to the grid or other shapes. For some shapes, the alignment box doesn't match the shape's outline, because that's how the shape should align in that diagram type. For example, the Bridge shape on the Road Shapes stencil is a 1-D group with a customized alignment box that makes it easier to connect the shape to road shapes.

Controlling Shape Behavior in Groups

If you want to know why a Visio-made group acts the way it does, or if you want to design your own groups, you can investigate the group behavior options. Group behavior includes the way shapes in a group are resized when a group is resized, the order in which shapes can be subselected in a group and whether they can be subselected, and other rather esoteric options designed with professional shape programmers in mind.

To define the behavior for a group, select the group, and then choose Format, Behavior. The Behavior tab of the Behavior dialog box includes options that apply to groups, as Figure 22-28 shows.

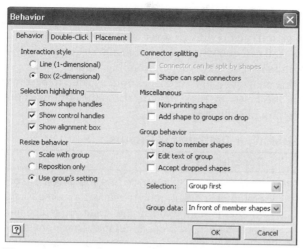

Figure 22-28. The Group Behavior settings in the Behavior dialog box are available only when you select a group.

The sections that follow tell you which options to use and when.

Controlling How Shapes Are Sized in Groups

The Resize Behavior options are useful when you're working with shapes that represent real-world objects. You probably wouldn't need these settings in a flowchart, but an office layout is another matter. The classic example used in Visio documentation is a kitchen countertop with appliances. You can group the appliances and countertop so that you can move them around as a unit in your house plan. You can even resize the group because you want the countertop to be longer. However, you wouldn't want the shapes in the group—the stove and sink—to stretch out of proportion. They represent industry-standard sizes. Table 22-3 describes the options.

Table 22-3. Resize Shape Behavior Options for Groups

Option	Description
Scale With Group	This setting means that shapes are sized proportionally when the group is resized.
Reposition Only	The shapes are repositioned as the group is resized; the individual shapes do not change in size (as in the kitchen countertop and appliances example).
Use Group's Setting	This option is the default for most Visio shapes and specifies that the shape will behave as the group does.

Chapter 22

Controlling How Shapes Are Added to Groups

Among the intriguing things you can do with groups is specify whether new shapes can be added to a group, and how. You can quickly add a shape to an existing group by selecting both the shape and group, and then choosing Shape, Grouping, Add To Group. However, you can set a behavior option that allows you to drag shapes onto a group to become part of the group. You can also prevent this behavior. Table 22-4 describes the options in the Behavior dialog box for controlling group membership.

Table 22-4. Add Shape Behavior Options for Groups

Option	Description
Add Shape To Groups On Drop	When selected, this option lets you drag a shape or group on top of another group to make it a member of the group. For this to work, though, the group you're adding to must have the Accept Dropped Shapes check box selected. This check box appears in the Miscellaneous section.
Accept Dropped Shapes	When selected, this option allows a group to accept as a member a shape or group that you drag on top of it, provided that the Add Shape To Groups On Drop check box has been selected for the prospective member shape. This check box appears in the Group Behavior section.

Controlling How Shapes and Groups Are Selected

When you click a group, what happens? The Behavior dialog box provides options that let you determine the answer to this question. Most of the time, when you click a group, the group is selected. You click again, and one of the shapes in the group is subselected. However, selection behavior doesn't have to work this way. Some Visio groups are set so that you can't subselect the component shapes. For example, the Bridge shape on the Road Shapes stencil includes this behavior, because the group doesn't contain any shapes you're likely to want to edit. Table 22-5 describes the options in the Behavior dialog box that control how groups and shapes are selected.

Table 22-5. Selection Behavior Options for Groups

Option	Description
Group Only	When selected, this option means that no matter how many times you click a group, you'll select only the group. You cannot subselect shapes in the group. If you clear this check box, you can subselect the group's shapes.

Table 22-5. **Selection Behavior Options for Groups**

Option	Description
Group First	When selected, this option specifies that the first time you click a group, the group is selected. The second click selects the shape you're pointing to. This is the behavior you encounter most of the time with Visio shapes.
Members First	When selected, this option specifies that the first time you click a group, the shape you're pointing to is selected. The second click selects the group if you're pointing to the group's bounding box; otherwise, the text insertion point appears in the shape. This setting is useful when the priority is access to the shapes in a group.

Controlling Group Text and Display

Because a group is an object, it has properties, including text, that are independent of the shapes in the group. Visio shape designers often take advantage of this fact to create master shapes that are easy to type in. Table 22-6 summarizes the options for controlling the display of group attributes, such as text.

Table 22-6. **Group Behavior Options**

Option	Description
Edit Text Of Group	This check box lets you control whether or not you can edit the text of a group.
Hide	This option in the Group Data list hides a group's text. You can type in a group for which this option is selected, but the text won't appear on the screen. The text is stored with the group and reappears if you choose a different behavior. This option makes it easier to type in shapes with multiple text boxes and makes it more likely that the text will end up in the right place. The Hide option does not hide a group's connection points or control handles.
Behind Member Shapes	This option in the Group Data list places the group's text behind the other shapes in the group.
In Front Of Member Shapes	This option in the Group Data list is the default used by most Visio shapes and places the group's text in front of the shapes in the group.

Chapter 22

Controlling Glue in Groups

Some groups are designed to be connected to other shapes. For example, a door in an office layout is a group that you can connect to a wall, which is another group. When you create a group, you can control whether the component shapes in the group can be connected to other shapes or just the group. The default behavior for Visio groups is to enable snapping and glue for the component shapes, but, as in the case of the door and wall shapes, that might not be the behavior you want.

In the Behavior dialog box, the Snap To Member Shapes check box controls group snapping and gluing behavior. When this check box is selected, you can connect the shapes in a group to other shapes, and the shapes' connection points are visible. By clearing this check box, you ensure that connectors and other shapes can be glued to the whole group only. Connection points on the group's component shapes are hidden.

Chapter 23

Defining Styles, Patterns, and Colors

If you open a Microsoft Office Visio 2003 template and drag Visio master shapes onto a page to create a diagram, you typically don't need to think much about styles, patterns, or colors. Most everything is formatted for you—styles are already included in the template, and an instant color scheme is only a click away. If you're not content with the options Visio provides, however, you have a lot of leeway to customize, as this chapter describes.

When you want to change the way a shape looks, you probably click a formatting button. However, styles give you a faster way to consistently format all the shapes in a diagram. Shape designers need to understand style theory as well. What if a formatting button doesn't include a satisfactory pattern or the exact color you want? This chapter goes inside Visio style theory and explains how to customize styles, patterns, and even colors and color palettes.

Understanding Text, Line, and Fill Styles

If you've used styles in Microsoft Office Word 2003 to format documents, you understand what a time-saver they can be. You select some text, choose a style from the style list on the toolbar, and you're done. Styles in Visio work in much the same way to give shapes a consistent look and make them easier to revise. However, in Visio, you can apply styles to shapes as well as text. That difference makes Visio styles unique.

Think of a Visio style as a collection of text, line, and fill formats that have a name. For example, the Flow Normal style is applied to flowchart shapes to provide a consistent look. What the Flow Normal style actually applies is 8-point Arial text with 2-point margins, a black border with a specified thickness (line weight) around shapes, and solid white fill color in shapes. All Visio templates come with some styles built in. You can see the styles in the Style list on the Formatting toolbar, as Figure 23-1 shows. The five styles you always see are Guide, Normal, None, Text Only, and No Style.

Figure 23-1. The Style list on the Formatting toolbar displays all the built-in styles that come with a template; styles from the Basic Flowchart template are shown here.

Applying Styles from the Style Lists

Visio lists all styles in the Style list on the Formatting toolbar regardless of whether they apply a line, fill, or text format. However, Visio also includes style lists on the Format Text toolbar and Format Shape toolbar, which you can display by choosing View, Toolbars as Figure 23-2 shows. You can also apply styles using the Styles command on the Format menu. Unnecessary redundancy? As it turns out, there's a method to this madness. Depending on which style list you work from, different formats can be applied, which matters when a single style specifies text, line, and fill attributes, and you want to apply only one set of attributes.

Figure 23-2. For quick access to line and fill styles, you can display the Format Shape toolbar (top). To apply text styles, display the Format Text toolbar (bottom).

For example, the Flow Normal style appears in Text Style, List Style, and Fill Style lists, which are displayed on the Format Text and Format Shape toolbars, as Figure 23-3 shows. There is only one Flow Normal style, but its effects can differ depending on the list from which you select the style. Weird? Maybe, but it gives you flexibility. Here's how it works:

Figure 23-3. A Visio style can appear in the Text Style, Line Style, and Fill Style lists. The list's appearance shows you whether the style applies a text (left), line (center), or fill format.

- **Text Style** If you apply a style from this list, and the style also specifies line and fill attributes, Visio asks you whether you want to apply the line and fill formats.

- **Line Style** If you apply a style from this list, and the style also specifies text and fill attributes, Visio asks you whether you want to apply the text and fill formats.
- **Fill Style** If you apply a style from this list, and the style also specifies text and line attributes, Visio asks you whether you want to apply the text and line formats.
- **Style** If you apply a style from this list, all of the style's attributes—text, line, and fill—are applied to the selected shape, no questions asked.

Knowing how the style toolbars work will help prevent style mishaps . However, it's hard to tell from the style name alone which type of formatting will be applied. Visio helps you out with a message as Figure 23-4 shows. When Visio asks, "Do you want to apply all of the included formatting," you have two choices, and both result in something being formatted:

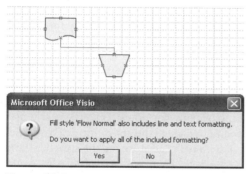

Figure 23-4.   If you select a style from the Fill Style list, Visio prompts you before applying the style's line and text formats to the shape.

- Click Yes to apply all formatting to the shape (and risk the possibility of unexpected behavior, such as a solid black shape).
- Click No to apply formatting for the single attribute identified by the name of the style list. That is, if you click the style in the Line Styles list, choosing No applies only the line attributes of the style.

With either option, some formatting will be applied. You can't cancel the action, but you can click Ctrl+Z to reverse the results.

Tip   Checking a style's attributes

To tell how many attributes a style applies, choose Format, Define Styles. In the Style list, select the style you're interested in. In the Includes area, you'll see a check mark beside each attribute that the style formats.

Chapter 23

Troubleshooting

Nothing happens when a style is applied to a shape

If you select a shape and apply a style, and nothing happens, the shape might be locked or guarded. Some shapes include built-in protections that prevent you from formatting them when the format might disrupt the shape's smart behavior. Sometimes you can work around these protections, and sometimes you can't. For details, see "Formatting Locked Shapes," page 687.

Formatting Versus Applying Styles

For most people, the difference between applying a style or manually formatting a shape is really just the command they use. For Visio, the difference between manual formats and those applied by a style is in how the change is stored. Now we're talking file mechanics, and this is an interesting topic only if you plan to design your own templates or want to understand how actions on the drawing page affect shape formats. The Visio term for the formats you apply manually is *local formatting*—"local" because the changes affect settings that Visio saves with each shape. You apply a local format when you select a shape and use a toolbar button or command on the Format menu to change the appearance of text, line, or fill. In contrast, a style applies a *global format*, because Visio stores all the style definitions for a diagram in one place—that is, globally. If you're working with a diagram that contains many shapes, you'll get better performance if you use styles rather than local formatting to format your shapes.

Troubleshooting

When you copy shapes to another Visio drawing file, their formatting changes

If you created or edited styles in your Visio diagram, and then copied it or parts of it to another Visio diagram, formats specified for the new diagram can override those in your shapes. This happens when the destination diagram has a style of the same name as the one you used to format your shapes. If the style in the new diagram is defined to format shapes differently, its styles will be applied to your shapes. To avoid reformatting, you can redefine your styles in the original Visio diagram to match those of the target diagram, or you can rename your Visio styles so that they don't match and your style will be used. For details, see "Creating and Editing Styles," page 688.

Comparing Color Schemes and Styles

Applying a color scheme is similar to applying a style in that it's a quick technique for making widespread changes in a diagram. Color schemes, however, are different from styles in the way they interact with locally formatted shapes. When you apply a color scheme in a diagram type that supports their use (most of the business diagram types do), all the shapes, titles, borders, and backgrounds adopt coordinating colors from the scheme—unless you have locally formatted a shape's line and fill colors. Visio ignores locally formatted shapes, including shapes you create, so the color scheme isn't applied to them. After you apply a color scheme, the diagram's shapes retain their original style assignments.

For example, a flowchart is a diagram type that supports color schemes. To apply a color scheme, right-click a page, and then choose Color Schemes. All the flowchart shapes you dropped into the diagram from the flowchart stencil will be filled with a color from the scheme—with the exception of any shapes that include manually formatted line and fill colors, as Figure 23-5 shows. Manually formatted colors remain unchanged.

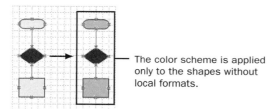

The color scheme is applied only to the shapes without local formats.

Figure 23-5. This flowchart's locally formatted Decision shape remains the same before and after applying a color scheme to the drawing.

What if you want all the shapes to adopt the color scheme colors? This is where styles and color schemes overlap to your advantage. If you restore the original styles to a shape, it will assume the color scheme automatically. To do this, see "Restoring the Factory Default Shape Formats," page 687.

Why does this work? The answer lies in how Visio really applies a color scheme. A color scheme maps new color values to existing style definitions. All shapes formatted with those styles adopt the new color scheme. That's why reapplying the master's format also applies the color scheme, and that's why some master shapes don't work with color schemes.

Inside Out

True color (32-bit) displays

If you have a true color (32-bit) display, you can see that the style definitions change to use the color scheme. After applying a color scheme, expand the Fill Style list on the Format Shape toolbar to see the new colors.

Overriding and Protecting Shape Formats

If you format a shape and then apply a style, you run the risk of losing the formats you applied. That's because applying a style resets all the formatting options that come with the style. In Visio terms, Visio *overrides* local formatting. This behavior can be a little unsettling

Chapter 23

685

if you're used to the way Word works. In Word, you can individually format one word in a sentence—for example, apply italics—and then choose a different style for the paragraph, and the italics format will be retained. Visio doesn't preserve individual, local formats as Word does unless you know a few tricks.

One trick is to use the Style command on the Format menu, rather than the style lists on the toolbars. Then you can apply a style and prevent it from overriding your local formatting by selecting the Preserve Local Formatting check box, as Figure 23-6 shows. If you don't select the Preserve Local Formatting check box, Visio applies the new style and overrides any local formatting.

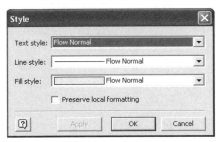

Figure 23-6.   The Preserve Local Formatting check box in the Style dialog box lets you save any manual formatting you've applied to a shape and still apply the style.

Another trick is to use the toolbar style lists, but choose carefully. For example, if you've manually formatted the text for a number of flowchart shapes but want to apply a style that changes their fill color, choose a style from the Fill Styles list. When Visio displays the message that asks you whether you want to apply the style's line and text formats as well, click No. That way, Visio applies only the fill formatting in the style, thus preserving your local text formatting.

Tip   **Format multiple shapes**

Of course you can also format multiple shapes by selecting them by either Shift+clicking on each in turn or lassoing them, right-clicking, and then selecting Format. The format you choose is applied to the selected shapes. By the same token, you can select a shape with the format you desire, double–click the Format Painter tool, and then click multiple shapes you wish to format. It's no fuss, and very little muss.

Inside Out

Checking for local formatting

How can you tell that a shape has been locally formatted? You can't—not if you look on the drawing page. However, if you look at the shape in the ShapeSheet window, the settings that represent local formats—that is, your edits to the shape—appear as blue formulas.

Restoring the Factory Default Shape Formats

You can remove local formatting from a shape and restore its original styles. One reason to do this is to make sure shapes look consistent when you're creating a new stencil or to make sure a shape adopts a diagram's color scheme. The Styles command provides an easy way to restore the styles that came with the master shape, as Figure 23-7 shows.

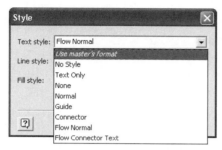

Figure 23-7. You can restore the default styles with the Format, Style command.

To restore default styles to a shape, first select a shape, and then choose Format, Style. Next, click the Text Style drop-down arrow, and then select Use Master's Format. Repeat for the Line Style and Fill Style lists, and then click OK.

> **Note** This technique works only when you're using shapes that you dragged from a stencil. If you created the shape on the page, it didn't come from a master, so nothing happens when you select Use Master's Format. Conversely, if you save the shape to a custom stencil, and subsequently use that stencil in another drawing, it becomes a master, with its own master properties.

Formatting Locked Shapes

Visio shapes can be protected against formatting. When you try to apply a style to a protected shape, you might see the error message shown in Figure 23-8, or you might see nothing at all. It depends on whether the shape was *locked* or *guarded*, two methods of protecting formatting that can affect your ability to interact with shapes on the drawing page. Shape designers usually have good reasons for locking a shape, but that doesn't mean you don't have an equally good reason for unlocking it. It's always fun to defeat shape protections and have your way, but be prepared for odd results. Sometimes those locked formulas can have a domino effect on shape appearance or behavior.

Shape protection and/or layer properties prevent complete execution of this command.

Figure 23-8. Visio prevents you from editing a shape that's been locked.

Removing Style Locks

To reset a shape so that you can apply a style, you must edit its ShapeSheet settings. To be on the safe side, make a copy of the shape first, and then edit the copy.

Follow these steps to unlock a shape:

1 Select the locked shape, and then choose Window, ShapeSheet.

2 Scroll down until you see the Protection section.

If you don't see this section, choose View, Sections, select the Protection check box, and then click OK.

3 Click in the LockFormat cell, type **0**, and then press Enter. The shape is now unlocked, because a value of 0 (or false) disables the lock. You can close the ShapeSheet window and then apply a style or format.

> **Tip**   The ShapeSheet-challenged among us might prefer to right-click on the locked shape. Next choose Format, Protection, and click None. Click OK, and you are done.

Formatting Guarded Shapes

Sometimes you try to apply a style or choose a format, and nothing happens—no error message, no format change, nothing. It might be that the shape includes guarded ShapeSheet settings that prevent you from making the change. If you're a shape programmer, the GUARD function is a useful way to protect your formulas. If you're a user who wants to format a guarded shape, there aren't any simple workarounds. Formulas are guarded so that they aren't overwritten when users interact with shapes, and usually that's a good thing. It keeps the shape behaving the way it's supposed to.

> For details about the GUARD function, see "Protecting Shape Formulas," page 745.

Creating and Editing Styles

You can edit existing styles, create your own from scratch, and delete styles you no longer need. Editing existing styles is a quick way to simultaneously format any shapes with that style in your diagram. Defining new styles is useful when you're building your own templates or can't find a style in the template you're using. You can revise, create, and delete styles by choosing Format, Define Styles, as shown in Figure 23-9.

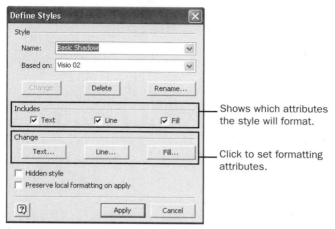

Shows which attributes the style will format.

Click to set formatting attributes.

Figure 23-9. Choose Format, Define Styles to display this dialog box, where you can edit, create, and delete styles.

The Define Styles dialog box is set up to make it easy for you to chug through multiple style definitions. You can edit or define a style and then apply your changes without closing the dialog box, so you can edit or define the next style. The dialog box also shows you whether a style defines more than one attribute: in the Includes area, a check mark appears beside the types of formatting defined by the style.

Note Because Visio tracks styles based on their name, you can't create a new style with a name that's already assigned to another style in the same diagram.

Visio saves your edited or new styles with the diagram. If you want your styles to be available in other diagrams, you can copy the styles to that diagram. For details, see "Copying Styles and Color Schemes to Other Diagrams," page 692. Or you can save your work as a template, which you can use again. When you save a diagram as a template, the styles will be included in every new drawing you create using that template.

Creating a New Text, Line, or Fill Style

Styles in Visio are always based on other styles. In effect, you're never starting entirely from scratch when you create a new style. Your custom style inherits baseline attributes from a "parent" style, which you specify in the Define Styles dialog box by choosing an option in the Based On list, as Figure 23-10 shows.

Chapter 23

Figure 23-10. A style is based on the attributes of the style selected in the Based On list.

The advantage to basing a style on another style is that you specify a particular attribute, such as 10-point Verdana text, only once. Then, as long as your new styles are based on the parent style with 10-point Verdana text, you won't have to keep repeating the Text settings every time you create a new style. If you suddenly decide that your diagrams would look better with 12-point Verdana text, you can edit the parent style definition, and all other styles based on the parent will inherit the new formats.

The disadvantage to basing one style on another is that if you delete the parent style, the remaining style will instead be based on the parent's parent. When you don't want to deal with style inheritance, you can base your style on one of the four built-in styles that cannot be deleted: Normal, None, Text Only, and No Style.

Basing a New Style on a Shape

A fast way to define a new style is to format a shape with all the attributes you want your style to have and then define a style based on the shape. That way, you can see the results of your choices.

To create a new style based on a shape, follow these steps:

1 Select a shape, and then use the buttons on the Formatting toolbar or the Text, Line, and Fill commands on the Format menu to specify all the attributes you want.

2 When your shape looks the way you want, choose Format, Define Styles.

3 In the Style area, in the Name list, select <New Style>. Visio fills in the attributes for the new style based on your selection. For example, if you formatted the selected shape with 12-point Verdana text, the new style is already set to 12-point Verdana text.

4 Click in the Name list, type a name for the style, and then click Add to add the style to the diagram. The dialog box stays open, so you can create a new style.

Defining a New Style from Scratch

Follow these steps to create a new style from scratch:

1 Make sure nothing is selected, and then choose Format, Define Styles.

2 In the Style area, in the Name list, type a name for the style.

3 In the Based On list, select an existing style that includes attributes you want to base the new style on. If you don't want to base your style on an existing one, select No Style.

4 In the Includes area, check the attributes that you want your style to apply.

5 In the Change area, click a button to specify the settings for that attribute. For example, click Text; specify font, paragraph, tab, and other settings; and then click OK. Then click Line and repeat the process, and so on for all the attributes you want your style to apply.

6 When the style contains the settings you want, click Add to add the style to the diagram.

7 If you want to apply the new style to any shapes that are selected, click Apply; otherwise, click Close.

Inside Out

Inside text, line, and fill

Although a style includes formatting attributes for text, line, and fill, these check boxes are really used by Visio to determine which of the toolbar style lists should include your new style.

Tip   **Choosing styles to display in the toolbar lists**
In the Define Styles dialog box, select the Hidden Style check box to prevent a style from appearing in any of the toolbar style lists. However, the style name still appears in the Define Styles dialog box and in the Drawing Explorer window.

Editing Existing Styles

An easy way to make sweeping changes across your diagram is to edit an existing style. All shapes formatted with that style are updated to reflect the changes you make to the style.

Follow these steps to edit a style:

1 Choose Format, Define Styles.

2 In the Name list, select the style you want to edit.

3 In the Change area, click a button to change formatting options for that attribute. For example, click Fill, specify the color and pattern settings you want, and then click OK.

4   Click Change to update the style definition and all shapes to which the style is applied.

5   To edit another style, select one in the Name list; otherwise, click Close.

Deleting a Style

Deleting styles is a clean-up task that helps keep your diagram file tidy. Mostly, this doesn't matter much unless you plan to save your diagram as a template, in which case you don't want extra styles lying around. Deleting styles is also a good way to change style inheritance, a concept introduced earlier. When you delete a style, any other styles based on that style will inherit from the deleted style's parent instead. If the new parent specifies different formatting attributes, you can see a ripple effect as new attributes are inherited by the remaining styles, and shapes formatted with those styles change.

Follow these steps to delete a style:

1   Choose Format, Define Styles.

2   In the Name list, select the name of the style you want to delete.

3   Click Delete, and then click OK.

> **Tip**   To undo the deletion and restore the style, press Ctrl+Z. However, if any other styles were based on the restored style, they might not regain all the inherited formatting that was lost when you clicked OK. You can reapply the style to restore their formats.

Copying Styles and Color Schemes to Other Diagrams

You can easily copy your customized styles to other diagrams. When you copy a shape with a style and then paste it in another Visio diagram, Visio also adds the style to the new diagram. You can then delete the shape, but the style remains in the new diagram.

The only hitch is if the new diagram already has a style of the same name. If it does, when you paste the shape, Visio applies the diagram's existing style. Similar behavior happens when you copy shapes that have a color scheme applied to them. When you paste the shapes into a diagram that does not use the same color scheme, the shapes change their fill color unless they're locally formatted.

Setting Default Styles for Drawing

If you're drawing your own shapes rather than using Visio master shapes in a diagram, you can ensure consistent formatting if you set up default styles for the drawing tools. That way, when you draw with the Pencil, Freeform, Line, Arc, Rectangle, and Ellipse tools or use the Text tool, Visio applies the default styles you have selected to your shape as you create it. For example, if you're creating a series of shapes, you can ensure that they all have the same line weight and text attributes by specifying the appropriate default styles before you begin drawing.

To specify default styles for the drawing tools, follow these steps:

1 Make sure nothing is selected on the drawing page.

> **Tip** Click a blank area on the page to be sure nothing is selected.

2 Choose Format, Style.

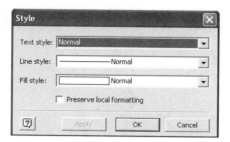

3 In each of the Style boxes, select the style you want to use as the default for that attribute. For example, if you're drawing a number of lines and want them all to have the same line weight, select a default in the Line Style box.

4 Click OK.

> **Note** Existing shapes on the page are not affected by this procedure. However, new shapes that you draw with the drawing tools will be formatted automatically with the default styles you selected. Hence, it's best to set these default styles before you begin the drawing.

Creating Your Own Line and Fill Patterns

If you want to use a fill pattern, line pattern, or line end not available in Visio, you can create your own. Custom patterns are powerful and peculiar. They work roughly like this: you create a shape and tell Visio to use it as a fill pattern, line pattern, or line end. You specify the attributes you want, and then Visio adds your pattern as an option in the Fill or Line dialog box. You can then apply the pattern to a shape in the usual way.

Understanding Pattern Philosophy

The pattern you design is a simple shape or group, as Figure 23-11 shows. The options you set for your pattern determine the way it looks when applied to a shape. The results can be dramatically different, as Figure 23-12 shows.

Chapter 23

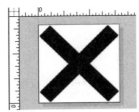

Figure 23-11. To create a custom pattern you design the single element that will be repeated when the pattern is applied; in this case it is a simple x shape.

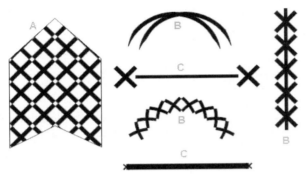

Figure 23-12. You can design a variety of fill patterns, line patterns, and line ends, and then apply them to shapes. The same simple pattern—the x shape—looks very different when applied as a fill pattern (A), line pattern (B), or line end (C).

The actual process for creating reliable patterns is somewhat complicated. That is, it's easy enough to draw a shape and define it to be a pattern, but it's an entirely different matter to get the results you want when the pattern is applied. That's where the "powerful and peculiar" come in. There are a lot of tricks to designing a shape that can be applied as a pattern, and Visio gives you many options to consider as well: Will the pattern ever be applied to shapes in a scaled diagram? Do you want the pattern to be tiled across a shape or stretched to fill it? What should happen to the pattern when a shape is stretched or a line is bent? The answers to these questions are the pattern's *behavior*, which you define when you create the pattern.

Methods of Creating a Pattern

The only way to create a pattern is through the Drawing Explorer window. To open it, choose View, Drawing Explorer Window. The Fill Patterns, Line Patterns, and Line Ends folders store new patterns that you create or other custom patterns that come with certain diagram types, as Figure 23-13 shows.

Figure 23-13. To create a new pattern, right-click a pattern folder, and then click New Pattern.

After you've created a pattern, you can apply it to other shapes as you would any of the built-in fill and line patterns. Depending on the type of pattern you design, your pattern appears as an option in the Fill or Line dialog box, as Figure 23-14 shows.

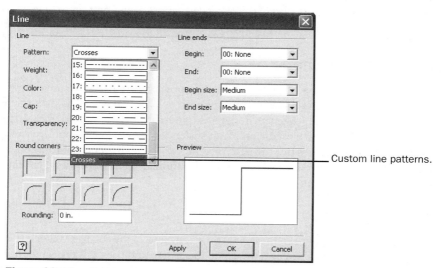

Custom line patterns.

Figure 23-14. Patterns you create appear at the bottom of the list of available patterns. Here, custom-designed line patterns are shown.

You can create a master pattern from a shape you create in Visio or a shape that already exists and set its properties, which affect how the pattern behaves. For example, you can choose how the pattern will appear when it's applied to a shape, how it responds when the shape is resized, or how it responds when the drawing page scale changes. You draw the pattern shape in a drawing window that Visio opens when you choose the Edit Pattern command by right-clicking a pattern in the Drawing Explorer window. The pattern's drawing page looks just like the regular drawing page or the drawing page for a master shape. When you work in the pattern's drawing page, the menus and toolbars display all the commands and tools you can use in designing your pattern. Table 23-1 lists the fundamental techniques to use and avoid when creating your own patterns.

Table 23-1. Dos and Don'ts for Creating Patterns

Do	Don't
Create a pattern as a single instance of the design that repeats. For example, you can design one square as a pattern that repeats to form a checkerboard.	Use multiple shapes in a pattern unless you group (Ctrl+G) or combine (choose Shape, Operations) them.
Use Visio's drawing tools.	Use Visio patterns in your pattern. For example, your pattern design cannot use a gradient (graduated color) fill.
Copy an existing shape.	Use a bitmap image or metafile in your pattern—they won't show up when the pattern is applied.
Design a pattern in black and white. Then, when you apply the pattern, you can click a new line or fill color to change the pattern color.	Use color in your pattern design unless you want the pattern to keep its color. For example, a green pattern stays green.

Designing a Pattern Shape

When you design a shape to use as a pattern, shape geometry is a big factor in how the pattern will be applied. You can choose different pattern behaviors that specify how the pattern is repeated on a shape, but when you design the pattern itself, you want to use a shape or shapes that will be positioned in a predictable way. Visio uses your pattern shape's *pin* and *alignment box* to determine where to put the pattern. A shape's pin is its center of rotation, a point that you can move. A shape's alignment box is its bounding edges, which don't have to match the shape's width and height.

Adjusting the Pin

Should the pattern's pin be in the center, on an edge, or in the corner? When you create a new shape, Visio automatically places the pin in the center, and uses it as the center of rotation. In a pattern, Visio uses the pin to align the pattern shape to the shape it's being applied to. If you move the pin, you can affect the position of the pattern as it is tiled along a line or repeated as fill, as Figure 23-15 shows. The easiest way to adjust pin position is to display the Size & Position window (choose View, Size & Position Window), and then use the Pin Pos option.

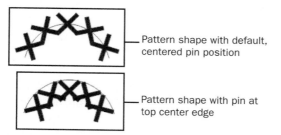

Pattern shape with default, centered pin position

Pattern shape with pin at top center edge

Figure 23-15. Visio repeats a line pattern based on its pin position.

Adjusting the Alignment Box

Should the pattern's alignment box tightly enclose the shape? Typically, a shape's alignment box is the same as its outer edges. In a pattern, Visio uses the alignment box to determine whether the pattern overlaps as it is tiled along a line. You can make the alignment box smaller or larger than the shape it encompasses. A small alignment box can produce a fish-scale effect. A large alignment box (shown in Figure 23-16) leaves spaces between repeating pattern elements.

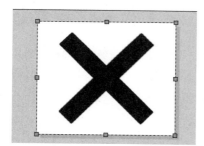

Figure 23-16. The alignment box for this pattern shape is slightly larger than the shape itself. When applied, the pattern will leave space around the repeating shape.

Changing the size of a shape's alignment box requires some fancy footwork. The easiest way is as follows:

1 Use the Rectangle tool to draw a shape in the size and position you want the alignment box to be.

2 Select the rectangle and your pattern shape, and then group them (press Shift+Ctrl+G).

3 Select the new group, and then choose Edit, Open Group to display the group window.

4 In the group window, delete the rectangle. Close the group window.

Now all that remains is your pattern shape, surrounded by the alignment box that was set by the size of the group.

Chapter 23

Inside Out

Seeing and editing patterns

Here's a technique borrowed from Visio shape developers that you can use to make it easier to see and edit patterns. After you've designed a pattern, on the pattern's drawing page, choose File, Page Setup. On the Page Size tab, select Size To Fit Drawing's Content, and then click OK. Visio reduces the page to the size of your pattern design, which makes it easier to see the pattern's alignment box and edit it later if necessary.

Designing and Creating a Fill Pattern

A fill pattern is applied to the interior of a closed shape. Visio can tile, stretch, or center a pattern to fit the shape, but the most common pattern behavior is to tile, or repeat, a pattern. That's how a single dot becomes polka dots and a single square becomes a checkerboard pattern. Figure 23-17 shows the three basic fill pattern behaviors.

Figure 23-17.   You can design a fill pattern that tiles when applied to a shape (A), is centered in a shape (B), or stretches to fill a shape (C).

How Fill Patterns Are Applied

Visio applies your pattern design differently depending on the behavior you select:

- **Tiled**   If your pattern is designed to tile, Visio can repeat the pattern up to 40,000 times or tile up to 200 by 200 pattern elements. The pattern's alignment box determines whether the pattern is overlapped, is tiled end to end, or includes space between design elements. When you stretch the shape, the pattern repeats to fill.

- **Centered**   If you want a centered fill pattern, Visio applies your pattern to a shape by aligning their pins. You can move the pin of your pattern shape for an off-center pattern. When you stretch the shape, the pattern isn't affected.

- **Stretched**   If you want to stretch your pattern to fill a shape, you don't have to worry about the shape's pin. When the pattern is applied to a shape, Visio stretches the pattern design in both directions to fill the shape. If the shape is resized, the pattern is resized, too.

Designing a Fill Pattern for Scaled Drawings

When you're designing a pattern for use in a scaled drawing such as a floor plan, you'll get better results if you set the pattern's drawing page to the same drawing scale. If the scales don't match, Visio will try to apply the pattern anyway. A tiled pattern can end up looking like solid black. If the scale of the pattern is more than eight times larger or smaller than the scale of the shape you're applying it to, Visio ignores the pattern's scale altogether. Unscaled patterns stay the size that you designed them to be. For example, if you create an unscaled pattern that's 1/4 inch in height, when you apply it to a shape in either a scaled or unscaled drawing page, the pattern design will still be 1/4 inch in height. Issues of scale and pattern size don't apply when you design a pattern with stretching behavior.

Designing Solid vs. Transparent Fills

When Visio repeats your pattern in a shape, the space between the repeating elements is transparent unless you design the pattern to use a solid color. For example, if your pattern looks like a black circle, and you apply it as a tiled pattern to a square, the square will be filled with solid-color polka dots with transparent areas between the dots. Anything behind the square shows through. You have replaced the shape's solid (white) fill with a new fill (polka dots). The solid fill is gone, so there is nothing to hide the background. Or you can think about those polka dots like this: you are tiling your shape with imaginary squares. Each square is the alignment box of a circle; it contains the circle, and nothing else. If you want dots with a white background, put a white square underneath your dot (with line pattern = None). If you want the white to stay white, make it RGB(254, 254, 254) instead of color index 1.

Creating Fill Patterns

To create a fill pattern, follow these steps:

1 If the Drawing Explorer window isn't open, choose View, Drawing Explorer Window.

2 In the Drawing Explorer window, right-click Fill Patterns, and choose New Pattern.

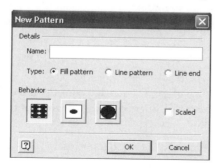

3 In the Name box, type a name for the pattern as you want it to appear in the Pattern box for fills.

4   In the Behavior area, select one of the following:

- Select tiled behavior, and the pattern will repeat to fill a shape.

- Select centered behavior, and the pattern will be centered on a shape.

- Select stretching behavior, and the pattern will stretch to fit a shape.

5   If the pattern will be used in diagrams with a drawing scale, select the Scaled check box.

6   Click OK to add the new pattern to the Fill Patterns folder in the Drawing Explorer window.

7   Right-click the new pattern in the Drawing Explorer window, and then select Edit Pattern to open a new drawing page, where you can create the pattern design.

8   Draw a new pattern, or copy a shape from the main drawing page and paste it on the pattern's drawing page. If your pattern includes more than one element, group them (Shift+Ctrl+G), or use a shape operation to combine them (Shape, Operations).

9   If you want a scaled pattern, choose File, Page Setup, and then on the Drawing Scale tab, set the pattern's drawing scale. Click OK.

10   When you're finished with your pattern design, click the Close button on the pattern's drawing page window. Visio displays a message similar to the following.

11   Click Yes to update the pattern design.

Tip   You can apply the new fill pattern as you would any fill: select a shape, and then choose Format, Fill. In the Pattern box, the new pattern is listed below the built-in patterns.

Creating a Line Pattern

When you design a shape to use as a line pattern, you need to consider the way that Visio will apply the pattern to both straight and curving lines of varying degrees of thickness. Visio applies a line pattern in one of the following ways:

- **Tiled and bent**   The pattern is tiled and distorted if necessary to follow the line's path.
- **Tiled and straight**   The pattern is tiled along the line's path, but not bent, much as bricks can be tiled to follow curving lines, but the bricks themselves aren't bent.

- **Stretched** A single copy of the pattern is stretched along the line. For example, if you stretch a triangle along a curving line, the result looks like a tail.
- **Beads on a string** The pattern is tiled at intervals along the line so that the original line remains visible, much like beads on a string.

How Line Patterns Are Applied

Visio uses the pin of your pattern shape (that is, its center of rotation) to align the pattern to a line. Figure 23-18 shows examples of each type of pattern behavior.

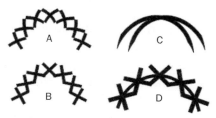

Figure 23-18.   The single, repeating element in each of these line patterns is an x shape. In pattern A the x is tiled and bent to follow the line. In pattern B the x is tiled but not bent. In pattern C the x is stretched along the line, and in pattern D the x is tiled at intervals like beads on a string.

Designing Line Patterns for Scaled Drawings

Each of the four line pattern behaviors has an additional option: scaled or unscaled. When you design a scaled line pattern, Visio resizes the pattern when it's applied—the height of the pattern shape's alignment box is set to match the line weight.

> **Note**   When you apply a line pattern, Visio can display up to 1000 instances of your pattern design along a line.

Creating Line Patterns

To create a line pattern, follow these steps:

1   If the Drawing Explorer window isn't open, choose View, Drawing Explorer Window.

2   In the Drawing Explorer window, right-click Line Patterns, and then select New Pattern.

Chapter 23

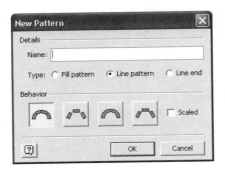

3   In the Name box, type a name for the pattern as you want it to appear in the Pattern list.

4   In the Behavior area, select one of the following:

- Select bending behavior, and the pattern bends as it is repeated around curves.

- Select brick-style behavior, and the pattern repeats without bending along a line.

- Select stretching behavior, and the pattern stretches along a line. Visio doesn't repeat the pattern design.

- Select beads-on-a-string behavior, and the pattern resembles strung beads.

5   If the pattern will be used in diagrams with a drawing scale, select the Scaled check box.

6   Click OK to add the new pattern to the Line Patterns folder in the Drawing Explorer window.

7   Right-click the new pattern in the Drawing Explorer window, and then choose Edit Pattern to open a new drawing page, where you can create the pattern design.

8   Draw a new pattern, or copy a shape from the main drawing page and paste it on the pattern's drawing page. If your pattern includes more than one element, group them (Shift+Ctrl+G), or use a shape operation to combine them (Shape, Operations).

9   When you're finished with your pattern design, click the Close button on the pattern's drawing page window. Visio displays a message asking whether you want to update the pattern and all of the shapes that might be using it as a pattern. Click Yes to update the pattern design.

Tip   If you apply a line pattern or line end pattern and it doesn't look the way you expected it to (for example, it's too small to see), try increasing the line weight.

Creating a Line End Pattern

Most people think of line ends as arrowheads, but many technical drawing types use unique line ends to convey meaning. For example, line ends in software and database models define relationships between objects, whereas in piping diagrams, they show the direction of flow. Line ends are easier to design than fills or line patterns, because they're really just shapes stuck on the ends of a line. The behavior options you have boil down to the direction in which your line ends will point. Visio provides two options, as Figure 23-19 shows:

- **In-line** When a line is moved or rotated, the line end rotates to point in the same direction. The line end shape is flush with the line—that is, no space appears between the pattern and the line (depending on the size of the pattern's alignment box).

- **Upright** When a line is moved or rotated, the line end remains upright with respect to the page. The pattern doesn't rotate. For example, a right-facing arrow will always point to the right regardless of where the line points.

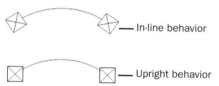

Figure 23-19.   You can design line ends to rotate in-line with the line to which they're applied or remain upright despite the line's direction.

How Line End Patterns Are Applied

Visio aligns the pin of your line end shape to the endpoint of a line. If you move the pin to the edge of the line end that you want to attach to the line, and then specify the in-line behavior, you can get the same effect as the built-in, solid arrowhead line ends in Visio. In addition, how you draw the line end pattern affects its application. Do the following to ensure your line ends behave as you want them to:

- Draw your line end pattern from left to right.
- If the line end implies direction, make it point to the right. That way, Visio can figure out how to orient the ends correctly when they are applied to either the begin point or endpoint of a line.

Designing Line End Patterns for Scaled Drawings

Whether the line ends are in-line or upright, they can be scaled or unscaled, which affects their size when applied to a line, as Figure 23-20 shows. If your pattern represents a real-world object in a scaled drawing, design the line ends to be scaled. When the line end is applied to a line, the Size and Weight settings in the Line dialog box will have no effect on the size of a scaled line end. If your pattern isn't scaled, Visio can resize the line end when it is

Chapter 23

703

applied—the height of the pattern shape's alignment box is set to match the line weight. For this behavior to work, you must set the Begin Size and End Size to Medium (the default) in the Line dialog box when you apply the line end pattern. If you choose any other Size setting, from Very Small to Colossal, the line end is sized in the usual manner.

 Unscaled line end

 Scaled line end

Figure 23-20. An unscaled line end sizes with the line weight. A scaled line weight remains the size you created it, regardless of line weight settings.

Troubleshooting

A custom line end pattern doesn't appear when you apply it to a line

If your line end isn't visible after you apply it, and you designed it to be unscaled, adjust the line weight. Select the line, choose Format, Line, and then in the Weight box, scroll down to select Custom. Type a thicker line weight, such as 12 pt. or .25 in.

Creating Line End Patterns

To create a line end pattern, follow these steps:

1 If the Drawing Explorer window isn't open, choose View, Drawing Explorer Window.

2 In the Drawing Explorer window, right-click Line Ends, and choose New Pattern.

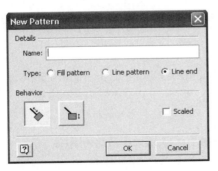

3 In the Name box, type a name for the pattern as you want it to appear in the Begin and End boxes for line ends.

4   In the Behavior area, select one of the following:

   ■ Select in-line behavior, and the line end points in the same direction as the line.

   ■ Select upright behavior, and the line end stays upright as the line is moved.

5   If the pattern will be used in diagrams with a drawing scale, select the Scaled check box.

6   Click OK to add the new pattern to the Line Ends folder in the Drawing Explorer window.

7   Right-click the new pattern in the Drawing Explorer window, and then choose Edit Pattern to open a new drawing page, where you can create the pattern design.

8   Draw a new pattern, or copy a shape from the main drawing page and paste it on the pattern drawing page. If your pattern includes more than one element, group them (Shift+Ctrl+G), or use a shape operation to combine them (choose Shape, Operations).

Tip   If your pattern implies direction, make sure it points to the right.

9   When you're finished with your pattern design, click the Close button on the pattern's drawing page window. Visio displays a message asking whether you want to update the pattern and all of the shapes that might be using it as a pattern. Click Yes to update the pattern design.

Applying Line End Patterns

The next step is to get the line end to show up at an appropriate size on a line. If you've designed an unscaled line end, and you apply it to a Visio line of the default size, the line ends probably won't be visible. You'll have to adjust the line weight.

Follow these steps to apply your line end pattern:

1   Select a line on the drawing page, and then choose Format, Line.

2   To apply a line end to the begin point, click the drop-down arrow in the Begin list, scroll down, and select the name of the pattern you created.

3   To apply a line end to the endpoint, click the drop-down arrow in the End list, and choose the name of the pattern you created.

4   If the line end is unscaled, make sure that Medium is selected in the Begin Size and End Size lists.

5   Click Apply. Verify that the line ends have been applied in the way you want on the drawing page. Move the Line dialog box out of the way if you need to.

Chapter 23

> **Tip**   If a line has rounded ends (the default style), a gap might appear between the end of the line and the line pattern. To specify flat ends, in the Line dialog box, choose Square in the Cap list.

6   If the line ends are too small to be easily visible (which can happen if the line ends are unscaled), click the drop-down arrow in the Weight list, and choose Custom.

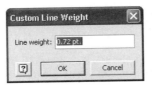

7   Type a heavier line weight (using any unit of measure Visio supports, including points, inches, and metric units), and then click OK. Visio redraws the line in the Preview area.

8   Verify the results, and adjust the line weight again if necessary. Click Apply in the Line dialog box for a better view of the result. When you like what you see, click OK.

> **Tip**   If you customize the line weight to make an unscaled line end more visible, enter a line weight that's equal to the height of the pattern shape you created. For example, if your pattern is 1/4 inch tall, enter **.25 in.** for the line weight.

Working with Color in Visio

Veteran Visio users will be glad to know that starting with Visio 2002, the product now supports 32-bit color, after a fashion. The Visio engine reserves the first 24 bits to specify 16.7 million colors and uses the remaining 8 bits to handle transparent colors, a new feature. This section provides additional background information about color management.

How Visio Applies Color to Shapes

You can apply color to a shape using either the Visio color palette or a custom color that you define. There is a distinct difference in how Visio tracks the two, and if you're designing your own shapes or writing ShapeSheet formulas, you need to know the difference. Visio can record a shape's text, line, and fill colors as an *index* to the color palette or as a specific RGB (red, green, blue) value. The numbered colors that appear in the Text, Line, and Fill dialog boxes refer to indexed colors, as Figure 23-21 shows. If the color at a particular index changes—which happens if you edit the color palette or copy the shape into a document with a different color palette—the shape can change color.

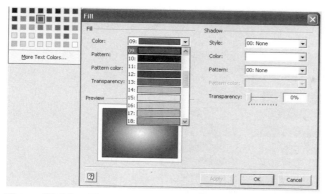

Figure 23-21. The default, indexed colors in a Visio diagram appear in the toolbar palettes and as the numbered options in the Color lists of the Text, Line, and Fill commands.

For example, if you select a shape and then choose red fill color from the toolbar, all Visio knows is that the shape is color 2. Although color 2 is by default red, someone could edit the palette to display a different color at index 2; then, if the red shape were copied into the drawing with the edited palette, the shape's color would change.

Visio also tracks color as specific RGB values. If a user applies a color scheme or chooses a custom color from the Colors dialog box, Visio records the exact color as a formula that specifies the RGB values, as Figure 23-22 shows. A similar formula can be used to specify colors as HSL (hue, saturation, luminosity) values instead. These formulas appear in the ShapeSheet window for cells having to do with color, such as the FillForegnd cell of the Fill Format section and the LineColor cell of the Line Format section.

Figure 23-22. Visio records custom colors and color scheme colors in the ShapeSheet window as exact RGB values, as the formula in the FillForegnd cell shows.

Tip   Use transparent colors

With the transparent fills and shadows in Visio, you can create shapes with see-through color. Where two transparent shapes overlap, their colors mix the way you would expect them to. You can vary the level of transparency, from fully opaque to fully transparent. However, you can't make a shape's lines transparent, only fills.

Editing the Color Palette

You can edit any of Visio's indexed colors so that a different color appears at that index with the Color Palette command, as Figure 23-23 shows. Perhaps you want to use the exact corporate blue in your diagram, and you would like it to appear in the toolbar color palettes for easy access. That's a good reason to edit an indexed color, but remember that your changes affect only the diagram you're working in. If you copy a shape formatted with the new color

Chapter 23

to a diagram without an edited color palette, the shape inherits the color assigned to the index of that document.

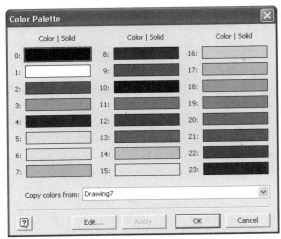

Figure 23-23. With the Color Palette command, you can edit the color palette associated with a Visio drawing file.

To edit the indexed colors that appear in a diagram, follow these steps:

1 Choose Tools, Color Palette.

2 Select the indexed color you want to change.

> **Caution** Do not edit index 0 (black) or 1 (white). Doing so will have far-reaching consequences, because Visio uses the indexed black and white colors as the default line and fill colors for a drawing.

3 Click Edit to open the Edit Color dialog box.

4 Choose one of the basic colors or define a custom color, and then click OK. The new color appears in the Visio color palette at the selected index.

5 In the Color Palette dialog box, click OK.

Visio changes the color of any shapes formatted with the edited index color. The new color is displayed in the Color lists of the Text, Line, Fill, and Shadow dialog boxes.

Changing or Restoring the Color Palette

You can use a different color palette altogether in a diagram or restore the original Visio colors. Maybe you're creating Visio diagrams that will be copied into a Microsoft Office Excel 2003 spreadsheet (or vice versa). For better compatibility between programs, you can use the Excel color palette in your Visio diagram. Visio includes a couple of built-in palettes, or you can copy a color palette from one Visio diagram, stencil, or template file to another Visio file.

To use a different color palette or restore the default Visio palette, follow these steps:

1 If you want to copy the palette from one Visio file to another, open both Visio documents.

2 In the diagram you want to change, choose Tools, Color Palette.

3 In the Copy Colors From list, select the palette you want to use. Visio lists any other Visio files that are open as well as the built-in palettes.

4 Click OK to add the new palette to the diagram. Make sure to save your changes.

Troubleshooting

When you copy shapes to another Visio drawing file or Microsoft Office document, they change color

Like the attributes of a style, the definition of a color can be overridden when shapes are copied between Visio and Office documents. If the new document uses a different color palette, it can override the colors used by your shapes. Visio uses the same color palette as other Microsoft Office XP programs, but conflicts can occur—particularly with Microsoft Office PowerPoint 2003. Here are some options for fixing the problem:

- If you're using Visio shapes on a PowerPoint slide, Visio can take on the presentation's color scheme. For details, see "Applying PowerPoint Colors to a Visio Diagram," page 349.

- You can copy the target document's color palette to your Visio diagram. For details, see "Changing or Restoring the Color Palette," page 708.

- You can make sure that Visio colors stay intact by applying a *nonindexed* color to shapes. Any color you apply from one of the color buttons on the Formatting toolbar is indexed, as is any color in the Text, Line, or Fill dialog box that is prefaced by a number. Choose a color that does not have a number, or choose More Colors to apply a custom color. For details about indexed and custom colors, see "Editing the Color Palette," page 707.

Chapter 23

Connecting Diagrams and Databases

Besides making great presentation graphics, Microsoft Office Visio 2003 diagrams are visual repositories of shape information. You can export that information to a database or spreadsheet program or update that information based on the contents of a database or spreadsheet program. For example, suppose you want access to the furniture dimensions stored in an office layout to add to a planning database. You can export shape data, such as dimensions and other properties, to a database, which is a one-way procedure. Or suppose you want to associate shapes that represent parts with the specification data stored in a manufacturing database. You can also create a two-way link between database records and shapes. This latter feature gives you the ability to create dynamic diagrams that respond to data from an external source. In effect, your diagram becomes a visual front end to your database.

This chapter discusses the way Visio works with databases so that you can export shape properties and link shapes to databases.

About Visio and Databases

Shapes are a visual representation of what can be considered a flat-file database. That is, each shape represents one record. Each shape property (including custom properties and Shape-Sheet properties) represents one field in a record. A property value corresponds to the value of a field in a shape record. If you're more accustomed to thinking in spreadsheet terms, each shape is like a row, each custom property or ShapeSheet cell is like a column, and each value is a cell's contents. Because Visio organizes shape information in this fashion, it's easy to export data from shapes as well as link external data sources to shapes.

Visio includes several commands and wizards for exchanging data. This chapter focuses primarily on two options:

- **Export To Database**   With this command, you can export data from shape properties to a database or file. This command does the same thing as the Database Export Wizard, which is complicated by its multiple-screen approach.

- **Link To Database**   With this command, you can create a two-way link between database records and shape properties. Two-way means that changes you make in Visio can be written back to the original database, and changes to database records can be used to update shapes. This command provides most of the functionality of the Database Wizard but in one dialog box instead of many wizard screens, which makes it easier to use.

Visio is compatible with any database that supports the Open Database Connectivity (ODBC) standard, which includes Microsoft Access as well as Microsoft Excel.

Inside Out

For those without Access

You don't actually need to have a database program to take advantage of Visio's database connectivity tools. Visio can read information from a database file through ODBC whether or not you have a program, such as Access or Microsoft SQL Server, installed on your computer. You can still export shape data in a database format and link to records in a database; you just can't open the database to edit it. Visio even includes a sample Access file (Dbsample.mdb) that you can use for testing the database linking feature. The sample file is installed by default in C:\Program Files\Microsoft Office\Visio11\1033.

Understanding Shape–Database Connections

Whether you link database records to shapes or export shape data to a database, you work with the cells and values in the ShapeSheet window. If the drawing page represents the graphical view of a shape, the ShapeSheet window represents the spreadsheet view of the same shape. Thus, Visio regards custom properties as yet another shape property that you can view in the ShapeSheet window. It just so happens that custom properties have another interface—the Custom Properties window. When you export data or link to a database, you specify ShapeSheet cells that contain the values you want to use—including custom properties and their values. If you don't typically work in the ShapeSheet view, linking or exporting data forces you to become more familiar with its nomenclature.

Visio stores a custom property in the Custom Properties section of the ShapeSheet window. Visio's internal name for properties—and the name you see when you use the Export To Database or Link To Database command—differs from the name displayed in the Custom Properties window, as Figure 24-1 shows. For example, if you create a property named Manufacturer, Visio refers to the property by the name prop.Manufacturer in the ShapeSheet and uses this name when you export or link properties.

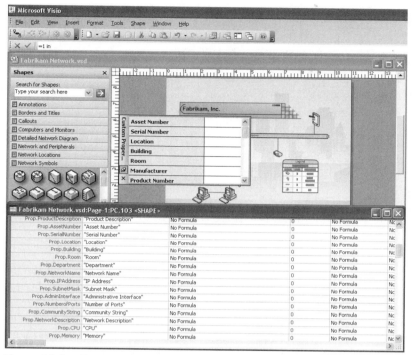

Figure 24-1. The Custom Properties window displays the property labels, which are stored in ShapeSheet cells along with their value and other settings.

For details about creating custom properties, see "Defining Custom Properties," page 175.

Exporting and Linking ShapeSheet Information

You can export or link to any of the built-in shape properties that are stored in the Shape-Sheet window for a shape. Besides shape size and position properties, such as width and height, you can export and link to formatting properties, such as fill color or shape text. If you're unfamiliar with the ShapeSheet window, it helps to remember that most ShapeSheet cells have a one-to-one correspondence with a command option or dialog box setting that is familiar. For example, the FillForegnd cell corresponds to the Color setting in the Fill dialog box, as Figure 24-2 shows.

For details about how Visio represents colors in the ShapeSheet, see "How Visio Applies Color to Shapes," page 706.

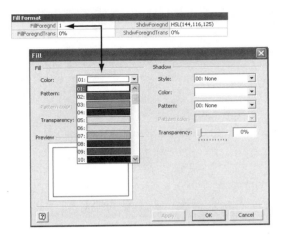

Figure 24-2. The FillForegnd cell reflects the setting (1, or white) in the Color box of the Fill dialog box.

The ability to export or link to shape formatting properties offers a great deal of flexibility. For example, you can export the Width property for all the dimension lines in an office layout to create a record of room dimensions. Or suppose you have a database of equipment that includes the color of a part. You could link the color records to shapes by specifying the FillForegnd cell so that the database controls the color of a shape.

> **Tip**   To find out what a ShapeSheet cell controls, click a cell, and then press F1. Visio displays the help topic about that cell.

When you connect Visio shapes to a database, Visio requires a unique field to associate each shape with the appropriate database record. By default, Visio uses the *shape ID* that it creates when you add a shape to the drawing page. The shape ID is a sequential number based on the order in which the shape was created on the page. In a drawing where identical shapes can represent different database records, as in a space plan or piping and instrumentation diagram, you can specify an internally generated unique ID called a *globally unique identifier* (GUID), which looks something like this:

{2287DC42-B167-11CE-88E9-0020AFDDD917}

A GUID is a unique null-terminated, 128-bit number assigned to each shape when you export its data. No two shapes in the same drawing file will have the same GUID.

Connecting to an ODBC Data Source

When you use the Export To Database or Link To Database command for the first time, you must set up and select an ODBC data source. Although you can use the Control Panel to set up an ODBC data source before exporting or linking, you don't have to—Visio provides all the options you need. A data source is simply the particular database file you want to connect to. You need to tell Visio where to find the database program, which ODBC drivers can communicate with it, and which database file (or *object*) to use. Through this process, you create a file called a data source name (DSN), which saves the settings used to create the connection.

You can create different types of DSNs depending on whether you want to share the connection with other users. The following procedure creates a *file-based DSN*, which means the DSN is portable—you can copy it to any other computer, such as a laptop or another user's computer. For added security, you can also specify a user or system DSN, both of which limit access to the DSN file to the user of your computer.

> **Note** The following procedure assumes that a data source already exists. If you are creating a new DSN and a new database or spreadsheet, you must first create a new database or spreadsheet file and save it before proceeding.

Follow these steps to create a new ODBC data source:

1 Choose Tools, Export To Database or Tools, Add-Ons, Visio Extras, Link To Database.

2 Click Create.

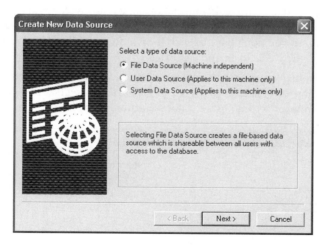

3   Select the File Data Source (Machine Independent) option, and then click Next.

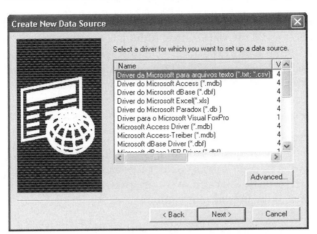

4   In the list of ODBC drivers under Name, select the driver for the database you want to connect to, and then click Next.

Tip   If you know structured query language (SQL), you can click Advanced, and then type the DSN parameters you want to use.

5   Type a name for or browse to the DSN file. It's a good idea to specify the program and database name. For example, if your data source is an Excel workbook with employee information, type a name such as **Excel-Employee**. DSN files are saved to a default system location, so you don't have to click Browse to specify a folder location unless you want to store the DSN file in another place.

6   Click Next to display a summary of your choices. Click Finish. Based on the ODBC driver selection you made in step 4, Visio displays a dialog box that contains driver-specific options for setting up the database program.

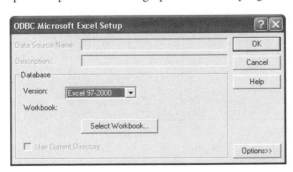

7   If you're connecting to Excel, specify the version, and then click Select Workbook to locate and select the particular file (.xls) you want to connect to. Click Options to expand the dialog box, clear the Read Only check box, and then click OK to return to the dialog box from step 1.

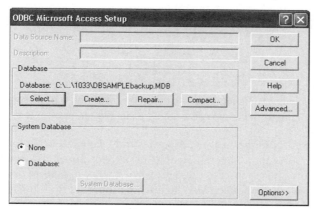

8   If you're connecting to Access, click Select to locate the specific database file (.mdb) that you want to use, and then click OK to return to the dialog box from step 1. The options for other databases are similar.

Tip   In the Export To Database or Link To Database dialog box, the DSN you created is listed in the Name box, and the tables contained in your data source are listed in the Table list box.

Exporting Shape Properties to a Database

When you export shape properties, you can choose the custom properties and ShapeSheet cells to export either from selected shapes or all the shapes on a drawing page. The Export To Database command on the Tools menu works with the ODBC Data Source Administrator, which is part of the operating system, to connect you to a data source or create a new one. After you have established an ODBC connection, you can export shape properties to an existing database table or to a new table in an existing database, as Figure 24-3 shows.

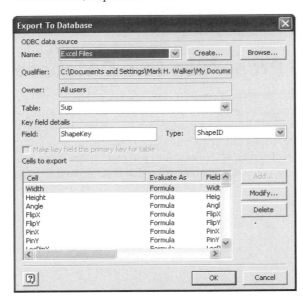

Figure 24-3. When you export shape properties, Visio creates a new table in an existing database or a NewTable worksheet in an existing Excel file, as shown here.

By default, Visio exports all the custom properties and ShapeSheet cells for each shape. At a minimum, Visio exports approximately 30 built-in size, position, and formatting properties. If you want to export only a subset of these properties, you can remove properties from the list in the Export To Database dialog box. Removing properties from the list doesn't delete them from the shape.

Follow these steps to export shape properties:

1 If you want to export properties for certain shapes only, select the shapes you want. Otherwise, cancel all selections to export properties from all shapes on the page.

2 Choose Tools, Export To Database.

3 In the Name list, select the ODBC data source that you want to export to.

   If you select Excel Files, the Select Workbook dialog box appears. Locate the file (.xls) that you want to use, and then click OK.

> For details about creating a data source, see "Connecting to an ODBC Data Source," page 715.

4 If your data source supports multiple databases, type the database you want in the Qualifier list. To limit the number of tables that Visio displays, type or select the name of a database creator in the Owner list.

> **Note**   If your data source is Excel, Access, or another program that creates a single database, the Qualifier box displays the database name and the Owner box defaults to All Users.

5 In the Table list, select the specific table to which you want to export the properties. To export to a new table, select NewTable, and then type a name for the new table.

6 In the Field box, type a new name for the field that Visio will create to uniquely identify each record. By default, Visio creates a field called ShapeKey, the value of which is the shape's internally generated ID number. To use a shape's GUID as the unique identifier instead, select GUID from the Type list box. To mark this field as the primary key for your table, select the Make Key Field The Primary Key ForTable check box.

> **Note**   Not all ODBC drivers can create primary keys.

7 To limit the number of properties that Visio exports for each shape, select an unwanted property in the Cell column, and then click Delete.

8 To export a property using a different name or data type, select the property, click Modify, make the changes you want, and then click OK.

9 To export the properties, click OK.

 Inside Out

Database Export Wizard

The Export To Database command is a more streamlined version of the Database Export Wizard. If you prefer to step through multiple screens, you can use the wizard, which does offer the ability to select shapes by layer for export. To start the wizard, choose Tools, Add-Ons, Visio Extras, Database Export Wizard.

Chapter 24

Troubleshooting

The Add button is not available in the Export To Database dialog box

By default, Visio lists all the exportable shape properties in the Cells To Export table of the Export To Database dialog box. The Add button appears dimmed because there are no other properties you can export—they're all listed. However, if you delete properties from the list, you can click Add to add them back. In the Add dialog box, the Name list under Cell Details lists the available shape properties. The options under Field Details indicate how to map the property to the data source. For details about these options, see the next section.

Mapping Shape Properties to an Existing Database

When you export shape properties, you can specify a field in an existing database table into which Visio writes property values. You can also change how Visio maps data when it exports shape properties and specify a data type to use. In the Export To Database dialog box (Cells To Export section), you can click Modify to display options for changing exported properties and specifying database fields, as Figure 24-4 shows. The next sections describe how to use the options in the Modify dialog box.

Figure 24-4. When you export shape properties, you can change how Visio maps property names and values to database fields.

Changing How Property Values Are Exported

The way that Visio exports a shape property reflects the way that data is stored in the ShapeSheet. In the Modify dialog box, you can specify how you want a value to be exported in the Evaluate As list, which provides a long list of options that boil down to three choices:

- **Value** Visio exports the contents of a custom property or ShapeSheet cell as a value—a text string such as an employee name, a number–unit pair (such as 1 inch), a date, or some other value.

- **Formula**   A ShapeSheet cell can contain a formula, that is, an expression that can include constants, cell references, functions, and operators that evaluate to a value. In the ShapeSheet window, the default view displays cell contents as formulas (on the View menu, Formula is selected). When you export a property as a formula, Visio exports the expression in a cell without evaluating it. For example, the width of a shape can be a formula such as .5 * Height. If the shape's height is 4 inches, the value of the Width cell will be 2 inches, but if you export the cell's contents as a formula, Visio exports .5 * Height.

- **Measurement unit**   Many shape properties are dimensional. For example, a shape's height is represented by a number and a unit of measure, such as 4 inches. You can export a value using an explicit unit of measure by selecting a unit in the Evaluate As list. If you don't specify a unit, Visio exports a value using the default units defined for the property.

Changing How Properties Are Mapped

When you export shape properties to an existing database table, you can map the property values to existing fields. In the Modify dialog box, under Field Details, you can type the name of a field in the Name box, and then specify the field's data type by selecting an option in the Type list. Visio writes the value of the shape property you select in the Export To Database dialog box to the field you specify in the Modify dialog box.

If the existing field is of variable length, type the size in bytes in the Length box. If the selected type supports decimal numbers, you can specify the precision by typing a number to indicate the number of decimal places in the Decimal box.

Exporting to a Specific Excel Worksheet

When you specify an Excel file as the data source, Visio can create a new "table" with the Table option in the Export To Database dialog box. Visio uses this option to add a new worksheet to an Excel file (if you're connecting to Excel 5 or later). Visio marks the records as a named range. If you want to export shape properties to an existing worksheet in an Excel file, ODBC requires that you create a named range in the Excel file that includes all of the rows and columns in the worksheet. Visio can then use the text in the first row of the named range as the table's column names.

Linking Shapes and Databases

Visio can link shape properties to database records with a two-way connection that you can keep up to date. In programmatic terms, the link is persistent, which means that after you set up the link between shapes and database records, the connection remains in effect as long as both the drawing file and database exist. When you change the value of linked shape properties, you can refresh the database with the values. Likewise, when the database changes, you can update shapes. Clearly, this functionality is a powerful way to tie drawings and data

Chapter 24

together. Your drawing file can become a dynamic catalog of information that accurately reflects the contents of a database. At a minimum, you can create a shape-to-database link to import values into custom property fields.

Linking Limitations

There are limits to what Visio can do when it creates a link between a shape and a database record. Be aware of the following limitations:

- **String size** You cannot store ODBC strings larger than 64-KB characters in Visio cells and fields.
- **Primary key type** You cannot specify a field of type SQL_TIMESTAMP as the primary key.
- **Replication IDs** You cannot update replication IDs from an Access database.
- **Timestamp fields** You cannot update Timestamp fields from an Informix database.
- **Binary field size** You cannot store ODBC binary fields larger than 32 KB in Visio cells and fields.

Note Visio stores numeric values as double floating-point numbers. If your database contains numbers with a large degree of precision, Visio stores them as approximate values.

Using the Link To Database Command

Follow these steps to link shape properties:

1. Select the shapes you want to link, and then choose Tools, Add-Ons, Visio Extras, Link To Database.

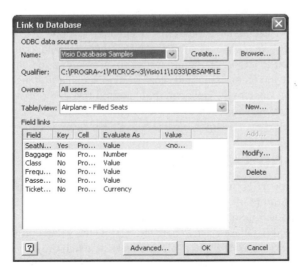

2 In the Name list, select the ODBC data source that you want to connect to.

For details about creating a data source, see "Connecting to an ODBC Data Source," page 715.

If you select Excel Files, the Select Workbook dialog box appears. Locate the file (.xls) that you want to use, and then click OK.

3 If your data source supports multiple databases, select the database you want in the Qualifier list box. To limit the number of tables that Visio displays, select the name of a database creator in the Owner list box.

> **Note** If your data source is Excel, Access, or another program that creates a single database, the Qualifier box displays the database name and the Owner box defaults to All Users.

4 In the Table/View list, select the table that contains the records and fields to which you want to link. To list fields from a system table or alias name, click Advanced, select an option under Link To, and then click OK. To create a link and a new table, click New, define the options you want, and then click OK.

5 To limit the number of fields that Visio links to shape properties, under Field Links, select an unwanted field in the Field column, and then click Delete.

6 To link a field to a different property or change the way Visio evaluates the database value, select the field, click Modify, make the changes you want, and then click OK.

Inside Out

Primary key field

In the Link To Database dialog box, make sure the field specified as Key (that is, the primary key) contains meaningful values in your data source. To change the field designated as the primary key, select a field, and then click Modify. In step 8, Visio displays the values of the primary key field in the Select Database Record box. It's simply easier to select a record based on a meaningful name (such as employee name, part type, room number, and so on) rather than an index or abstract ID number.

7 To link the database fields and shape properties, click OK.

8 To associate a linked shape with a specific record, right-click the shape, and then choose Select Database Record. Or, if you added links to a master shape, drag the master onto the drawing page, and then choose Select Database Record.

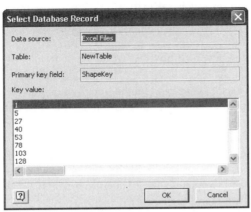

9 In the Key Value list, select the record you want, and then click OK to add its values to the corresponding custom properties or ShapeSheet cells.

Linking Master Shapes

You can select any shape on the drawing page and link it to a database record, but you get a more efficient result when you link master shapes instead. Each shape or master shape must be linked individually, so setting up links can be a time-consuming process no matter what type of shape you link. However, the advantage of linking master shapes is that you can drag the master onto the page to create many instances of the shape, and each instance can be linked to a different record in the database.

You can open a master for editing, and then use the Link To Database command to link it to a database record. Or you can link a shape on the drawing page and then drag it to a stencil to create a master that includes links. Remember, however, that you cannot edit masters that ship on the Visio 2003 stencils. You must first save them to a custom stencil by right-clicking the master, choosing Add to My Shapes, and saving it to a custom stencil. You can also right-click any stencil, choose Save As, and save it as a custom stencil by renaming it. You may set your master so that dragging the shape onto the page causes the Select Database Record dialog box to open as shown in Figure 24-5. To do so, you must click the Advanced tab in the Link To Database dialog box and then select the Select Record check box under Shape Drop Event.

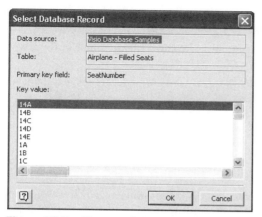

Figure 24-5. You may link database shapes to records in an Access database (Dbsample.mdb) stored in the same folder as the stencil if you wish to test your database shape-making knowledge.

Adding Shortcut Commands to Linked Shapes

By default, Visio adds commands to the shortcut menus for linked shapes so that you can more easily manage the database connection. When you use the Link To Database command, however, you can specify which actions and events you will be able to control from the shortcut menu. *Action* and *event* are Visio programming terms. An action in this context means a command that causes an action to occur, such as refreshing linked shapes. An event is simply something that happens, such as a user opening a drawing file. A *drop* event occurs when a shape is added to the page (copied and pasted or dragged from a stencil). In the LinkTo Shapes dialog box, you can click Advanced to display the Advanced dialog box, which contains these additional options, as Figure 24-6 shows.

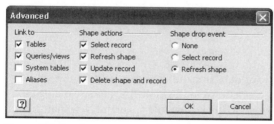

Figure 24-6. You can specify which shortcut commands Visio creates with the options under Shape Actions and Shape Drop Event in the Advanced dialog box.

You can specify the following actions:

● **Select Record**   With this command, you can associate a shape with a specific database record and add the record's values to the shape's properties.

- **Refresh Shape**   With this command, you can update the shape's property values based on the current database values.
- **Update Record**   With this command, you can write the shape's property values to the linked database record.
- **Delete Shape And Record**   With this command, you can delete a shape and the database record to which it is linked.

Troubleshooting

Copying a linked shape either copies the same link or doesn't copy any link

If you want to be able to copy and paste linked shapes—with links intact—you must specify an option that's available only when you click Advanced in the Link To Database dialog box. In the Advanced dialog box, the Shape Drop Event options control what happens when a shape is added to a page either through copying and pasting or by dragging a master from a stencil. If you select the Select Record option, Visio will prompt you to select a database record when you copy and paste a linked shape. That way, you can associate copies of shapes with new records. By default, the Refresh Shape option is selected, which means that copies of shapes are refreshed with the latest data from the same database record unless Select Record is also selected.

You can specify the following drop events:

- **None**   When you add a new shape to the page, nothing happens.
- **Select Record**   When you drop or paste a shape, Visio displays the Select Database Record dialog box, in which you can select a specific database record to link the shape to.
- **Refresh Shape**   When you drop or paste a shape, Visio updates its link and refreshes property values based on the latest database information.

Linking to a New Table

If you want to create a table in your database and define its fields at the same time you link those fields to shape records, you can do so in the Link To Database dialog box. Instead of selecting a table in the Table/View box, click New to display the New dialog box, shown in Figure 24-7. Here, you can name a new table and identify its fields and their data types. Visio creates the table in your database and displays its fields in the LinkTo Database dialog box.

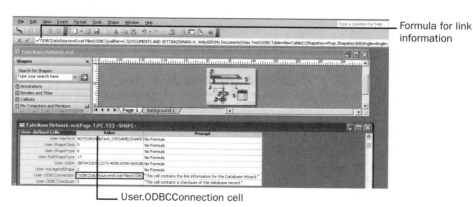

Figure 24-7. Rather than link to an existing table, you can create a new table in an existing database with the options in the New dialog box.

To create a new table, in the Table Name box type a name for the table that doesn't conflict with the names of other tables in the database. Then type the name of a field you want to include in the Name box, identify its data type in the Type box, and click Add. Make sure that at least one field is identified as a primary key, or Visio won't be able to refresh the link.

Understanding How a Visio Link Works

This section helps you understand exactly how Visio creates and stores the shape-to-database links that you create. After you link a shape to a database record, Visio creates a cell named User.ODBCConnection in the User-Defined Cells section of the ShapeSheet window. You can select a linked shape and then choose Window, Show ShapeSheet to see this cell and its contents, as Figure 24-8 shows.

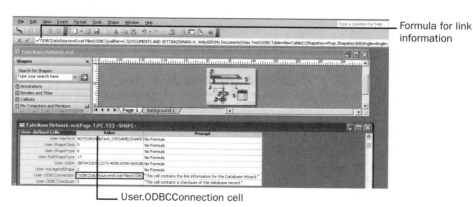

Formula for link information

User.ODBCConnection cell

Figure 24-8. Visio stores the information about a shape–database link as a formula that specifies the primary key, field, and most recent value.

Generating Shapes from a Database

The Link To Database command doesn't include one option that the Database Wizard does: the ability to generate new master shapes based on information contained in a database. This feature is particularly useful for organizations that maintain large databases of inventory or specification information. You can generate shapes that represent each type of part or each size of item in your database. However, to take full advantage of this option, you might want to design your own master shapes and then program them to respond to the database input.

The formula in the User.ODBCConnection cell is a very long line of code that looks a lot more straightforward when you break each line at the vertical bar like this:

```
ODBCDataSource=Visio Database Samples
ODBCQualifier=
ODBCTable=Office - Card Details
1
Name=Prop.Name
3
Department=Prop.Department=0
Extension=Prop.Extension=0
Title=Prop.Title=0
```

This example is taken from the Office Card shape on the Sample Database Shapes stencil. Here's what Visio records with each parameter:

- **ODBCDataSource=**<*name*>   This parameter stores the name of the data source used to link the shape. In the example, the data source is Visio Database Samples, which specified a table in an Access database.

- **ODBCQualifier=**<*name*>   For a data source that includes multiple databases, this parameter would specify the specific database. In the example, the Access data source doesn't support multiple databases, so the parameter doesn't include a value.

- **ODBCTable=**<*name*>   This parameter identifies the table in the database to which the shape is linked. In the example, the shape is linked to the Office – Card Details table.

- <*Number*>   This parameter shows the number of key fields that have been specified. In the example, only one key field is used. You can select multiple key fields when you link shapes using the Database Wizard rather than the Link To Shapes command.

- **Name=**<*name*>   This parameter identifies the custom property or ShapeSheet cell that stores the key field. In the example, the Prop.Name custom property is the key field.

- <*Number*>   This parameter identifies the number of fields that are linked to shape properties. In the example, three fields are linked. Each field is then described in the remaining parameters.

● *<Field name>=<cell name>=<number>*   Each of the remaining parameters identifies a specific field, the name of the cell where Visio stores its values (cells that represent custom properties are prefaced with "Prop."), and the manner in which Visio evaluates the current value of the property. In the example, the Title field is linked to the Prop.Title cell. The number 0 reflects the setting for the Evaluate As options and refers to a string. In programming terms, this number is a constant. Its possible values are shown in Table 24-1.

Table 24-1. Constants for Units of Measure

Constant	Unit of Measure	Constant	Unit of Measure
0	String (text)	66	Feet
1	Formula	68	Miles
32	Nondimensional number	69	Centimeters
33	Percent	70	Millimeters
40	Dates	71	Meters
50	Points	72	Kilometers
51	Picas	75	Yards
53	Didots	76	Nautical miles
54	Ciceros	81	Degrees
63	Default page units	83	Radians
64	Default drawing units	84	Minutes (of an angle)
65	Inches	85	Seconds (of an angle)

Managing Linked Shapes

If you never refresh a shape or update a database after creating a link, your shapes will represent a snapshot of the database. However, if you want to keep shapes in sync with the records they're linked to, Visio makes it easy. When you use the Link To Database command, Visio adds four commands to each shape's shortcut menu that you can use to manage and update the link, as Figure 24-9 shows. Visio always refers to updating shape properties as *refreshing* the shape, whereas using the shape's values to change the database is referred to as *updating* the database. To refresh or update an individual shape or a database record, right-click a shape, and then choose the command you want.

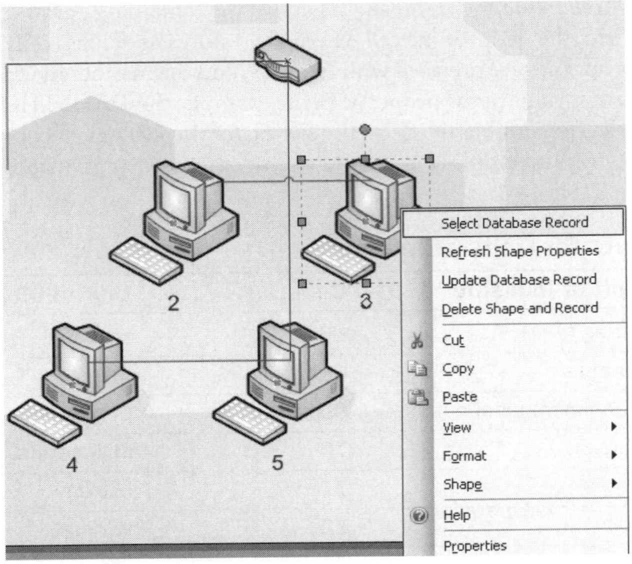

Figure 24-9. When you link a shape to a database record, Visio adds four commands to the shape's shortcut menu for controlling the connection.

You can also refresh or update all the shapes on a drawing page at once as follows:

● To refresh all the shapes, choose Tools, Add-Ons, Visio Extras, Database Refresh.

● To update the database with changes made to the shapes, choose Tools, Add-Ons, Visio Extras, Database Update. Visio prompts you before writing over existing records with a message such as the following:

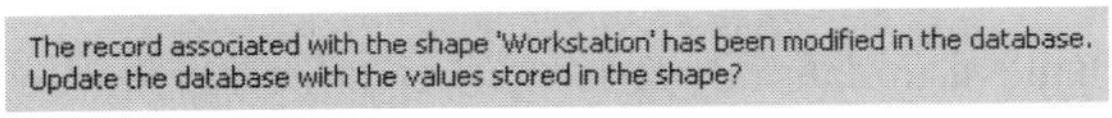

> The record associated with the shape 'Workstation' has been modified in the database.
> Update the database with the values stored in the shape?

Note You must have write access to a database for Visio to update the database based on changes in a drawing file.

Troubleshooting

Deleting records from a linked Excel worksheet causes an error

The ODBC driver for Excel does not support row deletion. According to the Database Wizard Samples Readme.txt file provided by Microsoft, Visio circumvents this problem by setting text fields to #ROW DELETED# and numeric fields to 0.

Adding Commands to Update All Shapes at Once

For convenience, you can add commands to the shortcut menu of a page so that you can manage the links for all the shapes on the page instead of those for individual shapes only. The Link To Database command doesn't provide this option, but the Database Wizard does. If you've already used the Link To Database command to set up the links, you can use the Database Wizard to add actions and events to a drawing page. The Database Wizard provides the following options for adding actions and events:

- **Refresh Shapes On Page**   This action adds the Refresh Shapes command to the shortcut menu of the page. When you right-click the page and choose the command, Visio refreshes all the linked shapes on the page.

- **Update Shapes On Page**   This action adds the Update Shapes command to the shortcut menu of the page. When you select the command, Visio passes along to the database any changes made to the value of shape properties.

- **Refresh Linked Shapes On Document Open**   The Open event is technical jargon for when a user opens a drawing file. In this case, you can have Visio refresh all property values for linked shapes every time you open the drawing file.

- **Periodically Refresh Based On NOW Function**   The NOW function is programming code that creates an event that happens continuously (until you specify otherwise). In this case, the event is refreshing the linked shapes based on database values. If you select this option, Visio adds the Start Continuous Refresh command to the shortcut menu of a page. When you select this command, you create a live link between the drawing file and the database that continues to transfer data until you right-click the page again and choose Stop Continuous Refresh.

Follow these steps to add actions or events to the shortcut menu of a page that contains linked shapes:

1   Choose Tools, Add-Ons, Visio Extras, Database Wizard.

2   On the first wizard screen, click Next.

3   On the next screen, choose Create A Linked Drawing Or Modify An Existing One, and then click Next.

4   On the next screen, choose Add Database Actions And Events To A Drawing Page, and then click Next.

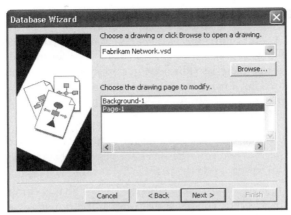

5　In the drop-down list, choose the drawing file (.vsd) that contains the linked shapes. If the drawing file is not open, click Browse, locate the file you want, and then click OK.

6　Under Choose The Drawing Page To Modify, select the page for which you want to modify the shortcut menu, and then click Next.

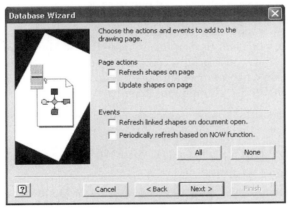

7　Select the actions or events you want to add to the page's shortcut menu, and then click Next.

8　Review your choices, and click Back to change an option if necessary. Click Finish to add the selected actions and events to the page's shortcut menu.

Updating Shapes Automatically

You can update linked shapes automatically at regular intervals based on changes that are made to the database. Visio monitors the database at regular intervals called the *refresh interval*, which you specify in seconds. If the connection takes longer to update than the time you set, Visio adjusts the refresh interval.

> **Note**   When you specify a refresh interval, it applies to all shapes that are connected to a database through the same DSN. Visio refers to this as a "global" setting for this reason.

Follow these steps to update shapes at regular intervals:

1   Choose Tools, Add-Ons, Visio Extras, Database Settings.

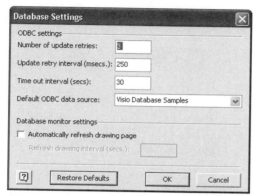

2   Select the Automatically Refresh Drawing Page check box.

3   In the Refresh Drawing Interval (Secs.) box, type the number of seconds in the interval, and then click OK.

Chapter 24

Making Shapes Smart

It's not a simple task to describe what makes a shape smart. The problem is that a truly smart shape requires no thought from the user. A door shape snaps into place on a wall. A background sizes to fit a page. The shape simply works as expected. So how do you describe something so transparent? The fact is, shape designers think long and hard about how to improve shape functionality, and often the smartest shapes in terms of the way they're programmed are the easiest to use. That's the SmartShapes conundrum.

However, anyone with a better idea about how a shape should work can make a shape smart. The place to start is in the ShapeSheet window, the Microsoft Office Visio 2003 built-in spreadsheet for defining all the properties of a shape—its size, position, format, behavior, and interactions with other shapes. This chapter takes you beyond the drawing page and into the ShapeSheet window, where smart shapes are created.

Using the ShapeSheet Window

In other parts of this book, the ShapeSheet window has been introduced as a way to complete certain tasks that can't be done on the drawing page. But what exactly is the ShapeSheet window? "Shapes are ShapeSheets, and ShapeSheets are shapes," said one of the authors of the ShapeSheet interface, who regards the window as simply another view of a shape. The graphical view is the shape you see on the drawing page. The ShapeSheet view looks beneath the surface to describe the geometry, formatting, and other settings that make up a shape, as Figure 25-1 shows. A *section* describes a particular behavior of a shape. For example, the Shape Transform section describes a shape's general position.

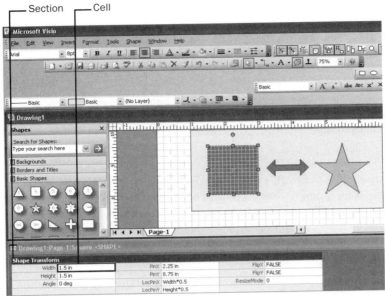

Figure 25-1. The ShapeSheet window contains cells and formulas that control the geometry, formatting, and other characteristics of shapes.

The ShapeSheet window is in essence a spreadsheet of rows and columns with a macro language not unlike that of other Microsoft Office programs. When you select a cell in a section, the cell's contents appear on the formula bar at the top of the window. Cells contain the instructions that Visio uses to create a shape. Moreover, you can edit these instructions to control a shape's appearance and behavior.

Tip Add a ShapeSheet command to the shortcut menu
For easy access to the ShapeSheet window, you can add a shortcut command that appears when you right-click a shape. Choose Tools, Options. On the Advanced tab, select Run In Developer Mode, and then click OK. This command also adds the Add-Ons command to the Tools menu.

Inside Out

Showing the ShapeSheet properties

When you choose Window, Show ShapeSheet, Visio displays the ShapeSheet properties for the currently selected object in a new window. If you select a second object on the drawing page and repeat the command, the new object's properties are displayed in a new window. However, you can display a new object's properties in the same ShapeSheet window. Choose Tools, Options. On the Advanced tab, select the Open Each ShapeSheet In The Same Window check box, and then click OK.

Visio can represent any of the following objects in the ShapeSheet window: shape, guide, guide point, object from another application, master shape, group, each member of the group, or drawing page. Table 25-1 describes how to display the ShapeSheet window for each type of object.

Table 25-1. Techniques for Opening the ShapeSheet Window for an Object

Object	Procedure
Shape, guide, guide point, or object from another application	Select the object, and then choose Window, Show ShapeSheet.
Group	Select the group, and then choose Window, Show ShapeSheet.
Shape in a group	Subselect the shape, and then choose Window, Show ShapeSheet.
Master shape	Open a custom stencil for editing or open the Document stencil. Right-click a master, and then choose Edit Master. Select the master shape, and then choose Window, Show ShapeSheet.
Page	Make sure nothing is selected, and then choose Window, Show ShapeSheet.

Viewing ShapeSheet Sections

Depending on the type of object you select, the ShapeSheet window will include a subset of the 34 possible sections. Most objects include a Shape Transform section, but, for example, only 1-D shapes include a 1-D Endpoints section. Visio adds the section it requires to build an object; other sections appear only if you explicitly add them. For example, the Scratch section, which programmers can use for their own formulas, doesn't appear in the ShapeSheet window unless you add it. You can also show and hide sections by choosing the Sections command on the View menu, as Figure 25-2 shows.

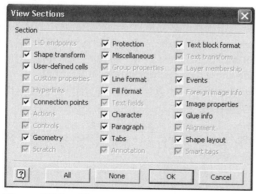

Figure 25-2. The ShapeSheet window for the selected shape displays all the available sections, as the check marks in the View Sections dialog box indicate. Options that are dimmed represent nonexistent sections, some of which are irrelevant for the object.

> **Note** The Sections command is available only when the ShapeSheet window is open.

If a section doesn't appear, you might be able to add it. Some sections don't apply to the selected object, but others provide you with additional options. For example, you can add the Actions section to the ShapeSheet window to add commands (actions) to an object's shortcut menu.

Follow these steps to add a section:

1 With the ShapeSheet window active, choose Insert, Section.

2 Select the sections you want to add.

3 Click OK.

> **Tip** You can collapse ShapeSheet sections so that you can see more sections at once by clicking a section name.

Touring the ShapeSheet Sections

Given the number of different ShapeSheet sections, it's not practical to describe them all here. However, Table 25-2 describes a subset of sections that are useful to know about, particularly if you want to gain a deeper understanding of shape behavior. When you tour the ShapeSheet window, remember that most cells have a one-to-one correspondence with an option that you've probably seen elsewhere. For example, most of the Shape Transform cells have counterparts in the fields of the Size & Position window, and cells in the Line Format section reflect the options in the Line dialog box.

> **Tip** To display help for any ShapeSheet cell, select a cell, and then press F1. Microsoft Visio Developer Help opens and displays the topic for that cell.

Table 25-2. Common ShapeSheet Sections

Section	Description
1-D Endpoints	Cells in this section describe the exact position of each endpoint on a 1-D shape.
Custom Properties	This section stores the labels and values of a shape's custom properties if it has any. You can add properties in the ShapeSheet window by choosing Shape, Custom Properties.
Fill Format	Cells in this section reflect the settings of the Fill command on the Format menu.
Geometry	This section defines the exact position of each shape vertex as an x- and y-coordinate and shows the type of lines and segments that make up the shape. A shape with multiple paths will include a Geometry section for each path.
Group Properties	In a group, the settings specified by the Behavior command on the Format menu are stored in this section.
Line Format	Cells in this section reflect the line formatting and line end settings specified with the Line command on the Format menu.
Miscellaneous	This section contains an assortment of shape settings that control shape selection and visibility, most of which can be set with the Behavior command on the Format menu.
Paragraph	Cells in this section reflect the paragraph formatting settings specified with the Paragraph command on the Format menu.
Protection	This section reflects the protection lock settings specified with the Protection command on the Format menu. However, this section includes a few locks that the Protection command doesn't, such as LockFormat, LockTextEdit, and LockGroup.
Shape Transform	This section stores the shape's size, position on the page, and orientation and reflects the settings shown in the Size & Position window.
Text Transform	Like the Shape Transform section, this section contains size and position information—but only for the shape's text block.
User-Defined Cells	Many Visio shapes include this section, which doesn't correspond to any commands on the drawing page. Instead, it provides a work area for any type of formula. Microsoft shape designers store keyword information used by the Find Shapes command in this section.

Chapter 25

Writing ShapeSheet Formulas

ShapeSheet cells can contain either a *value* or a *formula*, and you can alternate the view to show one or the other. A formula is the expression in a cell that evaluates to a value. Visio adds some default formulas to shapes; a shape inherits other formulas from a master shape. And then there are the formulas that you can create by typing in a ShapeSheet cell or on the formula bar, as Figure 25-3 shows. A formula always starts with an equal sign, which Visio inserts automatically.

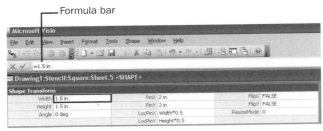

Figure 25-3. When you select a cell, its formula is shown on the formula bar. You can type directly in cells or use the formula bar to enter and edit formulas.

When you edit a cell's formula, you change the way that Visio calculates the value of the cell. The result is that shape behavior changes. For example, you can edit the formula in the TxtAngle cell of the Text Transform section by typing **45 deg.** and then pressing Enter. The result is that the angle of the shape's text block is rotated 45 degrees on the drawing page. You can accomplish the same feat with the Text Block tool, so what's the difference? Editing formulas becomes much more interesting when you realize that you can calculate a shape's geometry or appearance dynamically. That is, you can write formulas to adjust the value of one cell based on the value of another. This feature is the heart of SmartShapes programming.

Inside Out

Default formulas

When you draw a shape, Visio creates default formulas for the shape. To see what default formulas look like, draw a simple shape (such as a rectangle, ellipse, or straight line), and then take a look at its ShapeSheet.

Contents of a Formula

A Visio formula can contain the following elements:

- **Coordinates**   Most formulas are expressed as coordinates for controlling the position and size of a shape. A coordinate describes the position of a vertex with respect to the origin of a shape and to the origin of the group or page that contains the shape.

- **Numbers**   In a formula, numbers specify a wide range of values, such as measurements and angles. *Constants* are numbers that map to predefined Visio settings, such as those used to represent styles and colors. A number can include a plus (+) or a minus (–) sign and can be entered in exponential notation (for example, 1.2E-6) or as a fraction (for example, 5 1/16).

- **Units of measure**   Because many values in Visio are dimensional (for example, width in inches or angle in degrees), many formulas include measurement units after a number. If you don't specify a unit of measure, Visio uses default units of measure in cells that require a unit of measure.

- **Cell references**   A formula can contain the name of another cell, the value of which is used in the formula.

- **Functions**   Like Microsoft Excel functions, Visio functions perform a task. Visio includes mathematical, trigonometric, logical, date and time, statistical, and other functions.

- **Operators and parentheses**   Formulas typically include mathematical operators (+ for addition, – for subtraction, * for multiplication, / for division) and parentheses that control the order of operation. Formulas can also contain the Boolean expressions TRUE and FALSE.

- **Strings**   A string is simply text in a formula usually set off with quotation marks.

For example, the default formula that Visio enters for the position of a shape's pin (its center of rotation) is stored in the LocPinX and LocPinY cells and looks like this:

```
LocPinX=Width*0.5
LocPinY=Height*0.5
```

Learning to Write SmartShapes Formulas

The Microsoft Developer Network (MSDN) Web site includes resources for shape designers and programmers. At *http://msdn.microsoft.com/visio*, you'll find articles about Smart-Shapes programming as well as the text of the *Developing Microsoft Visio Solutions* programming guide, sample code, and information about training resources. If you want to learn more about SmartShapes programming and using other programming languages to extend Visio's functionality, the instructor-led training courses in Visio development are well worthwhile. Visio is an idiosyncratic program, and its development environment is quirky but very powerful. Visio is a full-fledged development platform that organizations have used to create some pretty amazing applications. The example applications on the MSDN Web site will show you some of the possibilities.

What does this tell you? In the top formula, the LocPinX cell represents the x-coordinate of the pin—that is, its horizontal location. *Width* is a cell reference and refers to the Width cell in the Shape Transform section and defines a measurement, such as 1 inch. The asterisk (*) symbol is the operator for multiplication. So, the horizontal location of the pin is the point that is half the value of the Width cell. In short, it's in the middle. The formula in the LocPinY cell is similar but defines the vertical distance of the pin in terms of the shape's height. Suppose you select the Rotation tool on the drawing page and use it to move the pin, thereby changing the shape's center of rotation. Visio writes new formulas into these cells to describe the pin's new position.

Creating and Editing Formulas

To create a formula, you can select a cell and type, just as you can select a shape and type. Similarly, you can double-click a cell to display the insertion point so that you can edit a formula. You can also use the formula bar, which works much like the one in Excel. It's somewhat easier to type on the formula bar, because you can see more of your formula at once.

> **Note** If you click a cell and type, you overwrite the existing formula entirely. To add to or edit the formula in a cell, double-click the cell or select it, and then press F2.

Follow these steps to type a new formula for a cell:

1 In the ShapeSheet window, click a cell to select it and display its formula on the formula bar.

2 Type the formula.

3 To accept the formula, click the Accept button (the blue check mark) on the formula bar or press Enter. If the number or formula contains an error, Visio displays a message.

Accept

4 In the message box, click OK. Visio highlights the error on the formula bar.

5 Correct the error, and then click Accept or press Enter.

> **Tip** When you're typing in a cell or on the formula bar, you can cancel your changes by clicking the Cancel Change button (the dark red X) on the formula bar or by pressing the Esc key.

You can edit formulas on the formula bar, much as you do in a spreadsheet. Table 25-3 describes how.

Table 25-3. Techniques for Editing on the Formula Bar

Task	Technique
Place the insertion point.	Click where you want the insertion point to appear.
Move the insertion point.	Press the Left or Right Arrow key.
Delete the character to the left.	Press Backspace.
Delete the character to the right.	Press Delete.
Select text.	Drag the mouse over the text.
Extend or reduce the selection to the left.	Press Shift+Left Arrow.
Extend or reduce the selection to the right.	Press Shift+Right Arrow.
Select a word.	Press Ctrl+Shift+Right Arrow or double-click.
Select to the end.	Press Shift+End.
Select to the beginning.	Press Shift+Home.

Tip You can copy the contents of a cell by selecting the cell and pressing Ctrl+C. You can paste these contents into a cell by selecting the new cell and pressing Ctrl+V.

Creating a Cell Reference in a Formula

Cell references provide a powerful way to create interdependent behavior in a shape. You can set one cell to a particular value based on the setting in another cell—in the same ShapeSheet or in the ShapeSheet for another object, including the page. You must follow Visio's naming *syntax*, which describes the rules for correctly referring to another cell. It's easy to refer to another cell in the same ShapeSheet. When you're typing a formula, you can click in another cell to add a reference to that cell in the formula, as Figure 25-4 shows.

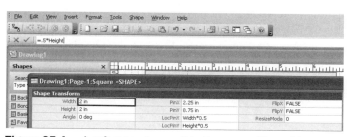

Figure 25-4. A reference to a cell in the same ShapeSheet specifies only the cell name, such as Height.

It gets a little trickier when you want to refer to another object's ShapeSheet cell. Then you must know the object's identifier or name and use an exclamation point (!) to separate the object name from the name of the cell like this:

```
Sheet.12!Width
```

Visio displays an object's identifier or name on the title bar of the ShapeSheet window, but you can also select an object, and then choose Format, Special, to display the identifier or name. An object's identifier, such as Sheet.12, doesn't change unless you move the object to another page or document.

> **Note** For more information about cell references, choose Help, Developer Reference. Click Microsoft Office Visio ShapeSheet Reference, expand Concepts, and then click About Cell References.

Entering Functions

You can perform a variety of calculations by using a function. Functions are really just predefined formulas that use specific values, called *arguments*, in a particular order. For example, the SUM function adds a series of numbers, and the UPPER function transforms text into uppercase letters. The structure of a function (that is, its syntax) requires you to use parentheses around the arguments. For example, the GOTOPAGE function uses the following syntax:

```
GOTOPAGE(pagename)
```

The GOTOPAGE function creates a link to another page specified by the pagename argument. You can use the name that appears on the page tabs at the bottom of the drawing page window. Because the page name is a string, you must enclose it in quotation marks. A valid formula using the GOTOPAGE function would look like this:

```
GOTOPAGE("page-2")
```

Follow these steps to quickly add a function to a ShapeSheet formula:

1 Double-click the cell, and then click where you want to insert the function.

2 Choose Insert, Function.

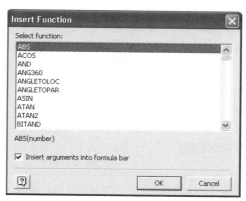

3 Scroll the Select Function list, if necessary, and then select a function.

4 Select the Insert Arguments Into Formula Bar check box, and then click OK.

5 In the cell, type over the argument placeholders to insert the arguments you want to use, and then click the Accept button (the blue check mark) or press Enter to enter the formula.

> **Tip** You can press the Esc key to cancel the changes when you edit a formula.

Protecting Shape Formulas

In other chapters, Visio's built-in protections have been discussed—features such as protection locks and other safeguards that prevent you from making changes to shapes. The equivalent mechanism in a ShapeSheet formula is the GUARD function, which prevents an expression from being overwritten by changes that occur on the drawing page. For example, when you click the Fill Color button and apply a new color to a shape, Visio records your action by changing the formula in the FillForegnd cell. If you want to prevent a shape's fill color from changing, you can guard the formula in that cell with the GUARD function. Many Visio shapes are guarded in this way to prevent SmartShapes formulas from being inadvertently changed. The syntax for the GUARD function looks like this:

GUARD(*expression*)

You most often see the GUARD function used in the Width, Height, PinX, and PinY cells of the Shape Transform section in Visio shapes. For example, when you drag a shape from the Backgrounds stencil, Visio sizes the background to fit the drawing page and guards the formulas that control size and position, as Figure 25-5 shows. The width and height of the background shape is set to match the page's width and height. The PinX, PinY, FlipX, and FlipY cells use the GUARD function to prevent the shape from being repositioned or flipped.

Figure 25-5. The GUARD functions in these formulas prevent the expressions from being replaced with other values. In effect, you cannot change the shape's width, height, position, or orientation on the drawing page.

Exploring Shape Geometry

If you want to design your own shapes and add SmartShapes formulas, you need to understand specifically how the drawing tools operate on shape geometry. When you strip away the formulas and formatting, shapes are just geometry—that is, lines, and arcs—and that's how Visio represents them internally. Every time you draw a new shape, Visio records your actions in a ShapeSheet spreadsheet for the shape. Every shape has a Geometry section in its ShapeSheet that defines each point that makes up the shape, as Figure 25-6 shows.

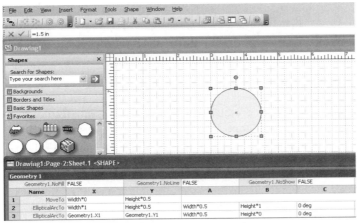

Figure 25-6. Every shape is described in the Geometry section of its ShapeSheet.

Depending on the tool used to create a shape, the Geometry section can describe points on a line, arc, ellipse, or spline. You can even convert one type of segment to another with the Change Row Type command on the Edit menu. Much of what the ShapeSheet records about shape size and position is also displayed in the Size & Position window and on the status bar at the bottom of the Visio window.

Visio defines shape geometry dynamically in terms of a shape's width and height by using default formulas. The first point on a shape—that is, the first point created by a drawing tool—is described in the MoveTo cell of the Geometry 1 section. The formula in the X column of this cell frequently looks like this:

```
=Width*0
```

This formula multiplies the value of the Width cell by zero to describe the horizontal starting point of the first line segment, which is the far left side of the shape. A similar formula in the Y column of the MoveTo cell multiplies the value of the Height cell by zero, which is the bottom of the shape. Therefore, the shape's origin, or 0,0 point in coordinate terms, is the bottom, left corner. If you click either MoveTo cell while the drawing page is visible, you'll see that Visio confirms this coordinate by selecting the lower left vertex, as Figure 25-7 shows. The subsequent rows in the section reveal the type of segment: line, arc, circular arc, elliptical arc, and so on.

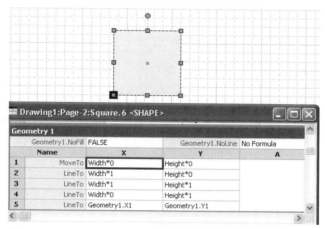

Figure 25-7. In the Geometry section, selecting a cell also selects the corresponding vertex on the shape.

Defining Double-Click Actions for Shapes

An easy way to make a shape smart is to have it do something when you double-click it. For most Visio shapes, the built-in double-click behavior is to open the shape's text block so that you can type. However, Visio provides several options that you can specify with the Behavior command on the Format menu, as Figure 25-8 shows. For example, you can configure a shape so that the Report dialog box opens when you double-click the shape.

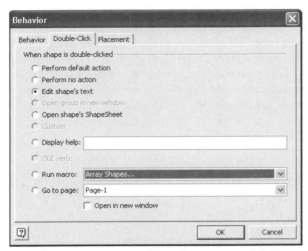

Figure 25-8. On the Double-Click tab, you can define what will happen when the shape is double-clicked.

Tip You can add double-click behavior to objects from another application that you've linked or embedded in Visio. The OLE Verb option in the Behavior dialog box is available only when you select a linked or embedded object.

Displaying a Help File for a Shape

One of the double-click behaviors that you can define for a shape is Display Help. This option is really designed for professional shape developers who want to link shapes to custom Windows help files (.hlp or .chm files). If you fall into this category, you must identify the help file and a topic in that file using the following syntax:

filename!keyword or *filename*!#Number

Filename is the name of the help file, such as MyShape.hlp or MyShape.chm. To locate a specific help topic in the file, you can specify either a keyword that is associated with the topic, or the ID number that is referenced in the MAP section of the help project file.

Follow these steps to set a shape's double-click behavior:

1 Select the shape that you want to change.

2 Choose Format, Behavior, and then click the Double-Click tab.

3 Choose the action you want to happen when the shape is double-clicked. See Table 25-4 for a list of options and what they do.

4 Click OK.

5 To test the new behavior, double-click the shape.

Troubleshooting

The Custom option is not available, or nothing happens when you select a double-click action

If the Custom option is selected but appears dimmed, the shape already includes a custom double-click formula, which is defined in the ShapeSheet window. If you select a new option on the Double-Click tab, you can overwrite the custom behavior. However, if a custom formula is protected (such as by the GUARD function), specifying a different behavior on the Double-Click tab will have no effect. Visio ignores your setting when you click OK. No error message appears; your change is simply not implemented.

Table 25-4. Double-Click Options for Shapes

Option	Description
Perform Default Action	Choose this option to use the default double-click action defined for the shape.
Perform No Action	Choose this option to remove double-click behavior from the shape.
Edit Shape's Text	Choose this option to open the shape's text block with the insertion point.
Open Group In New Window	Choose this option to open the group in the group editing window. This option is available only if you select a group. It has the same effect as choosing Edit, Open Group.
Open Shape's ShapeSheet	Choose this option to display the ShapeSheet window for the shape.
Custom	This option indicates when a custom formula has been defined in the ShapeSheet window for the shape and always appears dimmed.
Display Help	Choose this option to display a custom help topic for a shape. For details, see the sidebar on page 748, "Displaying a Help File for a Shape."
OLE Verb	Choose this option for a linked or embedded option to add an OLE command, such as Edit or Open.

Table 25-4. Double-Click Options for Shapes

Option	Description
Run Macro	Choose this option and select a macro or add-in to run the macro or add-in. The list box includes all the available add-ins, many of them built-in Visio wizards or tools, such as Report and Color Schemes.
Go To Page	Choose this option and select a page number to display that page. Select the Open In New Window check box if you want to display the new page in a separate drawing page window.

Adding Shortcut Commands to Shapes

If you like to put Visio commands at your fingertips, you can define commands that appear when you right-click a shape. All Visio shapes already include on their shortcut menus a number of commands for formatting and editing, and if you know how to program in the ShapeSheet, you can write your own command to do anything you want. However, with a minimum of ShapeSheet knowledge, you can add a shortcut command to do any of the actions provided by the Double-Click tab in the Behavior dialog box. In addition, this section shows you how to program a ShapeSheet function for putting any Visio command on a shape's shortcut menu.

When you want to add a command to a shape's shortcut menu, you must display the Actions section of the ShapeSheet window. For some shapes, this section already appears in the ShapeSheet window. For other shapes, you have to add it. The Actions section includes cells that define the names of commands as they appear on a shape's shortcut menu (the Menu cell) and the action to take when the command is selected (the Action cell), as Figure 25-9 shows.

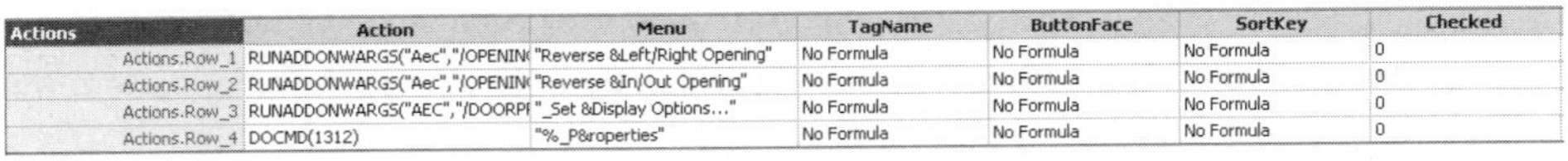

Actions	Action	Menu	TagName	ButtonFace	SortKey	Checked
Actions.Row_1	RUNADDONWARGS("Aec","/OPENIN	"Reverse &Left/Right Opening"	No Formula	No Formula	No Formula	0
Actions.Row_2	RUNADDONWARGS("Aec","/OPENIN	"Reverse &In/Out Opening"	No Formula	No Formula	No Formula	0
Actions.Row_3	RUNADDONWARGS("AEC","/DOORPI	"_Set &Display Options..."	No Formula	No Formula	No Formula	0
Actions.Row_4	DOCMD(1312)	"%_P&roperties"	No Formula	No Formula	No Formula	0

Figure 25-9. This door allows users to reverse its left/right and in/out openings and set display options from its shortcut menu. (An ampersand in the name defines the command's keyboard shortcut.)

Follow these steps to display the Actions section:

1 Select a shape, and then choose Window, Show ShapeSheet.

2 Scroll down in the ShapeSheet window until you see the Actions section.

3 If you don't see it, choose Insert, Section. Select the Actions check box, and then click OK.

The new Actions section doesn't do anything as is. To create a command, you have to type a label enclosed in quotation marks in the Menu cell, and then define the action to take in a formula in the Action cell. However, you can let Visio write the formula as the following section explains.

> **Tip** You can add additional rows in the Actions section by right-clicking a cell and selecting Insert Row.

Adding a Predefined Action

You can use the Action command, which is available only in the ShapeSheet window, to add a right-click action to a shape. The Action dialog box provides the same options as the Double-Click tab of the Behavior dialog box, as Figure 25-10 shows. The difference is that Visio creates a command on the shortcut menu instead of defining a double-click action.

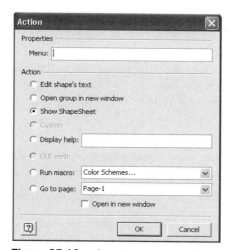

Figure 25-10. Just as you can define a double-click behavior for a shape, you can add a shortcut command for a shape in the Action dialog box.

Follow these steps to add a predefined action:

1 Display the Actions section for a shape as described in the previous procedure.

2 If the shape already includes actions, you must insert a new row as follows: click in the last Menu or Action cell to select it. Then right-click the cell and choose Insert Row (if there is currently only one row in the section) or Insert Row After (if there is more than one row).

3   Click the blank Menu or Action cell, and then choose Edit, Action.

4   In the Menu box, type the name of the command as you want it to appear on the shortcut menu.

5   Under Action, choose the action you want the command to take, and then click OK.

6   To test the new command, click the Close button in the ShapeSheet window to return to the drawing page. Then right-click the shape, and choose the new command.

Adding a Smart Tag to Your Shape

Visio 2003 allows users to not only add Smart Tags to their shapes, but enable the tags to trigger the same functions normally associated with shortcut menus. Smart Tags normally appear when the mouse is passed over the shape, but can be set to either appear when the shape is selected or remain permanently visible. To add a Smart Tag to a shape, follow these steps:

1   Select the shape and choose Window, Show ShapeSheet.

2   Select the ShapeSheet and select Insert, Section. Select the Smart Tags check box. A Smart Tag section and one Smart Tag row appear in the ShapeSheet window.

Actions	Action	Menu	TagName	ButtonFace	SortKey
Actions.Row_4	DOCMD(1670)	"Size & Position Window"	No Formula	No Formula	No Formula

3   Choose a display mode in the DisplayMode cell of the Smart Tags section for the Smart Tags row that you are working on. These are the modes: 0 indicates that the tag appears when cursor is passed over shape; 1 indicates that the tag appears when the shape is selected; and 2 indicates that the tag always remains on screen.

4   Type a name in the TagName cell. This name will link your SmartTag to an action in the Action section of the ShapeSheet. Choose something simple like Tag1.

5   Display the Actions section for a shape as described in the previous procedure.

6   If the shape already includes actions, you must insert a new row as follows: click in the last Menu or Action cell to select it. Then right-click the cell and choose Insert Row After.

7   Click the blank Menu or Action cell, and then choose Edit, Action.

8   In the Menu box, type the name of the command as you want it to appear on the Smart Tag drop-down menu.

9   Under Action, choose the action you want the command to take, and then click OK.

10   In the TagName cell enter the name in the Smart Tag's TagName cell. For example, if you entered Tag1 in the Smart Tag's TagName cell, you would enter Tag1 here.

11   Close the ShapeSheet window.

Now, when you click on the shape's Smart Tag, a menu appears that displays the name just chosen. Clicking the name executes the action.

Note   One action can apply to numerous tags. For example, you can link the Color Scheme action to the *color* TagName. Each Smart Tag with the *color* TagName will have this option in its menu.

Adding a Visio Command

For more options, you can program the action that takes place when the shortcut command is selected. Although this book isn't a programming guide, there is one particularly useful formula that you can use in the Actions section to place a Visio command on the shape's shortcut menu. For example, you can add shortcut commands for changing the zoom level or displaying the Pan & Zoom window, as Figure 25-11 shows.

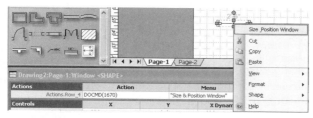

Figure 25-11.   This shape includes a custom formula in the Actions section of the ShapeSheet that displays the Size & Position window.

Visio includes a function called DOCMD (for "do command") that causes a command to be executed. When you add a DOCMD function to a formula in the Action cell of the ShapeSheet window, you can add a Visio command to a shape's shortcut menu. The DOCMD function takes as its argument an identifier that maps to a command on a Visio menu. These identifiers are documented for programmers in the Visio Type Library, which you can display with the Object Browser in Microsoft Visual Basic for Applications. For the purposes of this book, a handful of identifiers for useful commands are provided. For example, you can display the Size & Position window with the following formula, where 1670 identifies the Size & Position Window command:

```
=DOCMD(1670)
```

> **Caution** The downside of the DOCMD function is that it can get you into trouble—it executes a command without regard for other actions that are taking place in Visio. For example, you can use the DOCMD function to add the Change Spelling command to a shape's shortcut menu, but the command won't do anything, because it doesn't work outside of the context of the Spelling command. In past versions of Visio, users were actively discouraged from using this function by a lack of documentation. Still, you can safely use the DOCMD function for commands that do not require particular data to be available, such as displaying the Custom Properties window or changing zoom level.

Follow these steps to add a Visio command to a shape's shortcut menu:

1 Display the Actions section for a shape as described in an earlier procedure.

2 If the Actions section doesn't include a blank row, select the last Menu or Action cell. Then right-click the cell and choose Insert Row After.

3 Click the Menu cell in the row you inserted to display its formula on the formula bar at the top of the screen. The current formula looks like this:

=""

4 Click the insertion point between the two quotation marks. Type the name of the command as you want it to appear on the shortcut menu. The command name must appear between the quotation marks. Press Enter or click the Accept button (the blue check mark) to add the formula.

5 Double-click the Action cell in the same row to edit its formula (which is currently 0).

6 Type **DOCMD** followed by parentheses and a command identifier. (See Table 25-5 for a list of useful commands and their identifiers.)

7 Press Enter or click the Accept button. The new row in the Actions section should look something like this:

8 To test the new command, click the Close button in the ShapeSheet window to return to the drawing page. Then right-click the shape, and choose the new command.

Table 25-5. Command Identifiers for Use with the DOCMD Function

Command	Identifier	Command	Identifier
View, Size & Position Window	1670	View, Zoom, 75%	1034
View, Drawing Explorer Window	1721	View, Zoom, 100%	1035
View, Pan & Zoom Window	1653	View, Zoom, 150%	1036
File, Print Preview	1490	View, Zoom, 200%	1037
View, Zoom, 50%	1279	View, Zoom, 400%	1280

Part 7

Inside Technical Diagrams

Managing Facilities with Space Plans

Because Microsoft Office Visio 2003 can integrate information with graphical symbols, it has the potential to streamline tasks where you need to see the big picture as well as track countless details. Planning office space, moving employees, and managing facilities are examples of this type of task. In Visio, a space plan provides both a visual representation of a facility as well as up-to-date information about its contents that you can use to locate an office or other space, a piece of equipment or other physical asset, or even a person.

Managing office space and facility moves is a complex business, and the tools that Visio Professional provides—though always improving—are not entirely intuitive. However, they have been made easier with the addition of a new feature in Visio 2003—the Space Plan Startup Wizard.

This chapter explains how to use the Space Plan Startup Wizard, or set up your own model of a facility by preparing an existing floor plan and importing or adding facilities data. Then the chapter describes all you need to know about formatting and working with your space plan.

> **Note** The space plan functionality is included only with Visio Professional. It is not available in Visio Standard.

About Space Plans

Space plans can start out a lot like other floor plans and office layout diagrams. However, the Space Plan template is an application unto itself, and, frankly, this chapter only begins to describe its possibilities. The diagram you create might look like other Visio diagrams inasmuch as you can work with shapes. However, you're probably better off thinking of space plans as a different entity altogether, because you're not only creating a diagram, you're building a *model* of a facility. Part of the model is visible in the shapes on the drawing page, but the heart of the model is behind the scenes in the associations you create between shapes, spaces, people, and assets.

In fact, you can take a regular floor plan or any Visio diagram and convert it to a space plan. The result is a visual database—a picture of your facility with an extra layer of tools underneath the diagram that let you track information about people, space, equipment, and assets, as Figure 26-1 shows. That information is probably something your organization already has in the form of an operations or human resources database. Visio can link your existing data source to shapes in a floor plan diagram. Shapes don't have to be linked to an external data source; you can use Visio to enter information directly. In either case, with the facilities data, a floor plan becomes a model that can represent your office spaces, employees, network equipment, workstations, modular furniture, and more.

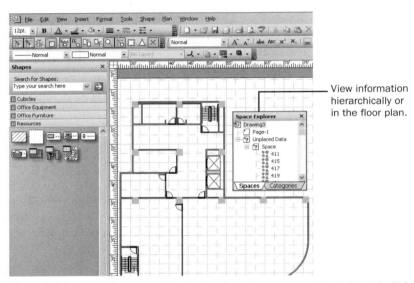

View information hierarchically or in the floor plan.

Figure 26-1. A Visio space plan looks like a floor plan but includes a built-in database of information about an organization.

Whenever you bring external data into the picture, you add power but also a layer of complexity to the diagramming task. Working with databases is a specialty, just as drafting or diagramming floor plans is a specialty. What Visio Professional provides is a way to tie the two specialties together. The Space Plan template is really designed for an applications developer or IT person in a facilities department, who can set up a model in Visio that represents his or her organization. Once a space plan is set up, it's designed so that anyone can use it to locate people and assets. If you're not a technician and you want to link your space plan to an existing database, you might require the services of your local database guru during the setup phase. On the other hand, Visio's new Space Plan Startup Wizard, which we cover later in this chapter, simplifies the process, but it is not intended to be a solution to all your space plan needs.

In general, you set up a space plan as follows:

1   Open the Space Plan template in the Building Plan folder, and then create, import, or copy a floor plan into the diagram.

2   Define the spaces for which you want to track information. For example, each office in a floor plan can be a space. To designate an area as a space, you can use a space shape or import data.

3   Identify each space in your drawing with a unique identifier (the space ID) and a name. You can type these values in Visio or import the information.

4   Add the assets, equipment, and people you want to track in the plan. You can add shapes to do this and then enter the information manually using the Custom Properties window. You can also import existing information from a spreadsheet or database.

5   Associate the assets, equipment, people, and other resources with spaces. Visio can make these associations automatically if you import the information from a data source that includes location information, or you can indicate what goes where manually.

As you can see, a lot of flexibility is built into Visio's space plans—you can use shapes, you can import data, or you can type information. More options usually means more complexity, and space plans aren't exactly straightforward to set up. The five general steps just outlined translate into quite a few more specific steps, even if you opt for the more automated technique and import data. The sections that follow steer you through the winding paths you must take to get from a floor plan to a fully functioning, data-rich space plan. Then it does get easy: you relocate people and assets simply by dragging shapes in your plan. You can also create reports that show how assets are allocated or how different departments use space.

Using the Explorer Window

A space plan includes a unique Explorer window that displays all the information included in your facility model. In fact, the Explorer window can actually display more information than the facility drawing can. Everything you see in a floor plan—assets, people, equipment, and so on—is listed in the Explorer window, but the reverse is not necessarily true. You can store information about your facility in the Explorer window without using a shape to represent it on the drawing.

The Explorer window provides two views of your facility information, as Figure 26-2 shows:

●   **The Categories tab**   This tab lists all the information in your space plan according to the following categories: Asset, Boundary, Computer, Equipment, Fixture, Furniture, Person, Printer, and Space.

●   **The Spaces tab**   This tab lists all the physical spaces you've set up and the assets, people, and information associated with a particular space.

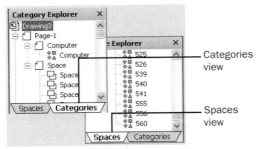

Figure 26-2.   You can track resources in your floor plan by category or by space in the Explorer window. Click a tab to switch views.

You can use the Explorer window to show where people and things are located in a floor plan, as Figure 26-3 shows. Right-click an item on the Categories or Spaces tab, and then choose Show. Visio pans the floor plan and selects the shape associated with the space, asset, or person. In addition, you can use the Explorer window to rearrange furniture and equipment and even move a person from one office to another—the drawing automatically reflects the changes.

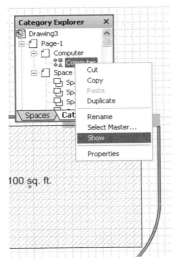

Figure 26-3.   You can locate people, spaces, and assets listed in the Explorer window with the Show command on the shortcut menu.

Like other windows in Visio, you can dock the Explorer window against an edge of the drawing page, or you can move it into the stencil area or above or below the drawing window to give you more space to view the floor plan.

> **Tip**   Merge windows in space plans
>
> You might want to dock the Custom Properties window inside the Explorer window, because space plans can include facilities data in the form of custom properties. To do this, drag the Custom Properties window into the Explorer window. The Custom Props tab then appears with the Spaces and Categories tabs for easy access to all the information stored with a space plan. The easiest way to undock a window is to drag it by its tab to a new location.

Understanding Shape Categories

When you drag shapes, such as furniture or computers, onto the drawing page, Visio automatically assigns them to one of the default categories. The exception is if you use a shape from a stencil not included with the Space Plan template; then you must assign it to the appropriate category with the Assign Category command. Unless shapes are assigned to categories, they don't appear in the Explorer window and Visio doesn't recognize them as resources in your facility.

> For details, see "Assigning a Category to a Shape," page 788.

> **Note**   Visio's default categories aren't flexible; you can't rename them or define your own. Perhaps this will change in a future release, but for now Visio tracks everything by these category names.

Understanding Unplaced Data

Resources in a space plan are *placed* when they appear on the floor plan drawing and are *associated* with a space or person. For example, you can drag a computer shape into the space that represents office 4N111 to place the computer and associate it with that office space, as Figure 26-4 shows. The Explorer window also includes a category named Unplaced Data. Sometimes when you import facilities or employee information from an external data source, the information is added to the underlying model as unplaced data but doesn't appear on the floor plan drawing.

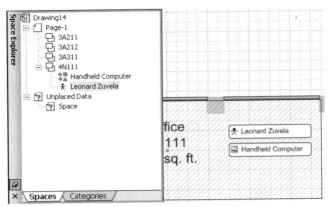

Figure 26-4. Placed resources—such as the handheld computer and the employee in this office—appear in the drawing. Because they're associated with office 4N111, they are also listed under the appropriate space in the Explorer window.

Placing and associating resources are key concepts to working successfully with the model of your facility that the Visio drawing file represents. The Explorer window shows all the information in your space plan; the floor plan drawing might not. You can drag an item from the Unplaced Data list in the Explorer window onto the page to create a shape for it and "place" it. The Explorer window is then updated to show where you've placed it. If you move shapes around in the drawing, such as moving a person shape to a new office, the data in the Explorer window is also updated.

Note If you delete a shape in the drawing, it's deleted from the Explorer window and doesn't return to Unplaced Shapes.

Displaying a Floor Plan in a Space Plan

Whether or not your space plan includes facilities data from a database, it must include a floor plan. You can create one in Visio, of course, or import an architectural drawing created in another program, such as a computer-aided design (CAD) program. You can also use a graphic file in any format that Visio can import. For example, if you have a hand-drawn version of your floor plan, you can scan that into your computer, save it as a TIFF or BMP file, and import that into Visio.

The floor plan doesn't have to be especially detailed to be used for tracking facilities information. You can even draw rectangles and other shapes using Visio's drawing tools and use the results as a rough space plan. If your space occupies more than one floor, display each floor on a separate page of the same drawing file. You can also split floors across pages for easier viewing. However, if your space occupies more than one building, use separate drawing files for each building.

Whether you use a Visio floor plan or an imported one, you must add Visio shapes to take advantage of the space plan features, as Figure 26-5 shows. Visio can store facilities and asset information for rooms in the floor plan only if you attach a space shape to each room. The space shape provides a unique identifier, such as a room number, which Visio requires for tracking information. The identifier is a custom property of the space shape.

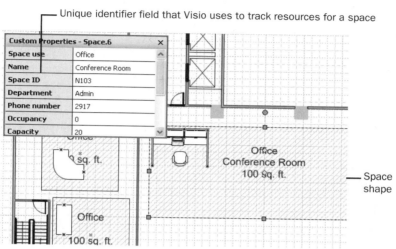

Figure 26-5.   To track information in a floor plan, rooms must be uniquely identified and associated with a space shape.

Starting a Space Plan from Scratch

Although any Visio Professional drawing can be converted into a space plan, you can start a new space plan from scratch with the Space Plan template in the Building Plan folder. This template creates a new, scaled drawing on standard letter-sized paper with a drawing scale of 1/8 inch (in.) = 1 foot (ft.). The drawing includes the Plan menu, which features commands specific to managing facilities information as well as the commands included with all of the Building Plan templates for working with rooms and walls. The template also opens the following stencils, many of which are familiar if you've used any of the other templates in the Building Plan folder:

- Cubicles
- Office Equipment
- Office Furniture
- Resources

Inside Out

The Resources stencil

The Resources stencil contains shapes that are unique to space plans. You use these shapes to represent the resources (people and physical assets) that you want to track in the plan.

For details about creating a floor plan in Visio, see Chapter 18, "Laying Out Floor and Site Plans." Follow the instructions for retaining space shapes with rooms.

Using a CAD Drawing

To use a drawing created in a CAD program as your floor plan, you need to insert it into an existing drawing. The simplest way is to start a new drawing with the Space Plan template, which sets up a standard, letter-sized page. Depending on the size of the CAD drawing you're using, you might want to enlarge the drawing page before you import. In addition, it's best to specify a drawing scale in Visio that matches the one used by your CAD drawing. When you import the CAD drawing, Visio provides options for you to set the page size and scale so that everything will fit.

Tip The new Space Plan Startup Wizard gives users the option of starting their space plan with either an existing Visio drawing, an imported CAD drawing, or an imported image file—a .bmp file, for example.

Inside Out

Converting a CAD drawing for viewing

Although you can manually convert a CAD drawing into a Visio drawing, so that each CAD object becomes a Visio shape, the Visio designers don't recommend it. Each line segment or arc in a CAD drawing becomes a separate Visio shape, which causes long redraw times that can make working with the drawing quite tedious. Before you import or convert a CAD drawing, review the information in Chapter 17, "Using CAD Drawings in Visio."

To start a space plan and insert a CAD drawing, follow these steps:

1. In Visio Professional, choose New, Building Plan, Space Plan.

   The Space Plan Startup Wizard opens. Press cancel to manually add a CAD drawing. We cover the Space Plan Wizard later in this chapter. Visio opens a new, scaled drawing page where 1/8 in. = 1 ft. The page size is 8.5 by 11 in., which allows for a space of 68 ft. by 88 ft. The Plan menu is added to the menu bar.

2   Choose Insert, CAD Drawing. Select the CAD drawing you want to use, and then click Open.

> **Tip**   Visio 2003 stores sample CAD drawings at C:/Program Files/Microsoft Office/ Visio11/Samples/1033.

3   Review the settings for your CAD drawing, and click OK. If the drawing scale of the CAD drawing doesn't match the scale set for the page, the CAD Drawing dialog box appears.

> For details about the options in the CAD Drawing dialog box, see "Importing CAD Drawings in Visio," page 476.

> **Tip**   If the CAD drawing includes more details than you need for a space plan, consider displaying only the layers or levels that contain the outline of offices and other spaces in the floor plan.

4   In the CAD Drawing dialog box, choose the option you want for fitting the CAD drawing to the Visio page, and then click OK to insert the drawing.

> **Note**   If you don't get the results you want, you can delete the inserted image and then start over using different settings in the CAD Drawing Properties dialog box. For details about your options, see "Importing CAD Drawings in Visio," page 476.

5   In the inserted CAD drawing, you may drag spaces from the Resources stencil to the drawing. As an alternative method, outline each office or area with the Rectangle tool, and then convert the rectangles to space shapes using the Assign Categories command on the Plan menu.

> For details, see "Using Shapes to Add Spaces to a Floor Plan" page 772.

Using an Existing Visio Drawing

If you've created a floor plan or rough space sketch in Visio Professional, it's easy to create a space plan from it. You can go about it in one of three ways:

● Run a macro that converts the existing floor plan to a space plan.

● Copy the existing floor plan, and then paste it into a new drawing created with the Space Plan template.

● Import the floor plan using the Space Plan Startup Wizard. We cover this method later in the chapter; maximizing the Startup Wizard's usefulness entails more than just simply importing a floor plan.

It doesn't particularly matter which way you do it. Converting an existing plan entails adding the space planning tools to the drawing, which is a simple, one-step process, but then you have to open the space plan stencils manually. When you copy and paste a floor plan or use

Chapter 26

the Space Plan Startup Wizard, you have the added security of retaining the original drawing, plus you get all the space plan stencils.

If you created a floor plan with the Floor Plan, Home Plan, Plant Layout, Reflected Ceiling Plan, or Site Plan template, the Plan menu already appears. When you use the Enable Space Plan command, Visio adds asset management and other commands to the Plan menu and provides access to the Explorer window, which displays information about the space plan.

To convert an existing drawing to a space plan, first choose Tools, Add-Ons, Building Plan, Enable Space Plan. Visio adds the space planning commands to the Plan menu, as Figure 26-6 shows.

Open Shapes

To open the Resources stencils, click the Open Shapes button on the Standard toolbar, and then select Building Plan, Resources.

Figure 26-6. After you use the Enable Space Plan command, the Plan menu includes commands for working with space and assets.

You might want to open additional stencils as well. The Space Plan template automatically opens several stencils, many of which are included with other building plan drawing types. The Resources stencil, however, is unique to space plans.

To create a space plan and add an existing Visio drawing to it, follow these steps:

1 Choose File, New, Building Plan, Space Plan. Click Cancel to close the Space Plan Startup Wizard.

Visio opens a new, scaled drawing page where 1/8 in. = 1 ft. The page size is 8.5 by 11 in., which allows for a space of 68 ft. by 88 ft. The Plan menu is added to the menu bar.

2 Choose File, Page Setup. On the Page Size tab, verify that the drawing uses the size settings you want, and make any changes. Then click the Drawing Scale tab, and verify that the scale is the one you want, and make any changes. Click OK.

> For details about setting up page size and drawing scale, see "Setting Up Measurements in a Diagram," page 421.

3 Choose File, Open, and then locate and select the existing Visio drawing containing the floor plan you want to use. Click OK to open the drawing in a new window.

4 With the existing floor plan drawing open, choose Edit, Copy Drawing.

5 Select Window, and then click Drawing1:Page-1 (or click the name of the new space plan drawing you created in step 1).

6 To paste the shapes on the current page, choose Edit, Paste.

7 Choose File, Save As to save your changes to the new space plan diagram.

Importing a Graphic to Use as a Floor Plan

A space plan can use just about any type of picture of your facility. If you don't have time to draw a floor plan in Visio, or don't have access to the original CAD drawings of the building, you can use any picture of a floor plan that comes in a Visio-compatible graphic format. You can even scan a drawing directly into Visio or import the drawing using the Space Plan Startup Wizard. For example, you can scan a floor plan sketch, save it in a graphic format such as GIF or JPEG, and then import the file into Visio. Make sure you know the name of the graphic and where it's stored on your computer or network.

Follow these steps to import a drawing for use in a space plan:

1 Choose File, New, Building Plan, Space Plan.

Click cancel to close the Space Plan Startup Wizard. We explain how to import graphic files with the Startup Wizard later in the chapter. Visio opens a new, scaled drawing page where 1/8 in. = 1 ft. The page size is 8.5 by 11 in., which allows for a space of 68 ft by 88 ft. The Plan menu is added to the menu bar.

2 Choose File, Page Setup. On the Page Size tab, verify that the drawing uses the size settings you want, and make any changes. Then click the Drawing Scale tab, and verify that the scale is the one you want, and make any changes. Click OK.

> For details about setting up page size and drawing scale, see "Setting Up Measurements in a Diagram," page 421.

3 Choose Insert, Picture, From File.

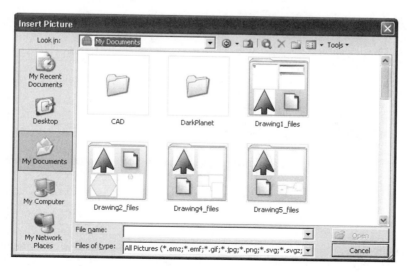

4 In the Insert Picture dialog box, locate and select the graphic you want to use, and then click Open.

After you import a graphic file, you must identify each office or area as a space. For details, see the following section.

For details about importing graphic formats into Visio, see "Importing Graphics," page 223.

Defining Spaces in a Floor Plan

For Visio Professional to track data in a space plan, you must uniquely identify each *space* with which you want to associate assets, equipment, people, and other resources. Even if your floor plan shows walls and rooms, you also need it to show space, as Figure 26-7 shows. This is a unique requirement of the Space Plan template that doesn't necessarily make intuitive sense, but it's how Visio keeps track of what goes where. The useful thing about tracking assets and people by space rather than by rooms or cubicles is that you can designate any area you want as space regardless of what your floor plan looks like.

After converting a Visio drawing to a space plan, open the Resources stencil.

Drag the Space shape into a room or area to enable asset tracking.

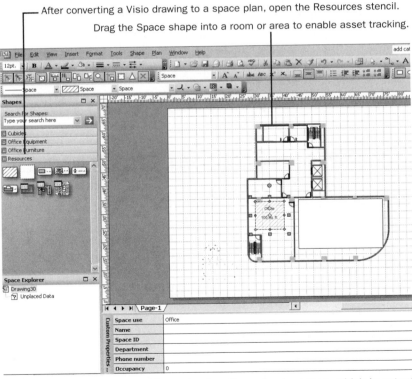

Figure 26-7. Visio tracks information in a floor plan by space, which is actually a separate shape that includes the custom properties used in associating resources with a location.

Chapter 26

Your drawing must include space, but what does that mean? In Visio terms, space in a floor plan is a shape—the Space shape. There are two general methods of adding space to a floor plan: either import it, or use space shapes. If you used the information in Chapter 18, "Laying Out Floor and Site Plans," to create a floor plan, you know that you can draw a floor plan in Visio that already includes spaces for every room. If, however, you imported a graphic or CAD file to use as a floor plan, you'll have to add space to the drawing. You can add space by dragging space shapes on top of rooms, or you can import a list of room numbers or other similar data to designate space in your floor plan.

The easiest method is to know from the outset that you need both rooms and space and then create a floor plan in Visio using wall and room shapes that include space shapes automatically. That method is described in "Using Space Shapes to Start a Floor Plan," page 512. However, that information doesn't particularly help you after the fact. The sections that follow describe how to add space to an existing floor plan that doesn't already have it.

Once your drawing includes space, each space must be uniquely identified. A unique identifier isn't anything fancy; typically, it's a room number. For example, to uniquely identify the space associated with a particular office, you could use 12-117 to specify office 117 on the 12th floor of a building. Depending on the method you used to add space to your drawing, you might need to manually identify each space. If you imported data, the space might already include a unique identifier. The value of unique identifiers for spaces is that they allow you to associate assets, people, and equipment with a given space.

> **Tip** If areas in your floor plan don't have room numbers, give them unique names that will make sense to people using the space plan, such as Kitchen 1 or Kitchen West.

 Troubleshooting

The Plan menu does not appear on the menu bar, or commands on the Plan menu seem to be missing

When you start a new drawing with the Space Plan template, Visio adds the Plan menu to the menu bar. The Plan menu includes all the commands needed to work with space and resources in a facility model. If you start a drawing with a different template, or open an existing floor plan that was based on a different template, the Plan menu might not appear, or, if it does, it might include only the Convert To Walls and Set Display Options commands. To add the Plan menu and all the space planning commands to a drawing, choose Tools, Add-Ons, Building Plan, Enable Space Plan.

Adding Space to a Floor Plan by Importing Information

If you already have a floor plan drawing, but haven't yet designated the spaces for which you want to track resources, you can import that information. If you have a spreadsheet, database, or other external data source that includes a column or record of room numbers or

Chapter 26

other unique identifiers, you can import that information with the Import Data Wizard (of course, you can also do this with the Space Plan Startup Wizard). Visio adds the information to the floor plan in the Explorer window, as Figure 26-8 shows, and then you can choose which spaces to show in the floor plan drawing.

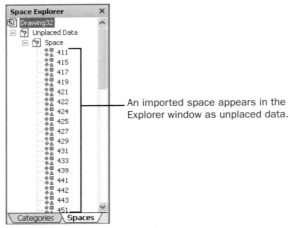

An imported space appears in the Explorer window as unplaced data.

Figure 26-8. You can define the spaces in a floor plan by importing room numbers or other information that uniquely identifies each space you want to track. To place a space in the floor plan, drag it from the Explorer window onto the drawing page.

The space data you import is stored as part of the facilities model that Visio maintains. This means that the information about a space is available and Visio can track assets for it whether or not it appears on the floor plan. The spaces are listed in the Explorer window under the Unplaced Data category. By dragging a space listed in the Explorer window onto the drawing page, you add a space shape to the floor plan.

Visio also tracks other attributes of a space as *custom properties* associated with the space shape. When you import room numbers or other space identifiers from a spreadsheet or database, you can also choose to import other information from your data source. Visio can create new custom property fields that store the values from your data source, or you can map the values to existing custom property fields. For example, space shapes already include a field called Space Use. If your data source includes a field or column of information about how a space is used—for example, Room Name—you can map the Room Name information from your data source to the existing Space Use field.

To import space information into a floor plan, follow these steps:

1 Choose Plan, Import Data to start the Import Data Wizard.

Chapter 26

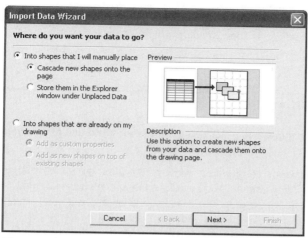

2 Choose where you want your data to go. Each selection provides a preview and explanation in the Preview section of the dialog box.

3 Follow the instructions on each screen to link to your data source and specify the fields containing space information.

For details about each wizard screen, see "Using the Import Data Wizard," page 776.

4 Click Finish. Visio imports the data. If you selected the Show Report check box, Visio opens your browser and displays the Import Data Report, which lists all the spaces it imported and the action it took. "Unplaced" means that the spaces were added to the Explorer window but not placed on the drawing page.

5 In Visio, click the Categories tab in the Explorer window.

Tip If you don't see the Explorer window, choose Plan, Explorer to open it.

6 Click to expand Unplaced Data, and then expand Space. The column data or fields you imported as space identifiers are listed.

7 Drag a space from the Explorer window onto the drawing and drop it on top of the room, office, or area that the space information corresponds to. Visio creates a space shape and sizes it to fit the room if the room was created with Visio shapes. If you're dropping space on top of nonwalled areas or an imported floor plan drawing, the space shape is not sized to fit.

8 If a space shape doesn't fit in an office or area, select the space, and then drag a selection handle to resize it manually. Make sure that space shapes don't overlap.

9 To see the properties that you imported with the space, choose View, Custom Properties Window, and then select a space on the drawing.

> **Tip** If the Custom Properties window is open, you can see the properties associated with each space as you select it. Then you can verify that the data you imported was added correctly.

Troubleshooting

After adding space shapes to a floor plan, all the furniture and other shapes have green stripes

If you drop space shapes on top of an existing floor plan, the space shapes will be displayed on top of existing shapes. You can move the space shapes behind other shapes so that their stripes don't obscure furniture, walls, and so on. To do this, select a space shape, and then select Shape, Order, Move To Back.

Chapter 26

Using Shapes to Add Spaces to a Floor Plan

Your floor plan probably already includes space if you see areas with green diagonal lines (the default fill style for the space shape), as Figure 26-9 shows. If your Visio floor plan doesn't have space shapes, though, or if you're using a CAD drawing or graphic for your floor plan, you can add space shapes to the drawing manually. The technique is simple but it can be time-consuming, particularly if your floor plan contains many rooms or offices. After you've added a space shape for every room in the floor plan, you need to assign a room number or other unique identifier to each space. You use the space shape's custom properties to do this. That means manual data entry, another time-consuming process, but you do it only once.

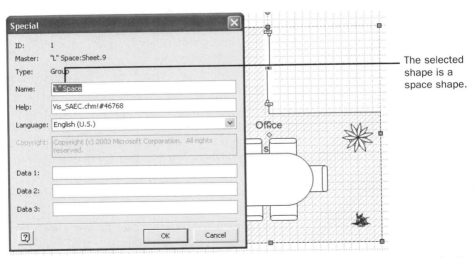

The selected shape is a space shape.

Figure 26-9. The Special dialog box reveals the name of the master used to create the shape shown in the Name box. By default, space shapes in a Visio floor plan look like areas with green diagonal lines.

Inside Out

Spaces in Visio floor plans

If you're using a Visio floor plan, you might already have a space shape for each room in the floor plan. To verify, select a shape, and then choose Format, Special. If it is a space shape, you'll see Master: Space at the top of the Special dialog box. Visio adds a space shape automatically when you use the Room shape to create a room. In addition, when you start a floor plan by designating spaces, you have the option to create space shapes when you convert the spaces to walls.

Follow these steps to manually add space to a floor plan:

1 Drag the Space shape from the Resources stencil onto a room.

If you're using a Visio floor plan, the Space shape snaps to the room's dimensions. However, Visio doesn't recognize the static vector lines in the background on a CAD drawing or graphic, so you'll have to resize the space shape for rooms in each of those types of drawings yourself.

Note Don't overlap space shapes. Visio can't track assets for overlapping areas.

2 To adjust the size of a space, drag a selection handle on the space shape. For example, you can trace a CAD floor plan in this way to create a mosaic of space shapes on top of it.

3 Repeat steps 1 and 2 to add a space shape to every room in the floor plan.

Tip Rather than use a space shape, you can draw with one of the drawing tools and convert the results into space. Select the shape, select Plan, Assign Category, and then choose Space from the Category list. Click OK.

4 If the Custom Properties window is not already open, choose View, Custom Properties Window.

5 To add an identifier to a space shape manually, select a space shape on the drawing page to display its properties in the Custom Properties window.

Chapter 26

Custom Properties - Space	☒
Space use	Office
Name	
Space ID	
Department	
Phone number	
Occupancy	0
Capacity	0
Space height	
Base elevation	
Zones	
Calculated area	100 ft.^2

`\ Categories / Spaces \ Custom Props /`

6 In the Space ID field, type a unique name or identifier for the space, and then press Enter. For example, type the office room number. The value for Space ID for each space must be unique within the drawing file, particularly in a multiple-page drawing where each page represents a different floor in a building.

7 Select the next space in the drawing, and then repeat step 6 until all the spaces are identified.

You can type in the other fields for each space shape, but the Space ID is the one field that Visio requires to associate assets and resources with spaces. If you type a value for the Name field, the text is displayed on the space shape unless you've specified different display options with the Label Shapes command on the Plan menu.

> **Tip**   Hide background images in a floor plan
> After you position space shapes on an imported CAD or graphic floor plan, you can hide the layer that contains the CAD or the graphic image so that your drawing is less cluttered. To hide the layer, choose View, Layer Properties, and then uncheck the Visible column for the graphic or CAD drawing layer.

Defining Boundaries Around Areas

When you're setting up space in a floor plan, you can designate special areas by using the Boundary shape on the Resources stencil. The Boundary shape is useful for calculating square footage for areas that include multiple rooms or spaces. You can also use it to denote spaces that belong to a particular department or function. The Boundary shape just gives you another way to track information in your space plan. It's listed in the Categories view of the Explorer window and appears on the page as a dotted line that encloses the spaces you specify, as Figure 26-10 shows.

Chapter 26

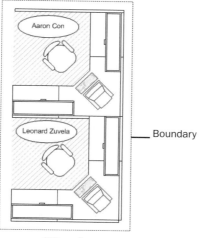

— Boundary

132 sq. ft.

Figure 26-10. You can use the Boundary shape to visually identify multiple spaces as a unit in a floor plan.

You can't associate people or assets with a boundary, but you can use a boundary to track space usage. Boundary shapes include custom properties for space use, name, department, phone number, occupancy, and capacity. In addition, you can give a boundary a unique space identifier.

To add a boundary around spaces in your floor plan, follow these steps:

1 Drag the Boundary shape from the Resources stencil onto the drawing page near the offices or areas you want to put a boundary around.

2 Drag a selection handle on the boundary shape to stretch the shape so that it encloses the area you want.

3 If the area you want to enclose isn't rectangular, edit the boundary shape. To do this, select the Pencil tool, Ctrl+click the edges of the boundary to add vertices, and then drag the vertices to reshape the shape.

> For details about editing with the Pencil tool, see "Editing Shapes with the Pencil Tool," page 639.

4 If you want to indicate the purpose of the bounded space, display the boundary's custom properties, and then type in the Space Use field. To display the boundary's properties, you can either open the Custom Properties window (choose View, Custom Properties Window), or right-click the boundary, and then click Properties.

5 To enter a name for the bounded area that appears in the Explorer window, type in the Name box.

6 To display a name on the boundary shape, select the boundary, choose Plan, Label Shapes, and then select a property to use for the name.

For details about labeling shapes, see "Displaying Labels on Shapes," page 794.

Troubleshooting

Text looks fuzzy after adding Boundary shapes to a floor plan

The Boundary shape includes a 70 percent transparent fill that is barely discernible but has the side effect of making shapes underneath look somewhat washed out. If shape text looks less readable after adding a Boundary shape to your floor plan, you can try one of the following:

- **Move the shape behind the others**   Select the Boundary shape, and then choose Shape, Order, Send To Back.
- **Remove the fill**   Select the Boundary, click the Fill Color button on the Standard toolbar, and then click No Fill.

Using the Import Data Wizard

Imported data can bring a space plan to life, but you don't need it to create a space plan in Visio. However, if you have a floor plan of some type and a spreadsheet or database of facility and employee information, you can bring the two together in Visio Professional. The Space Plan template includes the Import Data command on the Plan menu, which starts a wizard that you can use to import the information you want to include. It's easiest to import data from a Microsoft Excel spreadsheet, but you can import information from Microsoft Exchange Server, Microsoft Active Directory, or any ODBC-compliant database, which includes most popular database programs.

Note   ODBC stands for *open database connectivity*, a standard that Microsoft created to help you import database information into many different kinds of applications. If you aren't sure whether your database is ODBC-compliant, check its documentation.

The one piece of information your data source should include is a space identifier, as Figure 26-11 shows. The wizard uses the space identifier to figure out where to put the imported data in your floor plan. If you're importing information about spaces, the space identifier is the field in your data source that uniquely identifies each space—typically, a room number. If you're importing information about people or equipment, the space identifier is the field in your data source that matches the identifier already assigned to the space shapes in your drawing. For example, you can import an employee list so that your floor plan shows who sits where. In addition to employee names, your employee list must also include a space identifier that matches the spaces you've set up in your floor plan. Then, when the employee names are imported, the wizard can automatically associate people with spaces.

Managing Facilities with Space Plans

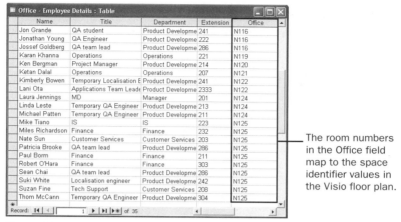

The room numbers in the Office field map to the space identifier values in the Visio floor plan.

Figure 26-11. When you import employee names from a Microsoft Access table, the wizard automatically places the names in the correct offices.

> For details about assigning identifiers to space shapes, see "Defining Spaces in a Floor Plan," page 768.

For details about assigning identifiers to space shapes, see "Defining Spaces in a Floor Plan," page 768.

If your data source doesn't include location information or a space ID, you can still import information from it, but you'll have to place the imported items in your floor plan manually where you want them. For example, if you have a database of computer equipment owned by different departments in your organization, you can import the data into your floor plan. To show where the equipment is located, you must drag individual computers from the Explorer window into the offices or rooms of your floor plan.

Starting the Import Data Wizard

The Import Data Wizard works like this: you point the wizard to your data source and indicate which columns or fields to import and where to put the data in your floor plan. The wizard imports the information and displays it in the Explorer window, from which you can choose the items you want to add to your floor plan. You might not want to display all of the data you import in the drawing, but you can always view and work with it in the Explorer window. You can use the imported data as criteria for color-coding spaces, and you can change which data is displayed at any time. To begin importing data with the Import Data Wizard, select Plan, Import Data. The sections that follow describe each screen in the wizard.

> **Tip** The Import Data Wizard can place people and assets in their correct locations, as long as each space shape in your drawing includes a space identifier (such as an office number) and your external data source includes the same identifier.

Preparing to Use a Database

Visio is able to link shapes in a floor plan to external data through the shapes' custom properties. The link is one-directional—that is, from the data source to the Visio shapes. You can refresh your floor plan with the latest information from your data source, but changes you make to facilities information in Visio cannot be written back to your data source. If you plan to work with an external data source, it helps to do the following before you start:

- **Create a data source**   If you're using a database other than Exchange Server or Active Directory, make sure that you have a data source for it. A *data source* is a file with the extension .dsn that allows you to connect to a data provider. You might already have the necessary data source on your computer, or an information systems technician or database expert can create one for you. If you don't know whether you have a data source, you can start to set up your space plan, and then determine whether a data source for your database is listed when you attempt to import data. You can use the Windows Control Panel to set up ODBC data sources.

- **Ensure that you have access to the data source**   To import data from a corporate or shared database, you might need specific permissions and network access. If database access requires a password, make sure you have the right one.

Inside Out

Exporting data from other formats

Even if your database isn't ODBC-compliant, you can probably export data from it into a format that Visio can import, such as tab-delimited or comma-delimited text, which are common output formats supported by most database programs. Then you can set up an ODBC data source for the exported file. The bottom line is that if you need to pull data in from a proprietary or legacy data source, you probably can—but you might need to have a professional prepare your data.

Step 1: Selecting Where You Want Your Data to Be Placed

On the first screen of the Import Data Wizard, you must select where you want your data to go, as Figure 26-12 shows. The options are as follows:

- Import the data into shapes that you will manually place. Choose this option to either create new shapes and cascade them onto the drawing page or create new shapes and store them in the Explorer Window under Unplaced Data.

- Import the data into shapes that are already on the drawing. If you choose this option you can choose to either add the data as a custom property or as a new shape on top of an existing shape.

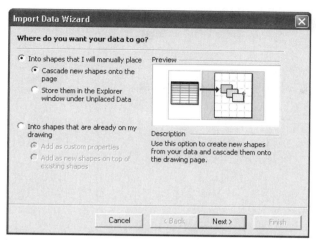

Figure 26-12. The first screen of the Import Data Wizard allows you to select where you want your data to go.

The category choices are Person, Space, Boundary, Computer, Printer, Asset, Equipment, Fixture, and Furniture. The shapes associated with each category are shown on the Resources stencil. Use the Space and Boundary categories to import information about locations and the Person category to import lists of people. Use the Computer, Equipment, Fixture, Furniture, and Printer categories to track these types of assets. The Asset category is useful for anything else not covered by the other categories.

After you have made your choice, click Next to proceed to the next screen in the wizard.

Step 2: Attaching to a Database

On the second screen of the Import Data Wizard, you identify the external data source you want to use. In the Type box, choose the type of database or spreadsheet that contains your space information. Depending on your choice, the options differ as follows:

- If you choose Excel, click Browse, locate the spreadsheet file, and then click OK, as Figure 26-13 shows. The name of the file will appear in the Name box. You can also use the Name box drop-down list to choose a name.

Chapter 26

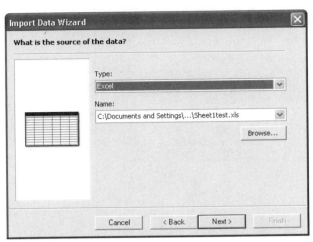

Figure 26-13. When you choose Excel for Source, the Name and Browse options are available. Click Browse to locate the spreadsheet you want to use as your data source.

- If you choose Active Directory or Exchange Server, click Next to log on to the appropriate server.

- If you're using any other kind of database or spreadsheet (such as an Access database, a proprietary human resources system, or an Oracle database), choose ODBC, and then click Next. On the screen that appears, select a data source name (DSN) in the Data Source box. A Select Database dialog box opens, where you locate a specific database file and then click OK. In the Import Data Wizard, Visio then lists the database's catalogs and tables, as Figure 26-14 shows. Select the one you want to use.

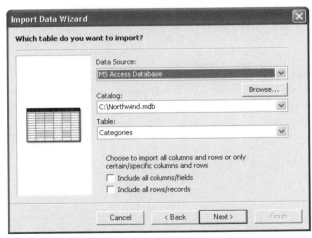

Figure 26-14. After you select a data source, you can choose the catalog and table that contain the information you want. This Access database doesn't support catalogs, so the wizard displays its file name instead.

When you've specified the file from which to import data, click Next to continue with the wizard.

Step 3: Identifying the Name and Location Information

On the next wizard screen (see Figure 26-15), you can choose to import all columns/fields and rows/records or none. If you choose to import all of both, skip to step 4 below. If you leave either or both boxes blank, the next screen allows you to choose specific columns or rows that you wish to import. This is critical, because in these two steps you specify the fields in your database that provide the information that the Import Data Wizard needs to match the data to the right space. The wizard needs to be able to name a record, match it to a space in the floor plan, match it to that space in the correct building, and link the database records to the space plan. If you choose to specify the fields, you can choose from the list of data fields present in your database in the next two screens.

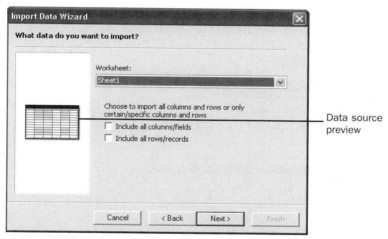

Figure 26-15. The wizard allows you to choose all of the data fields in this dialog box. If you leave either check box unselected, you will be allowed to choose specific fields on the next couple of screens.

Step 4: Finishing Up

The next screens differ depending on whether you chose to import the data into shapes that you would manually place or shapes that are already on your drawing. Let's look first at the options available if you chose to import data into shapes that you would manually place or import data into shapes on top of existing shapes.

● After you choose the data fields to import, the Import Data Wizard asks you to select which shape you want to import the data to. If you don't see a shape that you wish to use, click Browse to locate more shapes.

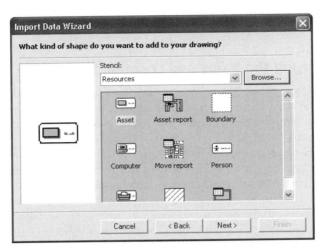

- Choose the field that you wish to label and color the shapes. For example, if you choose to label with the Name field, each shape will be labeled with the data string in Name (usually individual names).

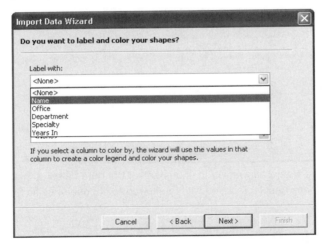

- The next screen asks you to choose which column in your data contains unique identifiers. This is usually Name or ID. The unique identifier is the key that ties a row of data to a specific shape. This identifier must be unique for each row of data (for example, a room number). Click Next and the Import Data Wizard imports the data and presents a drawing update summary, as Figure 26-16 shows. The drawing update also provides an Import Data Report link. Clicking the link displays a Hypertext Markup Language (HTML) file of the imported data.

Chapter 26

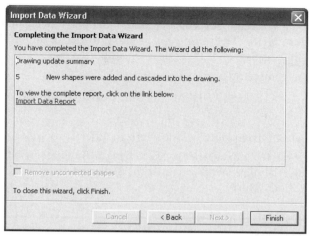

Figure 26-16. The drawing update summary summarizes Visio's actions and provides a link to view the Import Data Report.

Now let's look at how to import data as custom properties of existing shapes:

- After choosing the data fields to import, choose the field that you wish to label and color the shapes. For example, if you choose to label with the Name field, each shape will be labeled with the data string in Name (usually individual names).

- Next, choose into which shapes' custom properties you wish to import the data.

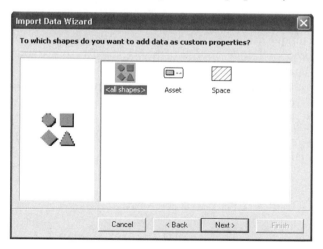

- Next the Import Data Wizard asks you to choose a property that uniquely identifies the shape to which you wish to import the data. Choose from the drop-down menu. The usual identifier is Space ID, but you can choose whichever identifier you like.

- On the next screen you choose a column in your data that has matching values. For example, if you chose Space ID in the previous step, then perhaps the Office column in your data would have matching data (that is, the name of the office/space ID).

Chapter 26

Visio will use this information to link your data to the proper shapes. Click Next and the Import Data Wizard imports the data and presents a drawing update summary, as shown in Figure 26-16. The drawing update also provides an Import Data Report link. Clicking the link displays an HTML file of the imported data.

- Click Finish to complete the wizard.

If your data was imported as Unplaced Data, you can associate it with a location in one of two ways:

- Drag an item from the Explorer window into an office or room.
- On the Categories tab, expand the Space list. Drag an unplaced item onto a space in the Space list. This is a little easier if you resize the Explorer window so that Unplaced Data and Space are both visible.

Troubleshooting

The Refresh Data command does not update the information in the space plan

The Refresh Data command works only if you imported data from a data source that includes a field that uniquely identifies each record and you mapped this field to a key in the Import Data Wizard.

Refreshing the Data

If you want to update the data in your drawing when your database changes, you can as long as you identified a unique field when you imported the data. Updating, or refreshing, the data is a one-way process: Visio reconnects to the original data source and imports the fields and their current values, which overwrites the information in your current drawing. If you've made changes to your space plan—for example, if you've moved employees around or real-located resources—your changes might be lost after you refresh.

Choose Plan, Refresh Data to refresh the data in your drawing. Visio refreshes the data and displays a drawing update summary, as Figure 26-17 shows. Like the Import Data Wizard, this dialog box contains options to remove unconnected shapes and to show a report of the import activity.

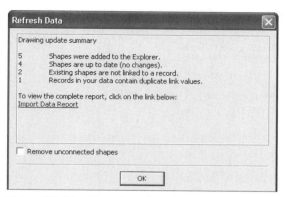

Figure 26-17. To update the information in your floor plan, choose Plan, Refresh Data. Visio reimports the data, overwriting the values in your model, and displays this dialog box.

Troubleshooting

Refreshing the data in the space plan overwrites changes that were made to the diagram

If you want to refresh the data in your facility model without losing the changes you've made in the drawing, the only way to do this is to make the same changes to the original data source. For example, if you move a person in a floor plan based on an imported spreadsheet of employee names, you must record the new location in the spreadsheet. If you aren't sure whether you made changes that will be overwritten, make a backup copy of your drawing before you refresh the data. That way you can compare the drawings later.

Another trick for keeping the information in sync between a space plan and your data source is to check the Unplaced Shapes listing. It can serve as a red flag for identifying problems in your data source. You can print a list of unplaced shapes for your database administrator to use in correcting the data.

If Visio can't locate your data source, it displays a message. If you click OK in the message box, a Login dialog box appears, from which you can reconnect to the data source.

 Using the Space Plan Startup Wizard

Although manageable, importing data to a space plan can be somewhat tedious. However, Visio 2003's Space Plan Startup Wizard makes the process much easier—at least when starting a new site plan from scratch. The wizard guides you through the process with minimal fuss. Here's how to use it:

1 Select File, New, Building Plan, Space Plan.

2 Select the type of file or floor plan you want to base your space plan on. Choose None if you wish to construct your space plan from scratch.

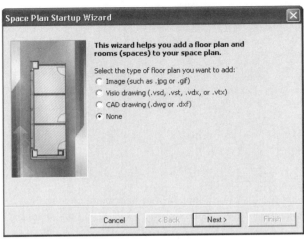

3   Browse to and select the file you chose in the previous step using the provided selection windows.

4   In the next window select how you want to add room numbers to your drawing. There are three methods: from an existing spreadsheet, from a new spreadsheet, and manually. If you choose an existing spreadsheet, you can select the Excel worksheet in the following dialog box. Also select the column in the selected spreadsheet that contains the room numbers from the drop-down list. These numbers are used to identify the created spaces. The Space Plan Startup Wizard imports the data and displays the Completing The Space Plan Startup Wizard screen. Click Finish to exit the Space Plan Startup screen.

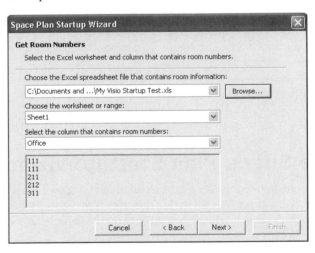

Note   You can only import data from an Excel worksheet in the Space Plan Startup Wizard.

5 If you choose to add the room numbers to your drawing from a new spreadsheet, Excel opens with a sample spreadsheet that you can use to enter your data. When you are finished entering data, save the spreadsheet and close Excel. The Space Plan Startup Wizard imports the data and displays the Completing The Space Plan Startup Wizard screen. Click Finish to exit the Space Plan Startup screen.

6 If you choose manual addition, Visio whisks you away to the Completing The Space Plan Startup Wizard screen. Click Finish to exit the Space Plan Startup Wizard screen.

Adding and Associating Resources

You can add people, space, computers, equipment, and other resources to your space plan without ever linking to a database or spreadsheet. Visio can act as a visual data entry screen where you use shapes to specify the resources you want to track. You can drag shapes from the Resources stencil to add people, equipment, fixtures, and other assets to a floor plan drawing, as Figure 26-18 shows.

Figure 26-18. To add people, equipment, and other assets manually to a space plan, drag a shape from the Resources stencil into a space on your floor plan.

When you use a shape from the Resources stencil, Visio adds it to the plan with the default shape name (for example, Person, Equipment, Computer, and so on). This is the name that appears in the Explorer window. If you add five printers to a floor plan, the Explorer window will display five resources named Printer. To provide a unique name, right-click the resource in the Explorer window, choose Rename, and then type. You might find it easier, however, to use the Custom Properties window, where you can type in the Name field. Both windows use the same name, so it doesn't matter which one you use; whatever you type will appear in the other window as well, as Figure 26-19 shows.

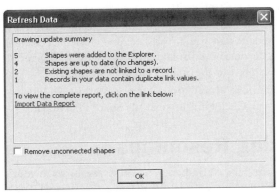

Figure 26-19. You can identify a resource by typing a name in the Custom Properties window or by right-clicking a resource in the Explorer window, and then choosing Rename.

Assigning a Category to a Shape

The resources you track in a space plan—assets, furniture, equipment—can appear as shapes in your floor plan drawing and as items within categories in the Explorer window. As long as you're using the shapes that open with the Space Plan template, Visio can categorize information correctly. However, if you draw a shape or use a shape from some other stencil, it won't appear in the Explorer window, and Visio won't recognize it as a resource in your facility model, even though you can see the shape on the page.

To add a shape to the model and have it listed in the Explorer window, you must assign the shape to a category. The categories are Space, Boundary, Person, Computer, Printer, Fixture, Furniture, and Equipment. For example, you can use the Laptop shape from the Basic Network Shapes stencil to show which employees have departmental laptops. If you want the laptops to be listed with other computers in the Explorer window, you must assign them to the Computer category, as Figure 26-20 shows.

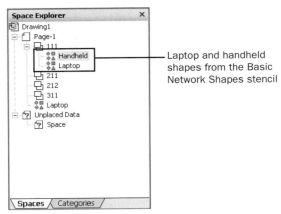

Laptop and handheld shapes from the Basic Network Shapes stencil

Figure 26-20. When you assign shapes to a category, they are listed on the Categories tab.

Visio also assigns the same set of custom properties to all the shapes in a category. That way, you can track the same information for all equipment, all fixtures, all furniture, and so on. When you assign a shape to a category, Visio adds the category's properties to the shape so that you can enter location and other information. This has two useful results:

● If you're using a shape that didn't come from a space plan stencil, you can assign it to a category as a way of quickly adding a set of consistent custom properties.

● If you want a space plan shape to track different information, you can reassign its category, which adds the new category's properties.

If your shape already includes custom properties with valuable data that you don't want to lose, you can map the shape's properties to the space plan properties that Visio recognizes.

To assign a shape to a category, follow these steps:

1 Select a shape or multiple shapes, and then choose Plan, Assign Category.

2 In the Category list, select the category that contains the properties you want to add to the shape. If you're not certain which category to choose, click Properties. Custom properties for the selected category are shown in the Category Properties list.

3 If your shape already includes custom properties that you want to keep or map to the category's properties, click Properties.

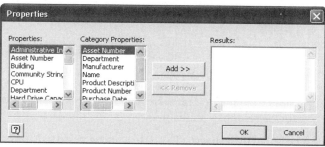

4 To match the shape's properties to the category's properties, select an existing shape property in the Properties list, select its match in the Category Properties list, and then click Add. When you're finished, click OK to return to the main Assign Category dialog box.

5 Click OK to close the Assign Category dialog box.

You can drag the Printer shape from the Resources stencil onto your site plan and use the shape to find a printer in the directory or browse for a printer. After you have found the printer, you can set it as the default printer or open the print queue. Just click on the printer's Smart Tag drop-down menu and choose the appropriate action.

Associating Spaces, Assets, and People

When you want your floor plan to show that a person goes in a particular space, or an asset belongs to a particular person, you can *associate* the resources. Associating resources means that the Explorer window will display the resource in the right place, as Figure 26-21 shows. Resources that are associated with a specific space are listed under that space on the Spaces tab of the Explorer window.

Figure 26-21. On the Spaces tab of the Explorer window, you can see the resources that are associated with a particular space. Here, the space named 111 is associated with a handheld, a printer, and a laptop.

One way that people and assets can be associated with spaces is by importing. When you specify a space ID in the Import Data Wizard, Visio knows to import the person or asset into a particular space. However, if you want to show that a person has moved to a new location, or if you're using shapes from the Resources stencil to add new information to the floor plan, you need to associate the resources manually:

- **Associate a person with a space** To do this, drag a person shape onto a space shape.
- **Associate an asset with a space** You can do this by dragging an asset shape onto a space shape. An asset shape includes the shape called Asset but also any of the other shapes that you're using to represent assets in your floor plan.

Chapter 26

Troubleshooting

After you have added network or other shapes to a space plan, they don't appear in the Explorer window

You can add shapes from stencils that aren't opened with the Space Plan template, but Visio won't recognize them as resources in your plan until you assign them to the appropriate category (for example, Person, Equipment, Computer, Space, and so on). For details, see "Assigning a Category to a Shape," page 788.

Formatting the Data in Your Space Plan

If you want just a simple seating arrangement, your space plan might be complete as is. However, you can refine the drawing to serve other purposes as well. You can color-code spaces to show at a glance how they're used, which employees are full-time, or even which rooms contain printers. And you can use the labeling feature to change the wording that appears on shapes. For example, if the IT department wants to see which computers in a floor plan need to be upgraded, you could label each office space with the amount of RAM in its computer.

Color-Coding Shapes

Suppose you want to see where different departments are located on a floor or which offices contain a particular type of equipment. If you've entered custom property data for the resources in your space plan, you can take advantage of the Color By Values command on the Plan menu to add color to shapes automatically. For example, space shapes include a custom property for department. You can use the value of that property to specify the color of spaces, so that shapes representing employees in the Administrative department appear in green and those in Engineering appear in blue, as Figure 26-22 shows. In addition, you can add a legend to your floor plan that shows the meaning of each color you use. Visio places the legend in the lower right corner of the drawing.

Chapter 26

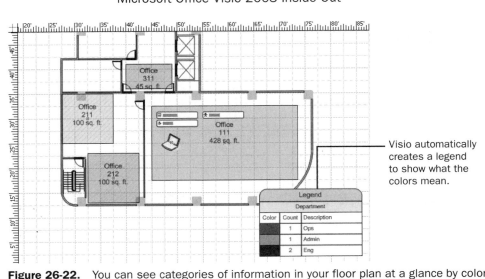

Visio automatically creates a legend to show what the colors mean.

Figure 26-22. You can see categories of information in your floor plan at a glance by color-coding different areas.

To color-code your space plan, follow these steps:

1 Choose Plan, Color By Values.

2 In the Color By list, select the category for the shapes that you want to color-code. Depending on the category you choose, different custom properties become available to use for color-coding in the Shape Type list. Click Import Data if you wish to import data before color-coding.

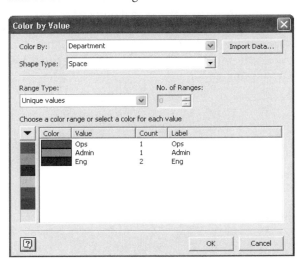

3 In the Shape Type box, select the custom property you want to use. The unique values for the selected property appear in the box below. If the custom property has no values—which is the case if you haven't entered or imported data—<NoValue> appears.

4   To apply different colors to the values shown in the sample area, click the color adjacent to the value and choose a new color. Click OK to apply the colors. Visio fills the appropriate shapes and places a legend on the page.

Note   If you drop a shape on the drawing after you've applied the colors, or if you change the value of a shape, the shape's color is not changed automatically to match the legend. You must choose Color By Values again.

Editing a Legend

You can edit the legend if you'd like it to take up less room or use a different font. The legend is really a grouped shape. You can drag a selection handle to resize the shape, or subselect the shapes containing the title text, property text, and colors to change them, as Figure 26-23 shows. You can also ungroup the shapes to make them easier to move around (Shift+Ctrl+U). When you have the legend the way you want it, regroup it to ensure that it moves as a unit.

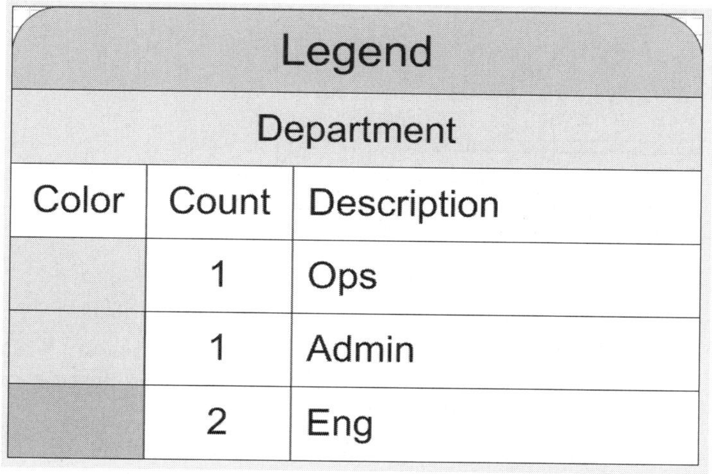

Legend		
Department		
Color	Count	Description
	1	Ops
	1	Admin
	2	Eng

Figure 26-23.   You can edit the shapes that make up a legend to customize its appearance.

For details about all the ways you can edit groups, see "Working with Groups," page 668.

Saving a Legend Shape

If you customize the legend shape and want to save your changes to use on other pages of your space plan or in other drawings, you can create a master shape from the legend. Just drag the legend onto the Document stencil. Then, when you're ready to color a different drawing, drag the shape from the Document stencil to the page. The legend shape "remembers" which category and custom property to look for and how to color each shape for its value.

Chapter 26

Displaying Labels on Shapes

Shapes in a space plan display a name, which might or might not be the name you want to show. For example, space shapes display the name Office by default, and equipment shapes don't display a label. Fortunately, space plan shapes are smart enough to display any custom property value as their label, and you can choose which one will appear in the Label Shapes dialog box, as Figure 26-24 shows. You can change the label for one shape, or select several and change them all.

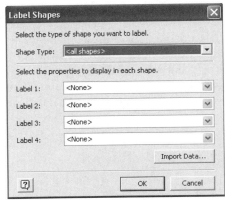

Figure 26-24. You can display the value of any custom property as a shape's label.

Follow these steps to specify how a shape is labeled:

1 Select a shape or shapes, and then choose Plan, Label Shapes.

2 In the Shape Type list, select the type of shape that you want to label.

3 In the Property list, select up to four custom properties that contain the value you want displayed in the label. For example, you might choose Product Description for an equipment shape, or E-Mail Alias for a person shape.

4 Click Import Data if you wish to import data into your space plan.

5 Click OK. Visio adds a label (or labels) to the shape.

6 To reposition the label, drag the control handle (the yellow diamond) to a new position.

Troubleshooting

Shapes and text in a space plan are too large

Because floor plans usually represent a large area, they're typically drawn to a small scale. When you add resource shapes to a room or office, the shape or its label might take up too much space. If the shapes aren't formatted the way you want them to be, the simplest thing to do is edit the master shape on the document stencil, which updates all the shapes in your drawing that are based on that master shape. To display the document stencil, choose File, Shapes, Show Document Stencil. To edit a master shape on the stencil, double-click the one you want. For details about this technique, see "Editing Multiple Shapes at Once," page 48.

You can also edit an individual shape's text if you want it to differ from the others. For example, you might make an administrative assistant's title more prominent on an employee shape to help new employees find resources. To do this, select a shape, choose Format, Text, and then specify the options you want. For details about working with text, see "Formatting Text," page 110.

Finding and Moving People and Resources

You can use the Explorer window to locate and relocate people and assets. For example, if you want to show that an employee has taken a job in a new department, you can move the person from one department to another in the Explorer window. You can also place unplaced shapes on the page. Just remember that the changes you make here aren't reflected in your database. If you make changes in your drawing that you want to be permanent, you must enter them separately in your database.

Finding People and Assets in a Floor Plan

You can use the Explorer window to locate any person or asset that has been placed in a floor plan. To do this, right-click a person, asset, or space, and then choose Show. Visio finds the person or asset in the floor plan, as Figure 26-25 shows.

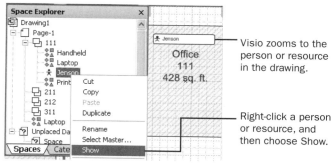

Figure 26-25. You can use the Explorer window to quickly locate people and other resources in your space plan.

Moving People and Assets

When you want to show that an employee has moved to a different office, or that an asset has been reassigned to a new person, you can easily do it. You can move a resource in the Explorer window or on the drawing page. Either way, Visio updates your facility model and reflects the change in both places.

To move people and assets, follow these steps:

1 Click the Spaces tab in the Explorer window.

2 Expand the space that shows the name of the person or resource you want to relocate.

3 Drag the name of a person or asset to the space you want to associate it with. When you drag items in the Space Explorer window, the shapes on the drawing page are relocated automatically.

Saving Space Plans on the Web

If you're the only one who needs to see a space plan, you can work with it in Visio, where you'll have access to the custom properties for each of the shapes. However, if you want to share the space plan—perhaps a manager needs to know where her reports are sitting, or the local computer expert needs to update virus protection software in certain offices—you have several options:

● You can save the space plan in a Web-compatible format, as Figure 26-26 shows. When you publish the space plan on your intranet or Internet site, others can interact with the drawing and use it to locate people. To export a space plan for use on the Web, choose File, Save As Web Page. For details, see Chapter 5, "Using Visio Diagrams on the Web."

The Custom Properties pane displays the information stored in the drawing.

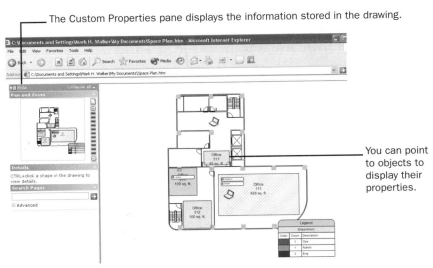

You can point to objects to display their properties.

Figure 26-26. When you save a space plan as HTML and use Vector Markup Language (VML) format, you can interact with the drawing using Microsoft Internet Explorer 5 or later.

- You can save your plan in a static graphic format that can be added to an existing Web page, such as GIF or JPEG. To do this, choose File, Save As, and then choose the format you want in the Save As Type list. For details, see "Exporting Shapes and Diagrams," page 217.

- You can also publish your Visio drawing in a shared workspace where others can look at it with the Visio viewer available at *http://www.microsoft.com/visio*.

In addition, facilities management software developers can use Visio as their graphic engine for Web deployment. Space plans and the data that goes with them can be saved in Extensible Markup Language (XML) format and integrated into other software programs. Exactly how to do this is beyond the scope of this book. However, Microsoft provides developer documentation for Visio that includes information about programming and XML. For details, search *http://msdn.microsoft.com/visio* for information about a Visio XML reference, which was not yet available at the time this book was being written.

Creating Space and Asset Reports

Although Visio includes many types of built-in reports, the Space Plan template includes two special reporting shapes. When you drag the Space Report or Asset Report shape from the Resources stencil, Visio reads the custom property data in the space plan and automatically generates a table that summarizes the information.

A space report provides subtotals and totals of the square footage in your floor plan based on the size of the space shapes, as Figure 26-27 shows. The report calculates the area by department and then adds the areas together. For each space shape in your floor plan, the report lists the space name, department, use, and area. If you haven't entered or imported data for the space shapes' custom properties, these fields will be blank in the report.

Space Report			
Department	Name	Use	Area
Sales	4N107	Office	1920. FT
Marketing	4N108	Office	1200. FT
Sales	4N109	Office	1200. FT
Sales	4N110	Office	1200. FT
Sales	4N112	Office	588. FT
Sales	4N113	Office	576. FT
Marketing	4N114	Office	576. FT
Sales	4N116	Office	2160. FT
Sales	4N117	Office	1200. FT
Sales	4N118	Office	1200. FT
Sales	4N119	Office	1200. FT
Total			16584 FT

Figure 26-27. Use the Space Report shape on the Resources stencil to generate a report similar to this one.

An asset report lists all the fixed assets in each space of your floor plan: computers, equipment, fixtures, furniture, and other assets represented by asset shapes. For each asset, the report displays the values of the category, name, and manufacturer custom properties, as

Chapter 26

Figure 26-28 shows. As with the space report, this report displays a blank cell for any custom properties that don't have a value.

Asset Report			
Belongs To	**Category**	**Name**	**Manufacturer**
4N106	Computer		Gatweway
4N109	Computer	Erik's Laptop	Toshiba
4N110	Computer		Dell
4N111	Computer		Gateway
4N111	Computer	Handheld 2	Palm
4N112	Computer		Gateway
4N113	Computer		Dell
4N113	Computer	CIS Laptop	Toshiba
4N114	Computer	QA Laptop	Sony
4N115			Xerox
4N116	Computer		Gateway
4N117	Computer		Gateway
4N117	Computer	Handheld 1	Palm
4N118	Computer		Dell
4N119	Computer		Sony
4N121	Computer		
4N121		4505	
4N122	Computer		
North Conference Room			Proxima
North Conference Room			Proxima
North Conference Room			Dell

Figure 26-28. Use the Asset Report shape on the Resources stencil to generate a report like this one.

Among other things, the reports are a great way to double-check your data entry. If a custom property doesn't have a value, the report will show a blank cell. If the cell should contain a value, you can select the space shape associated with the blank data, display the Custom Properties window, and then type the information. If you imported the property values from an external data source, the report tells you that your database or spreadsheet is missing some information.

Editing Space and Asset Reports

You can edit the report—they're simply Visio table shapes. Right-click a cell in the table to display a shortcut menu with options for editing the table.

You can also change the contents by editing the report definition that Visio uses to generate the space and asset reports. For example, if you want an asset report to include Asset Number rather than Category, you can edit the definition of the asset report to include the custom properties you want. The report shapes on the Resources stencil are only shortcuts for using the Report command in Visio. Rather than drag a shape onto the page, you can generate the same report as follows:

- **Create a space report** Choose Tools, Report. For Report Definition, choose Space Report. You can then run the report or click Modify to edit the report definition and change the properties that appear.
- **Create an asset report** Choose Tools, Report. For Report Definition, choose Asset Report, and then select the options you want.

For details about using the Report command, see "Defining a Custom Report," page 194.

Creating Reports in Different Formats

If you want to output a space or asset report as a separate file rather than as a table shape in your drawing, you can use the Report tool. You can still opt to create the report as a Visio shape, and it will appear on the page just as it would if you dragged the Space Report shape to the page. However, you can also choose to output the report to HTML, Excel, or XML format.

Follow these steps to output your report as a separate file:

1 Choose Tools, Report.

2 Under Report Definition, choose Asset Report or Space Report, and then click Run.

3 In the Run Report dialog box, select the output format you want, and then click OK.

For details, see "Running a Report," page 191.

Chapter 26

Diagramming for Mechanical, Electrical, and Process Engineering

Microsoft Office Visio 2003 Professional is a drawing and diagramming tool used by people in many different disciplines, but arguably the product's greatest strength is in engineering schematics. Visio makes it easy to represent and connect all kinds of symbols—whether they represent circuits, semiconductors, pneumatic equipment, ball bearings, or pipes. Smart-Shapes symbols are uniquely suited to symbolic or logical 2-D diagrams.

The engineering templates in Visio Professional offer tools to help you quickly create diagrams that communicate your plans or your existing setup in a way that others will understand. This chapter won't tell you all you need to know to be a successful engineer. We're assuming you're the expert on that part of the task. However, this chapter will help you make the most of the engineering shapes and tools in Visio Professional.

> **Note** The engineering templates are included only with Visio Professional. They are not available in Visio Standard.

Engineering Solutions in Visio Professional

Often, the tasks that engineers need to solve visually are quite complex and integrate data in the form of specifications or tolerances. Chemical industry workers need to see material streams moving between vessels; an engineering team needs to generate electronic equipment specifications and schematics. Although Visio shapes snap together quickly to present a flat picture of your world, shapes can also store and in some cases respond to real-world data so that your diagram becomes an accurate model of your system, process, or plant. For example, dimension line shapes automatically display accurate measurements. Custom properties can store additional attributes for shapes.

Most of the engineering drawing types in Visio Professional can be assembled using the "drag-drop-done" approach: drag shapes from stencils, connect as appropriate, add text, and then save your work. The process engineering templates, however, take a model-based approach to the diagramming task, as explained later in this chapter. Table 27-1 lists the engineering drawing types included with Visio Professional.

Table 27-1. Engineering Drawing Types in Visio Professional

Folder	Templates
Electrical Engineering	Basic Electrical Circuits And Logic Industrial Control Systems
Mechanical Engineering	Fluid Power Part And Assembly Drawing
Process Engineering	Piping And Instrumentation Diagram Process Flow Diagram

Creating Mechanical Engineering Drawings

You can use the mechanical engineering templates to create part and assembly drawings for manufactured products as well as fluid power and valve assemblies and equipment. Part and assembly drawings and hydraulic system schematics don't necessarily have much in common outside of Visio Professional, but on the drawing page, you use the shapes in much the same way. Many of the shapes include intelligent shortcuts for creating specific types and sizes of components, so you don't have to draw them yourself. For example, the drawing tool shapes help you draw precise circles, arcs, and other geometry. Nuts, bolts, springs, washers, and other shapes include custom properties for specifying size, tolerances, and other attributes.

Using the Part And Assembly Drawing Template

Part or detail drawings show each part contained in a product. Assembly drawings show how the parts fit together. The Part And Assembly Drawing template is a catch-all of mechanical engineering symbols for welding, springs, bearings, fasteners, and a variety of annotation and dimensioning shapes. You can draw parts, as Figure 27-1 shows, and include precise dimensioning instructions with engineering dimension line shapes.

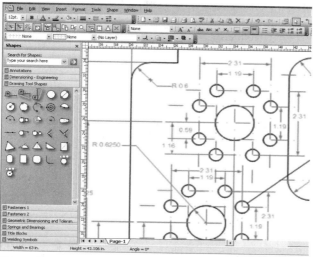

Figure 27-1. You can draw machined parts with the tools included with the Parts And Assembly Drawing template.

To start a drawing based on this template, choose File, New, Mechanical Engineering, Part And Assembly Drawing. When you select the Part And Assembly Drawing (US Units) template, Visio Professional creates an ANSI B-sized page (17 in. by 11 in.) with a drawing scale of ¼ in. to 1 in. The metric version of the template uses a drawing scale of 1:10 and sets up an ISO standard A3-sized page (420 mm by 297 mm). Both templates open the following stencils:

- **Annotations** This stencil includes callouts and reference note shapes.
- **Dimensioning – Engineering** This stencil contains intelligent dimension lines that measure length, height, radius, volume, area, and more.
- **Drawing Tool Shapes** This stencil includes geometric shapes with built-in customization features for drawing accurate lines, arcs, and so on.

Note The Annotations, Drawing Tool Shapes, and Dimensioning – Engineering stencils are stored in the \Shapes\Visio Extras folder. The other stencils are stored in the \Shapes\Mechanical Engineering folder.

- **Fasteners 1 and Fasteners 2** These stencils offer a variety of resizable fasteners, including nuts, bolts, pins, and rivets.
- **Geometric Dimensioning And Tolerancing** This stencil contains annotation shapes that indicate geometric dimensions and mechanical tolerances.
- **Springs And Bearings** This stencil includes resizable shapes for designing machine tools and mechanical devices.

- **Title Blocks** This stencil provides shapes for creating drawing frames and revision notes.
- **Welding Symbols** This stencil contains annotation shapes that identify welding operations.

For details about customizing the page size and orientation, the ruler and grid resolutions, and the drawing scale, see Chapter 16, "Measuring and Dimensioning with Precision."

Using Springs and Fasteners

Many of the shapes in the Springs And Bearings and Fasteners stencils are sized according to industry standards and can be used to represent different sizes. After you drag the shapes onto the drawing page, you can right-click and select Set Dimensions to enter thread diameter, length, and other dimensions for the shape, as Figure 27-2 shows.

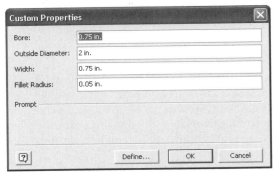

Figure 27-2. Some shapes display the Custom Properties dialog box when you add them to the page so that you can specify dimensions.

By default, these shapes are locked so that you can't accidentally resize them using the control handles. When you want to resize a spring or fastener shape, right-click the shape, and then choose Properties to display the shape's custom properties. However, if you prefer to resize a shape using its selection handles, you can remove the locks. To do this, right-click the shape, and then choose Resize With Handles from the shortcut menu, as Figure 27-3 shows.

Tip Add a title block to a background page
If you are creating a drawing that contains multiple pages, create a background page and add your title block to the background page so that it appears on every page of the drawing. To create a title block, drag shapes from the Title Blocks stencil. For details, see "Adding a Title Block to a Diagram," page 134.

Figure 27-3. Some shapes include options on their shortcut menu, including the Resize With Handles option.

Drawing with the Drawing Tool Shapes

You don't have to be creating a parts drawing to take advantage of the shapes on the Drawing Tool Shapes stencil. These shapes were designed by a mechanical engineer as a shortcut for creating the precise geometry required by many types of engineering drawings. The shapes in this stencil give you greater control than the drawing tools on the Standard toolbar, making it possible to create object outlines. For example, you can use the Arc Tangents shape or the Circle Tangent shape to draw belt systems, and you can represent a vessel or a tank using the Rounded Rectangle shape.

To draw the outline of an object for which there isn't a predefined shape, drag a shape from the Drawing Tool Shapes stencil onto the drawing page. Most of the shapes include built-in resizing and reshaping behavior, so you shouldn't just drag a selection handle. For example, you can move a vertex of the Triangle: Free shape by dragging a control handle. To see what a control handle does, hover the pointer over it until a ScreenTip appears, as Figure 27-4 shows.

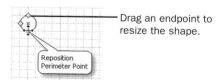

Figure 27-4. Pause the pointer over a control handle to display a ScreenTip.

There are several ways to edit the shapes in the DrawingTool Shapes stencil:

- Drag endpoints, control handles, or selection handles, as Figure 27-4 shows.

Chapter 27

● Right-click a shape, and then choose an option from the shortcut menu. For example, you can show the complimentary tangent for the Opposite Tangent shape, as Figure 27-5 shows.

Figure 27-5. Some drawing tool shapes include commands on a shortcut menu that you can use to reconfigure or edit the shape.

The following shapes have unique resizing behavior:

● **Arc – Numeric** To specify the angle of the arc, select the shape, and then type the angle measure in degrees.

● **Sector – Numeric** To specify the angle of the sector, select the shape, and then type the angle measure in degrees.

● **Rt. Triangle: Angle, Hyp** To specify the angle of the triangle, select the shape, and then type the angle measure in degrees.

If you want to combine the geometry of several drawing tool shapes to create a more complex object, or subtract areas to create holes, you can use the shape operation commands. Choose Shape, Operations to see your options.

For details about working with shape operations, see "Merging Shapes to Create New Ones," page 660.

Inside Out

Sizing and positioning shapes

To draw accurate assemblies and precise tolerances, you'll want to take advantage of the tools that Visio Professional provides for sizing and positioning shapes. For example, use shape extension lines to display reference lines that show tangent, perpendicular, and other lines. Choose Tools, Snap & Glue, enable Drawing Aids, and then specify options on the Advanced tab. You can also dock the Size & Position window on the screen and align shapes to guides and guide points. For details, see Chapter 16, "Measuring and Dimensioning with Precision."

Using the Fluid Power Template

To show the relative locations of equipment and piping valves, you can create a diagram based on the Fluid Power template. This template is intended for creating annotated drawings of pneumatic and hydraulic systems, fluid power assemblies, flow control, flow path, valves and valve assemblies, and fluid power equipment, as Figure 27-6 shows.

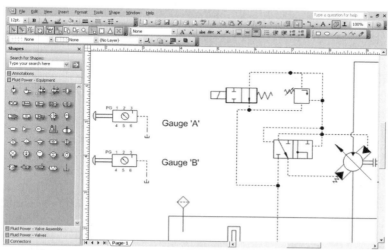

Figure 27-6.   The Fluid Power template opens stencils of shapes that make it reasonably easy to assemble a pneumatic or hydraulic control diagram.

To start a new diagram based on this template, choose File, New, Mechanical Engineering, Fluid Power. The template opens a standard, letter-sized drawing page with no drawing scale and the following stencils:

- **Fluid Power – Equipment**   This stencil includes shapes for pumps, motors, air compressors, meters, and other equipment.
- **Fluid Power – Valve Assembly**   This stencil contains shapes for pressure and flow regulators, flow direction indicators, and controls and symbols to design flow paths.
- **Fluid Power – Valves**   This stencil comes with a variety of shapes for pneumatic and hydraulic valves.
- **Connectors**   This stencil includes smart connector shapes that create specific types of branching and angled lines.
- **Annotations**   This stencil provides callouts and reference note shapes.

Connecting a Fluid Power Diagram

In Visio terms, fluid power drawings are a type of connected schematic. Valve shapes include *connection points* (the blue xs) that you connect to other shapes with lines called *connectors*. The number of connection points on a valve depends on the number of ports. Each port

Chapter 27

represents an opening through which pneumatic or hydraulic fluid passes. To show how the fluid is transported, you use shapes or draw lines with the Connector tool to represent pipes.

Although there are several techniques for connecting shapes in Visio, the fluid power shapes are designed to work with the shapes on the Connectors stencil. The general method is to drag the valve and equipment shapes into place and then connect them as follows:

Connector tool

1   Click the Connector tool on the Standard toolbar.

2   Click the Connectors stencil to bring it to the top.

3   Click—don't drag—a connector master shape.

4   On the drawing page, drag with the Connector tool from a connection point on one shape to a connection point on another. Visio draws a connecting line that routes between the shapes according to the master shape you selected on the Connectors stencil.

> For details about connectors and how they work, see Chapter 3, "Connecting Shapes."

Using Fluid Power Shapes

Fluid power valves can have several positions, ports, and controls in any combination. Many of the valve shapes include alternative configurations. For example, you can right-click a switch/transducer (on the Fluid Power – Equipment stencil) to display the symbol for pressure switch, limit switch, or transducer. Because shapes include display options, it's a little hard to know whether the shape you need already exists or not.

To reposition or connect some shapes, you use their control handles—the yellow diamonds you see when you select a shape. For example, to slide the piston for a valve, drag its control handle, as Figure 27-7 shows.

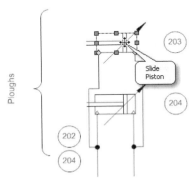

Figure 27-7.   To see what a shape does, pause the pointer over the control handle to display a ScreenTip.

Although most of the fluid power shapes don't include custom properties, a couple of shapes do. The properties are used to configure the shape's appearance, not to track data, as is the case with other diagram types. For example, the pump motor shapes on the Fluid Power – Equipment stencil include properties for displacement, flow directions, and rotation directions. To see these options, right-click a pump motor, and then choose Set Pump/Motor Properties.

Creating Electrical Schematics

The Electrical Engineering templates in Visio 2003 make it possible to create electrical and electronic schematic diagrams, as well as wiring diagrams, as Figure 27-8 shows. Among other things, you can draw integrated circuit and logic circuit schematics, general electrical diagrams (schematics, one-line, and wiring), industrial control system schematics, and printed circuit board drawings. The process for creating any of these diagram types is more or less the same—only the stencils from which you drag the shapes are different. Because all of the electrical engineering diagrams rely on default Visio shape and connection behavior, this section presents an overview of applicable techniques. All of the information presented in the first seven chapters of this book applies.

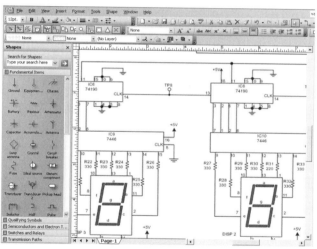

Figure 27-8. With the electrical engineering templates, you can create logic diagrams, circuit diagrams, and other schematics.

To start a new diagram based on one of the Electrical Engineering templates, choose File, New, Electrical Engineering, and then choose the template that sounds most like what you're trying to create. It doesn't particularly matter which template you choose; all create a standard, unscaled, letter-sized page. They differ primarily in the stencils that they open. Here are your choices:

● **Basic Electrical**   This template is used for one-line, wiring, and other general electrical schematics. It opens with the Fundamental Items, Qualifying Symbols, Semiconductors And Electron Tubes, Switches And Relays, and Transmission Paths stencils.

- **Circuits And Logic**   This template is used for integrated circuit and logic circuit schematics. It opens with the Analog And Digital Logic, Integrated Circuit Components, Terminals And Connectors, and Transmission Paths stencils.

- **Industrial Control Systems**   This template is used for control system schematics. It opens with the Fundamental Items, Rotating Equip And Mech Functions, Switches And Relays, Terminals And Connectors, Transformers And Windings, and Transmission Paths stencils.

- **Systems**   This template is used for printed circuit boards. It opens the Composite Assemblies, Maintenance Symbols, Maps And Charts, Switches And Relays, Telecom Switch And Peripheral Equip, Terminals And Connectors, Transformers And Windings, Transmission Paths, and VHF-UHF-SHF stencils.

If there's a trick to working with the electrical engineering shapes, perhaps it's finding the one you want. Not only are there 15 different stencils with more than 400 shapes to choose from, but individual shapes can often be configured to represent different symbols or settings, as Figure 27-9 shows. Right-click shapes to determine whether they include options. Visio uses custom properties to make these shapes configurable. If you dock the Custom Properties window on the screen, Visio displays a shape's properties in the window as you select the shape, which makes it easy to see which ones can be configured.

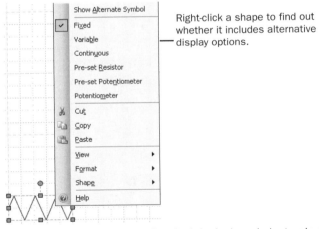

Figure 27-9.   Many of the electrical, logical, and electronic shapes can be used to represent multiple symbols and settings, such as this Resistor shape from the Fundamental Items stencil.

Connecting Electrical and Electronic Shapes

The efficient way to create a diagram that shows a lot of connections is to start with the fixed shapes and then connect them. For example, drag the logic gates onto the page, arrange and distribute them, and then use the Connector tool to connect them. Or start with resistors and capacitors, and then drag lines between them.

Use the Connector tool to connect components, as Figure 27-10 shows: select the Connector tool on the Standard toolbar, and then drag from a connection point on one shape to a connection point on another shape. Visio attaches the line to the shapes with *point-to-point* (or *static*) glue. When you move shapes, the connecting line might be rerouted, but the same two points stay connected.

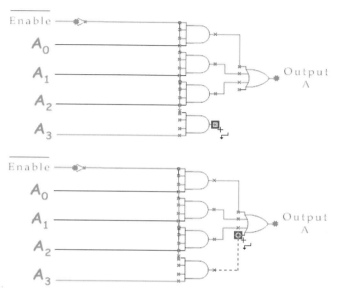

Figure 27-10. Because connector lines have a beginning and an end, use the Connector tool to drag in the direction you want the line to flow.

Inside Out

Shape-to-shape glue

If you drag the endpoint of a connector toward the middle of a shape, a red box appears around the entire shape to indicate that *shape-to-shape* (or dynamic) glue is in effect—which is probably not what you want. With shape-to-shape glue, you can move components on the page, and Visio automatically reroutes the connector to the closest connection points between the two shapes. If your goal is to show the circuit at pin 2, you want to ensure you're gluing at points, not gluing entire shapes.

Another handy reason for using the Connector tool is that the resulting line includes a shortcut menu with options for rerouting, as Figure 27-11 shows. A connector can also imply direction. It draws a line with a beginning and an end—the square endpoints you see when you select it. To show directionality in your diagram, such as the flow of electricity from a junction to the ground, always drag from the initiating point to the terminating point using the Connector tool.

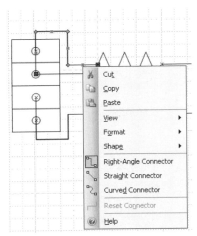

	Cut
	Copy
	Paste
	View ▶
	Format ▶
	Shape ▶
	Right-Angle Connector
	Straight Connector
	Curved Connector
	Reset Connector
	Help

Figure 27-11. You can right-click lines drawn with the Connector tool to display a shortcut menu with commands for controlling the line's routing behavior.

The way Visio automatically reroutes lines in a drawing can be mysterious. The best advice is usually to try a routing option and see if it does what you want. If not, press Ctrl+Z to undo the results and try something else.

For details about layout and routing options, see "Laying Out Shapes Automatically," 70.

Where Is the Netlist Generator?

Previous versions of Visio Technical included the Netlist Generator, an add-in that listed all the components in a circuit, the nodes to which each component was attached, and the value of each component. It sounds useful, but in practice, the information it produced was limited, and its output format was incompatible with most commonly used circuit simulation programs. As a result, Microsoft pulled the add-in from Visio Professional 2002. You might, however, be able to replicate some netlist-type functionality by creating a custom report definition. Using the Report Definition Wizard, you can generate a list of properties associated with shapes on the drawing page automatically, including width, height, and endpoints.

Tip Connect shapes as you add them

If it's okay not to connect shapes at specific points, you can quickly connect a series of components as you add them to the page. To do this, select the Connector tool, and then drag a shape onto the drawing page. With the shape selected, drag the next component onto the page. The shapes are automatically connected using shape-to-shape (dynamic) glue.

Labeling Components

The electrical engineering shapes rely primarily on Visio's default text-handling capabilities. That is, to add text to a shape, select the shape, and then type. You can control the position of the shape's text by dragging the control handle on the shape, as Figure 27-12 shows.

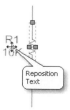

Figure 27-12.   To move the label on a component, drag the control handle.

For details about formatting text, see "Formatting Text," page 110.

The quickest way to format labels is probably to edit the EE Normal style, which is applied to all the electrical engineering shapes. By editing the style, you can establish a consistent format for your shapes. To edit a style, choose Format, Define Styles, select the EE Normal style, and then use the Change options to specify different text formats.

For details about editing styles, see "Editing Existing Styles," page 691.

Using the Process Engineering Template

The Process Engineering template is really a set of templates and shapes for creating piping and instrumentation diagrams (P&IDs) and process flow diagrams (PFDs). Unlike the other engineering diagram types mentioned in this chapter, P&IDs and PFDs can represent a true model of your system. Not only can you create a diagram that represents your system, shapes in the diagram can store physical specifications about components, such as line and valve sizes as well as manufacturing data such as model numbers. Visio organizes related diagrams and components into a cohesive *model* and displays windows unique to this drawing type for organizing model information.

Several other Visio Professional drawing types also create models. What these solutions have in common is a different perspective on the use of shapes. The shape itself isn't the important thing in a model, but rather what the shape represents. For example, you can use the Major Pipeline shape to connect to a pump, but the more interesting information is that the shape represents pipeline P-25-6-10 with a design pressure of 60 that connects Pump-6.

If you haven't used the Process Engineering template since the Visio 2000 Technical Edition, you'll find that the new version in Visio Professional has been revamped dramatically. You don't have to set up a separate project for your files any longer—instead, you make each related diagram a separate page in a single drawing. Microsoft made these changes to improve performance and simplify the solution so that anyone familiar with process flow and piping schematics can quickly assemble a diagram. In addition, third-party developers can

Chapter 27

much more easily access the functionality through external programs, which means that they can customize and automate diagrams. For example, Cadcentre, DataViews Corporation, ICARUS, and Technical Toolboxes have all created deeper process engineering tools based on the shapes in the Process Engineering template.

The good news is that if you've created process flow diagrams or piping and instrumentation diagrams in Visio 2000 or Visio 2002, you can convert them to Visio 2003, which is almost identical to Visio 2002, without losing any information. The rest of the topics in this chapter discuss how to create a model in the Process Engineering template. The following are some of the things you can do:

- Produce P&IDs and PFDs using shapes that represent pipelines, valves, instruments, and other equipment.
- Integrate drawings with critical data, such as codes, standards, and design details. Visio stores component-specification data as custom properties of the shapes.
- Convert other shapes and computer-aided design (CAD) symbols into intelligent process engineering symbols.
- Create pipeline lists, valve lists, and other reports based on the specification data stored with shapes.

Using a Diagram as a System Model

The Process Engineering template makes it possible to create P&IDs and PFDs. These diagrams not only show how a system of pipelines connects industrial process equipment, they also store data about the components in the diagram.You can also use P&ID schematics to document the instruments and valves that control the flow of materials through the pipelines, as Figure 27-13 shows. For any pipe segment or component in your diagram, Visio can show you its location, connections, and attributes. For example, you can display a list of all the valves connected to a particular pipeline, or locate a particular piping segment based on its tag.

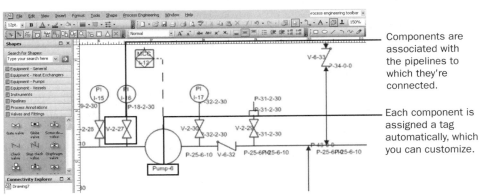

Components are associated with the pipelines to which they're connected.

Each component is assigned a tag automatically, which you can customize.

Figure 27-13. When you start a new drawing with a process engineering template, the Process Engineering menu is added to the Visio window.

Chapter 27

Diagramming for Mechanical, Electrical, and Process Engineering

Although shapes on the page are powerful as visuals, the heart of your model is shown in the Component Explorer, Connectivity Explorer, and Custom Properties windows, as Figure 27-14 shows. The Component Explorer and Connectivity Explorer are unique to process engineering diagrams and provide a hierarchical view of components. The Custom Properties window replaces the datasheets used by the previous version of the process engineering solution in Visio 2000. These windows are designed to work specifically with the process engineering shapes in the following ways:

Displays all components by category—equipment, instruments, pipelines, and valves.
Lists each pipeline by tag number and the components connected to it.

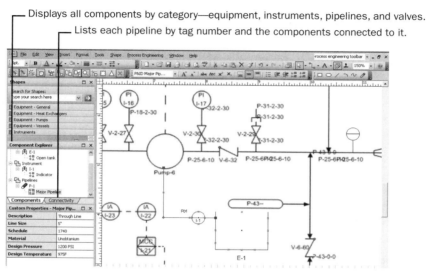

Figure 27-14. Valuable details about the model represented by component shapes are displayed in the Component Explorer and Connectivity Explorer, which you can dock in any convenient location on the screen.

- **Component Explorer** This window organizes components hierarchically in *categories*: equipment, instrument, pipeline, or valve. Within a category, every component in your diagram is listed by its tag number, and within a component, each shape used to represent that component is identified. Right-click a tag number, and then choose Select Shapes to select the component in the diagram. Right-click a shape name, and then select Go To Shape to pan the diagram to that shape.

- **Connectivity Explorer** This window is all about your diagram's pipelines. It lists each pipeline's tag number and the components connected to it. Right-click a pipeline or component, and then choose Select Shapes to select the shape represented by that tag in the diagram.

- **Custom Properties window** This window displays the specific attributes of a selected shape, such as the component's manufacturer and model or design pressure and line size.

Although these windows work in a similar fashion to the Drawing Explorer in Visio, the Component Explorer and Connectivity Explorer give you a different perspective on the pipelines and components in a P&ID or PFD. Sometimes it's simply easier to manipulate information in an outline view, particularly if components and the shapes that compose them are on multiple pages in the drawing. These windows show you the entire system model represented by the shapes on all pages of your Visio diagram.

By default, the Component Explorer and Connectivity Explorer windows are opened when you start a new drawing with one of the process engineering templates. You can quickly display and close the windows using the commands on the Process Engineering menu. To display the Custom Properties window, choose View, Custom Properties Window. These windows can be docked, floated, and tabbed inside one another.

Starting a New Process Engineering Model

To gain access to the tools and intelligent process engineering shapes, you must start your diagram with the appropriate template. When you choose File, New, Process Engineering, you can select the Piping And Instrumentation Diagram template or the Process Flow Diagram template. As it happens, both templates do pretty much the same thing. They open a new, unscaled drawing page set to ANSI B size (17 in. by 11 in.) and the Process Engineering menu is added to the menu bar, as Figure 27-15 shows. Diagrams started with these templates also display the following stencils:

- Equipment – General
- Equipment – Heat Exchangers
- Equipment – Pumps
- Equipment – Vessels
- Instruments
- Pipelines
- Process Annotations
- Valves And Fittings

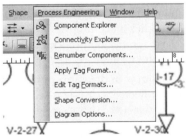

Figure 27-15. The Process Engineering templates add the Process Engineering menu.

Converting Visio 2000 Diagrams to This Version

If you created a process engineering project in Visio 2000 Technical Edition, and you want to continue working with it in this version of Visio Professional, you must *migrate* or convert your project. Only by converting your Visio Technical project can you take full advantage of the new solution's features, such as custom properties for tracking component specifications and the tag customization tools. When you open a P&ID or PFD project file created in Visio 2000 Technical Edition, Visio prompts you to convert it with the message shown in Figure 27-16. When you convert a Visio 2000 project to Visio 2003, each diagram in the original project is converted to a separate process engineering diagram on its own page in a single drawing file.

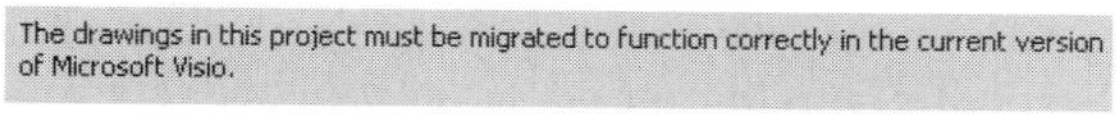

> The drawings in this project must be migrated to function correctly in the current version of Microsoft Visio.

Figure 27-16. Because the tools for process engineering diagrams have so radically changed since Visio 2000, P&IDs or PFDs that you created in Visio 2000 Technical Edition must be migrated—that is, converted—to work in the new format.

Process engineering diagrams are self-contained starting with version of Visio 2002 Professional. They don't require sets of diagrams and documents, compiled into projects, as they did in Visio 2000. There is no project file, project database, or supporting set of templates to manage. Instead, the data is stored in the diagram itself, making the diagram more portable and easier to control while still maintaining an accurate model of your system or plant through the use of custom property data.

Here's what to expect when you convert a project to a Visio Professional process engineering file:

- All master shapes and shapes will function as Visio Professional shapes.
- All pipelines are converted to Visio Professional pipelines.
- Information from datasheets is moved into custom properties for the components in the diagram.
- Datasheet field definitions are converted into custom property sets, which are applied to the appropriate shapes.
- Intelligent tags remain with the appropriate shapes.
- Automatic label shapes are converted to custom callout shapes.

> **Note** Your original Visio 2000 project files aren't changed in any way. If you save the Visio Professional file in the same destination folder as the Visio 2000 project folder, the Visio Professional files are given slightly different file names so that the original Visio 2000 files are not overwritten.

Follow these steps to convert a Visio 2000 process engineering project to Visio Professional:

1. If you want to save the converted project in a new folder (recommended), create a destination folder using Windows Explorer or another file manager.

2. Start Visio Professional, choose File, Open, and then locate the Visio 2000 process engineering project (.vsd file) that you want to convert. Click Open. Visio displays a message about Microsoft Visual Basic for Applications (VBA) macros. The migration relies on the macros saved with the diagram, which define the shapes' intelligence.

Chapter 27

3 Click Enable Macros.

4 In the message box, click Yes to convert all drawings. If you click No, you can still open the diagrams in Visio Professional as read-only drawings that can be printed.

5 In the Browse For Folder dialog box, select the destination folder you created in step 1. You can store the converted project diagrams in the same folder as the original diagrams. Visio renames the converted files to differentiate them from the originals.

When you click OK, Visio Professional begins to convert the shapes and data into the new format. Now is a good time to get a cup of coffee; the migration process can take several minutes, depending on the number of diagrams in your project and the speed of your computer. When the migration is successfully completed, the following message appears:

Migration of the Visio 2000 Process Engineering project is complete.

Creating P&IDs and PFDs

Each pipeline, valve, instrument, and other physical instrument or equipment in your factory or plant is represented in a Visio diagram by a component shape. Piping shapes lay out the direction of flow. Minor pipelines connect to major pipelines. Pipe endpoints connect to equipment shapes. Valves rotate into position on pipes, splitting a pipeline into two pipes, each of which is glued to the valve and tagged with the same number. Instruments also attach to the components they monitor. What holds everything together is *glue*. You know that shapes are glued when you drag one toward another and a red square appears around a selection handle or connection point, as shown in Figure 27-17. When shapes are glued, they move together. For example, you can drag a pipeline to reroute it, and valves glued to the pipe move with it.

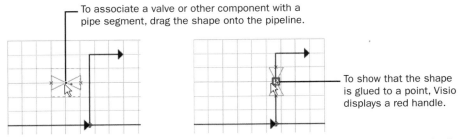

Figure 27-17. Drag valves on top of pipelines; they rotate into position automatically.

> **Tip** You can connect a pipeline to any point on the outside of an equipment shape—a connection point is automatically created at that point if one isn't there already.

The quickest way to connect components and pipelines in a P&ID or PFD is to work as follows:

1   Add the primary pieces of equipment to the diagram. For example, drag vessel and pump shapes from the Equipment stencils onto the drawing page.

2   Click the Connector tool on the Standard toolbar.

3   Click the Pipelines stencil, and then click (do not drag) the pipeline shape you want to use.

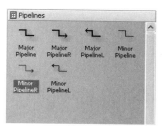

4   In the diagram, use the Connector tool to drag from one component shape to another to draw a pipeline between them. Visio draws the pipeline using the shape you selected on the Pipelines stencil. To change the type of pipeline that the Connector tool draws, click a different master shape on the Pipelines stencil.

5   Apply line styles to a pipeline to indicate its type. For example, you can display symbols for a capillary tube on a major pipeline by formatting the line with the P&ID Capillary Tube line style. For details, see the next section, "Working with Pipelines."

6   Drag valves from the Valves And Fittings stencil onto pipelines. When you position a valve, it rotates to match the orientation of the pipeline and attaches itself to the pipeline so that the two move together.

7   Drag instrument shapes from the Instruments stencil into position next to the pipelines, valves, or equipment they monitor. Drag an instrument shape's control handle to a component to show an association.

 Inside Out

Dragging pipelines onto the page

If this method of drawing and connecting pipes doesn't appeal to you, you can simply drag pipeline shapes onto the page. Glue the pipelines' endpoints to connection points on other component shapes. When a pipeline is glued to a shape, its endpoint turns red.

Working with Pipelines

When you connect a pipeline to another pipeline, Visio splits the original pipeline into two shapes. Each of these shapes has the same tag and continues to be tracked in the model as part of the original pipeline component. The shapes that represent the pipeline segments share custom property data, because they represent the same component. If you make changes to properties for either of the shapes, the properties are updated for the other shape.

When a valve is dropped onto a pipeline, the pipeline splits into two pipelines, each glued to the valve. Again, the split pipelines continue to represent the same component in the model, as Figure 27-18 shows.

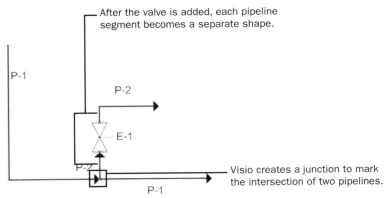

Figure 27-18. Dropping a valve onto a pipeline splits the pipeline into multiple shapes. However, each shape continues to represent a single component and displays the same tag.

Technically, Visio inserts a *junction* where two pipelines meet. The junction is represented as a shape, but it doesn't appear in the diagram. It's worth mentioning primarily because you sometimes see Junction listed as a shape in other dialog boxes of the Process Engineering template. You can specify which shape you want to use to represent pipeline junctions, although it's hard to say what the advantage of doing so would be.

Still, if you need to change it, you can: choose Process Engineering, Diagram Options. In the dialog box, specify the shape you want in the list labeled Use This Shape To Represent Pipeline Branches.

If you remove the component that caused the pipeline to split—for example, if you delete the valve or junction—the line is "healed" (Visio's term) and appears as a single pipeline shape again. Of course, if you remove a valve or a junction from two pipeline shapes that weren't originally part of the same pipeline, the shapes remain separate.

Showing Pipeline Connections

The Connectivity Explorer shows all the pipeline components in the drawing and everything they are connected to, as Figure 27-19 shows. You can see which components are connected to pipelines, but you cannot change their connections in the Connectivity Explorer. To do that, you must drag shapes in the diagram.

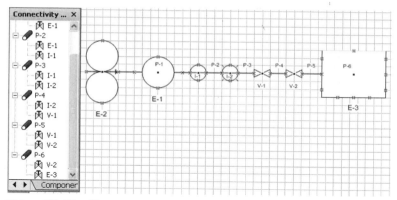

Figure 27-19. You can use the Connectivity Explorer to see which components are connected to a pipeline and to locate individual components in the diagram by selecting them.

If a pipeline and its vessels are connected, only one pipeline segment is listed in the Connectivity Explorer. If they've been disconnected or split, though, the Connectivity Explorer displays two pipeline segments with the same name.

You can use the Connectivity Explorer to find shapes in the diagram. Double-click a component, or right-click the component, and then choose Select Shapes. All the shapes associated with that component are highlighted in the diagram.

Changing Pipeline Appearance and Behavior

When you drag pipeline shapes from the stencil onto the drawing page, Visio applies the default pipeline style—a solid black line. However, these shapes are designed to represent a range of pipes and instrument lines, from capillary tubes to electromagnetic lines. The correct way to represent different types of pipelines is to apply a line style, as Figure 27-20 shows. To do this, select a pipeline, and then use the Style command on the Format menu, or display the Format Shapes toolbar, which contains the Line Styles list.

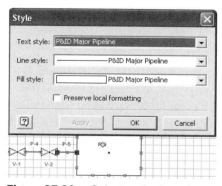

Figure 27-20. Select a pipeline shape, and then choose Format, Style to change the type of line used in the diagram. Process engineering diagrams include many custom styles for representing common industry line patterns.

For details about how styles work in Visio, see "Applying Styles from the Style Lists," page 682.

If Visio doesn't have the style to represent the type of line you need, create your own custom line pattern. For details, see "Creating Your Own Line and Fill Patterns," page 693.

Pipeline behavior is a function of Visio's built-in line layout and routing functionality. In a process engineering diagram, routing options that apply to pipelines are conveniently located on the shapes' shortcut menu when you right-click a pipeline. To specify a default routing behavior for all the pipelines in your diagram, choose Process Engineering, Diagram Options. In the Diagram Options dialog box, you can specify whether pipelines will be split around components or when branches are created, whether pipelines can be "healed," and which shape to use at pipeline branches, as Figure 27-21 shows.

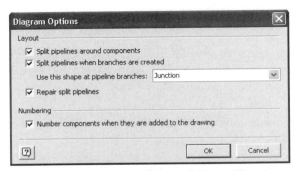

Figure 27-21. Use the Diagram Options dialog box to specify line routing options for pipeline shapes.

Associating Shapes with Components in the Component Explorer

In the Component Explorer, you can easily see and rearrange the way shapes are associated with components. Components are identified by their tags; shapes are listed by the master shape name. Visio assumes that each component is represented by a unique shape in the drawing—except pipelines. When you drop a valve on a pipeline, Visio splits the pipeline shape in two and represents each shape as a single pipeline component in the Component Explorer. For example, P-25-6-10 might represent a single pipeline composed of many shapes, each of which represents a segment of the pipeline. The shapes are listed under the pipeline's tag by shape name, such as Major Pipeline.83. The number at the end (83) represents the shape instance; in this case, the eighty-third instance of the major pipeline shape in the drawing file. You can create the same behavior for other shapes by assigning shapes to components in the Component Explorer.

You can locate a shape in the diagram by right-clicking it in the Component Explorer and choosing Go To Shape. You can also create, rename, or delete components within the Component Explorer. You can apply new model properties (category, property set, or tag format) to a component by right-clicking a category and choosing Model Properties. Most conveniently, you can drag and drop shapes in the Component Explorer to change the way they are associated with components.

> **Note** If you delete a shape from the drawing, it's also deleted from the Component Explorer.

Using Multiple Shapes to Represent a Component

The same component can appear in multiple places in a diagram. For example, say you want a pump to appear in both a system view and a detail view, which are represented as separate pages of the same drawing file. Although the pump is represented by two different instances of the same shape, it's the same pump in the real world. Your model reflects this by recognizing the pump as a single component. Changes made to the properties of a component on one page are reflected for all the shapes that represent that component in the drawing file.

To indicate that multiple shapes correspond to the same component, you can drag shapes in the Component Explorer to a component, as Figure 27-22 shows.

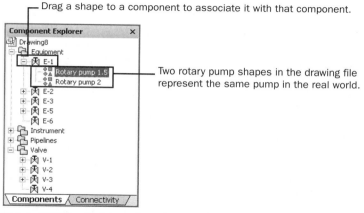

Drag a shape to a component to associate it with that component.

Two rotary pump shapes in the drawing file represent the same pump in the real world.

Figure 27-22. You can show that multiple shapes represent a single component in the Component Explorer.

Visio requires you to associate shapes with components in the Component Explorer. All shapes belonging to a component must be of the same category and have the same custom property set. When you close a drawing, Visio deletes components that are not associated with shapes.

Troubleshooting

A new shape in a PFD or P&ID does not show up in the Component Explorer or Category Explorer

Unless you add shapes from the stencils opened by a process engineering template, the shapes won't work with the commands on the Process Engineering menu until you convert them. If you copy a shape from a previous version of Visio, draw a shape, or add a shape from another stencil, Visio doesn't recognize it as a component in the model. To apply model properties to shapes that aren't based on process engineering masters, you can use the Shape Conversion command on the Process Engineering menu. For details, see "Converting Shapes and CAD Symbols into Components" page 835.

Adding Data to Components

In a process engineering diagram, components come with an integrated group of custom properties, called a *set*, that allow you to store detailed information. For example, you can include model number or line size with an instrument or valve. Adding data to components is as simple as typing in the Custom Properties window. But what if the properties don't represent your organization's standards? You can add, edit, and delete custom properties to better reflect the attributes you want to track with your diagram.

Visio assumes that you want to track the same information for similar components. The process engineering shapes you drag onto the page include default custom properties based on the kind of information you're likely to want to track for that component type. For example, all valves include a Line Size field, but only pipelines include a Design Pressure field. These default custom property fields appear when the Custom Properties window is open. Table 27-2 lists the properties associated with each category's custom property set.

Table 27-2. Properties Assigned to Process Engineering Shapes

Category	Custom Properties Included
Equipment	Description, material, manufacturer, model
Instrument	Description, connection size, service, manufacturer, model
Pipeline	Description, line size, schedule, material, design pressure, and design temperature
Valve	Description, line size, valve class, manufacturer, and model

Adding Component Data

To add component data, you can type in the Custom Properties window, as Figure 27-23 shows. The Custom Properties window displays the properties for a selected shape. For details about typing in the Custom Properties window, see "Entering Data in Shapes," page 174.

Type in the fields to specify component attributes.

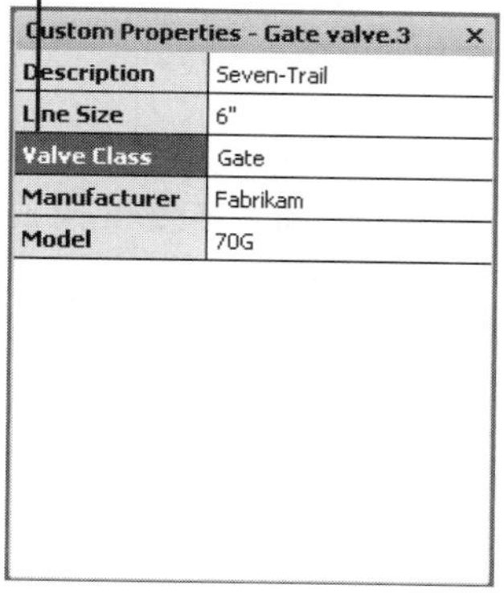

Custom Properties - Gate valve.3	×
Description	Seven-Trail
Line Size	6"
Valve Class	Gate
Manufacturer	Fabrikam
Model	70G

Figure 27-23. You can track detailed component information with each shape in a diagram. The Custom Properties window displays values for the selected component.

In a model of any size, it would be impractical to type specifications for each component. That's when you want to take advantage of Visio's data importing capabilities. You can import custom property values from ODBC-compliant databases as well as comma-delimited text files.

For details about importing custom properties, see "Linking Shapes and Databases," page 721.

In addition to model-tracking properties, such as Model or Design Pressure, some process engineering shapes use custom properties to change a shape's appearance. For example, the PLC shape on the Instruments stencil can be configured to show the type of flow meter required, as Figure 27-24 shows.

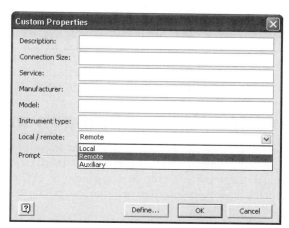

Figure 27-24. You can configure the appearance of many shapes by choosing options in the Custom Properties window.

For details about Visio's philosophy of custom properties, see "Using Shapes with Custom Properties," page 167.

Editing Custom Properties

Although you can add, remove, or edit a custom property for a specific component, the process engineering shapes are specifically designed to work with custom property sets, so you're better off editing custom property sets to include the properties you want, and then applying the set to all the master shapes on a custom or document stencil.

Tip You can use the Component Model Properties command on the Process Engineering menu to create and apply custom property sets to process engineering shapes.

Custom property sets are created and managed in the Custom Properties Window. Simply click the Prop Sets tab in the window. After you create a set, you can apply it to shapes of your choosing. Custom property sets are stored with the process engineering diagram in which they are created.

For details about creating and applying custom property sets, see "Using Custom Property Sets," page 180.

Inside Out

Sharing custom property sets

If you create custom property sets in one diagram that you want to use in another, you can, in effect, copy the sets from one to the other. To do this, both Visio documents must be open. Select Add in the Custom Property Sets window. This displays the Add Custom Property Set dialog box. Choose Create A New Set From An Existing Set, specify the Visio diagram or document (such as a stencil) that contains the sets you want to use, and click OK.

For details, see "Defining a New Set Based on Existing Custom Properties," page 182.

Labeling, Tagging, and Numbering Components

Each component can include an identifying *tag*, which can be hidden or customized. In addition, component shapes can include properties that store real-world data, such as a component's temperature rating or the line size of a pipeline, as Figure 27-25 shows. You can display custom property data on the drawing page as part of a component's tag or as a custom text label called a callout shape.

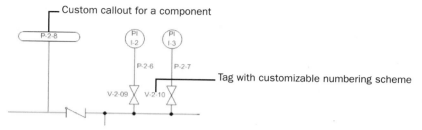

Custom callout for a component

Tag with customizable numbering scheme

Figure 27-25. You can use intelligent callout shapes to label the components in your diagram.

Labeling Shapes with Component Data

When you associate a callout shape with a component, you can specify the value to use as a label, as Figure 27-26 shows. Visio updates the callout's label if you edit the component's properties.

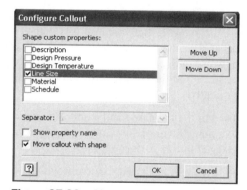

Figure 27-26. You can display component information using custom callout shapes on the Process Annotations stencil.

Follow these steps to set up a callout:

1   Drag a custom callout shape from the Process Annotations stencil onto the drawing page.

2   Drag the callout shape's control handle to any point on the shape for which you want to display data.

3   In the Configure Callout dialog box, select the custom properties you want to display in the callout shape.

4   To display more than one custom property, select the check boxes you want. To change the order in which properties appear on the callout shape, select a property and click Move Up or Move Down.

5   If you are displaying more than one custom property in the callout shape, separate the values to ensure that they're readable. To do this, select an option from the Separator list. (The Separator option is not available if you display only one custom property.)

6   Click OK.

Tip   You can change the settings for a callout shape any time by right-clicking it, choosing Configure Callout, and selecting different custom properties.

You can also display information about a shape directly in the shape's tag, or label. By default, the shape's tag is displayed. You can hide it by right-clicking the shape and choosing Hide Tag; and you can show it by right-clicking the shape and choosing Show Tag. For details about setting up a tag format to display the values for specific properties, see the next section, "Tagging Components."

Tagging Components

Each component has a unique tag that Visio Professional uses to identify and track it. When you first drag a shape to the drawing page, Visio labels it with a unique component tag based on the tag format associated with the master shape. If there are multiple shapes associated with a component, each of those shapes has the same tag. For example, when you drop a valve on a pipeline, the pipe is split into two shapes, one on either side of the valve, but both pipe segments have the same tag. This ensures that the correct information is listed for each of the shapes when one of the shapes is updated.

By default, the component tag is composed of the tag name and a one-digit counter. So, for example, if you drag a pump shape onto a new drawing, the pump is tagged Pump-1. If you drag another pump onto the page, it is tagged Pump-2.

You can change the tag for a shape by editing the shape's text manually, which isn't a particularly efficient method of tagging large numbers of components. Visio provides a more efficient way to write tags quickly and consistently. You can apply a *tag format* to shapes. The tag format, composed of alphanumeric text and component data, provides the rules that Visio Professional follows when tagging a component. If the existing tag formats don't meet your needs, you can customize them.

You can apply a tag format to an individual shape, multiple selected shapes, or a master on a custom or document stencil, which is the quickest way to update all the shapes in a drawing.

To apply a tag format to one or more shapes on the drawing page, follow these steps:

1   Select the shapes you want to tag by doing one of the following:

   ■   To tag specific shapes in the diagram, select the shapes you want.

Tip   Press Shift+click to select multiple shapes.

   ■   To tag all the components that are represented by the same shape—for example, all the gate valves—don't select anything.

2   Choose Process Engineering, Apply Tag Format.

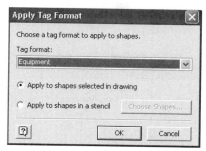

3   In the Tag Format list, select the tag format you want to apply.

4   Do one of the following:

■   If you're applying the format to selected shapes, select the ApplyTo Shapes Selected In Drawing option, and then click OK to complete the task and apply the new tag format.

■   If you're applying the format to all the components represented by a particular shape, select the ApplyTo Shapes In A Stencil option, and then click Choose Shapes.

5   In the Shapes list, select the component shapes you want to apply the format to. Shapes are listed in alphabetical order by the name of the master shape that represents them. Click OK.

6   In the Apply Tag Format dialog box, click OK to apply the new format.

Defining Component Tags

To customize the tagging scheme used in your diagram, you can create and edit the tag format Visio applies to component shapes. Tags can be pretty smart—you can display the value of custom properties in a tag, automatically number component tags in sequence, and display more than one line of information. With the Edit Tag Formats command on the Process Engineering menu, you can revise the format used for existing tags, as Figure 27-27 shows.

Or you can create a new tag format, which you can apply to shapes with the Apply Tag Format command.

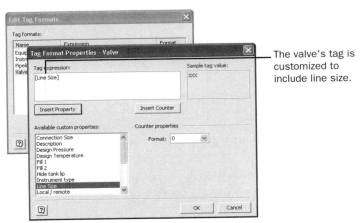

The valve's tag is customized to include line size.

Figure 27-27. You can use the Edit Tag Formats command to customize the appearance of tags.

The format for a tag is based on a *tag expression*, which is similar to the Visio text fields that insert file information. A tag expression can include punctuation and fields that are set off in square brackets ([ ]) as you can see in Figure 27-27. Visio evaluates the value of the field to display the tag on the shape. For example, if a tag expression includes the custom property Line Size, Visio inserts the value for the shape's Line Size custom property. If you haven't entered a value for Line Size, the tag displays nothing.

To number components, you can add a counter to a tag expression. Visio increments the counter field in one of two ways:

- If you select shapes and then define a tag expression with a counter, the selected shapes are numbered according to their stacking order (the order you added them to the page).
- If no shapes are selected, Visio numbers shapes as you add them.

By default, a counter includes only one digit, but you can specify two or more digits. Visio inserts leading zeros to fill the number of digits you specify. For example, if you specify two digits, the first pump in a diagram is labeled Pump-01 and the hundredth pump is labeled Pump-100.

To delete or rename an existing tag format, choose Process Engineering, Edit Tag Formats, which opens the Edit Tag Formats dialog box, as Figure 27-28 shows. Select the tag format, and then click Delete or Rename. If you're renaming the tag format, type a new name and then click elsewhere in the dialog box. Click OK to close the dialog box.

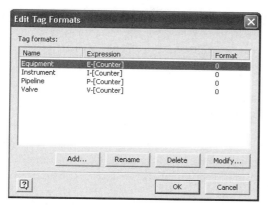

Figure 27-28. To revise or create a tag format, use the Edit Tag Formats command on the Process Engineering menu.

Follow these steps to create a new tag format:

1 Choose Process Engineering, Edit Tag Formats to display the Edit Tag Formats dialog box, and then click Add.

2 In the Name box, type a name for the new tag format as you want to identify it in the Apply Tag Formats dialog box.

3 Do one of the following:

   ▪ To base the new tag format on the default tag format, select the Create A New Format option.

   ▪ To base the new tag format on an existing format, select the Create From An Existing Format option. Then, from the Document list, select the document or stencil that contains the existing tag format you want to use. The tag formats included in that document or stencil are listed. From the Format list, select the tag format you want to base the new tag format on.

4 Click OK to return to the Edit Tag Formats dialog box.

Chapter 27

5   In the Tag Formats list, select the tag you just added, and then click Modify to display the Tag Format Properties dialog box.

6   In the Tag Expression box, type or edit the text to change any letters or punctuation that appears.

Tip   To create a tag that has more than one line, click to place the insertion point in the tag expression, and then press the Enter key.

7   To insert a custom property in the tag, click in the tag expression where you want to insert the field, select a custom property in the Available Custom Properties list, and then click Insert Property. Visio inserts a field enclosed in square brackets. For example, [Material].

8   To specify the number of leading zeros for a counter, select an option in the Format list.

9   When the tag expression is formatted the way you want, click OK to return to the Edit Tag Formats dialog box, and then click OK.

Renumbering Components

To help you distinguish one pump or valve from another, Visio assigns each component a number when it's added to the diagram. For example, the first pump you drag to the page is tagged Pump-1, and the second is Pump-2. You can change the way components are numbered automatically with the Renumber Components command, as Figure 27-29 shows. Tag numbers are incremented as you add shapes, and the format of the number itself is determined by the tag format as described in the previous section. However, if you've deleted components or want to count different kinds of components separately, Visio can renumber component shapes based on criteria that you provide. After you renumber components, new component shapes are numbered incrementally where the last component numbers left off.

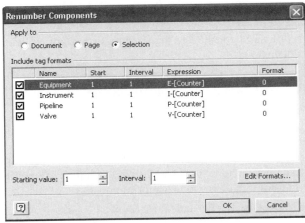

Figure 27-29.   You can specify how you want Visio to renumber component shapes.

Follow these steps to renumber components:

1 Select specific components you want to change or cancel all selections to renumber all shapes, and then choose Process Engineering, Renumber Components.

2 Under Apply To, select an option. You can renumber all components in the entire drawing file (Document), just those on the currently displayed page (Page), or selected shapes only (Selection).

3 To limit the renumbering to shapes that use a particular tag format, such as pumps or valves, under Include Tag Formats, clear the tag formats you don't want to include. By default, all tag formats are selected, which means that all tags that include a counter will be renumbered.

4 In the Starting Value box, type or select the first number to start counting with.

5 In the Interval box, type or select a number by which the counter is incremented.

6 Click OK to reset the counter in the component tags.

Note To prevent Visio from automatically numbering components you add, choose Process Engineering, Diagram Options, and clear the Number Components When They Are Added To The Drawing check box.

Creating Pipeline, Valve, and Other Reports

Engineering drawings often accompany reports, such as a bill of materials or parts list. One of the best features in Visio Professional is its ability to generate reports of all kinds based on the data stored with your drawing. For P&IDs and PFDs in particular, Visio includes several built-in reports that you can run to create components lists based on the custom properties stored with process engineering shapes. If you're working with one of the other engineering templates, the built-in report definitions probably don't apply to your diagram type. However, you can create your own report definitions that include the information you want.

For details about reports, see "Defining a Custom Report," page 194.

Generating Component Lists

Visio includes several built-in reports that you can run to create a list of all the pipelines, equipment, instruments, or valves in your process engineering model diagram, as Figure 27-30 shows. The built-in process engineering reports are based on custom property values and include the following lists:

● **Equipment List** This report includes tag number, description, material, manufacturer, and model.

● **Instrument List** This report includes tag number, description, connection size, service, manufacturer, and model.

- **Pipeline List** This report includes tag number, description, line size, schedule, design pressure, and design temperature.
- **Valve List** This report includes tag number, description, line size, valve class, manufacturer, and model.

	Pipeline List						
2	Displayed Text	Description	Line Size	Schedule	Design Pressure	Design Temperature	Quantity
3	P-1						1
4	P-10						1
5	P-11						1
6	P-12						1
7	P-13						1
8	P-14						1
9	P-15						1
10	P-16						1
11	P-17						1
12	P-18						1
13	P-19						1
14	P-2						1
15	P-20						1
16	P-21						1
17	P-22						1
18	P-23						1
19	P-3						1
20	P-4						1
21	P-5						1
22	P-6						1
23	P-9						1

Figure 27-30. The built-in pipeline list report can be generated as a Microsoft Excel file for further analysis. You can also generate reports in HTML, XML, and other formats.

Even if your diagrams don't include custom property data for shapes, you can run these reports to get a list of components by their tag number, because Visio tags process engineering shapes automatically. Reports are easy to customize as well. If you want to display different properties in a report, you can modify the report definition. For example, you can select theValve List report definition in the Report tool and then edit it so that the Description field is not included.

To generate one of the built-in reports, choose Tools, Report. In the Report dialog box, select a Report Definition, and click Run.

For details, see "Running a Report," page 191.

Customizing Process Engineering Reports

To make reports more useful for your process engineering group, you can also create customized reports. You can either modify an existing report definition or create one from scratch. The built-in report definitions (Equipment List, Instrument List, Pipeline List, and Valve List) include all the custom properties for a component shape, but you can create a custom report definition that includes only the shapes you want to list and the criteria you want to use.

The Report Definition Wizard isn't designed to accommodate the modeling behavior of process engineering diagrams. Therefore, it reports on shapes, not components. The built-in report definitions filter out duplicate shapes so that each component's data is reported only once. However, if you create your own report definition, make sure you also filter out duplicate shapes.

Follow these steps to create a custom report definition that filters out duplicate process engineering shapes, so that you only get the information for each component once:

1. Choose Tools, Report. If you want to base the new report definition on an existing definition, select the existing definition in the Report dialog box.

2. Click New, and then choose the option for the shapes on which you want to report.

3. Click Advanced to define the criteria for the report. In the Limit Selection dialog box select PEComponentTag from the Property list, Select Exists in the Condition list, and Select TRUE in the Value list.

4. Click Add to put this condition in the defined criteria list, and then click OK.

5. Click Next in the Report Definition Wizard.

6. Select <Displayed Text> to report on the component tag. Select any other properties you want to report on, and then click Next.

7. Click Subtotals. In the Subtotals dialog box select <Displayed Text> in the Group By list, and then click Options. Select the Don't Repeat IdenticalValues option, and then click OK to close each dialog box until you return to the wizard.

8. Click Next, complete the information to save your report, and click Finish.

> For details about the options in each screen of the Report Definition Wizard, see "Defining a Custom Report," page 194.

Converting Shapes and CAD Symbols into Components

Process engineering shapes don't work like other Visio shapes. They have categories, tag formats, and other attributes that make your diagram more valuable. However, you might need to create your own shapes or modify existing Visio shapes to complete your diagram. To take full advantage of the Visio Professional Process Engineering solution, you can convert other Visio shapes or even CAD symbols (from an AutoCAD .dwg or .dxf file) to process engineering shapes so that they will appear in your model. The Shape Conversion command on the Process Engineering menu applies the necessary component information to any shape or symbol, as Figure 27-31 shows.

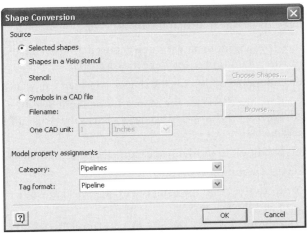

Figure 27-31. You can convert shapes from other sources, including AutoCAD files, to process engineering components with the Shape Conversion command.

The results of the conversion vary depending on the source of the shapes:

- **Shapes on the drawing page** If you convert selected shapes on the page, Visio applies a category, custom properties, and tags to each shape so that it appears in the appropriate model windows. Each shape links to a new master on the document stencil.

- **Shapes from a stencil** If you convert an existing stencil, all the master shapes are updated with a category, custom properties, and tags. When you drag a converted shape from the stencil onto the drawing page, it appears in all the appropriate model windows.

- **Shapes from an AutoCAD file** If you convert the symbols from a .dwg or .dxf file, Visio creates a new stencil and adds a master shape for each converted symbol with the appropriate category, custom property, and tag information. To save the new stencil, click its title bar, and then choose File, Save.

To convert shapes into process engineering shapes, follow these steps:

1 If you're converting individual shapes on the drawing page, select the shapes.

2 Choose Process Engineering, Shape Conversion.

3 Under Source, select one of the following:

- If you're converting shapes on the Visio drawing page, choose the Selected Shapes option.

- If you're converting shapes on a Visio stencil, choose the Shapes In A Visio Stencil option, and then click Choose Shapes. Select the stencil, select the shapes you want to convert, and then click OK.

> **Tip** To convert the shapes on the current diagram's document stencil—that is, all the shapes based on master shapes that you've added to a diagram—in the Choose Shapes dialog box, select the name of the file in the Documents list.

- If you're converting AutoCAD symbols, choose the Symbols In A CAD File option. Type the name and path of the CAD file in the Filename box, or click Browse to locate an AutoCAD file. In the One CAD Unit boxes, indicate the units of measure that you want to use. This setting establishes the drawing scale in Visio.

4 In the Category list, select a category for the converted shapes.

> **Note** All the selected shapes will be assigned to the same category unless you click Advanced and specify different categories for individual shapes.

5 In the Custom Property Set list, select a custom property set for the converted shapes. All the custom properties in the set will be added to each of the selected shapes.

6 In the Tag Format list, select the tag format to use in labeling the converted shapes.

7 Click OK to start the conversion. Visio converts the shape on the drawing page or on a stencil. If you converted CAD symbols, they are added as a new stencil of master shapes.

> **Note** If you convert a stencil or CAD symbols, make sure to save the changes to the master shapes on the stencil. To do this, right-click a stencil title bar, and then choose Save or Save As.

Troubleshooting

An equipment shape in a P&ID or PFD no longer works—its tag and other information have been deleted

Some operations in Visio can cause a process engineering shape to lose its data-tracking attributes, and you must use the Shape Conversion command to reapply the lost functionality. For example, if you ungroup a grouped shape, or use a shape operation command (choose Shape, Operations) with process engineering shapes, Visio discards the shape's custom property, tag, and category information. You can reapply the information by converting the shape.

Chapter 27

Part 8

Appendixes

Installing Visio 2003

This appendix tells you how to install and customize setup options for Microsoft Office Visio 2003 on an individual computer. If you're installing Visio for yourself, you'll probably find what you need in this appendix, which tells you how to customize options during Visio setup and describes known installation issues.

Installation Features

Table A-1 lays out the installation features of Visio 2003, most of which are primarily of interest to information technology professionals who are responsible for installing software for organizations.

Table A-1. Visio 2003 Installation Features

Feature	Description
Systems Management Server (SMS) deployment	Support for SMS simplifies installation. You can deploy Visio 2003 to selected personal computers on the local network and at remote sites.
Improvements to Windows Terminal Server installation	Windows Terminal Server is an extension to the Windows NT and Windows 2000 Server product line that allows multiple, concurrent users to access Visio in a secure Windows environment through terminal emulation. Among the improvements is faster performance time for users of Visio.
Install on demand	You can defer installing features until you need them. Later, if Visio detects that a particular feature is needed, it displays a message so that you can install the feature immediately—without restarting the product.
Self-repair	If Visio encounters a missing, corrupted, or unreadable file, it can repair the defect. Visio reinstalls the failed component automatically from the original source of the installation.
Group Policy support	Through Group Policy support, you can now secure registry settings for Visio 2003 so that users cannot change Visio behavior.

Installing Visio 2003

Microsoft recommends that you first uninstall any previous versions of Visio before installing Visio 2003 to prevent potential conflicts between the programs. This step is not entirely necessary—the Setup program can uninstall previous versions, or you can choose to retain a previous version of Visio.

> **Caution** Before installing Visio 2003, uninstall any beta versions of Visio.

Step 1: Start Setup

To install Visio on an individual computer, first exit all other programs, including e-mail and virus detection programs. Insert the Visio 2003 CD-ROM into the computer's CD-ROM drive and then wait for the Setup program to start and display the first screen, as Figure A-1 shows. If the Setup program does not start automatically, click Start, choose Run, and then in the Run dialog box, type **d:\Setup** and click OK (or type the drive letter for your CD-ROM drive).

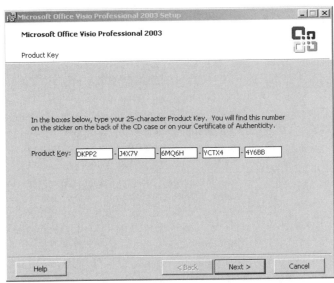

Figure A-1. To proceed with the Setup program, you must type the 25-character product key into the boxes of this screen.

If you provide the correct product key and click Next, the Setup program displays the license agreement, which you must agree to before you can proceed. Select the I Accept The Terms In The License Agreement check box at the bottom of the screen, and then click Next. Fill in your personal data, such as name, on the next screen.

Step 2: Choosing Your Installation Type

On the next screen, as shown in Figure A-2, you choose your type of installation. The Typical Install option is recommended and installs the options most users need. Selecting Complete Install installs all Visio 2003 files and selecting Minimal Install installs the minimum files that you need to run the program. With a minimal install, you can install the files that you need the first time that you run them. A custom install lets you install the files that you choose.

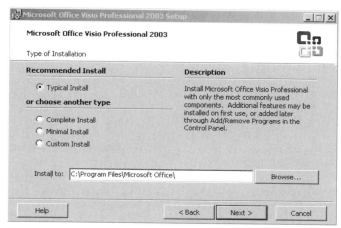

Figure A-2. Choose which type of installation you need on this screen.

If you choose to use a custom install, you can now choose which features you wish to install.

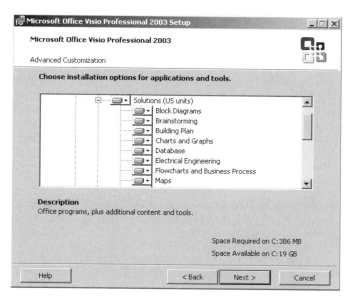

You can choose which templates to install and options for how you would like each template installed. The options are as follows:

- **Run From My Computer**   The selected feature will be installed on your hard drive and run from your computer.
- **Run All From My Computer**   The selected feature, and all its options, will be installed and run from your computer.
- **Installed On First Use**   The template will be installed the first time that you need to use it. This requires the CD to install it.
- **Not Available**   Don't install the template. It won't be available.

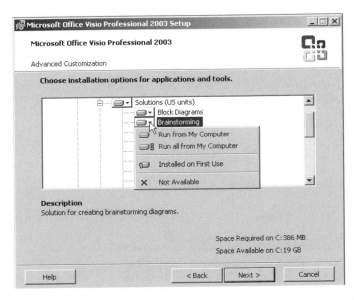

Note   If you're installing Visio from a network location rather than from the Setup CD, the Installed On First Use option is a great way to hedge your bets about features you're not certain you'll need. It's quick and easy to install the feature later. However, if you install from the Setup CD, you will be prompted for the CD if that feature ever becomes necessary, which could be inconvenient if your CD doesn't happen to be near your computer at that moment.

You can also choose where you wish to install Visio on the Type Of Installation screen. Just type in a path in the Install To text box or browse to the location using the Browse button to the right of the Install To text box.

> **Note**   If the file path you specify in the Install To text box is longer than 120 characters, the Setup program displays an internal error message. If this happens, click OK, and then type a path name that contains fewer characters. For example, the default installation location (C:\Program Files\Microsoft Office\Visio11) contains 41 characters (including the space characters).

Step 3: Installing with a Previous Version of Visio

What happens next depends on whether or not you have a pre-existing version of Visio on your computer. If the Setup program detects a previous version of Visio, the screen shown in Figure A-3 appears.

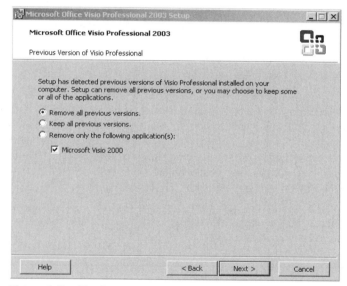

Figure A-3.   You have several options if Visio discovers an earlier version on your computer.

You can choose to remove the earlier version and install Visio 2003, choose Remove All Previous Versions, or choose to remove a specific version, and then click Next.

If you want to keep other versions of Visio, select Keep All Previous Versions or choose the specific version that you wish to retain. You'll need to specify a different installation path in the Setup Wizard on the next screen. Visio 2003 is supposed to be compatible with earlier versions of Visio, but problems can occur when you run different versions of Visio on the same computer.

Step 4: Installing Visio

When you click Install, the Setup program proceeds to copy all the program files to the selected location. Before you click Install, you can click Back to go over your choices and make changes if necessary. After you click Install, you can still stop the proceedings by clicking Cancel, but then you'll have to restart the Setup program when you want to install Visio.

Inside Out

Template versions

Visio includes two versions of each template and add-in: one that uses U.S. (imperial) measurement units and one that uses metric units. The Setup program analyzes your system configuration to determine which set of templates and add-ins to install given your locale and makes that set the default. The templates and add-ins are identical in every way except for the measurement units. If you want to include both versions, you can specify that you want to install all the Solutions (Metric Units), Add-Ons (Metric Units), Solutions (U.S. Units), and Add-Ons (U.S. Units).

One thing you can't customize is exactly which template or stencil to install. You can choose only sets of templates (and their associated stencils) based on the folder that Visio installs. For example, you can install all of the templates in the Block Diagrams folder or none of them, but you can't selectively install the Block Diagram template but not the Block Diagram With Perspective template. You do have the choice of installing certain annotation, border, background, callout, pattern, and symbol shapes, most of which are installed in the Visio Extras folders. These options appear under the Add-Ons feature.

Note For details about the templates included in each solution folder, see Appendix B, "Template and Stencil Reference."

Activating a New Installation of Visio

After you install Visio, you must *activate* it within the first 10 starts of the program. Activation is a method for ensuring that you've installed a certified Microsoft product, not an illegal copy, in accordance with the software license. When you activate Visio, you can also register the product, but you don't have to. Microsoft prefers that you register your copy of Visio, but in fact, the only information you need to provide when you activate Visio is your country or region.

The Microsoft Office Activation Wizard starts automatically the first time you run Visio. To activate Visio, follow the instructions in the wizard.

The wizard generates a hardware identification number that becomes the unique fingerprint for your configuration. You only have to activate Visio once (unless you rebuild your computer), but you must activate it to continue using the full functionality of the product.

> **Tip** If the Microsoft Office Activation Wizard is not running, you can start it by choosing Help, Activate Product.

Failing to Activate Visio

If you don't activate the product, the 11th time you start Visio, it enters what Microsoft calls *reduced functionality mode,* a highly inconvenient phase during which you can open and close existing drawing files, but you can't edit or save them or create new drawings. The following key features are shut down during reduced functionality mode:

- **Open and Save**   You cannot use the Save command to save changes to an existing drawing. You cannot use the Open, Insert, or Save commands to import or export files.
- **New**   You cannot create a new drawing.
- **Stencils**   You cannot open stencils or drag shapes from a stencil.
- **Editing**   You cannot use the Cut, Copy, Paste, or Paste Special commands, which also disables linking and embedding features.
- **Custom Properties**   You cannot use the Properties command.
- **Windows**   You cannot open any anchored windows (Pan & Zoom, Custom Properties, Size & Position, and Drawing Explorer).

In addition, the following advanced features are disabled:

- **Macros**   You cannot use the Macros command to run or create macros and add-ins.
- **Visual Basic for Applications (VBA)**   You cannot launch VBA.
- **Show ShapeSheet**   You cannot use the Show ShapeSheet command.
- **Automation**   The Visio automation model is disabled.
- **Doc Watson**   Visio disables Doc Watson so that activation-related errors are not automatically submitted to Microsoft.
- **Event handling**   No Visio object will call an event-handling procedure provided by client code.
- **Application object registration**   An unlicensed instance of Visio won't register itself as the active Visio.Application object.
- **CreateObject**   The class factory of an unlicensed Visio program won't provide an Application object in response to the CreateObject("Visio.Application") function.
- **Add-ins**   An unlicensed instance of Visio won't load or run add-ins (or "add-ons," as Visio refers to them).

No existing Visio drawing files are changed as a result of the reduction in product functionality; you just can't make changes.

To restore full functionality, run the Microsoft Office Activation Wizard, which appears automatically each time you start Visio when reduced functionality is in effect. You can also choose Help, Activate Product to start the wizard.

⚙ Inside Out

The Activation Wizard

The Activation Wizard in Visio is part of a larger set of features associated with the Mandatory Office Activation Wizard. Together with some other activation features, this technology is aimed mainly at supporting alternative methods of licensing of the Microsoft Office System. However, in Visio, only the antipiracy features are implemented. Mandatory Office Activation Wizard technology helps prevent product piracy by recording the unique combination of a hardware ID and product ID. The same product ID cannot be used to activate more than two hardware IDs—which means that you can't activate Visio on more than two machines at once.

Activating Visio on Terminal Server

If you log onto Windows NT with administrator privileges and install Visio on Terminal Server, you must activate Visio before any clients can run it. If users attempt to run Visio before you have activated it, the users will see a general failure message and Visio shuts down.

Running the Setup Program to Maintain Visio

After you install Visio, you can run the Setup program at any time to enter what's called maintenance mode, as Figure A-4 shows. You can use maintenance mode to reinstall a feature that's not working properly, to add and remove specific features, or to uninstall Visio.

Installing Visio 2003

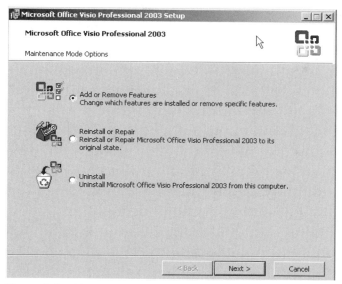

Figure A-4. You can run the Visio Setup program whenever you want to add, remove, or reinstall features or remove Visio from your computer.

To start the Setup program in maintenance mode, run the Setup.exe program from the Visio CD or the network installation point, or open Control Panel, and then choose the Add/Remove Programs option. Select Microsoft Visio 2003 and then click Change.

Appendix B

Template and Stencil Reference

This appendix lists all the templates that are installed by default with your Microsoft Office Visio 2003 product and the stencils that are opened by them. Visio installs each template and its stencils in a Solutions folder (by default, C:\Program Files\Microsoft Office\Visio 11\ 1033\). The templates in this appendix are listed in alphabetical order.

Templates and Stencils in Visio Standard

Visio Standard includes the core set of business diagramming templates that are also provided in all other versions of Visio. Table B-1 lists the templates available in Visio Standard and the stencils that each template opens.

Table B-1. **Visio Standard Templates and Stencils**

Template	Stencils Opened by the Template
Block Diagram Templates	
Basic Diagram	Backgrounds, Basic Shapes, and Borders And Titles
Block Diagram	Backgrounds, Blocks, Blocks Raised, and Borders And Titles
Block Diagram With Perspective	Backgrounds, Borders And Titles, and Blocks With Perspective
Building Plan Templates	
Office Layout	Cubicles; Office Accessories; Office Equipment; Office Furniture; and Walls, Doors And Windows
Flowchart Templates	
Basic Flowchart	Arrow, Backgrounds, and Basic Flowchart Shapes
Cross-Functional Flowchart	Arrow, Basic Flowchart Shapes, and Cross-Functional Flowchart Shapes Horizontal
Map Templates	
Directional Map	Landmark Shapes, Metro Shapes, Recreation Shapes, Road Shapes, and Transportation Shapes
Directional Map 3D	Directional Map Shapes 3D

Table B-1. Visio Standard Templates and Stencils

Template	Stencils Opened by the Template
Network Templates	
Basic Network	Backgrounds, Borders And Titles, Computers And Monitors, and Network And Peripherals
Organization Chart Templates	
Organization Chart	Backgrounds, Borders And Titles, and Organization Chart Shapes
Organization Chart Wizard	Backgrounds, Borders And Titles, and Organization Chart Shapes
Project Schedule Templates	
Calendar	Calendar Shapes
Gantt Chart	Backgrounds, Borders And Titles, and Gantt Chart Shapes
PERT Chart	Backgrounds, Borders And Titles, and PERT Chart Shapes
Timeline	Backgrounds, Borders And Titles, and Timeline Shapes

Templates and Stencils in Visio Professional

Visio Professional installs all the templates and stencils listed earlier—that is, everything in Visio Standard is also in Visio Professional. In addition, Visio Professional installs a variety of templates for technical professionals that aren't included with Visio Standard. Tables B-2 and B-3 list the templates available in Visio Professional and the stencils that each template opens.

Table B-2. Visio Professional Templates and Stencils

Template	Stencils Opened by the Template
Brainstorming Templates	
Brainstorming Diagram	Brainstorming Shapes
Additional Building Plan Templates	
Electric And Telecom Plan	Annotations, Drawing Tool Shapes, and Electrical And Telecom
Floor Plan	Annotations; Building Core; Dimensioning – Architectural; Drawing Tool Shapes; Electrical And Telecom; and Walls, Shell And Structure
Home Plan	Annotations; Appliances; Bath And Kitchen Plan; Building Core; Cabinets; Dimensioning – Architectural; Drawing Tool Shapes; Electrical And Telecom; Furniture; Garden Accessories; and Walls, Shell And Structure
HVAC Control Logic Diagram	Annotations and HVAC Controls

Table B-2. Visio Professional Templates and Stencils

Template	Stencils Opened by the Template
HVAC Plan	Annotations; Building Core; Drawing Tool Shapes; HVAC Ductwork; HVAC Equipment; Registers, Grills And Diffusers; and Walls, Shell And Structure
Plant Layout	Annotations; Building Core; Dimensioning – Architectural; Drawing Tool Shapes; Electrical And Telecom; Shop Floor – Machines And Equipment; Shop Floor – Storage And Distribution; Vehicles; Walls, Shell And Structure; and Warehouse And Shipping
Plumbing And Piping Plan	Annotations; Drawing Tool Shapes; Pipes And Valves – Pipes 1; Pipes And Valves – Pipes 2; Pipes And Valves – Valves 1; Pipes And Valves – Valves 2; Plumbing; and Walls, Shell And Structure
Reflected Ceiling Plan	Annotation; Building Core; Drawing Tool Shapes; Electrical And Telecom; Registers, Grills And Diffusers; and Walls, Shell And Structure
Security And Access Plan	Alarm And Access Control; Annotations; Initiation And Annunciation; Video Surveillance; and Wall, Shell And Structure
Site Plan	Annotations, Dimensioning – Architectural, Drawing Tool Shapes, Garden Accessories, Irrigation, Parking And Roads, Planting, Site Accessories, Sport Fields And Recreation, and Vehicles
Space Plan	Cubicles, Office Equipment, Office Furniture, and Resources
Business Process Templates	
Audit Diagram	Arrow Shapes, Audit Diagram Shapes, Backgrounds, and Borders And Titles
Basic Flowchart	Arrow Shapes, Backgrounds, Basic Flowchart Shapes, and Border And Titles
Cause And Effect Diagram	Arrow Shapes, Backgrounds, Borders And Titles, Cause And Effect Diagram Shapes
Cross Functional Flowchart	Arrow Shapes, Basic Flowchart Shapes, and Cross Functional Flowchart Shapes Horizontal
Data Flow Diagram	Arrow Shapes, Backgrounds, Borders And Titles, and Data Flow Diagram Shapes
EPC	Arrow Shapes, Backgrounds, Borders And Titles, Callouts, and EPC Diagram Shapes

Appendix B

Table B-2. Visio Professional Templates and Stencils

Template	Stencils Opened by the Template
Fault Tree Analysis Diagram	Arrow Shapes, Backgrounds, Borders And Titles, and Fault Tree Analysis Shapes
TQM Diagram	Arrow Shapes, Backgrounds, Borders And Titles, and TQM Diagram Shapes
Work Flow Chart	Arrow Shapes, Backgrounds, Borders And Titles, and Work Flow Diagram Shapes
Charts and Graphs Templates	
Charts And Graphs	Backgrounds, Borders And Titles, and Charting Shapes
Marketing Charts And Diagrams	Backgrounds, Borders And Titles, Charting Shapes, Marketing Shapes, and Marketing Diagrams
Database Templates	
Database Model Diagram	Entity Relationship and Object Relational
Express-G	Express-G
ORM Diagram	ORM Diagram
Electrical Engineering Templates	
Basic Electrical	Fundamental Items, Qualifying Symbols, Semiconductors And Electron Tubes, Switches And Relays, and Transmission Paths
Circuits And Logic	Analog And Digital Logic, Integrated Circuit Components, Terminals And Connectors, and Transmission Paths
Industrial Control Systems	Fundamental Items, Rotating Equip And Mech Functions, Switches And Relays, Terminals And Connectors, Transformers And Windings, and Transmission Paths
Systems	Composite Assemblies, Maintenance Symbols, Maps And Charts, Switches And Relays, Telecoms Switch And Peripheral Equip, Terminals And Connectors, Transformers And Windings, Transmission Paths, and VHF-UHF-SHF
Additional Flowchart Templates	
Data Flow Diagram	Arrow, Backgrounds, Borders And Titles, and Data Flow Diagram Shapes
IDEF0 Diagram	IDEF0 Diagram Shapes
SDL Diagram	Backgrounds, Borders And Titles, and SDL Diagram Shapes

Table B-2. Visio Professional Templates and Stencils

Template	Stencils Opened by the Template
Mechanical Engineering Templates	
Fluid Power	Annotations, Fluid Power – Equipment, Fluid Power – Valve Assemblies, Fluid Power – Valves, and Connectors
Part And Assembly Drawing	Annotations, Dimensioning – Engineering, Drawing Tool Shapes, Fasteners 1, Fasteners 2, Geometric Dimensioning And Tolerancing, Springs And Bearings, Title Blocks, and Welding Symbols
Additional Network Templates	
Active Directory	Active Directory Objects, Active Directory Sites And Services, and Exchange Objects
Basic	Backgrounds, Borders And Titles, Computers And Monitors, and Network And Peripherals
Detailed	Annotations, Borders And Titles, Callouts, Computers And Monitors, Detailed Network Diagram, Network And Peripherals, Network Locations, and Network Symbols And Servers
LDAP Directory	LDAP Objects
Novell Directory Services	NDS Additional Objects, NDS GroupWise, NDS Objects, NDS Partitions, and NDS ZENworks
Rack Diagram	Annotations, Callouts, Free-Standing Rack Equipment, Network Room Elements, and Rack-Mounted Equipment
Process Engineering Templates	
Piping And Instrumentation Diagram	Equipment – General, Equipment – Heat Exchangers, Equipment – Pumps, Equipment – Vessels, Instruments, Pipelines, Process Annotations, and Valves And Fittings
Process Flow Diagram	Equipment – General, Equipment – Heat Exchangers, Equipment – Pumps, Equipment – Vessels, Instruments, Pipelines, Process Annotations, and Valves And Fittings
Software Templates	
COM And OLE	COM And OLE
Data Flow Model Diagram	Gane-Sarson
Enterprise Application	Enterprise Application
Jackson	Jackson
Program Structure	Memory Objects and Language Level Shapes
ROOM	ROOM

Appendix B

Table B-2. **Visio Professional Templates and Stencils**

Template	Stencils Opened by the Template
UML Model Diagram	UML Activity, UML Collaboration, UML Component, UML Deployment, UML Sequence, UML Statechart, and UML Static Structure
Windows XP User Interface	Common Controls, Icons, Toolbars, Windows And Dialogs, and Wizards
Web Diagram Templates	
Conceptual Web Site	Backgrounds, Borders And Titles; Callouts; Conceptual Web Site Map Shapes; and Web Site Map Shapes
Web Site Map	Web Site Map Shapes

Table B-3. **Visio Extras Templates**

Template or Stencil	Description
Custom Line Patterns	This stencil contains industry-standard CAD line styles, including dashed, dotted, and divided lines for representing border, edge, dividing, property, and center lines.
Custom Patterns – Scaled	This stencil contains industry-standard, scaled CAD hatch and fill patterns for denoting masonry, brick, and tile patterns.
Custom Patterns – Unscaled	This stencil contains standard CAD hatch and fill patterns, including architectural hatch patterns (for walls, floors, and roofs), topographical and landscape hatch patterns, and masonry hatch patterns.

Index to Troubleshooting Topics

E

F

G

I

L

Index to Troubleshooting Topics

M

N

O

P

Index to Troubleshooting Topics

R

S

Index to Troubleshooting Topics

T

U

W

Index

J

K

L

P

P&IDs. *See piping and instrumentation diagrams (P&IDs)*
packages
    defining, 586–87
    elements grouped into, 585
page. *See drawing page*
page breaks, 295–96
page coordinates
    guide point position and, 448
    for shape position, 439
Page Info field, 142
Page Setup dialog box
    overview of, 49–50
    setting drawing scale in, 423–24
page size, 280
palette
    changing/restoring, 708–9
    editing, 707–8
panning
    with hyperlinks, 300
    overview of, 20–21
paper space text, 90
paragraph
    text block *vs.*, 113
    text, formatting, 113–16
parent tables
    foreign key and, 575
    relationships, specifying, 575–76
    role text on relationships, 577
Parent To Category shape, 572
Parking And Roads stencil, 547–48
Part And Assembly Drawing template, 802–4
password, 408–9
Paste As Hyperlink command, 152
pasteboard, 50
pasting
    diagram on PowerPoint slide, 351–53
    text, 92–93
    without embedding, 216–17
patterns
    creating new, 693–96
    line, 701–3
    methods for creating, 694–96
    pattern shape, designing, 696–98
PC Report, 388
PDF format, 221–22
Pencil tool
    curve symmetry adjustment with, 656

Pencil tool *(continued)*
    drawing arcs with, 657
    drawing closed shapes with, 645–46
    for drawing connections, 374
    drawing curves with, 655
    drawing lines with, 646–47
    editing shapes with, 639–40
    for measuring perimeter/area, 460
    shape selection with, 637–38
    shape types with, 638
people
    associating in floor plan, 790
    space plans and, 795–96
perimeter, calculating, 458–60, 520
perspective, 319–20
PERT Chart template, 334–35
PERT (Program Evaluation and Review Technique) charts, 324, 334–36
PFDs. *See process flow diagrams (PFDs)*
physical data types, 573
pictures, 357–58
pin
    pattern, 696–97
    positioning shapes with coordinates, 439–40
Pin Pos box, 440
Pipeline List report, 192, 834
pipelines
    appearance/behavior of, 821–22
    connecting components to, 818–19
    connections, showing, 820–21
    Process Engineering template for, 814–16
    working with, 819–20
Pipelines stencil, 819
Piping And Instrumentation Diagram template, 816
piping and instrumentation diagrams (P&IDs)
    creating, 818–24
    Process Engineering template for, 813–18
    reports for, 833–35
piping shapes, 541
placeable shapes, 70
plans. *See floor plans; landscaping plans; site plans*

Plant Layout template, 503
Planting stencil, 547
PLATINUM ERwin, 556
plow settings, 71–72
Plumbing And Piping Plan template, 539
plumbing layout
    drawing, 539
    piping shapes, 541
    plumbing equipment, 540
    rotating fixtures, 541
point-to-point glue, 811
portable data types, 573
positioning shapes
    coordinates for, 439–41
    dynamic grid to center shapes, 438–39
    with guides, 443–49
    Move Shapes add-in, 441–43
    snapping shapes for automatic alignment, 436–38
PowerPoint. *See Microsoft PowerPoint*
presentations, PowerPoint, 345–47
preview, diagram, 235–36
preview, print, 255–58
primary key
    column defined as, 569
    defining/customizing, 571
    exporting shape properties and, 719
    linking limitations on, 722
    linking shapes to databases and, 723
Print option, 468
Print Preview window, 256–57
Print Setup command, 257–58
Printer shape, 790
printing
    centering diagrams before, 248–51
    diagrams, 242–43
    to a file, 254–55
    guides, 449
    multiple-page drawings, 251
    previewing before, 255–58
    selected shapes/pages, 251–54
    tiled drawings/diagrams, 244–48
process engineering diagrams
    converting shapes/CAD symbols into components, 835–37

About the Author

Mark H. Walker has written numerous computer-related books and software user manuals, including the Visio Bible. He has also authored numerous articles on Visio and general computing for a variety of companies and publications, including *Visio Smart Pages*, *Interaction* magazine, SoftSeek, Deep Canyon, Smart Solutions, Alaska Airlines, and Informant Communications.

Microsoft Press

Learn how to get the job done every day— *faster, smarter, and easier!*

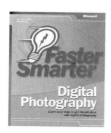   

Faster Smarter Digital Photography
ISBN: 0-7356-1872-0
U.S.A. $19.99
Canada $28.99

Faster Smarter Microsoft® Office XP
ISBN: 0-7356-1862-3
U.S.A. $19.99
Canada $28.99

Faster Smarter Microsoft Windows® XP
ISBN: 0-7356-1857-7
U.S.A. $19.99
Canada $28.99

Faster Smarter Home Networking
ISBN: 0-7356-1869-0
U.S.A. $19.99
Canada $28.99

Discover how to do exactly what you do with computers and technology—faster, smarter, and easier—with FASTER SMARTER books from Microsoft Press! They're your everyday guides for learning the practicalities of how to make technology work the way you want—fast. Their language is friendly and down-to-earth, with no jargon or silly chatter, and with accurate how-to information that's easy to absorb and apply. Use the concise explanations, easy numbered steps, and visual examples to understand exactly what you need to do to get the job done—whether you're using a PC at home or in business, capturing and sharing digital still images, getting a home network running, or finishing other tasks.

Microsoft Press has other FASTER SMARTER titles to help you get the job done every day:

Faster Smarter PCs
ISBN: 0-7356-1780-5

Faster Smarter Microsoft Windows 98
ISBN: 0-7356-1858-5

Faster Smarter Beginning Programming
ISBN: 0-7356-1780-5

Faster Smarter Digital Video
ISBN: 0-7356-1873-9

Faster Smarter Web Page Creation
ISBN: 0-7356-1860-7

Faster Smarter HTML & XML
ISBN: 0-7356-1861-5

Faster Smarter Internet
ISBN: 0-7356-1859-3

Faster Smarter Money 2003
ISBN: 0-7356-1864-X

To learn more about the full line of Microsoft Press® products, please visit us at:

microsoft.com/mspress

Self-paced
training that works
as hard as you do!

Information-packed STEP BY STEP courses are the most effective way to teach yourself how to complete tasks with the Microsoft Windows operating system and Microsoft Office applications. Numbered steps and scenario-based lessons with practice files on CD-ROM make it easy to find your way while learning tasks and procedures. Work through every lesson or choose your own starting point—with STEP BY STEP'S modular design and straightforward writing style, *you* drive the instruction. And the books are constructed with lay-flat binding so you can follow the text with both hands at the keyboard. Select STEP BY STEP titles also prepare you for the Microsoft Office User Specialist (MOUS) credential. It's an excellent way for you or your organization to take a giant step toward workplace productivity.

Microsoft Press also has STEP BY STEP titles to help you use earlier versions of Microsoft software.

- **Home Networking with Microsoft® Windows® XP Step by Step**
  ISBN 0-7356-1435-0

- **Microsoft Windows XP Step by Step**
  ISBN 0-7356-1383-4

- **Microsoft Office XP Step by Step**
  ISBN 0-7356-1294-3

- **Microsoft Word Version 2002 Step by Step**
  ISBN 0-7356-1295-1

- **Microsoft Project Version 2002 Step by Step**
  ISBN 0-7356-1301-X

- **Microsoft Excel Version 2002 Step by Step**
  ISBN 0-7356-1296-X

- **Microsoft PowerPoint® Version 2002 Step by Step**
  ISBN 0-7356-1297-8

- **Microsoft Outlook® Version 2002 Step by Step**
  ISBN 0-7356-1298-6

- **Microsoft FrontPage® Version 2002 Step by Step**
  ISBN 0-7356-1300-1

- **Microsoft Access Version 2002 Step by Step**
  ISBN 0-7356-1299-4

- **Microsoft Visio® Version 2002 Step by Step**
  ISBN 0-7356-1302-8

microsoft.com/mspress

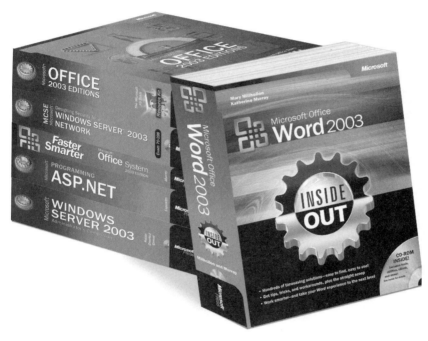

Your fast-answers, no jargon guides to Windows XP and Office XP

Get the fast facts that make learning the Microsoft® Windows® XP operating system and Microsoft Office XP applications plain and simple! Numbered steps show exactly what to do, and color screen shots keep you on track. *Handy Tips* teach easy techniques and shortcuts, while quick *Try This!* exercises put your learning to work. And *Caution* notes help keep you out of trouble, so you won't get bogged down. No matter what you need to do, you'll find the simplest ways to get it done with PLAIN & SIMPLE!

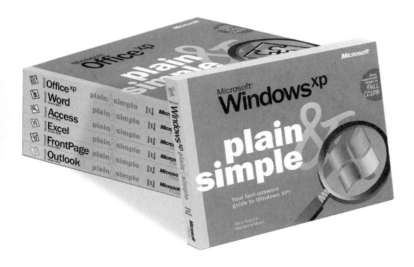

Microsoft Windows® XP Plain & Simple
ISBN 0-7356-1525-X

Microsoft Office XP Plain & Simple
ISBN 0-7356-1449-0

Microsoft Word Version 2002 Plain & Simple
ISBN 0-7356-1450-4

Microsoft Excel Version 2002 Plain & Simple
ISBN 0-7356-1451-2

Microsoft Outlook® Version 2002 Plain & Simple
ISBN 0-7356-1452-0

Microsoft FrontPage® Version 2002 Plain & Simple
ISBN 0-7356-1453-9

Microsoft Access Version 2002 Plain & Simple
ISBN 0-7356-1454-7

U.S.A.	**$19.99**
Canada	**$28.99**

Microsoft®
microsoft.com/mspress